Deciphering Diverse Liberative Readings in Indian Biblical Studies

Deciphering Diverse Liberative Readings in Indian Biblical Studies

A Festschrift in Honour of
Prof. Rev. Dr. Kondasingu Jesurathnam

Editors
Varaprasad Gosala
Jeeva Kumar Ravela

Christian World Imprints
Society for Biblical Studies in India
Theos Publishers

First Published in 2024 by

Christian World Imprints
Christian Publishing & Books from India
A-71 Group, Wazirpur Industrial Area
Delhi-110052
cwidelhi2017@gmail.com
www.ChristianWorldImprints.com
Phone: +91 11 41526079

&

Society for Biblical Studies in India
63 Miller Road, Benson Town
Bangalore-560046
sbsindia1416@gmail.com
Phone: +91 9483743497

In Collaboration with Theos Publishers, Hyderabad

ISBN: 978-93-6065-180-0

The cover picture and background colours denote the presence of God in various forms. The doves indicate the presence of the Holy Spirit. The hand from above indicates that God is always amidst the suffering people to help. The eye with tears and multiple colours indicates human suffering in various forms. The wounded hand indicates God's experience of suffering through Jesus that breaks the chains of oppression, which is God's liberating presence.

Cover art: Denin Sweety BD (2024-2025) UTC, Bangalore.

Printed in India.

Prof. Rev. Dr. Kondasingu Jesurathnam
Friedmann Golka Professor of Old Testament,
the United Theological College, Bengaluru.

Contents

Section - Three: Bible, Politics, Religion and Theology

Section - Four: Bible, Ecology, Women and Mission

Acknowledgements

This Festschrift has been a collaborative effort, and we are deeply grateful to everyone who has contributed to its realization. The journey of bringing this Festschrift to life has been an enriching experience made possible by the contributions of many individuals. We would like to express our heartfelt gratitude to the contributors of this volume, whose thoughtful and insightful essays are a fitting tribute to the life and work of Prof. Rev. Dr. Kondasingu Jesurathnam. Their dedication and scholarly engagement with his legacy have made this Festschrift a witness to his profound impact on academia and beyond.

First and foremost, we are indebted to Bishop Rt. Rev. Dr. Royce Manoj Victor, Bishop in CSI Diocese of Malabar and President, UTC Society, for graciously writing the foreword despite his busy schedule. His thoughtful insights and reflections have added immense value to this work. We are thankful to Patricia Welsch and Nr, Garland Gates for their tributes, sharing their friendship and fellowship with Prof. Jesurathnam over the years. The tributes have added cheerfulness to the celebrations of the 60th birthday of Prof. Jesurathnam.

We would also like to sincerely thank the cover page designer, Ms. Denin Sweety Y, who is currently pursuing her BD studies at UTC, Bangalore, for creating a beautiful and meaningful cover page that perfectly captures the spirit of this Festschrift.

We are thankful to the United Theological College, Bengaluru for encouraging and allowing Dr. Jeeva Kumar to work on this project. We also express our profound appreciations to Andhra Christian Theological College, Hyderabad. Our heartfelt thanks go to Christian World Imprints for their guidance and collaboration throughout the editorial process in printing this high-quality publication. We also thank the Society for Biblical Studies in India (SBSI) for their invaluable collaboration in this venture. Their support has been crucial in bringing this project to fruition. We sincerely thank Theos Publishers for taking on this project. Their dedication and commitment have been instrumental in making this Festschrift a reality. To all those mentioned and to the many others who have supported this effort in various ways, we extend our sincere gratitude. We are grateful to a few individuals for their encouragement and support that they have extended in different ways to this project.

We are especially indebted to Prof. Dr. Jesurathnam himself, whose life of service, scholarship, and commitment to justice has inspired many students, colleagues, and communities. His tireless advocacy for Dalit rights and his theological contributions have left an indelible mark, and it is an honour to celebrate his legacy.

Finally, we would like to acknowledge our family members and close friends for their unwavering encouragement and patience during the long hours of work that this project required. Their belief in the significance of this volume has sustained us throughout this process. This Festschrift is a labour of love, scholarship, and collective effort. May it serve as a meaningful tribute to Prof. Rev. Dr Jesurathnam's influence and inspire future generations of scholars and students.

Varaprasad Gosala
Jeeva Kumar Ravela
Editors

Foreword

It is an immense privilege to write forward to the *festschrift* in honour of my friend, colleague and fellow minister in God's vineyard, Rev. Dr. Kondasingu Jesurathnam, whose profound scholarship and commitment to the liberation of the marginalized through Biblical interpretation has significantly shaped theological discourse in India and beyond. On the auspicious occasion of his 60th birthday, 'Shashtipoorthi,' it is fitting that we reflect on his groundbreaking work and celebrate his invaluable contributions to Old Testament studies and the cause of justice.

Dr. Jesurathnam's approach to the scriptures is distinctive in its deep concern for the oppressed, especially the Dalit and subaltern communities. His interpretations, always rooted in the socio-political realities of the marginalized, challenge traditional readings of the Bible and open up fresh avenues for liberative thought. Through his meticulous scholarship, Dr. Jesurathnam has revealed the multifaceted ways in which divine revelations can be understood in contexts of suffering, offering hope and transformative possibilities for oppressed peoples.

The theme of this festschrift, "Deciphering Diverse Liberative Readings in Indian Biblical Studies", aptly reflects Dr. Jesurathnam's life and ministry. His focus on the plurality of divine revelations in the Bible and his insistence on reading the Scriptures through the lens of marginality have inspired a generation of theologians, pastors, and students to engage more deeply with the liberative potential of the Bible. His influence has been profound, and this collection of essays, contributed by his friends, former students, and colleagues, serves as a testament to the far-reaching impact of his work.

As we honour Dr. Jesurathnam, we are reminded that Biblical scholarship is not merely an intellectual endeavour but a calling to speak truth to power and to stand in solidarity with the oppressed. Dr. Jesurathnam has embodied this calling with grace and courage throughout his distinguished career. It is my sincere hope that this *festschrift* will inspire new generations of scholars and students to continue in his footsteps, exploring the depths of God's revelations and their implications for a world yearning for justice and reconciliation.

May this volume serve as both a tribute to Rev. Dr. Jesurathnam's legacy and a source of inspiration for the ongoing theological task of liberating Biblical interpretation.

Rt. Rev. Dr. Royce Manoj Victor, Ph.D.
Bishop in CSI Diocese of Malabar &
President, UTC Society

Tributes

In 2008 when Dr. Jesu was on sabbatical leave in the United States, it was the delight of my husband and me to host him for four nights. During that time, Dr. Jesu preached in one of our United Churches of Christ, met with a small group of share information about the Dalit community, shared a meal and spoke with another of our churches, and toured one of our local farms as well as a local food pantry.

At each of these gatherings, Dr. Jesu spoke powerfully and passionately about the social, economic, and theological issues facing the Dalit community. He spoke openly about not only the community as a whole but also his own experiences within it. My husband and I were honored to be a part of each of these gatherings, to be enlightened and moved by Dr. Jesu's understanding and faithfulness to the cause of exposing the need for justice among the Dalit and other oppressed communities. It was clear that he was speaking from his faith in God's love and justice as rooted in scripture.

As Dr. Jesu was still writing his book on the prophet Jeremiah from a Dalit perspective, we shared enjoyable and fruitful conversations about his thoughts and my own responses. It was my delight to receive a copy of his published work. Several of Dr. Jesu's thoughts found their way into my sermons and other conversations. Thank you, Jesu, for your careful reflections. It is an honor to know you and celebrate your 60 years.

Rev. Patricia Welsch and Nr, Garland Gates
PATRICIA is a retired minister of United Church of Christ, USA. Currently they are residing at Vermont, USA

Introduction

This book, marking the celebration of Prof. Rev. Dr. Kondasingu Jesurathnam's 60th year, consists of several articles and essays, mostly from his colleagues and students, and provides an array of views that inform the perception and place of God's liberative acts in the Ancient texts and modern thoughts. The book's title explains polyphonic voices that uphold the liberation of God in multiple contexts of human life in the ancient biblical texts. At the same time, the hermeneutical principles employed lead its readers to discover the liberative acts of God in their contexts of life. It also informs various vantage points that unpack the liberative potentialities of the Bible.

The book is divided into five sections. Section One presents Prof. Jesurathnam's life, ministry, and academic contributions, highlighting interesting turns in his pastoral and teaching ministry. The two essays by Varaprasad Gosala and Jeeva Kumar Ravela take a glimpse into Prof. Jesurathnam's life and ministry, emphasizing his journey through pastoral and academic ministries.

Section Two talks about the biblical interpretative contexts in an Indian church, inviting and influencing the reading communities with the subaltern, Dalit and Tribal interpretations of the Bible. David Joy, in his article, *Towards an Indian Subaltern Hermeneutics*, while evaluating the immense collection of biblical interpretative methods and models, challenges the present reading communities and native scholars to consider the sociocultural, political and religious realities to read and interpret the biblical texts to navigate the subaltern communities in their search for a just society. The Biblical hermeneutics must reach out to the faith communities to accentuate the significance of the Bible in the day to day life. B. Lalnunzira, in his article *Hidden Story of the Subalterns in the Healing of Naaman*, examines the complex relationship between the Assyrian and Israelite empires during the 9th century B.C.E., focusing on the healing narrative of Naaman, an Assyrian military officer, as described in 2 Kings 5:1-14. By applying a socio-literary approach with a subaltern perspective, the article aims to reveal the hidden stories of these subaltern figures, which have often been neglected in interpretations throughout history.

Sam P. Mathew, in his article, *A subaltern reading of Mark 10: 46-52*, expounds a paradigmatic story of the liberation struggle of the subalterns of society. It reinforces the point that the subalterns need to throw away the mantle of victimhood and play an active role as agents not only in initiating their liberation but also in remaining steadfast in persisting with the liberation struggle amid adversities to become independent, affirming their agency, dignity and self-worth. Johnson Thomaskutty, in his article, *Reading the Scripture in 'Groaning': A Contextual Biblical Hermeneutic in India Today*, examines the development of a defensive hermeneutic among Christian communities in India in response to the dominant Hindu nationalism. It highlights how biblical readers, particularly the marginalized, employ a "hermeneutic of groaning" to understand and respond to persecution, political marginalization, and communal conflicts while maintaining their faith and identity within the broader socio-political context. Varaprasad Gosala, in his article *The Weeping Prophet and the Dyche: Lament, Resilience and Quest for Justice* draws a parallel between the experiences of the biblical prophet Jeremiah, known as the Weeping Prophet, and the life of Dalits in India. Just as Jeremiah endured physical, emotional, and spiritual challenges, Dalits faced caste-based discrimination and oppression. The essay emphasizes that expressing sorrow can foster unity and drive social change while recognizing Dalits' strength and determination in their ongoing fight for equality and justice. Jeeva Kumar's article *Culture of Knowledge in the Book of Job: Exploring Dalit Cultural Interpretation* explores the culture of knowledge that the Book of Job presents as its central argument. The views of Job and his friends show how ancient communities struggled to understand and establish various views by using cultural and moral values through the discourses of knowledge. By venturing into Dalit cultural interpretation, this article argues that Dalit cultural discourses must initiate discovering the culture of knowledge that Dalit communities possess to counter the hegemonic cultural discourses that humiliate and marginalize Dalits.

Section Three focuses on the political thoughts and historical problems that the margins like Dalits, Palestinians and Tribals go through. Y. T. Vinay Raj, in his article *Post-secular Philosophy of Religion: Taking a Cue from Ambedkar,* finds Ambedkar as an appropriate philosopher of Religion in India who upholds the significance of Religion in the transformation of society and thereby brings the tapestry of the Religion of the oppressed into our debate on religion-in-society. Laurence Culas' article *Freedom in*

Galatians and Indian Constitution: A Comparative Analysis concentrates on one of the core values: Liberty or Freedom. The Preamble secures an assertion that liberty of thought, expression, belief, faith and worship are for all people of India. The Constitution of India secures for its citizens the freedom that everyone, without bias, has the right to think and express their views without harming other's liberty. John Mohan Raju, in his essay *Militant Judaism and Jewish Zionism- Israel's War against the Palestinians: A Case in Point*, critically reviews the present Israel-Palestine war situation. The power politics, the military prowess of the so-called powerful nations like the U.S.A. and Israel and its coalition for power and control over the resources of the Middle East resulted in an ongoing war and bloodshed. Raju asks, 'Why did they become so irresponsible for such a bloodthirsty war-mongering mentality of a few nations that destroy humanity in this twenty-first century? He urges that no one has the right to use and quote the Bible for their bloody actions in the name of regional security and holy land constructions.

David Chalcraft, in his article *Dalits, Missionaries, Tourists and Flaneurs: 'Free Movement' in India before Dalit Literature'* reads a few kinds of literature of Western missionaries, Bishops who worked in Indian Churches, and native poets who inform the pathetic and oppressive condition of Dalits through their experiences in a narrative style. They unpacked the unnoticed experiences of the Dalits. David understands that Dalits cannot be flaneurs in their land as the purity-pollution schema obstructs their freedom of movement and living. However, he poses questions to native biblical exegetes about whether their voices can provide hope for the Dalits as they navigate their lives in the context of stigma and marginalization.

Joseph P. Titus, in his article "*Her Judges are Evening Wolves" (Zeph. 3:3): A Critical Study of Israelite Judiciary in 8th and 7th cent B.C.E. and India Today*," examines the judicial system of ancient Israel and contemporary India, focusing on justice and integrity. It explores the role of judges in ancient Israel, who were seen as God's representatives, and the critiques of corrupt judges by prophets such as Amos and Isaiah. Finally, it highlights challenges in India's modern judiciary and proposes moral standards for judicial reform.

Wungtei Buchem, in his article "*International Politics and Colonial Dynamics in 2 Kings 22-23: A Voice from the Space of Liminality*," asserts that biblical themes should be interpreted from the perspectives of marginalized readers, particularly Christian tribes in Northeast India (NEI) while maintaining the essence of the text. It emphasizes a "hermeneutics of voice" that values indigenous experiences over Western interpretations rooted in colonialism. By following Sugirtharajah's concept of vernacular hermeneutics, the study critiques hegemonic readings that erase native worldviews and advocates for interpretations that reflect marginalized voices, enabling these communities to connect with the God of the Bible and resonate with its themes.

Esther's article *The Sabbath in the Early Postexilic Period: Negotiating Social Identity and its Implication* for the Indian Churches explores the role of the Sabbath in negotiating social identity during the early Postexilic period. Focusing on Isaiah 56: 4-5, it examines how Sabbath observance functioned as an identity marker for eunuchs, a marginalized group in the postexilic Jewish community. The study reveals that Sabbath observance, rather than physical attributes, was critical in integrating eunuchs into the community, affirming their relationship with Yahweh, who offered them a lasting legacy.

In his article "*Delving into the Chronicler's Narrative: An Examination of its Key Themes and Significance*," Lalawmpuia Hauhnar argues that the Chronicler's historiography, written during Persian domination, served as a tool of resistance for the subjugated people, offering hope and resilience against oppressive powers, much like how marginalized groups in India today can reinterpret their history and theology for liberation.

Rohan Gideon's article "*Stirring up Rooted Solidarity while Living alongside Children*" explores how solidarity with children can advance their agency. It draws on theological perspectives of solidarity with marginalized groups and applies them to the context of empowering children. It highlights the need for adults to navigate the moral challenge of supporting children's autonomy while avoiding the entitled mindset that traditionally impinges on their potential for agency.

In his article, '*Sacred and Fetishized Narratives: Certain Receptive Practices of the Bible*," Allan Samuel Palanna argues that the Church should continuously examine its actions and beliefs to ensure they align with moral and ethical principles. Additionally, the Bible should be viewed as a dynamic and ever-evolving source of inspiration relevant to addressing the needs of the marginalized and the environment.

Section Four is devoted to various concerns of the Church and its missional activities, including ecological issues, women and mission. In his article, *Image and Likeness in Genesis 1: 26-28*, Vasantha Rao reads the creation narrative with environmental concerns. His reading of Genesis 1:26-28 emphasizes that humankind must evaluate its role in the ongoing exploitation and abuse of the creation. God has placed the image and likeness in humanity not to enjoy the privilege and exploit nature but to take care of the creation as a steward. Vasantha Rao once again reminds us of the responsibility of Christian communities towards nature.

Laila Vijayan's essay *Dalit Reading of Holiness in the Revelation Narrative of Exodus 19* argues that people's experience of God and the mighty acts of God mirror the divine revelations in various contexts and life situations. Exodus 19 provides the priestly holy concerns that unwittingly create the boundaries of sacred and unholy, which eventually cause cultural and social divisions. The faith communities must challenge the oppressive elements of creating borders and divisions among humankind, and it should never be the guideline for the practice of the Church and society.

Nongthombam Alifina, in her article "*Resonance of Women's Resistance: The Exodus Women and the Meira Paibis of Manipur*," highlights the often-overlooked role of women in the Exodus narrative, emphasizing their crucial contributions alongside Moses and Yahweh in the liberation movement. It focuses on figures like the Hebrew midwives, Moses' mother, Miriam, and Pharaoh's daughter, who displayed moral courage and solidarity by resisting Pharaoh's genocidal orders. Furthermore, it connects historical narratives to contemporary struggles for justice and community protection, drawing parallels with the efforts of the Meira Paibis in Manipur, where they face vulnerabilities due to state failures.

B. Silpa Rani's article "*Purity and Pollution in the Dead Sea Scrolls: A Dalit Perspective*" explores the concept of "purity and pollution" in the Dead Sea Scrolls through an Indian Dalit perspective. By examining the Qumran community's beliefs and practices during the Second Temple Period, the article highlights parallels between the scrolls' notions of ritual cleanliness and moral conduct and the systemic discrimination faced by the Dalit community in India. Ultimately, it aims to illuminate how the caste system's ideologies of purity and pollution contribute to social exclusion and marginalization.

Subramani, in his article, *Prophetic Movement during the Period of Hosea and its Relevance in Today's Context,* explores how God protects God's people despite infidelity and rebellious activities that people are involved in. The book of Hosea spoke to those exiled and those listening to false prophecies and practising idolatry. The practice of idolatry was alarming because the prophets shared the message of God to the people. They were to convey the message to the people going astray, to direct them and warn them about God's impending judgment.

In his article "*Reclaiming a Compassionate God: Conceptualizing a Theology of Ahimsa*," Arun Kumar Wesley argues that theology is not static but evolves based on the context in which it is practised. Throughout history, it has emphasized different aspects of faith and belief, adapting to the needs and preferences of various cultures and societies.

Swami Raju's essay *"Christian Impact on the Modern Indian Renaissance*" focuses on how Christians contributed to the rise of a Renaissance in India during the modern era of our country, particularly during the 19th and 20th centuries C.E. Perhaps it is an attempt to access the impact of Luther's Reformation and modern Christian missionaries.

Jevi, in her article "*Rhetorical Reading of Psalm 13:1-6 and Leshe: Its Significance of Deciphering Divinity in Laments*," explores Psalm 13:1-6 to understand how lament psalms can reveal divine intervention in human suffering. It challenges the common perception that suffering is merely a punishment for sin. It emphasizes that laments, through their unique rhetorical and literary styles, offer deep insights into the relationship between humanity and God. Using rhetorical criticism, the researcher aims to show how laments like Psalm 13 and Leshe unveil divine presence in times of grief, loss, and despair.

Premvardhan, in his article, *The Necessity of Agroecological Prophetism: Hope for the Agriculture*, argues that the agrarian prophets of ancient Israel, particularly in the eighth century, offer a valuable model for evaluating the failures of ancient communities. The eighth-century prophets stood firmly against imperial ideologies and policies that created social injustice and ignored essential agroecological principles for sustaining justice and righteousness in society. Amid these failures, the prophets also offered a vision of hope, promising restoration if the community returned to agroecological principles.

Section Five delineates the Dalit and Tribal readings of the Biblical texts. The authors have chosen several texts from the Bible, employing Dalit and Tribal liberative hermeneutics. Lydia Bujem, in her article "*Voice of Dissent against the Whitewashed Walls: Deciphering Divine Revelation for the Contemporary Indian Churches*", emphasizes the critical role of "Dissent" in the prophetic ministry of the Church, urging boldness to challenge deceptive narratives as seen in Ezekiel 13:10-16. It highlights the need for an alternative imagination grounded in truth, inspired by K. Jesurathnam's work on Dalits as righteous dissenters.

Gnanam David's article *Deciphering the Divine Revelation in Isaiah 27: Reifying Dalit Apocalyptic Vision for Justice and Social Liberation* explores the apocalyptic imagery in Isaiah 27 and its resonance with Dalit Apocalyptic Thought. By examining symbols such as Leviathan and the vineyard within this framework, we honour Jesurathnam's legacy and contribute to the ongoing discourse on divine justice, social transformation, and the role of memory in shaping collective identity.

Sam T Rajkumar's article "*From Exile to Emancipation: Dalit Resonances in Psalm 137*" explores Psalm 137 as a powerful expression of the Jewish people's yearning during their Babylonian exile, highlighting themes of longing for home, cultural identity, and faith amidst adversity. By employing hermeneutics of suspicion and retrieval, the article underscores the psalm's potential for liberation, providing a voice of lament and resistance that empowers the oppressed to assert their dignity and rights in the face of injustice.

Jeevan Sagar's article *Divine Revelation and Marginalization: A Liberative and Social Identity Reading of 1QHa XII:6-10 in Dialogue with Dalit Struggles* focuses on a specific passage of 1QHa XII: 6-10, examining it through textual analysis, Social Identity Theory, and Liberative Hermeneutics. The Hodayot (Thanksgiving Hymns), with their obscure mixture of personal lamentation and communal expression, present a complex representation of a group transforming its identity in the face of observed opposition and divine favour. This tension between human marginalization and divine approval raises fascinating questions about the nature of religious identity and the experience of the sacred in the context of social exclusion.

Monalisa, in her essay, *Administrative Pattern of Joseph in Genesis 47:13-26: A Dalit Perspective on Historical and Contemporary Inequities* presents that Dalit reading of Genesis 47:13 26 exposes conniving Joseph's administrative policies, reinforcing structural inequality, exploitation, and systemic oppression. This reading invites reflection on how marginalized people, like the Dalits, navigate systems of power and oppression and what ethical responsibilities leaders have to challenge unjust structures rather than uphold them.

Daniel, in his essay *Ideological Critique of the Construction of the Jerusalem Temple and its Implications for Dalit Christian Communities in India*, reveals how Solomon's Temple, driven by dominant ideologies, benefited the elite while imposing economic burdens on the ordinary people. Similarly, in the contemporary case presented, the Dalit Christian community is burdened by financial strain due to the construction of a grand church. John Mathew's reading of the book of Jeremiah, *A Geo Trauma Reading of Jeremiah 12: 7-12: Reclaiming the Importance of the Land and Wounded Psyche of the Margins*," deals with the use of trauma theory as an interpretive framework to explore challenging biblical texts, mainly focusing on Jeremiah's portrayal of land loss and grief. The article examines how trauma impacts marginalized people and raises questions about land ownership, authority, and rights.

Hukholu's essay "*From Exclusion to Embrace*: *Dissecting Deuteronomy 10:17-18 through Tribal Lenses* signifies the theological move from systemic exclusion and marginalization towards embracing divine justice and compassion. This work delves into the social, cultural, and spiritual realities of tribal communities while juxtaposing them with the Biblical call for impartiality, justice, and the protection of the vulnerable.

In his article *A Dog's Life Better than a Dead Lion: A Dalit Liberative Reading of Ecclesiastes 9:1-6, Sam Thomas* read Ecclesiastes with a Dalit

Lense. Being alive like a dog assures the Dalits that they can strive to live life to the fullest and make amends to acquire knowledge and wisdom. The dominant Hindu sacred texts and its system of education restricted the Dalits, and the dominant castes exploited them. There was a massive disparity between the priestly caste and the untouchables and outcastes, having limited access to scriptures. Unlike ordinary people, the priests and the sages can access all this knowledge to know God. They denied such knowledge to the Dalits. Wilson's essay 'Empowering Spirit of Yahweh: Reading the Story of Othniel in the Book of Judges' informs that the story of Othniel assures the strength of the Spirit of Yahweh to the Dalits, women, Adivasis and Tribals to fight against oppression and humiliation. As the Spirit of Yahweh moves Othinel to take part in liberating work, it works among the suffering people even today to empower and strengthen them to achieve liberation and justice.

Section - One

A Glimpse into the Life, Ministry and Academic Contributions of Prof. Rev. Dr. Kondasingu Jesurathnam

1

A Glance Through the Life and Ministry of Prof. Rev. Dr. Kondasingu Jesurathnam

Varaprasad Gosala

Rev. Dr Kondasingu Jesurathnam, Professor at the United Theological College (UTC), Bangalore, has gained great acclaim as a scholar and theologian. In 2010, when I secured admission to the doctoral programme at UTC, I was informed that Dr. Jesurathnam would be my guide. I was initially petrified as Dr. Jesurathnam is well known for his discipline and punctuality, though on the other hand, I was happy as his scholarship and critical acclaim speak volumes about his passion and keen study of the scriptures. Thus began a guru-shishya relation and journey, the best part being I was Dr. Jesurathnam's first doctoral student.

During my master's program at UTC during 2005-2007, Dr. Jesurathnam was on study leave for his Doctoral studies at the University of Edinburgh and just returned to UTC, Bangalore, during our last semester in 2007. Therefore, during my M.Th. studies, especially towards the end of the program in the last semester of 2007, we just got acquainted and would come across one another either at the Chapel, Library, community programmes or Telugu Fellowship.

But it was only during my Doctoral studies that I had the opportunity and privilege to have and know Professor Dr. Jesurathnam as a guru, mentor, scholar, well-wisher, prayer partner, a man of great faith and also a trusted friend. Initially, my guru sat me down and took me through the guidelines for doctoral studies, explained the expectations regarding my work and progress and also helped me establish my goals and deadlines. Over the days and months I realized how passionate, dedicated and keen Jesu Sir was towards theological scholarship - especially towards articulating and producing scholarly content and articles. I also realized he not only expected me to submit my study material on time but he too would give his valuable feedback and guidance well in advance so that we would never lose time. This, in turn, was a great motivation for me too.

Our friendship and fellowship continue even today. I offer this Festschrift as a token of love and appreciation…

Prof. Rev. Dr. Kondasingu Jesurathnam was born to a humble Hindu family on November 1, 1963, in Chennai, then known as Madras. His parents, Kondasingu Pothuraju and Kotamma were deeply rooted in their traditions and upbringing. His father worked as a class IV employee in the Southern Railway, initially employed as a Gangman responsible for maintaining railway tracks between Chennai Central and suburban areas such as Pattabiram and Sullurupeta. The family's early economic life was defined by hardship and modest means. In 1955, when Dr Jesurathnam's father started his railway job, he earned a meagre salary of Rs. 25 per month. As years passed, through dedication and laborious effort, he was transferred to the Perambur Wagon Works and rose to the position of a fitter, retiring in 1990 with a monthly salary of Rs. 2000. His mother, Kotamma, was a devoted homemaker, who despite being illiterate, played a critical role in supporting the family and ensuring that her sons received an education.

Despite these financial challenges, the Kondasingu family valued education deeply. His father, who had studied up to the fifth standard in a village school near Ongole, Andhra Pradesh, was determined to provide his children with opportunities he had been denied. His mother's illiteracy did not prevent her from being a powerful influence, nurturing their dreams with hope and sacrifice. Growing up in poverty, Dr. Jesurathnam and his younger brother faced numerous obstacles, but their parents' resilience ensured that they were able to pursue an education.

Dr. Jesurathnam began schooling at the Madras Corporation School, where he studied until the fifth standard. He then transitioned to a Hindu Brahmin school for his intermediate studies. These years were marked by financial struggle, with the family relying on scholarships and mid-day meal schemes to meet basic needs like school fees and lunch. Dr. Jesurathnam's academic journey continued at Loyola College in Madras, where he pursued his undergraduate studies in Zoology. Throughout this time, he took on various temporary jobs to support his family financially, embodying the values of diligence and perseverance instilled in him by his parents.

In 1983, he graduated with a Bachelor of Science degree in Zoology, receiving a gold medal from the University of Madras in recognition of his academic excellence. Following his graduation, Dr Jesurathnam took up a job as a salesboy, going from shop to shop selling goods. His hard work and determination paid off when he was promoted to the position of sales representative in a leading Ayurvedic medical firm.

In 1985, Dr. Jesurathnam received a divine call to full-time ministry. This was a turning point in his life. For nearly 12 months, he wrestled with this calling, torn between the prospect of a lucrative career as a sales executive, which his father strongly encouraged, and the pull he felt toward serving God. His father, aware of the family's financial struggles, was keen for him to pursue the sales executive position, seeing it as a way to secure a stable future. However, Dr. Jesurathnam's maternal uncle, Rev. T. Punnaiah, played a significant role in guiding and encouraging him to follow his calling. His uncle's influence and spiritual guidance were instrumental in helping him embrace his vocation with confidence. Dr. Jesurathnam knew that God had a definite plan for his life, and his calling to ministry was unmistakable.

In 1986, Dr. Jesurathnam enrolled in the Bachelor of Divinity (BD) program at the United Theological College (UTC), Bangalore. From the very beginning of his time at UTC, he felt the unmistakable hand of God leading him toward success in his studies and ministry. As an independent student without denominational backing, he faced numerous challenges, yet his faith sustained him through it all. He graduated with a BD in first class, further solidifying his commitment to theological education and ministry.

In 1994, he embarked on a new academic journey by pursuing a Master of Theology (M. Th) in the field of Old Testament at UTC. His passion for the subject was palpable, and his dedication to studying the Old Testament propelled him to excel in his coursework. Dr. Jesurathnam's enthusiasm for the scriptures and intellectual curiosity helped him develop a deep understanding of the field. Upon completing his M. Th, he began teaching in 1996, an opportunity that opened new doors for him professionally and spiritually.

After working for about four years in various capacities, Dr. Jesurathnam was invited to join the faculty at UTC in 2000. His previous work experience and academic achievements allowed him to transition into his new role easily. In 2003, Dr. Jesurathnam embarked on another transformative chapter of his life, pursuing a PhD in Old Testament studies at the University of Edinburgh, United Kingdom. This period was marked by intense scholarship and reflection as he delved deeply into the complexities of the Old Testament.

Prof. Dr. Jesurathnam has been associating with Society for Biblical Studies in India for several years, contributing to its growth and development over the years. He has been a constant member, and later served as the

Treasurer, and the Secretary leading this prestigious Indian biblical society with his outstanding leadership and scholarship. I had the privilege to work with him in the Executive Committee of SBSI as a member and later as the Treasurer for a few years. At present he is the president of the Society, bringing together the scholars of all the generations from both Catholic and Protestant background which surely enrich learning mutually.

Currently, Dr. Jesurathnam serves as the Friedemann Golka Professor of Old Testament at UTC, Bangalore, where he has spent over 25 years imparting knowledge and mentoring students. His contributions to the field of Old Testament studies are well-regarded both nationally and internationally. He has guided numerous postgraduate and doctoral research scholars, exploring new avenues in biblical scholarship and fostering a greater understanding of the scriptures.

One of his key areas of contribution has been Dalit Biblical Hermeneutics, where he has used his expertise to address issues of social justice and equity through the lens of the scripture. His work has inspired many, both within India and beyond, as he continues to challenge traditional interpretations and advocate for the marginalized.

Over the years, Dr. Jesurathnam has had the privilege of teaching at various institutions in the United States and other countries, further broadening his influence and scholarship. His dedication to his work, his unwavering faith, and his commitment to justice have left an indelible mark on the field of theological education.

His wife, Beatrice Veena, a former Nursery School teacher, is currently a homemaker. His son David Sunil Wesley Raju is currently an Assistant Professor of English at St. Joseph's College of Commerce, Bangalore.

2

Contextual Challenges and the Enterprise of Hermeneutics A Glimpse into the Writings of Prof. Rev. Dr. K. Jesurathnam

Jeeva Kumar Ravela

Prof. Rev. Dr. Kondasingu Jesurathnam is a well-known academician, ardent reader, sincere writer and an influential teacher. Prof. Jesurathnam is preparing a generation of students, supervising many research scholars and influencing people around him to understand and read the Bible considering contextual challenges. It is my pleasure and honour to write this essay to explain,though briefly, his profound writings and scholarly interventions in reading the Old Testament. As I was in a situation looking for a supervisor to help me complete my research work, I had the privilege to finish it under his guidance. He is rigorous and vigorous in his academic ventures, persuading his students to be involved in academic activities without any compromise. He influences me with his profound scholarly contemplations and writings that focus on the real struggles of oppressed communities. It is candid in his writings that he keeps the Indian context integral and relevant, which navigates his students and people like me to rejuvenate the efforts to read and interpret the Bible with relevance to the present faith communities' lives. At the same time, he is friendly, approachable, and humorous. He cracks jokes with his students and colleagues, generating a lot of laughter. As a senior colleague in the Department of Biblical Studies at the United theological College, his guidance and support are the sources of inspiration. His friends, colleagues and contemporaries fondly call him 'Jesu' a short form of his name that creates vibes of friendship and companionship among his friends.

Prof. Jesurathnam's Dalit interpretation of the biblical texts over three decades offers his students and colleagues an academic feast to relish several delicious thoughts and views that he prepared for the welfare and wellbeing of the church and society. His thoughtful insights provoke and prepare his readers to act upon the realities around. He affirms that a reader cannot escape the influence of one's socioeconomic and religious world while interpreting a biblical text from a distant past.[1] Such an affirmation shows his rooting in the realities of the reading communities, Dalits in (t)his case, to inform the liberating message of God. By doing so, he comes out with intense curiosity to stimulate the ecclesiological community that should reinvent the meaning of the word of God to the present-day realities.This essay attempts to unravel his contributions, focusing on the methodological orientation that he employed in the past years. Presumably, it may be a partial explication of what his methodological frameworks provide, but it aims to introduce and highlight his profound writings that blended both theory and praxis. I hope and believe such elucidation would give a glimpse into the core of his writings to inform Indian academia about the area of Dalit contextual hermeneutics.

Liberative Potentiality of the Bible

Prof. Jesurathnam understands and believes that the Bible, the holy scriptures of the Christian faith community, promotes the essence of liberation to the oppressed communities. Such a liberating potential embedded in the sacred scriptures is a significant view of the feminist and Latin American liberation theologians and interpreters of the Bible. His intense research of reading the Old Testament from a Dalit perspective commences with the book of Psalms. Prof. Jesurathnam emphasizes the book of Psalms to resonate with the Dalit struggles. He writes, 'Psalm 22 appropriates the interpretative keys available that resonate and discover the liberation potential of Psalm that converges with the Dalit liberation. Prof. Jesurathnam recognizes that 'the liberative hermeneutics is the common ground and concern in our quest to see interrelatedness between Biblical and Dalit worlds. The important objective in the liberative praxis for Dalits is their liberation from socio-cultural oppression. The Dalit liberative praxis-oriented hermeneutics is

1 K. Jesurathnam, "Methodological Issues and Trends in Old Testament Studies with Special Reference to Dalit and Queer Interpretation," in *Methodological Issues in Theological Research: An Exploration*, Vol-4 (Serampore:Department of Research /SATHRI, 2020), 7.

geared towards liberating Dalits from psychological, cultural and social oppression and empowering them to organize their struggles for freedom.'[2] Prof. Jesurathnam is confident that the Bible promotes and provides a liberating message to suffering communities. His innumerable articles continue to accentuate this academic vigour in presenting the Bible's liberating message to oppressed and marginalized communities.

Prof. Jesurathnam contributed many academic articles and books to the theological students and teachers. His book, Old Testament Theology: History, Issues and Perspectives, offers many insights and invaluable theological directions to engage with the Hebrew Bible, considering the contextual and contemporary challenges of faith communities. He attempts to unpack inventive ways of explaining the Old Testament Theology utilizing the gains of 'descriptive and integrated' approaches in dealing with the theology of the Old Testament, covering the historical debates and its relevance to the modern church. Employing an 'integrated' approach to expound upon the theology of the Old Testament is an atypical attempt that he has made in this work. Discerning the essence of Old Testament theology in terms of its historical arguments and vivid discussions around different concepts and concerns is not only an academic interest for the students of the Hebrew Bible but also a faithful commitment to grapple with the profound theological debates. The study of the history of the Old Testament theology reveals that it is an unending process of various scholars craving for rich theologies embedded in the Old Testament, determining to describe its definite meaning and distinct scope, which keeps on sprouting new vistas and innovative views to rekindle the ideological debate on the usage of the Old Testament theology for the benefit of the faith community across the world. Prof. Jesurathnam's passion for illuminating the historical debates on the theology of the Old Testament and his rigorous hard work to facilitate the intricacy of the Old Testament theology for contemporary readers is commendable.

Human Pathos and Divine Ethos

Prof. Jesurathnam contributed several writings on the Dalit contextual issues, interpreting the biblical texts focusing on Dalit pathos. Very much inspired by the Dalit theological discourses, Prof. Jesurathnam chooses to locate God in the struggles of pathetic human conditions. Presumably, his conversations with Old Testament scholars across the globe and vivid writings equipped him to commit to a pertinent reading of the Hebrew Bible. For him, God's inevitable actions console and liberate the oppressed communities in ancient

2 K Jesurathnam, *Dalit Liberative Hermeneutics: Indian Christian Dalit Interpretation of Psalm 22* (Delhi: ISPCK, 2010), xvi.

and modern times. He affirms that the oppressed communities look for God's rigorous actions against the oppressor and that divine involvement in human pathos is candid in the scriptures.

His seminal work, 'Dalit Reading of Psalm 22', opens a new vista in the realm of contextual biblical hermeneutics in the Indian context. He asserts that readers' influence can play a vital role in interpreting a biblical text and conveys a thoughtful inclination towards contextual hermeneutics. He writes: 'Dalit interpretation, in spite of sharing much in common with its non-Dalit partners, differs at certain points in its interpretation of Psalm 22. The distinctive reading of Psalm 22 features a Dalit reading that comes not only because of difference in context but also because of a deep commitment to the Bible as a guide to their struggles in the world.'[3]While interpreting a biblical text from a distant past, one cannot escape the influence of one's socioeconomic and religious world. With the help of contextual hermeneutics, readers can bring out various meanings of texts that could explore an array of meanings to their readers. He affirms that the message of Psalm 22, with its form and rhetorical critical interpretation, brings out 'the nuance that God's liberating action is certain amid distress and agony expressed in the Psalm. Thus, the Dalit interpretation shares a similar nuance of God's liberating transformation.' When contextual readings encounter existential interpretations, the reader's views in their context predominantly guide the interpretative strategy. Prof. Jesurathnam is convinced that the reader's role and participation in deriving meaning from the scriptures is essential. One must pay attention to readers' deep desire when they come to the scriptures for a specific sense of the text to address their contextual challenges. In his writings, deciphering divine revelation and transcendence is crucial in informing what God is to the struggling community, even in the modern world.

Voice of Dissent and Quest for Justice:

Prof. Jesurathnam provokes his readers by challenging them to consider the realities of faith communities' socioeconomic, religio-cultural and political situations. As he hailed from a simple and humble Dalit family context, Prof. Jesurathnam's writings touch upon the real struggles of Christian faith communities, especially Dalit Christians. His commentary on the book of Jeremiah from a Dalit perspective invites one to gather the prophetic voices for Justice and human rights. His deep commitment to interpreting the scriptures persuaded him to search for praxiological sensibilities that could bring forth messages of hope and liberation to the Dalits. He writes,

3 K. Jesurathnam, *Dalit Liberative Hermeneutics: Indian Christian Dalit Interpretation of Psalm 22* (Delhi: ISPCK, 2010), 275.

'Jeramiah's daring and glaring message on divine judgment and hope can be estimated as of high quality in terms of stirring up the consciousness of the people of Judah starting from the ruling class until the ordinary folk who were robbed and oppressed by the ruling elite.'[4]Examining judges, kings, prophets, sages, and apocalyptic writings in the Old Testament and the Indian context is an exciting area that Prof. Jesurathnam introduced in his study of the Old Testament. According to the Old Testament, the pattern of leadership with the values of Justice and ethics that God of Israel designed, governed, and handed to the selected people to lead God's chosen race in times of difficulties and hostility. A historical overview of how Yahweh manifested His (sic) plan for the people of Israel through the above-mediated roles guides readers in understanding the theological significance of leadership that the Old Testament elucidates.

The prophetic struggle for Justice and their relentless fight for rights of the margins in ancient society give an impression that the prophetic discourses contribute to God's unfathomable social values, economic ethos and political rights for the victims and oppressed in society. Prof. Jesurathnam coins the word 'Dalit prophets' to designate the prophets of ancient Israel for their committed prophetic vocation that informs a great deal of divine profound concern for the most marginalized communities in the ancient context. In the same way, he juxtaposes the prophetic message of ancient Israel with the Dalit literature in the present context in which he discovers 'Dalit Prophetic voices' that condemn injustice and call for a just society.

Out of his heartfelt commitment to the cause of Dalit liberation, Prof. Jesurathnam places an interaction between prophetic literature and Dalit literature. It is an innovative way of dealing with Dalit literature. It illustrates the pain and pathos of the oppressed and promulgates their courageous voices that resist the hegemonic forces in the Indian context. He intersects the prophetic voices with the Dalit voices. He gallantly envisages that Prophets in ancient Israelite society and Dalit literature in the present context dedicated to dethroning unjust structures and 'their voices of protest continued untiringly despite the hard circumstances'.

His reading of the ancestral narratives, legal codes and exodus events reflect faith communities' sincere efforts in receiving and disseminating the liberating message of God to the world. The splendour sparks in his articulation of fusing the impressions of the Old Testament with the Indian legal systems to produce and promulgate various spiritual ethos

---

4 K. Jesurathnam, *Exploring Dalit Liberative Hermeneutics in India & the World Based on an Ancient Hebrew Prophet, Jeremiah of Anathoth* (Delhi: Christian World Imprints, 2015), xv.

and democratic values. It would be challenging to take an integrated approach unless one has a thorough knowledge of 'the context' that can probe biblical themes and issues into a given context. Prof. Jesurathnam is very much conscious of this integrated perspective using the German scholarship developed in the mid-18th century, where the Bible was read as an ancient text to reconstruct a new civilization in the context of European fanaticism and religious violence. He boldly says it is a complementary approach to dealing with the Old Testament themes 'based on the canonical, chronological, theological and thematic perspectives to get a comprehensive and integrated treatment on the subject.'[5]. Prof. Jesurathnam firmly affirms that God encourages and accepts righteous dissent and anger that intends to change the existing hegemonic structures into harmonious human relationships.

Praxiological Agenda: An Interpretative Strategy

From ancestral narratives to apocalyptic literature, Prof. Jesurathnam provides an array of Dalit readings of biblical texts in all realms of Dalit socio-cultural, economic, and political contexts. He considers the context of the ancient text and the context of the readers, Dalits as hypertext, for meaningful conversation to create a hypotext that will directly have an influence on the hypertext. His recent book on the introduction to the Old Testament approves his methodological orientation in interpreting the Old Testament.[6] He employs a cluster of Bible reading strategies that consider comparison, contextualization, conversion, intersection and interaction as viable interpretative pathways that can lead one to produce a praxiological agenda for the faith communities. Appropriating biblical messages and notions for Dalits and other marginalized communities' liberation, Prof. Jesurathnam sturdily affirms that biblical messages can be a beacon of hope in the context of hopeless and hapless human-made social structures which continue to produce inequality and inhumane social and cultural structures in society. Many of his writings opened new vistas for the contextual interpreters of the Bible to consider socioeconomic, religious, cultural and political contexts when they approach the biblical texts.

To conclude, the gamut of his writings provides an array of scholarly interpretations and pastoral expositions to academia in the Indian context that can reinvigorate the thrust of reading the Bible in our contexts. Prof. Jesurathnam's interpretative strategies, his thoughtful writings on divine

---

5 K. Jesurathnam, *Old Testament Theology: History, Issues and Perspectives* (New Delhi: CWI, 2016), 74.

6 K. Jesurathnam, *Introduction to the Old Testament: A Dalit Liberation & Hermeneutical Perspective* (Delhi: Christian World Imprints, 2023).

pathos and ethos, his commitment to unravel the liberating potentiality of the scripture, his voice of dissent and quest for Justice, and his praxiological agenda in his profound writings are a few that could notify the enterprise of hermeneutics of what his contributions have made to the academia in Indian and global context. Though challenging to give an elaborative account of his writings, it provides a gist of Prof. Jesurathnam's prime agenda and pivotal points to approach and interpret the Old Testament. As he celebrates his 60th birthday, it is our prayer and wish that God would continue to use Prof. Jesurathnam to read and interpret God's word for the welfare and wellbeing of all. May God continue to bless and use Prof. Jesurathnam to prepare generations of young men and women for the ministry of the church and society.

Section - Two

Biblical Interpretative Contexts

3

Towards an Indian Subaltern Hermeneutics

C. I. David Joy

Rev. Prof. Dr. K. Jesurathnam and I have been journeying together for the last four decades as UTC BD students and as theological educators. It gives me immense pleasure to join with others and appreciate Dr K. Jesurathnam for his years of hard work and significant contributions as a prolific writer. The Indian biblical scholarship is indebted to him as his contributions are vital in developing a possible hermeneutical paradigm for biblical interpretation in India. I wholeheartedly appreciate his diligent mentoring of MTh and DTh students. I wish him God's blessing as he reaches 60!

Introduction

A global endeavour to rekindle prophetic imagination in the study and interpretation of the Bible is an encouraging fact that enables students of the Bible to move beyond the traditional methods of biblical interpretation. Given the socio-cultural environment, Hermeneutics is defined significantly by using contemporary language to understand the Bible. In the same way, a possible understanding of subaltern hermeneutics is proposed by taking the insights from the leading readers of the Bible who could use subaltern and subversive experiences as a tool for defining the meaning of the Bible. Subaltern biblical hermeneutics is an umbrella term used to bring all reading strategies and tools to interpret the Bible from the point of view of the people on the edges. This paper, therefore, will look at various aspects of biblical interpretation given the swift changes and challenges in studying the Bible both in academia and church.

Navigating Hermeneutics

Hermeneutics is the science of interpreting written text. However, it is today understood as a method of reading the text with the help of historical realities of faith communities, including cultural shifts in society. Even though Hermeneutics explains religious texts in the general sense, it is "a mixture of hermeneutics of faith and suspicion."[1] I argue that Hermeneutics should motivate us to enter the hermeneutical circle and become part of "an endless stimulation to further inquiry and conversation."[2] As a reading tool, the biblical hermeneutics travelled through several significant stations, namely Rabbinic interpretation, medieval hermeneutics, the age of romanticism, historical-critical methods, and contextual readings. In this process, it is essential to recognise the contributions of many Schleiermacher, Westcott, Bultmann, Heidegger and Ricoeur. I want to mention their attempts for clarity briefly. The significant contribution of Friedrich Schleiermacher (1768-1834) is the presentation of epistemology in the study of the Bible. According to him, epistemology is a reflective thought pattern of the nature of knowledge, and he kept piety and intellectualism as central to his hermeneutics.[3] By placing himself in Schleiermacher's thought pattern, Rudolf Bultmann (1884-1976) proposed a straightforward process of demythologising as the core of hermeneutics. His 1950 essay "The Problem of Hermeneutics" is an excellent starting point for understanding his wavelength of reading the text to uncover the meaning of human existence.[4] In an accurate and careful reading of Bultmann, I understand that the interpreter's affinity with the text is vital in understanding the text. While B.F. Westcott focused on the commentary form of biblical interpretation, and Heidegger and Ricoeur offered unassuming patterns of biblical interpretation, namely mystical reading and textual reading.[5]

Jacques Derrida (1930-2004) initiated postmodern directions in hermeneutics by offering contemporary ideas about presenting the meaning of the text. He is remembered for his proposal of a theory of deconstruction

1 David Jasper, *A Short Introduction to Hermeneutics* (London: Westminster John Knox, 2004), 23.

2 David Jasper, *A Short Introduction*, 21.

3 David Jasper, A Short Introduction, 84.

4 Rudolf Bultmann, "The Problem of Hermeneutics", in R. Bultmann, *Essays Theological and Philosophical* (London: SCM Press, 1955), 234-261.

5 Rudolf Bultmann, "The Problem of Hermeneutics", 110-113.

of the text.[6] According to him, deconstruction is not all about imagination but allowing "counter coherance perceived in hitherto neglected voices in the text", such as female and subaltern voices, as "the texts themselves are inherently deconstructive of the very meanings that they might seem to promote and embody". [7] Jasper concludes, " Postmodernism, it seems, is the final abandonment of logic and reason and their long reign in the ordered world of hermeneutics."[8]

A postmodern study of the Bible is very significant in today's context. Hence, I have preferred *The Postmodern Bible Reader*, a 2001 book, as a foundational one to initiate the study.[9] The Postmodern Bible is a rich and insightful attempt of the late twentieth-century reading strategies to maintain the significance of the Bible in a postmodern context. I argue that the same pitch is relevant for understanding the church if the term ecclesia is courageously used as a verb; as a verb, ecclesia can offer us a feeling of movement and warming.

The process includes seven major reading strategies: Reader-Response Criticism, Structuralist and Narratological Criticism, Poststructuralist Criticism, Rhetorical Criticism, Psychoanalytic Criticism, Feminist and Womanist Criticism, and Ideological Criticism.[10] The directions and insights offered by the outstanding Western theorists, namely Derrida, Kristeva, Egleton and Cannon, have been meaningfully adapted and adopted by leading biblical readers. The biblical scholars include David Jobling, Tina Pippin, Julia Kristeva, Hillis Miller, Robert Allen Warrior, Zakia Pathak and Gayathri Spivak.

When I entered my theological education vocation in 1998, it was a time of contextual reading of the Bible and a precise transition from the historical-critical method to contextual hermeneutics. Within one decade, the scenario had changed radically as several postmodern reading strategies were used in the academy. As a theological teacher whose context was primarily the church, my interactions and conversations promoted some postmodern hermeneutical patterns in the documents prepared to study the people of God at large. Through those conversations and interactions, I also gained a new horizon of understanding of the interpretation of the text. Thus, postmodern hermeneutical principles have become inseparable in the

---

6 Barry Stocker, *Routledge Philosophy Guidebook to Derrida on Deconstruction* (London: Routledge, 2006).

7 Rudolf Bultmann, "The Problem of Hermeneutics", 114.

8 Rudolf Bultmann, "The Problem of Hermeneutics", 113.

9 David Jobling, Tina Pippin and Ronald Schleifer, eds., *The Postmodern Bible Reader* (Oxford: Blackwell Publishers, 2001).

10 David Jobling, and Eds, *The Postmodern Bible Reader*, VIII.

discourse. At United Theological College, Bangalore (1999-2019), I had the privilege of having regular academic interactions with biblical scholars and theologians who could demonstrate tremendous potential and possibility in collaborating postmodern insights in the process of hermeneutics by adapting Indigenous hermeneutical elements critically and reflectively. In this context, it is worth noting the views of Anthony Thiselton: He wrote:

> The goal of biblical hermeneutics is to bring about an active and meaningful engagement between the interpreter and the text, thereby reshaping and enlarging the interpreter's horizons.[11]

Postmodernism is flexible, and it is possible to use postmodernism to fix a clear privileged starting point for any interpretation of the text, as there is no centre point to begin the process. The text was once studied by focusing on the reality of God revealed in Jesus and recorded in the Gospel and is now analysed by taking the cultural shifts in the reader's context. Many scholars could brilliantly portray the transition from historical-critical to postmodern methods. Among them, A.K.M. Adam offered a specific focus on postmodern biblical interpretation. Adam stated:

> Postmodernism is antifoundational in that it refuses to posit any one premise as the privileged and unassailable starting point for establishing claims to truth. It is antitotalizing because postmodern discourse suspects that any theory that claims to account for everything is suppressing counter examples or applying warped criteria so that it can include recalcitrant cases. Postmodernism is also demystifying: it attends to claims that certain assumptions are 'natural' and tries to show that these are, in fact, ideological projections.[12]

One of the best volumes I have recently encountered on hermeneutics is Darren Sarisky's 2016 book *Theology, History, and Biblical Interpretations: Modern Readings.*[13] It is a dependable volume mainly because of Darren Sansky's analytical and reflective skills in presenting a very relevant collection of essays for our further study. He claims: "The freedom in interpretation has to do with the fact that the purpose of the biblical message is to speak, time and again, to new people in new situations and to be interpreted in new ways in their lives. The proclamation and activity of Jesus

11 Anthony C. Thiselton, *The Two Horizons* (Exter: Paternoster Press, 1980), xix.

12 A.K.M. Adam, *What is Postmodern Biblical Criticism?* (Minneapolis: Fortress, 1995), 5.

13 Darren Sarisky, *Theology, History, and Biblical Interpretations: Modern Readings* (London: Bloomsbury, 2016).

establish the freedom which we see at work in the later actualisations."[14] In this regard, an attempt to propose a possible theological interpretation of the Bible seems significant as it can address the question of the central idea of theology in a text. The central idea should emerge from a rigorous and systematic attempt to study scripture in a meaningful fashion with the help of the available tools and methods to exposé the meaning of the Bible for the building of the people of God.

However, there is a tendency among recent biblical scholars to exegete any text by keeping an overarching theme of the Bible, such as Christology, eschatology and so on. This interpretation may limit the possibility of evaluating the text in a contextually relevant manner. Kevin J. Vanhoozer's outstanding book *Is there a meaning in this text? The Bible, the reader and the morality of literary knowledge* raise several relevant concerns for developing a possible reading of the Bible.[15] He has brought together almost all contemporary hermeneutics for a conversation and dialogue, and his proposal is well appreciated by Anthony C. Thiselton and D.A. Carson. I am fascinated by his proposal to opt for faith-seeking interpretation; in other words, interpreters could maintain an interpreter-believer relationship.[16] These are clear pointers to the direction we need to travel as the expositors of the word of God. What should be the centre point of possible hermeneutics today? is a billion-dollar question we encounter. Though many answers have emerged over the years, for Christians, revisiting Gospel-centered Hermeneutics in its broader sense is absolutely necessary. Graeme Goldsworthy has done some solid reading in this regard.[17] While analysing basic evangelical presuppositions such as grace alone, Christ alone, scripture alone, and faith alone, Goldsworthy advocates a more spectacular hermeneutical framework by considering the person and work of Christ. It is also essential to survey the early interpretations of the Bible, including the sub-apostolic period. Why there are multiple foci other than the Gospel-centered views is a valid concern that should be part of our discourse and conversation. Goldsworthy stated:

> The tendency to move away from the centrality of the gospel to a greater emphasis on Christian behaviour was not a new phenomenon. As the New Testament letters clearly indicate,

---

14 Darren Sarisky, *Theology, History, and Biblical Interpretations: Modern Readings*, 287.

15 Kevin J. Vanhoozer, *Is there a meaning in this text? The Bible, the reader and the morality of literary knowledge,* (Leister: Apollos, 1998).

16 Kevin J. Vanhoozer, *Is there a meaning in this text? The Bible, the reader and the morality of literary knowledge*, 467.

17 Graeme Goldsworthy, *Gospel-Centered Hermeneutics: Biblical-theological foundations and principles*, (Nottingham: Apollos, 2006).

> legalism and moralism were always dangers in the early church. If this sudden collapse of apostolic gospel-centricity in the sub-apostolic period seems inexplicable, it may help if we remember that the apostolic scriptures were uniquely prop.[18] hectic.[19]

As the sub-apostolic period witnessed most of the features of the apostolic age, it is essential to study in detail the hermeneutical developments. Many non-canonical documents emerged in the sub-apostolic period. The memory of the life and ministry of Jesus and the twelve had been fresh in the era. Many contemporary voices advocate for theological hermeneutics in order to define Christian doctrines in a relevant way. Mark D. Thompson, in his 2006 book *A Clear and Present Word: The Clarity of Scripture,* emphasises the need for developing theological hermeneutics by considering various theological themes in the Bible coherently.[20]

Towards Contextual Hermeneutics

I want to state that Richard Bauckham's 1989 book *The Bible in Politics: How to Read the Bible Politically* created a wider and deeper interest among biblical interpreters across the globe in terms of initiating new horizons and avenues of biblical interpretation. The interest in political reading of the Bible by the majority of the world was incomparable. Such an incredible atmosphere of freshness and support pushed the political hermeneutics forward. Richard Marsden, after a careful evaluation of the role of Christianity in European states and politics, argued:

> In a cultural world that made little separation between religion and politics, interpretation of the Bible reflected institutional developments and broad intellectual, as well as theological concerns and, in turn, acted to shape the culture. The overall trend was a move from the cloister to the school and from the Bible as a focus for spiritual rumination to the Bible as a resource for study and teaching.[21]

The origin and development of contextual hermeneutics, which is the basis of subaltern hermeneutics, are associated with two clearly convincing views: the interpretation of the Bible using liberation theology

---

18 Richard Bauckham, *The Bible in Politics: How to Read the Bible Politically* (London: SPCK, 1989).

19 Richard Bauckham, *The Bible in Politics: How to Read the Bible Politically*, 93.

20 Mark D. Thompson, A Clear and Present Word: The Clarity of Scripture (Illinois: IVP, 2006).

21 Richard Mardsen and E. Ann Matter, eds., *The New Cambridge History of the Bible from 600 to 1450* (CUP: Cambridge, 2012), 10.

and cross-cultural missions, such as Protestant missions in India.[22] A proper hermeneutical engagement is desirable for any advanced study of the Bible. It is noted that the time frame we live in is a mixture of post-conservative, post-evangelical, and post-liberal theological thinking. Mark D. Thompson, in this regard, argues:

> In a postmodern world, Christian evangelism and apologetics need not be constrained by modernist notions of proof and evidence. Reflection means so much more than thinking, and theology means so much more than arguments about biblical texts and their implications. Postmodernism retains its flavour of protest even in the theological sphere, challenging authoritative traditions of exegesis and doctrine and calling on us not to choose comfort and closure over authentic Christian existence.[23]

This notion has empowered many theological schools to promote a contextual reading of the Bible, taking the living context of the readers into account while interpreting the Bible for the sustenance of faith communities. I recently came across a very interesting book published by SBL in 2022 entitled *Race and Biblical Studies: Antiracism Pedagogy for the Classroom.*[24] This volume is a welcome change in biblical studies as, at the global level, scholars now consider contextual hermeneutics as a proper alternative to propose a paradigm shift in hermeneutics. For the teachers of the Bible, mainly in the classroom setup of the seminaries, it is suggested that we understand the potential of classroom teaching in bringing transformation in our multi-cultural and multi-lingual environments. The book mentioned above claims:

> A classroom as a teaching and learning community should mean that everyone, including the teacher, can learn from other members. Sources and resources for learning and teaching can come from many unexpected places and persons, even those not institutionally or professionally legitimated. Classrooms as communities are temporary, but the racial effects and effects that occur in classrooms can be long-term. Teaching, like religion, is generative and worldmaking. The question is what kind of a

22 Paul Hiebert, 'Critical Contextualization', in ed., J. I. Packer, *The Best in Theology* (Carol Stream: Christianity Today, 1987), 387.

23 Mark. D. Thompson, *A Clear and Present Word: The Clarity of Scripture*, 44.

24 Tat-siong Benny Liew and Shelly Matthews, eds., *Race and Biblical Studies: Antiracism Pedagogy for the Classroom* (Atlanta: SBL Press, 2022).

> world we are making for and with our students in and beyond biblical studies classrooms.[25]

An effective conversation in the classroom will happen only with the help of proper reading materials and lecture notes provided by the teachers. The Western Academy notes that most of the world or the Global South is not adequately represented. For instance, while discussing Dalit hermeneutics, instead of discussing the literature produced by the native scholars, the diaspora scholars receive priority as they have better visibility and representation in the global bodies. I state this as I am a board member of SBL-ICI and an editorial board member of SBL-IVBS and have been able to assess many documents produced by SBL. My arguments in no way underestimate the contributions of diaspora scholars, but I would like to argue for appropriate space for native and diaspora scholars. SBSI can surely take the initiative by collaborating with Asian and African biblical forums to prepare sufficient materials for our classroom teaching. Unless and until the global biblical bodies recognise the plurality of reading methods and tools that emerged from Asian and African contexts, there will not be a proper paradigm for biblical interpretation.

Paula Gooder, an Anglican theologian who was also my PhD supervisor in Birmingham, recently compiled an introductory book on hermeneutics, including outstanding New Testament scholars of our time. She advocates:

> The introductory guide offered in this book to the different possible methods of biblical interpretation is designed to provide you with a guide to the major issues that will allow you to explore these questions for yourself and to decide where you place yourself in the debate on what the text meant vs. what it means. This book is introductory in the extreme but seeks to open your eyes to the issues involved in interpreting the New Testament and to what has already been achieved in New Testament interpretation, and also to encourage you to continue this search for meaning.[26]

Edgar W. Conrad expressed a view that both the Bible and its dominant interpretative tools are predominantly the West's construct and used extensively in the process of colonisation. However, the Bible has been offering a clear meaning of solidarity for the people on the edges regarding their struggle towards freedom, justice, equality and peace. It is significant

25 Tat-siong Benny Liew and Shelly Matthews, eds., *Race and Biblical Studies: Antiracism Pedagogy for the Classroom*, 18.

26 Paula Gooder, *Searching for Meaning: An Introduction to Interpreting the New Testament* (London: SPCK, 2009), xxi.

to note that contextual reading of the Bible is vital for developing a meaning for the building up of the reign of God. Conrad states:

> Meaning does not lie embedded in a text to be extracted from it like ore from the ground. Rather, meaning arises when readers bring interpretative strategies to the text. Readers and not texts are active in making the text speak. The reader is a kind of "author". Shaping the texts, creating the conditions in which interpretative strategies can be successfully employed.[27]

Until this aspect is taken seriously in our theological education and interpretation of the Bible, meaningful interpretation of the Bible will not be possible. For a meaningful contextual understanding of the Bible, a basic knowledge of philosophical hermeneutics is essential, as is philosophical hermeneutics and biblical hermeneutics, as conversation and dialogue offer sufficient space for people on the edges to engage in biblical interpretation.[28] Emmanuel Levinas vividly stated this challenge as he viewed "the scriptures consist of a unique mode of being whereby the history of each piece of writing counts less than the lessons it contains, and where its inspiration is measured by what it inspires."[29]

Legitimising An Indian Subaltern Hermeneutics

Today, it is noted that religious practices across the globe demand many things depending on the politics and culture of the region/s. People always try to draw insights to develop a hermeneutical grammar from the West. Despite the explosion in knowledge and information technology, Western countries and educational centres possess and own the monopoly of scientific data, even in the field of humanities. Therefore, it is assumed that many recent attempts in India to develop subaltern biblical hermeneutics were ditto of some Western reading strategies. At the same time, some efforts were initiated by Indian readers in the light of native scriptures and religious texts, which were not well accepted by the famous religious communities that acted as interpretative communities. As a hermeneut, I searched for a foundational element to justify and legitimise the quest for Indian subaltern hermeneutics. Even though I could see some traces of legitimisation in

27 Edgar W. Conrad, " How the Bible was colonised", in ed., Philip L. Wickeri, *Scripture, Community, and Mission: Essays in honor of D. Preman Niles* (London: CWM, 2003), 95.

28 B.H. McLean, *Biblical Interpretation and Philosophical Hermeneutics* (Cambridge: CUP, 2012), 178.

29 Emmanuel Levinas, *Beyond the Verse: Talmudic Readings and Lectures* (London: Continuum, 2007), 130.

the writings of Christopher Rowland, Monica Melanchthon, and R. S. Sugirtharajah, B.H. McLean's statement is compelling. Mclean argued:

> Therefore, we, as "nomadic" interpreters, need not ask what a biblical text means (as if it were a semantic container), or look for a historical author or historical content by which to restrict its meaning (as if it were a mere residue of vanished authorial presence). Rather the nomadic interpreter, abounding in productive desire, seeks out all that the text functions with and all that it transmits its own intensities to. Such a hermeneutic strategy transforms textual interpretation from an archaeological dig into an exploration of how both the text and interpreter function within a unified, pulsating world ontology.[30]

It is significant to recognise the published papers of SBSI biennial meetings since 1962, either in a book form or in *Bible Bhashyam,* as those contributions are the signposts of the theological literature in terms of developing a hermeneutical paradigm for our context. Jamesy Massey's dream project, *Dalit Bible Commentaries*, should be recognised and evaluated by the scholarly world as they could offer many insights for path finders in hermeneutics. I am reminded of the great struggle and encounters in the European Reformation in proposing a new framework for studying the Bible in a more contextually relevant manner.

Alister E. McGrath in his 2004 book *The Intellectual Origins of the European Reformation,* brilliantly expressed this arduous process.[31] According to him, tradition, text translation, scholasticism, and humanism played remarkable roles in pushing towards reformation and interpretation of the Bible. The exact process is repeated in our context as many of our secular movements for the dignity and human rights of the people make an impact in redefining the interpretation process of the Bible. Though there were endeavours to interpret the Bible by the lay people and the congregations to highlight the meaning of the Bible about the life of the ordinary people in their actual living contexts in the twentieth century, the benchmark of the interpretation of the Bible remained with the theological academy for various reasons. Andrew Village made a substantial study in 2007 entitled *The Bible and Lay People: An Empirical Approach to Ordinary Hermeneutics,* highlighting the role of the interpretative communities in

30 B. H. McLean, *Biblical Interpretation and Philosophical Hermeneutics*, 301.

31 Alister E. Mcgrath, *The Intellectual Origins of the European Reformation* (Oxford: Blackwell, 2004).

studying the scripture.[32] Stanley Fish, in his 1980 book *Is There a Text in this Class?*, proposed the idea of interpretative communities in the interpretation of texts.[33] His famous assumption about the role of the readers in studying the text is that readers create meaning in the act of reading. Having evaluated Stanley Fish, Andrew Village wrote: "This act is so strongly governed by the reader that, the text does not exist as an independent entity until it is read."[34] This is the philosophical basis for contextual reading and re-reading the Bible across the globe. It is necessary to affirm that many factors influence the readers while reading the Bible. I think Gerald O. West's influence is crucial in many ways, as academic scholars in India have widely used his writings to develop a paradigm for interpreting the Bible. It is not easy to estimate the level of influence in terms of offering foundational elements to define the format and purpose of the interpretation of the Bible in India, specifically an Indian Subaltern reading.

Recently, I have heard many people in the academy and the church publicly discussing the significance of re-reading the Bible, given the spiritual stagnation in Christian religious practices. All of us know and are convinced that Christian spirituality is not a form of entertainment, as untrained pastors and preachers in India have unfortunately misunderstood. Therefore, it is a timely task to keep things right as it would be done when it has been meant to be carried out by the appropriate persons and communities. I underline the significance of the communities as the role of the interpretative communities should be vital in the process. In this regard, Richard Bauckham's observations on the role of Bible interpreters are remarkable. He stated:

> The Peril of blindness to the influence of our interests on interpretation can also be countered by attention to the work of interpreters whose political and economic circumstances are different from our own. ..All this reminds us that in the end the task of contextualising Scripture today is the task of the whole church, and must take place in the dialogue between Christians whose varied cultures, conditions and Chrisitan traditions can alert them to aspects of Scripture which others may miss..The Bible's meaning for today cannot result automatically from the correct use of a set of hermeneutical principles. It requires in the

32 Andrew Village, *The Bible and Lay People: An empirical approach to Ordinary Hermeneutics* (Ashgate: Hampshire, 2007).

33 Stanley Fish, *Is there a Text in this Class?* (Harward: HUP, 1980).

34 Andrew Village, *The Bible and Lay People: An empirical approach to Ordinary Hermeneutics*, 128.

> interpreters' qualities of insight, imagination, critical judgement, and expert knowledge of the contemporary world.[35]

Given this clear affirmation of the validity of contextual interpretation, it is suggested that we offer some vivid insights for formulating a set of principles for Indian subaltern hermeneutics. In this connection, I would like to present some major insights and thoughts from Gerald O. West's book *The Academy of the Poor: Towards a Dialogical Reading of the Bible.*[36] Though West began with a deep understanding of the liberation hermeneutics, his conversations with other contextual hermeneutical patterns, such as Minjung, Dalit, Tribal and womanist, influenced him to offer a hybrid pattern of contextual reading of the Bible with a precise dimension of participation of the people in the reading or re-reading of the Bible. I understand West introduced the term "socially engaged biblical scholars" to the academy and the church. This space is fantastic as many people across the globe, specifically in the majority world, could connect their biblical spirituality with the ongoing struggles and confrontations of the people of God. This is extremely significant as in the era of economic empire in the world, there is hope based on the Bible, and a possible re-reading of the Bible will surely motivate many to offer embodied solidarity to the broader world. Gerald West summarised his arguments:

> Because socially engaged biblical scholars are already actively engaged in collaborative work of various kinds with poor and marginalised communities, they are often drawn into local Bible reading practices when it is found that they have Bible reading resources.[37]

Indian subaltern biblical hermeneutics may equip the readers of the Bible with alternative epistemology in terms of motivating faith communities to formulate a space for solidarity and fellowship in its radical sense. It is, therefore, noted that in India, British colonialism and its impact on the practice of Christianity has been addressed by some readers of the Bible who effectively used the subaltern reading strategy to expose the nexus between race, gender, caste, class and power both in the governance of the churches and institutions. One cannot evaluate recent developments in the mainline churches in terms of structural adjustments as most of those issues connect with the wrong notion of handling power in the churches

---

35 Richard Bauckham, *The Bible in Politics: How to Read the Bible Politically*, 18.

36 Gerald O. West, *The Academy of the Poor: Towards a Dialogical Reading of the Bible* (Sheffield: SAP, 1999).

37 Gerald O. West, *The Academy of the Poor: Towards a Dialogical Reading of the Bible*, 11.

without considering the colonial debris, which is still part of the structure of the Indian church. When I state this courageously, I am aware of the non-inclusion of sufficient modules and courses in the syllabus of BD courses to address these issues. A careful and systematic attempt to equip the candidates in tune with the possibility and potential of subaltern reading strategy will surely enable them to use the Bible to address and encounter significant hurdles and challenges they would face in this regard. Very often, it is noted that most leaders cannot handle leadership roles with honesty, integrity, and transparency; instead, they might opt for ugly practices and shelters of corruption and misuse of power. As Indian subaltern hermeneuts, we need to develop a strategy to use the Bible meaningfully to create an atmosphere of honesty, integrity and transparency.

Conclusion

As the world remains amid unpredictable and incomparable conflicts and struggles, it is essential to create a scaffold of solidarity for the people who experience oppression and marginalisation in many ways. This article presented a contemporary caricature of biblical hermeneutics and even evaluated the history of biblical interpretation up to the postmodern era. Then, the article highlighted the origin and foundations of contextual hermeneutics, which became a path finder for Indian subaltern biblical hermeneutics.

4

Hidden Story of the Subalterns in the Healing of Naaman

B. Lalnunzira

Introduction

In the 9th century BCE, the two empires, namely Assyria and Israel, engaged in an intricate relationship. One case showing their relationship is found in the book of 2 Kings 5:1-14. This text is often read as the healing story of an Assyrian military officer with the aid of the Israelite prophet Elisha. The narrative is characterized by a literary artistry with the character profiles of certain personalities - Naaman, Naaman's wife, a little girl, servants of Naaman, and Elisha, a combination of episodes. The story also appears to be characterized by power and socio-cultural conflicts of the time. According to traditional readings, healing occurs through a process designed by the king of Israel and the prophet Elisha. However, a careful reading of the story unearths a healing story of a leprous officer with the heroic acts of a captivated girl, wife of Naaman, and servants of Naaman. Those marginalized, however, are not exposed correctly in the text and in the interpretation of the text through centuries. This article attempts to draw out the hidden story of the Subalterns preserved in the text hitherto neglected by interpreters.

In this study, a Socioliterary approach with subaltern reading will be employed. A socio-literary approach is popularized by scholars such as Norman K. Gottwald and others, who call for common ground in literary criticism and social scientific criticism in Biblical studies. Gottwald explains how literary criticism and social scientific criticism function in a common ground:

> "While literary criticism shifts attention from religious systems and historical reconstructions to the Hebrew Bible as a literary world, social scientific criticism shifts attention from the history and religion by concentrating on the Hebrew Bible as a residue of social worlds in which real people lived in social networks and fought out social struggles that were highly influential in the environment of the biblical writers, and which are attested in social data and allusion in biblical texts."[38]

As a sociological analysis, we will examine the social structures or systems that are either explicit or implicit in 2 Kings 5.[39] Thus, the text will be analyzed in its context regarding the social realities of Israel in the 9th century BCE. As a literary analysis, we take the text as it stands and analyze its overall structure and theme to discern how the speeches in the text function within their context.[40] Most interpreters look into 2 Kings 5:1-14 as Naaman's healing through Elisha's miraculous power. By applying subaltern studies, we will explore the roles and functions of characters in the text much deeper.

Subaltern studies "analyzes the 'binary relationship' of the subalterns and ruling classes, and thus studies the interplay of dominance and subordination in colonial systems, most notably India, though the methods of the movement have since been applied to other nations, spaces, and

---

38 Norman K. Gottwald, *The Hebrew Bible- A socio-literary Introduction.* (Philadelphia: Fortress Press, 1985), 29–30.

39 According to Gottwald, Sociological exegesis tries to situate a biblical book or subsection in its proper social setting, considering the literary and historical relations between the parts and the whole. See Gotwald, *The Hebrew Bible*, 28-29. According to Hens-Piazza, there are three areas of scholarly investigation in the approach of social scientific studies of the Bible, viz: (1) The social history of Israel, (2) the structures and systems of Israelite society, and (3) the social contexts of the biblical writings. See Gina Hens-Piazza, *Of Methods, Monarchs, and Meanings: A Socio-rhetorical Approach to Exegesis OSTI* (Macon, Georgia: Mercer University Press, 1996).

40 Paul R. House states that Literary criticism that took its seeds in the years 1969-1974 has its roots between 1974-1981 flowered in the work of Robert Alter's book, *The Art of Biblical Narrative* (1981). Currently (1989), literary criticism of the Old Testament stands on fairly firm ground. See Paul R. House, "The Rise and Current Statues of Literary Criticism of the Old Testament," *Beyond Form Criticism: Essays in Old Testament Literary Criticism*, edited by Paul R. House (Winona Lake, Indiana: Eisenbrauns, 1991), 3-22.

historical moments."[41] This study, applied to literary works, focuses on the 'subalterns' known as 'inferior ranks' documented in the texts, whose roles, though massive, are yet silenced.[42] By doing biblical interpretation using this method, we identify the people and their voices embedded in the text, which have been silenced by dominant discourses. It involves both rereading and redefining of texts, proposing that every text, knowledge, and information is a product of an affiliation, politics and agenda. By applying subaltern reading, this study explores the hidden story of the Subalterns (marginalized) in the narrative of 2 Kings 5:1-14.

The Story in Its Sociopolitical Context

The healing narrative of Naaman found in this text may be placed in the context of the ninth century BCE Israel. D.N. Premnath argues that the accession of the Omrides to the throne of Israel signifies a systematic watershed in the history of the Northern Kingdom in the ninth century BCE.[43] According to Premnath, there is a strong political and military establishment, development of building projects at urban centers, and a strong bond of relationship with foreign nations, especially with the Phoenicians marks this century.[44] On the other hand, Israel's expansion was restricted by the rise of neighbouring nations, the Arameans, the Assyrians and the Moabites.[45] Inter-state conflicts also posed serious problems in the

---

41 https://www.google.com/search?q=subaltern+studies&client=firefox-b-e&sca_esv. Accessed on 4th Sept.2024.

42 The term 'subaltern' is a synonym for people 'of inferior rank.' Antonio Gramsci adopts the term to refer to those groups in society subject to the hegemony of the ruling classes. The term's semantic range has evolved from its first usage by Ranajit Guha, following Gramsci, to refer solely to peasants who had not been integrated into the industrial capitalist system. Subaltern studies aim to hear people and their voices, which were silenced by the colonial and dominant discourses, making them speak in their language, the language of protest, resistance and negation. For discussion on Subaltern Studies, See Ranajit Guha (ed) *Subaltern Studies: Writing on South Asian History and Society* (*Vols. I-VI*). Also See Ranajit Guha, *Elementary Aspects of Peasant Insurgency in Colonial India* (Delhi: Oxford University Press, 1983).

43 See D.N. Premnath, *Eight Century Prophets – A Social Analysis* (St. Louis, Missouri: Chalice Press, 2003), 38. There are various evidences proposed by researchers to illustrate the rise of monarchy in the 9th century BCE. Apart from the record of the Old Testament, there have been epigraphic evidences such as the ostraca, archeological excavations, near eastern texts relating to the Old Testament, etc.

44 Premnath, *Eighth Century Prophets*, 38-40. Cf 1 Kings 10:26; 16:31; 18:5.

45 In the 9th century BCE, the Arameans rose into power under the leadership of Ben-haddadI (880-842), and they managed to emerge as the dominant power in the region, eventually replacing Israel. In the meantime, the Assyrian power headed by Asshur-nasir-pal II (884-864) and Shalmanesser (859-825) extended their campaign westward, which posed a constant threat for the Arameans, Israel, and Judah. Israel also suffered

land.[46] It appears that a well-established domination of the Omrides was about to decay with the coming of King Jehu with whom Elisha had an important affair.[47] However, Israel remained stable until the fall of Samaria in 722 BCE. The strong political system and development of urban centers with many building projects in ninth-century BCE Israel resulted in conflicts between the monarchy and the common people of the time.[48] Likewise, the cultural syncretistic attitude of Israel's kings irritated the devout Israelites, including the prophets (cf. 1 Kings 16:31). This resulted in the evolution of Elijah/Elisha stories through various editions and evolved around the socio-political realities of the 9th century BCE. According to T.M. Renteria, the stories engage or reflect the concerns and experiences of the powerless-egalitarian ideology against the dominant-elite monarchic type of society.[49]

Literary Structures

Though many scholars maintain the unity of the healing of Naaman as found in 2 Kings 5, some critics find three literary units in the chapter. Majority of commentators agree with the internal unity of the passage. However, scholars agree with progression and purposeful shifts in the foci with three units characterized by three scenes, themes, and characters – Elisha (1-14), Naaman (15-19), and Gehazi (20-27).[50] The first unit of the passage contains the coming of Naaman, an Aramean officer for healing to Elisha. This story is narrated interestingly with roles played by different characters, including the king and prophet Elisha, and women folks and servants, whose roles have rarely been noticed. As our concern is to explore the marginalized and their voices in 5:1-14, we will concentrate on the episode's literary features

---

the incessant threat of Moabites. See detailed discussion in John Bright, *A History of Israel*, 3rdEdn. (Philadelphia: Westminster Press, 1981), 236-239; also see Tamis Hoover Renteria, "The Elijah/Elisha Stories: A Socio-Cultural Analysis of Prophets and People in Ninth-Century BCE Israel," *Elijah and Elisha in a Socioliterary Perspective,* edited by Robert B. Coote (Atlanta, Georgia: Scholars Press, 1992), 84-95.

46 See 1 Kings 20; 22; 6:5-7:20.

47 See 2 Kings 9:1-13 cf. I Kings 19:16. Critics such as Marsha C. White and Tamis Hoover Renteria consider that the Elijah/Elisha stories are counter-hegemony or tale of resistance against the Omride dynasty, appropriated probably by the Jehuites to the purpose of the new regime (of Jehu dynasty). See Marsha White, *The Elijah Legends and Jehu's Coup* (Atlanta: Scholars Press, 1997), 3-43.

48 See Renteria, "The Elijah/Elisha Stories," 75-126.

49 See Renteria, "The Elijah/Elisha Stories," 81.

50 SeeCohn, "Form and Perspective," 171-172. This is also advocated by Hens-Piazza. See Gina Hens-Piazza, *1 and 2 KingsAbingdon Old Testament Commentaries* (Nashville, TN: Abingdon Press, 2006), 258.

explaining the period's social context. The development of the scene in the episode may be observed in a two-chiastic pattern of parallel stages:[51]

First Stage (2 Kings 5:1-7)

v. 1 First Character – Naaman - Note of tragedy of Naaman (A)

2-3 Second Character – A young girl (hr[n) from Israel – came and reported to Naaman's wife concerning the prophet in Samaria who could heal leprosy. (B1)

Third Character – Wife of Naaman – the two characters told about the prophet to Naaman (B2)

4 Report of Naaman about the news of healer Elisha the prophet to king of Aram (C)

5-6 Fourth character – Aramean king – went (וילך), brought gifts and sent letter to king of Israel (disappears after doing his obligation) (D)

7 King of Israel – reacted with suspicion and fright (he disappeared from the story) (E)

Second Stage (2 Kings 5:8-14)

v. 8 First Character – Elisha – Note of healing for Naaman (A^{I})

9-10 Second Character – Naaman from Aram – came to Elisha reported about Elisha who could heal leprosy) (B1^{1})

The third Character – Messenger of Elisha – said to Naaman about Elisha's word (B2^{2})

11 Speech of Naaman about his disbelief and anger toward his servants (יבדים) (C^{I})

12-13 Fourth Character – Servants (יבדים) of Naaman – brought their challenge repeating Elisha's word (disappear after doing their obligation) (D^{I})

14 Officer of Aram – Naaman – went down וילך with obedience and humbleness and was healed like a lad (נער) (he continued to appear in the next scene). (E^{I})

Narration of the Healing of Naaman in 2 Kings 5:1-14

The healing of Naaman (2 King 5:1-14) represents a form of narrative with distinctive characteristic features. No less than four characters each, or groups of characters, appear in the cast. There is Naaman, his wife, her maid, the king of Syria, the king of Israel, Elisha, servant of Elisha, Naaman's servants. According to Cohn this unit (1-14) is the longest of the three units

---

51 The arrangement is also shared by T.R. Hobbs but without detail arrangement. See T.R. Hobbs, *2 Kings – Word Biblical Commentary* (Waco, Texas: Word Books Publishers, 1985), 58-59.

and most complex one.[52] The tale begins with Naaman's leprosy in verse 1 and ends with the healing of the leprosy in verse 14. Between these verses, we see carefully constructed plots of characters from problem to solution. Our process of analyzing the text will be both a detailed examination of the passage and investigation of the literary patterns of the verses (1-14) in its social setting in a coherent whole. For our analysis we will follow two stages of literary structures.

First Stage (vv. 1-7)

If we look into the first stage of the episode, we encounter two major characters—Naaman and the king of Israel. We also find three minor characters—a little girl, Naaman's wife, and the king of Aram. We will see how these characters play important roles in the scene.

The story begins with the character profile of Naaman,[53] an Aramean general whose greatness is explained with laudable characteristics – great man (גדול) and lifted up. So, he is a man who ranks high not only in position but also in respect and honor.[54] The description of Naaman's profile poses certain questions: Why does the story about Israel's prophet open with such a lavish and positive appraisal of Israel's enemy, an Aramean officer? Why does the Lord grant victory to Aram in his account?[55] Moreover, to make the matter more complex, he suffers from leprosy.[56] Here leprosy is a major defect in an otherwise perfect resume.[57] The sharp contrast between Naaman's greatness and his illness is correctly introduced by a participial phrase מצרע—'being leprous' or 'being struck with leprosy'.[58] The narrative does not give any information about the exact nature of Naaman's disease

---

52 Cohn, "Form and Perspective," 173.

53 The name 'Naaman' signifies 'pleasantness,' or 'charm.' See detailed explanation of the meaning of the name of Naaman in J.M. Ward, "Naaman," *IDB* vol. III, ed. George A. Buttrick (Nashville: Abingdon Press, 1962), 490.

54 Rick Dale Moore, *God Saves: Lessons from Elisha Stories* JSOTS 95 (Sheffield: Sheffield Academic Press, 1990), 71.

55 Overhalt observes a pro-Yahwistic ideology in this aspect, and from the very beginning of this story, the narrator tells us that Naaman was a great commander because Yahweh had given him victory. See Thomas W. Overhalt, "Elijah and Elisha in the Context of Israelite Religion," in *Prophets and Paradigms*, ed. Stephen Breck Reid (Sheffield: Sheffield Academic Press, 1995), 107.

56 See more on these questions raised in the opening of her comments on Naaman's character in her exegetical analysis: "Elisha Cures Naaman," in Hens- Piazza, *1 and 2 Kings,* 258-259.

57 Lai Ling Elizabeth Ngan, "2 Kings 5," *Review and Expositor* 94 (1997), 590.

58 See the etymological meaning of צרע in *BDB*, 863.

or the social consequences resulting from this affliction.[59] Cohn describes this contrast as ironic for readers as the careful description underscores the distinctiveness of the subject Naaman, which, however, consists of his disease.[60] The contrast creates narrative tension. At that point, the narrative suspends us and leaps ahead to introduce a second character.

The Israelite captive girl is introduced into the story almost indirectly (v. 2). Here are two contrasts: (1) **Grammatical contrast** – the little girl is a direct object in the narrative, and Naaman is the subject of the sentence. (2) **Actual contrast** - a little girl being the object of military conquest (captivated) and Naaman the subject of military conquest.[61] Hobbs defines a little girl and Naaman's wife the two subsidiary characters that help move the plot along, and then disappear.[62] Here, the reader is given a decisive indication that a comparison between these two characters is intended. Naaman is described as a great man before his lord; the Hebrew נער (lass) is called a little girl, and she was before Naaman's wife.[63] An entire series of contrasts are listed: great (גדל) vs. small (קטן), Aramean vs. Israelite, conqueror vs. captive girl, male vs. female, adult vs. child, and ruler vs. servant.[64] A little girl is reported to have served Naaman's wife. Gray suggests a girl to be captivated by semi-nomad Aramean tribesmen because of border raids.[65]

In verse three, we see the role of a nameless servant girl set in motion a series of events. If we look back to verse two, we see the description of the parallels between Naaman and the little girl. This heightens the contrast between them. While he is a great man, she is a little girl; he is a commander; she is a captive; he is a Syrian; she is from the land of Israel; as he is

59 One being struck by leprosy is barred from public participation according to the Levitical laws (Lev. 12-13). Smith argues that Namaan's disease seems to be *leuke*, a whitening, or discoloration of the skin pigment instead of the more severe Hansen's disease. See W. Allan Smith, "Naaman and Elisha: Healing, Wholeness, and the task of Religious Education," *Religious Education* 89/2 (Spring 1994), 208.

60 Cohn, "Form and Perspective," 173.

61 See Moore, *God Saves*, 71.

62 Hobbs, *2 Kings*, 59.

63 Cohn recognizes parallel and contrast as this story demonstrates a ruler-servant antithesis which opens up the literary aesthetic dynamics of the entire story. See Cohn, "Form and Perspective," 174.

64 See Moore, *God Saves*, 72'

65 Gray elaborates on the account of warfare between the Arameans and Israel at the time. He suggests that there were border raids by bands, probably by semi-nomad Aramean tribesmen, who also sold their booty in the market of Damascus, the capital city of the Arameans. See Gray, *I & II Kings*, 506.

before his lord, she is before the wife of Naaman.[66] Yet, despite her lowly position, her remark to Naaman's wife begins the series of communications that resulted in Naaman's cure. It establishes a pattern that will dominate the first movement of the story: help and solution for the great one will be mediated through lowly persons.[67] She reports to Naaman's wife concerning the 'prophet of Samaria' who could heal the leprosy.

Here, Elisha is called נבי (prophet), and he is in Samaria, where he had the opportunity to interpose the word of God in affairs of the state.[68] Moreover, he has a power to heal (אסף). The root אסף is associated with an impersonal object, e.g. – wrath, light, peace, meaning 'to rid, remove.'[69] Gray considers that in its present context the verb suggests Akkadian *asapu* – 'to practice exorcism.'[70] Paul J. Kissling, who calculates the magnitude of Elijah's miracles, concludes that Elisha is very much like Yahweh in that he has the power to kill and make alive, to wound and to heal.[71] It is certain that Elisha is a professional prophet who has a good reputation as a healer in the capital city of the Northern Kingdom. The story is given national dimensions. An uneasy peace exists between Aram and Israel. During the ninth century BCE, Aram is obviously in a position of military superiority. Yet the narrative is careful to include another background in detail. Yahweh stands behind Aram's military success. This is further narrated in the next verse.

The words of Naaman's wife, though hidden in detail travel very fast and reach Naaman very quickly.[72] To emphasize the power of the words, the narrator skips over the transmission of the message from Naaman's wife to Naaman and does not repeat the message when Naaman reports it to the king (v. 4).[73] According to Gina Hens-Piazza, the series of interchanges that lead up to the meeting are related with brevity and little detail.[74] Moore observes the use of the preposition 'before' (לפני) as having a pregnant meaning: It is

66 See more detail in Cohn, "Form and Perspective," 174.

67 This is noted by Moore, *God Saves*, 72.

68 One can assume that *Nabi*in the capital city is a cultic prophet or official prophet whose status is therefore much higher and more influential than among the various local prophetic-communities.

69 Gray, *I and II Kings*, 505.

70 Gray, *I and II Kings*, 505.

71 Paul J. Kissling, *Reliable Characters in the Primary History: Profiles of Moses, Joshua, Elijah and Elisha.*JSOTS 224 (Sheffield: Sheffield Academic Press Ltd, 1996), 193.

72 Renteria concedes that the inclusion of women as interacting with prophet Elisha (directly or indirectly) suggests a propaganda campaign for women's role as prophetic patronesses and as mothers. See more in Ranteria, "Elijah/Elisha Stories," 121-125.

73 See Cohn, "Form and Perspective," 174.

74 Hens-Piazza, *1-2 Kings*, 259.

used twice directly to Naaman. Naaman is before his lord; if only he were before the Israelite prophet.[75] Literally, it may imply 'in the presence of' 'at the face of.'[76] However, this preposition could also be understood in another sense, as illustrated in v. 2 when applied to the little girl. Here לפני conveys the idea of 'being in the service of' or 'being under the authority of.'[77] Hence, the preposition conveys a double meaning: the great Naaman, who is under the authority of the king of Aram, will receive his healing if and only if he comes under the authority of God's prophet. The little Hebrew girl, then, is unconsciously pronouncing the condition upon which Naaman's healing will be predicated.[78] Cohn also rightly points out that here the lowest of the low, the great king of Assyria heeds a female Israelite captive.[79]

After the rapid transfer of the message to the king, he announces his intention to send Naaman with a letter of introduction to the king of Israel, presumably king Jehoram (v.5-6). Then the narrator reports about the preparation of Naaman with gifts of silver, gold, and garments. These represent the Aramean's effort to gain his healing. The royal mission to the king of Israel recalls similar correspondence between kings in the Amarna tablets on the same subject.[80] Aram's king has commissioned Israel's king to cure Naaman of his leprosy. Volkamar Fritz comments that sending a letter to the king of Israel suggests that he did so as his peer.[81] Aram's king was likely respecting the Israelite monarch's prerogative to commission the prophet to do great deeds in his name.[82] It appears that making relationship with the neighboring country with gifts had been a means of making strong bond of relationship in the ninth century BCE.[83] The original suggestion,

75 See Moore, *God Saves*, 72-73.

76 See *The Brown-Driver-Briggs Hebrew and English Lexicon* (*BDB*), ed. Francis Brown, S.R. Driver, and C.A. Briggs (Peabody, Mass: Hendrickson Publishers, 2004 eighth printing), 816.

77 See *BDB*, 817.

78 Moore, *God Saves*, 73.

79 Cohn, "Form and Perspective," 175.

80 This is a letter to king Amenhotep III (of Egypt), Tusratta of Mitani (King of Syria), stating that he has sent the statue of Astarte of Nineveh, which was held to have healing propensities to the Pharaoh. See detail in Gray, *I & II Kings*, 505.

81 See Volkamar Fritz, *1 & 2 Kings: A Continental Commentary*, trans. Anselm Hagedon (Minneapolis: Fortress Press, 1989), 259.

82 See discussion in Hens-Piazza, *1-2 Kings*, 259.

83 This in mainly found in the period of Ahab when strong relationship was built between Israel and Phoenicia by import and exchange of valuable ornaments. For a more extensive discussion, see Premnath, *Eighth Century Prophets*, 38-40.

that Naaman to go the prophet, appears to be forgotten which causes panic to the Israelite king.[84]

When the letter is delivered, the reaction is dramatic. The king, intimidated by what he understands to be a challenge to him, rips his garment and cried, "Am I God to kill and to make alive?" (v.7). The outcry registers not only the king's helplessness but also the underlying assumption that God does indeed wield sufficient power.[85] The flow of the narrative reflects to verse six where we find the king of Aram sending Naaman to be healed by the king of Israel. One may assume that in the mind of the king of Aram, the miraculous curative powers of which the Israelite maiden spoke must surely he found under royal auspices. In fact, her identification of Elisha as 'the prophet, who is in Samaria,' the Israelite royal city would signal to the king of Aram that this prophet operated under royal patronage.[86] The king interprets the request in the letter (v.6b) as a threat. He reacts as though confronting deep troubles, pleads his powerlessness, and invokes the politics of international suspicion.[87] Long comments thus: The narrator portrays the king as if he consults his advisers because he impugns the Arameans' intention without the slightest trace of diplomatic delicacy.[88] Here the author mocks the impotence of royal authority, which points to conflict between prophets and monarchy.

Second Stage (vv. 8-14)

If we look into the second stage of the episode, we encounter two major characters – Naaman and the Elisha. We also find three minor characters – servants of Naaman and messenger of Naaman perhaps Gehazi or unnamed. We will see how these characters play important acts and how the literary features are developed negating the first stage of the story.

The story resumes in verse 8, and we see that Elisha initiates the action. The narrator assures us that Elisha is a man of God. Perhaps tension is built up here. Suddenly, the prophet, who has seemed somehow inaccessible to Naaman, intervenes in the impasse. Elisha thus sends a message chiding the king for his wrongheadedness.[89] Bergen finds that the Naaman story characterizes the power relationship between the king and the prophet,

84 Thomas L. Brodie, "Towards Unraveling the rhetorical Imitation of Sources in Acts: 2 Kings 5 as one Component of Acts 8:9-40," *Biblica* 67 (1986):41-67.

85 Moore, *God Saves*, 75.

86 See more detail comments in Cohn, *Form and Perspective*, 175.

87 The reaction of the king of Israel runs as, "that he sought an occasion (to trouble) with me."

88 See Long, *2 Kings*, 70.

89 This is noted by Long. See Long, *2 Kings*, 71.

that prophetic power is different from monarchic power as it controls an international confrontation.[90] One can assume that the king of Aram requested the king of Israel to guide Naaman to Elisha for healing. However, the present story seems designed to depict the prophetic breaking through the royal authority; the author shifts the emphasis from the cure to the source of the cure; not the king but the prophet holds sway. So he said, "let him come to me that he may know that there is a prophet." Here the young girl's word is recalled (cf. v.3). As elsewhere in the Elijah-Elisha story, the king of Israel is depicted as ineffectual and powerless.[91] The prophet issues orders to the king of Israel, not the reverse. The king now fades from the scene and the prophet control.[92] We can also observe the chiastic parallel between the note of tragedy of Naaman (v. 1) and the hope of healing for Naaman (v. 8). The scene is cut short with the absence of details about the action of Israelite king in relation to Elisha's words. Here we see (v. 9) Naaman's journey to Elisha's house with symbols of status 'horses an chariots.' The fact that Naaman was able to drive up in his chariot to the house of Elisha indicates either that Samaria under Omri and Ahab had been more spaciously laid out that the normal eastern city, or more probably, that Elisha lived either in an isolated house or in the proximity of the official quarters.[93] Like many other characters in the book of Kings, Naaman seems to believe that he has a responsibility to please Elisha as superior to him.[94] Therefore, he obeys by coming to Elisha's door to be healed.

The same pattern repeats in Elisha's next communication with Naaman (c. 10). Though Naaman stands at the door, Elisha sends a messenger to him announcing what he must do to be cured. Cohn argues that here, Elisha uses courtly behavior, summoning (v. 8) and communicating (v. 10) through an intermediary.[95] We may also observe the author's implicit contrast of impotent king (Naaman) and the confident prophet (Elisha) in this scene. The word of Elisha to wash seven times[96] in the river Jordan reflects the tradition of rites of purification.[97] It has also been suggested that the washing

---

90 See Bergen, "The Prophetic Alternative," 131.

91 See 1 Kings 21; 22; 2 Kings 1

92 This is the observation of Cohn. See "Form and Perspective," 176.

93 Gray, *I & II Kings*, 506.

94 Cf. 1 Kings 22:13; See also Iain W. Provan, *1 and 2 Kings – New International Biblical Commentary* (Peabody, Mass: Hendrickson Publishers, 1995), 192.

95 Cohn, "Form and Perspective," 176.

96 The same number of times the Shunamite woman's son sneezed before he finally began to breathe again. The number seven anticipates fulfillment or conveys he sense of successful completion in the biblical tradition. (Cf. Lev. 14:7; 16, 27, 51).

97 See Leviticus 14:1-9. Here we see rite of purification. It is sprinkling blood of slaughtered bird, dipped in water seven times upon the leprous.

for ritual cleansing in rivers such as the Jordan had its origin in the primitive worship of river gods in the ancient near east.[98] Nevertheless, this is denied by the fact that there is little parallel of the story with Naaman story.[99]

Naaman's protest or reaction is quite revealing (v.11). "I thought to me he would surely come out." The sentence shows a grammatical emphasis of infinitive absolute יצאיצוא, which signifies emphasis and reinforcement of the verb's mood as well as its action.[100] Not only this, the sentence shows emphasis from the anterior positioning of 'to me.' [101] Naaman's expectations are also observed: "he will call the name of Yahweh his God;" "he will waive his hand upon the place." The interpretation of 'the place' (המקום) is different and debatable.[102] For some commentators, using definite objects connotes the place where Naaman stands.[103] Whatever is the indication, the story tells that Naaman expects something dramatic, something visible, and something that was done to him rather than something he would have to do.[104]

In v. 12, Naaman expresses his indignation in a rhetorical question, repeating the predicates used by Elisha's messenger: "Could I not wash in them (the Aramean rivers) and be clean?" He cannot fathom how the puny Jordan waters of Israel can have curative powers superior to those of the mighty rivers of Damascus. According to Qere, Syriac, and Targum, the first of the two rivers Abanah is Amana.[105] This river is identified with the modern Barada River, which flows east from the anti-Lebanon mountain range to Damascus.[106] Mordecai Cogan also argues the correctness of the identification in the light of Assyrian writings and geographical

---

98 See discussion in W. Allan Smith, "Naaman and Elisha: Healing, Wholeness, and the task of religious education," *Religious Education* 89 (1994), 208.

99 Hobbs, *2 Kings*, 64.

100 See Allen P. Ross, *Introducing Biblical Hebrew* (Grand Rapids, Michigan: Baker Academic, 2001), 167. See also J. Weingreen, *A Practical Grammar for Classical Hebrew* (Oxford: Clarendon Press, 2nd Edition; 1959), 79.

101 Moore studies the rhetorical exposure of the literary feature, and argues that he (Naaman) is his (Elisha) superior and deserves the prophet's obeisance. See Moore, *God Saves*, 75.

102 For Kittel and others, it is the sanctuary where the prophet would invoke Yahweh. Some have argued that it would mean the disease was expected to be exorcised in some particular place. See Gray, *I & II Kings*, 506-507.

103 So, Sanda proposes that the use of definite article indicates that it is not the part affected by leprosy, but the place where Naaman was standing. Cited in Gray, *I & II Kings*, 506.

104 This is noted by Hens-Piazza, See *1 & 2 Kings*, 261.

105 See *BHS*, Regum 2:12 footnote. See also Mordecai Cogan and HayimTadmor, *II Kings Anchor Bible* (USA: Doubleday & Company, INC., 1988), 64.

106 Hobbs, *2 Kings*, 65.

investigation.[107] The river el-Auwaj, which is south of the city of Damascus, may be the Pharphar.[108] Naaman is quite convinced in his own mind that the rivers of Damascus rare much better than other rivers. Therefore, it would be possible to translate "Surely the rivers back in Damascus, the Abana and the Pharphar, are better than any river here in Israel. I could have been healed by washing in them."[109]

After Naaman's turning and storming away, his servants approach him with a rhetorical question of their own, 'If the prophet had enjoined you to do some great thing,' they ask, 'would you not be doing it, how much rather then when he says to you 'Wash and be clean?' (v.13). Provan analyzes the Hebrew meaning עַף כִּי־עָמַר (Has he really said?) as in Gen. 3:1; and suggests that the servants seek to undermine a false interpretation of Elisha's words.[110] However, this interpretation is unlikely as the servants (עבדים) called him 'father' אבי, which is an unusual address of a servant to his lord. Therefore, it may convey personal concern of Naaman's servants for their lord;[111] or it may be a persuasive voice.[112] The question beautifully penetrates to the heart of Naaman's hang up, which aimed at the reasonableness of Elisha's request. It is addressed in the opposite of Naaman's case that something small is easier to perform then something great. Thus, Moore comments: "This great man left Aram prepared to do something great, and if Elisha had asked him to do a great thing,

107 According to Cogan, review of the textual evidence and an inspection of the historical map of the Lebannon confirms the correctness of the identification (255).The river Baada, which flows from the Anti-Lebanon to water the whole of the Damascus plain (The Ghouta), is most certainly the river Amanah. It rises in the two heights, which are known as Mt. Amanah since the ancient times. Mt. Ammananu in the inscription of TiglathPilesar III is identical with Amanah. See Mordecai Cogan, "From the Peak of Amanah," *Israel Exploration Journal* 34 (1984): 255-259.

108 Modecai Cogan and HayimTadmor, *II Kings AB*, 64.

109 Translation proposed by Roger L. Omanson and John E. Ellington, *1-2 Kings* Volume 2 (New York: United Bible Societies, 2008), 810.

110 Provan, *1 and 2 Kings*, 195.A conjunction אַף is used more frequently in poetry to introduce emphasis, especially when introducing a new thought. It can be translated as 'indeed' 'even' 'really.' See *BDB*, 64.

111 This is suggested by Mordecai Cogan and HayimTadmor, See *II Kings AB*, 65.

112 Thus, Naaman's servants politely strike the target with a 'persuasive voice.' See Long, *2 Kings*, 73.

indeed his servants [113] are right, he would be doing it."[114] Like the young girl, the servants' words prompt Naaman to act and change the course of the story.

The words of his servants transformed Naaman's thinking, and he went down (ירד) to the Jordan River (v.14). The verb ירד (go down) expresses more than physical descent. Naaman is also descending from his attitude of superiority.[115] This demonstrates his humility and obedience to Elisha. It is significant that Naaman's comparison to a 'little girl/servant (נער קטן) immediately follows the observation that he has acted according to the word of the man of God. By bringing himself under the authority of the word of the man of God, he has made himself a servant (נער).[116] Cohn summarizes the healing process as:[117]

> The young maiden (נערהקטנה) initiates the action, which results in the figurative transformation of Naaman into a young boy (נער קטן). Moreover, he, who is now described as a young lad, was initially introduced in v.1 as a great/big man. Our last view of Naaman thus contrasts dramatically with the first view. On the way to a cure from leprosy, the great military hero has been forced into submission to the prophet whose reputation had lured him like a magnet but whose methods, conversely, repelled him. Yet as he heeded the wish of the Israelite maiden, so too, he yields to the urgings of his servants and "goes down" to the Jordan as Elisha instructed.

The healing of Naaman is found in 2 Kings 5:1-14; thus, there are two stages of development. It is arranged in a chiastic pattern from the problem (vv. 1-7) to the solution (vv. 8-14). Naaman gets his flesh restored after completing the pattern that began at the outset. One can observe that healing of Naaman is achieved with the lowly sources. A captain servant (captivated) girl, a woman (Naaman's wife), a prophet's servant, and servants of Naaman serve as instruments of healing.

---

113 For the meaning and significance of the term עבד see Schultz, Richard. "Servant/Slave," *New International Dictionary of the Old Testament and Exegesis* Vol. 4 edited by William A. Van Gemeren et.al (UK: Paternoster Press, 1996), 1183-1198.

114 Moore, *God Saves*, 76.

115 This is noted by Hobbs and Moore, See Hobbs, *2 Kings*, 65; Moore, *God Saves*, 76.

116 This is investigated by Moore, See *God Saves*, 76-77.

117 Cohn, "Forms and Perspective," 177.

Conclusion: The Hidden Subalterns are Dignified

The healing of Naaman found in 2 Kings 5:1-14, which is placed in the ninth century BCE, helps us to see the impressing and powerful characters of the marginalized people whose actions, however, are appended in a very clandestine manner. The prophetic role of Elisha in the story gives us a glimpse of socio-political conflicts in the period of king Jehoram of Israel. One could have a conclusion that the story of the healing of Naaman is purposefully crafted as a campaign against the hegemonic ideology of the elite - that is, both the Arameans and the monarchy that undermines the marginalized group of people like servants, slaves and women. We could make the following observations:

1) The Healing of Naaman was set during the reign of King Jehoram (Israel), during which the relationship between Israel and Aram was intricate. The narrative evidently critiques the oppressive nature of the Aramean power over Israel.
2) There was tension between monarchy and prophetism in Israel, and the healing of Naaman shows prophetic authority and power over monarchy. The fear and perplexity in the royal court may be translated into knowledge that 'there is a prophet in Israel.' The story illustrates that an attempt to establish the healing of Naaman through official channels is unsuccessful.
3) It was the courageous and thoughtful acts of the lowly –a captive girl, Naaman's wife, servant of Elisha, and the servants of Naaman that caused the healing of Naaman and a great transformation of a haughty warrior to a lowly servant.
4) A literary analysis of the text reveals that the healing narrative is carefully designed to demonstrate how the lofty (Naaman) becomes like a young boy, the exalted becomes the lowly, and the rivers of Assyria are inferior to river Jordan.
5) While dominant reading of the text often points to exaltation of Israelite monarchy over Assyrian counterpart or Elisha's miraculous healing power. The marginalized actors are missed out. However, a closure and truthful reading demonstrates that the Subalterns are the real actors in this healing process.

5

A Subaltern Reading of Mark 10:46-52

Sam Peedikayil Mathew

Introduction

The Bible comes alive in interaction with real life-situations. The text of the Bible produces many colours when it passes through the prism of varied contexts of contemporary times. Reading the Bible from the perspective of the subalterns, the most marginalized and oppressed communities, who constitute the majority of Christians in India, can bring forth fresh meaning to the Biblical texts. Therefore, this essay will attempt to read Mark 10:46-52 through the eyes of the subalterns, employing subaltern biblical hermeneutics. The first part will outline the methodology and method of subaltern biblical hermeneutics. The second part will delineate the literary and social contexts of the passage. The third part will bring out some insights from the passage through the lens of the subalterns.

Methodology and Method of Subaltern Biblical Hermeneutics[118]

The Bible's nature as a book of the subalterns, addressed to the common people of different times and places, and the contemporary subaltern context of India call for a subaltern reading of the Bible.[119]

118 This section draws on Sam Peedikayil Mathew, "Paradigm Shift in Indian Biblical Hermeneutics: Towards a Subaltern Biblical Hermeneutics", *Religion & Society* Vol. 68 (No.4, December 2023), 73-82.

119 See for details of the rationale for a subaltern reading, Mathew, "Paradigm Shift in Indian Biblical Hermeneutics," 73-74.

Methodology of Subaltern Biblical Hermeneutics

1. Spivakian Notion of 'Subaltern'

The Oxford English Dictionary defines a 'subaltern' as someone of inferior rank or status. For Ranajith Guha, 'subaltern' is a "name for general attribute of subordination in South Asian society whether this is expressed in terms of class, caste, age, gender and office or in any other way."[120] Guha classifies Indian population as 'elites' and 'subaltern' groups, which are further divided into three: 1) 'dominant foreign groups', 'dominant indigenous groups at the all India, regional and local levels', representing the elite; 2) the social groups and elements included in the terms "people"; and 3) "subaltern classes," representing the demographic difference between the total Indian population and all those whom we have described as the "elite."[121] Gayatri Chakravorty Spivak[122] criticizes Guha's essentialist construct of people as "identity-in-differential" and insists that "the colonized subaltern subject is irretrievably heterogeneous."[123] Although Spivak explains subalterns as "those removed from lines of social mobility," she states that the subalterns are not victims but agents.[124]

Against Fredric Jameson's definition of 'subalternity' as "the experience of inferiority," Spivak stresses the notion of "the subaltern inhabiting a space of difference."[125] She further says, "For the (gender-unspecified) "true" subaltern group, whose identity is its difference, there is no unrepresentable subaltern subject that can know and speak itself; the intellectual's solution is

---

120 Ranajith Guha, ed., *Subaltern Studies* Vol. I. (Delhi: Oxford University Press, 1982), vii. Italian Marxist thinker Antonio Gramsci was the first one to use the concept of 'subaltern social groups.'

121 Guha, *Subaltern Studies* I, 4, 8. See also Ranajith Guha, ed. *A Subaltern Studies Reader*. Minneapolis: University of Minneapolis Press, 1997.

122 Although Gayatri Chakravorty Spivak, a famous cultural and literary theorist, is considered one of the 'Postcolonial Trinity' along with two other theorists, Edward Said and Homi Bhabha, she rejects the label 'postcolonial' since, in her view, postcolonialism overemphasizes past forms of colonialism and is inadequate to criticize the impact of contemporary global economic domination of the economic agencies of the West on the economies and societies of the global South. See for details Stephen Morton, *Gayatri Chakravorty Spivak: Ethics, Subalternity and the Critique of Postcolonial Reason* (London: Polity Press, 2007), 2. Cited in V. T. Vinayaraj, *Theology After Spivak (*Delhi: ISPCK, 2016), 17, n.13.
Spivak, *A Critique of Postcolonial Reason,* 273.

123 Gayatri C. Spivak, *A Critique of Postcolonial Reason: Towards a History of the Vanishing Present* (Cambridge & London: Harvard University Press, 1999), 270-71.

124 Gayatri C. Spivak, *Other Asias* (Oxford: Blackwell, 2008), 22, 12-13.

125 Fredric Jameson, "Marx's Purloined Letter," *New Left Review* 209 (1994), 95. Cited in Spivak, *A Critique of Postcolonial Reason,* 271, n.118.

not to abstain from representation."[126] Spivak insists that, "simply by being postcolonial or the member of an ethnic minority, we are not 'subaltern'. That word is reserved for the sheer heterogeneity of decolonized space" and the idea of subalternity is a political position – a 'decolonized space' – which means 'without a place in the colonial scheme.'[127] Denying that the term subalternity is a synonym for 'oppressed' or any identitarian personality, because not all the oppressed are subalterns, Spivak understands subalternity as "a position without identity."[128]

2. Spivakian Theory of Subalternity

a) The unspeakability of the subaltern: Spivak argues against the *Subaltern Studies Collective* that there cannot be an 'essentialist subaltern subject' to speak against the colonial/postcolonial (native) representation. Spivak put forward the thesis that 'the subaltern cannot speak themselves'.[129] She argues that the voice of the subaltern cannot be heard because its language cannot be heard within the dominant discourse: "The subaltern cannot speak means even when the subaltern makes an effort to the death to speak, she is not able to be heard, and speaking and hearing makes the complete speech act."[130] Subaltern speech is nothing but the represented speech through which the elites speak for the subaltern. Therefore, according to Spivak, the real voice of the subaltern is cauterized. This phenomenon explains 'the unspeakability of the subaltern.'

Spivak further explains that the unspeakability of the subaltern and the non-audibility of the subaltern women are not a failure of articulation but the result of the failure of representation.[131] The subaltern speaks, but it cannot be heard. She argues that while the intellectuals claim that the subalterns can speak for themselves, they assume the position of 'proxy', and the voice of the 'true' subaltern remains *aporia*.[132] Spivak proposes "strategic use of positive essentialism in a scrupulously visible political interest," as subalternity is a political space of alterity and difference which has nothing

126 Spivak, *A Critique of Postcolonial Reason,* 272.

127 Spivak, *A Critique of Postcolonial Reason,* 310.

128 Gayatri C. Spivak, *An Aesthetic Education in the Era of Globalisation* (Cambridge/ Massachusetts/ London: Harvard University Press, 2012), 432; Spivak, *A Critique of Postcolonial Reason,* 310

129 Spivak, *A Critique of Postcolonial Reason,* 273.

130 Donna Landry and Gerald McLean, eds., *The Spivak Reader: Selected Works of Gayatri Chakravorty Spivak.* New York and London: Routledge, 1996), 292.

131 Spivak, *A Critique of Postcolonial Reason,* 72-74.

132 Gayatri C. Spivak, *In Other Worlds: Essays in Cultural Politics* (New York: Methuen, 1987), 205.

to do with identitarianism.[133] Thus, Spivakian theory of subalternity does not support any essentialism or identitarianism.

Spivak further clarifies, "If the subaltern can speak, ... then the subaltern is not a subaltern anymore."[134] As Landry and McLean explain, when Spivak says that the 'subaltern cannot speak' she means that the subaltern as such cannot be heard by the privileged. "If the subaltern were able to make herself heard... her status as a subaltern would be changed utterly; she would cease to be a subaltern. And this is the goal of the ethical relation Spivak is seeking and calling for – that the subaltern, the most oppressed and invisible constituencies, as such might cease to exist."[135] Spivak considers subalternity as a 'rhetorical space' that cuts across any essentialist position regarding caste, class, gender and geography. If the subaltern speaks, it is an echo,[136] a 'secrete' which is impossible for any gazing, cognition, or representation without deconstruction. Spivakian subalternity destabilizes the 'epistemic violence' of 'othering' of the subaltern, and it postpones the 'truth' of subalternity in order to rescue it from any representation or 'worlding' in history, culture, politics and theology.[137]

b) Marginality: Spivak's marginality notion further clarifies her subalternity idea. As in the case of subalternity, marginality signifies a 'rhetorical space' that denies its obligation to the centre. In the Spivakian understanding of marginality, the notion of centre crumbles and thus, the margin becomes a non-margin. Spivak theorizes a non-essentialist, heterogeneous and contestatory location of marginality that erupts at the centre. Marginality, just like subalternity, is an *aporetic* space of impossibility that cannot be represented or assimilated. Spivak argues that "when a cultural identity is thrust upon one because the centre wants an identifiable margin, claims for marginality assure validation from the centre."[138] Thus, for Spivak, marginality is not a fixed location that demands validation from the centre; instead, it is a deconstructive space that upholds its 'irreducible singularity' and alterity, which signals the ethical repositioning of oneself in relation to the 'other.'

---

133 Vinayaraj, *Theology After Spivak,* 16.

134 Gayatri C. Spivak, "The New Historicism: Political Commitment and the Postmodern Critic," in *The Postcolonial Critic: Interviews, Strategies, Dialogues*, edited by Sarah Harasym (London and New York: Routledge, 1990),158.

135 Landry and McLean, *The Spivak Reader,* 5-6.

136 According to Spivak, 'Echo' is an attempt to give women a space to deconstruct her out of the representation, however imperfectly. See Spivak, 'Echo,' in Landry and McLean, *The Spivak Reader,* 177.

137 Vinayaraj, *Theology After Spivak,* 17.

138 Spivak, *Other Asias,* 17.

c) Representation of the Other: Both Spivakian subalternity and marginality problematize the representation of the other and re-imagine it in terms of alterity and irreducible difference. When privileged people speak for the other, it, in fact, further cauterizes the Other. She questions the ability of the 'self' to empty itself to represent the Other. Alluding to Derrida, she challenges us to keep trying to learn from below. However, learning the Other without keeping the self-ego intact is impossible. In other words, unravelling the hegemonic system that constructs the Other and the self is complex. Drawing on Derrida, Spivak contends that learning from below requires *teleopoiesis*. For Derrida, *teleopoiesis* becomes the process of creating an ever-distant future. By adding the question of space, contrary to Derrida, Spivak defines it as the process of creating a distant future with a "distant other."[139] As William Simmons says, “It suggests that the gap between the ego and the Other will never be bridged. Awareness of this distance leads to humility and suspension of certainty.”[140]

d) Pedagogy of the Subaltern. Spivak considers the subaltern the teacher while speaking about the pedagogy of aesthetic education in a globalized era. This pedagogy has two dimensions: first, one must “learn to learn from below, from the subaltern, rather than study him (her)….”; second, one must “learn to unlearn one’s privileges.”[141] Spivak says, “Our privileges, whatever they may be in terms of race, class, nationality, gender and the like, may have prevented us from gaining a certain kind of Other knowledge.”[142] The purpose of learning from the subaltern is “to be able to devise a philosophy of education that will develop… “the habits of democratic behaviour” or “intuition of public sphere.”[143]

Learning to learn from below as pedagogy means living in a ‘radical imagination’ where the Other is revisited, and the sacred is detranscendentalized. It is to live in an ethical responsibility and a subject position of ‘quite-other’ - to live in the marginal space where the impossible subaltern unspeakable voices speak.[144] It is an apocalyptic space where the self, the Other, the community, and the tradition unveil themselves and touch the infinite – the radical transcendent – the radical Other. For Spivak, the bottom line of being human is radical alterity, “being-in-the ethical relation”, since “by definition we cannot – no self can – reach the

139 Vinayaraj, *Theology After Spivak,* 19.

140 William Paul Simmons, *Human Rights Law and the Marginalised Other* (New York: Cambridge University Press, 2011),142.

141 Spivak, *An Aesthetic Education* 439.

142 Landry and McLean, *The Spivak Reader,* 4.

143 Spivak, *An Aesthetic Education,* 439.

144 Vinayaraj, *Theology After Spivak,* 19.

"quite other."[145] Before the pedagogy of learning or listening, the challenge is whether it can supplement this gap between the self and the "quite other." This education challenges training in the imagination where the 'othering' and the 'worlding' of the 'colonized other' is moved towards an ethico-political responsibility without romanticizing the Other. "It is a kind of counter-pedagogy to educate the educator by learning to learn from below."[146]

Stephen Morton's observation on two main functions of Spivakian pedagogy of the subaltern in the case of human rights workers is instructive for the subaltern biblical interpreter also: 1) to foster a critical intelligence about the power structure that prevents the political participation of the subalterns in parliamentary democracy at a local and national level; 2) to recognize the ways in which dominant discourses are implicated in a relationship of ethical responsibility with the subaltern, which Spivak names 'subordinate cultures of responsibility.'[147] These 'subordinate cultures of responsibility' "provide the critical, cultural, linguistic, and ethical resources for the invention of a subaltern counter-public in which the asymmetrical power relations between subaltern and intellectual, educator and educated are radically reconfigured."[148]

For Spivak, the task of pedagogy of the subalterns involves "suturing the torn and weak responsibility-based system into a conception of human dignity as the enjoyment of human rights."[149] Since subalternity is a position without identity, Spivak stresses the need to "think of building infrastructure for the agency," meaning the effort to establish, implement, and monitor structures that allow subaltern resistance to be located and heard."[150] Thus, subaltern Biblical hermeneutics is an ethical-political practice.

Method of Subaltern Biblical Hermeneutics

Applying the hermeneutics of suspicion to texts that promote hegemony, subaltern reading interrogates the culture and politics of the ruling elites in light of the subalterns' resistance to domination.[151] It attempts to bring to

145 Spivak, "A Moral Dilemma", cited in Ritu Birla, 'Postcolonial Studies: Now That's History' Can the Subaltern Speak: Reflections on the History of an Idea, ed. Rosalind C. Morris (New York: Columbia University Press, 2010), 98.

146 Vinayaraj, *Theology After Spivak,* 24.

147 Stephen Morton, "Subalternity and Aesthetic Education in the Thought of Gayatri Chakravorty Spivak," *Parallax* 17 (No.3, 2011), 81; Spivak, *Other Asias,* 36-37.

148 Morton, "Subalternity and Aesthetic Education," 81.

149 Spivak, *Other Asias,* 51.

150 Gayatri C. Spivak, *An Aesthetic Education in the Era of Globalisation* (Cambridge/ Massachusetts/London: Harvard University Press, 2012) 439, 440.

151 See, for example, Guha, *Subaltern Studies* I, 5-7.

the forefront the hidden faces of the victims of domination and oppression by interrogating the public transcript of the dominant. Subaltern biblical hermeneutics employs critical tools such as hermeneutics of suspicion and reconstruction from the perspective of the subalterns, informed by socio-historical realities of the text and contexts within the methodological framework of Spivakian notion of 'subalternity.' Subaltern hermeneutics is a hermeneutics of resistance to hegemony and affirms the identity, dignity and agency of the most marginalized and the oppressed. The following guidelines are helpful in Indian subaltern biblical interpretations:

Identify the subalterns in the present context, the Biblical context, and the text.

Understand the condition of the subalterns in the light of the cultural and political hegemony in the text and its context using social scientific methods.

Listen to the subalterns in the text; locate and listen to their resistance.

Learn to learn from the subalterns.

Learn to unlearn one's privileges.

Listen to the self-representation of the subalterns in solidarity with them to represent their subjectivity, agency, and resistance.

Contexts of the Passage

1. Literary Context of the Passage: The episode of the Healing of a Visually Challenged Man (Mk. 10:46-52) is the last healing miracle Jesus performed before entering Jerusalem. It is placed between Jesus' criticism of the Gentile rulers in Mk: 10:42-45 and the entry of Jesus into Jerusalem in Mark 11. When there was a power struggle among the disciples, Jesus is depicted in Mk. 10:42-44 as vehemently criticizing the nature and practice of power by Roman rulers (referred to as 'Gentile rulers'). Jesus observes that the Gentile rulers "lord it over them" and "their great ones are tyrants over them" (Mk. 10:42). Jesus disapproves such understanding and exercise of power and does not want the disciples to follow that pattern of oppressive and hierarchical power. In Mk. 11:1-10 Jesus' entry into Jerusalem riding on a colt shows that his understanding of power differs from that of the Jewish liberation leaders, like the Maccabeans, who exhibited their power in pomp and glory, riding on horseback as war heroes. Thus, the immediate literary context of the passage seems to shed some light on Jesus' understanding of power and its

exercise among the most vulnerable sections of society, such as the visually challenged beggar in Mk. 10:46-52.

2. Social Context of the Passage: To understand the socio-cultural location of the visually challenged man, it is essential to locate him within the purity system of Judaism of Jesus' time. Purity is an integral part of a group's cultural system and organizing principle. "It provides a map or series of maps which diagram the group's cultural system and locate a place for everything and everything in its place."[152] Using Mary Douglas' anthropology, Neyrey has provided Jewish 'purity maps' for things, places, persons, and times. He quoted Mishnah and Tosefta, which classify and rank the people of Israel in the order of Holiness.[153]

Avoiding contact with what is either too holy or unclean or reinforcements of boundaries and purity concerns is the appropriate strategy in this type of world. People who continually have contact with sinners, lepers, blind, lame, menstruants, corpses and the like are seen as spurning the map of people. Those who show no respect for holy places, such as the Temple, disregard the map of places. People who disobey the Sabbath are crossing the dangerous lines on the map of times. All those who disregard the map of persons, places, things or times would be judged in some way as rejecting the system and would be rated as unclean, thereby becoming a source of pollution.[154] As Füssel has observed, the purity system of Judaism always strengthened the class system since the 'pure Jews' always belonged to the wealthy class.[155] The strictness required for ritual purity and pollution, the difficulty in complying with it and the danger of transferring ritual impurity led to the stratification of the Jewish society. The profusion of the purity laws and the difficulty in observing them led to the exclusion of many people.[156] John H. Elliott has summarised the situation created by the purity system: "According to the system of economic and social

152 J. H. Neyrey, "The Idea of Purity in Mark's Gospel," in *Semeia* 35, ed., John H. Elliot (Decatur, GA: Scholars Press, 1986), 93. Sam P Mathew, *Temple Criticism in Mark's Gospel: The Economic Role of the Jerusalem Temple in the First Century CE* (Delhi: ISPCK, 1999), 85.

153 See *M. Kelim* for places (1:6-9) and things listed in order of ascending Holiness; T. Megillah 2:7 rank persons and *M. Moed* for order of Holiness of time (Neyrey, "The Idea of Purity in Mark's Gospel," 95-96, 99).

154 *Ibid.*, 105. Mathew, *Temple Criticism in Mark's Gospel*, 86

155 K. Füssel, *Drei Tage mit Jesus im Tempel: Einfürung in die materalitische Lektüra der Bibel* (Münster: Editon Liberación, 1987), 34. Mathew, *Temple Criticism in Mark's Gospel*, 86

156 A. Oppenheimer, *The 'Am Haaretz: A Study of the Social History of the Jewish People in the Hellenistic-Roman Period* (Leiden: E. J. Brill, 1977), 18; Mathew, *Temple Criticism in Mark's Gospel*, 86 also J. Jeremias, *Jerusalem in the Time of Jesus: An Investigation*

stratification legitimized by purity classifications, the rich were ranked above the poor, the clergy above the laity, the urban dwellers (especially in Jerusalem) above the rural peasantry (especially in distant Galilee), men above women, married above unmarried, healthy above the ill, conformists above deviants."[157]

Those who were physically blind were not permitted to enter the Temple at Jerusalem. As J. Jeremias has pointed out, the Septuagint of II Sam. 5:8 adds to the proverb, "The blind and the lame shall not come into the house", the words, 'of the Lord.'[158] The blind who came to Jesus in Jerusalem did so in the court of the Gentiles (Mt. 21:14).[159] The blind is not allowed to make any offerings to the Lord (Lev. 21:18; 22:22). The Qumran documents that existed in Jesus' time also reflect the linking of blindness and purity concerns. These documents say that the blind and the deaf are not pure because they cannot hear or, see or observe the Law (4QMMT 56-57). Temple Scroll directs that the blind should be barred from the Temple and the holy city (11QTemple 45:12-14).[160] The social and religio-cultural implications of healing of the blind and the lame are evident in the prophetic literature where the healing of the blind, the deaf and the lame were used as a literary paradigm to announce the restoration of the people of God.[161] This would mean that the blind had a very low social, economic and religious status in the Jewish society stratified by the purity laws. It is no small wonder that most of the visually challenged people were driven to begging. Thus, the visually challenged person is clearly presented as a subaltern in the time of Jesus.

Reading Mk.10:46-52 from a Subaltern Perspective

The Encounter of the Visually Challenged Man with Jesus

Subalternity of the Visually Challenged Man:

The narrative begins with the Markan comment, "As Jesus and his disciples and a large crowd were leaving Jericho, Bartimaeus son of Tamaeus, a blind beggar was sitting by the roadside." (Mk. 10:46b) The marginal existence

---

into Economic and Social Conditions During the New Testament Period, translated by F. H. & C. H. Cave. London: SCM, 1969, 271-358.

157 J. H. Elliott, "Temple Versus Household in Luke-Acts: A Contrast in Social Institutions," in *The Social World of Luke-Acts: Models for Interpretation*, ed. J. H. Neyrey (Peabody, Massachusetts: Hendrikson, 1991), 222. Mathew, *Temple Criticism in Mark's Gospel*, 86

158 Jeremias, *Jerusalem in the Time of Jesus,* 117.

159 Jeremias, *Jerusalem in the Time of Jesus*, 118.

160 S. Guijarro, "Healing Stories and Medical Anthropology: A Reading of Mark 10:46-52," *Biblical Theology Bulletin* 30 (3, 2000), 109.

161 Guijarro, "Healing Stories and Medical Anthropology, 109.

of the visually challenged person as a dishonourable person is indicated by the fact that he was on the periphery of the city of Jericho ("were leaving Jericho"), "sitting on the roadside" and "begging", engaged in a shameful act. Jericho, the city of trade and commerce full of pilgrims and priests, did not help the impoverished and marginalized man in any way. It is noteworthy that only Mark mentions his name (see Mk. 10:46; cf. Mt. 20:29; Lk.18:35). The mention of his name as 'Bartimaeus' (*bar Timaeus* 'son of Timaeus' meaning 'son of honourable') and the dishonourable conditions of the man point to the religious and social stigma associated with this man. The mention of the father's name and family is intended to indicate that the family was affected by his situation and the inability of the family to bring healing to this blind man.[162]

When Jesus called the visually challenged beggar sitting on the roadside, he threw away his mantle - everything he had - and came to Jesus. What the rich man in the previous episode (Mk. 10:17-22) refused to do, i.e., parting with his riches, this impoverished man did. Material things or riches were not his priority. He wanted only to regain his sight. Till now, he was dependent on the charity of others. Now, he wants to be independent and stand on his legs. He threw away his economic crutches and wanted to be self-reliant and independent. Thus far, his livelihood has been earned at the mercy of others. His economic and physical dependence on others diminished his dignity and self-worth. Now, he wanted to regain his lost dignity, so he threw away whatever things were attached to a life without dignity.

It is noteworthy that the visually challenged man replied to Jesus' question, "I want to see again." It indicates that he had physical vision in the past and is now lost. Perhaps he lost his ability to see due to sickness, malnourishment or political oppression. Gauging eyes was a form of punishment in ancient times during Roman colonial rule. Though we are not sure about the exact reason for his condition of blindness now, it is clear that socio-economic and political reasons could have caused it. Thus, several indicators in the passage point to the fact that visually challenged people experience subalternity in the social, economic, and religious spheres.

Self-representation of the Subaltern Man

The visually challenged beggar was neglected by the politically influential religious leaders of his time. Since the southern district of Judea, under Roman imperial rule, was allowed to have its self-government under the leadership of the Sanhedrin headed by the High Priest, the religious leaders were also political rulers. The social historians of Palestine inform us that

162 Guijarro, "Healing Stories and Medical Anthropology, 109.

most priests in Jesus' time lived in Jericho. This man was on the Jericho road to Jerusalem. Despite the presence of many members of the priesthood and the ruling class, no one helped this man.

It is significant that he addressed Jesus as "Son of David" twice. The man was echoing the popular expectation of a political Messiah who would come in the Davidic line to liberate the Jews. Like any other Jew, he believed that there would be wholeness (*shalom*) in the Messianic time. More importantly, he identified Jesus as the expected Davidic Messiah, clearly a political ruler of Jews. This is clear in his first address, "Jesus, Son of David."

The impoverished man was expecting 'mercy' from Jesus and he cried out, "Have mercy on me." When the political and religious leadership of his time did not show any mercy, he begs Jesus for mercy. However, Jesus goes beyond showing mercy or charity and empowers this subaltern by asking, "What do you want me to do for you?" The politics of Jesus consists not only of doing acts of mercy but also of rendering justice to the most oppressed people by listening to the self-representation of the subaltern despite opposition from the powers that be. Thus, Jesus gave the most marginalized person an opportunity to represent himself and his dire need instead of representing the subaltern man.

Affirmation of Self-identity and Subjectivity

The visually challenged man was oppressed not only physically and economically, but also socially. He had physical blindness that affected him at some point in his life. He must have been already poor, and his disability made him further impoverished. All this made him a beggar, living solely at the mercy of others. Since he was visually handicapped, he was considered impure, according to the purity laws of Judaism, as we saw above. Mark seems to underline the class and race contrast between Bartimaeus's discipleship and the rich man's non-discipleship. As Ched Myers comments, "The rich man could not liquidate his fortune, but poor Bartimaeus throws away his garment, his sole element of his livelihood."[163] By throwing away his garment, which he used for begging, the man dared to discard the identity imposed on him and ventured to create his own new identity and affirm his subjectivity.

As we saw above, visually challenged persons were considered as outcasts who were beyond the pale of Jewish religion due to their inability to fulfil the requirements of the Law. Therefore, it is natural that they are rejected and despised by others. Their plight is further worsened by the

163 Ched Myers, *Binding the Strong Man: A Political Reading of Mark's Story of Jesus* (Mary Knoll, New York: Orbis Books, 1988), 252.

belief that the sins of the sufferers cause sicknesses and handicaps. This misconceived notion of associating sin and sickness made the sick and the suffering targets of ridicule and scorn by healthy and wealthy people. The social ostracism and oppression of the visually challenged man is evident in the way others silence the man. When he cried out for mercy from Jesus, "many sternly warned him to be quiet." The mainstream of Judaism and those who were close to Jesus tried to silence the cry of the blind beggar for mercy on the roadside. Nevertheless, the man refused to be silent, overcame his attempts to silence him, and shouted all the more. He rose above the rejection, ridicule, exclusion and oppression in society, especially by the religiously powerful people, by demonstrating his self-determination and requesting help from Jesus.

Although the impoverished, visually challenged man was very close to Jerusalem and Temple leadership, amid the pilgrims passing through the road of Jericho, which was only fifteen miles away from Jerusalem, he was outside the ambit of religion. The ordinary priests and the pilgrims heading to Jerusalem Temple did not have any mercy or genuine concern for the poor blind man on the roadside. The man was reduced to a recipient of occasional charity of some kind-hearted passerby.

The poor man begins by associating the widespread Davidic messianic expectation with Jesus. Gradually, he rises to the expected level of a disciple not only by acknowledging Jesus as his rabbi ("my teacher") but also by recognizing the central focus of Jesus' ministry (see Luke 4:18-19), namely "to give sight to the blind", and longing for receiving his sight. The sight that Jesus gives is physical sight but also spiritual and social, establishing a proper relationship with God and fellow humans.

Finally, he receives his sight and performs the ideal action of a disciple, namely, following Jesus "on the way." In the Markan redaction, special emphasis is placed on the healed man's following Jesus "on the way," since only Mark's Gospel mentions this (Mk. 10:56; cf. Mt. 20:34; Lk. 18:43). The healed man identified himself with the community established by Jesus, the people of the way, by following Jesus. He started his long journey with Jesus' borderless, broker-less, open and dynamic community of equals. Thus, he became an ideal disciple of Jesus. Indeed, it has long been noted that this passage is "a paradigmatic story of discipleship."[164] However, a subaltern reading of the episode shows that it is a paradigmatic story about the discipleship of a liberated subaltern.

---

164 Paul J. Achtemeier, "And He Followed Him: Miracles and Discipleship in Mk. 10:46-52", *Semeia*, 11(1978), 115–116.

The Response of Jesus to a Most Marginalised Person

Jesus' Use of Power: A New Praxis of Power

When the passage is read against the context of the previous episode that deals with the disciples' craving for power (Mk. 10:35-45), a new understanding of power in action could be seen here. Jesus' initial response to his two disciples (James and John) and to the blind beggar is the same: "What do you want me to do for you?" (Mk. 10:36,51). When the disciples asked for seats of power, Jesus gives a new interpretation of power. For Jesus, power lies not in dominating and oppressing others, but in serving others and giving oneself for others: "Son of Man came not to be served but to serve and to give his life as a ransom for many" (Mk. 10:45). In the episode that follows, Jesus presents himself at the service of a visually challenged beggar on the roadside – a most marginalized and impoverished person, by stopping by to listen to the subaltern, giving a visible demonstration of his power.

Unlike the rich and the powerful of society, who do what they want to do for those in the margins, Jesus asks the visually challenged man, "What do you want me to do for you?" subverting the way power is usually exercised. Instead of imposing his ideas and views about the needs of the most impoverished and marginalized man, Jesus asks him what he wants, making a sincere attempt to understand the needs and aspirations of this subaltern. Here, Jesus tries to get into the real world of the subaltern man. Jesus wants to see the main problem of the impoverished man through the eyes of the most oppressed, prioritizing his dire need as he sees it. In other words, Jesus problematizes the problem of the subaltern from the perspective of the subalterns.

Jesus' Understanding of Power: A New Epistemology of Power – Learning to Unlearn One's Power

In this passage, as in most other cases in the Gospels, we find Jesus venturing into the periphery, to those living on the margins – to villages, seashores and the fields in the small townships. In Jericho, a centre of trade and commerce and where pilgrims and priests passed through, Jesus focused on the most vulnerable and marginalized among them, those who struggle for survival. Whereas the focus of attention of the political and religious elite was on the centres of power and those who wield power and influence, Jesus' attention in this episode is directed to the most powerless and the vulnerable, just as the main focus of Jesus' mission practice in the Gospels is among the subalterns.

In contrast to the disciples around Jesus, who tried to shout the poor man down and silence him, Jesus stops and listens to the distress call of the subaltern on the roadside. In the hustle and bustle of the traders, pilgrims and priests in the great crowd, Jesus was sensitive to the cry of a subaltern in dire need. Jesus not only heard his cry but also stopped by and called him. Jesus seems to understand power as the ability to listen to the cries of those in distress and pain. Such a perception was a counter-cultural understanding of power since the rich and the powerful often not only ignored the distress calls of the impoverished and the most marginalized but also suppressed and silenced them through their henchmen. This is because "lording over" others involves silencing the voices of the oppressed and the exploitation of society through brute force, as mentioned in the previous passage. Jesus begins to unlearn his power and privilege as the therapeutic conquering Davidic Messiah[165] and locates the power to heal in the faith of the subaltern man.

Jesus' Method of Liberation: Listening and Learning to Learn from the Subaltern

Through listening to the cry of the visually challenged man and calling him, Jesus affirms the personhood and importance of the marginalized man. In a context in which the subaltern man was utterly neglected and despised, Jesus sent the signal that the impoverished beggar on the roadside is essential and deserves attention. This act of Jesus must have increased the self-worth of the dejected and the distressed beggar. By lending listening ears to the silenced one in distress, Jesus makes the first positive response to the initiative of the impoverished man in his longing for a dignified identity and life.

Jesus affirms the dignity and identity of the visually challenged beggar by trying to learn from the subaltern what he wished: "what do you want me to do for you?" Though he cried out for mercy twice, Jesus' question helps him precisely articulate his request. By doing this, Jesus communicated to him that clear articulation of his views and aspirations or self-representation is essential. He respected the needs of the man in distress. Instead of treating his problem superficially, Jesus enables him to go into the root or source of his situation, namely begging and blindness and encourages him to seek remedy from the root problem of social exclusion and shame.[166] Whereas the

165 Numerous traditions depict David's son Solomon as a miracle-worker and exorcist with control over demonic activity. [Wisdom of Solomon 7:17-22; Josephus, *Ant.* 8.45-49; esp. Testament of Solomon. See D. C. Duling, "Solomon, Exorcism, and the Son of David,' *HTR* 68 (1975), 235-52; D. C. Duling, "The Therapeutic Son of David', *NTS* 24 (1978), 392-410] [Warren Carter, "Matthean Christology in Roman Imperial Key: Matthew 1:1", in *The Gospel of Matthew in Its Roman Imperial Context*, eds. John K. Riches and David C. Sim (London & New York: T & T Clark International, 2005), 162, n.69)]

166 Guijarro, "Healing Stories and Medical Anthropology", 110.

purity system of Judaism excluded the blind and sick, Jesus' strategy was to erase all signs of exclusion and strive for their inclusion.[167] Thus, Jesus becomes a catalyst who empowers the subaltern man to come out of his socio-economic and religo-political exclusion and shame by representing himself.

Jesus accepted the Christological address, "Son of David," repeated twice by the suffering man. This indicates that Jesus recognized the poor man's theological resources. However, by attributing the healing to the faith of the visually challenged man ["your faith has made you well" (Mk. 10:52)], Jesus appreciates his religious resources and gifts as well.

Instead of attributing the restoration of sight of the visually challenged man to Jesus' power, Jesus surprises everyone by saying that the man's faith made him well. It has been observed that this pericope is narrated from the perspective of the beggar in such a way that the central focus is not Jesus but Bartimaeus and his faith, although Jesus' name is mentioned six times: "Die Perikope von Anfang an so erzält, daβ Bartimäus und seine Glaube – nicht Jesus – im Mittelpunkt steht, obvohl dessen Name sechsmal vorkommt, wie sie auch perspektivisch vom Standpunkt des Bettlers aus berichtet."[168] By putting the subaltern and his faith in the centre, Jesus is presented as learning to unlearn his privileges as the healing Davidic Messiah.

Jesus subverts once again the dominant understanding of the source and direction of power, i.e., power flows from top to bottom – from the Davidic Messiah to the subaltern. Jesus asserts that the power of faith lies among the subalterns, and such faith of the excluded ones can bring wholeness or well-being. Jesus seems to bring out the innate power of faith in God vested in every human being to bring physical and social healing to oneself - to those suffering and excluded. The marginalized man was led to realize his full potential. Thus, Jesus exposed the source of power and the resource of faith in the subaltern. Jesus accepted and commended the power in the agency of a subaltern on the street who was considered as 'powerless' in a position without identity by forging a relationship of ethical responsibility with the subaltern.

Jesus Enables the Margins to Erupt at the centre

It is significant to note that the site of the healing of a subaltern is on the "roadside." The liberating activity takes place in the very place where the subaltern suffered, right in front of the people who discriminated and despised him. It is a wonder that the healed man decided to remain "on the

---

167 Guijarro, "Healing Stories and Medical Anthropology, 110-11.

168 J. Gnilka, *Das Evnagelium Nach Markus (Mk 8,27-16,20)*, EKK II/2 (Düsseldorf: Benziger/ Neukirchner, 1994), 109.

way" following Jesus. Jesus enabled him to liberate himself and become a catalyst of liberation, following Jesus' method of liberation. Jesus' way of liberation enabled and empowered the 'powerless' man to affirm his dignity and personhood and to discover his resources and potential, leading to the fullness of life. Thus, the gaining of sight of one of the most marginalized visually challenged men and his joining the liberation movement of Jesus shows that the margins are demolished and erupted at the centre. Since the subaltern man's voice is heard and his agency and subjectivity are affirmed through his healing, fostering full participation in the movement of Jesus, he ceases to exist as a subaltern.

Conclusion

To sum up, our reading of Mark 10:46-52 from the perspective of the subalterns shows that this episode is a paradigmatic story of the liberation struggle of the subalterns of society. It reinforces the point that the subalterns need to throw away the mantle of victimhood and play an active role as agents not only in initiating their liberation but also in remaining steadfast in persisting with the liberation struggle amid adversities in order to become independent, affirming their agency, dignity and self-worth. There is an urgent need to join forces with the catalysts of liberation who toil hard for the liberation of the subalterns and work out a synergy with them to achieve social inclusion and wholeness. An effective liberation of the subalterns is possible only when they represent their problems and propose solutions with their resources, inherent power and faith. This calls for a re-imagination of how power is understood and practised by adopting the pedagogy of the subaltern - learning to learn from the subaltern and learning to unlearn one's privileges. The final goal of the liberation of the subalterns is not only the liberation of subalterns from the forces of physical and social oppression but also joining the new caste-less, class-less community to form liberated communities where the subalterns cease to exist, and the margins erupt at the centre.

6

Reading the Scripture in 'Groaning'
A Contextual Biblical Hermeneutic in India Today

Johnson Thomaskutty

Introduction

There is a reversed defensive mechanism that develops when the majority community of India defends its nationalistic voice and the minority communities defend their faith and ethos in groaning. The Hindu nationalism in India is defensive to the Bible mission. A defensive hermeneutic is embedded in the day-to-day affairs of the Christians against the Hindu nationalistic forces. This study has a double benefit: first, it helps us to understand the popular perception of the Bible and the reason for the hostility toward the Bible mission; and second, it sheds light on how Christians use hermeneutical tools to negotiate their existence in the hostile society. A missional mechanism developed by the Christian communities in India that takes into account the existent Hindu nationalism and the resultant minority struggles. In such a context, the churches and the Christian communities develop a hermeneutic in groaning. It is important to consider the ordinary, local, contextual, and dynamic day-to-day faith reactions of the Bible readers. As a voiceless community, the followers of Jesus look at issues, understand their existence, reflect upon their faith realities, and respond to social and national issues through the lens of the Bible. The prism of the Bible enables them to keep the faith alive within themselves, identify themselves with the faith communities inscribed within the scripture, control their emotions, and express their sentiments as per the demands. A reader of the scripture embraces the down to earth realities where human existential stories are unfolded with an emphasis on oral and folkloric aspects. As a reader identifies her/himself with the biblical characters in times of struggle, the biblical settings, characterization, themes, plot developments, focalization, dialogues, monologues, and other literary and hermeneutical dynamisms become their own.

Submerging her/himself into the Biblical story-world, the reader develops ordinary hermeneutics that reiterates a hermeneutic of groaning, lament, and biblical accommodation. In such contexts, a reader of the Bible responds as follows: first, the majority and minority conflicts emerged with a political agenda alerts the reader to keep a safe balance between the threatening majority voice and the existent minority ethos and pathos; second, when the communal and fundamentalist agenda of the majority group flourishes, the minority Christians employ a hermeneutic of groaning;[169] Third, in the context of persecution and marginalization, readers seek texts of perseverance, and fourth, common readers replace transcendentalism with a hermeneutic of normalcy and ordinariness. The response of the reader is defensive as s/he chooses methods as per the demands of the time and space.

I congratulate my senior colleague in UTC, Rev. Dr. Kondasingu Jesurathnam, who celebrates his sixtieth birthday this year. After referring his academic works, especially on Old Testament theology, Dalit Biblical Hermeneutics, and Contextual Biblical Interpretation, I could see his groaning heart as a member of the minority religious community, as a prophet of Dalit liberation, and a scholarly interpreter of the Scripture with a keen interest of the realities of the people groups in India. Dr. Jesurathnam reveals his groaning heart not only through his theological writings but also through his involvements in the class lectures, chapel worship services and sermons, academic engagements, and various other ecclesial and social activities. His groaning heart, coupled with his prophetic imagination, enabled him to brainstorm, conceptualize, and foreground the ground realities of the suffering and the marginalized communities in India. By keeping Dr. Jesurathnam's hermeneutical model in mind, let us read the following paragraphs and sections.

Necessity for a Hermeneutic of Groaning

A hermeneutic of groaning is a silent but powerful responsive cry of the oppressed in the midst of subjugation and dehumanization. In India, the

169 We see a difference between the words such as 'lament' and 'groaning': while a 'lament' is a more organized internal voice, a 'groaning' is an unorganized voice created within a reader in the context of suffering and pathos. An unorganized 'groaning' can be developed into an organized 'lament.'

emerging Hindu nationalism with its new agenda suppresses the minority voices with a claim that Christianity and Islam are foreign religions and external forces in the country. Frykenberg comments that the term 'anti-national' has been used "to implicate Indian Christians as being alien, anti-national, and unpatriotic, or subject to forces from outside of India."[170] This impression about the Christian community is widely propagated irrespective of the long-standing and historical connections and associations of the community within the nation. The foreign relationships and invasions provided a fertile ground for the Bible to be connected to the Indian realities and the thought-world.[171] The foreign Bible societies did their best to translate the Bible into various dialects of the country.[172] The new political scenario of the country attempts to interpret Christians as 'anti-nationals,' Christianity as a 'foreign religion,' and the Bible as a 'foreign [religious] book.' It affected the pervasive and active involvement of Christianity in various sectors of society.[173] Though Bible is reckoned as a 'Holy' book, as in the case of Indian religious scriptures, it was often treated as an alien scripture. In Christian mission schools/colleges, medical institutions, charity homes/ organizations, and other places, Bible lessons are taught to inculcate the ethics and values of the scripture irrespective of people's caste, class, religion, race, gender and other human-made boundaries. Moreover, as the Bible is freely distributed by several ecclesiastical and mission organizations, the message of the Bible is accessible to the general public. Thus, the anti-Christian attitude from the Hindu nationalists, the Christian heritage in the country, and the accessibility of the Bible among the masses provide a new platform for interpreting the Christian scriptures with new eyes.

The Hindu nationalistic movements like Rastriya Swayamsevak Sangh (RSS), Vishwa Hindu Parishad (VHP) and others claim that 'India is a Hindu nation.'[174] Over against the secularism propagated by the Indian

---

170 Robert Eric Frykenberg and Alaine Low, eds., *Christians and Missionaries in India: Cross-Cultural Communication since 1500: With Special Reference to Caste, Conversion, and Colonialism*, Studies in the History of Christian Missions (Grand Rapids: Eerdmans, 2003), 7-8; quoted in Manohar James, *Religious Conversion in India* (Eugene: Wipf & Stock, 2022), 15.

171 Louis Jacolliot, *The Bible in India: Hindoo Origin of Hebrew and Christian Revelation* (New York: Carleton, Publisher, 1870), 15-18.

172 See J. S. M. Hooper and W. J. Culshaw, *Bible Translation in India, Pakistan and Ceylon* (Oxford: Oxford University Press, 1963).

173 Abraham Vazhayil Thomas, *Christians in Secular India* (Rutherford: Fairleigh Dickinson University Press, 1974), 89-99.

174 Mohan Bhagwat, "All People Living in India are Hindus," *The Indian Express* (28 November 2022), see https://indianexpress.com/article/india/all-people-living-in-india-

constitution, the Hindu nationalists popularize the *Hindutva* ideology to get support from the masses. The Hindu nationalism, the ideology of *Hindutva*, the Sangh Parivar and the politics and policies under the current regime foster a new socio-political profile in the Indian context.[175] Today religion is treated as politics and a politics of religion is at the core of human realities.[176] This is the context in which the minority religious communities are persecuted, their voices are suppressed, and their freedom is curtailed.[177] Christian participation in nation-building through educational, medical, and charity missions is threatened by the so-called nationalistic movements.[178] The irony is that Indian Christianity is nationalistic in its very nature and presence, as it is rooted in the ethos and ethics of the nation of India. Christianity in India has its own peculiarities as a nationalistic religion in comparison to other Christian communities in different parts of the world. Tracing the history of Christianity in India back to the Apostle Thomas, affirming its roots in the cultural, contextual, and conceptual framework of India, and developing a distinct mode of faith and praxis in closer affinity with the Indian religions, Indian Christianity is nationalistic in its conceptual and ideological framework.[179] This is the very soil in which an Indian interpretation of the Bible was/is widely practiced by the Indian Christian theologians and the Indian church.[180]

Historically, Christianity is very much part of India, has contributed much to the development of the nation, and is nationalistic in its outlook. However, the Hindu nationalistic movements often treat Christians as

---

are-hindus-mohan-bhagwat-8294874/, accessed on 3 May 2023.

175 Christophe Jaffrelot, *Modi's India: Hindu Nationalism and the Rise of Ethnic Democracy* (Princeton: Princeton University Press, 2021), 7-30.

176 Suhas Palshikar, "Toward Hegemony: The BJP Beyond Electoral Dominance," *Majoritarian State: How Hindu Nationalism is Changing India*, eds. Angana P. Chatterji, Thomas Blom Hansen, and Christophe Jaffrelot (New York: Oxford University Press, 2019), 101-116.

177 Johnson Thomaskutty, "Reading John's Gospel as a Jewish-Christian Conflict Narrative: A Paradigm for Contemporary India," *Religious Freedom and Conversion in India*, eds. Aruthuckal Varughese John, Atola Longkumer, and Nigel Ajay Kumar (Bengaluru: SAIACS Press, 2017), 139-161.

178 See M. M. Thomas, *Christian Participation in Nation Building: The Summing Up of a Corporate Study on Rapid Social Change* (Bengaluru: NCCI/CISRS, 1960).

179 For more details, see Chad M. Bauman and Richard Fox Young, eds., *Constructing Indian Christianities: Culture, Conversion and Caste* (London/New York/New Delhi: Routledge, 2014).

180 See Augustine Thottakara, ed., *Indian Interpretation of the Bible: Festschrift in Honour of Joseph Pathrapankal* (Bengaluru: Dharmaram Publications, 2000).

strangers in the nation.[181] The contributions of Christianity through educational, healthcare, and charity involvements, societal engagements, and participation in nation-building are ignored by the majoritarian nationalists to suppress the voice of Christ's followers.[182] This movement against minorities and, especially against Christianity is aggressive in the contemporary socio-political scenario. It is the very context in which the Christian community in India develops a hermeneutic of groaning. A hermeneutic of groaning is derived from the oppressive situation of Christ's followers and the Bible readers. The word 'groaning' can mean 'a low, deep sound that continued for a while and that emerges in someone who is suffering from pain or unhappiness' or 'a complaining noise or phrase.'[183] These expressions can amply demonstrate the current situation of the Christian communities in India. They are denied the freedom that was constitutionally provided to them, and now they are in a voiceless situation. This is the critical juncture in which the minority voice of the Christian communities develops in the form of deep groanings.

The expression 'groaning' and its derivatives are widely used in the Bible in the sense that it is a pain that goes beyond mere physical pain. In Exo 2:23, it is stated that the children of Israel (Jacob) groaned and sighed because of the bondage (also see Exo 6:5; Psa 5:1; 6:6; 12:5; 22:1; 31:10; 32:3; 38:9; 79:11; 102:5, 20; Lam 1:4, 21; Eze 7:16; Mark 8:12; John 11:38; Acts 7:34; Rom 8:22; Heb 13:17).[184] Groaning is an inner cry of people [or non-human beings and the creation] due to the rising societal evils. In a majority-minority, powerful-powerless, elite-poor, and higher-lower hierarchical structure, the underprivileged are marginalized, and their voice is suppressed. Though they have their own voice, the system does not allow people to raise their voice. The only way is to suppress their anger, voice, and frustration at their own deeper levels. The word for groaning in Hebrew is *'anāḥāh* from the root word *'ānaḥ* which is a sigh, a sigh of mourning. Renn states that "The 'groaning' of God's people in exile after the destruction of Jerusalem is indicated in Lam 1:4-6; signifying their 'anguish.'"[185] In

181 Rebecca Samuel Shaw, "Saving the Soul of India: Christian Conversion and the Rise of Hindu Nationalism," *Christianity in India: Conversion, Community Development, and Religious Freedom*, eds. Rebecca Samuel Shaw and Joel Carpenter (Minneapolis: Fortress Press, 2018), 3-22.

182 Asghar Ali Engineer, ed., *They Too Fought for India's Freedom: The Role of Minorities* (Gurgaon: Hope India, 2005), 194-210.

183 A. S. Hornby, *Oxford Advanced Learner's Dictionary of Current English* (New York: Oxford University Press, 2000), 566-567.

184 Stephen D. Renn, ed., *Expository Dictionary of Bible Words* (Peabody: Hendrickson Press, 2005), 454.

185 Renn, ed., *Expository Dictionary of Bible Words*, 454.

that sense, the expression indicates a pressure and a screaming deep within, but no one hears that screaming except God. The Greek verb *stenadzō* is roughly an equivalent to the Hebrew terms expressed above (cf. Mark 7:34; Rom 8:23; 2 Cor 5:2, 4). While *anastenadzō* is a rare variant of *stenadzō* denoting the 'deep sighing' of Jesus (Mark 8:12), another variant *systenadzō* refers to creation 'groaning' like a woman in labor (Rom 8:22).[186] Another variant *stenagmos* indicates 'groaning' of the Israelites during their bondage in Egypt (Acts 7:34) and 'groaning' of the Holy Spirit within the believers (Rom 8:26). The Biblical authors through various derivatives denote it as a deep, emotional, and painful cry of human/non-human beings or the creation due to the dehumanizing and ostracized situations around.

In antagonistic contexts, Bible engagement enables a reader to develop a reverse defensive mechanism. The powerless and suppressed voices of the Indian Christians can be empowered by the power dynamics of the scripture.[187] A reader can submerge her/himself into the story-world and the ideological framework of the text to be empowered from deep within. The cravings of the heart are the starting point of hermeneutical and theological interplay in a haphazard situation. The Book of Exodus delineates the divine engagement in the life of the people of God. God utters to Moses: "I have indeed seen the misery of my people in Egypt. I have heard them crying out because of their slave masters, and I am concerned about their suffering. So, I have come down to rescue them from the land of the Egyptians and to bring them up out of that land into a good and spacious land, a land flowing with milk and honey" (3:7-8a).[188] Here, the God of Israel addresses the groanings of the people in an imperial hegemonic context. Similarly, the Nazareth Manifesto of Jesus in the Gospel of Luke outlines a groaning situation of the people. Jesus proclaims to them: "The Spirit of the Lord is on me, because he has anointed me to preach good news to the poor. He has sent me to proclaim freedom for the prisoners and recovery of sight for the blind, to release the oppressed, to proclaim the year of the Lord's favor" (Luke 4:18-19).[189] In the above texts, the groanings of the people frame a context for divine intervention. A hermeneutic of groaning emerges when people of God are left with complete hopelessness and despair in the world. Identifying the heart language of the people of God is the starting point

186 Renn, ed., *Expository Dictionary of Bible Words*, 454.

187 For more details, see Elisabeth Schüssler Fiorenza, *The Power of the Word: Scripture and the Rhetoric of Empire* (Minneapolis: Fortress Press, 2007), 7.

188 John F. Craghan, "Exodus," *The International Bible Commentary*, ed. William R. Farmer (Bangalore: Theological Publications in India, 1998), 465-466.

189 Filip Noël, "Luke," *The International Bible Commentary*, ed. William R. Farmer (Bangalore: Theological Publications in India, 1998), 1456-1457.

of a hermeneutic of groaning. A contemporary reader can look back to the text and accommodate the implied and suppressed voices as her/his own. Thus, a paradigmatic and specified reading of the text is at the core of this hermeneutical strategy.

A hermeneutic of groaning is a powerful tool to instill the persecuted and the ostracized in times of dehumanization, threatening dominant voices, and marginalization. The following things are suggestive when someone frames a hermeneutic of groaning: first, the minority communities can engage into the Biblical story-world and articulate new voices based on the 'in front of the text' realities;[190] Second, in the process of engagement, a reader identifies paradigmatic stories and concepts within the textual horizon to idealize the contemporary struggles;[191] Third, while engaging the scripture, a reader first of all comfort her/himself and then articulate the resilient groanings as silent but communicative voices to strengthen all others; and fourth, paradigmatic figures in the Biblical story-world can be identified as they develop their strugglesome situations to transformative movements.[192] A hermeneutic of groaning is framed out of a reader's dynamic engagement with the scripture to identify suppressed voices within the story world and align them with her/his contextual realities. A rhetoric of resilience is part and parcel of a hermeneutic of groaning.

Bible Engagement and Its Wider Impact

In India, Bible engagement is practised both in the public and private spheres of human life. As the hard copies of the Bible are widely available in public through the ecclesiastical authorities and the mission organizations and the soft copies are accessible through the internet, it has a readership beyond the Christian circles. Hindu intellectuals like Arun Shourie and RSS leaders like Mohan Bhagwat engage with the Bible from a *Hindutva* perspective. Shourie argues that "it [the Bible] had been collected through four centuries after Christ with the intention of helping conversion."[193] Shourie and others from the recent Hindu nationalistic movement level their criticisms toward the Bible not as "objective reports but as propaganda" and they drew attention

190 Johnson Thomaskutty, "A Polyvalent Hermeneutic of John 2:13-25: Theoretical and Exegetical Considerations," *HTS Theological Studies* 79/1, a8157, 3-4.

191 Thomaskutty, "A Polyvalent Hermeneutic of John 2:13-25," 3-4.

192 A "behind," "in," and "in front of" the textual and hermeneutical dynamism is at the centre of a hermeneutic of groaning.

193 See https://www.indiatoday.in/magazine/society-and-the-arts/books/story/20000117-book-review-of-arun-shourie-harvesting-our-souls-776921-2000-01-16, accessed on 5 May 2023.

to the problem of the historicity of Jesus Christ.[194] As a response, Vishal Mangalwadi critiques Shourie, stating that "Mr. Shourie was right in seeing the Bible as the most dangerous intellectual challenge to Hindutva."[195] On the other hand, there are several positive interpretations of the Bible by other figures in history. A brief account of some of the Christian and non-Christian figures and their engagement with the Bible are outlined hereafter.

Bible translation was one of the significant initiatives during the Protestant Missions in India that facilitated the transmission of the texts in the vernacular dialects: the Tranquebar Mission translated the Bible in Tamil; the Serampore Mission under William Carey translated it into twenty-nine languages either in full or in fragments; the Basel Mission involved in the task of translating the scripture into Kannada and Tulu; Hermann Gundert and Benjamin Bailey translated it into Malayalam; and the like.[196] Bartholomäus Ziegenbalg (1682-1719) and his colleagues initiated a mission theology that prioritized a life-affirming, people-oriented, and faith-centered interpretation of the scripture.[197] For Ziegenbalg and his colleagues, "[T]he Bible was always at the center of their lessons, though the missionaries also taught literacy, rhetoric, medicine, geography, and several other subjects."[198] Their engagement with the scripture and with the Indian contextual realities enabled them to be groaning in their hearts. Out of their groaning hearts, they facilitated the translation of the scripture and interpretation of the text into the 'in front' realities and inspired the people to develop groaning hearts within themselves. William Carey (1761-1843), as a Baptist Missionary to the Bengali context, learned the truths of the scripture with a committed heart, realized the social taboos such as Sati, child marriage, female infanticide, poverty, human struggles, and translated the scripture in vernacular styles.[199] Reading the scripture and understanding the life realities of the people of Bengal and vice versa enabled him to groan

---

194 Sebastian C. H. Kim, "Hindutva, World Evangelization and the Question of Conversion in India," *News of Boundless Riches: Interrogating, Comparing, and Reconstructing Mission in a Global Era*, Vol 1, eds. Mack L. Stackhouse and Lalsangkima Pachuau (New Delhi: ISPCK/UTC/CTI, 2007), 167.

195 Vishal Mangalwadi, *The Book that Made Your World: How the Bible Created the Soul of the Western Civilization* (Nashville: Thomas Nelson, 2011), 157.

196 M. Stephen, *A New Mission Agenda: Dialogue, Diakonia, and Discipling* (Delhi: ISPCK, 2007), 71.

197 See David Bosch, *Transforming Mission: Paradigm Shifts in Theology of Mission*, Twentieth Anniversary Edition (Maryknoll: Orbis Press, 1970/2011), 259-261.

198 Katharine Gerbner, *Christian Slavery: Conversion and Race in the Protestant Atlantic World* (Philadelphia: University of Pennsylvania Press, 2018), 144.

199 Johnson Thomaskutty, *The Gospel of John: A Universalistic Reading*, Biblical Hermeneutics Rediscovered 25 (New Delhi: CWI, 2020), 20-24.

deep within and take steps to translate the scripture into people's language.[200] Bible engagement motivated him to groan within himself and get involved in social works to urge the government to outlaw practices such as sati and child marriage.[201]

Raja Ram Mohan Roy (1772-1833) was a Hindu reform leader and a social activist. In his 1820 work entitled *The Precepts of Jesus: The Guide to Peace and Happiness*, he placed the four gospels alongside the *Upanishads*.[202] It was published anonymously; no author's name was printed in the book.[203] His primary intention with his booklet on the Gospel was to give his compatriots, both Hindus and Muslims, an idea of the teaching of Jesus.[204] To underscore that intention, the English text had to be accompanied by translations in Sanskrit, the holy language of the priests, and Bengali, the language of the people.[205] Schouten comments that,

> It is personal, congenial work, and we can clearly see what Ram Mohan Roy is doing. In order to persevere in life, he begins, a person needs two things. First, there is the understanding that there is a Creator and Preserver of the universe. That belief in God is passed on and taught to us, and we can also discover this by carefully studying the miracles of nature. The second thing that people need is the law, which teaches us to treat others as we ourselves would like to be treated. Ram Mohan writes that the law is partially present in all religions but principally taught by Christianity.[206]

As a Hindu reform leader, Ram Mohan Roy placed Jesus as a guru and Sermon on the Mount as an apex level of teaching for social transformation. He blended the message of Jesus with the Hindu teachings and derived a new way forward for morality in the Indian context.[207] The groanings of the Indian masses during a context of sati, female infanticide, colonialism, poverty and oppression is well represented in his hermeneutic of groaning. By hiding his identity in the masterpiece, he was trying to make the voice as

200 Thomaskutty, *The Gospel of John: A Universalistic Reading*, 15-36.

201 https://www.britannica.com/biography/William-Carey, accessed on 5 May 2023.

202 For more details, see Raja Ram Mohan Roy, *The Precepts of Jesus: The Guide to Peace and Happiness* (San Francisco: BiblioLife, 2008).

203 Jan Peter Schouten, *Jesus as Guru: The Image of Christ among Hindus and Christians in India* (New York/Amsterdam: Rodopi, 2008), 14.

204 Schouten, *Jesus as Guru*, 16.

205 Schouten, *Jesus as Guru*, 16.

206 Schouten, *Jesus as Guru*, 16-17.

207 Schouten, *Jesus as Guru*, 18-24.

of all the Indians in that critical juncture. Ram Mohan's incorporation of the message of the Bible with a special focus on Jesus's teachings aimed at the silent cry of the people of Bengal. He acclaimed the powerful voice of the scripture in the context of colonialism and dehumanization.

Narayan Vaman Tilak (1861-1919) was a remarkably influential poet of Maharashtra who used indigenous Christian ideas. As an ardent reader of the Bible, he referred to himself as 'a Tukaram and a St. Paul blended together.'[208] As he was part of British India, he was groaning for freedom and cultivated a great love for his country. His poems reflect the passionate love of a true patriot, rising above the bondage of caste and creed. As Tilak was reading the Sermon on the Mount and its words of love, he was attracted to the way of Christianity that attuned him to compassion and truth. After an extensive study of the Bible, he concluded that Christ was the teacher whom India and the world needed. He conglomerated the teachings of the Bible and his personal experiences.[209] Tilak's ardent devotion, passion and enthusiasm enabled him to groan for the freedom of the marginalized sections of society. In spite of the threat of poverty, loss of employment, loss of friends and the separation from his family for a number of years, he was immersed in the love of Christ and groaned for the freedom of the nation of India. Plamthodathil S. Jacob comments, "Tilak's perception of the Bible was mainly experiential and not necessarily a scholarly study of the Bible in the conventional sense. Tilak was neither a theologian nor a biblical scholar in traditional meanings of the terms. Nevertheless, one can find an Indian cultural learning in his interpretations of Biblical themes."[210] Tilak introduced his innovative ideas of Christian living by blending together the 'otherworldliness' of the Indian saintly approach to spirituality and yet being rooted in the human world of daily living. He was attracted to Christ's love and suffering, resurrection as power of transformation and hope, and 'majestic sweetness of God crowned in Christ.'[211] As a Biblical and Christian poet, he embraced a hermeneutic of groaning that is derived from his devotion to Christ and his liberating musings based on the 'in front of' the textual realities.

---

208 Plamthodathil Samuel Jacob, "Narayan Vaman Tilak and the Bible—Part I," *New Testament Scholarship Worldwide*, https://ntscholarship.wordpress.com/2013/01/28/narayam-vaman-tilak-and-the-bible-part-i/, accessed on 24 April 2023.

209 Jacob, "Narayan Vaman Tilak and the Bible—Part I," https://ntscholarship.wordpress.com/2013/01/28/narayam-vaman-tilak-and-the-bible-part-i/, accessed on 24 April 2023.

210 Jacob, "Narayan Vaman Tilak and the Bible—Part I," https://ntscholarship.wordpress.com/2013/01/28/narayam-vaman-tilak-and-the-bible-part-i/, accessed on 24 April 2023.

211 Plamthodathil Samuel Jacob, "Narayan Vaman Tilak and the Bible—Part II," *New Testament Scholarship Worldwide*, https://ntscholarship.wordpress.com/2013/01/30/narayam-vaman-tilak-and-the-bible-part-ii/, accessed on 24 April 2023.

Pandita Ramabai (1858-1922) was a convert from Brahminical Hinduism to Christianity. The longing for social reform that would improve the lot of women in areas such as child marriage, literacy and education grew ever stronger in Ramabai.[212] Her experience in the London Rescue Home and her reading of the story of the Samaritan woman (John 4:1-42) persuaded her to groan deep within herself concerning the underprivileged women in Maharashtra and across India. In 1889, her groanings developed into action and she founded the Mukti Mission for destitute orphans, widows and single mothers.[213] With an extension of Christian love, she rescued thousands of young girls and widows. Though there was a Marathi Bible translation already in existence during the early part of the nineteenth century, she developed a translation from the Hebrew and Greek texts to address the ordinary levels of the Marathi readers. Her translation had a specific audience: uneducated women of lower castes.[214] A hermeneutic of groaning was at the heart of Ramabai as she read the scripture through the eyes of the destitute women and did her best to liberate the voice of the dehumanized in society.

The next significant figure who engaged with the Bible was Mahatma Gandhi (1869-1948). Gandhi, his accusers declared, was 'a Christian in secret.'[215] Emilsen quotes Gandhi, "There have been many times when I did not know which way to turn. But I have gone to the Bible, and particularly the New Testament, and have drawn strength from its message."[216] Gandhi revered Jesus's Sermon on the Mount in almost equal terms with *Bhagavat Gita*.[217] Gandhi's ideals, such as *Satyagraha* (truth-seeking) and *ahimsa* (non-violence), go much closer to the teachings of Jesus in the Sermon on the Mount and in the Gospel of John.[218] Emilsen says, "Both Matthew's gospel and Gandhi's emphasize readiness to suffer, poverty, lowliness, renunciation of worldly honour and service, and those who withstand the test and show themselves approved in these matters receive the promised

---

212 David Morgan, "Pandita Ramabai: A Pioneer Bible Translator," *Wycliffe Bible Translators* (29 August 2022), see https://wycliffe.org.uk/story/pandita-ramabai, accessed on 23 April 2023.

213 Morgan, "Pandita Ramabai," *Wycliffe Bible Translators*, see https://wycliffe.org.uk/story/pandita-ramabai, accessed on 23 April 2023.

214 Morgan, "Pandita Ramabai," *Wycliffe Bible Translators*, see https://wycliffe.org.uk/story/pandita-ramabai, accessed on 23 April 2023.

215 William W. Emilsen, *Gandhi's Bible* (New Delhi: ISPCK, 2018), xix.

216 Emilsen, *Gandhi's Bible*, v.

217 M. K. Gandhi, "Speech at Missionary Conference, Madras" (14 February 1916), *C.W.*, 13, 220.

218 Emilsen, *Gandhi's Bible*, xxxi-xxxiii.

reward in the Kingdom of God."[219] Gandhiji argued that Europe mistook 'the bold and brave resistance full of wisdom by Jesus of Nazareth for passive resistance.'[220] In his reading of the New Testament, Gandhi detected no passivity or weakness in Jesus.[221] In a context in which India was under colonialism, and the people of the nation underwent suffering, Gandhi read the Bible alongside other scriptures with a preferential option to the suffering Indians.[222] In his reading, he groaned for justice, truth, and freedom and hence he followed the path of Jesus.[223] In his *The Story of My Experiments with Truth*, Gandhi emphasizes the aspects of love, truth, non-violence, integrity and morality.[224]

Mother Teresa (1910-1997) was a reader of the Holy Scriptures and in 1946 she received what she would later describe as a "call within a call." She said Jesus spoke to her and told her to work in the slums of Kolkata, aiding the city's poorest and sickest people.[225] She took vows of chastity, poverty, obedience, and to give "wholehearted free service to the poorest of the poor."[226] Mother Teresa's reading of Matthew 25:40 is phenomenal. She says, "[Jesus] makes Himself the hungry one, the naked one, the homeless one, the sick one, the one in prison, the lonely one, the unwanted one, and he says: 'You did it to me.' He is hungry for our love."[227] The Gospel is about loving; first, it is about loving Jesus, and second, it is about loving others for his sake.[228] Another Scripture that inspired her was Psalm 113:7-9.

---

219 Emilsen, *Gandhi's Bible*, xxxv.

220 Emilsen, *Gandhi's Bible*, xxxvi.

221 M. K. Gandhi, "Letter to Yvonne Privat" (29 November 1947), *C.W.*, 90, 129.

222 See Johnson Thomaskutty, *The Gospel of John: Contemporary Readings* (Bengaluru: Omega Book World, 2023), 19-20.

223 Thomas Weber, *Gandhi, Gandhism and Gandhians* (New Delhi: Roli Books, 2006), 123-139.

224 See M. K. Gandhi, *The Story of My Experiments with Truth* (Ahmedabad: Navajivan Publishing House, 1968); cf. Thomaskutty, *The Gospel of John: Contemporary Readings*, 13.

225 Joe Carter, "Nine Things You Should Know about Mother Teresa," *The Gospel Coalition* (3 September 2016), https://www.thegospelcoalition.org/article/9-things-you-should-know-about-mother-teresa/, accessed on 24 April 2023.

226 Carter, "Nine Things You Should Know about Mother Teresa," https://www.thegospelcoalition.org/article/9-things-you-should-know-about-mother-teresa/, accessed on 24 April 2023.

227 Scott G. Hefelfinger, "Matthew 25:40 with St. Teresa of Calcutta," *Faith and Culture: A Journal of the Augustine Institute* (8 February 2021), https://www.faithandculture.com/home/2020/8/21/matthew-2540-with-st-teresa-of-calcutta, accessed on 24 April 2023.

228 Hefelfinger, "Matthew 25:40 with St. Teresa of Calcutta," https://www.faithandculture.com/home/2020/8/21/matthew-2540-with-st-teresa-of-calcutta, accessed on 24 April 2023.

Mother Teresa's Bible engagement enabled her to groan deep within herself to develop a divine perspective about the marginalized sections of society.

The above details demonstrate how Bible engagement impacted the wider spheres of the church and society. The Bible is a storehouse of human expectations for transformative and liberative living. While the scripture was translated into several languages and dialects, it was influential among communities to create groaning hearts. A hermeneutic of groaning is a rhetoric that persuades people to get involved in the existential struggles of the community in the socio-religious and politico-cultural realms. In that sense, a 'groaning' heart inspired by the Biblical paradigms is the starting point of societal engagement and nation-building. As the personalities discussed above, like Ziegenbalg, Carey, Mohan Roy, Tilak, Ramabai, Gandhiji, Teresa, and many others who engaged into the textual world with a consciousness about the contemporaneous struggles, developed a bleeding heart within themselves, and engaged in the life realities of the people, a reader of the Bible can conceptualize and understand the significance of a hermeneutic of groaning in the contemporary realities of the world. A hermeneutic of groaning is a slow, silent, and individualistic voice at its outset, but it can develop as a rapid, powerful, and communitarian voice while it is properly triggered.

A Hermeneutic of Groaning in the Sociopolitical Context of India

The Hindu nationalistic trajectory under the current regime creates two or even more levels of citizens in India.[229] While the Hindu religious community is treated as the owners of the nation, minorities like Muslims, Christians and others are treated as secondary citizens or even as non-citizens.[230] While the Hindus enjoy the status of the superior religious community, who are considered as people really rooted in the cultural ethos of the country and receive all the legal provisions, the minority communities suffer vulnerable situations.[231] This is the context in which the Christian community wrestle for their survival. The advocates of Hindu nationalism do not recognize the Christians of the country as a nationalistic community but rather as followers of a foreign religious ideology.[232] The defensive attitude of the

---

229 Jaffrelot, *Modi's India*, 7-30.

230 For more details about the citizenship aspects, see Mohammed Girma, "Citizenship: A Christian Conception," *Christian Citizenship in the Middle East: Divided Allegiance or Dual Belonging?*, eds. Mohammed Girma and Cristian Romocea (London: Jessica Kingsley Publishers, 2017), 23-42.

231 Christophe Jaffrelot, *Religion, Caste and Politics in India* (New Delhi: Primus Books, 2010), 170-188.

232 Kirsteen Kim, "Indian Christian Ideological Responses to Political Hinduism," *Nationalism and Hindutva: A Christian Response, Papers from Tenth CMS Consultation*,

majoritarian nationalistic movement toward the Christian ideology brings tension within the socio-cultural realities of the country.[233] It is in this context the Christian community of the nation delves reversive defensive mechanisms through a hermeneutic of groaning. This movement is silent, invisible, and undercurrent in its very nature. But the silence is louder, invisibility is visible, and undercurrents are powerful in the contemporary context.

Bible engagement is widely practiced in the socio-religious and politico-cultural context of India. As a multi-religious and pluralistic context, people of the nation have varied responses toward the Bible and its message, especially based on their backgrounds.[234] The North-Eastern part of the country was fostering a Biblically-centered cultural dynamics as majority of the people were connected to the ecclesiastical bodies. The relationship between the church and the state in Mizoram and in Nagaland facilitate a Bible-centered culture that influences the people and the society at large. The ethics and ethos of the people were usually derived from the Bible as the communities accepted it as the measuring rod both in the church and in the society.[235] But under the new regime of government, the influence of the Bible belt in the North-Eastern states slowly waned as the Hindu nationalistic movement established its grip in that region. It is a Hindu nationalistic agenda to place the Bible and the culture in opposition to adopting an anti-minority ideology. The Bible culture that is promulgated in several parts of the country, like in Karnataka, Uttar Pradesh, Chhattisgarh, Odisha, and other parts, face opposition from the Hindu nationalistic movements.[236] Many missionaries are persecuted due to their faith and practices based on the Bible. In this critical juncture, the Biblical message of groaning remains as a hermeneutical key and as a counter defensive mechanism. While Mohammed Girma suggests a hermeneutic of memory as a starting point to deal with the politically induced trauma in the African context,[237] I find

---

ed. Mark T. B. Laing (Pune/New Delhi: CMS/UBS/ISPCK, 2005), 162-176.

233 For more details, see Ashutosh Varshney, *Ethnic Conflict and Civic Life: Hindus and Muslims in India* (Grand Rapids: Yale University Press, 2002).

234 Carver T. Yu, "The Bible and Culture in the Shaping of Asian Theology," *Christianity and Cultures: Shaping Christian Thinking in Context*, Regnum Studies in Mission, eds. David Emmanuel Singh and Bernard C. Farr (Carlisle: Regnum Books International, 2008), 51-62.

235 Zhodi Angami, *Tribals, Empire and God: A Tribal Reading of the Birth of Jesus in Matthew's Gospel* (London: Bloomsbury T&T Clark, 2017), 23-76.

236 Sarbeswar Sahoo, *Pentecostalism and Politics of Conversion in India* (Cambridge: Cambridge University Press, 2018), 120-157.

237 Mohammed Girma, "From Painful Memories to Restorative Nostalgia," *The Healing of Memories: African Christian Responses to Politically Induced Trauma*, ed. Mohammed

a hermeneutic of groaning as a significant starting point in the context of Hindu nationalism in India. While memory guides the interpreter toward past experiences, groaning guides a reader toward the present and immediate experiences of the people.[238] A groaning heart enables a reader to look back to the text and to look in front for hermeneutical application or vice versa. The message of the Bible empowers the Christian communities to remain disciplined irrespective of the opposition and persecution orchestrated by the majoritarian power-structures.

The current government promulgates a new political agenda that is anti-Christian in its very nature. The nationalistic agenda of the current regime silences the voices of the minorities in the country. Though the minority communities are part and parcel of the country and their identities are derived out of the ethos of the nation, they are projected as aliens and as second-class citizens in the country.[239] While the power structures are exercised by the majoritarian nationalistic groups, the minority communities are forced to the periphery, and they are at the receiving end of the afflictions delved from above. While the new regime remains aggressive in its political agenda, it regards the Bible as a foreign religious document. However, a thorough historical investigation enables us to understand that the minority communities of India hold the ethics and ethos of the nation. Hence, "Indian Christianity" can be considered as a distinct identity in the global Christendom.[240] This liminal space of the Indian Christians makes them vulnerable as they neither belong to this nation nor belong to other nations. Hence, they groan for identity, righteousness, and justice in their own land.

Girma (Lanham/London: Lexington Books, 2018), 3-16.

238 See Girma, "From Painful Memories to Restorative Nostalgia," 3-16.

239 Chad M. Bauman and James Ponniah, "Christian Responses to Repression in India and Sri Lanka: Religious Nationalism, Legal Restriction, and Violence," *Under Caesar's Sword: How Christians Respond to Persecution*, eds. Daniel Philpott and Timothy Samuel Shah (Cambridge: Cambridge University Press, 2018), 259-297.

240 Paul Joshua Bhakiaraj, "Being Indian, Becoming Christian: Towards a Theological Vision for Identity Formation," *Indian and Christian: Changing Identities in Modern India, Papers from the First SAIACS Consultation*, eds. Cornelis Bennema and Paul Joshua Bhakiaraj (Bangalore: SAIACS Press, 2011), 95-113.

Some of the Biblical paradigms are important in the process of developing a hermeneutic of groaning. In the Old Testament, the people of God groaned over the evils of society by relying on divine wisdom. The suffering people groaned and Yahweh heard their sighs.[241] The early Christian communities considered the person and works of Jesus as paradigms to develop a reverse defensive mechanism and thus to shape a hermeneutic of groaning. The ordinariness of the human realities and the existential struggles of their day-to-day affairs persuaded them to remain groaning.[242] The Matthean, Markan, Lukan, and Johannine communities placed Jesus as the paradigmatic figure to interpret new ways forward in their socio-religious and politico-cultural lifestyle.[243] The liberative words of Jesus enabled the people of God to groan in the phase of growing atrocities around them.[244] In the Pauline communities, Paul being influenced by the crucified Christ and the resurrected Lord groaned within himself to implement a transformative living.[245] The Book of Revelation reveals how a hermeneutic of groaning works well. The Christian community in Rome was suffering from persecution and emperor worship. Mitchell G. Reddish states that "Emperor worship involved the offering of divine honors, including sacrifices, to the emperors, either living or dead."[246] The Christians who denied worshipping the emperor had to undergo severe persecution. The people of God were placed between their faith in God and the compulsion and persecution from the Roman Empire. They relied on the words of Jesus and groaned deep within themselves. As the Book of Revelation uses Apocalyptic language in a colonial context in the first century CE, a new Apocalypticism is in progress in the context of cult, chaos, terror, vanity, seizure, and disunion in the Indian context.

---

241 G. H. Haas, "Slave, Slavery," *Dictionary of the Old Testament: Pentateuch*, eds. T. Desmond Alexander and David W. Baker (Downers Grove: Inter-Varsity Press, 2003), 778-783.

242 See Dibyesh Anand, *Hindu Nationalism in India and the Politics of Fear* (New York: Palgrave Macmillan, 2011).

243 Edwin Jebaraj and Johnson Thomaskutty, "The Gospel of Mark," *An Asian Introduction to the New Testament*, ed. Johnson Thomaskutty (Minneapolis: Fortress Press, 2022): 75-101.

244 Johnson Thomaskutty, "Culture Dynamics in the Johannine Community Context," *One Gospel, Many Cultures: Doing Theology in Context*, ed. Arren Bennet Lawrence (Minneapolis: Fortress Press, 2022), 138-142.

245 Michael J. Gorman, *Participating in Christ: Explorations in Paul's Theology and Spirituality* (Grand Rapids: Baker Academic Press, 2019), 29-52.

246 Mitchell G. Reddish, *Revelation: Smyth & Helwys Bible Commentary* (Macon: Smyth & Helwys, 2001), 11.

In India, Bible readers' groaning hearts persuade them to get involved in the Dalit, Tribal, and Adivasi liberation, emancipation of the women, and transformation of all other ostracized in the society.[247] The Dalit Christians in India read the Bible for liberative power and they appropriate their struggles in alignment with the pain and pathos of the people of God inscribed in the scripture.[248] Though the Dalit Christians are 'ordinary people,' they keep the Bible close to their life situations and apply its meaning to their day-to-day realities and struggles.[249] The Dalit Christians consider the Bible as their life and daily bread and the very foundation of their existence in the world, even when they are in dehumanized situations. They often suffer vulnerability in society due to their status as 'Dalits,' and especially as 'Christian Dalits.' But the message of the Bible gives them the power of resilience, and they sigh deep within themselves, irrespective of the growing atrocities around them.[250] The groanings of the Dalit Christians in India are powerful means to orchestrate a hermeneutic that facilitates a liberative mission.

Just as C. S. Song treated the Bible as a storybook and not as a textbook,[251] The tribal communities of the northeastern Indian states treat the Bible as a story book.[252] Yangkahao Vashum says, "The Bible is a story book. It is filled with the stories of people of faith. They are stories about how God has been faithful to them, how God has been leading and guiding them. They are stories of relations, liberation and life in abundance."[253] The Bible is placed close to the liberative visions of the tribal communities. The recent conflicts between the Meitei and Kuki communities in Manipur proved that it is an issue between the majoritarian Hindu ideology and the minoritarian Christian community. The tribal Christians of the province

---

247 Jeeva Kumar Ravela and David J. Chalcraft, "Encountering the Bible: Listening to the Voices of Madiga Christians," *A Biblical Masala: Encountering Diversity in Indian Biblical Studies*, eds. David J. Chalcraft and Zhodi Angami (New Delhi: Christian World Imprints, 2021), 196.

248 Ravela and Chalcraft, "Encountering the Bible," 196.

249 A. P. Nirmal, "Doing Theology from a Dalit Perspective," *A Reader in Dalit Theology*, ed. A. P. Nirmal (Madras: Gurukul Lutheran Theological College and Research Institute, n.d.), 142.

250 Ravela and Chalcraft, "Encountering the Bible," 215-217.

251 C. S. Song, "In the Beginning were Stories, not Texts," *Madang International Journal of Contextual Theology in East Asia*, Vol. 14 (15 December 2010), 7-16.

252 Yangkahao Vashum, "Introduction," *Tribal Theology and the Bible: A Search for Contextual Relevance*, Tribal Study Series 19, ed. Yangkahao Vashum (Jorhat: Tribal Study Center, Eastern Theological College, 2011), 1-9.

253 Vashum, "Introduction," *Tribal Theology and the Bible*," 2. Also see Hrayr Jebejian, *Bible Engagement: The Discovery of Faith, Hope and Self* (Lebanon: Bible Society in the Gulf, 2019), 115-116.

suffered massive attacks, violence, and vandalism inflicted upon them by the powerful nationalistic regime. Under the BJP-led central and state governances, the Meitei community found it easier to inflict attacks on the Kuki community. But the groanings of the Kuki community are powerful to develop a reverse defense in the socio-political situation of the state.[254] The Biblical concept that 'God is warrior' can be well adjusted to the tribal aspirations of the Northeasterners.[255] The Creator God of the Bible can be an all-inclusive reality who can encompass the tribal groanings.[256] As discussed above, the majoritarian politics and its nationalistic agenda under the current regime of government silence the voices of all the 'other' sections of people in the Indian context. The Christian communities are always at the end of suffering. A hermeneutic of groaning rhetorizes the minority sighs for liberative praxes.

Concluding Remarks

The above discussion foregrounds the wider impact of the Bible engagement and a hermeneutic of groaning in the sociopolitical context of India. A reversed defensive mechanism develops among the Indian Christians over against the burgeoning Hindu nationalistic agenda under the current regime. The current Indian government defends its anti-minority activities and silences the 'other' voices. The hostile attitude of the BJP government is obvious through its negative approach to the Bible mission. It is in this context a hermeneutic of groaning negotiates between the anti-Christian voices in the country and the silent voices of the marginalized communities.[257] A hermeneutic of groaning visualizes the ordinary and contextual faith-reactions of the Bible readers. In a hermeneutic of groaning, the Biblical contexts and characterizations are aligned with the day-to-day affairs of the suffering and marginalized communities. Rev. Dr. Kondasingu Jesurathnam's engagements with the Scripture and his alignment of the "behind," "in," and "in front of" the textual realities demonstrate his groaning heart coupled with his prophetic imagination. In that process, two story-worlds are submerged and interlocked in a dynamic way: that is, interlocking the 'in front of' the textual realities with the 'behind' and

254 See https://currentaffairs.adda247.com/manipur-violence-understanding-the-conflict-in-manipur/, accessed on 8 May 2023.

255 Tremper Longman III and Daniel G. Reid, *God is a Warrior*, Studies in Old Testament Biblical Theology (Grand Rapids: Zondervan, 1995), 31-47.

256 See https://ntscholarship.wordpress.com/2012/02/27/reading-jesus-paradigmatically-into-the-northeastern-indian-tribal-context/, accessed on 8 May 2023.

257 Gerald O. West, *Reading Other-wise: Socially Engaged Scholars Reading with Local Communities* 62 (Atlanta: Society of Biblical Literature, 2007), 3.

'in' the textual horizons.[258] In the context of majority-minority issues and the Hindu-Christian conflicts, a reflective and contextually-aligned reading shall yield fruits and it may lead the wider community to liberative action and transformative living. In that sense, a hermeneutic of groaning is an internal sigh of the reader of the text with a vision of a sociopolitical transformation. Gerald O. West states, "within a liberation paradigm praxis involves ongoing action and reflection, with reflection being a requisite component of emancipatory action."[259] Such a model is significant in the contemporary missional and ministerial engagements in India.

258 Thomaskutty, "A Polyvalent Hermeneutic of John 2:13-25," 3-4.

259 West, *Reading Other-wise*, 3.

7

The Weeping Prophet and the Dyche
Lament, Resilience and Quest for Justice

Varaprasad Gosala

Introduction

Lament, resilience and quest for Justice are the significant factors that surface from the life experiences of Jeremiah, also known as the Weeping Prophet. Similarly, parallel attributes can be drawn from the experience of being a Dalit. The inter-connectedness between the Prophet Jeremiah and the Dalit experiences helps us to understand how historical injustices still affect Dalits today. It allows us to explore the underlying themes within the gamut of life situations - the highs and the lows, the need to vent out emotions of anguish and despair, an unwavering conviction for resilience in the face of difficulties, and a categorical quest for justice and equality.

The prophetic vocation of Jeremiah, as depicted in the Hebrew Bible, encompasses a spectrum of experiences: physical, emotional, and spiritual. The book of Jeremiah, particularly 20: 1-18, offers a poignant portrayal of human emotions, resonating with themes of lament, resilience, and the unwavering pursuit of justice. This paper argues that these expressions find parallels in the experiences of Dalit youth in India who face the brunt of caste-based discrimination, oppression, rejection, and humiliation. Instead of giving up, Jeremiah strives in the pursuit of justice, which is not only a vital characteristic but also indispensable to integrate and secure a just society.

This essay explores these crucial themes, showing how expressing sorrow can bring people together and push for change. It also looks at Dalits' strength in continuing to fight for their rights despite challenges. Additionally, it examines the ongoing battle for justice, both in the past and present, as Dalits strive for equal treatment and respect.

Jeremiah's Lament (Jeremiah 20: 1-18) in Historical Context

Jeremiah 20:1-18 offers a glimpse into one of the most intense and personal moments of anguish in the Bible. After being publicly humiliated—beaten and imprisoned by Pashhur, the chief officer in the temple—Jeremiah finds he overwhelmed by the weight of his calling. The pain he feels is not just physical; it's emotional and spiritual. He pours out his heart in a raw, unfiltered lament, filled with anger, deep despair, and a sense of hopelessness. Jeremiah is so distraught that he questions his very purpose, even cursing the day he was born (Jeremiah 20:14-18).[260]

The text in Jeremiah 20 captures a deeply turbulent time in the prophet's life, as he finds himself torn between the demands of God, the hostility of the people, and the threats from his enemies. It's a moment of personal crisis, where Jeremiah is frustrated with the burden of being chosen as a prophet. He is caught in a painful struggle, questioning why God would put him in this position. J.R. Lundbom suggests that this moment happened around 605-604 BCE, shortly after King Jehoiakim threatened Jeremiah's life for preaching the Temple Sermon.[261] Meanwhile, Carroll connects the passage to the destruction of Jerusalem and Judah in 587 BCE, noting the stark reference to cities destroyed without mercy—recalling the devastation of Sodom and Gomorrah. This period of Jeremiah's life is marked by profound disillusionment, as he wrestles with the cost of his prophetic calling amid the collapse of his world. [262]

Weiser interprets this text as Jeremiah's personal confession, offered in front of the religious community, allowing his raw emotions to be seen publicly. On the other hand, Reventlow suggests that it may not be an account of Jeremiah's actual experiences but rather a crafted speech for a religious ceremony, with Jeremiah speaking as a representative of the people. Clines and Gunn take a slightly different perspective, proposing that Jeremiah is publicly asserting that his words are from Yahweh, even though he feels reluctant to prophesy. They see his message emerging from

260 Jack R. Lundbom, "The Double Curse in Jeremiah 20: 14-18" *JBL* 104/4 (1985): 591.

261 Lundbom, "The Double Curse in Jeremiah…," 589.

262 Robert P. Carroll, *Jeremiah: A Commentary. The Old Testament Library* (Philadelphia: Westminster Press, 1986), 239

a personal struggle against opposition, highlighting the tension between his inner hesitation and the divine compulsion to speak.[263]

Diamond suggests that the imagery of the prophetic call and the sense of being compelled to speak in this passage paints a picture that goes beyond the simple role of a messenger. It reveals the deep inner struggle Jeremiah faces as he grapples with his mission. His relationship with his calling is complicated—it's not just about delivering a message, but about the emotional and spiritual weight that comes with it. This passage can be seen through different lenses, showing how Jeremiah's experience with his prophetic duty is far from straightforward.[264]

In the Bible, lament is a way of dealing with the pain and sadness of life while still believing in God. It helps people express their feelings and ask God why bad things happen. Even though they may feel angry or confused, they still hope for a better future. The Bible has many examples of people who lamented, like Jeremiah and Job. They talked to God about their problems and showed how strong they were despite their suffering. By lamenting, people can show that they won't just accept things the way they are. They want God to help them and make the world a better place.

The Function of Lament in the Hebrew Bible

Lament is a powerful and recurring theme throughout the Hebrew Bible, often serving as a way for individuals and communities to confront the profound tensions between their suffering and their faith. Through lament, people express their raw emotions—anger, sorrow, and confusion—in response to injustice and suffering. Lament serves as an active and courageous expression of resilience, a refusal to accept pain or injustice in silence. This dynamic tension between grief and hope makes lament a vital part of the biblical tradition.

The Hebrew Bible presents numerous examples of laments, where individuals openly confront God with their pain. One of the clearest examples is found in the correct it as book of Psalms, a book filled with prayers of lament. Psalm 13, for instance, begins with the cry, "How long, O Lord? Will you forget me forever?" (Psalm 13:1). Here, the psalmist is not merely expressing personal despair but is actively seeking a response from God, questioning why God seems distant or silent in the time of suffering.

263 Cited in J. A. Clines and D. M. Gunn, "Form, Occasion and Redaction in Jeremiah 20", *ZAW* 88 (1976): 400.

264 R. Diamond, *The Confessions of Jeremiah in Context: Scenes of Prophetic Drama,* edited byDavid J. Clines and Philip R. Davis, JSOT Supplement Series 45(Sheffield: Sheffield Academic Press, 1987), 108.

The psalmist's cry for deliverance is an act of faith, grounded in the belief that God listens to human anguish and can ultimately provide relief.[265]

A significant example of communal lament is found in the Book of Lamentations, which mourns the destruction of Jerusalem and the suffering of the Jewish people following the Babylonian exile. The city's devastation is described in painful detail, as the author asks, "Is it nothing to you, all who pass by? Look and see if there is any sorrow like my sorrow" (Lamentations 1:12). Here, lament becomes a way for the community to collectively grieve over their loss and express their sorrow to God.[266]

Lament also serves as a protest against injustice. One of the most powerful examples of this is found in the book of Habakkuk. The prophet Habakkuk begins his dialogue with God by questioning, "O Lord, how long shall I cry for help, and you will not hear? Or cry to you 'Violence!' and you will not save?" (Habakkuk 1:2). Habakkuk is outraged by the rampant injustice he sees around him and challenges God to act against it. His lament is not passive but a direct confrontation with God, calling for divine intervention and justice.[267]

When Job faces unimaginable personal suffering, he does not simply accept it or remain silent. Instead, he boldly challenges the unfairness of his situation and demands answers from God. Job's grief and pain drive him to question why the innocent must endure such hardship. Even as his friends urge him to accept his fate without questioning or doubting God, Job refuses to go along quietly. His lament becomes an act of defiance, a powerful expression of his need for clarity and justice. In his anguish, Job doesn't turn away from God but confronts the injustice of his suffering head-on.[268]

While lament often begins with sorrow and questioning, it frequently transitions toward hope and trust in God's ultimate justice and deliverance. In Psalm 22, the psalmist begins by crying out, "My God, my God, why have you forsaken me?" (Psalm 22:1), but by the end of the psalm, there is a shift to praise and confidence in God's faithfulness: "For he has not despised or scorned the suffering of the afflicted one; he has not hidden his face from him but has listened to his cry for help" (Psalm 22:24). This movement from

265 Claus Westermann, "The Role of the Lament in Theology of the Old Testament, *Interpretation* (1974), 23.

266 Westermann, "The Role of the Lament…," 24.

267 Rickie Dale Moore, "Tracking the Burden of Habakkuk: The Prophetic Path," *The Living Pulpit* (2002): 26.

268 Yung Suk Kim, "Job's Lament: How to Understand," *Currents in Theology and Mission* (2023): 31.

despair to hope shows how lament can serve as a transformative process, where grief is acknowledged but not allowed to define the future.[269]

Jeremiah's Lament: A Journey through Darkness

Jeremiah's words in Jeremiah 20:7-18 are some of the most powerful and emotional cries of pain in the Bible. It's more than just complaining; He is questioning everything – who he is, why God seems to have left him, and what the point of it all is. He is not just sad for himself, but feels like God has turned away from him. But instead of hiding from his pain, he faces it head-on. It's a powerful reminder that even when things are really tough, we can still be honest about how we feel and find strength in facing our pain.

Many scholars highlight the existential nature of Jeremiah's lament, noting that it goes beyond his immediate circumstances to question the very meaning of his existence and calling. Walter Brueggemann, emphasizes that Jeremiah's lament is not just a personal outcry but a crisis of vocation. Jeremiah feels deceived by God, expressing this in his bold statement, "You deceived me, Lord, and I was deceived; you overpowered me and prevailed" (Jeremiah 20:7). For Brueggemann, this accusation of deception reveals the prophet's deep frustration with the divine, as Jeremiah grapples with the unbearable weight of his prophetic mission. The tension between his calling and the suffering it creates an existential crisis, as Jeremiah questions the very purpose of his life.[270]

Similarly, Abraham J. Heschel, discusses Jeremiah's deep sense of alienation, not only from his community but also from God. According to Heschel, Jeremiah's lament encapsulates the experience of being abandoned by the very God he serves, a divine betrayal that compounds his personal trauma. The depth of this feeling is evident when Jeremiah curses the day of his birth (Jeremiah 20:14-18), signaling that his pain has reached an existential level where life itself feels unbearable. Heschel argues that Jeremiah's lamentation is emblematic of the prophet's profound sense of isolation, both spiritually and socially.[271]

Jeremiah's words about feeling alone and misunderstood are something everyone can relate to. Claus Westermann says that these kinds of prayers of pain are important because they help us connect with God in a real way. Jeremiah's words remind us that even people who are really close to God can feel abandoned and rejected. His question, 'Why was I ever born to see

269 Richard D. Patterson, " Psalm 22: From Trial to Triumph," *Journal of Evangelical Theological Society* (2004): 216.

270 Walter Brueggemann, *The Prophetic Imagination* (Minneapolis: Fortress Press, 2018), 110.

271 Abraham J. Heschel, *The Prophets*, (New York: Harper Collins Publishers, 1962), 150.

trouble and sadness and die in shame?' is something many people have asked throughout history when they have felt lost and alone. Westermann says that Jeremiah's words are not just about him; they show us how everyone feels sometimes. They remind us that it's okay to be honest about our pain when we're trying to find meaning and justice in life.[272]

Jeremiah's words are full of deep emotions, from the pain of personal loss to feeling abandoned by God, and his refusal to hide his feelings. Scholars agree that he was going through a really tough time, questioning everything about himself and his faith. Others say that his words are about something everyone goes through: suffering and being strong. By being honest about his pain, Jeremiah shows us that even when you believe in God, you can still suffer. It takes courage to be honest about how you feel, but it's also a way to be strong.

Dyche and its Manifestations

M. C. Raj introduced the concept of 'Dyche' to describe the psychological impact of oppression on Dalits. He argues that the Dalit psyche was not always wounded. Before the arrival of Aryans in India, Dalit people, whom Raj refers to as 'Adijan,' possessed a resurgent and proactive psyche. However, due to external forces imposed by the migrants (Aryans), the Dalit psyche became broken or wounded (Dyche). These external forces were likely designed by the Aryans to establish their own comfortable existence. The dominating attitude of Aryan's wounds the healthy Indigenous psyche of Dalits and creates a psyche of worthlessness in them.[273]

Raj points out that the Dyche (psyche of Dalit people) can be comprehended not just through clinical analysis but also by carefully observing its various expressions in different behavioural situations. Thus, M.C. Raj explains that the manifestations of Dyche in the various behavioural contexts of the Adijan people are the result of his meticulous and sensitive observations. In Dyche, the authors identify the underlying cause of the abnormal reflections of Dyche as the dominating attitude of Aryans and offer possible suggestions for healing the wounds of the Dalit, aiming for their liberation and empowerment of the nation.[274]

M. C. Raj asserts that the denial of rights to Dalit people has transformed their psyche into one of dependency. Due to the authoritarian attitude of the Aryans, the Adijan psyche of generosity has been altered into a psyche of craving. This natural inclination to give has been subverted into

272 Westermann, "The Role of the Lament…," , 35.

273 M. C. Raj and Jyothi Raj, *Dyche, the Dalit Psyche: A Science of Dalit Psychology* (Tumkur: Ambedkar Resource Centre, 2008), 255.

274 M.C. Raj and Jyothi Raj, *Dyche, the Dalit Psyche…*, 255.

a Dyche characterized by compulsive craving, resulting in vulnerability within the Dyche. Consequently, a self-sufficient psyche has been changed into a dependent one.[275]

The Dalit Experience: Lamenting Injustice in Modern India

Caste-based Oppression and its Psychological Impact on Dalit Youth

For generations, Dalits in India have endured deep-rooted discrimination and social exclusion. The caste system, woven into the fabric of society, pushes them to the margins, denying them opportunities for education, decent jobs, and even basic respect. This kind of oppression leaves a significant mark on Dalit youth, who carry the weight of the rejection and humiliation they face daily. Over time, these experiences can take a heavy toll, leading to mental health challenges like depression, anxiety, and a deep sense of hopelessness. Sadly, in some cases, it can even drive young Dalits to consider taking their own lives, with studies showing a troubling rise in suicides among Dalit youth.

The Suicidal Crisis among Dalit Youth: A Call for Attention

The number of Dalit young people committing suicides is rising dangerously in India. This is because of the unfair treatment they face due to their caste, poverty, and the lack of social support. Many young people feel hopeless and see suicide as a way to escape their problems.

Dalit suicide has emerged as a significant social problem in contemporary Indian society, particularly among students. Numerous studies have linked these suicides to social discrimination and lack of opportunities. Notable cases include Rohith Vemula (2016), Muthukrishnan (2017), Anitha (2017), and Payal Tadvi (2019), whose suicides highlight the severe impact of the caste system. While these cases do not represent the overall trend, they underscore the pervasive harassment and denial of opportunities faced by Dalits. This ongoing trauma often leads to the tragic outcome of suicide.[276]

In 2023, several Dalit students ended their lives by suicide at India's top universities, which led to renewed discussion about caste-based discrimination in institutions of higher education:[277]

A former student at the Indian Institute of Technology (IIT) Madras, Vaibhav Jadhav, tweeted in February 2023 about being cornered by a group of seniors during his first year. "Seeing that I was not one to fall in line, one

275 M.C. Raj and Jyothi Raj, *Dyche, the Dalit Psyche…*, 255

276 https://www.intechopen.com/chapters/77988 (accessed on 27th June 2024).

277 https://article-14.com/post/-caste-on-campus-dalit-students-face-exclusion-alienation-in-india-s-higher-education-institutions--642b88a7149fe (accessed on 27th June 2024).

of them asked me my rank, wrote Jadhav. "I gave my SC (scheduled caste) category rank, to which he replied, "Sala SC hone ke baad bhi itna attitude dikhata hai! (Showing so much attitude despite being an SC)." Jadhav further said humiliation based on his case continued throughout his five years at one of India's premier educational institutions. Jadhav is one of dozens of students admitted to top educational institutes across India who have spoken out in recent months about enduring caste-based discrimination.[278]

Apeksha Priyadarshini, 31, a PhD scholar at New Delhi's Jawaharlal Nehru University (JNU), said faculty members tended to make "subtle observations" on reserved category students' performance, even though no overt casteist comments were made. "Nonetheless, you can detect the faculty's consistent treatment of students from marginalized communities," said Priyadarshini.[279]

An 18-year-old Dalit student, Darshan Solanki, from IIT Bombay, reportedly died by suicide. His family alleges he faced caste-based discrimination while at the prestigious institute. Solanki, a first-year Chemical Engineering student, reportedly jumped from his hostel building.[280]

Darshan Solanki's sister, Jhanvi, claims her brother experienced a shift in his friends' behaviour after they learned of his Dalit caste. She says they stopped talking to him and socializing. Darshan's mother believes he felt tortured by this isolation and took his own life due to the distress. His father, unaware of the severity of the situation, mentioned a seemingly normal conversation just before the reported suicide.[281]

A Dalit village development officer, Trivendra Kumar Gautam, in Lakhimpur Kheri, Uttar Pradesh, allegedly committed suicide by hanging. Gautam's family reported he had been repeatedly subjected to humiliation and casteist remarks.[282]

In November 2023, Mr. Mahesh died by suicide following his arrest by police in Dommeru village, Kovvuru. His family alleges that he was

278 https://article-14.com/post/-caste-on-campus-dalit-students-face-exclusion-alienation-in-india-s-higher-education-institutions--642b88a7149fe (accessed on 04th October 2024).

279 https://article-14.com/post/-caste-on-campus-dalit-students-face-exclusion-alienation-in-india-s-higher-education-institutions--642b88a7149fe (accessed on 27th June 2024).

280 https://scroll.in/latest/1043916/dalit-student-death-no-indication-that-it-was-linked-to-caste-bias-says-iit-bombay (downloaded on 27th June 2024).

281 M.C. Raj and Jyothi Raj *Dyche, the Dalit Psyche*..., 255.

282 https://www.indiatoday.in/india/story/up-young-dalit-officer-commits-suicide-after-farmer-body-humiliates-him-uses-casteist-slurs-1596614-2019-09-07 (downloaded on 27th June 2024).

mistreated and humiliated while in custody. The arrest was connected to a dispute involving the removal of a YSRCP flex banner.[283]

Dalit youth in India endure a detrimental life spoiled by systemic caste-based discrimination and oppression. They face constant rejection and humiliation, leading to severe emotional and psychological distress. The social stigma and lack of opportunities exacerbate their plight, often pushing them towards extreme measures, including suicide. The traumatic life experiences faced by Suicides among Dalit youth is a growing social issue that demands urgent attention on the pertinent psychosocial problems.

The above real-life situations witnessed in this reading indicate the lack of solid support systems vital for the existence of the marginalized, especially in an inclusive approach. Moreover, the particular reference here to the lack of support systems implies several aspects, including a lack of coherence between various institutions, mechanisms and laws. However, if duly addressed and corrective measures are taken and applied, the confidence of the Dalits can be strengthened, and their dignity and identity can be positively enhanced. Also, strengthening the law enforcing mechanisms will clearly drive the essential message to the oppressors and enable the oppressed community to seek justice and live peacefully.

Interweaving Jeremiah's Lament and Dalit Experience

Jeremiah's lament in 20:1-18 finds deep resonance with the experiences of Dalit youth in India. Both Jeremiah and Dalit youth experience intense rejection, humiliation, and oppression. Both struggle with feelings of hopelessness and despair. Yet, both also demonstrate resilience in the face of overwhelming adversity. Jeremiah's refusal to remain silent in the face of his pain provides a model for Dalit youth to confront their own suffering and seek justice.

One of the key insights from Jeremiah's lament is the importance of having spaces and channels for emotional expression. For Dalit youth, creating such spaces is essential to addressing the psychosocial consequences of caste based oppression. Schools, religious institutions, and community organizations must prioritize mental health support and create environments where Dalit youth can express their emotions without fear of judgment or further rejection.

Jeremiah's voice, though filled with sorrow and despair, is not just about giving up. It's a cry for help, a plea for justice. His unwavering

283 https://www.thehindu.com/news/national/andhra-pradesh/kin-of-kovvur-dalit-youth-who-died-by-suicide-over-humiliation-by-police-given-house-site-patta-job/article67719496.ece (downloaded on 27th June 2024).

commitment to justice and his refusal to give up on his prophetic calling demonstrate a profound resilience in the face of suffering'

For young Dalits, this can be a real inspiration. It shows that even when things seem hopeless, there's still a way forward. Lamenting the injustices they face is not just about feeling sorry for themselves. It's the first step in standing up and demanding change.

Jeremiah's resilience, despite his suffering, offers a powerful lesson for Dalit youth. His ability to continue his prophetic mission, even in the face of physical and emotional pain, serves as a model of endurance and perseverance. This resilience does not come from a denial of suffering but from an honest engagement with it. For Dalit youth, embracing their pain and finding ways to articulate it can be a first step towards building resilience in the face of systemic oppression.

Lament is not merely an individual act of emotional release; it is also a public call for justice. Jeremiah's lament was directed not only towards God but also towards the unjust structures of his society. Similarly, the laments of Dalit youth must be heard as a demand for systemic change. Addressing the root causes of caste-based discrimination and creating pathways for social mobility are essential components of a just society. Lament, in this sense, becomes a powerful tool for advocacy and social transformation.

Conclusion

The prophetic vocation of the prophet Jeremiah encompasses a prism of experiences physically, emotionally and spiritually. This text (Jeremiah 20: 1-18), in particular, encapsulates human expressions resonating with lament, resilience and the quest for justice. The similarity in these emotional outpours with the Dalit expressions amidst caste-based discrimination, oppression, rejection and humiliation is brought to the fore especially among the Dalit youth in India.

Interweaving through the challenges and personal trauma faced day in and day out, a majority of the Dalit youth succumb to psycho-social problems, even to the extent of committing suicide, which is an emerging social problem. Taking into purview, the above context among the Dalit youth, Jeremiah's lament in 20: 1-18 is considered a relevant text that narrates Jeremiah's expressions. Jeremiah's lamentation shows that it is better to vent one's emotions and feel deeply, even in despair. Thus, the present study takes into account the gamut of psychosocial repercussions, especially the nature of suicidal tendencies among Dalits, by drawing implications from Jeremiah 20: 1-18, especially spaces and channels of expression for individuals as well as community.

The striking similarities between the experiences of the prophet and the Dalit youth, especially about one's identity, social alienation, intense conflict and frustration, come out of multilayered internal and external environments. Some of these practices have existed for several eras and have resisted change. Multi dimensional conflicts are borne out of social, economic, psychological, and political inequalities, as access to promoting one's life, ambitions, and goals is limited. These limitations pose a threat to one's identity, resulting in extremity to the point of suicidal attempts and eventually ending lives. There is a dire need to address suicide prevention and develop strong network support and access to resources like counseling.

8

Culture of Knowledge in the Book of Job
Exploring Dalit Cultural Interpretation

Jeeva Kumar Ravela

Introduction

Throughout the book of Job, there is a dispute among sages over different ways of talking and expressing their views over a range of themes such as suffering, sin, piety, life, wickedness, knowledge/wisdom and justice of God. Job, an innocent sufferer, encounters the traditional understanding of God and wisdom while talking about suffering and injustice, whereas Job's friends, Elihu and the Yahweh speeches, come up with a different stock. The expressions in various voices compete with one another and stand against one another as it is the way the book has been composed (4:12-13; 6:4; 8:8-10; 11:6-9; 15:8-10; 22:3-5; 28:12-14; 32:11-14; 38:2; 39:1-2; 42:1-4). Contention over the arguments reveals the ancient social world's cultural values and morals and the knowledge that those cultural value systems purport. The unending debate presents the way sages perceive and deliberate various views. Such an understanding leads one to raise the following questions: Can one unveil the cultural nuances that designed and deliberated over the pressing needs of innocent suffering and justice in the Joban community? Have the views of various protagonists come from learned wisdom that informs a culture of sages who held traditional knowledge? If so, do Job's views in the dialogue part reveal a collective voice of unexpressed and undisclosed cultural wisdom for the sufferers in the Joban community? According to the debates in the book, is wisdom an unchanged way of life and a fixed system of values by the divine?

The rival discourses in the book of Job can be juxtaposed with contemporary discourses of the postmodern cultural world in general and the Dalit cultural world in the Indian context in particular. The Book of Job presents a confluence of traditional wisdom and heterodox arguments that eventually unfold possible alternative views in understanding multiple voices embedded in the arguments. Dalit readings are counter readings in nature seeking alternative voices to make known and heard. Dalit interpretation primarily works with the reader-oriented approach that considers both diachronic and synchronic approaches in a balanced way. Prof. Jesurathnam is the pioneer of such a study in the Indian context and contributed a lot to reading the Bible, considering the struggles of Dalits in this country. Dalit cultural interpretation takes into consideration the cultural discourses that question and criticize the dominant cultural worldviews which impinge on the lives of Dalits for ages. Such a reading will unravel the dominant traditional views that rational views can subvert.

Dalit Cultural Interpretation: Methodological Considerations

In the postmodern context, there is a rivalry between traditional beliefs and rational questions. Sociocultural studies invigorate the social structures and cultural systems of human communities. Sociology focuses on the nature and function of societal structures and different aspects of society, with all the changes occurring due to various social factors such as social mobility and changing social patterns. Cultural studies examine accepted and followed human behaviour along with its custom of belief systems that influence human communities over a period of time. Furthermore, it is a study of the way of life of a community, the structure of a system of symbols and a set of adaptive strategies for community life.[284] Cultural studies affirm that every culture is embedded in a worldview, sustaining a notion of life, knowledge, economy, philosophy, political consciousness and even spirituality. At the same time, it is to notify that every religion produces and promulgates a specific cultural worldview. The religious ideologies influence cultures that shape, govern and guarantee a culture's sustenance in any society.[285] At the same time, cultures sustain a set of values, which can be considered a system of knowledge embedded in them.

284 S. M. Michael, "Cultural Studies and Theologizing on the Empowerment of Dalits in India" in *Frontiers in Dalit Hermeneutics*, ed, James Massey and Samson Prabhakar (Bangalore: BTESSC, 2005), 74ff.

285 Max Weber, *Protestant Ethic and the Spirit of Capitalism* (New York: Charles Scribner's Sons, 1958), quoted in S. M. Michael, "Cultural Studies and Theologizing on the Empowerment of Dalits in India" in *Frontiers in Dalit Hermeneutics*, 78.

Cultural interpretation of the Bible is well-received in scholarly interactions. Brian Blount makes an effort to frame and employ cultural interpretation in a context where racial oppression is a painful memory among oppressed communities.[286] Considering the categories of text-linguistic inquiry that utilizes 'textual, ideational and interpersonal' and taking the aid of the sociological model that works through 'interpreter's worldly setting', Brian reads the biblical texts to unravel various nuances that inform vivid meanings of the text. What is interesting about Brian's proposal is that every interpreter can blend his/her social context into the inventive interpretation of a text for a deeper meaning to be embedded in it. One can assert that it is part of contextual, cultural interpretations of a text as an interpreter reads a text from a specific sociocultural context.[287] Contextual interpretations in the Indian context read a text in a specific context, informing what the scripture proposes to face and fight against discrimination. However, continuing such a textual and ideational reading, cultural interpretation emphasizes the reader's cultural context to interpret the text for a different meaning as a response to the present context. Taking such a cue from Brian's cultural interpretation, this essay uses his idea of merging the sociocultural context of the readers to read a biblical text to affirm the deep-seated meanings in the text.

In the Indian context, while the age-old teachings of religions maintain their dominance, impinging a culture of knowledge, rationale questions try to subvert the dominance of traditional values through centrifugal arguments. For instance, the traditional Hindu culture produced the existence of a caste system as the religio-cultural norm. It projects that caste cultures have to be subservient to the given traditional culture of knowledge. On the contrary, the Dalit discourses as indigenous voices raise rational questions, nullifying the traditional caste culture and initiating cultural discourses to discover the inherent values in the marginalized communities. Such a rivalry leads to the discovery of knowledge in all cultures. Dalit cultural interpretation considers the cultural values available through the cultural lives and production symbols of Dalits that the cultural discourses unveil when they talk about the cultural knowledge of Dalits.

286 Brian K. Blount, *Cultural Interpretation: Reorienting New Testament Criticism* (Minneapolis: Fortress Press, 1995), 7–17.

287 K. Jesurathnam understands that contextual readings use the reader-centred method. It empowers the readers as 'ideologues' as their preunderstanding of a text influences one's interpretation of the text. See, K. Jesurathnam, *Dalit Liberative Hermeneutics: Indian Christian Dalit Interpretation of Psalm 22* (New Delhi: ISPCK, 2010), 3-5.

In the Indian context, the cultural discourses attract everyone's attention as they propel to speak out the cultural rivalry between Hindu and non-Hindu cultures. Hinduism continues to sustain an oppressive sociocultural structure in the form of a caste system, which is being buttressed by its religious teachings. In the recent past, sociocultural discourses in the Indian context point out that there is a fundamental difference between the culture of Hinduism and the cultures of indigenous communities. Kanch Ilaiah argues that indigenous communities like Dalits and Tribals sustain a productive culture, which is rooted in the tasks of production and agriculture. In contrast, Hindu culture does not know productive culture and its ethics.[288] Brahmins, the legitimators of Hindu culture, claim that their knowledge originated in the divine and that whatever they speak is divine. Ilaiah criticizes such a dominant culture as parasitic, and it does not engage in critical thinking about specific issues. Mainly, productive cultures of Dalits engage in working for the good of society despite the suffering and marginalization due to caste stigma and oppression imposed by the dominant Hindu religion and its culture. Ilaiah considers knowledge in the cultures of Dalit-Bahujan[289] is immense as it comes from the living nature of the Dalits and backward communities in the Indian context. Indigenous Dalit cultural discourses claim that the dominant caste culture of Hinduism overrides the fundamental values of Dalit-Bahujan cultures, undermining their rich cultural values and philosophies. As Ilaiah argued, Hindu cultural knowledge has not contributed to the Indian social spectrum's growth to be a better society over the years.

The essential point for our discussion is that Dalit cultural resources contribute a vast array of social values which are hitherto neglected and undermined. Those cultural resources unfold the cultural knowledge of Dalit communities, labelled as polluted and maligned. The Dalit cultural discourse unearths Dalit knowledge rooted in their daily living as a sociocultural community. Hence, the following is the lens one can use to read the biblical text to understand rivalry in the discourses on culture and cultural knowledge. Dalit cultural interpretation of the Bible asserts that every human culture sustains a system of knowledge that promotes equality and human dignity; one needs to understand that social stabilization must be the point of cultural knowledge; Dalit cultural discourses criticize manipulative mechanism of dominant cultures, and strive to unearth rich social values, economic ethos and political principles for the good of

288 Kanch Ilaiah, *Post-Hindu India: A Discourse on Dalit-Bahujan Socio-spiritual and Scientific Revolution* (New Delhi: Sage Publications, 2009), x - xi.

289 Dalit-Bahujan is a term that informs a collective expression of Dalits and other backward communities in the Indian context.

humanity. This essay keeps these views pivotal, and attempts to look at the discourses on the notion of knowledge to comprehend the rigorous debate in the book it can facilitate an amicable intellectual discussion among the communities for an exchange of knowledge that can ensure a sociable living in a plurality of religions and cultural communities of Indian society. Hence, this paper attempts to examine the following: First, it examines the idea of knowledge, Job, and friends exchange through the dialogue part. Second, it investigates rivalry in the discourses of Job and his friends, identifying the sources of knowledge they bring forth; finally, how and what the discourses in the book of Job inform and shape the Dalit cultural arguments and the idea of knowledge in the cultures of marginal communities.

Sociocultural World of the Book of Job

The wisdom traditions in ancient Israel show that wise men or sages (*hakam*) played a vital role in inculcating wise teachings through family/clan, royal court, and schools. Robert Gordis long ago argued that the social world of wisdom literature can be viewed in the lives of sages, who sustained both conventional and unconventional wise sayings over centuries.[290] These sages represent two types of schools of thought: One is the main school, which taught conventional wisdom, wherein Yahweh, the God of Israel, was the centre of the origin of wisdom, and second, the school of dissidents, where the cultivation of heterodoxism was rampant. These two schools maintained certain antagonism in their arguments over various concerns of life.[291] R. N. Whybray views that the social world of wisdom literature is caught up in the complex history of ancient Israel through the pre-exile, exile, and post-exilic periods, as each wisdom book can be identified with specific social concerns in Israel's history.[292] As wisdom books present numerous teaching materials, each book’s cultural ideology is undoubtedly different from one another to a certain extent.

Among the books of wisdom literature in the Old Testament, the book of Job is unique, encompassing a profound discussion about the traditional given knowledge on suffering, injustice, the life of wicked and righteous, and justice of God. The book presents a deep contemplation over the conventional wise teachings, interrogating various issues through dialogue and argument. While the book poses innumerable questions about its place

290 Robert R Gordis, “The Social World of the Wisdom Literature”, *Hebrew Union College Annual*, 18 (1944): 82.

291 Robert Gordis, “The Social World of the Wisdom Literature”, 83f.

292 R. N. Whybray “The Social World of the Wisdom Writers” in *The World of Ancient Israel: Sociological, Anthropological and Political Perspectives: Essays by Members of the Society for Old Testament Study*, ed, R. E. Clements (Cambridge: CUP, 1991): 229-247.

in the socio-historical and religio-cultural life of ancient Israel, the history of composition adds complexity to understanding the purpose and purview of the book in the life and faith of ancient Israel. The book of Job has a long composition history from the pre-monarchic period through the post-exilic period. Nevertheless, most scholars place the book during the horrible exilic experiences and completed its composition in the early post-exilic period. The book is a combination of prose and poetry. The prose part (1:1-2:13 and 42:7-17) is in narrative style, whereas poetry (3-31; 32-37; 38:1-42:6) is a dialogue (through dispute and exchange of thoughts) in its literary style.

Nevertheless, the book invites its readers to draw various insights when reading from a particular sociocultural context. One must grapple with two challenges while understanding the sociocultural world of the Book of Job. First, the social class of sages in the social structure of ancient Israel; second, the cultural ideologies of sages that they held on to. The social class of sages probably inform a range of their cultural worldviews. Robert Gordis views that sages were from the middle class and lived as independent wisdom teachers but reflected an upper-class orientation in their teachings. By examining the profound teaching of wisdom books, Gordis believes that sages uphold instructions of morality and teachings on faith through the wisdom schools.[293] Perhaps the discussion has been unending as there are contentions about identifying the social class of sages. One can assert that sociological studies help unravel the social class of sages. Norman K. Gottwald's sociological study informs the class society of ancient Israel as follows: ruling class group, middle layers and exploited classes. Gottwald views sages as part of state scribal activities as they wrote the records, preserved the royal decrees and maintained official kingdom records.[294] In this social setting, he locates scribes and authors of wisdom literature as a layer within the ruling class group.

Mark R. Sneed informs that the aid of the sociology of knowledge would assist in assessing the social stratification of ancient Israelite society, in which sages can be notified. Seeing the ancient Israelite society as a master-slave society, Mark R Sneed understands that sages belong to a middle-class layer as an appendage of the master class, who occasionally

293 Robert R Gordis, "The Social World of the Wisdom Literature", *Hebrew Union College Annual*, 115f.

294 Gottwald examines various social class theories according to the study of sociology. He is convinced of the economic category influenced by Marx's theory of stratification, which emphasizes that economic standards define class systems in a society. Norman K. Gottwald, "A Hypothesis about Social Class in Monarchic Israel in the Light of Contemporary Studies of Social Class and Social Stratification" in *The Hebrew Bible in Its Social World and In Ours*, ed, Norman K. Gottwald (Atlanta: Scholars Press, 1993), 160.

came up with criticism of power structures in biblical literature.[295] Thus, Sneeds maintains that the sages were a 'retainer social' class in the ancient world. In other words, they were the intellectual body in the master class, ameliorating the intricacies of sensitive views for social justice and social welfare in literature. They were responsible for producing various required materials for the benefit of the royal administration, carrying multiple responsibilities such as documenting and teaching wisdom.[296] So, the sages worked in different capacities in the ancient royal courts, producing a wide range of wisdom material. They would have perceived the knowledge and wisdom from different sources in their social context. Moreover, at the same time, sages would have taken a stand to support the ideology of the dominant notions of piety and prosperity. Thus, sages can be seen as a social class in the middle layers, which supports the ideology of the ruling elite class. It is undoubtedly a difficult task to identify the sociocultural world of the Book of Job as it needs to give a clue about its socio-historical location in the life and faith of ancient Israel. In addition, it is challenging to identify the sociocultural background of the book, as there is no indication of social history in it. Nevertheless, utilizing the given literary evidence in the book, scholars made impressive attempts to understand the cultural worldviews of sages and their profound thoughts over several factors like suffering, piety, life, injustice and justice of God.

Samuel Terrien understands that the sage in the book of Job is a master of unconventional wisdom, employing a wide range of linguistic, stylistic, rhetorical and thematic elements to point wisdom. Terrien also sees that 'the Joban poet was thoroughly acquainted with the literature of ancient Israel, but he lived amid a cultural and cultic vacuum that fits neither the last days of the Kingdom of Judah in the sixth century B.C.E. nor the earl days of Restoration in the fifth and fourth centuries.' Thus, he considers the *Sitz im Leben* of the Book of Job, mostly the dialogue part, to be most likely that of the first generation of the exile, between 585 and 570 B.C.E.[297] Albertz Rainer conducts a thorough literary analysis of the book and assumes that sages hold different religio-cultural worldviews. According to Rainer, sages belong to an ideal group of learners who taught elite pious

295 Mark R. Sneed, “Middle Class in Ancient Israel?” in *The Concept of Class in Ancient Israel*, 64f.

296 Mark R Sneed, *The Social World of the Sages: An Introduction to Israelite and Jewish Wisdom Literature* (Minneapolis: Fortress Press, 2015), 286. Also see Mark R. Sneed, "The Social Setting of the Wisdom Literature" 18.

297 Samuel Terrien, “Job as a Sage” in *The Sage in Israel and The Ancient Near East*, eds, John G. Gummie and Leo G. Perdue (Winona Lake: Eisenbrauns, 1990), 239-240.

communities during crises and socio-political calamities like exile.[298] He believes that Job and his friends come from the guild of pious sages. They are primarily concerned about comforting Job (Job 2:11) in his present predicament. However, as the exchange of arguments is rigorous, they cling to conventional wise teachings, the culture of knowledge of sages. On the other hand, Job maintains unconventional wisdom from his experience as an innocent suffering. Rainer's study convinces one to realize vivid views of sages over a range of concerns that unfold the book's richness in holding a culture of conventional and unconventional knowledge that ancient wise taught and practised. The following discussion focuses on the dialogues between Job and his friends to further delineate how the culture of traditional knowledge and unconventional wise teachings meet at the matrix of intense debate over knowing the secrets of wisdom as the knowledge they share.

Discourses of Knowledge: Arguments in the Book of Job

The Book of Job is a literary platform that unfolds the culture of knowledge of pious sages who hold both conventional and unconventional wise teachings. As the book of Job contains an intense debate over various views on piety, suffering, injustice and justice of God, one can see that Job and his friends as sages differed on many issues. Job's friends hold the traditional wisdom, which reflects a culture of knowledge that sustains conventional teachings and clings to the dominant ideology of retributive principle. On the contrary, Job embraces unconventional arguments, countering and encountering the traditional culture of knowledge of friends. With this view, we examine some of Job's arguments and his friends' arguments to understand the dispute over various issues concerning knowledge.

The word '*dayat*' means knowledge or knowing something deeply or profoundly. *It* comes from the word *yadah*, which means proper perception of things or knowing things purely and aptly with moral quality (Genesis 2:9, 17).[299] In its prose tale (Chaps 1-2 and 42:7-17), the book of Job affirms that a righteous person will be rewarded despite suffering and destruction if he endures in his life. Job is declared righteous and upright, but he was tested to see whether he holds his faith in the face of severe oppression and suffering. The story continues to inform that he has not sinned against God despite the suffering he goes through (2:10). The traditional retributive principle, which says that the righteous will be rewarded and the wicked will be punished, dominates the prose part of the book. The poetry presents

298 Rainer Albertz, "The Sage and Pious Wisdom in the Book of Job: The Friends' Perspective" in *The Sage in Israel and the Ancient Near East*, eds, John Gummie and Leo G. Perdue (Winona Lake: Eisenbrauns, 1990), 247-248.

299 Francis Brown, *The Brown-Driver-Briggs Hebrew and English Lexicon*, Ninth ed, (Peabody: Hendrickson Publishers, 2005), 395.

a dialogue part through various voices of Job and his friends (Chaps 3-26) that rationale questioning of such a tradition is inevitable as it has to respond to the interrogations of the righteous about the suffering and injustice of God and the world. There comes the hot debate among Job and his friends, enquiring who knows (*dayat* – 5:24-27; 8:9-10; 9:1, 21; 10:7, 13; 11:11; 13:2; 15:9; 19;) what. The word knowledge (*dayat*) is an essential and multifaceted view in the book of Job, as Job, and his friends represent it from different vantage points. James L Crenshaw understands that the ancient Israelite world practices three ways of gaining knowledge: observing nature and human behaviour, learning through creed and reality, and encountering the transcendent one.[300] Crenshaw's views inform that tradition and revelation play crucial roles in knowing things. However, along with tradition and revelation, experience is also vital in expressing knowledge about various things. Jan Dietrich rightly observes that tradition, revelation, and experience are three standard modes of justification in arguments in the book of Job.[301] The central part of the poetry is the dialogue between Job and his friends over suffering, life, piety and justice. One can see that the dialogue part argues about the prose tale in all possible ways, enquiring about the traditional wisdom and knowledge that Job and his friends affirm and uphold. Job comes up with unconventional wisdom, but his friends hold on to the traditional perception of knowledge that Job needs to learn and understand. The following is a brief presentation of the essence of knowledge that Job and his friends have used to counter one another. It also attempts to see whether knowledge implies culture and its moral world. This paper tries to understand the arguments of Job and his friends to examine the way they claim knowledge they have over many things.

Culture of Knowledge in the Speeches of Job and His Friends

Job responds to the calamity that befell him with words that have a heterodox tone. Job curses the days he was born. The phrase ‘let there be darkness’ in 3:3 calls the reversal of the call of God when God says ‘let there be light’ (*Genesis 1:3*). Such a view of Job hints that the dialogue part in the book begins with a view that takes a stand against the notions of traditional belief of the Joban community about God's creation and its order. Job continues to talk about various things in the creation and world that invite Job’s friends to respond with traditional wisdom sayings (Chapters: 4-5; 8; 11; 15; 18; 20; 22; 25). Job confirms that his friends are aware that he is not guilty.

300 James L. Crenshaw, “The Acquisition of Knowledge in Israelite Wisdom Literature” in *Urgent Advice and Probing Questions: Collected Writings on Old Testament Wisdom*, ed, James L. Crenshaw (Georgia: Mercer University Press, 1995), 292–299.

301 Jan Dietrich, “Modes of Argumentation: The Epistemology of Arguments in the Book of Job” *Hebrew Bible and Ancient Israel* 12/3 (2023): 266.

However, they are unable to express the source of deliverance that he can receive (10:7). Job also realizes that friends' knowing of things is not to propose an alternative path of knowledge that he is seeking about divine but scarcely terrifying him for his current situation (10:13). Job struggles to understand God's ways of dealing with the righteous. He does not see any serious divine purpose in his suffering. Job confirms that whatever his friends know (13:2), he also knows it. Probably, it is to counter Eliphaz, who affirms that no one knows of God's purposes in one's life except receiving God's provisions (5:24f). Job's current situation as suffering, his experience of losing social privilege, human dignity and unconsolable words from his friends perturb him that he could not resist raising his voice against the traditional and given views about suffering and injustice. He confirms that 'for the arrows of the Almighty are in me; my spirit drinks their poison; the terror of God are arrayed against me' (6:4). Metaphorically, Job expresses that the knowledge that friends bring forth disturbs, humiliates and marginalizes him. Eventually, he sarcastically says that he has become a laughingstock to his friends (12:4). Abbigail Pelham rightly argues that several metaphorical paths lead one to attain wisdom differently.[302] Perhaps Job's argument proclaims that friends' knowledge of several things leads him to fruition, which Abigail counters by saying that there are innumerable paths to learn wisdom, as the book upholds in its very argument. So, can one state that Job's knowledge over several things that happen to him do not matter to his friends?

Job's friends claim that they have received wisdom from the traditions, God's revelation, and profound personal observations in their learning. The following briefly explains the position of the knowledge they espouse. First, rooted in the traditional retributive principle, Job's friends claim that their experiences (4:8; 15:17; 5:27) gave them critical thought about what they observe in life. When Job questions the validity of their experience, the friends occasionally take up proverbs and call upon honoured traditions (8:8; 15:18; 20:4). Friends' experience of wisdom comes with a rich and traditional knowledge that Job has lost. Eliphaz maintains that I have seen it (4:8), a word came to me (4:12), what do you know that we do not know (15:9); Bildad holds that 'for inquire now of bygone generations, and consider what their ancestors have found (8:8), and consider, and then we shall speak (18:2b); Zophar says that 'I hear censure that insults me, and a spirit beyond my understanding answers me (20:3). The rhetoric of knowing things deeply reverberates in their speeches. Katherine J Dell rightly observes that Job's friends are the vanguard of transmitted advice.

302 Abigail Pelham, "Metaphorical Paths and the End of Wisdom in the Book of Job" *Word & World* 31/4 (2011): 381-387.

Further, they thought Job had lost the way of traditional wisdom and must be drawn back to the traditional wisdom fold.[303] Second, they also emphasized a tradition of learning or being taught in different stages of life. They may have thought about ancient wisdom traditions (15:17-20) that taught and nurtured many generations. For instance, Eliphaz claims that he will show what sages have told and the ancestors have passed onto them (15:17). Such a view inevitably invites one to understand that the reason for a dispute between Job and his friends over knowledge is a traditional knowledge that comes up with inherited authority. Jan Dietrich maintains that Job's friends' main point is that they come up with the 'argument with the authority of tradition'.[304] Dietrich calls such authoritative knowledge trans-generational, typical of inherited wisdom that they passed on to their listeners, like Job.[305] It appears that Job's friends gain such a knowledge by the inherited traditions that provide them social authority and honourable position in their society. In other words, they claim that the knowledge is authoritative and they have right to respond.

Third, Job's friends including Elihu claim they have received wisdom through divine revelation (4:12-21; 33:14-18, 36:7-12). The epistemology of knowledge that friends espouse lies in the 'argument from divine authority'.[306] At the same time, it is evident that Job's personal experience criticizes traditional arguments that claim authority. Job's personal experiences come to the fore, which leads to an explicit critique of inherited wisdom.[307] Here, personal experience differs from the traditional perspective about the tight nexus between deeds and consequences. Thus, the Book of Job, over the argument of knowledge, vows to the moral perception and cultural world of the ancient community. One can unearth nuances of traditions and their authoritative waves that the ancient sages uphold and offer in the Book of Job. Carol A Newsom argues that the Book of Job is a contest of moral imagination that tries to establish the moral values and ethics of interlocutors from their moral worlds.[308] The voices in the book

303 Katherine J. Dell, "Representing Tradition: Exploring the Epistemology of the Friends in the Book of Job" *Hebrew Bible and Ancient Israel* 12/3 (2023): 283.

304 Jan Dietrich, "Modes of Argumentation: The Epistemology of Arguments in the Book of Job", 267.

305 Jan Dietrich, "Modes of Argumentation: The Epistemology of Arguments in the Book of Job", 267f.

306 Jan Dietrich, "Modes of Argumentation: The Epistemology of Arguments in the Book of Job", 268.

307 Jan Dietrich, "Modes of Argumentation: The Epistemology of Arguments in the Book of Job", 268.

308 Carol A Newsom, *The Book of Job: A Contest of Moral Imagination* (Oxford: Oxford University Press, 2003), 24.

of Job compete with one another, expressing a sociocultural authority over what they have learned, received and passed onto the generations. Yahweh speeches extend the horizon of knowledge by introducing the order of the world that God established in the creation. Abigail rightly maintains that 'God directs Job's vision out along a multiplicity of paths, showing him that there is a great variety of ways of being in the world and that God's creation is too diverse and multifarious to be so reduced.'[309] The book culminates with an impression that the multiple ways of knowledge is in the structure of God's creation. God calls Job and his community to realize such an ambiguous and yet, an amicable created order in the creation.

The Book of Job and Dalits: Discourse on Knowledge and Culture

With the above brief examination of the argument of Job and his friends, one can assert that Job comes up with a personal experience that contradicts the traditional, authoritative and divine granted wisdom and knowledge. Further, as a sufferer, Job's observation of life upholds self-thinking and self-imaginative views that claim over against the trans-generational and traditional authority of knowledge. Job's friends, on the other hand, as the wise teachers in the Joban community, affirm that they have an authenticity to teach and that their teachings have divine legitimacy. Life is futile; one should accept whatever comes in the way of one's life. Submission to and humbling before God would bring peace and comfort. Job's friends maintain hierarchy and dominant views about God and justice but never try to address unjust suffering with a view of rationality and criticality by considering socio-economic and political situations.

The Dalit cultural discourses critically view the culture of knowledge the dominant religion promotes in the Indian context. The Indian cultural fabric and its knowledge orientation cling to cultures of parasitism and production. The traditional caste system in India divides human communities into intellectual races and untouchable masses. Kancha Ilaiah criticizes the dominant culture of Brahmins as they claim that their source of knowledge originates from Brahma. They label Dalits and their culture as polluted and insignificant.[310] Dalit sociocultural realities are enormous and they remain intact through the oral traditions of art, music, folk dance, and their simple lifestyle. Approaching Dalit cultural symbols like dappu, music, dance, art, and folklore are not uncommon in Dalit theological discourses. Even theologians have identified the Dalit Sahitya movement (Dalit Literature) as a vital resource that could awaken Dalits to uphold protest and social change

309 Abigail Pelham, "Metaphorical Paths and the End of Wisdom in the Book of Job", 387.

310 Kanch Ilaiah, *Post-Hindu India: A Discourse on Dalit-Bahujan Socio-spiritual and Scientific Revolution*, 26.

as focal points, inspiring Dalits to voice for equality and justice in caste-ridden societies.[311] The traditional occupations they take up reveal their skills and knowledge, which help one to understand the culture of knowledge they possess and practice.[312] One can assert that Dalit cultures embedded in the cultural life of Dalits miss the knowledge dimension in the Dalit cultural discourses. In addition, cultural symbols drive ethics and democratic values systems, which cultural discourses need to unpack. Sporadically attempted cultural studies affirm that biblical cultural worldviews, have revolutionary potential in empowering Dalits in India.[313] S. M. Michael initiates such a thoughtful study, holding that the biblical cultural worldview can counter the oppressive caste culture of Hinduism. While agreeing with Michael's robust attempt to revisit the cultural oppression of Hinduism with the potentiality of the Biblical cultural world that could curb the hegemony of caste oppression, he did not take the structure of Dalit sociocultural life into consideration when construing the biblical message of liberation. Instead, he considered the Dalit's wretched condition as an object to be braced by the biblical cultural world.

The cultural struggle of Dalits resonates with the Joban community's cultural struggle to understand knowledge and truth. Such knowledge eventually lays a path to liberation. S. Lourdunathan tried to invigorate a philosophy of liberation against the philosophy of cultural domination that the Hindu caste system has been safeguarding for many years. Using Ambedkar's deconstructive and reconstructive discourse, Lourdunathan addresses the problem of caste and its despotism that created 'other' (Dalits) in Indian society and produced a philosophy of domination as it is the core of caste culture. To deconstruct such a hegemonic philosophy of domination, Dalits must progress in the realms of 'the intellectual, the cultural, the

311 P. G. Jogdand, "Dalit Sahitya Movement: Hermeneutic Perspective" in *Frontiers in Dalit Hermeneutics*, ed, James Massey and Samson Prabhakar (Bangalore: BTESSC/SATHRI, 2005), 65-70.

312 Kancha Ilaiah enumerates the cultural life of Tribals and Dalits, viewing several values and ethics in it. In his valiant attempt to redefine the cultures of the Dalits and Bahujan of this country, Ilaiah calls Tribal communities are unpaid teachers for teaching how to live; he calls Madigas, one of the Dalit communities in the Telugu context, Subaltern scientists; he calls Malas, another Dalit community, productive soldiers. The point that Ilaiah makes here is that each caste community has productive knowledge that has helped them to survive and fight over the oppression of Hindu culture and its caste structure. Kancha Ilaiah, Post-Hindu India: A Discourse on Dalit Bahujan, Socio-Spiritual and Scientific Revolution, 1ff.

313 S. M. Michael, "Cultural Studies and Theologizing on the Empowerment of Dalits in India", 90ff.

economic, the religious, the political and even the spiritual'.[314] It is apparent in Lourdunathan's argument that Dalits must endure a philosophy of resistance and liberation while encountering the caste hegemony and evil structures that caste culture has produced. To endure such a philosophy of resistance and liberation, Dalits must use the cultural knowledge that their cultures provide. At this juncture, the core argument of the book of Job on knowledge invites one to cling to its rich argument and polyvalent discourses to fetch vivid views about knowledge.

The Book of Job provides a significant view informing that the culture of knowledge has several sources and modes of acquisition. Traditional knowledge, passed on to the next generations, has a significant role in the lives of ancient communities. The book also informs that divine revelation is the source of receiving knowledge, but the book contests the discourses on traditional knowledge. The book also discusses experiential knowledge that contests traditional, transgenerational knowledge. Such interpretations would provide ample space for Dalit communities to argue against the culture of knowledge that the dominant castes continue to spread using religion as a defence. The Dalit cultural discourses can become a beacon of hope for Dalits to energize their discourses rooted in their social living, cultural values and economic ethos they practise in their everyday life. An empirical study about the Dalits' sagas, beliefs, values, customs, and traditions will reveal how the dominant caste culture and the knowledge discourses undermine the Dalit culture of knowledge in the Indian context. The Book of Job invites deprived communities to affirm that a culture of knowledge must inculcate morals that can help suffering communities overcome the burden of injustice and marginalization. This paper creates a plausible space for marginalized communities like Dalits to revisit the discourses in the book of Job to gain profound and enriching insights about the knowledge of ancient communities in their contexts.

Conclusion

Based on the argument above, one can make the following remarks:

First, the Book of Job, through the arguments of Job and his friends, presents that the conversation over the culture of knowledge is rooted in the perception of morality and belief systems. There is a moral contest among the interlocutors, and there are no fixed views about the knowledge that the book offers. *Second*, though the traditional perception of knowledge has gained momentum in the discussions, it engages in the discourse of the

314 S. Lourdunathan, "The Cultural Context for Evolving a Philosophy of Dalit Emancipation" in *Frontiers in Dalit Hermeneutics*, ed, James Massey and Samson Prabhakar (Bangalore: BTESSC/SATHRI, 2005), 242.

knowledge as the ancient communities place a plurality of voices alongside to interrogate the moral and cultural worlds of ancient faith communities. *Third*, the Book of Job offers and complements the cultures of knowledge maintained by various interlocutors like Job and his friends, providing space for cultural discourses for further learning of knowledge that emerge from their respective contexts of life. *Fourth*, Dalit cultural discourses can invigorate its culture of knowledge by bringing forth their values, customs and beliefs. They can generate the counterarguments of knowledge that the dominant caste system perpetuates by clinging to the traditional and orthodox intellectual theories backed by religion and culture.

Section - Three

Bible, Politics, Religion and Theology

9

Postsecular Philosophy of Religion
Taking a Cue from Ambedkar

Y. T. Vinayaraj

Being included in the festschrift volume dedicated to Rev. Dr. Kondasingu Jesurathnam, a visionary Christian leader in India and a seasoned biblical teacher, is a great honour and privilege for me. Dr. Jesurathnam is always passionate about connecting the Bible to Dalit life experiences and starts fresh conversations about Dalit biblical hermeneutics. I want to take this opportunity to express my gratitude to him for his contributions to the ministry of the Christian Institute for the Study of Religion (CISRS) during his two years as a member of the executive committee (2023–2025). As he embarks on an incredible chapter in his life, I send him my best wishes for prosperity and blessings.

Introduction

Religion is a social force - Ambedkar 1987b, 23 and Ambedkar, B.R. 1989. *Babasaheb Ambedkar: Writings and Speeches,* Vol. 7. Bombay Education Department, Government of Maharashtra, 471-2.

There is a general renewed interest in the significance of Religion in society. The role of Religion in creating responsible citizens, rebuilding society around equality, justice, and fraternity, and reimagining the state as a democratic and egalitarian space is widely recognized and validated in today's post-secular or post-religious context. India has reached a critical juncture where all available resources are vital and indispensable for restoring our social guild. Regardless of Religion or ideology, Romila Thapar reminds us that in order to oppose the forces of totalitarianism and unitarianism and maintain our hope and faith in the process of democratizing democracy, we must find and gather all the voices of dissent ingrained in our national historical consciousness.[1] In the same line of reasoning, Arundhati Roy exhorts us to mobilize our cultural and religious counter resources in order to confront the increasingly prevalent aspects of imperialism and communalism in our shared civil life: "Our strategy should be not only to confront empire but to lay siege to it. To deprive it of oxygen. To shame it. To mock it. With our art, our music, our literature, our stubbornness, our joy, our brilliance, our sheer relentlessness – and our ability to tell our own stories. Stories that are different from the ones we're being brainwashed to believe."[2]

We discuss the role of Religion in the process of society's transformation not in the days of normalcy, but in the "new normal" in which totalitarian forces use religions, ideologies, and cultures for their political ends. In the current Indian context, religions are being used to spread hateful ideologies and serve as instruments for dividing communities. The victims of this condition have one face: the face of the disenfranchised and marginalized, the people who exist on the periphery of Religion and state. This situation increases violence, violation, and virulence in society. In this critical era of violent Religion and biased politics, we attempt to analyze and identify the opportunities and difficulties facing Indian religious philosophy. This paper, however, focuses on how those on the periphery of faith and state perceive Religion as a whole rather than offering an in-depth and comprehensive discussion of the Indian philosophy of Religion. This essay locates Ambedkar's philosophy of Religion and investigates the possibility of characterizing Religion as an ethical-political practice of justice in India's "religion of the oppressed."

Babasaheb Ambedkar provided a methodical religious philosophy based on the experiences of India's marginalized population. Ambedkar defines Religion as a social force of transformation through dialogue with contemporary philosophical traditions such as Marxism and engagement with the ancient Indian materialist philosophical traditions (1987:23). In contrast to Karl Marx, he acknowledges and affirms the social phenomenon of Religion's fertility as a means of ensuring social revolution and the social emancipation of the marginalized. "Religion is not opium as some hold," he said, acknowledging that it is a part of one's inheritance. Any positive traits I possess or the advantages my education has brought to society, I owe

1 Romila Thapar, *Voices of Dissent* (Gurgaon: Penguin Books, 2020).

2 A. Roy, *Ordinary Person's Guide to Empire* (New Delhi: Penguin Books, 2013).

them to my religious beliefs. I want Religion, but I do not want hypocrisy in the name of religion".[3] Ambedkar is a devout follower of Religion, but he also sharply criticizes the religious rites and practices that support injustice, discrimination, and poverty. This paper finds Ambedkar as an appropriate philosopher of Religion in India who upholds the significance of Religion in the transformation of society and thereby brings the tapestry of the Religion of the oppressed into our debate on religion-in-society.

Philosophy of Religion

Etymologically speaking, philosophy is an investigation into reality (Bouvert Regulas 2015: 5). It looks into the fundamentals of existence and knowledge. It improves our ability to think by enhancing perception and comprehension. The word "Darshan," from the East, reveals its profound significance and alternative reality perception. The philosophy of Religion deals critically with the tenets, doctrines, and rituals of Religion. It facilitates a better understanding and comprehension of Religion. According to Maheshwarappa, the philosophy of religion "is an examination of what religion or theology stands for, like the belief in the existence of God, life beyond the empirical world, rituals and ceremonies that emerged in the long process of social development, divine authority over moral standards, infallibility of the sacred book, the immortality of the soul and its transmigration".[4] The philosophy of Religion offers techniques and procedures for analyzing a religious experience rather than being an adjunct to any religion, religious ideology, or theology. It assesses a community's religious life in light of the state of humanity and society. Studying religious philosophy entails using "critical reason" to analyze the world's significant faiths' tenets, standards, rituals, and behavioural patterns. It considers general human interests when assessing them. The study of the applicability of a given religion's social and moral precepts and how they impact collective human existence is the focus of the philosophy of Religion. The variety of philosophers who study Religion encompasses theists, atheists, agnostics, and theologians; as such, it necessitates an intersectional and multidisciplinary approach. Therefore, all of the main branches of philosophy and other pertinent disciplines like natural science, psychology, sociology, history, and theology are all incorporated into the philosophy of Religion.

What is Religion, however? According to its etymology, Religion is a necessary bond or relationship between God and the universe. It is an act of community that reconciles God and the world. Scholars have

3 D. Keer, *Dr. Babasaheb Ambedkar Life & Mission* (Bombay: Popular Prakashan, 1954).

4 M. Maheshwarappa,"Dr. B.R. Ambedkar Views on Religion: A Philosophical Analysis." *IJCAR*, Vol.7, Issue 8, August (2018).

offered numerous definitions of Religion. According to the Concise Oxford Dictionary, phenomenologists define Religion as "the human recognition of a superhuman controlling power, especially of a personal God or gods entitled to obedience and worship." Phenomenology examines Religion as a phenomenon, covering the full range of religious concepts, practices, organizations, traditions, and symbols. Sociologist Clifford Geertz saw religious tradition as a system of symbols. For him, Religion is a phenomenon of symbols connected to myths and rituals (Geertz 1973:90). Psychologists define Religion as "individual men's feelings, acts, and experiences in their solitude, to the extent that they understand themselves to be about whatever they may regard as divine" (William James). "A set of beliefs, practices, and institutions which men have evolved in various societies" is how sociologists define Religion (Talcott Parsons). Emil Durkheim, Karl Marx, and Max Weber—three contemporary sociologists—challenged Religion's *sui generis* character and upheld its sociological and multidisciplinary implications. Marx, in contrast to Durkheim and Weber, revealed the ideological fabrication of religious symbols to serve the interests of the wealthy and powerful. Marx's critique of Religion, particularly Christianity, has reduced Religion from its "heavenly abode" to the world of the oppressed and disenfranchised. G. Aloysius correctly states that "they all exposed the concealed character of the historic-social dimension of the religious beliefs and practices," regardless of whether it was Weber or Marx.[5]

Marx was an adherent of the Spinozian materialistic tradition, which revealed the materialistic basis of our existence and evolution. Feuerbach defined God as a human project of emancipation and Religion as a social force of transformation, situating Schleiermacher's theory of experience in the materialist backdrop of the social relationship. Slavoj Zizek characterizes Religion as a social movement of love, adopting the Lacanian framework and adhering to this materialistic critique of Religion. Zizek views Religion as a social movement of radical faith that opposes the systems of social hierarchies and marginalization by rejecting the metaphysical content of Christianity and God.[6] Refuting the dichotomy between thinking and being, being and becoming, and God and world, Gilles Deleuze, in the contemporary continental philosophical tradition, envisages a monistic philosophy of life, which is immanent, materialistic, and political in content. The Deleuzian notion of life envisioned a new materialistic thinking prominent in the contemporary postsecular philosophy of Religion.

---

5 G. Aloysius,*Religion as Emancipatory Identity: A Buddhist Movement among the Tamils under Colonialism* (New Delhi: New Age International Publishers, 1998), 3.

6 S. Zizek & J. Millbank, *The Monstrosity of Christ: Paradox or Dialectic*? (New York: MIT Press, 2011).

As a political philosophy of Religion, postsecularism reaffirms the place of Religion in public life, opposing secularism's privatization of Religion. Following the new materialist tradition that relocates Religion in post secularity, Kimerer L. LaMothe defines Religion as "an ongoing rhythm of bodily becoming." New materialists define Religion as a social movement and a social power that "empowers resistance to unsustainable modes of production that exhaust life" (LaMothe 2016:33). In the Indian context, it was Babasaheb Bhimrao Ambedkar (1891-1956) who initiated the process of defining Religion as the process of being and becoming social and political. Interrogating the metaphysical content of the Vedic religiosity that validated the caste system as a divine program and thus substantiated the marginalization and discrimination of Dalits in India, Ambedkar offered a postsecular philosophy of Religion.

Philosophy of Religion in India

India's religious philosophy encompasses heuristic and intuitive knowledge/ experience traditions. This can be seen in the development of Indian religious traditions and ideologies, from the struggle between the Lokayata and Vedic epistemologies in antiquity to the Gandhian and Ambedkarite religious philosophies of the present. The primary focus of the Vedic religious tradition, also known as the *Sanatan Sanskriti*, is on ritualistic practices, or *yajnas*, of sacrifice, intended to appease God or gods who fulfil a function in their favour according to their cosmic significance. However, Rajeev Bhargava reveals the two elite classes, the Brahmins and the Rajanyas, who dominate the ritualistic practices ingrained in this ancient Religion.[7]Lokayata critiqued the Vedic theology, which upholds the hierarchy of the sacred against the profane and thus validates the untouchables' subjugation, and presented a materialistic philosophy that validates the material process of change and transformation. Lokayata refuted the existence of any transcendental idea that would support social hierarchies. It was a political epistemology to challenge the Vedic teachings that substantiated the profanation of Dalit bodies and spaces. Based on its anti-Vedic philosophy and ideology, scholars such as Chattopadhyaya, Debi Chatterjee, and Romila Thapar discovered epistemological continuity between Buddhism and Lokayata.[8] On the other hand, Religion was defined differently from the traditions of (Brahminic) Hinduism by the Bhakti traditions within Hinduism, the Sufism of the Mughal traditions, Sikhism, and Jainism.

7 R. Bhargava,*Reimagining Indian Secularism*(London: Seagull Books, 2023), 6.

8 D. Chattopadhyaya, 1992. *Lokayata: A Study in Ancient Indian Materialisms* (New Delhi: People's Publishing House, 1992), and D. Chatterjee, "Dalits and Religion: Anti-caste Movements in India," in Knut A. Jacobsen (ed.), *Routledge Handbook of South Asian Religions* (London and New York: Routledge, 2021).

In revealing the connection between Lokayata and Buddhism, Sunil Sardar critiques the Vedic ideas of Indian social order in order to show how Buddhist philosophy envisioned a religion of the oppressed.[9] The ethical and rational practice of Religion, as opposed to the hierarchical, hypocritical, and bigoted social order promoted by (Brahminic) Hinduism, was greatly influenced in this country by the teachings of the Gautama Buddha. Buddhism is a protest and heterodox tradition where marginalized groups can struggle against various forms of ritualism, superstitions, and priest craft in favour of moral rectitude and intellectual transparency.[10] Buddhism was not concerned with proving the existence of God or justifying any sacred social structure. It was concerned about the existence of human beings and their relief from sufferings and bondages in the world. Locating in a postsecular framework, Ambedkar sees himself as part of this materialistic tradition and envisions Buddhism as having a contemporary theory of social suffering. Revising the Buddhist narrative of suffering in terms of *parivraja* (leaving home by seeing a sick and an old person), Ambedkar saw *dukkha* as a core feature of humans' social condition. The most prominent features or background of suffering for him were 'inhumanity' and 'injustice' (Ambedkar 1992:126). The Buddhist word for Religion, Dhamma, gave him the means to deal with these suffering socio-political and economic situations in the era of colonial modernity. Ambedkar envisioned Navayana Buddhism, a revised form of Buddhism that continues to spur the definition of Religion as a political strategy for social emancipation.

Postsecualr Philosophy of Religion: Taking Cue from Ambedkar

Ambedkar investigated the prospect of democratizing Indian social order as an interlocutor of colonial modernity, grounded in the counter-socio-political and religious morality that stems from the combination of Indian and Western materialist philosophical traditions. Ambedkar developed a modern political philosophy in support of the untouchables and the marginalized in India due to the influence of Deweyan pragmatism. Ambedkar appropriates Deweyan pragmatism's liberal-scientific thinking from the Western Enlightenment to modernize Indian society and refute irrational Brahminic-Hindu knowledge and customs. Karl Marx was another important interlocutor for Ambedkar. Ambedkar defines class as a collective identity that emerged from the social, political, and economic experiences of the exploited and their shared vulnerabilities for marginalization. Unlike Marx, Ambedkar contends that

9 S. Sardar, "The Socio-Spiritual Slavery of Shudras: A National Agenda for their Liberation." In *The Shudras Vision for a New Path*, edited by Kancha Ilaiah Shepherd and Karthik Raja Karuppusamy (India: Vintage, 2021), 23.

10 G. Aloysius,*Religion as Emancipatory Identity: A Buddhist Movement among the Tamils under Colonialism* (New Delhi: New Age International Publishers, 1998), 210.

the untouchables' labour is already defined as defiled and impure in the Indian context, so it has no value or count.Nonetheless, Ambedkar refers to Dalits as Dalit Varga, a socio-political category, and employs the Marxian concept of class to denote their ability to organize. Through Marx, Ambedkar interacts with Buddhism in a renewed framework to overcome the secular state's failure to address the marginalization of Dalits in India. According to Kancha Ilaiah, Ambedkar, under the influence of Marxism, re-constitutes Buddhism by defining God as a political philosopher and the human self as a futurist and becoming through political engagement (1996:135).

Religion as the Moral Consciousness

As a political thinker in India, Ambedkar recognizes an inherent problem in the epistemological foundation of the Indian socio-political order, which excludes most people based on a social practice—caste. Ambedkar was convinced of the inconsistency in the political understanding of the Indian casteist social order in which the majority of people are permanently excluded and of their struggle to enter into the political domain. In the Indian context of caste discrimination, Ambedkar argues, it is not only the absence of a political conscience but also the absence of a moral conscience that becomes significant. According to him, this moral conscience reorganizes society in favour of justice and equality through the religious content of social structure. Religion, in his opinion, promotes both societal advancement and personal growth. It is a revisionist view of contemporary Western morality based entirely on secular logic and scientific rationality. The supernatural powers, God or his prophets, or heavenly revelations do not impose their will on Religion. It is an important role that stems from the necessity of defending society's weak and preserving harmony among the various tribes, groups, classes, and castes. Religion is nothing more than a morality predicated on the law of love, which is the law of life(Thumma (1999:3). Ambekar was convinced about the limitation of the law of the state to inculcate the moral consciousness in society.

On the contrary, he asserts that social and religious revolutions have always come before political revolutions.[11] But as he correctly pointed out, the issue with India is that Brahminic Hinduism, which is essentially corrupt and evil, acts as a mediator between the moral consciousness of the people and the society. The moral consciousness of India is based on a mischievous and unethical caste system. His criticism of Hinduism stems primarily from this.

---

11 B. R. Ambedkar,*Babasaheb Ambedkar: Writings and Speeches,* Vol. 7 (Bombay Education Department, Government of Maharashtra, 1989), 43.

Ambedkar critically discusses Brahminical Hinduism, which solidifies caste consciousness in society. According to him, caste and social inequality in Hinduism have a "divine basis" and are approved by Religion.[12] It led him to look for a religious foundation for the removal of the caste system and the establishment of a more egalitarian value system.[13] Ambedkar was persuaded of the importance of Religion in upholding moral and egalitarian standards and values and in providing for the needs of the populace. He was convinced that the untouchables required a different discipline to change their caste-based behaviour and mentality.Ambedkar struggled to understand how social actors' dispositions and the perpetuation of the social structure are related.[14] He argues that the exclusivist and enslaving ideology and theology of Vedic religiosity make it morally unacceptable. The majority of Indians are enslaved and have their freedom severely restricted by the authoritarian Hindu social order. The victims of the caste system are outcasts and untouchables, and they are excluded from society's socio-political and economic resources. Ambedkar adopts a moral religiosity and argues for reconstructing the social order based on the contemporary liberal values of justice, equality, and fraternity. He is aware that Hinduism's exclusivist caste epistemology and theology render it incapable of offering an ethical, social life. Here, Ambedkar raises the issue of religious conversion as a Dalit political tactic for achieving social democracy and freedom.[15]

Ambedkar believed Buddhism had the innate capacity to be a moral society founded on political ethics and reasoning. Buddhism has a history of theologically and politically challenging caste epistemology in India, in contrast to Islam and Christianity. Ambedkar thought that the Semitic religions, being alien faiths, could not provide the Dalits with a strong national identity within India. The main goal for India in achieving Dalit participation in Indian politics was to work toward national and political unity within the Indian nation-state. Ambedkar disapproved of all other theistic religions because of their monolithic and irrational theological underpinnings. He engages with the Buddhist philosophy of ethics critically and redefines it as Navayana Buddhism, in which Ambedkar discovers fecundityAmbedkar's ideal community is to be established by the moral conversion of an individual from caste status to political subjectivity, in

12 B. R. Ambedkar, *Babasaheb Ambedkar: Writings and Speeches*, 69.

13 B. R. Ambedkar, *Babasaheb Ambedkar: Writings and Speeches*, 471.

14 M. Fuchs, "Dhamma and the Common Good: religion as Problem and Answer—Ambedkar's Critical Theory of Social Relationality" in *Religious Interactions in Modern India*, edited by Martin Fuchs and Vasudha Dalmia (New Delhi: Oxford University Press, 2019), 373.

15 E. Zelliot,*Ambedkar's World: The Making of Babasaheb and the Dalit Movement* (New Delhi: Navayana, 2004), 76.

opposition to the Marxist understanding of class. Ambedkar thinks that reformed Buddhism has the potential to start this moral transformation because of its anti-casteist epistemological heritage and the moral philosophy of political becoming through the *Sangha* (community). He promoted the idea that a new socio-cultural-political community should be the criterion instead of the state's law since it can create moral unity and social consciousness. Ambedkar's conversion to Buddhism was part of his political agenda to envision a political theology of community and counter-symbolic space that would challenge the casteist social order and advance political subjectivity for the marginalized in Indian society.

The Dhamma as True Religion

Ambedkar defines Religion as a political philosophy of Dhamma, or the ethical-political practice of justice, in accordance with Buddhist philosophy. He makes a distinction between Dhamma and Religion (Dharma). In his view, Dharma, or Religion, is personal, while Dhamma is social. Ambedkar claims that Hinduism, as a modified version of Brahminic philosophy, is ritualistic and thus creates subjectivities and enslaves people. Dhamma, on the other hand, is synonymous with righteousness or having a proper relationship with everyone. Dhamma demands that people have a sociopolitical relationship with one another. The Dhamma is indispensable to society. Dhamma brings about justice and liberty. The elements of Dhamma are *karuna* (compassion) and *prajna* (reason). Our social life remains morally upright and democratic because of this understanding of ethics and compassion. Ambedkar identified four categories for Religion: "Religion in the sense of morality must, therefore, remain the governing principle in every society, Religion it is to function must be in accord with the region which is merely another name for sciences; its moral code must recognize the fundamental tenets of liberty, equality and fraternity; unless a religion recognizes these three fundamental principles of social life, Religion will be doomed; and Religion must not sanctify or ennoble poverty (Ambedkar 1943: 23).Ambedkar, like Buddha, believed that while Dhamma is to reconstruct the world, Religion is linked to disclosing the origin of things or the beginning of things. While Religion is based on transcendence, Dhamma is based on immanence because it is morality. Here, Ambedkar bases his ethico-political practice of faith and spirituality on the Buddhist conception of the *Dhamma-Vinaya* (doctrine & discipline). According to Ambedkar, morality is an attachment to Religion because it is associated with the idea of a foundation that is "beyond" God or transcendental; in contrast, morality replaces God in Dhamma, although there is no God in Dhamma (Ambedkar 1992: 322). In the Dhamma, morality is independent of divine approval or validation from outside of itself (transcendence). It emerges from the social desire for liberty, freedom, and justice in human relationships. Ambedkar clarifies: "Morality in Dhamma arises from the direct necessity for man to love man. It does not require the sanction of God. It is not to please God that man has to be moral. It is for his good that man has to love man" (Ambedkar 1992:323). Even though Ambedkar pushes God aside, he considers morality sacred. Its tendency to favour the weak and the vulnerable makes morality sacred. Ambedkar believed that Religion was true because ethics was sacred. According to Gail Omvedt, Ambedkar's interpretation of the sacred nearly resembles Durkheim's (Omvedt 2003: 260).

Since morality in the Dhamma promotes the defence of the weak, it is revered. The social imperative underlying morality is the survival of the weakest (Ambedkar 1992: 323–50). The politics or morality of the weakest people surviving determines the socio-political life's sacrality. Sacredness does not establish a hierarchical social structure within or outside of socio-political life. In contrast to Religion, social morality governs Dhamma, which upholds the sacred in society rather than through ceremonies, rituals, and liturgies. He sees the Dhamma as practical and thus internally political, not merely rhetorical. Our efforts to make society more moral and ethical determine what is holy in social life. Dhamma is the pursuit of an ethical, compassionate, and fraternal social life rather than faith in a supernatural entity. God is viewed as the ultimate ethos of responsibility that calls us to constantly strive for an ethical-political community of love and justice, not as a point of legitimation. The political construction of just relationships within the community is what embodies the transformation of society, not any transcendental logic. Here is where Giorgio Agamben's post-continental philosophy holds that "the world itself, as it is thus, and insofar as it is absolutely and irreparably profane, is God." Ambedkar's political theology of (no) God converge (Agamben 1993:90). Agamben contends that the materialist and politically charged "being thus" of things contains God as the divine potentiality within. Naturally, this is where Catherine Keller's adage—"If God is immaterial, God does not matter"—becomes more important (2006:91). Christian theology is prompted by Ambedkar's political theory of (no) God to look for an embodied, enfleshed, and mattered God who is the "being thus" of all political practices of equality, justice, and freedom.

Conclusion

Ambedkar's political philosophy of Religion, which affirms the restructuring of Indian social order in favour of the weak and vulnerable, becomes crucially significant and relevant in the contemporary Indian political context where Hindutva ideology—the political philosophy of orthodox Hinduism—reinforces the age-old casteist and hierarchical social values and practices for the sake of retaining political power. Being an imperial ideology of transcendence, Hindutva substantiates the hierarchical ordering of society and thus validates the socio-political and economic exclusion of the Dalits in this country by legitimizing an "imperio-colonial sense" or "beyond" in the social order. It is interesting to observe how well-suited neo-capitalism and neo-liberalism are to sustaining political power and social resources in this neo-fascist ideology—two byproducts of modernity. Here, we witness the unholy coalition of neo-capitalists and religious fundamentalists that incite hatred and violence among different religious and cultural groups. The religious and cultural minorities can reinterpret Religion as a social force of emancipation rather than as a set of rites and rituals that validate spiritual and social hierarchy, thanks to Ambedkar's concept of Dhamma as the ethical-political practice of justice. Ambedkar provides a post-secular political philosophy of Religion that enables us to see beyond the dialectics between Religion and secularism and to envision an ethical community of equality and fraternity—"the radical democracy to come" (Jacques Derrida). Religion, after Ambedkar, is a political process that helps people become morally upright members of a "political society" (Partha Chatterji). Of course, Ambedkar envisages a postsecular religion that repositions it as an ethical-political practice of justice.

10

Freedom in Galatians and Indian Constitution
A Comparative Analysis

Laurence Culas

I am immensely grateful to contribute an article to the Festschrift in Honour of Rev. Dr. Kondasingu Jesurathnam on his 60th birthday. His profound biblical insights at SBSI gatherings were a source of inspiration. I am grateful to him for collaborating while I served as the Secretary and President of SBSI.

Introduction

The Preamble to the Indian Constitution underlines the core values: Justice, Liberty, Equality and Fraternity. This paper concentrates on one of the core values, namely Liberty or Freedom. The Preamble secures an assertion that liberty of thought, expression, belief, faith and worship are for all people of India. The Constitution of India secures for its citizens the freedom that everyone, without bias, has the right to think and express their views without harming other's liberty. Does this core value encapsulated in the Preamble and the Constitution appear consistent with Christian usage? This essay outlines Paul's understanding of Christian freedom in the Letter to the Galatians and then relates it to the freedom assured in the Indian Constitution.

Letter to the Galatians

Paul's letter to the Galatians is often characterized as the *Magna Carta* of Christian freedom because, in this epistle, Paul proclaims a new era in Christ. This section will answer the following questions: What is the context in which Paul speaks about freedom in Galatians? What is the meaning of freedom in Galatians?

Context

From the letter's content, it is evident that Paul's addressees are not ethnically Jewish. They are Gentiles, who probably remained in close relation with Jewish communities. They are "most likely among the descendants of Celts who had invaded western and central Asia Minor in the third century BC and had settled in the territory around Ancyra (modern Ankara, Turkey)."[16] Paul had travelled through this area during his second missionary journey (Acts 16:6). Again, during the third missionary journey, he had journeyed through this place (Acts 18:23). During Paul's visit, they would have stayed with the Jewish communities as thus received Paul's gospel.[17]

The Galatians had heard Paul preach Christ crucified (3:1). Thus, they had received the spirit (3:2) and had come to know God (4:9). But they were enticed by others – the Judaizers –[18]To add observances of the Jewish Law, including the rite of circumcision, to the cross of Christ as a means of salvation (5:2-3; 6:12-12). When Paul perceived the situation, he wrote this letter to defend his apostolic authority and the correct understanding of the faith. Paul argued that Christ is sufficient for salvation (3:1-5); Christians live by faith in the indwelling Christ (2:19-20; 3:22) or through the spirit by faith (5:5). In the context of such an argument, Paul uses the language of freedom.

---

16 Catherine Upchurch, *et al.* (eds.), *Little Rock Catholic Study Bible* (Bangalore: Claretian Publications, 2010), 2381.

17 For the chronology and date of the events written down in the letter, see Martinus C. de Boer, *Galatians: A Commentary* (Westminster: John Knox Press, 2011), 5-11; Richard N. Longenecker, *Galatians*, WBC 41 (Nashville: Thomas Nelson, 1990), lxxii-lxxxviii. See also Hans D. Betz, *Galatians: A Commentary on Paul's Letter to the Churches in Galatia*, Hermeneia (Philadelphia: Fortress Press, 1979); Robert Jewett, *A Chronology of Paul's Life* (Philadelphia: Fortress Press, 1979).

18 Those who propagated other interpretations of Christianity in Galatia are probably the converts from Judaism. The name "Judaizers" is sometimes applied to them. It has specifically been suggested that they were Jewish Christians who had come from the austere Essene sect. See C. Upchurch, *et al.* (eds.), *Little Rock Catholic Study Bible*, 2381-2382.

Freedom in Galatians

Freedom becomes "the basic concept underlying Paul's argument throughout the letter."[19] The Greek word *lutheri*e, which is translated as freedom, occurs more frequently in Paul's Letter to the Galatians than in any other NT writing.[20] In the letter, Paul uses the term "freedom" and its cognates ten times.[21] This term assumes equal importance in all occurrences in relation to the concept of the new identity in Christ (cf. 3:26-29; 4:21-31). For lack of space limitations, we consider two instances in Galatians where the phrase 'freedom in Christ' occurs.

Galatians 2

The first occurrence of the phrase is in the *letter's narratio*n, where Paul's historic call to preach the gospel is narrated (1:11-2:14).[22] In this narrative, Paul gives a retrospective view of his former life: his gospel is not of human origin (1:12-24), his gospel is approved by Jerusalem church leaders (2:1-10), and his gospel challenged Peter's inconsistency at Antioch (2:11-14). The incidence of the phrase, 'freedom in Christ,' is found in the micro-narrative, where Paul describes his second visit to Jerusalem church and the approval of his gospel by the leaders there (2:1-10), particularly in v 4: "But because of the false believers secretly brought in, who slipped in to spy on the freedom we have in Christ Jesus so that they might enslave us."[23]

In the particular pericope of Paul's meeting with Jerusalem leaders (2:1-10), Paul's mention of 'freedom in Christ' is reminiscent of situations in communities of Jewish and non-Jewish Christians in Antioch (cf. Acts 15:5), who were characterized by unity in Christ, until the arrival of the "false brothers" (Gal 2:4). These Judaizers pressed for the circumcision of Gentiles and their obligation to observe the Mosaic Law. But Paul

---

19 Hans D. Betz, *Galatians*,255.

20 Federico P. Ramos, *La Libertad en la Carta a los Gálatas* (Madrid: EAPSA, 1977).

21 Four times as the noun 'freedom': 2:4; 5:1, 13[2] and six times as an adjective 'free': 3:28; 4:22, 23, 26, 30, 31. See Abel Frantisek, "Freedom in Christ in Galatians: A Matter of Identity," *Communio Viatorum* 61 (2019) 235-255, 242.

22 Joseph A. Fitzmyer, "The Letter to the Galatians," in *New Jerome Biblical Commentary*, Raymond E. Brown, *et al.*, eds. (Bangalore, TPI, 1990), 780-790, 782 divides the letter into six parts: 1. Introduction (1:1-11); 2. *Narratio* (1:12-2:14); 3. *Propositio* (2:15-21); 4. *Probatio* (3:1-4:31); 5. *Exhortation* (5:1-6:10); 6. *Postscriptio* (6:11-18). For the various structures of the letter, see Martinus de Boer, *Galatians*, 11-15; Richard N. Longenecker, *Galatians*, c-cxix; Nils A. Dahl, "Paul's Letter to the Galatians: Epistolary Genre, Content and Structure," in *The Galatians Debate: Contemporary Issues in Rhetorical and Historical Interpretation*, Mark D. Nanos, ed. (Peabody: Hendrickson Publishers, 2002), 17-142.

23 Biblical texts refer to *New Revised Standard Version* (Bangalore: TPI, 1993).

emphasizes the significant point made in the Jerusalem meeting: the “pillar” apostles preached circumcision-free gospel (Gal 2:9 cf. Acts 15:6-15); the same gospel had been entrusted to him by God (2:7), even in the face of another faction, who are labelled the “false brothers.” These false brothers are advocates of circumcision for Gentiles.[24] Paul portrays the “false brothers” as spies who have "infiltrated our ranks’[25] to "enslave" the free citizens. They “slipped in to spy on the freedom we have in Christ Jesus” (2:4). “They were suspiciously observing the freedom with which Jews and Gentiles associated and worshipped together, including the celebration of the Lord’s Supper.”[26] Hence, 'freedom in Christ Jesus' refers to the equality of non-Jewish Christians among Jewish Christians (3:28).[27]

In Christ Jesus, the Gentiles have been freed from the Law. ‘The freedom we have in Christ Jesus’ is the Magna Carta of Galatians. In other words, Jewish and non-Jewish Christians’ ‘freedom in Christ’ entitles Jews to remain, Jews with Jewish traditions, and Gentiles to remain Gentiles with a new identity. They are "justified (legitimated) by the way of faith in Jesus Christ, by whom God has righteous Gentiles in the same way as Jewish people.”[28] Hence, freedom remains antithetical to slavery.[29] In the first appearance, “‘freedom’ refers to the unqualified association of Jewish and Gentile Christians, while ‘enslavement’ refers to the attempted imposition of circumcision on Gentile believers.”[30] Those who advocated circumcision on Gentiles were trying to enslave the Gentile Christians. But Paul refers to his stand at the Jerusalem Council as a reminder of 'the truth of the gospel'

24 Mark Nanos remarks, while referring to Peter Richardson, *Israel in the Apostolic Church* (Cambridge: Cambridge University Press, 1969), 91-96, that both texts (2:4-5; 2:12-13) “seem to indicate the possible involvement of Jews who do not believe in Christ in the various situations,” Mark D. Nanos, *Irony of Galatians: Paul’s Letter in Frist Century Context* (Minneapolis: Fortress Press, 2002), 146.

25 New International Version (NIV) translates it in this fashion.

26 Richard B. Hays, “The Letter to the Galatians,” in *The New Interpreter’s Bible*, L.E. Keck, *et al.*,eds., Vol. 9 (Nashville: Abingdon Press, 1995), 181-348, 225.

27 Martinus C. de Boer, *Galatians*, 113, interprets "freedom" as "specifically freedom from the imposition of circumcision and, by implication, of (the remainder of) the law." However, for Paul and other Jewish Christian followers, freedom does not mean abandoning Jewishness but considering oneself equal to Gentile-Christian followers. See Abel Frantisek, "Freedom in Christ in Galatians: A Matter of Identity," 246.

28 Mark D. Nanos, “What was at Stake in Peter’s ‘Eating with Gentiles’ at Antioch?,” in *Galatians Debate: Contemporary Issues in Rhetorical and Historical Interpretation*, Mark D. Nanos, ed. (Peabody: Hendrickson Publishers, 2002), 282-318, 316.

29 "Freedom" and "slavery" will reappear as a central theme of the epistle in 3:28; 4:1-11; 4:21-5:1 and 5:13.

30 Richard B. Hays, “The Letter to the Galatians,” 225.

(Gal 2:5)[31] will remain with the Gentiles as a whole. Paul, thus, wants to assure the Gentiles of equality in their status.

Galatians 5

The second occurrence of the phrase 'freedom in Christ' appears in the *exhortatio* proper (5:1-6:10).Paul's exhortation falls into three units: 1. Counsel: preserve the freedom you have in Christ (5:1-12); 2. Warning: walk not into the flesh, but according to the spirit (5:13-26); 3. Advice: the right way to use Christian freedom (6:1-10).[32] Paul's counsel to the Galatians begins with an imperative: "For freedom, Christ has set us free. Stand firm, therefore, and do not submit again to a yoke of slavery" (5:1).[33]

The imperative (5:1) condenses the letter's message into a powerful slogan.[34] The main emphasis is on Christ's actions: "For freedom, Christ has set us free" (cf. 3:13; 4:4-5). Here, freedom can be understood at least in two ways: negatively and positively. Negatively speaking, it is generally freedom from the Law, though there is an attempt to make freedom more encompassing, including freedom from sin, death, etc.[35] Positively, freedom

---

31 'The truth of the gospel' is closely tied to Paul's insistence on preaching a gospel free from legal and cultural prerequisites, a gospel that focuses on God's liberating initiative See Richard B. Hays, "The Letter to the Galatians," 225.

32 Joseph A. Fitzmyer, "The Letter to the Galatians," 789. For a detailed analysis of this section, see Charles H. Talbert, "Freedom and Law in Galatians," *Ex Auditu* 11 (1995) 17-25; Gordon D. Fee, "Freedom and the Life of Obedience," *Review and Expositor* 91 (1994) 201-217.

33 It flows directly out of the language about the two mothers in 4:31. In the original text, the first words in 5:1 were directly connected to the final words of 4:31 without a word or paragraph break (*Eleuthera te Eleuthera*, "... of the free woman for freedom ..."). See Gordon D. Fee, "Freedom and the Life of Obedience," 213. This is partly responsible for the several textual variations in 5:1, as scribes tried to show the connection between the two sentences. For a detailed study of textual variations in 5:1, see Assisi Saldanha, *The Concept of Freedom in Galatians: Its Subordination to the Truth of the Gospel, A study of Gal 5:1-12 in the light of the rhetorical analysis of the epistle* (Bangaluru: TPI, 2016), 177-360.

34 It is also suggested that Gal 5:1 sums up the doctrinal section of the letter: 'freedom in Christ' is not license but freedom from the Law and its material observances. See Joseph A. Fitzmyer, "The Letter to the Galatians," 789.

35 E. de Witt Burton, *A Critical and Exegetical on the Epistle to the Galatians*, ICC (Edinburgh: T & T Clark, 1988), 270 thinks that by freedom, Paul means freedom from Law. Heinrich Schlier, *Der Brief an die Galater*, KEK (Göttingen: Vandenhoeck, [4]1965), 229-230 understands that for Paul, the freedom from the Law includes freedom from sin as well. Hans D. Betz, *Galatians*, 256 speaks of the Christian experience of freedom which amounts to liberation from the elements of the world and their tyrannical regime of evil (Gal 1:4; 4:1-10), from slavery under the Law and sin (cf. Gal 2:19; 3:13, 25; 4:5), from death (cf. Gal 2:20; 3:11; 5:25; 6:8), from ignorance of God (Gal 4:8-9), from superstition (Gal 4:8-10) and from social oppression and religious-cultural discrimination

denotes the freedom of the children of God.[36] In other words, freedom is "belonging to the heir, the mature son, the child of the free woman."[37]

Since Christ has set us free from Law and placed us as children of God, the Galatians are to take a firm stand in the freedom that they have been given. Paul had already decided to stand for freedom at Jerusalem Council (2:4-5). Now, Paul urges the Galatians to take their stand. In the given context, it would mean that the Galatians should take a firm stand against the Judaizers, who had come to the church of Galatia as missionaries and insisted the Gentile Christians follow the teachings of the Law. But Paul authoritatively exhorts the Galatians to live according to the new identity of 'freedom in Christ.'

To submit to the Law is equivalent to falling into slavery.[38] Paul considers this submission to law "a yoke of slavery." The image of "yoke" is sometimes described positively as the discipline provided by the teaching of the Torah.[39] The Judaizers "may have spoken of the Law as a yoke in these terms, as a gracious divine gift."[40] But Paul portrays the "yoke" as a symbol of enslavement. For Paul,Judaizers are treacherous slave masters who desire to bring the Galatians under the constraint of a new religio-cultural system of domination (cf. Acts 15:10).[41] Christ has delivered the Galatians from slavery. They are now righteous and free. Hence, under any circumstances, they should never fall subject to slavery again (cf. 4:8-9).

Meaning of Freedom in Galatians

The above brief analysis of the two texts from Galatians assists us in understanding the meaning of freedom in Galatians.

(Gal 3:26-28). For those who have become partakers of Christ and put on Christ (Gal 3:27), freedom includes liberation from the Law (cf. Gal 2:19; 3:25; 5:18).

36 Frederick F. Bruce, *The Epistle to the Galatians: A Commentary on the Greek Text*, NIGTC (Grand Rapids: Eerdmans, 1990), 226; J. Kürzinger, *Briefe des Apostels Paulus: Die Briefe an die Korinther und Galater*, Echter-Bibel (Würzburg: Echter, 1968), 108.

37 Ragnar Bring, *Commentary on Galatians*, E. Wahlstrom, trans. (Philadelphia: Muhlenberg, 1961), 234.

38 See Elsa Tamez, "Galatians," in *The International Bible Commentary*, William R. Farmer, *et al.*, eds. (Bangalore: TPI, 1998), 1728-1743, 1741.

39 *m. Abot* 3.5. In this sense, the yoke provides stability and guidance. Evangelist Matthew adapts this theme to the teaching of Jesus (Mt 11:29-30).

40 Richard B. Hays, "The Letter to the Galatians," 306.

41 See James D.G. Dunn, *The Epistle to the Galatians*, BNTC (Peabody: Hendrickson, 1993), 263.

Freedom: Equality of Jewish and non-Jewish Christians

Freedom in Christ involves the equality of Jewish and non-Jewish Christians. One of Paul's central concerns was the inclusion of Gentiles into God's New Covenant. Paul did not deem circumcision necessary but thought that God included Gentiles in his New Covenant through faith in Christ. Christian faith transcends barriers to make all free and equal. Paul tells the Galatians to stand for their freedom in Christ and to refuse to be circumcised; even though they were born as Gentiles, they have equal rights with Jewish Christians. The Gentiles are justified by faith in Christ like Jewish people are justified.

Freedom: Antithetical to Slavery

Before becoming Christians, the Galatians followed the traditions and cultures of Hellenistic religions.The Galatians were acquainted with powers that held them in bondage.[42] When they became Christians, they were liberated from these powers. However, the new Gentile Christians in Galatia were incited by the Judaizers to regard Jewish Law and its institutes as necessary to remain in communion with the Jewish Christians. According to Paul, it takes away the freedom Christ had given, and it replaces freedom in Christ with slavery to the Law.But the Christian experience of freedom amounts to a liberation from slavery under the Law and sin (cf. Gal 2:19; 3:13, 25; 4:5). "Christ has paid the ransom to set all believers free from their state of confinement and to become members of the family of God and gain elevation in status."[43] The Galatians are free through Christ Jesus' redemption. They must remain steadfast in their freedom and heirship.

Freedom from Law

By freedom, Paul means freedom from Law. Paul powerfully convinces the Galatians of the validity of the Law-free gospel. For him, the crucifixion of Jesus Christ (3:1) eradicated the credibility of Jewish Law (2:19-20). The crucifixion is as contra-circumcision (5:11).[44] The Galatians received the faith through the proclamation of the cross. Therefore, Paul concludes that faith does not need the Law; the Law is rendered unessential and ineffective by the spirit. The works of the Law are powerless to bring such freedom

42 According to Bernanrd H. Brinsmead, *Galatians: Dialogical Response to Opponents*, SBLDS 65 (Chico: Scholars Press, 1982), 190 "In Galatians, justification is particularly freedom from all enslaving powers."

43 C-W. Chang, 'Freedom in Galatians: A sociohistorical study of the slavery and adoption imagery,' in die Skriflig 56(1), 2022 a2883. https:// doi.org/10.4102/ids. v56i1.2883.

44 Cf. Louis Panier, "Parcours pour lire l'epitre aux Galate," *Semiotique et Bible* 54 (1989) 36-41, 38.

(2:16).[45] Freedom became a historical reality solely with the advent of Jesus Christ. With him, a new way of existence, known as the 'new creation,' came into being.[46] Hence, freedom of faith must not be destroyed by legalism.[47] "Jesus sets us free that we might serve one another, thus being in community."[48]

Freedom of Children of God

According to Paul, freedom also refers to the freedom of the children of God, a liberty that becomes possible because of the Christ event.[49]

> The Galatians had sought to become true Christians by being first called Abraham's sons through circumcision. Paul's reinterpretation of this argument makes circumcision unnecessary. The Galatians were already the heirs of promise when they belonged to Christ (3:29). The death of Christ had made this possible.[50]

Hence, the freedom held out by Paul's gospel is the freedom of the children of God.

The Indian Constitution

As stated in the introduction, the immediate context of our study of freedom in Galatians is the Constitution of India. Drafting the Indian Constitution took almost three years, and it is the largest in the world. The Indian Constitution is hailed as versatile because whatever we wish for a nation's prosperity, we find in it. The Indian Constitution is the soul of democracy. Initially, the right-wing forces were against formulating a written Constitution. The reason was that they wanted the *Manusmriti* tradition to reign supreme.[51] We

---

45 Daniel Patte, *Paul's Faith and the Power of the Gospel* (Philadelphia: Fortress Press,1983), 62.

46 David J. Lull, *The Spirit in Galatia: Paul's Interpretation of Pneuma as Divine Power*, SBLDS 49 (Chico: Scholars Press, 1978), 132.

47 Charles Kingsley Barrett, *Freedom and Obligation: A Study of the Epistle to the Galatians* (Philadelphia: Westminster Press, 1985), 71.

48 Jack Albright, "Stand Firm in Freedom: Summer Lections from Galatians," *Quarterly Review* (1995) 89-106,100

49 Assisi Saldanha, "The Core Values of the Preamble from a Biblical Perspective," in *The Preamble of the Indian Constitution: Biblical Perspectives*, Joy Philip Kakkanattu and Laurence Culas, eds., CBAI Seminar Papers 4 (Bengaluru: TPI, 2019), 51-74, 66.

50 Assisi Saldanha, *The Concept of Freedom in Galatians*, 213.

51 See Joe Tauro, "The Bible and the Preamble of Indian Constitution: Meeting Points," in *The Preamble of the Indian Constitution: Biblical Perspectives*, Joy Philip Kakkanattu and Laurence Culas, eds., CBAI Seminar Papers 4 (Bengaluru: TPI, 2019), 75-102, 96.

should be happy that our Constitution is written. The Preamble expresses our commitment.[52] It affirms commitment to securing:

- Justice to all citizens: political, economic and social justice
- Equality of all human beings in status and opportunities
- Liberty of thought, expression, belief, religion and against exploitation
- Fraternity among individuals, societies and nations

These values form the core message of the Constitution, which iswhy reaffirming the values of the Indian Constitution becomes particularly important.

Context

We, the Indians, in the sovereign, socialist, secular and democratic republic, were living peacefully, following the core values of the Constitution, affirmed in its Preamble: Justice, equality, liberty and fraternity. But now, there is a considerable force to undermine the peace and tranquillity experienced by the citizens of India.[53]The three distinct activities in every government through which the will of the people is expressed in a democracy, namely the Legislative, Executive, and Judiciary, are under serious threat. We know in what direction the Legislative is moving, how the Judiciary is being threatened, and how the Executive is progressively strengthening its control over the Legislature. In this context, it is imperative to reaffirm the freedom stipulated in the Indian Constitution.

Freedom in the Indian Constitution

The Preamble asserts that liberty of thought, expression, belief, faith, and worship is secured for all people of India. The Constitution of India secures for its citizens the freedom that everyone, without bias, has the right to think and express their views without harming others' liberty. They can convert to any religion, worship any god or goddess, or believe in any philosophy they want.

The freedom guaranteed by the Indian Constitution is stipulated in various Articles of the Constitution:

- Right to Freedom: Protection of 6 rights (art. 19) - Right to freedom of speech and expression, Right to assemble peaceably and

52 For a detailed study, see Assisi Saldanha, "The Background to the Core Values of the Preamble," in *The Preamble of the Indian Constitution: Biblical Perspectives*, Joy Philip Kakkanattu and Laurence Culas, eds., CBAI Seminar Papers 4 (Bengaluru: TPI, 2019), 23-49; Laurence Culas, "Core Values in the Preamble of Indian Constitution," *Prophetic Voice*13 (2022) 1-3.

53 Recall here how the intruders – Judaizers – brought problems to the church in Galatia.

without arms, Right to form associations or unions or co-operative societies, Right to move freely throughout the territory of India, Right to reside and settle in any part of the territory of India, Right to practice any profession or to carry on any occupation, trade or business; Protection in respect of conviction for offences (art. 20); Protection of life and personal liberty (art. 21); Right to education (art. 21A); Protection against arrest and detention (art. 22).

- Right to Freedom of Religion: Freedom of Conscience, Profession, Practice and Propagation (art. 25); Freedom to manage religious affairs (art. 26); Freedom from taxation for promotion of religion (art. 27); Freedom for attending religious instruction (art. 28).

Denial of Freedom

Despite the Constitution affirming the fundamental rights of its citizens, there are numerous instances of their denials in the country.

Denying Equal Status for Citizens

Freedom in Galatians primarily signifies the equality of Jewish and Gentile Christians. India's Constitution similarly encompasses provisions emphasizing complete legal equality for its citizens, regardless of their religion and creed, and prohibits religion-based discrimination. It also provides safeguards to religious minority communities. Nevertheless, minorities face discrimination and persecution due to a combination of overly broad or ill-defined laws, an inefficient criminal justice system and a lack of jurisprudential consistency. For example, Article 48 of the Indian Constitution and most Indian states (24 out of 29, as of 2015) significantly restrict or ban cow slaughter. Those found guilty of cow slaughter are subject to fines, imprisonment, or both. The cow protection laws are often mixed with anti-Muslim sentiment.

One of the clear examples of Muslim persecution through the politics of cow protection is the killing of Mohammad Akhlaq by Hindu mobs in September 2015. Mr. Akhlaq, age 50, was dragged from his home in the village of Bisara – 45 miles from the capital of Delhi – and beaten to death by an angry Hindu mob due to rumours that his family had been eating beef and storing the meat in their home.[54]

Matters related to caste-based offences and discrimination are dealt with under the Prevention of Atrocities Act (1989). However, India's National Crime Bureau statistics exhibit a steep rise in caste atrocities. 'Crime in

54 https://www.hrw.org/report/2019/02/18/violent-cow-protection-india/vigilante-groups-attack-minorities

India 2021' reveals crimes against Scheduled Caste and Scheduled Tribes increased by 13.1% and 14.3% respectively over 2021.[55]

Captivity versus Freedom

In Galatians, freedom is antithetical to slavery or captivity. But in India, one wonders: "Has the world's biggest democracy that assures freedom of speech and expression become an intolerant nation?"[56] India, the nation that gave birth to four religions and protects both secularism and freedom of speech in its Constitution, exhibited intolerance after the Hindutva brand of politics came into power at the centre. Such a thought proliferates out of a disturbing trend, namely, the prevention of freedom of speech. We have witnessed a spate of murders of Indian writers. A visitor to his residence gunned down the Kannada language scholar M.M. Kalburgi. His death followed the murder of Govind Pansare, a veteran Communist leader. Then, Gauri Lankesh, a prominent Indian journalist critical of Hindu nationalist politics, was shot dead.

The right to freedom of expression is crucial to the growth of a community and, eventually, a state. It is one of the most fundamental rights protected from government restriction or control. However, outspoken journalists, media outlets, actors and human rights activists are threatened and intimidated through the misuse of the Unlawful Activities Prevention Act (UAPA). In February 2021, Climate activist Disha Ravi was arrested for "sedition" and "spreading disharmony between communities" for sharing a social media toolkit to help farmers protest against three contentious farming laws.[57] In March 2021, Hidme Markam, a human rights activist from the Adivasi Indigenous community, was arrested under the UAPA for highlighting sexual violence against women by state security forces. In October 2020, Fr. Stan Samy, who was involved in promoting the rights of Dalits and Tribals in Jharkhand, was accused and jailed under UAPA for his alleged involvement in a blast case near Pune. He was jailed for no reason and was denied water and medical treatment, leading to his death.

Denial of Freedom of Religion

By freedom, Paul means freedom from Law. The Indian Constitution Article 25 entitles freedom of conscience and the right to profess, practise

55 https://timesofindia.indiatimes.com/india/crimes-against-scs-went-up-13-and-against-sts-by-14-3-in-2022-ncrb/articleshow/105790790.cms

56 Laurence Culas, "Contemporary Socio-Political Scenario," *Prophetic Voice* 10 (2019) 3-6, 3.

57 https://time.com/5939627/disha-ravi-india-toolkit-arrest/. More than 183 people were arrested for protesting against the three laws, which were passed by parliament in 2020 with minimal consultation. The laws were repealed in December 2021.

and propagate religion. But ten states have the Law known as "Freedom of Religion Act,' with hidden intent to curtail religious freedom: Odisha (1967), Madhya Pradesh (1968), Chattishgarh (2000), Arunachal Pradesh (1978), Gujarat (2003), Himachal Pradesh (2006), Rajastan (2008), Maharastra (2015), Jharkhand (2017) and Uttarakhand (April 2018).The Act presumes that the Christians forcibly convert the Adivasi and Dalit, the disadvantaged groups, from Hinduism.

However, no one was convicted in Odisha, the first state to introduce the anti-conversion Act in 1967.The basis of conversion is too vague and broad to harass any person, such as 'force,' 'allurement,' 'inducement', and 'fraud.' Even prayers for healing, offering water or medicine during natural disasters or teaching religious songs can be misinterpreted as per this Law as the basis for conversion. Hence, such acts are criminal acts. The conversion law categorizes women, Adivasi and Dalits as 'vulnerable/weak' in parallel to minors, not in a position to exercise their conscience.

Freedom of Citizens Denied

Galatians affirms the freedom of children of God. The Constitution establishes freedom of all citizens in various aspects. Scheduled Castes Presidential Order in 1950 gives only Hindus as recipients of affirmative action. The Presidential order added Sikhs and Buddhists, not Dalit Christians and Muslims. It has resulted in denying the basic fundamental rights and other entitlements as equal citizens enshrined in Articles of 14, 15, 16, 25, 26, 27 & 28 based on their religion. The denial has a huge impact on Dalit Christians and Muslims as it is deprived of their access to scholarship and social, economic and political representations. They are denied protection under another protection law that addresses the issues of atrocities – Scheduled Castes and Scheduled Tribes (Prevention of Atrocities) Act, 1986. The Dalits are deterred from converting to Christianity or Islam for fear of losing affirmative action. The moment they convert to the Indian-born religions, they have access to equal citizen rights and protection from the government. It is a violation of freedom of religion and belief by the state itself. It is crucial as 65% of Christians and an equal number of Muslims are from Dalit origins in India.

Conclusion

Both Galatians and the Indian Constitution emphasize freedom: equality of all, freedom from slavery or captivity, freedom from Law and freedom of children of God/citizens. However, there is a denial of freedom or rights, specified in the Indian Constitution, by central and state governments. So, to safeguard the freedom guaranteed by the Constitution, we have to engage in the following:

1. Know your Society

It is important to know our society. For this purpose, an effective assessment has to be carried out. SWOT analysis can be used here: a strategic assessment of the society's Strengths and Weaknesses, with an assessment of the Opportunities and Threats posed by various factors.

2. Know your Constitution

The Constitution stipulates a number of Rights/Entitlements. So, we have to know the rights prescribed by the Constitution. The Constitution outlines where government powers end by guaranteeing individuals' rights and freedoms. Therefore, "engage people with the Constitution of India and the common future it holds for all of us."[58]

3. Research, Lobbying, and Advocacy for Minorities

Every individual has to take up the role of human rights defenders in their capacities to ensure that the rights of national or ethnic, religious, and linguistic minorities are highlighted and taken into account. By working on guaranteeing their rights, our chief aim must be that no one will be afraid to self-identify as a member of a minority. Respect for the rights of minorities and the promotion of an integrated, multicultural society can help to ensure stability and peace in the country.

4. Counter Disinformation

Hoaxes and disinformation have long been a global threat to freedom and democracy. The development and widespread use of digital media allow for campaigns to spread quickly, making disinformation a more pressing problem. Strategic communication is one of the critical tools in the fight against disinformation and requires a broad approach.

5. Use of Social/Print/Electronic Media

Professional codes of ethics and self-regulation in journalism could promote intercultural dialogue and combat discrimination. Minorities' access to media professions and productions could be improved to propagate their Rights, protect their interests, report crimes against them, and create awareness about the freedoms in the Constitution.

6. Documentation

There is no Institute in India which researches or documents violence against Christians. Hence, documentation is essential. The Supreme Court

58 Pankaj Kumar Naik, "Indian Constitution: A Minority Perspective," *Prophetic Voice* 14 (2023) 10-14, 14.

of India, in 2022, postponed the hearing of a plea seeking protection from and investigations into rising attacks on Christians and their institutions across the nation. The United Christian Forum (UCF), a New Delhi-based rights group, in its annual report, called 2021 the "most violent year" in terms of targeted violence against Christians.

7. Linkage with Social/Gender/Minority/Peoples' Movements

In the recent past, the country has witnessed a significant rise in human rights violence against marginalized social groups and minorities alike. A number of socio-religious-political movements are working for the safety and development of these deprived communities. We have to take the initiative to associate with them.

We hope for a better India as the famous Sanskrit mantra envisions:

Om Sarve Bhavantu Sukhinah
Sarve Santu Niraamayaah
Sarve Bhadraanni Pashyantu
Maa Kashcid-Duhkha-Bhaag-Bhavet
Om Shaantih Shaantih Shaantih
May all be happy!
May all be free from illness!
May all see what is auspicious!
May no one suffer!
Peace, Peace, Peace!

11

Militant Judaism and Jewish Zionism - Israel's War Against the Palestinians A Case in Point

John Mohan Razu

Jesu is a good friend of mine for decades. I'm indeed happy to note that as a mark of respect to their guru especially on Jesu's sixtieth birthday—Varaprasad and Jeeva have taken the initiative to come out with a Festschrift. I commend them—a gesture of this sort to Prof. Dr. K. Jesurathnam is apt and fitting. He is one of the eminent Old Testament scholars in the country and widely known in the academia across the globe. Known for his nuanced Dalit Hermeneutics by taking up some difficult texts in the prophetic literature and others as well. Jesu has produced a commentary that is potentially a revolutionary and ground-breaking. I'm grateful to the editors for asking me to write a piece in honor of Jesu. May God continue to use Jesu as he is involved in the teaching and writing vocation

Post-war II scenarios candidly posited a bipolar world where the United States of America (USA) emerged as the leader of one group of nations that comprised Northern America and Western European countries. At the same time, the former Union of Soviet Socialist Republic (USSR) became the leader of East European countries. To keep the countries under its control, both the empire builders, as part of their strategy, had created two blocks, i.e., NATO and WARSAW, symbolizing friendship, cooperation, and assistance. In due course, those countries that came under the USSR became autonomous and independent and are still under the dictate of Russia.

Consequently, WARSAW was disbanded, while the then East Germany merged with West Germany. Between the 1950s and 1990s, the world was dominated by these two powers—the Cold War.

A few countries are vying to become major powers, but they are tied up by showing their support to one of them openly, but a few subtly. Israel is the most-liked confidant of the United States, enjoying absolute support financially and militarily. It is also a nuclear power. Dominating production of susceptible AI-driven gadgets and military armaments, Israel wants to expand its territories—an inclination to become an empire-builder. It is part of the far-extreme-right party's vision, which is insulated in its Zionist ideology. Narratives and rhetoric such as 'From River to Sea' and 'Greater Israel' clearly show Israel's ambition to become a superpower. It is built into the psyche of the majority of the Israelis who favor Jewish Zionism. As part of its empire-building, the State of Israel continues its occupation of the territories of the Palestinians, with genocidal intent and massacres, decimating Gaza, East Jerusalem, and West Bank and changing the geographical landscape of Palestinian land. Currently, Israel is using America out and out as part of its empire-building ambitions. Towards this end, PM Netanyahu is desperately trying to wipe out the Palestinians or at least wants to purge the Palestinians to neighbouring countries such as Egypt or wherever they want to go. For Israel, it is a war to establish its regional dominance. If everything goes well, Israel in due course of time, if the neighbours in the Middle East are not vigilant, Israel will take over and thus become one of the empire-builders.

2

In the past, the West, built empires, invaded countries of the two-third world, and, in the process, colonized and thus brought every country under its dominion. Empires and colonizers plundered all the raw materials from their colonies and then converted those to products and used the colonies for marketing. To that end, they used cheap labour and the system of 'slavery' for the construction of railways, shipyards, infrastructures, and many more for their developments and advancements. The decadent West and technologically advanced 'developed nations' continue to use the erstwhile colonies in subtle ways. If we glance through the post-war II scenarios, what happened and has been happening around us currently portrays and sheds lots of light on the underlying meanings and nuanced reasons. Take, for instance, the West's war against Afghanistan, Iraq, and now Palestine; if we go down and deeply analyze all these wars that the West went to wars against these nation-states with all kinds of assertions, justifications, and several false narratives that brought ruins and destructions to the people of these countries.

Post-War II brought independence to almost all the countries of the world from their colonies. Free and independent countries blossomed worldwide, some of them merit mentioning. India became independent from British colonialism without bloodshed via non-violence; Fidel Castro fought the Spanish, the colonizer and later the United States for free Cuba; Nelson Mandela fought apartheid against white supremacy employing Gandhian-non-violence. Some more like Che Guevara contributed to change from imperialists to colonists, dictators, and anti-democrats.

Who was involved in the killing of Col Gadafi of Libya and Saddam Hussain of Iraq? The United States is the root cause of all these problems and is the culprit. For example, who is responsible for the creation of Al-Qaida and its leader Osama-bin-Laden? Osama-bin-Laden was picked up and trained by the CIA, but came to know the motive behind the American administration, who turned against the Western forces attacking the installations and businesses of the West and then planned an attack which rocked the entire world, popularly known as 9/11. Another theory which is currently occupying the centre stage amidst the current conflict in the Middle East is the emergence of Hamas and its taking over Gaza.

Yasser Arafat, emerged as a natural leader of Palestine, who used violence as a tool and means towards the establishment of an independent Palestinian State. He founded *the Palestine Liberation Organization* (PLO) as a revolutionary movement along with a political party called *Fatah*. Arafat later, through the persuasion of other Arab leaders for the sake of statehood for Palestinians, agreed to peace in exchange for a two-state formula. At that time, Israel's PM Yitzhak Rabin was also for peace and freedom for all and achieved their goals. Acknowledging their contribution to world peace, the peace committee awarded the Nobel Peace Prize to Chairman Yasser Arafat, Israel's then-prime minister Yitzhak Rabin, and its foreign minister Shimon Peres. Rain was the PM of Israel between 1974-77 and 1992 until his assassination. Within hours of his assassination, the Israelis occupied the West Bank. Then, the peace talks and two-state formula seemed to become a distant reality – a Maya or illusion. In the absence of Rabin and Arafat, everything went to a toss and lost its focus and purpose. There was a political vacuum, particularly in Gaza, which Fatah failed to fill, and Hamas occupied its place, whose ideology is 'force'. Parallel to these developments, Israel flung towards far-rightism in its polity and this climate, a 'Jewish hawk' who believes and thus underlines Zionism as a foundational doctrine of Judaism, belonging to the Likud party, Israel's longest-serving PM who has drastically changed the contours of politics and vision of Israel.

3

The footage and snapshots of the Israel-Palestine conflict exposit nerve-chilling and mind-boggling images. A question that arises is that, after all these attacks and bombardments, has Israel achieved its objective? For Israel, 'end Hamas'/'destroy Hamas completely' has been Israel's foremost agenda and narrative that includes its allies right from day one—since Oct 7, 2023. However, we should reckon with the fact that Hamas is part of the Palestinian society, so destroying or marginalizing Hamas is a remote possibility for Israel. Further, separating the civilians from Hamas in densely populated Gaza for the Israeli army could result in not just collateral damage but beyond.

Israel is an apartheid state premised on racist overtones in nature and manifestation. Its architecture of occupation is purely built around the safety and security of the Israeli people to control, monitor, and surveil the Palestinians. All these are visible in how Israelis have constructed their residential complexes and the landscape on which they have been raised against the Palestinian landscape, where their structures portray packed multistoried tenements standing close to narrow roads and by-lanes. Israel army can barge into any Palestinian home without a search warrant and arrest anyone. If the military or police come across during their search of Palestinians any houses that are locked, they break open and ransack everything.

Israel, along with those attacks on all fronts, is simultaneously employing the architecture starvation. 2.4 million of Gazans are living in hunger and starvation. With great difficulty for the last four days, the UN got permission from Israel to allow about 30-40 trucks, whereas every day, to meet the hunger of millions of Gazans, about 300 to 400 truckloads of foodstuffs are required. The governments of Israel, the United States and those countries that support Israel in the EU are responsible for using starvation as a weapon of war, which is antithetical to humanitarian laws that fall under the UN convention. It is 'genocidal' and certainly comes under war crimes.

4

Having lost its goal of the 'war', the State of Israel is engaged in the architecture of destruction. Israel, as of now, has not achieved its desired goal. It is involved only in the demolition mode of Palestinians' lives and their domiciles and not Hamas. The American establishment is embarrassed as mounting pressure keeps growing from within and outside. Israeli forces have thus far killed about 40,000 people; in the occupied West Bank, 1,400 people have been arrested.

Enforcing a pause to send billions worth of sophisticated armouries is a gimmick employed as a deterrent for Israel not to enter Raffa to silence those voices who support the Palestinians and their freedom. Corroded with ferocity, the Jewish lobby in the United States, in collusion with a far-right Jewish caucus, would never allow for a 'ceasefire' or 'cessation of war'. Rage is such that far-right Jewish extremists are waging war against Hamas—a terror organization that wants to wipe out Gaza. Joe Biden went to the extent of offering the Israeli citizens that the Jews do not require visas to enter the United States—a rare privilege extended to a community. How could this happen? It shows the proximity between Jews and the White House. Power works on corridors, between four wails and over phone calls. While deliberating on power, Foucault maintains "In hypothesizing "that power is war, a war continued by other means". Foucault makes clear that he seeks not to deny but to expand Clausewitz's relevance: It may be that war as strategy is a continuation of politics." Netanyahu of Israel wants to stay in power to tide over the current political turmoil. For Joe Biden, the Israeli-Palestinian War is a showcase for his 2024 re-election bid. As of now, the majority of Americans want the perpetrators of this episode to be eliminated. The Western mainstream media shows images that bewilder its audience, while the narratives present stories that support the images.

5

The United States has always been a war-mongering nation, and Israel is an occupying power. Both have joined together in such frenzy ways, refusing to see reason. The current PM Netanyahu has aligned with Biden, and the EU keep escalating the crisis by demolishing Gaza. Dominant powers cannot contain the rights, dreams, and aspirations of the Palestinians forever. Israel, along with the United States, kept dominating and reigning over Palestine for decades. Palestinians have been living under 'permanent starvation and hunger' for decades. Violations and ill-treatment of the Palestinians by the Israelis have now blown up beyond proportions.

Israeli's ruling class believes that the military and besiege are the only solution. Israel does not believe in conversation and dialogue for peace. Military reprisals are not the solution, but they ought to be political, which means whatever is due to the Palestinians should be given to them. Hamas should come forward for the conversation because it is a major actor. There must be a difference between military and military conceptions about the current impasse.

In this war, Projecting America again as an arbitrator, guarantor, or honest broker has disappointed and failed. The United States, in the war, is a major party along with Israel. Palestinians have the right to live on their land. Laws have rules. There cannot be two set rules—one for Israel and the other for Palestinians. What Hamas did was wrong and will have to be brought under war crimes. Similarly, Israel continues to bombard and, in return, kill more than 5000 innocent citizens that cross many times than Hamas. And so, the State of Israel, by all means, should be branded as a 'war criminal' too. Two wrongs will never make one right.

Anti-Semitism and Islamophobia will escalate as the days and weeks go by across the world. The United States claims to be a free democracy allowing dissent, but when hundreds of demonstrators descended on a congressional building in Washington demanding a ceasefire in the Israel-Hamas war, it resulted in an estimated 300 arrests and restricted access to Capitol Hill. Two Jewish anti-Zionist groups organized the rally. Jewish Voice for 'Peace and If Not Now', and about 400 of their members assembled inside the dome of the Cannon House Office Building, led by about 25 rabbis reading testimonials from Palestinians in the Gaza Strip and reciting prayers.

Outside, hundreds more chanted, "ceasefire now." Demonstrations are not permitted inside congressional buildings. The world is still human because some people live by their moral conscience. Indeed, UN Secretary-General, in his speech before the foreign ministers and foreign secretaries on the war between Israel and Palestine at the United Nations in New York two days ago, said that the "Hamas attack did not happen in a vacuum". It simply means he said, "56 years of Israel's suffocating occupation", candidly underlines several factors that ought to be examined, analyzed, and evaluated. In tune with this, a State Department official in the bureau that oversees arms transfers resigned a few days ago in protest of the Biden administration's decision to continue sending weapons and ammunition to Israel.

6

In his resignation letter, Josh Paul, who has been the director of congressional and public affairs for the State Department's Bureau of political-military Affairs for over 11 years, said that the Biden administration's "Blind support for one side" was leading to a policy decision that were "short-sighted, destructive, unjust and contradictory to the very values we publicly espouse." "The response Israel is taking, and with it the US support both for response and for the status quo of the occupation, will only lead to suffering for the Israeli and the Palestinians people," he wrote." Those with a moral conscience would act in this way. They live by what the conscience says and abide by ethical principles. That makes them unique because they go beyond others abiding by moral authority.

Israel has not only violated UN laws and conventions but also has failed to follow what the Torah teaches them. Love among human beings is one of the core commandments of Judaism. Without mincing, one of the core commandments of Judaism is "Love your neighbour as yourself" (Leviticus 19:18) . The commandment stands at the centre of the central book of Torah. Many Hebraic scholars pointed out that this is the central commandment of the Torah. The ruling regime of Israel has not demonstrated this command in its governance. Paradoxically, the Israel government is acting in a rage filled with vengeance. Prime Minister Netanyahu wants to change the demography of Palestine in favour of Israel through Israeli settlements. It is part of an 'apartheid program' leading to 'ethnic cleaning'. Israel wants to eradicate the Palestinians from the face of the earth by conspiring with the United States—which is Zionist ideology.

All these years and decades, the top wigs in the ruling dispensation somehow scuttled the peace process and two-state solution. And PM Netanyahu, for his political and leadership continuation, has somehow managed to fool the Israelis for some time and indeed not all the time. By the time the dust settled, the people of Israel were going to ask him whether he had given enough safety and security to the Israelis. This question will determine his future in politics. That is why he wants to go on full-stream for ground operations. That is why Netanyahu is against cease-fire. Increasingly, he is under pressure from within and outside for total de-escalation.

But in his war committee, there are differences because it might lead to more causalities even for the Israelis and would risk the lives of the hostages. Over and above, whether the Jews like it or not, the Palestinian problem ought to be addressed by all means, and hopefully, there should be a two-state solution. It is their land, and therefore, they have all the rights to live in freedom and with dignity. In this war, there are no winners and no losers –Israel or Hamas. The losers are those young children and others who were killed in the conflict. We, as spectators and others as participants in the war, are responsible for this fiasco. What we have lost is 'humanity' in the process.

7

The State of Israel, being a small country, ranks as one of the largest weapon exporters, earning $12.5 trillion. Its earnings show a sizable per cent of the money the State of Israel earns via arms production and sales. It is also evident that Israel is investing quite a considerable amount towards R & D. Israel's military apparatus is mind-boggling. The Jewish State is one of the major arms exporters; thus, it sells its armaments to 140 countries. Israel is the 10th largest arms exporter, showing its technological strength in the production of weapons.

Israel has been using its machinery to perpetuate violence against the Palestinians who have been living in Israel's occupied land. Since Oct 7, 2023, Israel has increasingly weaponized the Gaza Strip, West Bank, and East Jerusalem. Israel is currently regarded as a high-tech superpower. The State of Israel is involved in the manufacture of high-tech production of arsenals and is also engaged in high-tech solutions. Israel is known for the production of military intelligence employing sophisticated apparatus.

In addition to these, Israel is the largest exporter of military drones. Its AI is known for generating targets. In 1975, Israel sold arms to the white regime that perpetuated apartheid in South Africa. Its automated drones are known for mass assassination, and its intelligence plays a pivotal role in espionage. Israel's prowess in technology can generate enormous targets with precision. Its arms buyers are spread across the world, numbering 130 countries. Israel is using all its latest armaments, land, air, and water, against the Palestinians. In its recent attack in the occupied Hebron, drones came with the slogan 'Do not resist'. 2/3 happened to be drones that Israel uses.

In Israel's exports of military technologies and spyware, drones occupy the central place because two-thirds of its exports are drones. Since 1948, Israel has been attacking and causing all forms of dehumanization, which is the central ideology of the Zionists because many Israelis think that Palestinians are not equal people. It is also known for its spyware. Israel hardly follows any ethical guidelines, and so it is indeed complicit. This is what the Zionist Israel stands for. Many may eulogize the State of Israel for all that is said above, but its behaviour has deeper darkness and black holes.

The United States, even during the war against the Palestinians, has offered billions of dollars and supplied arms and ammunition. The military prowess of Israel cannot be matched with its Middle-Eastern neighbours. However, Hamas's strategic strike on Oct 7, 2023, has changed Israel's confidence in its weaponary. It is also true with the United States as Israel's closest ally. That is why both countries, at all costs, want to destroy Hamas and drive Palestinians from the Gaza Strip, West Bank, and East Jerusalem. After months of experience on the ground, Israelis, especially PM Netanyahu's war cabinet, must have realized it is not possible to wipe out Hamas because it is an idea and ideology. Further, having massive and powerful weaponry alone would not win a war—Vietnam is the classic case.

8

With Hamas's sudden ambush on Oct 7 2023, on a music festival farming community, those visitors wanting to participate in the fest and army outposts in southern Israel were drowned in shock, unbearable grief, totally awestruck, and pushed to be drowned in disarray. Israelis could not digest the ambush of the Hamas. The rage and fury indicate how Israeli forces pounded, pulverized, and destroyed everything, including 40,000 human lives, out of which children number more than others, hospitals, schools, infrastructure, and UN shelters. The occupying power consolidated the journalists, medical doctors, paramedics, and UN staff involved in humanitarian initiatives/efforts. Gazans were pushed to run helter-skelter-like rates and cockroaches from Gaza North to Central, South, and Rafah. The government of Israel keep advising them to evacuate from one place to another; rescuers dig through smouldering piles of concrete, stone and dust, looking for survivors of airstrikes and shelling. Never in its 75 years of existence has the State of Israel become so vulnerable and shaken.

This conflict is supposedly the worst since the 1948 Nakba. Generations both in Israel and Palestine would have experienced psychological drama. Jewish Zionists and Christian Zionists are located in Israel, Europe, the United States, and other parts of the world. Rohini Hensman summarises that "Anti-Semitism is racism against the Jews. Zionism is racism against the Palestinians, Arabs and Muslims." Ironically, the countries that support the state of Israel are Christians, especially the Christian West, which has created the problem for decades and thus endorsed the genocidal project of Israel. Though many nation-states expressed their position for a ceasefire, nothing has happened thus far. People worldwide have continued their demonstrations for millions in the last hundreds of days, expressing their protests and shouting slogans against their political dispensation to enforce the ceasefire. These visuals seem to have fallen into the deaf years. India, like others, is engaged in covert deals with Israel.

It is a catastrophe. The land of Palestinians has become a graveyard. 40,000 Palestinians have been killed, hundreds and thousands wounded, and the entire population is under the grip of famine. President Joe Biden and his administration, the most trusted ally of PM Netanyahu and his far-right-wing administration, have promoted him by offering all kinds of arsenals, aid, and money and extended all kinds of support to go ahead since October, 7, 2023 till now. Netanyahu went ahead without any pause, killing, destroying, plundering, intimidating, arresting and all kinds of this against the Palestinians. Palestinians started vacating, instead fleeing from North Gaza to the Southern and the Centre as per Israelis warning.

Wherever they went, Israeli forces kept pounding and killing. At last, 1.5 million Palestinians, having no other choice, are sheltering in Rafah. It is indeed the only remaining place for them to escape the ongoing bombardments and assaults of the Israeli forces. PM Netanyahu kept warning that there would be attacks on Rafah so that the tunnels where Hamas hangs on would be wiped out. American administration has been begging PM Netanyahu not to carry out because the results would be catastrophic, and the war could spill over to the region. For over a month, Biden has threatened Netanyahu to show restraint in Rafah's operation. Still, Netanyahu has not been listening and wants to proceed with the next phase.

One and a half million are sheltering, and 1.1 million Gazans are on the brink of famine. The equations have changed. Who is dictating who? Who is controlling who? Netanyahu created the United States, and Biden was more responsible for the current affairs. Netanyahu has now turned out to be a Frankenstein. For him, it's survival—do or die. Ceasefire negotiation, though, is going on; Frankenstein would like to dodge and keep pushing and threatening. Netanyahu, the Frankenstein, has defied everyone, including Biden, UNO, and others. No one seems to be having the guts to overpower. Netanyahu, the Frankenstein of Israel, be bound. He is dangerous to our world. Like him, there are a few Frankensteins around the world. The extreme-right Zionist party headed by Netanyahu has lost its objectives on the following counts: PM Netanyahu neither brought back the hostages nor wiped out Hamas. The state of Israel is failed and rogue. As Brazil's President Lula rightly called that, the current government of Israel under Netanyahu is genocidal and thus involved in the Holocaust. Millions and billions of people across the countries and continents show their anger, holding demonstrations and protests in varied ways. Apparently, on Feb 25, 2024, a US Air Force personnel died after setting himself on fire in front of the Israeli Embassy in Washington DC on Feb 25, 2024, shouting "Free Palestine".

9

The United States and Israel are known for their contradictions. Presently, in Israel's war against the Palestinians, the USA has shown its inhumanity and collaboration by supporting PM Netanyahu, the butcher of the Palestinians, for the last year by killing and destroying everything that belongs to them. It has led to the unprecedented suffering of more than 1.5 million Palestinians without food and basic needs. The State of Israel, though it has a few entry points, has decided not to open but is determined to push the Palestinians to Egypt's Sinai as refugees.

US President Joe is the co-supporter to PM Netanyahu (Bibi) in this war. Having failed to agree to the open, the corridors that Israel is controlling have decided to drop from the skies over the Gaza Strip American food pallets. It's such a farce that Joe has used the same skies to deliver bombs to Israel, which in turn uses the skies to pound the Palestinians living in the Gaza Strip, West Bank, and East Jerusalem. Joe Biden thinks that he could keep fooling the world, delivering death and life, trying to find balance in an unbalanced Middle-East war. Is it possible to find an elusive balance between supplying bombs on the one side and delivering food packs from the skies on the other?

Many Americans who belonged to the democratic party and represented the US Senate and Congress were disgusted with his behaviour in this war. One of the Congressmen representing California Ro Khanna said: "You can't have a policy giving aid and giving Israel the weapons to bomb the food trucks at the same time." In an interview the day after the speech of Joe Biden, he said: "There is inherent contradiction in that. And I think the administration needs to match the genuine empathy and moral concern that came out last night for Palestinian civilian lives with real accountability for Netanyahu and the extreme right-wing government there."

Critics point out that the supplies floating down by parachute hardly meet the needs and only highlight the moral conflict in Biden's approach to the war, which started when a Hamas terrorist attack killed about 1,200 people in Israel on Oct 7, 2023, and prompted an Israeli response that has killed more than 40,000 people in Gaza. Yousef Munayyer, the head of the Palestine-Israel program at the Arab Center, said: "It doesn't make any sense." Israelis and their supporters reject that logic, saying, "Why are they at cross purposes?" Justifying Joe's act, Eyal Hulata, former national security adviser to former PM Naftali Bennett, said, "The message is – and I strongly support Bidden for doing so – that he supports the elimination of Hamas, which is the source and cause of all those atrocities, while at the same time putting a lot of emphasis on assisting the civilian population of Gazza." Joe Biden's response to the current impasse is with a number of contradictions—perhaps alludes to 'Christian conscience'.

10

Aaron Bushnell, 25, was taken to hospital after Secret Service officers extinguished the flames. Before setting himself alight in what he called an "extreme act of protest", he said that "he would no longer be complicit in genocide". He did inform several reporters and posted on a few websites before committing that act that "Today, I am planning to engage in an extreme act of protest against the genocide of the Palestinian people". Aaron Bushnell conveyed a clear message to the world at large that those with conscience shall never accept the massacres and bombardments going on in the land of Palestinians. Images that we see and hear stories have been so powerful that they prick those with conscience emanating from a deep spirituality. Aeron Bushnell, an American young man with a great future ahead, had decided to let flames consume his mortal body, but his soul and spirit continued to live. Aeron Bushnell is a martyr who listened to his conscience and thus decided to end his life for a cause. His conscience did not allow him to be a passive onlooker to the ongoing massacre.

Before and after immolating himself in front of the Israeli Embassy, he kept shouting to stop the killing. He continued till he was fully consigned to flames. Aeron Bushnell listened to his conscience and must have deeply examined it before resorting to an act, knowing well he would die. As a young Air Force officer, he listened to the voice and acted accordingly. He gave his life for a definitive purpose. Binding an evil, which consumed more than 33,000 lives, several hundred journalists, UNRAW staff, doctors, paramedics and a host of others, is difficult.

A catastrophe that the world has been witnessing for the last year. Israel's war on Palestinians is nothing but a rage, mayhem, indiscriminate slaughtering and butchering of humans at alarming levels. It is definitely the worst in modern history, wherein such blatant butchering is happening despite the world coming out openly against the state of Israel. PM Netanyahu went ahead with a rampage, not heeding to including his closest ally, Joe Biden, the president of the United States.

11

On Apr 8, 2024, Israeli forces killed seven aid workers in an air strike that the military called 'an operational accident'. This incident has stoked anger in the West, as the Israeli forces slayed the World Central Kitchen (WCK) staff, including Australian, British, and Polish nationals, along with a US-Canadian dual national. Israeli leaders shed crocodiles and came out with all sorts of narratives, such as it was a 'misidentification' and 'unintended' of a WCK at night in a combat zone. But those who witnessed the ambush said that the convoy was attacked thrice at different points from the air despite having coordinated its route in advance with the military. Still, the military control suspected and thus ambushed.

Israel cannot get away from this attack. Since those belonging to Israel's closest alleys got killed, they want an investigation that should be transparent, comprising of members belonging to those who the State of Israel killed. WCK's founder, chef Jose Andres said he believed his food delivery team had been "systematically"; whereas Israeli spokesperson Raquela Karamson said: "This was unintended". Israel's ruling class is known for all kinds of lies and denials. Israel's ruling dispensation has lost its credibility and morality. This has totally changed the scenario that existed in the past six months wherein Joe Biden Joe) called Netanyahu (Bibi) and told him enough is enough and better fall in line.

He instructed to open the corridors that the Israeli government closed for long months so that entry of essential goods could reach Gaza. Not complying would lead to devastating consequences. Biden said Israel has "not done enough to protect civilians" in its war in Gaza." He was "outraged and heartbroken" by the death of the workers. From the legislators and civil society organizations both in England and the United States, more pressure has started to mount, pressurizing the heads of governments to stop sending the sale of weapons and weapon systems to Israel. Lawyers, retired judges, academicians, and policymakers wrote letters to refrain from aiding the State of Israel. The lives of all nationals matter, not just the lives of the West.

Usually, those who think that they're 'too smart' somewhere fail. Bibi's military overacted by killing the staff of World Central Kitchen (WCK) that carried nationals from North America, Europe, Australia, and one Palestinian. For Biden & co, six lives matter because it changed the trajectory of Israel's war on Palestinians. The WCK incident marks the first international causality. Since the Israeli army killed citizens of Western countries, Israel has to go through a problematic situation responding to those countries. The US and UK governments are under pressure to supply arms to Israel. Delivering food aid in war zones is a brave work for humanity. Killing aid workers who risked their lives for humanity is the most heinous, inhuman, barbaric act.

During the pandemic, natural catastrophes, and other disasters, religious and secular organizations engaged in relief works and food distribution, risking to save humanity. Likewise, WCK, founded by celebrity chef Jose Andres, helped those struggling for food in Palestine and Ukraine. As Andres says, "Food is not a weapon of war, and yet that is what the war has turned into in Gaza. Israel cannot keep arguing, "It happens in war," as its actions starve Gazans to death. But who'll make the Israeli government eat its own words?" The entire Gaza Strip, East Jerusalem, and West Bank smells as Elie Wiesel says in *Night*: **"That night, the soup tasted of corpses."**

12

In this case, Israel's war on Gaza candidly exhibits and shows that militant Judaism and crony capitalism go hand in hand. Max Weber proved this in his seminal work entitled *Protestant Ethics and Spirit of Capitalism,* Max Stackhouse's book *God and Globalization,* and Karl Marx's *das Capital.* These public intellectualswent deep into the roots of religion, especially the first two, showing Christianity and capitalism have a symbiotic nature, thus mutually enriching and growing. Zionism is the central ideology of far-right fundamentalists. Zionists believe in militant Judaism, which is a nationality vis-à-vis Israelism as well as a religion.

Jews trace their nationhood back to the biblical kingdoms of David and Solomon. In contrast, modern Zionism is built on Jewish yearning for a 'return to Zion' visualized in the 19th century and is gaining momentum now in militant ways. The far-right Zionists and Christian Zionists are the significant actors. Zionism per se encompasses encapsulating the Jewish character of the Israeli state, meaning that Jews have privileges and others don't. Zionism is a species of colonialism and racism aimed at appropriating Palestinian land systematically and occupying with the Israeli settlement – a grand expansionist plan of Greater Israel.

Zionism, in the words of the UN in 1975, is "a form of racism and racial discrimination." This definition has subsequently been repealed. Nonetheless, Israel is indeed a colonial settlement project. Judaism is grounded in the first five of the Holy Bible, the Torah. It exhaustively describes the Israelis' lineage and movement, captivity, struggles, exodus, and settlement. Pseudo-Judaism has reverted everything and wants to establish premised on Zionists political premises. As promised in the Torah, Israelis believe that their God, Yahweh, brought them as covenanted to the 'Promised Land', flowing with milk and honey. The underlying factor has been that Israelis as Yahweh's 'chosen race and people'.

A beautiful picture epitomizes in Torah that along with the desert terrains, i.e., from the coast of the Mediterranean Sea to the Jordan River, everything shall eventually transform into fertility and, in due course of time, transform the desert into a livable and blessed habitat. Jews are hard-working people endowed with innovative and technical know-how. Jews scattered across the world at the time of World War II holocaust. They thus reached top positions—whatever reasons attributed to finance, innovation in science, technology, and finance that pushed them to enter into economy and polity in their respective countries. They influence American academia, finance, and politics. The current interpretation of militant -Judaism enjoins blessings to prosperity and well-being of a race at any cost with an assumption that Yahweh blessed with wealth and well-being at any cost—means and ends hardly matter.

For the Zionists, crony capitalism as an economic creed pushed the Jews, Zionists and Israelism to such levels of fury and rage. Zionist Jews and Zionist Christians have negated the core ethical values and moral principles that the Torah and the Holy Bible prescribe. Judaism is a prophetic religion, while on the other, crony capitalism believes in the 'ends', and not the 'means'. For Jewish Zionists and Christian Zionists, ends justify, not the means, which contradicts the core values of Judaism—which essentializes both means and ends are imperative. Billionaires and millionaires belonging to Jewish Zionists and Christian Zionists have invested vast sums of money in the oligopolistic corporations that manufacture armaments and weapons, spyware, AIs, drugs and pharmaceuticals, food chains, etc., for huge returns, which in turn invested or given as endowments to top universities across North America and Europe as well as in big mega transnational corporations.

These developments are visible in light of other problems, such as the Supreme Court of America's ban on affirmative action in admissions.

The tenure system for faculty is under heavy strain, as the teaching load spills over to the poorly paid adjunct instructors. The university's traditional commitment to free speech is gradually waning. Arrests, suspensions and recruitment boycotts have pushed the students to protest against the relentless assault in Gaza, slaughtering more than 40,000 human lives. This is how the ultra-Zionists have been controlling the American and European countries by employing diverse mechanisms against those who critique and counter the Jews/Israelis—all in the name of 'anti-Semitism' or branding them as anti-Semites. A vivid semblance of inter-play of crony capitalism and ultra-Zionism The way the Zionist Jews and Christian Zionists think and behave can be easily seen in the ongoing war in Gaza. They have completely forgotten the basic tenets and essence of Judaism and its value premises.More importantly, if they believe in biblical history, let me not take colonial history, only the biblical history that says that they were once enslaved people, captives, and nomads moving from one place to another. Oppressed and, exploited and ravaged by different regimes by not having their own identity. Having forgotten all those now gripped in domination, rage, and anger have taken over, their morality and spirituality are under scrutiny because their actions hardly concur with Judaism. Not bothered about their bankruptcy in moral principles and ethical code, these Zionists drive destruction, occupation, and expansionism. Power, domination, and expansion have become their war's central foci and objectives.

Michael Foucault's notion of the modern form of power is based on relations of domination, hierarchy, asymmetry and control. Therefore, liberation or freedom is impossible at the individual or collective levels. The Modern State of Israel and the ruling dispensation dominated by far-right Zionists use all the categories as exposited by Foucault. And yet the tool used by the Zionists that extend domination and the ones that leverage ought to be countered. In exceptional ways, university students in the United States found tools to locate the exploitative and oppressive modes. They now demand the administration to divest, withdraw, and enforce the ceasefire.

13

The West historically is known for imperialism, colonialism, apartheid, and ethnic cleansing. As part of the expansionist strategy, the government of Israel wants to annex all the territories from the River to the Sea. The countries in the West, the United States, and Israel keep invoking the Christian Scriptures to their advantage. Zionists, Jews, and Zionist Christians tend to invoke the Bible to justify their actions. They employ a reductionist approach, selecting and interpreting the verses that suit them. For example, "For lo, I will command and shake the house of Israel among all the nations, as one shakes with a slave, but no pebbles shall fall to the ground" (Amos 9:7). Zionist both the Jews and Christians take up from the same book verse 15 that "I will plant them upon their land, and they shall never again be plucked up, out of the land that I have given them, says the Lord your God."

Jewish and Christian Zionists have forgotten the core biblical message that 'God loves all nations'. PM Netanyahu, while justifying his war on Gaza, invoked a part of a verse from Ecclesiastes 3: 8b that "... a time for war, and a time for peace". Holy Scriptures are used left and right to justify the actions of those who failed to go through the essence of the texts. More importantly, the Christian Zionists invoke Revelation 16 and 19 in this regard.There is no longer Jew or Greek; there is no longer slave or free, there is no longer male and female; for all of you are one in Christ Jesus (Gal3:28).

Zionists should desist from quoting the Bible to justify the brazen killings of innocent people of any race. Israel could perhaps be a nuclear power state and is one of the significant producers of weaponry and spyware, but Gazans completely de-coded and thus exposed Israel. The genocide in Gaza is a testimony and proof of how a victor turned guest, then settlers, and finally, the predator can unleash terror on innocent civilians. People around the world are rattled by the ways that the nations support Israel's involvement in the collective punishment of the Palestinians, which shows fissures in deep spirituality. Invoking portions of the Christian Scriptures both by the Jews and the Christians show the moral bankruptcy and total spiritual blackout. Deviating from the basic biblical ethical and moral principles such as love, humanity, freedom, equality, human dignity and rights, shalom, justice, relational responsibility, and a host of others and by punishing in diverse ways out of rage and anger posits moral bankruptcy and ethical accountability. The core and root cause of all kinds of wars and conflicts happening in the world that we live in is religion. Therefore, religion is the core contesting point of all disputes, especially if we use Netanyahu's usage of the term 'war', which is embedded in 'religion', which drives all the actors involved in this so-called 'war' or 'conflict'.

Palestinians have been living under subjugation and enslavement for more than seventy-five years on their land. Israel has always been occupying power. Israel has a very close tie-up with the American administration. Whoever takes the reigns of Presidency of the United States will have to have a solid clout with the Jews because they have infiltrated into all facets—politics, economy, culture, religion, technology, public service, and many others. For example, Antony Blinken, the Secretary of State of the United States, is a Jew who is involved closely with the Israeli-Palestine War; Jared Kushner, Donald Trump's son-in-law, was the key in changing the American Embassy from Tel Avi to Jerusalem is Jew. Janet Yellin is the Secretary of Treasury, US Ambassador to India Eric Garcetti, and many in Biden's administration are Jews.

Media is playing the most crucial part in influencing its viewership. Israeli society is also polarized because it is Netanyahu's war. In a world of fluidities, we need to watch those who invoke anti-Semitism, Jihad, Islamophobia, xenophobia, and many other constructs so that we don't fall prey to their narratives. In a polarized world, religions play decisive roles. We must be cautious and apply a critical theory of 'suspicion' in our understanding and judgment. As part of the conclusion, Judaism is a prophetic religion and is now reduced to Zionism as the far-right and fundamentalist Jews and Christians have changed it to Jewish Zionism. This is what happens when religion is in the hands of far-right and fundamentalist Jews who would go to any extent to distort and misinterpret the Torah to suit their vested interests and to meet their Zionist ends. In the entire process, the core values of Judaism are betrayed.

14

Israel's war against Palestinians in its entirety has opened up the Pandora's box of those who invoke the Holy Scripture vis-à-vis Old Testament, especially the Torah, and thus interpret it as if the ownership and entitlement vests with the Jews. The so-called Zionist Jews and Christian Zionists somehow managed to push this theology against the Palestinians, justifying and perpetuating the atrocities of the Jewish Zionists and Christian Zionists. Their narratives and interpretations are getting exposed. The following illustrates whatever has been said.Tensions between Israel and the Vatican—the Catholic Church is escalating after a gathering of prominent catholic bishops called on Israel to end the occupation of Palestinian territories and to stop using the Bible to justify the occupation.

The bishops started a two-week special synod of bishops organized by the Vatican. Archbishop Cyril Celine Bustros is, the head of the Melchite Greek Catholic Church in the United States of America said: "It's actually clear for new on the purpose of as a sure the time that I tell promise this is clear for us the concept of the Promised Land cannot be used as the base for justification of the return of the Jews to Israel, and the displacement of Palestinians 4 to 5 million Jews have been brought in and 3 to 4 million Palestinians have been chased out of their land where they lived for 1400 to 1600 years." Therefore, what we want to say is it is a political question, but the justification for Israel's occupation of the land of Palestine cannot be based on sacred scriptures. Justifying apartheid, occupation, and keeping millions of Palestinians under siege without freedom, self-determination, fundamental rights, equality, and self-determination for about 75 years shall never be tolerated and justified by invoking Scriptures and interpreting in flimsy, partisan, and subjective ways to suit heinous, diabolical, and immoral acts.

The false narratives have been ripped open in the recent war with Israel, the occupying power of the Palestinian's land who are the original inhabitants. Zionist Jews and Christian Zionists, in covert and subtle ways, point to the Christian Scriptures saying all kinds of non-nonsensical and irrational things to suit their stories. It is a matter of politics and history. Negating politics and history and bringing in absurd arguments by lifting the Scriptures will no longer be accepted. Read the political history, the colonial history, and how the colonizers used Scriptures and power to justify their acts favouring a particular race. More such analyses and interpretations will surface over time. Do not fool the world by invoking the Scriptures to justify the nefarious actions. Remember, Jews and Israelis who were once enslaved people, refugees, and migrants.

12

Dalits, Missionaries, Tourists and Flaneurs 'Free Movement' in India before 'Dalit Literature'

David J. Chalcraft

'They do not figure in any of the so-called ancient Indian literatures- as though they have never talked, never walked; as though they never lived on this soil at all' (Kancha Ilaiah, Post Hindu India: A Discourse on Dalit-Bahujan, Socio-Spiritual and Scientific Revolution. New Delhi Sage, 2009: 26)

It is an honour and privilege to write this essay for a book to mark, with a Festschrift, the 60th birthday of Professor Jesurathnam. If my memory serves me right when I was visiting Professor of Old Testament Studies and Sociology at United Theological College Bangalore in the summer of 2014, Professor Jesurathnam was largely on sabbatical in the United States. Hence, we were not in direct daily communication, and I learnt of his work through reading his books. In no way could I fill his shoes whilst at UTC- and that was not the intention-but even so, given our meetings at other conferences, seminars and events over some years in India, he was kind enough to remark on my solidarity with his commitment to the life of the Dalits and the importance of biblical exegesis relevant to their context. He has consistently and effectively devoted his career to developing the liberative dimensions of Dalit exegesis.

Introduction

This essay considers aspects of the degrading social experience of Dalits by looking at narratives of free and restricted movement and travel in India.

Three narratives are utilised. First, *A South India Diary* (1951) by Lesslie Newbiggin[59] is considered, followed by an incident related in a report by Bishops Azariah and Whitehead[60] from 1930, and finally, in a justly celebrated and well-known short novel from 1935 by Mulk Raj Anand[61], entitled *Untouchable* (and I draw some brief comparisons between this text and Valmiki's *Joothan: A Dalit's Life*).[62] During my research on the history of Christianity and biblical exegesis in India, I have read these books over the years with increasing interest, and in some ways this essay is meant as an appreciation of them; at the same time, repeated reflection on them has led me to see how they portray differences of the experience of 'free movement' in India. This essay considers what these books can tell us about Missionary and Dalit movements through physical and public spaces in their context. This will provide a point of departure for considering briefly how texts about 'being unclean' in the Hebrew Bible might resonate or challenge Dalit hearers and readers of the biblical text today. Moreover, a firmer grasp of the 'authentic' Dalit voice can be achieved, and consideration given to the challenges a Dalit poetic poses to biblical exegesis.

In all three cases, the *direct* personal voice of the Dalit is *not* heard. The account of Lesslie Newbigin (1909-1998) describes for his audience of family, friends and well-wishers back home in the United Kingdom, his experiences and shares his knowledge of village life in South India, where the gradations of caste are precise and operative but which Newbigin arguably describes from a sanguine distance. The fictional narrative written by Anand (1905-2004), published before Ambedkar's *The Annihilation of Caste* (1936)[63] but after the Poona Pact (1932), it covers one day in the life of the untouchable Bakha from the sweeper caste. The incident recounted by Bishop Azariah (1874-1945) and Bishop Whitehead (1853-1947) in their *Christ in the Indian Villages* (1930) serves in my essay as a bridge between Newbiggin and Anand, providing an example of how the 'mass movement' of Untouchables converting to Christianity encouraged more profound knowledge of the life of Dalits.

Anand himself was from the Kshatriya varna, but his narrative evidences great empathy with the life of his fictional character. It is remarkable for the way in which it captures and expresses the depth of humiliation, anger and despair that characterises Bakha's experience. As such, it is an improvement

59 Lesslie Newbigin, *A South India Diary* (London: SCM Press, 1951).

60 V. Z. Azariah and Henry Whitehead, *Christ in the Indian Villages* (London: SCM Press, 1930).

61 Mulk Raj Anand, *Untouchable* (London: Penguin, 1935/2014).

62 Omprakash Valmiki, *Joothan: A Dalit's Life* (Kolkata: Samya, 2003).

63 B. R. Ambedkar, *Annihilation of Caste* Noida (UP: Maple Press, 1936/2023).

on the reportage of the Dalit experience presented by Newbiggin, but it is still not a vehicle of an authentic Dalit voice. For example, more authentic voices are found in the poems and short stories written by Dalits and in auto/biographies. One recent (2004) classic example is *Joothan*: *A Dalit Life* ('scraps') by Valmiki. Comparing *Untouchable* by Anand with the personal, vivid firsthand accounts of Valmiki in *Joothan* shows that Anand's *Verstehen* is very strong. The expression of the lasting and haunting trauma that humiliating and violent, and shocking encounters had on Valmiki are excruciatingly given in *Joothan* and bear comparison with Anand's imaginative reconstructions, for example. However, even while Anand described the squalor and material nature of human existence, through references to bodily functions, sex and sexuality, through the constant presence of the abject, it is *Joothan* that can shock the reader more with the sheer cruelty and violence that is metered out on the central subject. With the acts of sexual exploitation of women, and the ever presence of dirt, filth and excrement that is portrayed: all the senses are assailed.

Given the recent explosion in publication in both original languages and in translation (into English) of Dalit fiction, poetry, and auto/biography, it is now possible to hear more authentic Dalit voices. Within biblical studies, it is now possible to directly hear the voices of Dalit biblical scholars through their own exegesis.[64] In the absence of ethnographic data, the literature produced by Dalits can serve as a perfect proxy and lift the veil on Dalit experience and trauma that would otherwise remain closed to those not of Dalit origin. Lifting the veil on Dalit's experience prior to modern times is more complicated than it is today, but whenever Dalit's social worlds are encountered, the reader is challenged. One question that remains in the development of Dalit biblical exegesis within the field of theological and biblical studies is the extent to which the Christian Dalit writers and exegetes 'water-down' so to speak, and anaesthetize the Dalit experience, rendering it more anodyne in the interaction with the biblical text and the communication of its meaning to a Christian audience, and hence altering the full force of the Dalit poetic. The full voice of the Dalit can be best captured through ethnographic work in the field and in the capturing of first-hand life histories: this has only just begun.[65] Of course, the final voice

64 David J Chalcraft, "Strategies Past, Present and Future: The Context and Variety of Biblical Studies in Indian Culture and Society", inDavid J Chalcraft and ZhodiAngami, ed. *Encountering Diversity in Indian Biblical Studies: A Biblical Masala* (London: Routledge, 2023), 31-76, and the bibliography there.

65 Jeeva Kumar Ravela and David J Chalcraft, "Encountering the Bible: Listening to the Voices of Madiga Christians", in David J Chalcraft and ZhodiAngami,ed. *Encountering Diversity in Indian Biblical Studies: A Biblical Masala* (London: Routledge, 2023), 190-211.

to be heard is that of the oppressed in the Bible itself—the Dalits of the ancient world. What is the best procedure for retrieving these voices this is a pressing question in global and Dalit biblical hermeneutics.

1947: Partition and The Church of South India

It was events in 1947 that brought Lesslie Newbigin back to India. However, it was not on account of the Partition of India, which accompanied the Independence of India and the creation of Pakistan and East Bengal (Independence is dated August 15th, 1947). This tragedy caused one of the largest displacements of people in world history that has ever taken place. Any account of movement in India has to recognise its significance. A contemporary writer states: 'Whole worlds suddenly fell apart at the time of India's partition'.[66] It is estimated that between 12 and 16 million people were displaced. Numbers who died (or were murdered) during the transition is impossible to determine with figures as large and incomprehensible as 2 million. Many stories are related to the massacres of passengers on trains crossing the new borders either way, and there are memories of the long columns of people walking on foot in *kafilas* of up to 40,000 persons and caravans '45 miles long in places.[67] The legacies of Partition continue into the present day: the culture and social geographies of major cities like Mumbai, Kolkata and Delhi were dramatically altered by the sheer number of refugees and the need to assimilate people who were total strangers to their new surroundings, for example.[68] One historian observes that 'Partition had a wide-spread psychological impact which may never be fully recognised or traced...Some people went, quite literally, mad.'[69]

The experience of Indian Christians has not figured prominently in the historiography. Charitable aid for the refugees became a major preoccupation of Christian groups, but it is important to learn of the ways in which other ethnic/religious groups perceived Christian groups. There are occasions when Hindus and Muslims together attacked Christian and Parsi premises.[70] In other cases, the Indian Christians were seen as potential members of other communities- if it could be shown that Christians should be counted

66 Neeti Nair, *Hurt Sentiments: Secularism and Belonging in South Asia* (Cambridge, Massa: Harvard University Press, 2023), Kavita Puri, *Partition Voices: Untold British Stories* (London: Bloomsbury, 2022).

67 Yasmin Khan, *The Great Partition: the Making of India and Pakistan*, New edition, (New Haven: Yale University Press, 2017), 160.

68 Ramachandra Guha, *India After Gandhi. The History of the World's Largest Democracy*. 1st edition. London: Pan Book, 2007), 84-102.

69 Yasmin Khan,*The Great Partition: the Making of India and Pakistan*, 187.

70 Alex von Tunzelmann,*Indian Summer: the Secret History of the End of an Empire* (London: Pocket Books, 2007), 57.

as in alliance with Muslims, for example, the increase in the numbers could improve the claim to be a majority group in an area There are known cases in the Punjab where Christians were advised to clearly show their identity and affiliation through wearing red crosses or other symbols so that it was obvious that they were neither Hindu, Muslim nor Sikh and could escape the rioting, pillage, rape and murder.[71] Untouchables and Christian minorities were not directly catered for in the drawing of the maps of Partition.[72] In recent times, more attention is being paid to the diversity of experience of Partition, differentiating different castes.[73] However, at the present time, it is not possible to relate the experiences of Indian Christians and the routes they took during Partition and how these experiences of 'forced migration' impacted their biblical exegesis and theology, nor their social relations and psychology.

It is striking that whilst the Partition was taking effect in the North of India, in Southern India, within Christian communities, a process was taking place, bringing different religious parties together under the newly created Church of South India. The Church of South India was inaugurated in September 1947, bringing together the four denominations of Anglicans, Congregationalists, Presbyterians and Methodists. In the North, Partition was ripping communities apart and intensifying communal violence and murder, while in the South, attempts were being made to ecumenically combine various Christian denominations.This event in South India is found in histories of Christianity in India.

It would be a worthwhile project, in my view, if Christian responses, especially their use of biblical exegesis to address the issues of Partition, were to be examined and written about so as to have a complete history of the role of the Bible in Indian political, cultural and social life. Newbigin was on furlough as the war ended, and India and Pakistan achieved independence. There are no references to Partition in *A South India Diary*, and in his autobiography, for example, he only makes a passing comment and largely has a rosy, optimistic view of the achievement of Independence and attitudes toward the departing British Raj. His assessment of the achievement of Mountbatten certainly is not in agreement with more recent work.[74] He wrote: ‘On the wider political scene, there was much to bring zest and excitement into life. India, newly Independent, was full of development

71 Yasmin Khan, *The Great Partition: the Making of India and Pakistan*, 82.

72 Yasmin Khan, *The Great Partition: the Making of India and Pakistan*, 110.

73 For example, Banerjee and Sarbani discuss different identity formations in Bengal partition narratives by Dalit refugees. *Interventions: International Journal of Postcolonial Studies*. 19/4 (2017):550-565.

74 Alex von Tunzelmann, *Indian Summer: the Secret History of the End of an Empire*, 57f.

plans. The style Mountbatten had carried through his final actions had wiped out the bitterness of earlier years, and the British who remained in India basked in the sunshine of an unaccustomed popularity. Even the tragedy of Partition brought one good gift: the challenge of Christians in the south to go to the north and help with the terrible consequences of the murderous communal strife between Hindus and Moslems. The assassination of Gandhi by the hand of a Hindu zealot sent shock waves through the whole nation.'[75]

A South India Diary (Newbigin 1951)

As communities in Northern India were being wrenched apart by these geo-political processes, in South India, the Church of South India sought to bring several separate Christian denominations under one overarching constitution. The founding of the Church of South India and the installation of nine Bishops brought Lesslie Newbigin back to India. Newbigin is well known as a churchman, theologian, missionary, and writer committed to the Church of South India and grappling with the inter-cultural processes of communicating the word of God in a modern and post-colonial society. Newbigin was installed as Bishop of Maduria and Ramnad. He writes an account of this process and his involvement in it in his Diary. *A South India Diary* begins with an account of the ceremony held at St George's Cathedral in what was then Madras (today Chennai) in Tamil Nadu on September 27th, 1947. Newbigin was beginning his duties as the new Bishop, and he devoted himself in these first years to visiting as many of the 550 villages that are in the Diocese. The Diary is full of personal and lively descriptions of his experiences as he travels around his large diocese, travelling by bus, by car, as pillion on a motorbike, visiting as many village communities as possible, and offering his reflections on the enormity of the task, and the range of very challenging problems and issues that required his attention. Problems included intervening on behalf of striking Christians who were associating with communists, asking caste communities to allow Dalit access to their wells, baptising the children born from the union of men and the women that men of the Puliyan caste Christians had 'captured'; the impacts of Hindu boycott of Dalits recently converted, and establishing schemes for economic self-reliance.

Newbigin and 'The Country Bus'

If 'Travel Writing' can be very generally described as 'an encounter between self and other precipitated by movement' [76] then Newbigin's *ASouth India*

75 Lesslie Newbigin, *Unfinished Agenda: An Autobiography* (Grand Rapids, Michigan: Eerdmans, 1985), 108

76 Carl Thompson,*Travel Writing* (London: Routledge, 2011), 10.

Diary qualifies as an example of the genre, and we expect to find descriptions of the new impressions he sees and the 'negotiation between similarity and difference ' that takes place, which, through the narrative, reveals aspects of his self and the other. In what follows, I provide a passage from Newbigin's *A South India Diary*, one of my favourite pieces of writing by a European missionary and traveller in India. The passage runs as follows:

> 'The country bus sways and jolts along the road, scattering the poultry, cattle and pedestrians in front and leaving a long cloud of white dust for a hundred yards behind. It is a ramshackle affair, and there seems to be no reason why it should not fall to pieces at any moment. Inside it, there is a close-packed cargo of men, women, and children, as well as baskets, sacks, boxes, and babies. Those who do not get a seat squat comfortably on the floor. There is a continuous high-pitched crackle of conversation, easily heard above the engine's roar. We do not talk about the weather or anything so trivial. Money, marriages, village gossip, religion, politics- these all have their share of attention. The stranger is thoroughly catechized. Occupation, native place, monthly income, father's name and income, destination, object of journey- these questions have to be answered by way of introduction. The last question leads out into theological territory where everyone can join in. Even the V.I.P's. in the front seat beside the driver turn round to cock an ear at the conversation. There is every variety of responses, from the open-eyed wonder of the villager who has never heard of the Gospel to the blasé scepticism of the college graduate who has seen through it all.
>
> A prosperous-looking Brahmin begins a mocking imitation of a missionary preaching in Tamil: 'Ah, rascals, dolts, tramps and vagabonds, come to us and we will take you in'. Tamil has no words which mean to 'save sinners.' Apart from Christ, how could it? The Tamil Bible words could be translated as 'to provide free board and lodging for rascals'. That is one of the inescapable problems of evangelism. The Brahmin has made a good hit and gets a good laugh. I am wondering how to reply when an unexpected ally turns up. A young farmer, sitting behind the bench, leans forward and tackles the Brahmin. 'I know all your nonsense. "All religions are the same", you say. "All roads lead to God". It is not true. If you want to go somewhere you have to get into the right bus. If you get into the wrong bus you get to the wrong place. If you want salvation you have got to have the religion that gets you that. That's Christianity'. The Brahmin was

> not expecting this and is silenced. It is quite good fun teasing a missionary but decidedly less edifying to argue about religion with an obvious outcaste. The farmer tells me his story, how he became a Christian, how he learned to be a good farmer, how he has developed fruit farming. Here is his place now. There are his fruit trees over there. He shouts to the driver to stop and, gets down, shoulders his bundle, and tramps off through the fields to his house. The Brahmin is a little sorry for his attack, and we have a good talk.The bus is slowing up again at the signal of a group standing by the roadside. This is where I have to get down. The pastor, the village teacher, and some of the elders are waiting to greet me. The village deacon comes forward with one of the exquisitely beautiful garlands with which the Tamil expresses his greetings. We walk together to the village.[77]

This passage is full of life, and it's almost as if we can enter the bus ourselves, find a seat, join the ride and contribute to the conversation. It's a colourful cosmopolitan scene, and whilst there are individuals from different walks of life, of various castes and statuses (the front seat beside the driver is the reserve of the most important), the bus feels more like a republic of persons travelling in the same direction. Given that the European traveller and the missionary undertake many journeys and in a variety of vehicles, it is appropriate that this is one of the opening narratives of Newbigin's Diary. Newbigin, is fully conscious of his experience, and of its newness. His senses are alert, and he notices what is going on in detail. It some ways it is remarkable that Newbigin seems so relaxed since it was his being involved in a bus accident in the 1930's in which his legs were badly damaged that forced him to return to Scotland for medical treatment. During this period of recuperation after surgery on his legs, he learned Tamil, which explains the ease with which he converses with everyone on the country bus. The 'ramshackle affair' brings attention to the quality of the vehicle on which he is travelling. The 'miracle' of its staying together and functioning is noted, and he would not be surprised if it were to fall to pieces at any moment. There is a Madiga short story, translated from the Telegu, where, after only a short distance, the Dappu drummers who have boarded a bus to journey to the funeral where they will be paying their respects and playing their drums have to disembark since it has quickly broken down. Gogu Shyamala describes this as follows: 'The bus arrived after some time, and one by one, the old men, the young boys and their dappu climbed into it. They squeezed past passengers holding onto their dappu for dear life, crushing all and

77 Lesslie Newbigin, *A South India Diary*, 27-29.

sundry as they hurried towards empty seats. But the bus had not plied even a mile before it sputtered and hushed to a stop'.[78]

The bus journey in *A South India Diary* is the vehicle for conveying theological truths and church history. Modes of travel and the experience of types of movement are part of the consciousness of being in India, but they can also serve as symbols of spiritual journeys and of routes and pathways undertaken. Pathways through life, through places and even through texts. 'Movement' is a powerful metaphor that is not lost on Newbigin. Indeed, the 'Outcaste man' expresses the symbolic meaning of journeys and taking the 'right bus' or the right path to arrive spiritually and literally where you wish to end up. Challenging the Brahmin's idea that all roads lead to God he states: 'If you want to go somewhere you have to get into the right bus. If you get into the wrong bus you get to the wrong place. If you want salvation, you have to have the religion that gets you that. 'There is something realistic (since it brings to mind similar interchanges that one has experienced in India) about the way that people on the bus learn of Newbigin's background, status and purpose. As he says, he was 'fully catechized'. The use of the terms of religious formation merge here with the dimensions of identity that are of importance in Indian culture. The challenge of inclusion of Dalit members in the Christian Church is presented through the comic parodying of a Christian missionary by the Brahmin. Newbigin's humour and goodwill are not undone, and he does not fail to note that he and the Brahmin have a good conversation even after the comic and critical banter has occurred. The power of the Gospel to appeal to Untouchables, as well as the idea that through contact with Christianity, the self-respect of the Dalit is improved, is presented in the case of the farmer who has converted to Christianity and is now successful. Newbigin's interest and excitement in being in India, pursuing his vocation, and travelling joyously to his destination are clearly conveyed in the passage. Newbigin leaves the bus when he reaches his destination and is greeted by the village gatekeepers with the customary garland. Then they walk together to the village.

Azariah and Whitehead: *Christ in the Indian Villages*

Let's move from the almost holiday atmosphere of Newbigin's adventure, where we can almost feel the bumps in the road and the breeze coming through the open windows of the Country Bus, to a road in Kerala, and hear the report of a Christian traveller near Travancore, from 20 years before. A more painful picture of the relationship between the Dalit movement and the caste system is related in this pre-partition work by Bishops Azariah and

78 Gogu Shyamala, "Trace it/Jaada", in her *Father May be an elephant and mother only a basket but...*(New Delhi: Navayan, 2012), 27-38, the quotation is from p. 32.

Whitehead, in a chapter entitled 'Christ Among the Outcastes' in their *Christ in the Indian Villages*. They record the account of a visitor to Travancore who related:

> 'I was walking down a road one evening on the south west coast of India and a brahmin priest, a member of the highest caste, was behind me. Turning a corner, I came across about twenty outcastes coming in from their work in the fields. As soon as they caught sight of the Brahman they scattered about thirty or forty yards on each side of the road, cowered down in abject, servile fear in the mud and slush of the rice fields, put their hands to their mouths, lest their breath should defile the high caste man, and cried out in harsh pathetic tones, "unclean, unclean", to give warning of the pollution of their presence.'[79]

The 'unclean, unclean' refrain is a leit-motif of Dalit encounter.The account echoes some of the similar observations offered by Ambedkar in his *Annilihation of Caste*, where he seeks to present the reality of the tyranny against the Outcastes/Dalits in past and contemporary India and to give expression to the suffering, pain and humiliation of 'his people' and to argue for the need for social reform as well as political reform. Restrictions on Dalit movement and use of public highways and paths were and is a common situation (see paragraphs 2.8 to 2.12 for example[80]). The Dalits' situation, inability to move with freedom, and inattention along a common road in India that Azariah and Whitehead relate are completely different from the joyous freedom of travel recorded by Newbigin. In *A South India Diary*, we are told about some of the difficulties of travel that he faces. However, it is mainly in order of rugged terrain and inaccessible regions of his Diocese, given the spread of the jungle, the state of the roads, tracks and paths, or the fact that there is hardly any way to penetrate the interior or coast. In these latter examples, Newbigin presents himself as a pioneer missionary, exploring unknown and uncharted territory, where the people he encounters have such an undeveloped material culture that were an archaeologist in later times to seek material remains, there would not be anything to find. Nevertheless, despite the difficulties of travel and access, Newbigin finds a way to achieve his destination, relying on various forms of transport and the help of companions, guides and locals. It is the privilege of the white European missionary to be able so to wander and explore, to find and be immersed. He is pleased by what he finds, enjoys humane relationships with one and all, sings the Christian 'kummies', and appreciates the nature that

---

79 V. Z. Azariah, and Henry Whitehead, *Christ in the Indian Villages*, 22-23.

80 B. R. Ambedkar, *Annihilation of Caste* (Noida UP: Maple Press, 1936/ 2023).

surrounds him, whether that be a pool of refreshing water where he can bath, or vistas of village or coast seen from an impressive elevation. The caste system in the villages is described as well-functioning, and he expects change to come only slowly. When the changes begin to occur- precipitated by the coming of modernity, communications and Christianity- it is to be expected that caste Hindus will feel their world 'turned upside down'.[81]

Even though he is concerned with the various congregations and their spiritual and physical needs, and he makes sure to remember what resources or expertise might be required to improve their spiritual, economic or physical condition, one often gets the feeling that Newbigin is in the privileged position not to get, as it were, his Bishop's robes splattered with mud or blood or excrement, and whilst he certainly 'rolls up his sleeves' and devotes himself to the task at hand, he is able to leave and move on to other places or return after his tour to his relative haven back in Madurai. Newbigin, in many ways, is a Christian tourist. No such freedom or enjoyment of movement, or sense of new places or the possibilities of change are available to the Dalits that are observed cowering on the road side as the Brahmin walks through, in Azariah and Whitehead's account. Whilst the European visitor to India cannot fail but to notice, especially during the weeks of first encounter, all the variety of modes of movement in India, and the unique forms of transport that they will utilise as they travel to places, enjoying all the strangeness and uniqueness of the ride, it surely does not occur that movement for themselves is not possible. In theory, there is a belief that all places can be reached in one way or another. The Outcaste/Dalit does not share this 'free' experience of movement. The Dalit is no tourist, and as we shall see, neither does the Dalit have the opportunity to be a *Flâneur.*

Mulk Raj Anand's *Untouchable* (1935)

In this section, I consider a (fictional) account of Dalit (untouchable) life that gets closer to the social realities of caste in India. The central character, Bakha, is an untouchable sweeper and toilet cleaner. The narrative is one day in the life of this outcaste. One violent encounter during the day leads him to question his identity, destiny and fate severely. It is on this encounter that I want to concentrate.

Let's begin by walking through the local town with the outcaste, Bakha, the central character in Mulk Raj Anand's 1935 novel *Untouchable*. Bakha is of the sweeper caste, an outcaste, whose main occupation is to keep the latrines clean, with his bare hands and any broom he can make for himself. This is an inherited occupation, passed down through his caste. His father's

81 Lesslie Newbigin, *A South India Diary*,43-50.

duty of cleaning the streets of the local town, and also the Temple precincts, has to be conducted by Anand on this day. On the way from the outcaste colony to the streets, after three rounds of his cleaning of the latrines Bakha revitalises his senses, enjoys the sun on his face and limbs, buys cigarettes, begs a light from a Muslim, and is then consumed by observing all around him in the busy town. Anand describes all the variety of what he sees most colourfully and engagingly. Anand writes:

> 'Passing through the huge brick-built gate of the town into the main street, he was engulfed in asea of colour…and he couldn't help being swept away by the sensations that crowded in on him from every side. He followed the curves of the winding, irregular streets lined on each side with shops, covered with canvas or jute awnings and topped by projecting domed balconies…his first sensation of the bazaar was of its smell, a pleasant aroma oozing from so many unpleasant things, drains, grains, fresh and decaying vegetables, spices, men and women and asafoetida. Then it was the kaleidoscope of colours, the red, the orange, the purple of the fruit in the tiers of basket which were arranged around the Peshawari fruit seller, dressed in a blue silk turban, a scarlet velvet waistcoat, embroidered with gold, a long white tunic and trousers; the gory red of the mutton hanging beside the butcher who was busy mincing meat on a log of wood, while his assistants roasted it on skewers over a charcoal fire, or fried it in the black iron pan: the pale blond colour of the wheat shop; and the rainbow hues of the sweetmeat stall, not to speak of the various shades of turbans and skirts, from the deep black of the widows to the green, pink, the mauve and the fawn of the newly wedded brides, and all the tints of the shifting, changing crowd, from the Brahmins white to the grass cutters coffee and the Pathan's swarthy brown'.[82]

But then comes the dramatic interruption that will be the defining moment of the day and places all Bakha's feelings, past, present and future, in the wake of it. Like the experience of Bakha, the collision with the Brahmin breaks into our reader's world. Anand narrates,

> 'Keep to the side of the road, you low caste vermin!" he suddenly heard someone shouting at him. "Why don't you call, you swine, and announce your approach! Do you know you have touched me and defiled me, you cock-eyed son of a bow-legged scorpion! Now, I will have to go and take a bath to purify myself. And it

82 Mulk Raj Anand, *Untouchable*, 34-35.

> was a new dhoti and shirt I put on this morning.... "You swine, you dog, why didn't you shout and warn me of your approach!".[83]

The encounter has an immense physical and psychological effect on Bakha. It leaves 'a smouldering rage in his soul'.[84] He is slapped in the face, his turban is knocked off, the sweets he purchased are scattered on the dirty ground, surrounded by an accusing crowd, insulted over and over again by the Brahmin; he is utterly humiliated. Anand describes: 'Bakha stood amazed, embarrassed. He was deaf and dumb. His senses were paralysed. Only fear gripped his soul, fear and humility and servility.'[85]

The most significant development is the absolute consciousness of his own status, of his occupation, of his stigma, of his caste brought about by this event. 'I am untouchable, he said to himself, an untouchable...then, aware of his position, he began to shout aloud the warning word with which he used to announce his approach: *Posh, posh*, sweeper coming.'[86]

The Dalit *Flâneur*?

For a short while, especially if the reader is inattentive to all details, the reader becomes distracted, like Bahka, by the attractions of the scene, with all its colour and variety of things and people and activities. The reader admires the descriptions and Anand's manner of capturing the kaleidoscope of life, and they 'draw us in'. For a moment, Bakha is like the *Flâneur*, who practices *flânerie*. The *Flâneur* is the wandering detached character of European cities like Paris and Berlin, where the freedom of the street and its shops is open to the leisured individual (most usually a male), who can stroll through the environment without care. The *Flâneur* has been made famous by modernist poetry and contemporary sociology.[87] With Bakha, we leisurely take in all the sights, sounds, and smells as we walk with him. There is no care but only enjoyment and the consumption of sensation. Once he is shaken out of his reverie by the collision with the Brahmin, we too are taken unawares, but once shaken, we realise that throughout his tour of the town, Bakha has not been unaware of his caste status. For example, his shame means he does not return to the shop where he bought his cigarettes (a brand smoked by the sahib members of the Cantonment) to acquire matches but chooses to ask a Muslim since, not being a Hindu, the Muslim would be more sympathetic to him as an untouchable- such matters matter less to a Muslim than a Hindu. Also, when he buys the cigarettes and later

83 Mulk Raj Anand, *Untouchable*, 37.

84 Mulk Raj Anand, *Untouchable*, 41.

85 Mulk Raj Anand, *Untouchable*, 37.

86 Mulk Raj Anand, *Untouchable*, 42.

87 Keith Tester (ed), *The Flâneur* (London: Routledge, 1994).

the (cheap and rough) sweets he desires, he places his coin on the counter, but this payment will only be taken up by the Hindu shop owner once an assistant has washed them. We notice these things only when the Brahmin interrupts the flow of Anand's description with his cries and insults. Till then, we have been lulled into the comfort of the scene. In short, Bakha is no European *Flâneur*: such an option is unavailable for an Untouchable. Indeed, in Indian society, since all castes are so aware of each other and their status as compared with all others, it would appear that being a *Flâneur*is not available as a social practice in Indian public space. As was the case with the 'missionary tourist', the role of *Flâneur*, is also not available as an option for the Dalit as they move through social physical space. What is more, these experiences of restriction of movement are internalised by the Dalit characters and form part of their wounded psyche.

From the perspective of our concern with mobility and the restrictions on movement, it is striking that when Gandhi and his entourage come to Bakha's town to hold a meeting (arriving by train and then motor car), and everyone is rushing to gain a Darshan of the great man and hear something of his discourse, Anand describes how the crowd moves together, and caste is lost sight of. Just as the apparent message of Gandhi is one of a collective India where the treatment of untouchability is to be improved, the movement of the crowd creates a solidarity of identity between every individual: the focus on Gandhi means that acknowledgement of caste is lost. Anand describes the scene: '…there was everybody going to meet the Mahatma…And like Bakha they hadn't stopped to ask themselves why they were going. They were just going: *walking, running, hurrying*, occupied them. (my italics).[88]

Bakha's occupation is not revealed during this time because he is not carrying the tools of his trade, the symbols of his untouchability, namely, the broom and the basket. All persons present are occupied and moving, and there is no restriction of movement, the only hindrance to freely moving being the sheer number of people sharing a single purpose. However, at the end of the novel, Bakha's consciousness- which has brought home to him with piercing force- remains- that he is a sweeper, that he is Untouchable, and that he is, in the eyes of Hindu caste people, 'Unclean!'

Biblical Resonances of Being 'Unclean'

Bakha is brought to full consciousness, during the day in the life that Anand relates, that he is a sweeper, an untouchable, a Dalit. The Dalits in Aziariah and Whitehead's account are fully attuned to their polluting status and scatter immediately after the on-coming Brahmin is spotted. For Bakha,

88 Mulk Raj Anand, *Untouchable,* 120.

announcing his occupation, even when carrying the symbols of status and caste, is imperative. He, and the other untouchables in our sample, must announce that they are 'Unclean, Unclean'. If the Dalitforgets his status and occupation in public spaces through inattention, the consequences can be fatal.

From an outsider's point of view, a resonance suggests itself between the 'unclean' call of the outcaste on the road and in the urban streets, as narrated by Anand and recorded by the Christian writers Azariah and Whitehead, and the calling out of the leper as a warning to others that they are 'unclean' as found in Leviticus. Interestingly in Anand's novel, Bakha does come across a Leper, and he does not see an affinity between himself and the Leper. 'His attention was diverted to a black leper who sat swathed in tattered garments, exposing his raw wounds to the sun and the flies by the wayside, his crumpled hand lifted in beggary...Bakha had a sudden revulsion of feeling. He looked away from the man'.[89] This should alert us that the Dalit does not make the association. Bakha is repelled and feels revulsion. Rather, it is the treatment of the Leper by others and the demand to call out their stigma to others that creates the affinity. The Leper is individualised and made to live outside the camp in Leviticus. For the Dalits, the stigma applies to all, is inherited and is bequeathed to the next generation, and all are made to live in a colony outside the village. When the number of Lepers with incurable conditions warranted the need in Old Testament times, colonies of Lepers were established.

It is possible to speculate on what type of response such biblical texts would have on the outcaste who has read or heard (from the missionary, the pastor or a fellow literate outcaste). However, it is always a risk without data to speculate on what a text means to a group of people without being able to ask them. The risk of being inaccurate and non-historical is involved when we speculate on what a text might mean to a group of people from particular social contexts with particular social identities. Much less risky is seeking to uncover interpretationsof what the text has meant and may mean from the outcaste users of the biblical text themselves. Such an account might be found in the published work of Dalit biblical scholars, and in the absence of such published work, information could be gathered from fieldwork amongst the communities of bible readers and users to uncover their attitudes to this text in the context of their own lives. The ethnographic turn in biblical studies suggests these ways forward. I can only offer some observations on the role of Leviticus 13.45 in the life of Dalit users of the Bible.

89 Mulk Raj Anand, *Untouchable*, 118.

Leviticus 13:45 reads: 'The person who has the leprous disease shall wear torn clothes and let the hair of his head be dishevelled; and he shall cover his lip and cry out, "Unclean, unclean". He shall remain unclean as long as he has the disease; he is unclean. He shall live alone: his dwelling shall be outside the camp'.

Whereas a skin condition or a disease in Hebrew society rendered the person 'untouchable' and they were required to announce their presence and condition in wider society, and otherwise to 'live outside the camp'- their social status was affected only for the duration that they carried the stigma of the disease. In the case of the Dalits, caste determined their social status, and their stigma was a permanent one. The 'disease' of being oppressed could not be cleansed. There was no way to lose caste. They were treated as if they were diseased, like the incurable leper. Outcaste communities are found on the edges of the towns and villages where they reside. The colonies of the outcastes resemble the leper colony in this symbolic fashion. Contact with the unclean Dalit would mean the caste Hindu would have to undergo a series of ritual purifications to restore their cleanliness.

A Dalit response to the Leviticus texts could be to despair: that the way they have been treated in Indian society could be destined to be no different in any Christian setting that revered these texts; another possibility is to appreciate that there have been other communities and individuals, even in ancient Israel, who have experienced the stigma and humiliation of being 'unclean' (sociologically perhaps Dalit sensibility could be generalised to reconstruct the 'life of the leper in biblical times'); alternatively, some hope might be found in the fact that the chance of recovery and being restored is suggested (though the administrations and power of the priests would strike a sour note no doubt); a further response would be to appreciate that Jesus in the Gospels not only heals the Lepers but is friend to all outcastes. Finally, and this is probably a response that would be the most resonant in contemporary India and Dalit poetics and politics, namely, to refuse to accept the label and condition of being 'unclean' and being similar to a Leper in other settings. The Dalit would assert their humanity and resist their caste name, status and destiny.

Conclusion

To travel with Dalits, at least with those who have communicated their life stories through the prose and autobiographical accounts which have been published, is to travel through all the mire, gore, blood, excrement and dirt, to be insulted and constantly hear foul language. To travel through an unsanitary, non-salubrious, threatening environment and to listen to their everlasting pain and trauma, humiliation and ever-present fear. Dalit literature challenges the classical canons and their 'universal' rules of grammar and politeness, borne more of Brahmin and bourgeois respectability and (European?) Christian moral standards more than anything else. An authentic Dalit hermeneutic, it would seem, for biblical studies, in the light of this Dalit poetic, would be one where not only the quotidian but also the abject are brought to the fore. Can the Bible be read this way, the Dalit speak, and the voice be heard? Or will their journey through the text be restricted in movement and not be mobile?

13

"Her Judges are Evening Wolves" (Zeph. 3:3) A Critical Study of Israelite Judiciary in 8th and 7th cent B.C.E and India Today

P. Joseph Titus

It is with great pleasure that I contribute this essay to the *Festschrift* honoring Professor Rev. Dr. K. Jesurathnam. I am deeply indebted to him for providing me with the opportunity to teach at the *United Theological College* and become a member of the *Society for Biblical Studies in India* (*SBSI*). His guidance also introduced me to the world of ecumenism. This essay is a small token of my gratitude for his influence.

Introduction

The foundation of any society is the integrity of its judicial system. When the courts become so degraded that injustice, rather than justice, is meted out, society is on the brink of total decline. This article intends to examine the judicial system in ancient Israel of the 8th and 7th century B.C.E. and India today.

The term *šôpēṭ* derives from the Hebrew verb *šāpaṭ*, which encompasses various meanings such as 'decide,' 'judge,' 'rule,' 'govern,' 'vindicate,' and 'deliver.' This term can refer to both God and human judges.[90] In ancient Israel, God was considered the ultimate judge, not only of God's people but

90 Temba L. J. Mafico, "Judge, Judging," in *The Anchor Yale Bible Dictionary.* vol. 3, ed. David Noel Freedman (New York: Doubleday, 1996, c1992), 1104-1105.

of the entire world. God was the sole authority capable of restoring justice, harmony, and wholeness to society and the land. Human judges were appointed to act as God's representatives, judging "not on behalf of human beings but on the Lord's behalf; he is with you in giving judgment" (2 Chr 19:6). Within God's justice system, judges were granted authority to carry out His will and execute His divine justice.

The primary responsibility of ancient Israelite judges was to maintain harmonious relationships within the community. They adjudicated civil disputes (Judg 4:5; 1 Sam 7:15; cf. 2 Sam 15:4) and often focused on cases involving the welfare of the poor, widows, orphans, and foreigners (Ps 82; Jer 5:28-29; 22:15; Deut 1:16-17). While judges aimed to deliver just verdicts, their role sometimes extended beyond mere legal decisions. They frequently acted as mediators, working to restore *šālôm* (peace) and harmony within communities (Gen 16:5; 19:9; Judg 11:27). If individuals felt wronged by human judges, they could turn to Yahweh, the ultimate Judge, for intervention (Ps 6:7-9; 82:8). Yahweh's reputation for righteousness ensured that innocent individuals could appeal directly to Him for justice (Ps 26:1; cf. Judg 11:27).[91]

This essay is divided into four sections. The first section provides a brief overview of the judicial system in ancient Israel, tracing its development from the time of Moses. The second section examines the critiques of corrupt judges offered by 8th-century prophets Amos, Isaiah, and Micah. The third section analyzes Zephaniah's portrayal of corrupt judges as "evening wolves" in his prophetic writings. The fourth section explores the current state of the judicial system in India, highlighting challenges and potential areas for improvement. The essay will conclude by outlining the moral standards that should guide the judiciary.

Judicial System in Ancient Israel as Described in the Bible

In ancient Israel, if personal attempts at reconciliation failed, individuals could seek legal recourse through the court system. The biblical record reveals a diverse range of individuals qualified to serve as judges, from single judges to panels of varying sizes.[92]

1. Initially, Moses oversaw all legal matters. However, upon the advice of his father-in-law Jethro, he established in Exod. 18:13-22 a system of lower-level judges to handle less complex cases. Moses reserved judgment on more significant matters, such as

91 Mafico, "Judge, Judging," 1105.

92 Tikva Frymer-Kenski, "Anatolia and the Levant: Israel," in *A History of Ancient Near Eastern Law*, ed. Raymond Westbrook (Leiden: Brill, 2003), 2:992.

cases involving blasphemy (Lev 24:10-23),[93] the gathering of wood on the Sabbath (Num 15:32-36),[94] and the inheritance rights of the daughters of Zelophehad[95] (Num 27:1-11).[96]

2. Beyond the formal judicial system, local elders also played a crucial role in resolving disputes. Their authority can be traced back to Num 11:16-17, where the Lord instructs Moses to appoint seventy elders to assist him in governing the people.[97]
3. Extending this administrative system, the book of Deuteronomy begins by appointing tribal leaders to serve as judges in cases involving private disputes: "So I took the leaders of your tribes, wise and reputable individuals, and installed them as leaders over you, commanders of thousands, commanders of hundreds, commanders of fifties, commanders of tens, and officials, throughout your tribes. I charged your judges at that time: "Give the members of your community a fair hearing, and judge rightly between one person and another, whether citizen or resident alien" (Deut. 1:15-16 NRS). The exact relationship between the judicial systems described in Exod 18,[98] Num 11, and Deut 1 has been

93 Jacob Weingreen, "The Case of the Blasphemer, Leviticus XXIV 10 ff.," *VT* 22/1 (1972): 118- 23; Rodney R. Hutton, "Narrative in Leviticus: The Case of the Blaspheming Son (Lev 24, 10-23)," *ZABR* 3 (1997): 145-63; Rodney R. Hutton, "The Case of the Blasphemer Revisited, Lev. XXIV 10-23," *VT* 49/4 (1999): 532-41; Jacob Milgrom, *Leviticus 23-27: A New Translation with Introduction and Commentary* (New York: Doubleday, 2001), 2101-45.

94 Jacob Weingreen, "The Case of the Woodgatherer (Numbers XV 32-36)," *VT* 16/3 (1966): 361-64; Gnana Robinson, "The Prohibition of Strange Fire in Ancient Israel: A New Look at the Case of Gathering Wood and Kindling Fire on the Sabbath," *VT* 28/3 (1978): 301-17.

95 Jacob Weingreen, "The Case of the Daughters of Zelophehad," *VT* 16/4 (1966): 518-22; Josiah Derby, "The Daughters of Zelophehad Revisited," *JBQ* 25/3 (1997): 169-71.

96 John W. Welch, "Judicial Procedure in Biblical Times," in *The Legal Cases in the Book of Mormon* (Provo, UT; BYU Press/Neal A. Maxwell Institute for Religious Scholarship, 2008), 77-103, 83-84.

97 John W. Welch, "Judicial Procedure in Biblical Times," 83-84.

98 Even before Israel receives laws at Sinai, Exodus 18:13-22 tells how Jethro the Midianite advises Moses to establish judges, a unique origin story for the judicial system with no parallel in ancient Near Eastern law collections. Taking Jethro's advice to heart, Moses immediately implements his ideas for delegating judicial authority to dispense justice more efficiently (vv 24–26). Notably, the story of the establishment of the judicial system comes before the account of God's revelation of law to Israel at Sinai in chapters 19–24. This narrative sequence created implications for later readers of the text, already within ancient Israel. This presentation of the judicial administration in Exodus 18, before the revelation of the law in Mt Sinai, could be seen as downplaying the importance of divine revelation in Mt Sinai. This is problematic because it suggests that Israel's judicial system is foreign

a subject of scholarly debate for centuries, leading to various interpretations and configurations based on these precedents.[99] Cases involving public concerns, such as whether a manslayer who had sought refuge at the altar in one of the cities of refuge should be granted asylum, were heard by a local assembly composed, apparently, of groups of city elders in each city of refuge (Num 35:24).[100]

4. On other occasions, perhaps primarily in cases concerning family and property affairs, a group of ten town elders could be convened rather spontaneously at the town gate to witness and resolve

---

(Midianite) in origin and was established before the Sinaitic revelation, implying that the divine revelation is incomplete and reliant on external sources. Therefore, Deuteronomy revises the story to credit Moses with this idea after the revelation at Horeb. Deuteronomy 1:9-15 corrects the issues raised in Exodus 18 regarding the origin of the judicial system. Deuteronomy rearranges the sequence of events to prioritize the revelation of the law over the creation of the judicial system. It also omits the Midianite inspiration for the judicial system, attributing it solely to Moses. These revisions aim to emphasize the importance of divine revelation and the Israelite origins of the judicial system. See Marc Z. Brettler, *The Creation of History in Ancient Israel* (London: Routledge, 1995), 65–70; and Bernard M. Levinson, "Textual Reformulation and Resequencing by the Deuteronomistic Historian," *The Hermeneutics of Innovation: The Impact of Centralization upon the Structure, Sequence, and Reformulation of Legal Material in Deuteronomy* (Ann Arbor: UMI, 1991), 424–32. There is an immense amount of recent work on and debate about the formation of the Pentateuch and the sequence and relation of its sources to one another. Among the questions is, of course, the relative role of Numbers 11 in the evolution of the narrative discussed here. It goes beyond the scope of this article to do full justice to that debate. For a recent study with an excellent summary of the issues and full bibliography, see Jeffrey Stackert, *A Prophet like Moses: Prophecy, Law, and Israelite Religion* (New York: Oxford University Press, 2014), 137–65. The two passages differ only in the presence of the conjunction ו "and" before each element in the list in Deut 1:15; Exod 18:21 includes only one such conjunctive *waw*, before the final element in the list. These variations tell us little about the relationship between the two texts, however. Both types of lists, with a *waw* before each element and with a *waw* only before the last element, are attested in Biblical Hebrew. Moreover, the texts and versions of Exod 18:21 are themselves not consistent, meaning we cannot be certain that the version of Exod 18 to which the authors of Deuteronomy 1 respond lacked the conjunctions. The use of conjunctions in the Septuagint, Peshitta, Vulgate, Targum, Samaritan Pentateuch, and various other Hebrew manuscripts, including one from Qumran, all differ in one way or another from the biblical Masoretic text of Exod 18:21. See William H. C. Propp, *Exodus 1–18*, AB 2 (New York: Doubleday, 1999), 626. Editor's note: For another approach to this problem, see David Frankel, "Deuteronomy's Jewish Democratic and Egalitarian Agenda," *The Torah* (2014).

99 Hanoch Reviv, "The Traditions Concerning the Inception of the Legal System in Israel: Significance and Dating," *ZAW* 94/4 (1982): 566-75.

100 Welch, "Judicial Procedure in Biblical Times," 83-84.

legal matters (Ruth 4:2).[101] In some cases, local courts may have consisted of a single judge (Numbers 25:5; Deut 25:1-3), perhaps assisted by some of the elders; in other cases, they ("the priests and the judges") sat as a body (Deut 19:17), all together.[102]

5. In Israel, as elsewhere, ad hoc courts of various configurations were often the norm locally. Westbrook describes these local courts as "ad hoc assemblies" and notes that the term "judges" appears to refer to individuals distinct from official or council-based courts. He further states that it remains unclear whether the term designated a profession or merely a function and that these judges were not trained jurists in the modern sense.[103] Despite their informal nature, these judicial bodies wielded significant power and influence. [104]

---

101 Thomas Thompson and Dorothy Thompson, "Some Legal Problems in the Book of Ruth," *VT* 18/ 1 (1968): 79-99; Derek R. G. Beattie, "The Book of Ruth as Evidence for Israelite Legal Practice," *VT* 24/3 (1974): 251-67; Robert Gordis, "Love, Marriage, and Business in the Book of Ruth: A Chapter in Hebrew Customary Law'" in *A Light unto My Path: Old Testament Studies in Honor of Jacob M. Myers*, eds. Howard N. Bream, Ralph D. Heim and Carey A. Moore (Philadelphia: Temple University Press, 1974), 241-64; Baruch A. Levine, "In Praise of the Israelite Mispaha: Legal Themes in the Book of Ruth," in *The Quest for the Kingdom of God: Studies in Honor of George E. Mendenhall*, eds. H.B. Huffmon, F.A. Spina, A.R.W. Green (Winona Lake, IN: Eisenbrauns, 1983), 95-106.

102 Ze'ev W. Falk, *Hebrew Law in Biblical Times: An Introduction,* ed. John W. Welch, 2nd ed. (Provo, UT: Brigham Young University Press; Winona Lake, IN: Eisenbrauns, 2001), 49. See also Joachim Oelsner, Bruce Wells, and Cornelia Wunsch, "Mesopotamia: Neo-Babylonian Period," in Westbrook, *History of Ancient Near Eastern Law*, 2:919.

103 Raymond Westbrook, "Introduction: The Character of Ancient Near Eastern Law," in *History of Ancient Near Eastern Law,* ed. Westbrook, 1:30

104 Welch, "Judicial Procedure in Biblical Times," 85.

6. While kings often served as judges in Mesopotamia and Egypt,[105] this role appears to have been less common in Israel.[106] Kings naturally handled cases involving threats to their power, as exemplified by King Saul's treatment of Ahimelech, who was accused of conspiring against him (1 Sam 22:16). However, as illustrated by the cases of the Tekoite woman (2 Sam 14:4-11), and the two harlots before King Solomon (1 Kings 3:16-28), even the most vulnerable members of Israelite society could seek legal protection from the king. These vignettes, while potentially literary embellishments, demonstrate the king's role as a guarantor of justice.[107]
7. During the monarchy, kings held the authority to appoint both military and judicial officials. This suggests that the judges (šôpĕtîm) and officials (šôṭĕrîm)[108] mentioned in Deut 16:18-20 and 25:2 were likely royal appointees. King Jehoshaphat's

---

105 "The king was everywhere the supreme judge, although his judicial activity is more in evidence in some periods than in others. There was no formal machinery of appeal from a lower court; rather, a subject would petition the king to redress an injustice suffered by a lower court or official. The king could also try cases at first instance. Various law-code provisions suggest that certain serious crimes involving the death penalty were reserved for the king, but he is also found judging apparently trivial matters. Westbrook, "Introduction," *History of Ancient Near Eastern Law,* 1:30. In Mesopotamia, in the Old Babylonian period, "the king might deal with a case brought before him in one of three ways. He either tried the case himself and gave final judgment, decided a point of law and remitted the case to a local court for a decision on the facts, or remitted the entire case to a local court." Westbrook, "Mesopotamia: Old Babylonian Period," in *History of Ancient Near Eastern Law*, 1:367. In Egypt, "the pharaoh himself ... constituted the highest court," Ignacio Marquez Rowe, "Anatolia and the Levant: Canaan," in *History of Ancient Near Eastern Law,* ed. Westbrook, 1:739.

106 Margaret Elizabeth Bellefontaine, "Customary Law and Chieftainship: Judicial Aspects of 2 Samuel 14:4-21," *JSOT* 38 (1987): 47- 72; and Theodore J. Hoftijzer, "David and the Tekoite Woman," *VT* 20/4 (1970): 419-44.

107 Welch, "Judicial Procedure in Biblical Times," 86.

108 Though technically the term *šôṭĕrîm* derives from a root meaning "to write" or "to arrange," it is used commonly in the Old Testament to pertain to persons who decide legal cases and administer justice. F.C. Fensham, "The Judges and Ancient Israelite Jurisprudence," *OTWSAP* (1959): 15–22; J. Milgrom, "The Ideological and Historical Importance of the Office of Judge in Deuteronomy," in *Isaac Leo Seeligmann Volume: Essays on the Bible and the Ancient World*, eds. Alexander Rofe, Yair Zakovitch (Jerusalem: E. Reubinstein's Publishing House, 1983), 129–39; A. van Selms, "The Title 'Judge,'" *OTWSA* 2 (1950): 41–50. That was clearly the case here; in fact, even the "officials" mentioned may have been judges, taking the construction as a hendiadys to be construed as "judging officials" or the like. This finds support in the fact that the only function described here is judging (vv 18–20). Eugene H. Merrill, *Deuteronomy*, NAC, vol. 4 (Nashville: Broadman & Holman Publishers, 2001, c1994), 257-58.

appointment of subordinate judges (šôpĕtîm) to travel and adjudicate cases throughout the kingdom of Judah further supports this notion (2 Chr 19:5–11).

8. In Israel, priests played significant roles in the judicial system (Deut 17:9; 19:17; 33:10), particularly in cases involving oaths, ordeals, and purification rituals. For example, a husband who suspected his wife of adultery could bring her before a priest for a trial by ordeal, where her oath and consumption of bitter waters could determine her innocence (Num 5:15). Additionally, if a slain person was found outside a village without witnesses, the Levitical priests would resolve the matter by requiring all the men in the village to swear an oath of ignorance and innocence (Deut 21:5).[109]
9. While the judicial system evolved over time, the people remained a constant force (Jer 26:16). As Jacob Milgrom observed, "One factor remains unchanged. As the trials of Naboth and Jeremiah clearly demonstrate, the people, *'am*, persists as an integral element of the judiciary."[110]

Prophetic Critique of Judges in Israel

The prophetic criticism of judges in Israel during the 8th and 7th cent B.C.E. was a significant aspect of the religious and social discourse of the time. Prophets like Amos, Isaiah, Micah and Zephaniah denounced the moral and political corruption of the judges, accusing them of injustice, oppression, and idolatry. They delivered severe indictments addressed to "judges" in the plural.[111] The following prophetic criticisms over judges give us an idea about the moral degradation of the 8th and 7th cent B.C.E. judges in Israel:

i. "They sell the righteous for silver and the needy for a pair of sandals, they who trample the head of the poor into the dust of the earth and push the afflicted out of the way" (Amos 2:6-7).
ii. "You who afflict the righteous, who take a bribe, and push aside the needy in the gate" (Amos 5:10-12).

109 Welch, "Judicial Procedure in Biblical Times," 86-87.

110 Milgrom, "The Ideological and Historical Importance of the Office of Judge in Deuteronomy," 139. See Zeen Weisman, "The Place of the People in the Making of Law and Judgment," in *Pomegranates and Golden Bells* (Studies in Biblical, Jewish, and Near Eastern Ritual, Law and Literature in Honor of Jacob Milgrom), eds. David P. Wright, David Noel Freedman, Avi Hurvitz (Winona Lake, IN: Eisenbrauns, 1995), 407-20.

111 Delbert R. Hillers et al., *Micah: A Commentary on the Book of the Prophet Micah* (Philadelphia: Fortress Press, 1984), 42.

iii. "Ah, you who are heroes in drinking wine and valiant at mixing drink, who acquit the guilty for a bribe, and deprive the innocent of their rights!" (Isa 5:22-23).

iv. "Ah, you who make iniquitous decrees, who write oppressive statutes, to turn aside the needy from justice and to rob the poor of my people of their right, that widows may be your spoil, and that you may make the orphans your prey!" (Isa 10:1-2).

v. "Those who cause a person to lose a lawsuit, who set a trap for the arbiter in the gate, and without grounds deny justice to the one in the right" (Isa 29:21).

vi. "Listen, you heads (*rosh*) of Jacob and rulers (*qatzin*) of the house of Israel! Should you not know justice? [2] you who hate the good and love the evil, who tear the skin off my people, and the flesh off their bones; [3] who eat the flesh of my people, flay their skin off them, break their bones in pieces, and chop them up like meat in a kettle, like flesh in a caldron" (Mic 3:1-3).

vii. "Its heads (*rosh*) judge (*shapad*) for a bribe (*shohad*)" (Mic 3:11).

viii. "Their hands are skilled to do evil; the official (*haśśar*) and the judge (*haššōpēṭ*) ask for a bribe (*shillum*), and the great one (*haggādôl*) speaks (*dober*) the desire (*hawwat*) of his soul; thus they weave it together" (Mic 7:3).

The above prophetic texts, primarily from the prophets Amos, Isaiah, and Micah are primarily focused on how the judges along with the leaders of Israel perpetrated evils of corruption and injustice. The texts consistently depict those judges as using their power to exploit and oppress the vulnerable. They are accused of taking bribes, denying justice, and enacting unjust laws. Bribery is a recurring motif, with officials and judges often portrayed as accepting bribes to favour the wealthy and powerful over the poor and marginalized. The texts emphasize the suffering and injustice experienced by the poor and oppressed at the hands of the judges. They are depicted as being denied their rights, exploited, and even physically harmed. The prophets criticize in these texts the moral decline of the judges, accusing them of greed, cruelty, and a disregard for justice.

Zephaniah's Critique of Judges

Literary and Historical Contexts

Zephaniah's three chapters represent the collected oracles or divinely inspired sermons of the late seventh century B.C.E. prophet Zephaniah ben Cushi. Zephaniah's ministry, therefore, is best situated in the city of Jerusalem at the outset of Josiah's Deuteronomic reform movement, approximately between 630 and 620 B.C.E., contemporary with the prophet Nahum's oracles celebrating the fall of Nineveh in 612 B.C.E. (Zeph 2:13-15). For three-quarters of the seventh century B.C.E., the nation of Judah was in a state of profound religious and political decline.[112] The book informs us that Zephaniah received his prophetic call during the reign of King Josiah (640–609 B.C.E.). Given the vivid descriptions of the sins being condemned and the unwavering earnestness of Zephaniah's proclamation of the devastating day of the Lord, it is likely that he delivered his message during the gloomy period before Josiah's reform became apparent.[113] Since the book primarily addresses the sins of the people of Judah, most commentators place its date before the religious reform of 621 B.C.E.[114]

The Book of Zephaniah describes God's concern for righteous living among the nations and the people of Judah. Zephaniah's internal structure has traditionally been viewed as tripartite. The first chapter, and often the first three verses of the second, is considered to announce and describe judgment against the nations and the nation of Judah on "the day of the Lord" (1:7). Subsequently, the second chapter or 2:4–15 declares judgment against specific nations, including Philistia (vv 4–7), Moab and Ammon (vv 8–11), Cush (v 12), and Assyria (vv 13–15). Finally, the third chapter proclaims that out of judgment will emerge blessing and joy for a righteous remnant. The first eight verses of chapter 3 are sometimes considered part of the second division since they address judgment, specifically against Jerusalem, "the city of oppressors" (3:1).[115]

Perhaps no city on Earth is more beloved than Jerusalem. The psalmist aptly wrote, "Beautiful for situation, the joy of the whole earth, is Mount Zion … the city of the great King" (Ps 48:2). God declared, "This is Jerusalem; I have set her in the midst of the nations and countries that are round about her" (Ezek 5:5). Jerusalem is the city of God, the capital of Judah, the sanctuary of spiritual life, and the joy of the whole earth to the Jew. Never could Jerusalem's princes or people imagine its destruction, especially at the hands of her heathen neighbours. Here alone God placed His name and revealed His Law to the world. Here alone was God truly worshipped. And here alone stood the great Temple of Solomon, wherein dwelt God's shekinah glory. Yet, the stench of Jerusalem's moral depravity had reached the nostrils of the holy God. He could no longer tolerate the defamation of

---

112 For a current historical review see W. C. Kaiser, Jr., *A History of Israel* (Nashville: Broadman & Holman, 1998), 371–85. Kenneth L. Barker, *Micah, Nahum, Habakkuk, Zephaniah*, NAC, vol. 20 (Nashville: Broadman & Holman Publishers, 2001, c1999), 380.

113 Robert A. Bennett, "The Book of Zephaniah," *NIB*. Barker, *Micah, Nahum, Habakkuk, Zephaniah*, 379.

114 Barker, *Micah, Nahum, Habakkuk, Zephaniah*, 396.

115 Barker, *Micah, Nahum, Habakkuk, Zephaniah*, 386-387.

His holy name, the pollution of His sanctuary, and the oppression of the righteous. In vivid language, Zephaniah detailed Jerusalem's corruption and her impending judgment.

Zephaniah's prophecy against Judah and Jerusalem stands out for its stark depiction of impending divine judgment. The "Day of the Lord," a time of cataclysmic reckoning, is portrayed as a period of darkness, anguish, and utter devastation. Cities will be plundered, lives will be lost, and the very fabric of society will be torn asunder. At the heart of Zephaniah's condemnation lies Judah's transgression of worshipping foreign deities and the corrupt, oppressive leadership that has plagued the nation (3:1–4).[116] The prophet particularly lambastes the judges, labelling them "evening wolves" in Zeph 3:3 for their predatory and unjust behaviour.

4.2 Analysis of the Text

Her ***heads*** (*sarim*) in her midst *are* roaring lions, Her ***judges*** (*šôpĕtîm*) *are* evening wolves, they have not gnawn the bone in the morning. (Zeph 3:3)

1. Having issued a broad condemnation of the entire chosen city in Zephaniah 3:1-2, the prophet now turns in vv 3-4 his attention to the specific elements of leadership that have contributed to this moral decline. "Officials" or "princes" (שָׂרִים), "judges" (שֹׁפְטִים), "prophets" (נְבִיאִים), and "priests" (כֹּהֲנִים) are all implicated in the nation's corruption.[117] Zephaniah singles out officials and judges, perhaps due to the public's misplaced trust in these figures. Despite their positions of authority, these leaders have actively participated in the nation's rebellion against God. Instead of providing righteous guidance, they have become predatory and exploitative, resembling roaring lions and evening wolves that devour their flock. Their behaviour stands in stark contrast to the role of true shepherds, who are called to lead and nurture their people (see also Ezekiel 22:25; 22:27; Micah 3:1–3).
2. The "officials" (שָׂרִים) and "judges" (שֹׁפְטִים) mentioned in verse 3 are metaphorically portrayed as "roaring lions" and "evening wolves" to highlight their predatory nature and abuse of power.[118] This comparison to ferocious wild animals underscores their role as oppressors who prey

116 https://bible.usccb.org/bible/zephaniah/0 as accessed on 31 August 2024 at 14 pm.

117 O. Palmer Robertson, *The Books of Nahum, Habakkuk and Zephaniah*, NICOT (Grand Rapids, MI: Wm. B. Eerdmans Publishing Co., 1990), 319.

118 Marvin A. Sweeney and Paul D. Hanson, *Zephaniah: A Commentary,* Hermeneia (Minneapolis, Minn.: Fortress Press, 2003), 162.

on the vulnerable.[119] The phrase "evening wolves"[120] is also found in Hab 1:8 and Jer 5:6, further emphasizing the predatory nature of these corrupt leaders. This imagery echoes the description of Benjamin in Gens 49:27 as a "wolf" that devours prey. While Gen 49 criticizes the tribal leaders of the past, Zephaniah's use of similar imagery highlights the continuing pattern of corrupt leadership in his time.[121]

3. The "lions" (officials) and "wolves of the evening" (judges) represent different methods of predation. While the lions openly prey on the people, the wolves operate in the shadows, taking bribes under the cover of darkness at night. The mention of "morning" reinforces the idea of "evening" in the phrase "wolves of the evening." The Hebrew verb "*garam*" is typically understood to mean "gnaw a bone" (cf. Num 24:8; Ezek 23:34). In the context of Zephaniah's prophecy, this suggests that the judges are so voracious that they consume everything, leaving nothing behind by morning. This makes them even more predatory than wolves, who typically do not eat the bones of their prey.[122]

---

119 Adele Berlin, *Zephaniah: A New Translation with Introduction and Commentary* (New Haven; London: Yale University Press, 2008), 128.

120 A number of scholars have noted the parallel between Zeph 3:3–4 and Ezek 22:23–31, in which Ezekiel condemns the prophets, priests, and officials of Judah in language very much like that of Zeph 3:3–4; that is, Ezekiel compares the prophets to roaring lions who devour prey, states that the priests have done violence to Yahweh's Torah and profaned holiness, and compares the officials to wolves who also devour prey, shed blood, and take bribes. Because Ezekiel does not mention the judges that appear in Zeph 3:3–4, some have supposed that Ezekiel and Zephaniah are dependent on a third source that each reworked differently. It should be noted, however, that Ezekiel portrays the crimes of the officials as those of corrupt judges. Furthermore, the book of Ezekiel never refers to judges. In that the Mosaic tradition in Exod 18:21–23 makes very clear that judges are to be chosen from among the officials of the people, it would appear that Ezekiel 22 presupposes both Zeph 3:3–4 and Exod 18:21–23, especially since Ezekiel is well known as an erudite individual who constantly cites earlier texts and traditions from both the Bible and the general ancient West Asian world. Reference to judges in the context of Ezekiel 22 would be unnecessary, as they are already addressed by reference to the officials. E.g., Michael Fishbane, *Biblical Interpretation in Ancient Israel* (Oxford: Clarendon Press, 1985), 461–63; Walther Zimmerli, *Ezekiel 1: A Commentary on the Book of the Prophet Ezekiel, Chapters 1-24* (Philadelphia: Fortress Press, 1979), 465–70; D.H. Müller, "Der Prophet Ezechiel entlehnt eine Stelle des Propheten Zephanja und glossiert sie," *WZKM* 19 (1905): 263–70. Ehud Ben Zvi, *A Historical-Critical of the Book of Zephaniah* (Berlin, New York: de Gruyter, 1991), 204–5. Marvin A. Sweeney and Paul D. Hanson, *Zephaniah: A Commentary,* Hermeneia (Minneapolis, Minn.: Fortress Press, 2003), 162.

121 Berlin, *Zephaniah: A New Translation,* 128.

122 Berlin, *Zephaniah: A New Translation*, 128.

4. The nation's true representatives, those entrusted with upholding the law, have become predatory beasts. The judges, who should be impartial arbiters of justice, instead act like night-prowling wolves. Driven by insatiable greed, they pounce on their helpless victims under the cover of darkness. Their voracious appetites for the innocent leave nothing to be scavenged in the morning.[123] Zephaniah compares these judges to wolves hunting at dusk, a time when they would be particularly hungry.[124] Like these ravenous predators, the judges are consumed by greed, "picking the people clean" through their corrupt practices.[125] The city of Nineveh, once occupied by humans, has become a desolate wasteland inhabited by beasts (2:14a). Similarly, Jerusalem has fallen under the dominion of these predatory leaders, who have betrayed their people's trust and have become "*mis*leaders."[126]
5. The portrayal of government officials (*sarim*) and judges (*shophetim*) as animals vividly illustrates their cruelty, greed, and insatiable appetite for power and wealth. This passage depicts a climate of constant fear and terror that gripped the people like a deadly poison. The top officials and judges, whose duty was to protect and care for the lower classes, instead used terror as a tool of oppression. They wrongfully confiscated the property of others and instilled fear in those under their care. Power had corrupted them, eroding any sense of self-control. A relentless pursuit of profit and personal gain defined their lifestyle. The people viewed their governors as roaring lions, inciting terror and fear. The judges were likened to desert wolves, swift and voracious in their pursuit of prey. Such imagery is prevalent in the prophetic literature, highlighting the

---

123 The term *gāram* probably means "to gnaw or to crush bones" (cf. *gerem*, "bone"). This meaning is supported by Num. 24:8, where the phrase "he shall devour the nations his enemies" *(yō'ḵal gôyim ṣārāyw)* is paralleled by "their bones are crushed" *(aṣmōṯêhem yəḡārēm)*. The idea of "not gnawing in the morning" suggests that these ravenous wolves, prowling in the night, leave no morsel for the morning. Robertson, *The Books of Nahum, Habakkuk and Zephaniah,* 320.

124 D.J. Clark and H.A. Hatton, *A Handbook on the Books of Nahum, Habakkuk, and Zephaniah* (New York: United Bible Societies, 1989), 186.

125 Watts believes the Hb. means "since morning" and so can say: "These wolves have nocturnal hunting habits and begin their hunt in the evening when they are ravenous from an entire day without food" (*Joel, Obadiah, Jonah, Nahum, Habakkuk and Zephaniah,* 175). See Gen 49:27.

126 John Alec Motyer, "Zephaniah," in *The Minor Prophets: A Commentary on Zephaniah, Haggai, Zechariah, Malachi*, ed. T.M. McComiskey, vol.3 (Grand Rapids, MI.: Baker Academic, 2018), 943. Barker, *Micah, Nahum, Habakkuk, Zephaniah*, 477.

corrupt and oppressive nature of many leaders (Mic 3:1ff., 7:4; Jer 2:8, 5:31, 21:21-23; Ezek 22:23-31).[127]

> And I said: Listen, you, heads of Jacob and rulers of the house of Israel! Should you not know justice? you who hate the good and love the evil, who tear the skin off my people, and the flesh off their bones; [3] who eat the flesh of my people, flay their skin off them, break their bones in pieces, and chop them up like meat in a kettle, like flesh in a caldron (Mic 3:1-3 NRS).

> [25] Its princes within it are like a roaring lion tearing the prey; they have devoured human lives; they have taken treasure and precious things; they have made many widows within it. [26] Its priests have done violence to my teaching and have profaned my holy things; they have made no distinction between the holy and the common, neither have they taught the difference between the unclean and the clean, and they have disregarded my sabbaths, so that I am profaned among them.[27] Its officials within it are like wolves tearing the prey, shedding blood, and destroying lives to get dishonest gain.[28] Its prophets have smeared whitewash on their behalf, seeing false visions and divining lies for them, saying, 'Thus says the Lord God,' when the Lord has not spoken.[29] The people of the land have practised extortion and committed robbery; they have oppressed the poor and needy, and have extorted from the alien without redress (Ezek 22:25-29 NRS).

6. Zephaniah describes Judah's judges as "evening wolves" (verse 3). These magistrates entrusted with protecting the poor and innocent, instead aided and abetted injustice through political oppression (compare Amos 2:6-8; Hab 1:8). Wolves are cunning, ferocious, and merciless predators, always on the hunt for new victims. Like evening wolves that silently approach their prey under the cover of darkness, these judges, under the guise of law and justice, rapaciously devoured the wealth and property of those who came before them. Their greed is insatiable, akin to wolves that scour vast areas in search of food, risking their own lives to satisfy their hunger. The prophet states, "They gnaw not the bones till the morrow" (verse 3), implying that they consumed their prey entirely, leaving nothing behind. Like lawless wolves, these leaders manipulated

127 Mária Eszenyei Széles, *Wrath and Mercy: A Commentary on the Books of Habakkuk and Zephaniah,* ITC (Grand Rapids; Edinburgh: Eerdmans; Handsel Press, 1987), 102.

the law to their own advantage, accumulating wealth through corruption and oppression.[128]

Judiciary in India Today

The Indian judiciary, often lauded as the guardian of the Constitution and a beacon of justice, is not immune to the scourge of corruption. Allegations of corruption and nepotism have tarnished the judiciary's reputation, raising concerns about its credibility and integrity. This is particularly troubling given the judiciary's role as the last line of defence for ordinary citizens seeking justice.

Justice Venkataramiah, the 19th Chief Justice of India, who held office from June 19, 1989, to December 17, 1989, expressed deep concern about the decline in judicial standards. In an interview with the journalist Kuldip Nayar, he claimed on the eve of his retirement that many judges were susceptible to influence through lavish parties and gifts: "The judiciary in India has deteriorated in its standards because such judges are appointed as are willing to be 'influenced by lavish parties and whisky bottles'." The complainant, Vishwanath Palshikar, alleged that the judge had scandalized the court with this statement: "In every high court, there were at least four to five judges who were practically out every evening, wining and dining either at a lawyer's house or a foreign embassy and that the estimate of the number of such judges was around 90 and that practically in all the 22 high courts in the country, close relations of the judges were thriving."[129]

Former Chief Justice of India Venkataramiah revealed that in nearly all (then) 22 of India's high courts at the time, judges' relatives were thriving in legal careers. He alleged that these connections could influence certain judgments, even when the relatives were not directly involved in the cases. Venkataramiah claimed: "It is hard to disregard the reports that every brother, son or son-in-law of a judge, whatever his merit or lack of it as a lawyer, can be sure of earning an income of more than Rs 10,000 a month." In a 2001 speech, Chief Justice S.P. Bharucha lamented that 20% of Indian judges were corrupt. Justice Saldanha of the Karnataka High Court echoed this concern, estimating that 33% of the judiciary was compromised by corruption. Justice Krishna Iyer, in an open letter to then Congress General Secretary Rahul Gandhi in 2011, criticized the judiciary's own corruption: "The judicature, a sacred instrument with great powers to punish corruption, is itself corrupt. Not a single corrupt judge has been caught or punished."

128 https://israelmyglory.org/article/judgment-on-jerusalem-zephaniah-31-8/ as accessed on 31 August 2024 at 14 pm.

129 https://www.barandbench.com/columns/nine-former-judges-who-spoke-of-corruption-what-ag-kk-venugopal-hinted-prashant-bhushan-hearing as accessed on 31 August 2024 at 14 pm.

Iyer also wrote to President Pranab Mukherjee in 2013, calling for an investigation into those who are "suspect of moral deviance" among certain Supreme Court judges. He warned that the scourge of bribery, which had long plagued Indian politics, was now infiltrating the judiciary.[130]

Corruption is a pervasive problem in the Indian judiciary, affecting every stage of the legal process, from filing a case to obtaining a decision. A 2013 Transparency International Report found that 45% of surveyed households believed the judiciary to be corrupt or extremely corrupt, and 36% of those who had contact with the judiciary in 2012 reported paying a bribe.[131] This corruption has eroded public faith in the justice system, as evidenced by the massive backlog of cases pending in Indian courts: 59,867 cases in the Supreme Court, 44.75 lakh cases in high courts, and a staggering 3.14 crore cases at the district and subordinate level (as of November 2019).[132] The nature of corruption in the judiciary has reportedly shifted, with bribes now being demanded for even basic tasks like scheduling hearings or obtaining copies of orders. A 2018 CMS (India Corruption Study) estimated that the total amount of bribes paid in the Indian legal system in a single year is a staggering Rs 534 crore.[133]

Instances of Judicial Corruption and Scandals in India

The Indian judiciary has faced numerous allegations of corruption over the years. As of April 1, 2022, Law Minister Kiren Rijiju informed the Lok Sabha that there had been 1,631 complaints about the judiciary's functioning, including allegations of corruption. These complaints were forwarded to the Chief Justice of India (CJI) and the Chief Justices of the respective High Courts for internal investigation.[134]

In a significant development, Justice C.S. Karnan, a sitting High Court judge, was sentenced to six months in prison in May 2017 for making corruption allegations against Supreme Court judges. This was the first time in India that a sitting judge faced such punishment. In 2019, the Central Bureau of Investigation (CBI) accused Justice Narain Shukla, a sitting judge

---

130 https://www.barandbench.com/columns/nine-former-judges-who-spoke-of-corruption-what-ag-kk-venugopal-hinted-prashant-bhushan-hearing as accessed on 31st August 2024 at 14 pm.

131 https://www.firstpost.com/india/judicial-accountability-who-will-judge-the-judges-in-india-1405511.html as accessed on 31 August 2024 at 14 pm.

132 *FP_Source=FP_Hi_DT_TS_Wgt_1405511&FP_Medium=FP_Hi_Topstories_149874* as accessed on 31 August 2024 at 14 pm.

133 https://www.legalserviceindia.com/legal/article-2764-corruption-in-indian-legal-system.html as accessed on 31st August 2024 at 14 pm.

134 https://www.thehindu.com/news/national/over-1600-complaints-against-judiciary-rijiju/article65282517.ece as accessed on 31 August 2024 at 14 pm.

of the Lucknow bench of the Allahabad High Court, of corruption. The CBI alleged that Shukla had received illegal gratification in exchange for favouring a medical college in a case. The retired judge of the Chhattisgarh High Court, Ishrat Masroor Quddusi, and others were also implicated in the case.[135]

In 1949, Justice S.P. Sinha of the Allahabad High Court became the only Indian judge to be removed from office, based solely on his judicial decisions. In 1996, Calcutta High Court judge Ajit Sengupta faced controversy for routinely issuing ex-parte, *ad interim* stay orders on anticipatory bail pleas from smugglers linked to the Mumbai underworld. He was subsequently arrested for violating the Foreign Exchange Regulation Act (FERA) after his retirement. During the tenure of Chief Justice A.M. Ahmad (1994-1997), concerns arose about the "special" treatment his daughter, a Delhi High Court lawyer, received from certain judges. Attempts to ban lawyer relatives of judges from residing in the same house were thwarted by Chief Justice Ahmad's influence.[136]

In two separate incidents, Indian High Court judges were implicated in corruption scandals. In the Punjab and Haryana High Court, three judges sought the help of the disgraced Public Service Commission (PSC) chief, R.P. Sidhu, to ensure that their daughters and other relatives topped PSC examinations. Two inquiry panels indicted the judges, leading to the resignations of Justices Gill and Amarbir Singh. Justice M.L. Singh remains on the bench but has been assigned no work. In another incident, three judges of the Karnataka High Court, along with two women advocates were involved in a brawl with a woman guest at a resort. Despite police involvement, no action was reportedly taken. While a three-judge inquiry committee appointed by the Chief Justice of India (CJI) investigated the matter, it ultimately cleared the judges.[137]

In 2017, Justice C.S. Karnan, a sitting High Court Judge, made public allegations of corruption against Supreme Court Judges. This resulted in his sentencing to six months imprisonment for contempt of court.[138] In another high-profile case, a former junior Court Officer accused Chief Justice of India Ranjan Gogoi of sexual harassment in April 2019. She submitted

135 https://www.lawyered.in/legal-disrupt/articles/corruption-and-judiciary-dr-vinod-surana/ as accessed on 31 August 2024 at 14 pm.

136 https://www.legalserviceindia.com/legal/article-5419-a-sneak-peek-into-the-corrupted-indian-judiciary.html as accessed on 31 August 2024 at 14 pm.

137 https://www.legalserviceindia.com/legal/article-5419-a-sneak-peek-into-the-corrupted-indian-judiciary.html as accessed on 31 August 2024 at 14 pm.

138 https://www.legalserviceindia.com/legal/article-5419-a-sneak-peek-into-the-corrupted-indian-judiciary.html as accessed on 31 August 2024 at 14 pm.

supporting documents and wrote to 22 other Supreme Court Justices.[139] In November 2018, a judge in Telangana's Ranga Reddy District Court was arrested for possessing assets disproportionate to his known sources of income.[140] These cases highlight the ongoing challenges of corruption and misconduct within the Indian judiciary.

Reports of corruption and bribery in the lower ranks of the Indian judiciary continue to emerge from across the country, contributing to a negative public perception of the judicial system. For example, in April 2018, three judges of lower courts in Telangana were arrested for possessing assets that far exceeded their declared income. In Gujarat, two lower judiciary judges were arrested for allegedly accepting bribes to settle cases during their time at the Vapi court in 2014. In January 2018, a shocking development occurred when four sitting Supreme Court judges held a press conference to expose alleged corruption and wrongdoing within the judiciary.[141]

How does Corruption Take Place in the Judiciary?

Instances of judicial misconduct and corruption have contributed to a decline in public trust. To maintain its credibility, the judiciary must be an independent and impartial body committed to combating corruption. However, there are concerns that some judges may be abusing their powers for personal gain or under pressure from political leaders and bureaucrats. These allegations raise questions about the integrity of the judicial system and the extent to which corruption has infiltrated its ranks.

Corruption in the Indian judiciary manifests in various forms, including bribery, favouritism, nepotism, and political interference. The most prevalent form is bribery, where judges are allegedly offered bribes to deliver favourable judgments. This undermines the fundamental principles of justice and erodes public trust. Additionally, there have been instances of judges accused of favouritism and nepotism, showing bias towards individuals or parties based on personal connections. Corruption can also occur in the allocation of cases or the formation of judicial benches, potentially compromising the impartiality of the legal process.[142]

---

139 https://www.scobserver.in/journal/10-sexual-harassment-and-the-cji/ as accessed on 31 August 2024 at 14 pm.

140 https://www.hindustantimes.com/telangana/hyderabad-judge-arrested-in-corruption-case-for-having-assets-worth-over-rs-3-crore/story-ivF01re9Nf0nvxft7PcYyK.html as accessed on 31 August 2024 at 14 pm.

141 https://www.legalserviceindia.com/legal/article-5419-a-sneak-peek-into-the-corrupted-indian-judiciary.html#google_vignette as accessed on 31 August 2024 at 14 pm.

142 https://www.jyotijudiciary.com/corruption-in-indian-judiciary/ as accessed on 31 August 2024 at 14 pm.

Judicial corruption is a complex issue with no single cause. To effectively address this problem, it is essential to identify the specific factors contributing to corruption in different states before implementing reforms. The effects of judicial corruption are far-reaching and detrimental to the core principles of the rule of law, such as equality, impartiality, integrity, and propriety. A key issue is the systemic nature of corruption, which benefits all parties involved. While the harms may not always be immediately apparent, judicial corruption undermines the fairness of the judicial system and defeats its purpose of upholding justice. Those who lack the resources to participate in corruption are particularly vulnerable, as they lose the protection that the judiciary is meant to provide.

Conclusion

The judicial systems of both ancient Israel and modern India have faced significant challenges related to corruption and the erosion of public trust. In Israel during the 8th and 7th cent B.C.E., prophets like Amos, Isaiah, Micah, and Zephaniah denounced the moral and political corruption of judges, accusing them of injustice and oppression. Zephaniah's critique of the corrupt judges of his time as "evening wolves" was examined in detail. Similarly, the Indian judiciary today has been marred by allegations of corruption, nepotism, and political interference, raising concerns about its credibility and integrity.

The comparison between these two historical periods highlights the enduring nature of these issues. While the specific contexts and methods of corruption may differ, the underlying themes of abuse of power, disregard for justice, and the exploitation of vulnerable populations remain constant. In Israel, the corrupt judicial system along with the evil kings led to the collapse of Israel in 587 B.C.E.

To address these challenges in India, it is imperative to implement comprehensive reforms that promote transparency, accountability, and public trust in the judiciary. This may include measures such as strengthening judicial oversight mechanisms, increasing the independence of the judiciary, and improving the efficiency and accessibility of the legal system. By taking decisive action to combat corruption and restore public confidence, India can ensure that Her judicial systems serve as true guardians of justice and uphold the fundamental principles of democracy.

To conclude, it would be fitting to recall what the Bible requires of the judges when they were appointed in Deut 16:18-20. These principles provide a valuable framework for evaluating the conduct of Indian judges and serve as a call to action for those seeking to restore integrity and justice to the nation's judicial system:

> [18] You shall appoint judges and officials throughout your tribes, in all your towns that the Lord your God is giving you, and they shall render just decisions for the people.[19] You must not distort justice; you must not show partiality; and you must not accept bribes, for a bribe blinds the eyes of the wise and subverts the cause of those who are in the right [20] Justice, and only justice, you shall pursue, so that you may live and occupy the land that the Lord your God is giving you.

According to the above Deut 16:18-20, judges are held to a strict standard of righteousness in their judicial duties. This imperative is reinforced by explicit prohibitions against actions that compromise justice and fairness. Judges must avoid partiality, literally "recognizing faces," and must never accept bribes. These behaviours are considered incompatible with the Lord's character (Deut 10:17) and therefore unacceptable for those entrusted with administering divine justice. These instructions apply not only to judges but also to the broader community. The direct address, "You shall not pervert justice," underscores the collective responsibility to uphold fairness. The judicial system cannot function effectively if only judges adhere to these principles. All participants, including community members, must resist the temptation to compromise justice. The opening section of Deuteronomy emphatically emphasizes justice as an indispensable condition for life within the land (v 20), a call that resonates throughout the prophetic writings.[143]

143 Patrick D. Miller, *Deuteronomy,* Interpretation (Louisville: J. Knox Press, 1990), 143.

14

International Politics and Colonial Dynamics in 2 Kings 22-23
A Voice from the Space of Liminality

Wungtei Buchem

Introduction

This paper shows a keen interest in history before and during the Josianic Reformation. Reading the epoch from the marginalized space is found underrated but is all the more wanting. Two specific parameters from the Josianic reformation will show the prospective reading of 2 Kings 22-23 from the space of what I borrowed from Uriah Kim (*Decolonizing Josiah,* 2005) to call Space of Liminality. Reading this way, I will espouse the feasibility of defining the interpretation as *the hermeneutics of voice.* The deciphering of such reading made possible is what Professor Jesurathnam aspired to and contributed to the majority of his writing in his career. As his pupil myself, this paper attempts to emulate his approach to reading the chosen text, albeit inadequate to situate my discernment to his calibre.

History

During Josiah's reign, "Jerusalem developed greatly with the construction of Mishneh and Maktesh"[144] as a quarter in the western slopes of Jerusalem.

144 There was rapid demographic growth during Josiah's time. They were basically new refugee settlers from the territories of the North and West that had been annexed by the Assyrian empire. The names of the two that emerged are the Mishneh and Maktesh

These quarters are told to have served as industrial and commercial centres. Ezra 2 and Nehemiah 7 give accounts of the list of Judaean restoration and expansion and that these lists of territorial and popular expansions of Judah is attributed to the reign of Josiah (*Cf.*, Joshua 15, 18, 19)[145]

These territorial expansions and reorganizations did not stand on its own but were associated with the revival of the Israelite religious traditions. These are found expression in:

(i) The cultic purification in the worship life and the re-establishment of the Passover in Jerusalem (centralization).
(ii) The interpretation and authorization of the discovered Law Book became both as a religious and as a spiritual initiative. The possible decline of Assyrian power and the residual political imbroglio of the Judaean themselves prompted these reorganizations.

What was significant before and during Josiah's reign was the Assyrian force. The Assyrian power was already a great concern for the security of the Judaeans before Josiah. Tiglath-Pileser-III (745-727 BCE) who represented its political sway is said to have restructured the government and military expansions that would blanket the known world of the time.[146] The political situation changed when king Ahaz (732-716 BCE), a contemporary to Tiglath-Pileser-III reigned in Judah. The Assyrian territory is said to have come closer by twenty miles to Judah, and its security was threatened. Ahaz had only made things worse by offering to subject himself to the Assyrians in exchange for protection against the kings of Damascus and Northern Israel. Ahaz's clumsy diplomacy had serious socio-religious consequences for his people. Much of the Judaean territories were lost and a hefty slice of the royal revenue was squeezed.[147] In such a situation it was foreseeable that people would resort to any activities to look after themselves with no thought of the wider social and moral repercussions.

---

quarters. Mordechai Cogan, "Into Exile: From the Assyrian Conquest to Israel to the Fall of Babylon," in Michael David Coogan (eds.), *The Oxford History of the Biblical World* (Oxford: Oxford University Press, 1998), 325.

145 Pertinent Ephraimite cities like Jericho and Bethel, including Lydda/Lydea and Ona, are considered part of Judah. This relevant discussion is also borrowed by the (unknown) author after 2004 in "Josiah," accessed in https://www.jewishvirtuallibrary.org/josiah, on 19 May 2017. The author also seems to have depended mainly on Mordechai Cogan's 1998 article.

146 James I. Packer, William White and Merrill C. Tenney (eds.), *The World of the Old Testament* (Alton: Window Books, 1982), 151. John Drane, *Old Testament Story: An Illustrated Documentary* (Herts: Lion Publishing, 1983), 118.

147 John Drane, *Old Testament Story: An Illustrated Documentary* (Herts: Lion Publication, 1983), 122.

After Ahaz, Hezekiah (715-686 BCE) was still tempted to make his own bid.[148] He began by demolishing idols of the Assyrian gods and putting a stop to other alien forms of worship in Jerusalem (which were partly introduced by Ahaz). Knowing that many inhabitants of Jerusalem were from the old Israelite tribes, he made significant efforts to unify these tribes. Having also reorganized the army, his opportunity came in 705 BCE with the death of Sargon-II, and both the Babylonians and Egyptians attempted to form an alliance with him to help him overthrow Assyria. The Assyrian king Sennacherib (705-681 BCE) responded by marching through Palestine, causing Egypt and the Philistines to collapse at once, and subsequently moved against Judah, weakening Hezekiah's position. Instead of integrating the towns and villages of Judah into his empire, he handed them to various Philistine kings. Hezekiah was left with no supporters, and so Sennacherib moved him to Jerusalem to live like a bird in a cage.[149]

It is assumed that Sennacherib annexed Judah and the rest of the foreign nations by 701 BCE. Perhaps this is because Assyria saw its ambition achieved during Sennacherib's reign. He managed to crush Egypt and capture its capital city, Thebes. In such a context, Hezekiah's successor, Manasseh (co-regency 697-687 BCE; sole reign; 687-643 BCE) had no room to exercise either his nationalistic motives or religious reforms. He was no match for Assyria's power (2 Kings 21: 1-18).[150] Things changed with the Assyrians because of the feud between Ashurbanipal (668-627 BCE) and his brother Shamash-shum-ukin.[151] After Ashurbanipal (627 BCE) died, the Assyrians were fighting for survival against the Babylonians and the Medes. The Egyptians then emerged as a more potent force. The kingdom of Lydia and the Medes began to raid the territories of the Assyrians.[152]

In the wake of the weakening Assyrian power and the mushrooming of the kingdoms, the revival of national hope emerged in Judah. International relations and politics were fluid when Josiah became king of Judah. The Assyrian Empire was not as strong as the past. The Neo-Babylonian Empire was on the verge of taking the lead in international politics, although it was not an easy task. The Egyptians were recovering from the then Assyrian

148 Drane, *Old Testament Story,* 123ff.

149 Donald John Wiseman, *1 and 2 Kings: An Introduction and Commentary* (Leicester: InterVarsity Press, 1993), 33.

150 Wiseman, *1 and 2 Kings*, 31.

151 See, Donald John Wiseman, "Ashurbanipal King of Assyria," in ***Encyclopedia Britannica,*** available in HTTPS ://www.britannica.com/biography/Ashurbanipal, accessed on 12th July 2016.

152 Drane, *Old Testament Story,* 130.

hegemony. For this short period, Jerusalem was governed by the Judaeans themselves without intervention from outsiders.

Josiah took charge in Judah after the death of his father, Amon. He set about re-asserting his country's independence and identity. Archaeological evidence shows that he controlled as far as North of Galilee, and his sway extended east of the River Jordan into Gilead. In an excavation conducted by David Ussishkin at Tell ed-Duweir, Lachish, which, according to 2 Kings 18: 14, was demolished during the Sennacherib crisis (701 BCE) and had become the vassal region of the Assyrians, was rebuilt by Josiah.[153] Necho-II (610-595 BCE) was an Egyptian king when Josiah was on his religio-political mission in Judah.

According to Mordechai Cogan, it was in "the spring of 609 BCE that Pharaoh Necho-II led an army up to the Euphrates River to aid the Assyrian against the Babylonians."[154] However, by the time they were crossing Jezreel valley, Josiah's army blocked their forthcoming leading to a fierce battle between the two at Megiddo.[155] Having killed Josiah in his encounter at Megiddo, it is said that Necho-II then appointed his candidate to replace Josiah and made the successor pay tribute on behalf of Judah.[156]

The biblical accounts of the Judaean kings show that, even prior to Josiah's reign, kings had fervently risked their role to defend their power, land, rights and privileges of the kingdom and its people. We see that YHWH have secured lives and kingdom from a complete annihilation. Hope for the kingdom never failed. Similarly, the plan of YHWH for the exile remains itself a matter of deliberate discussions until the Judaeans return in 538 BCE under the Persian king Cyrus.

Two Parameters of Observations in Josianic Reformation

The Josianic period was intensively charged with ethnic consciousness, religious revivals and political resurgence. A study of the Deuteronomistic History cannot ignore the discussions of the exiles' ethnic consciousness which contributed to the creation of the Deuteronomistic community and its history. In this section, I will highlight two parameters concerning Josiah's background and reform. Based on these, I will argue for an interpretation of his confrontation with Necho-II within a hermeneutical paradigm of voice

153 John R. Bartlett, "Archaeology," in J. W. Rogerson and Judith M. Lieu (eds.), *The Oxford Handbook,* 64.

154 Mordechai Cogan, "Into Exile," 346.

155 Cogan, "Into Exile," 344-346.

156 "Necho-II King of Egypt," in *Encyclopedia Britannica,* available in https://www.britannica.com/biography/Necho-II, accessed on 12th July 2016.

and show the potential of reading centralization from a marginalized context of NEI.

i. Cultic Purity or Ethnic Unity

Just as the ambiguities that might linger on the books of the HB, the redactional composition of DH is ambiguous. If what we have as the final product of the DH comes from the hand of the Dtr(s), then this form of the work itself must be placed during the period of exile, at the time when once again, Israel was stateless and in need of an identity that would outweigh the threat of cultural and religious assimilation. In this connection, the Dtr's notion of "Israel" lay on the centrality of the covenant by which YHWH bound this people together.[157] Keeping the *covenant* to which the identity and uniqueness of Israel are attached with, Josiah's criterion of reformation can be argued in multi-faceted ways. Questions such as these can be asked: Does the reformation represent voice of the people to resist? Is the reformation purely religious? Is the reformation an attempt at reliving the past/remembrance? Or is it a fight for ethnic and cultural rights?

Two similar points can be noted from the arguments of John McKay, and Mordechai Cogan whose commentaries on the Judaeans' cultic lives are paradoxical:

(i) The Assyrians did not force the Assyrian cult to be established in Judaean territories. Yet, as John McKay argues, the influence and the endorsement of "Ashur worship on the defeated territories cannot be denied."[158]

(ii) Cogan talks about "the non-coercive religious attitude of the Assyrians or for cultural uniformity among the subjects."[159] However, considering Assyria's intrusion, the impact on Judah's socio-religious life cannot be denied.

Oddly, after two decades, Cogan produced another article seemingly contradicting his previous statements. This new phase in the argument was reached with an appraisal by Herman Spieckermann[160] where Cogan is reported to have stated:

157 Theodore E. Mullen, *Narrative History and Ethnic Boundaries: The Deuteronomistic Historian and the Creation of Israelite National Identity* (Atlanta: Scholars Press, 1993), 56.

158 John McKay, *Religion in Judah under the Assyrian 732-609 BC* (London: SCM Press, 1973), 67-68.

159 Mordechai Cogan, *Imperialism and Religion: Assyria, Israel and Judah in the Eighth and Seventh Centuries BCE* (Missoula: Scholars Press, 1974), 85-88, 95.

160 Herman Spieckermann, *Juda unter Assur in der Sargonidenzeit*(Gottingen: Vandenhoeck& Ruprecht, 1982), 371ff.

> There is no distinction between provinces and vassal states regarding religious practice; all areas under Assyrian hegemony were constrained to worship Assyria's gods.[161]

Furthermore, Cogan also mentions that Josiah's reform could be understood as a *coup d'état* against Assyrian imperial power.[162] Kim's thesis clarifies the nature of Assyrian imperialism and Josiah's reform in a more appropriate way:

> What is clear is that, whether Judah was affected by cultural imperialism or political coercion or both, Judah's history and culture had been over-written, erased, or ignored during the Assyrian domination. Therefore, part of Josiah's reform was to recover the Judaean 'inscriptions' which had been forgotten during Assyrian domination . . . some of the writings of Josiah's court also contained not only about the 'discovery of the book of Law' or Josiah's reform but much to do with the identity of the people living in Judah at that time.[163]

In studying the religio-political materials of Israel, one cannot deny the impact Assyrians had on the ethno-communal environment of the Israelites. Unlike other foreign nations of the time, Biblical Israel was a confederation of the ethno-tribal community. The conventional concept of ethnicity currently appears to be out of fashion, as it is now considered as a changing phenomenon involving the construction and reconstruction of social interaction. This results from a changed identity as groups encounter new environments and newer experiences.[164] This suggests that ethnicity is closely bound up with group identity. Interaction between groups involve hetero-cultural confrontations and, as it occurs, produce ideologies of similarities as well as of differences. S. Malesevic says, "Ethnicity is a social entity where social actors produce relations where each one perceives about themselves and others as a distinct cultural collectivities."[165] Biblical scholars define ethnicity in the Bible from the perspective of "groupness" or

---

161 Mordechai Cogan, "Judah under Assyrian Hegemony: A Re-examination of Imperialism and Religion," *JBL* 112 (1993): 403-414 (405).

162 Spieckermann did this study by showing that the gods mentioned in 2 Kings 23: 4-14, especially those known as the Assyrians and demonstrated that Assyrians imposed religious obligations on vassal states as well as provinces. Cited in Mordechai Cogan. "Judah under Assyrian Hegemony, 403-414.

163 Uriah Kim, *Decolonizing Josiah: Towards a Postcolonial Reading of the Deuteronomistic History* (Sheffield: Sheffield Phoenix Press, 2005), 227.

164 J. C. Miller, "Ethnicity and the Hebrew Bible: Problems and Prospects," *CBR* 6/2 (2008): 170-213 (172).

165 S. Malesevic, *The Sociology of Ethnicity* (London: SAGE, 2004), 4.

"group identity," where there is obvious discrimination against one ethnic boundary by the other. Generally, in socio-anthropological studies, "ethnic groups" are mostly seen as a minority group or a certain racial group.[166] Such groups contend for their rights and justice, challenging the dominant social order in order to safeguard cultures, worldviews and traditions.

Deuteronomy 1: 1-18 introduces the notion that Israel's identity was formed in Moab before crossing the Jordan.[167] This passage recounts the formation of an ethnic identity based on *the Torah*, indicating an *ideal* nation under Yahweh. Perhaps this has shaped an ideology that enhances social and political agendas after that. From this perspective, the Josianic discourse in 2 Kings 22-23 is befitting in that the *Israelite ethnic identity.*[168] is traced back. Like Malesevic, James C. Miller opines that the intensity of ethnic sentiments is situational. Therefore, he says the question about Israelites' identity can be answered by asking "to know how they understood themselves as well as others' perception about them given a particular point of time and space."[169] K. L. Sparks thinks that in the monarchic era, ethnic sentiments were intensified in the context of *peripheral groups.*[170] or the diaspora, Israelites were subjected to domination by more powerful imperialistic nations and kingdoms. The sentiments then were mostly aggressive and oppositional. Hence, the ethno-religious identity consciousness of Josiah's period is likely fostered because of two threats:

(i) Firstly, the fear of identity erosion came in a novel form of "ethnic indicia found primarily in the priestly writings, for instance, the Sabbath, circumcision and ritual purity."[171]
(ii) Secondly, the threat of unimaginable loss of ancestral inheritance regarding land, autonomy and culture triggered apprehensions.[172]

In this disposition, Sparks reckons that prophet Isaiah's theology was founded on the hegemonic Assyrian context, where the threat of universal rule over the weaker nation was the focal agenda of the former. This accord

166 Miller, "Ethnicity and the Hebrew Bible," pp. 170-213. Malesevic, *The Sociology of Ethnicity*, pp. 1-2. J. M. Hall, *Ethnic Identity in Greek Antiquity* (Cambridge: Cambridge University Press, 1997), 47.

167 Mullen, *Narrative History and Ethnic Boundaries*, 63-75.

168 Hall, *Ethnic Identity*, p. 25.

169 Miller, "Ethnicity and the Hebrew Bible: Problems and Prospects," 170-213.

170 K. L. Sparks, *Ethnicity and Identity in Ancient Israel: Prolegomena to the Study of Ethnic Sentiments and their Expression in the Hebrew Bible* (Winona Lake: Eisenbrauns, 1998), 21.

171 Priestly writings from the Holiness Code of Lev. 17-26. Sparks, *Ethnicity and Identity*, 314.

172 Miller, "Ethnicity and the Hebrew Bible: Problems and Prospects," 170-213.

takes the form of understanding that the Israelite ethnic identity sentiments were a response to Assyrian imperial rule.[173] Therefore, the Josianic policy of cultic purity reformation was inclusive of ethno-cultic reassertion.

Prior to James C. Miller, similar thoughts on ethnicity and identity of Israelites were propounded by Theodore E. Mullen, who argued that the ethno-cultic consciousness of the Israelites emerged after the devastation of the Temple leading to the phases of the Babylonian deportation. After this, the indigenous Israelites were distanced from their traditions and homeland and their dynastic lines were obstructed. Miller, in discussing common thoughts on ethnicity and identity with Mullen states:

> Within this scenario, Mullen contends that the DtrH presents the exile in Babylon with a host of 'memories' they can draw upon as part of the historical people. It presents the ideal, programmatic depiction of Israel's ethnic, religious and cultural distinctiveness, setting forth two key elements that serve as a basis for Israelite identity. *First,* in contrast to all other nations, Israel stands in a unique relationship with Yahweh. *Second,* Israel must maintain certain behavioural norms corresponding to their faith.[174]

Despite DH's ideological and theological points of view that seem to have a message representative of the death of hope for marginalized peoples, my interest is in unveiling these voices of the lived realities in these historical contexts. Read this way, readers from marginalized locations such as NEI can comprehend and identify themselves with the elements of the voice of the marginalized in the texts. Given the Assyrians as predators of the vulnerable nations and taken Israel as one, I would assume the role of Josiah, symbolising the voice of hope to the people. These aspects of roles for transformation, reassertion, realization, and self-consciousness would have intensified the cultic as well as ethnic unity and nation's prosperity.

ii. Josianic Reformation Conditioned by the State of Liminality

In light of the first parameter of the Josianic reformation discussed above, here in the second observation, I will look at the oppressive socio-political context that includes the pressure of assimilation. Mullen's idea of ethnic consciousness seems to have set the framework for Miller, who says ethnic consciousness is situational. These evaluations are convincing because the sentiments of self-worth do not arise in a vacuum but are situational, and the situation in the Josianic era is one of multiple crises. In this light, Sparks

173 Miller, "Ethnicity and the Hebrew Bible: Problems and Prospects," 170-213.

174 Mullen, *Narrative History and Ethnic Boundaries*, 56, 59–60, 72. Miller, "Ethnicity and the Hebrew Bible: Problems and Prospects,"196.

looks further back from the exilic situation to the times when imperial power of Assyria controlled Judah for over 60 years prior to Josiah's reign.[175] Assyria saw Judah and its people as the *Other*. Hence, Josiah's period that suffered multiple blows during the Assyria's regime cannot be overlooked in the study of the formation of ethnic consciousness of the Judaeans.

Building on these discussions, Kim's *Realpolitik of Liminality* will help us to read Josiah's context as one of ethnic crisis as well as consciousness *vis-à-vis* the reformation. The *Realpolitik of Liminality* is a phrase Kim used to discuss the Judaean fate before and during the Josianic era. In his view, even prior to exile, Judah was like a petty state wedged in the political and commercial matrix shaped by the Assyrians,[176] who were driven by the ideology of expansion and assimilation. Judah was positioned at the margin of the Assyrian empire, generally as a victim or as a witness of exploitation.[177] As a result, the uniqueness of Judaean ethnic identity was shattered. Judah had no control over her own resources, lacking in economic and political security. Fear and anxiety made the community miserable. The prime cause of this, then, is the Assyrian imperialism that compelled the Judaean community to live in the state of liminality.

The politico-ideological factor that formed the Neo-Assyrian empire's policy of expansion and subjugation implied that the prime task of a king was territorial expansion. The persistent idea which drove them was the motif of "heroic priority," in which "the king boasts that he had traversed a land none of his forefathers had heard of."[178] Sennacherib (704-681 BCE) is said to be the king who did not put into practice the hierarchical motif of "heroic priority." However, he saw himself as a powerful king who devastated,

175 Sparks, *Ethnicity and Identity*, 272-273, 281.

176 The Neo-Assyrian dynasty's intrusion into the region west of the Euphrates River, referred to as "Hatti" in the inscriptions of the Neo-Assyrian kings, began with Ashurnasirpal II's (883-859 BCE) desire for military expeditions across the Euphrates River. Shalmaneser III (858-824 BCE), son of Ashurnasirpal, not only continued his father's intrusions, but also conducted more systematic campaign designed to secure Assyrian commercial interests and territorial expansion until Tiglath-Pileser III (744-727 BCE). Finally, Sargon II (721-705 BCE) and his dynasty dominated and controlled the entire west for the next 100 years. Hayim Tadmor, "Assyria and the West: The Ninth Century and its Aftermath," in Hans Goedicke and J. J. M. Roberts (eds.), *Unity and Diversity: Essay in the History, Literature and Religion of the Ancient Near East* (Baltimore: The John Hopkins University Press, 1975), 36-48.

177 Kim, *Decolonizing Josiah,* 206.

178 Hayim Tadmor, "World Dominion: The Expanding Horizon of the Assyrian Empire," in L. Milano, S. de Martino, *et al.*(eds.), *Landscape Territories, Frontiers and Horizons in the Ancient Near East* (Pedova: Sargon, 1999), 55-62.

destroyed and burned the cities of his enemies.[179] It is said that when vassal subjects rebelled against Sargon II (722–705 BCE), he practised a policy of cooperation and solidarity with the subjects, but only to strengthen his hegemony over the provinces.[180] So he is known to have practised a double-edged policy of terror and benevolence. In such a context of the Judaeans' state of liminality and the ruthlessness of Assyrians' violence K. L. Young writes:

> If we accept the royal inscriptions' descriptions of what the Assyrians did to their enemies at face value, it is truly terrifying: flaying alive, impalement, cutting or excising, burning alive, smashing, heaping up of corpses or of heads, and so on. The king conducted exemplary punishments on those enemies 'who have shown a stiffer resistance.'[181]

S. Gitin points out that Israel and Judah were primary victims of such policies, especially the Northern kingdom after Tiglath Pileser-II. Human beings became an economic commodity for the Assyrians, who shifted the local people *en masse* to other provinces, which could obtain more profit for the Assyrians. Judah was downgraded to a relatively insignificant role in the broad economic policy of Assyria. As a result, Judah had to stand on its own while paying direct and crude means of taxation and tributes to the Assyrian empire, which had an unbalanced trade relationship with them.[182] These treatments prior to Josiah were ways by which the Assyrians instilled fear-psychosis in their subjects, which particularly affected the vulnerable nation. These led to deteriorating social and cultural conditions, shaken economic security, and compelled the populace to remain under the psychological control of the Assyrian empire.

This socio-political location of Josiah as one of the two observations confirms that Judah as a nation was helpless and voiceless. Irrespective of the harsh lived experiences, Josiah's persistence in bringing about reform

---

179 Julian Reade, "Neo-Assyrian Monuments in their Historical Context," in Frederick M. Fales (eds.), *Assyrian Royal Inscriptions: New Horizons in Literary, Ideological, and Historical Analysis* (Rome: Instituto Per l'Oriente, 1980), 163.

180 Giovanni Lanfranchi, "Consensus to Empire: Some Aspects of Sargon II's Foreign Policy," in H. Waetzoldt and H. Hauptmann (eds.), *Assyrienim Wandel der Zeiten*(Heidelberg: Heidelberger Orientverlag, 1997), 81-86.

181 K. L. Young, *Ancient Conquest Accounts: A Study in Ancient Near East and Biblical History Writing* (Sheffield: JSOT Press, 1990), 76.

182 S. Gitin, "The Neo-Assyrian Empire and its Western Periphery: The Levant, with Focus on Philistine Ekron," in Simo Parpola and R. M. Whiting (eds.), *Assyria 1995: Proceedings of the 10th Anniversary Symposium of the Neo-Assyrian Text Corpus Project* (Helsinki: The Neo-Assyrian Text Corpus Project, 1997), 78, 82, 84.

both in the religious and national life of Judah is the perspective of voice that I see in this narrative. In the discussions below, I will consider these two parameters as the background for looking at Josiah's motive in confronting Necho-II at Megiddo. This discussion will help me propose hermeneutics where Josiah's role is taken as a representative of voice, reading from the optic of a marginalized context of NEI.

Centralization Reform: Hermeneutics of Voice (2 Kings 22-23)

Besides what I have discussed on cultic unity and cultic purity concerning Josiah's centralization policies, I will briefly discuss Josiah's resistance to the foreign powers as a means of voice explainable using the preposition 'עַל. I am keen to look specifically at 2 Kings 23: 29 regarding 2 Chron. 35: 20 on the emendations and interpretation of 'עַל. There are similar translations of עַל, עָלָה and וַיֵּלֶךְ in 2 Kings 23: 29 and וַיֵּצֵא in 2 Chron. 35: 20, that is, Pharaoh Necho-II *went up to the king of Assyria* (NRSV) in 2 Kings 23: 29 and *fought at Carchemish* (NRSV) in 2 Chron. 35: 20. Consequently, causing Josiah to act against the Pharaoh. However, Cogan seems to have signified something different concerning Necho-II's expedition, which then makes the action of Josiah pitted for his death. Cogan writes:

> These days of glory on the home front did not stand him well on his day of reckoning, for Josiah met a sorrowful end. . . Egyptian Pharaoh Neco II . . . was rushing north **with aid for** Assyria.[183]

To go by the phrase "with aid for Assyria," which Cogan renders, the intentions of Pharaoh's expedition and Josiah's motive to confront the Pharaoh itself become paradoxically related to the political context of the time. So, my quest is whether Necho-II marched out *against* the Assyrians or, as Cogan renders, *to aid* Assyria.

Texts: 2 Kings 23:29

בְּיָמָיו עָלָה פַרְעֹה נְכֹה מֶלֶךְ-מִצְרַיִם עַל-מֶלֶךְ אַשּׁוּר-עַל-נְהַר-פְּרָת וַיֵּלֶךְ הַמֶּלֶךְ יֹאשִׁיָּהוּ לִקְרָאתוֹ
וַיְמִיתֵהוּ בִּמְגִדּוֹ כִּרְאֹתוֹ אֹתוֹ

> In his day, Pharaoh Neco, king of Egypt, **went up to the king** of Assyria to the river Euphrates. King Josiah went to meet him, but when Pharaoh Neco met him at Megiddo, he killed him (NRSV).

I would argue that words such as[184] עֵזֶר which is a noun masculine for *help* or לַעֲזוֹר with ל *(to)-infinitive of* עָזַר which is a verb for *help* or to *assist* is nowhere found in v. 29 and v. 20 of both the accounts. Moreover, the

183 Cogan, "Into Exile," 246-247.

184 Henry Browne, *Triglot Dictionary of Scriptural Representative Words in Hebrew, Greek and English* (London: Samuel Bagster& Sons Ltd., 1901), 7, 16, 185.

common word סיוע in Hebrew for *aid* or *assistance* is out of view in these texts. Like Cogan's emendation, there are also some English Bible translations that associates these texts with the idea that Pharaoh's political expedition to Carchemish was to *aid* or *help* the Assyrians.

As it is shown, the translation and perspective of Josiah's action in both accounts, however, is undisputed. With the same preposition being involved in these verses, it is clearly understood, Josiah *went* or *marched* to *fight against* Necho-II, that is, both Necho-II and Josiah march out 'על. In the case of Josiah, this is uniformly rendered 'against' the Pharaoh, but in the case of Necho-II, the preposition is apparently ambiguous. Since the translations of the prepositions are not uniform, the whole theo-political aspect of Josiah's death can be disputed. Contrary to Cogan, F. M. Cross and D. N. Freedman posit that since the destination is Carchemish, Necho-II's journey and his intention cannot be *to help* Assyrian king Ashur-Ubalit retake Haran, which lay across the Euphrates River.[185]

The translation of the preposition עַל in v. 29, which can either mean 'against' or 'for', becomes a determining factor here. I contend that considering the context of Josiah's reign, the connotation of the preposition 'על can best be read as *against*. Although I do not intend to study the Chronicler's emendation in detail, looking at the Pharaoh's words to Josiah in 35: 21b gives me an insight that the Pharaoh was on the move to *fight against* the Assyrians. The ill-fated animosity is clear among the kings, as expressed through the ironic words of Necho-II's warning to Josiah. Necho-II's words are ironic about what he had to say to Josiah but straightforwardly in the way he desired to become a superpower in the international politics of the time. Chaim Herzog and Mordechai Gichon observe that a plan to restrain Josiah was voiced by Necho-II when he tried to convince Josiah not to interfere with his progress to "fight" the Assyrians (v. 21).[186] Hence, the translation *to aid* or *to help* rendered by Cogan and various other Bible translations prove a slender emendation.

עַל as a Hermeneutical Principle for Reading Centralization

The Pharaoh's intention was seemingly political. I will substantiate this in the light of Josiah's earnest resistance as a voice *against* the Pharaoh's imperial march and as a voice that endorsed the centralization and security of the Judaeans.

185 Frank M. Cross and David Noel Freedman, "Josiah's Revolt against Assyria," *JNES* 13 (1953): 56-58 (57).

186 Chaim Herzog and Mordechai Gichon, *Battles in the Bible* (London: Greenhill Books, 1978), 214.

Considering Josiah's period's national and international socio-political and religious dynamics, Necho-II mirrors the imperial force, and Josiah represents the rebellious and resistant voice. Josiah resisted the tendency of the international politics that had the potential as a single force or in collective forces to subjugate the Judaeans.

(i) The context of the state of political affairs during Josiah's era changed ethnic consciousness for the Judaeans. Therefore, perspective of resistance can be best read as a voice *against* dominant forces of assimilation and subjugation.

(ii) Both Necho-II and Josiah's gestures in the narrative can signify their ideologies of defence and a contest for power. Hence, the confrontation is proof enough to be taken as the context in which Josiah, in his pursuit to defend the marginalized Judaeans, had become the victim of that *liminal*[187] socio-political location.

In these frameworks, the discussions of K. L. Sparks, Miller and Mullen have merit. Their arguments suggest a multifaceted uprising of the Judaeans who under Josiah emerged to restore cultic purity as well as cultic unity. Judah's rise in self-awareness of its distinctive identity and the need to defend this is conditioned by and through the essential response to the Assyrian imperial rule.

It might appear that Josiah's centralization policy contradicts Jeroboam's decentralization policy. My interest is on the plausibility of voices in the narratives for an interpretation that bespeaks for marginalized readers of NEI, irrespective of the chronology and thematic deviations. For instance, how will theological themes such as centralization as well as decentralization be interpreted from a marginalized reader's perspective of NEI? This is where the significance of the textual message becomes known within the lived realities of marginalized readers. To me, biblical texts of varying eras are the product of socio-historical phases of the lives of the people of biblical times. Given a motivation to garner hope for marginalized readers, approaching any text requires a perspective on how the texts might speak to the readers. In theory, the themes contradict one another, but in a realistic interpretation that favours marginalized readers, it is essential to consider reader-response in both the narratives. Robert Alter's statement can support my argument, "biblical narratives are approachable to contemporary readers in the way they relate characters and situations of the texts with their lived realities."[188] Similarly, Charlene van der Walt notes that "readers

187 Kim, *Decolonizing Josiah,* 221.

188 Robert Alter, *The World of Biblical Literature* (New York: Basic Books, 1992), 39.

of the texts can be involved with the stories within their specific reading strategies, irrespective of faith or non-faith."[189]

Josiah believes the Megiddo battle is a battle of defence: a voice for rights and identity, a voice against injustice and the threat to the land and its people. In this reading, to the Judaeans of that period, the actions of Josiah, both in his internal reform and in external resistance, represented undying courage and hope. In pursuit of a liberating reading of texts like 2 Kings 22-23, reading the Josianic approach as retrieving the formerly defeated heritage to reassert communal distinctiveness amid an imperial catastrophe is pertinent. It seeks cultural rejuvenation against the decline caused by cultural proselytization by the colonizers.

Identifying the pathos and ethos of the resistant Judaeans with marginalized readers like NEI becomes empowering. When the "worldview that sustained peoples' identity"[190] is muted, it is time for the marginalized to realize the possibility of destructing the colonial/hegemonic myth in the light of the Josianic model of resistive voice. Such a paradigm of an *underground*[191] In other words, a counter-reading that proceeds from the suppressed paradigm comes closer to the marginal reader. It is a reading paradigm that can encourage liberty rather than lowering hope. To me, being vulnerable must not be seen as an end of hope but as this vulnerability can be a means to hope. The *hermeneutics of voice* is one approach to realizing this greater end.

While it is possible to appreciate the positive contributions[192] of the Westerners, their ideological reality is that, consciously or not, I observe, they drew on biblical motifs of occupation to defend their cultural assault on tribal identities. The voice of the tribes in NEI runs as a counter to the legacy of the stereotypes that the Westerners have imposed on them. In the same way as the suppressed Judaeans of Josiah's time, the tribes in NEI

189 Charlene van der Walt, "Hearing Tamar's Voice- How the Margin Hears Differently: Contextual Readings in 2 Samuel 13: 1-22," in Athalya Brenner-Idan and Archie Lee (eds.), *Samuel, Kings and Chronicles*, Vol. I (London: T & T Clark, 2017), 4.

190 A. Wati Longchar, "Trends in Tribal Theology in Northeast India," in Samson Prabhakar and Kinwan Kown (eds.), *Dalit and Minjung Theologies: A Dialogue* (Bangalore: BTESSC/SATHRI, 2006), 65.

191 Ernst Bloch, *Atheism in Christianity: The Religion of the Exodus and the Kingdom* (London: Verso Press, 2009), xv. Original publication by New York: Herder and Herder, 1972.

192 It is without a doubt that missionaries came to the NEI with good intentions to propagate the gospel of Jesus Christ and they meant to be helpful and liberating. However, as Vashum concurs, "consciously", the Westerners preached the gospel in the pretext of the "White man's burden" and in the native's general assumption the White invaders were virtually immune from any wrongdoing and the Christian missionaries were uncritically acquiesced to as doers of good.

seek confidence in their distinctive socio-cultural identities from the rest of the country. Although tribes in NEI inhabit different regions, districts and villages, the familiar voice that they share is their aspiration to be who they are in their self-definition of identity, religion, rights, history and destiny, rather than living in a liminal state, suppressed by the ideology of Hinduization promulgated by the Indian policymakers. Just as with the subjective historiography of the Dtr that concealed the voice of the marginalized and privileged elite in the texts, the worldview of the tribes in NEI was veiled by the Western hegemony both religiously and politically. In response to this, it is in the curiosity towards *who we are* and *what is ours*, which fed into the hidden voices of tribal resistance, that a mode of liberative reading of the Bible is sought.

Conclusion

In this article, I contended that the interpretation of themes can be determined and examined *from the place* of the readers, although the essence of the theme remains as it is. The *hermeneutics of voice* that I attempt to articulate espouses the marginal mode of interpretation, taking the native eyes of the Christian tribes in NEI as the case. My argument went on to show the interpretive strategies identified with the aspirations, experiences, and lived realities of the marginalized against the backdrop of the interpretation by Western Christianity of the colonial era.[193] This then relates to Sugirtharajah's statement that "vernacular hermeneutics is about taking the text closer to the readers themselves."[194] Hence, the *hermeneutics of voice* depicted in my study counter-reads the Dtr's championing of the theme of doom, while placing the readers' experiences at the forefront of its interpretation.

The use of Bible from the hegemonic paradigm itself has at times been insensitively imposed על on the indigenous peoples of NEI. A reading from *above*[195] i.e. one that implicitly accepts and endorses the claims of the interpreters can lead to subjugation and annihilation of the native's

193 Also see, Laura E. Donaldson, "The Sign of Orpah: Reading Ruth through Native Eyes," in Sugirtharajah (eds.), *Vernacular Hermeneutics* (Sheffield: Sheffield Academic Press, 1999), 21.

194 Sugirtharajah categorizes the "Third World biblical hermeneutics into two categories: *liberation-focused* and *culture sensitive*." While the aspect of *liberation-focus* privileges liberation as a crucial hermeneutical key, *culture sensitivity* mobilizes indigenous cultural nuances for theological enterprises. Detailed readings in Sugirtharajah, "Vernacular Resurrections," in Sugirtharajah (eds.), *Vernacular Hermeneutics,* 11, 13.

195 L. H. Rawsea, "Indigenous Spirituality and Modernity: A Theological Response," in HrangthanChhungi (eds.), *Hearing the Voices of Tribals and Adavvasis* (Nagpur: NCCI publication, 2018), 253.

worldview and their stories, past and present. In this climate, a reading that endorses the texts' imperial rhetoric may readily distort the possibility of a marginalized readership identifying the God of the text as their God. However, a reading from *below* in the text, and the stories told of the lived realities by the people themselves, could help relate to the God of the Bible and the themes of the texts that are read are represented in the voice of the marginalized themselves.

15

The Sabbath in the Early Postexilic Period Negotiating Social Identity and its Implication for the Indian Churches

S. Esther Ao

Introduction

This article is dedicated to Prof. Rev. Dr. K. Jesurathnam, Professor of Old Testament at the United Theological College (UTC), Bengaluru, in recognition of his scholarly contribution to studying the Old Testament, Old Testament Theology, and Dalit Hermeneutics. I had the privilege of learning from him as a Master of Theology student. I was fortunate to have him as my thesis guide, an experience that deeply enriched my academic journey.

This article seeks to honour his life and remarkable contributions to the Church, theological academy, and the countless students he has mentored. His influence extends through his prolific writings, which sincerely affirm his Dalit identity, express solidarity with the struggles of the Dalit community, and challenge the discriminations and atrocities meted out based on this identity. In recognition of his effort to uplift marginalized identity, this article is dedicated to him, a scholar who advocates for and negotiates the identities of subordinated people. The issue of social identity is particularly pertinent for those who are marginalized and discriminated against based on the identity ascribed by society. To address this issue, K. Jesurathnam asserts that "all human beings must ask how their respective religious identities enrich or skew a vision of our shared humanity on this planet and explore the possible horizon of a shared witness to inhabiting the world today."[196] This perspective is crucial for understanding how biblical communities navigated social identity.

In this context, this article focuses on the role of Sabbath in negotiating social identity during the early postexilic period, a period of significant transformation for the Jewish community in Yehud marked by redefinition of communal and religious boundaries, specifically through the lens of Isaiah 56: 4-5.This work explores how Sabbath negotiates the social identity of eunuchs according to Isaiah 56: 4-5. Isaiah 56 speaks explicitly of the Sabbath and gives information regarding its observation and who can participate. This raises the question: How does Sabbath negotiate the circumstances in which the eunuchs could consider themselves as individuals or as a group in Israelite society? What does Sabbath observation mean for the 'identity' of eunuchs? How does the Sabbath extend their identity in the community? In this exploration,the first part of the article delves into the definition of social identity and the social identity approach. The second part examines the Sabbath as an identity marker and the 'identity' of eunuchs during the postexilic period. It then investigates how the Sabbath negotiates the social identity of eunuchs in Isaiah 56:4-5. Through the study, the work attempts to draw implications for the Indian churches about the challenges faced by sexual minorities, as Indian churches and their community play a vital role in defining the social identity of their members.

Social Identity

Identity is a complex phenomenon and a fundamental concept for human beings. Social identity refers to the "aspects of an individual's self-image that derive from the social categories to which he perceives himself as belonging."[197] It could also be defined as "that part of an individual's self-concept which derives from their knowledge of their membership of a social group (or groups) together with the value and emotional significance attached to that membership."[198] It involves an individual's sense of belonging that

196 K. Jesurathnam, "Quest for Identity in Community Formation: Ancestral Narratives for Model Communities in the Book of Genesis," in *Identity and Community in Biblical World*, ed. L. Lalnunzira and Varaprasad Gosala (Bangalore: Society for Biblical Studies in India, 2020), 20.

197 H Tajfel and H.C. Turner, "The Social Identity Theory of Intergroup Behavior," in *Psychology of Intergroup Relation*, ed. W.G. Austin and S. Worchel (Monterey, CA: Brooks/Cole, 1986), 22–37.

198 Henry Tajfel, *Human Groups and Social Categories: Studies in Social Psychology* (Cambridge: Cambridge University Press, 1981), 255.

comes from belonging to a particular group, playing a crucial role in the interaction between personal and group identities.[199]

Having a social identity provides a sense of belongingness to a group and also a sense of identity to its members. It shapes an individual's self-perception and worldview. However, social identity threatens individuals when an individual is excluded from a group or not accepted within it. They often internalize adverse feelings and become isolated. Presumably, social identity is a construct and fluid. J. T. Lamoreaux notes that in ancient times, religious rituals and practices were instrumental in establishing solid social boundaries around their own communities, defining who were insiders and outsiders.[200] These boundaries are identity markers that decide between the in group and the out roup.[201] In other words, religious rituals and practices create boundaries and serve as identity markers, distinguishing a person or group as an in group or out group. However, suppose boundaries define who belongs and who does not belong to the group, and religious rituals and practices create boundaries. In that case, religious traditions and practices also provide a process through which an individual can join the group.[202] In other words, while identity markers created identity, people were constantly subjected to negotiations to join the group and be part of that social identity. Taking note of the understanding of social identity and how religious rituals and practices are identity markers, the social identity of eunuchs and Sabbath as social identity markers will be examined.

Social Identity Approach in Biblical Studies

British Psychologist Henri Tajwel and his colleagues developed Social Identity theory in the early 1970s. It emerged after several decades of academic research to understand the relationship between the individual and society and the development of an individual's personal and social identities.[203] In the arena of biblical studies, P.F. Esler pioneered the use of Social Identity Theory. Since then, the Social Identity approach in biblical studies has aided innumerous insights.[204] The works showcase that it is a

199 Coleman A. Baker, "Social Identity Theory and Biblical Interpretation," *Biblical Theology Bulletin* 42, no. 3 (2012): 130.

200 J.T. Lamoreaux, "BTB Readers Guide: Ritual Studies," *Biblical Theology Bulletin* 39 (2009): 159.

201 Tajfel and Turner, "The Social Identity Theory of Intergroup Behavior," 17.

202 Baker, "Social Identity Theory and Biblical Interpretation," 131.

203 Henry Tajfel, "Social Identity and Intergroup Behavior," *Social Science Information*, no. 13 (1974): 65–93.

204 Baker, "Social Identity Theory and Biblical Interpretation"; P.H.W. Lau, *Identity and Ethics in the Book of Ruth: A Social Identity Approach* (Berlin: De Gruyter, 2011); Andrew M. King, *Social Identity and the Book of Amos*, Library of Hebrew Bible/ Old

helpful tool for analyzing biblical texts to understand the inter-group and intra-group dynamics and social identity formation.[205]

This approach also analyses how the texts aid in the negotiation of identity.[206] There is often an implied sense of identity within the texts, both for the author and the audience.[207] Social Identity theory helps explore the social identity embedded in the text, whether there is a subversion of "normal" inter-group processes by negotiating social identity in ways that "affirms yet chastens and transcends" specific group identity.[208] Isaiah 56:4-5, concerning the Sabbath and eunuchs, will be analyzed through this approach to understanding how Sabbath negotiates the identity of the eunuchs and, by doing so if it conforms or transcends "normal" inter-group identity.

Sabbath and the Negotiation of Social Identity

The Sabbath, with its prescribed practices and rituals, played a significant role in shaping the social identity of the Israelite community. These instructions influenced how people viewed themselves and behaved as members of society. By observing the Sabbath, individuals reaffirmed their relationship with God and negotiated their place within the community. The Sabbath allowed for the negotiation of identity within the community. While social identity defines people, negotiating identity is about defining relationships. Negotiating social identity takes place in social interactions. One of the principles of negotiating identity is that one should communicate clearly the desired identity and the relationship goals to the other. Another important aspect is honouring the identity that one negotiates with.[209]

The book of Isaiah captures the essence of postexilic Israel, a time when social groups formed distinct boundaries. As Andrew M. King explains, "The formation of social groups, necessitating group boundaries, allows group members to negotiate who they are." These groups not only defined their members but also shaped how they interpreted the world for their group members.[210] Among the various identities negotiated during this

---

Testament Studies 706 (London: T&T Clark, 2021); Aaron J. Kuecker, "The Spirit and the 'Other': Social Identity, Ethnicity and Intergroup Reconciliation in Luke-Acts," Library of New Testament Studies (London: T&T Clark, 2011).

205 Baker, "Social Identity Theory and Biblical Interpretation," 134.

206 King, *Social Identity and the Book of Amos*, 23.

207 King, *Social Identity and the Book of Amos*, 23.

208 Kuecker, "The Spirit and the 'Other': Social Identity, Ethnicity and Intergroup Reconciliation in Luke-Acts," 48.

209 S. Ting-Toomey, "Identity Negotiation Theory," in *Sage Encyclopedia of Intercultural Competence*, ed. J. Bennett, vol. 1 (Los Angeles: sage, 2015), 418–22.

210 King, *Social Identity and the Book of Amos*, 1.

time, the eunuchs, particularly highlighted in Isaiah 56:4-5, stand out. The observance of the Sabbath and how it facilitated the negotiation of their social identity is an exploration of the following lines

Sabbath as an Identity Marker During the Early Postexilic Period

Niels-Erik A. Andreasen notes that the history of the Sabbath has demonstrated that it has developed about the historical and religious process in ancient Israel.[211] Sabbath as a religious institution was known to Israel very early. Its observance is recorded in the pre-exilic writings (2 Kings 4:23; 11:4ff; 16:18; Isaiah 1:13; Hosea 2:13, Amos 8:5). By the postexilic period, the postexilic community was acquainted with the Sabbath. It was known that Sabbath keeping was one of the religious obligations of the covenant people (Nehemiah 13). The observance of the Sabbath was considered equivalent to the fulfilment of the statutes and the commandments. It ensured that the people sustained their lives (Isaiah 58:13f).[212]

At this point, the Jerusalem congregation was organized, and Sabbath observance was recognized as a distinctive obligation for its community members. Paul D. Hanson explains that during the postexilic period, the Sabbath emerged as "the emblem of Jewish Identity." Those who faithfully kept the Sabbath distinguished themselves as members of the people of Israel.[213]Thus, in the early postexilic period, the Sabbath was an important identity marker for the individuals and the community who observed it.

סרים (Eunuchs) as an "Identity" during the Early Postexilic Period

The term סרים etymologically denotes 'officials.' In Genesis 40:2, the term refers to officials who were not eunuchs. However, in Isaiah 56:4-5 the term סרים is "an identity label."[214] It referred to the eunuchs and their physical phenomenon. A eunuch was a man who was rendered impotent and sterile by an act of sexual mutilation. This mutilation had the motive of letting the eunuchserve as a royal servant, ensuring he was incapable of sexual involvement with women at court or even procreating children by them. It

211 Niels-Erik A. Andreasen, *The Old Testament Sabbath: A Tradition-Historical Investigation*, SBL Dissertation Series 7 (Montana: Society of Biblical Literature, 1972), 14.

212 Gnana Robinson, *The Origin and Development of the Old Testament Sabbath* (Delhi: ISPCK, 1998), 3.

213 Paul D. Hanson, *The Dawn of Apocalyptic* (Philadelphia: Fortress Press, 1975), 194.

214 Jacob L. Wright and Michael J. Chan, "King and Eunuch: Isaiah 56:1-8 in Light of Honorific Royal Burial Practices," *Journal of Biblical Literature* 131 (2012): 99–119.

also ruled out the possibility of an 'alternative dynasty' competing with the king's lineage.[215] They were also often referred to as 'sexually mutilated.'[216]

Niels-Erik A. Andreasen presumes that there were "undoubtedly many eunuchs" present during the postexilic period, particularly among the returning exiles from Babylon.[217] Katherine Southwood suggests that the eunuchs were excluded from the postexilic Yehud community due to the reinterpretation and reapplication of Deuteronomy 23, which prohibited eunuchs from assembling the postexilic Yehud community because of their 'bodily defect.'[218] It presupposes that some of the eunuchs were Israelites who were probably marginalized and excluded from the postexilic Yehud community.

Sabbath Negotiating Social Identity in Isaiah 56:4-5

Isaiah 56: 4-5 is part of the broadersection of Trito-Isaiah (Isaiah 56-66) and belongs to the smaller unit of Isaiah 56: 1-8, which originated in Jerusalem after the exile. These verses typically date to the late sixth century BCE or the early fifth century.[219] Generally, they might address concerns regarding the role of the eunuchs in Israel's "restored community."[220] Considering that negotiation could indicate the identity of the minority and opposition positions,[221] this passage explores the negotiation of the identity of the eunuchs who were at the margins of the postexilic Yehud community.

Relationship with Yahweh

Verse 4.Thus, Yahweh says, *"To eunuchs who keep my Sabbaths and choose the things that please me, and hold fast my covenant."*

Verse 4 begins with the message formula, כֹּה אָמַר יְהוָה 'For thus says Yahweh," in the form of words used by a messenger to relay the words of a king.It indicates that the community has to listen to Yahweh's message about

215 Jacob L. Wright and Michael J. Chan, "King and Eunuch: Isaiah 56:1-8 in Light of Honorific Royal Burial Practices," 119.

216 Joseph Blenkinsopp, "Isaiah 56-66," in *The Anchor Yale Bible* (New Haven: Yale University Press, 2003), 130.

217 Andreasen, *The Old Testament Sabbath: A Tradition-Historical Investigation*, 37–38.

218 Katherine E. Southwood, "' And They Could Not Understand Jewish Speech': Language, Ethnicity, and Nehemiah's Intermarriage Crisis," *The Journal of Theological Studies* 62, no. 1 (April 2011): 443.

219 Andreasen, *The Old Testament Sabbath: A Tradition-Historical Investigation*, 37–38. See Robinson, *The Origin and Development of the Old Testament Sabbath*, 219.

220 Andreasen, *The Old Testament Sabbath: A Tradition-Historical Investigation*, 37–38.

221 Blenkinsopp, "Isaiah 56-66," 139.

the eunuchs.[222] This verse delivers a reassuring message from Yahweh to the eunuchs. The repetition of the first-person pronouns speaks of a relationship in which the people love what God loves and keep the Sabbath not out of obligation but because they are God's Sabbaths.[223] The Sabbath symbolizes a relationship with Yahweh. This verse, which addresses the Sabbath and eunuchs, counters any claim made in Deuteronomy 23 that excluded the eunuchs who devoted themselves to Yahweh.[224] This unique relationship that Yahweh shared with God's people affirms God's covenant with them (Gen 9:9, Judges 2:1; Exodus 31:16).

Belongingness

Verse 4. Thus, Yahweh says, *"To eunuchs who keep my Sabbaths and choose the things that please me, and hold fast my covenant."*

In this verse, after pronouncing the blessing in v. 2, the prophet addresses the eunuchs in the Jewish community. The issue of membership in the postexilic community is an essential subject in these verses.[225] The concern is for the eunuchs generally excluded from the community (Deuteronomy 23:1-7). So, the negotiation of the social identity of the eunuchs comes with three conditions: (i) the observance of Sabbath, (ii) choosing what is pleasing to Yahweh, and (iii) holding fast to the covenant.

This statement contrasts with the priestly prescriptions found in the Pentateuch (Genesis 17: 9-14; Exodus 12: 43-49), which are sacral customs of Israel. The sacrificial lamp has to be without blemish, and so does the one officiating the sacrificial cult.[226] However, in this verse, obedience and faithfulness to the covenant are so important in relation to the Sabbath observation that they override ritual considerations such as 'bodily defect.' Sabbath observance, not circumcision, is the criteria for membership in the community.[227] By keeping the Sabbath, the eunuchs are assured of not being excluded from community membership but integrated into it. This verse also implies that the eunuch is already in alignment with the characteristics of the Sabbath. Therefore, on the part of the eunuchs, Southwood presumes through this verse that "a strong relationship of belonging is desired" by the

---

222 John Goldingay, "Isaiah 56-66," *The International Critical Commentary* (Oxford: Bloomsbury, 2014), 64.

223 John N. Oswalt, "The Book of Isaiah 40-66", *The New International Commentary on the Old Testament* (Grand Rapids: William B. Eerdmans Publishing Company, 1998), 458.

224 Goldingay, "Isaiah 56-66", 76.

225 Paul D. Hanson, "Isaiah 40-66", *Interpretation* (Louisville: John Knox Press, 1989), 194.

226 Hanson, *The Dawn of Apocalyptic*, 194.

227 Blenkinsopp, "Isaiah 56-66", 135.

eunuch.[228] This verse clearly shows that the eunuchs desired to belong to the community that worshipped Yahweh, and their actions pre-decided their identity. In other words, ultimately, it was their decision to make this social identity.

Recognizing the Social Identity and the Struggles of the Eunuchs

Verse 5."*I will give them in my house and within my walls a monument and a name better than sons and daughters; an everlasting name will I give them which shall not be cut off.*"

This verse addresses the belief that one's presence and personality will continue only through children, who are responsible for burying and caring for the parents. Since the eunuchs cannot have children, this verse offers an alternative which will not obliterate their memory, which is thought of as 'the real and final death' since the name and descendants (*zera*', "seed") are inseparable (Isaiah 66: 22). The assurance given to the eunuch is that their 'name' will live on "in my house and within my walls."[229] This implies that the eunuchs will be members of the Jerusalem community ("in my house"), which also comes with civic status.[230] This indicates that eunuchs are not only granted membership but also a recognized identity within the Jerusalem cult community when negotiating their identity. The above discussion reveals that Sabbath functioned as a significant social identity marker in the postexilic period. The Sabbath facilitated the negotiation of the eunuch's social identity, which had previously been marginalized. It highlights the fluid nature of the Sabbath. By observing the Sabbath, eunuchs were granted community membership and a renewed relationship with Yahweh. Yahweh promised to act on their behalf, recognize their struggles, and provide them with a lasting monument and name, affirming their identity and inclusion within the community.

Indian Churches and the Negotiation of the Social Identity of Sexual Minorities

Sexual minorities[231] are a group whose sexual identity, orientation or practices are different from the majority of those in the society. They comprise lesbian, gay, bisexual and transgender individuals.[232] In heteronormative

228 Katherine Southwood, "The 'Foreigner' and the Eunuch: The Politics of Belonging in Isaiah 56:1-8," *Biblical Interpretation* 30, no. 4 (2020): 453.

229 Blenkinsopp, "Isaiah 56-66," 139.

230 Blenkinsopp, "Isaiah 56-66," 139.

231 The article acknowledges that there are diverse experiences of sexual minorities; however, due to the limitation of space, it has addressed them as a group.

232 Report of PUCL (People's Union for Civil Liberties) human rights violation against sexual minorities in India. http://www.pucl.org/Topics/Gender/2003/sexualminorities.

societies, the male-female binary often conceals sexual diversity, leading to identity challenges. In India, the sexual minority community remain a stigmatized and largely invisible community. They face discrimination in employment, health issues and personal rights.[233] The Indian Journal of Medical Research notes thatdue to such stigma and discrimination, many sexual minorities develop and suffer from emotional disorders. The social exclusion, discrimination, stigma and atrocities they face impact their self-esteem and sense of social responsibility.[234] Sexual minorities in India face multiple challenges related to their identities, which stem from deeply ingrained social, cultural, legal, and religious norms.

The National Council of Churches in India (NCCI), the apex body of protestant and Orthodox churches across India, ecumenical organizations, regional councils and agencies, in order to address the challenges faced by the sexual minorities, affirmed its "faithful commitment to the liberating Gospel of Christ in accompanying the gender and Sexual Minorities in order to affirm their respect, equality and dignity." It envisions the Church as a 'Just and Inclusive Community', a community in which 'people who are stigmatized and demonized' are reached out and be a 'listening community.'[235] In this effort, NCCI has facilitated various programmes that encourage churches and organizations to foster inclusivity. Despite these initiatives, the issue of sexual minorities remains a sensitive subject both in society and the Church.

The Church's role in shaping identity of its members is crucial. Romal Laisram, a gay Christian, recalls his experience of growing up as a Christian. He states that the church community defined his being, and the Church was the centre around the Church. However, he also recollects hearing from the Pastor, before he discovered he was gay, that "the gay people are the reason the world is ending, for our trials and tribulations in the world, for global warming. Everything terrible in the world was because of the gay people." These expressions created in him the negative understanding that being gay "was far worse than being a murderer." So, when he discovered his sexual identity, he withdrew away from the Church.[236] Such an atmosphere

pdf (accessed on 16th/09/2024).

233 C.K. Faisal, "On the Margins with Full Equality Still out of Reach," *The Hindu*, June 28, 2021, https://www.thehindu.com/opinion/lead/on-the-margins-with-full-equality-still-out-ofreach/article35008220.ece. (accessed on 16/09/2024).

234 Suresh Bada Math and Shekhar P.S., "The Invisible Ones: Sexual Minorities," *Indian Journal of Medical Research* 137, no. 1 (January 2013): 4–6.

235 National Ecumenical Forum for Gender and Sexual Diversities (NEFGD. https://ncci1914.com/ncci-nefgsd/ (accessed on 16/09/2024).

236 Joshua Muyiwa, "Queer Christians in India cautiously rebuild relationships with their churches," in *queerbeat, https://www.queerbeat.org/stories/queer-christians-in-india-*

of disapproval and disdain has led many sexual minorities to distance themselves from their churches. Yet, some sexual minorities continue to seek solace within the Church, striving to understand their identity and to belong. In such a context, the churches must negotiate the social identity of sexual minorities and those who seek to be part of the Church and are trying to understand their identities and place in the world. In Isaiah 56:4-5, the context in which the eunuchs faced social stigmatization and the observance of the Sabbath negotiated the social identity of the eunuch, integrating them into the community of the people of God. From this, some of the implications that could be drawn for the Indian churches today:

Acknowledging and Affirming the Relationship between God and Sexual Minorities

Yahweh recognized the eunuchs who kept Sabbaths, chose the things that pleased Yahweh and remained steadfast to the covenant. In other words, Yahweh affirmed their relationship. The churches, too, need to acknowledge the faith of sexual minorities. Their relationship with God and commitment to continuing in this relationship deserve acknowledgement and encouragement.

Creating a Sense of Belongingness in the Church: The Sabbath negotiated and created a sense of belonging in the community where they were usually excluded. The observance of the Sabbath became the criteria for becoming a community member and belonging to it, not their bodies. Similarly, churches today, the churches should not allow the sexuality of the sexual minorities to overshadow the commitment and the personhood of the sexual minority. The Church must actively challenge stigmatization and exclusion. It is pertinent to create space where the sexual minorities feel welcomed inside the Church, worship, and liturgy.

Negotiating the Social Identity of Sexual Minorities*:* The address to the eunuchs about the Sabbath acknowledged the constructed social identity of the eunuchs and the fluidity of the social identity of the eunuchs. The churches also need to acknowledge the socially constructed identity of heteronormative sexuality and be willing to negotiate the identities of the sexual minority.

Identifying the Struggles of the Sexual Minority*:* For the eunuchs who observed the Sabbath, recognizing that they cannot have children to carry on their names and legacy, the Sabbath offered a monument and a name. Many sexual minorities today experience the internal conflict of self-acceptance and acceptance from society and the Church. This struggle often makes it difficult for them to accept their identities. Today, it is crucial for

---

cautiously-rebuild-relationships-with-their-churches(accessed on 17/09/2024).

the churches to respond with sensitivity, recognizing and addressing the struggles of the sexual minority.

Conclusion

This article explores the role of the Sabbath in negotiating social identity within the early postexilic period, focusing on its implications for contemporary Indian churches and their approaches to sexual minorities. By examining Isaiah 56: 4-5, the observation was how the Sabbath served as an identity marker for integrating eunuchs, whom the traditional society marginalized. The text also illustrates that the observance of the Sabbath, rather than physical attributes, was necessary for identity within the postexilic community. The Sabbath's role in negotiating social identity is significant. It offers eunuchs belongingness within the community. Its observation affirms eunuchs' relationship with Yahweh and Yahweh's affirmation of their identity, providing a lasting legacy. The implications drawn from this study challenge the Indian churches to affirm the faith and commitment of sexual minorities, creating inclusive spaces and addressing their struggles with sensitivity. Thus, the Church, too, could embody the Sabbath as negotiating identity for a transformative marker of identity and belonging. In Isaiah 56:4-5, the Sabbath offers lessons for addressing social identity and inclusion issues in contemporary Indian churches.

16

Delving into the Chronicler's Narrative
An Examination of its Key Themes and Significance

Lalawmpuia Hauhnar

Introduction

There is a popular dictum in the sphere of theological education that every theology has its own context. In the same manner, every history has its own context, which implies that each historical writing is greatly shaped by its own context. This is true of the Chronicler's History, which is sometimes considered a secondary block of the history of Israel when compared to the Deuteronomistic History. It should, however, be understood that these two blocks of writing have their own concerns and ways of writing in their contexts and that both of them have their own principles and values.

There is a traditional understanding that the Chronicler's History includes Ezra, Nehemiah, 1 Chronicles and 2 Chronicles. However, the vast majority of scholars today adhere to the view that Ezra and Nehemiah should be separated from the books of Chronicles.[237] The Chronicler's History appears to have been composed several years after the writing of the books of Ezra and Nehemiah. This history is mainly composed of historical narratives, speeches, prayers, lists and genealogies.[238] As the Deuteronomistic History had already been in use for such a long period of

237 Steven Schweitzer, *Reading Utopia in Chronicles*, Library of Hebrew Bible/Old Testament Studies 442 (New York/London: T&T Clark, 2007), 3.

238 Cf. Schweitzer, *Reading Utopia in Chronicles*, 5–6.

time when the Chronicler's History was put into writing, the Chronicler's History can aptly be considered as a rereading or rewriting of the history of Israel from a different perspective. This article will, therefore, put its focus on the major concerns of the Chronicler's History and will evaluate the same from the context of the margins in India today.

Key Themes of the Chronicler's History

There are several important themes mentioned and discussed in the Chronicler's History. In spite of the fact that those different themes can be treated separately, they are yet closely connected with each other. We shall try to identify and discuss the major concerns of the Chronicler's Historiography such as Davidic kingship, Jerusalem temple, all Israel, and immediate reward and retribution.[239] It is expected that our discussion of the major concerns of the Chronicler's History can help us to understand the main intentions and purposes of the Chronicler in writing this history.

(a) Davidic Kingship

One of the most important concerns of the Chronicler's History is its emphasis on the Davidic kingship. There are several places where the same is elucidated in order to show its legitimacy. In fact, the whole structure of the Chronicler's History revolves around the matters concerning the Davidic kingship and its related issues. It is clearly shown that God elected David and his descendants to be the rulers of his people (1 Chr 10.14; 11.2-3; 2 Chr 13.5). Since Solomon, the builder of the temple, which is another significant concern of the writing is given prominence in the Chronicler's History (1 Chr 28.5; 29.1; 2 Chr 9.8), there is an idea that this kingship can well be interpreted as "Davidic-Solomonic Kingship."[240] However, it is quite appropriate to refer to this kingship as Davidic kingship since other kings after David including Solomon were the descendants of David.

What would be the reason why Davidic kingship occupies a central position in the Chronicler's History? While there is an opinion that the Davidic kingship was given great importance in order to make grounds for the eschatological hope for the restoration of Israel to its former glory, there is another idea that the same was emphasized for the purpose of legitimizing the postexilic temple cult. The second one puts the kingship in a secondary position to temple worship. In view of the intrinsic connection between the

239 In his discussion on the central themes of Chronicles, Ralph W. Klein has identified essential themes such as kingship, temple and cult, Israel, reward and retribution, attitude toward the Persians, personal piety, and future hope. Ralph W. Klein, *1 Chronicles: A Commentary*, edited by Thomas Krüger (Minneapolis: Fortress Press, 2006), 44-48.

240 Steven L. McKenzie, *1-2 Chronicles*, Abingdon Old Testament Commentaries (Nashville: Abingdon Press, 2004), 47.

kingship and the temple, however, these two observations should not be seen as opposite ideas. They rather should be taken to have complemented each other in the sense that the kings had profound roles to play in the temple and that the Chronicler idealized the periods of David and Solomon as the golden age for Israel. The fact that David established the dynasty and Solomon, his son, built the temple at the place where David had prepared signifies the relationship between the kingship and the temple.[241]

As a matter of fact, the Chronicler deliberately avoided mentioning the negative portrayal of David and his sons in the Deuteronomistic History, including David's adultery (2 Sam 11-12), Absalom's revolt (2 Sam 13-20) and Solomon's negative accounts (1 Kings 11), because those negative depictions would tarnish the face of the Davidic dynasty. With this brief introduction, we shall now turn to the chosen text to throw more light on the Davidic kingship.

Text: 2 Chronicles 13.4-7

[4] Then Abijah stood on the slope of Mount Zemaraim that is in the hill country of Ephraim and said, "Listen to me, O Jeroboam and all Israel! [5] Do you not know that the LORD God of Israel gave the kingship over Israel forever to David and his sons by a covenant of salt? [6]Yet Jeroboam son of Nebat, a servant of Solomon son of David, rose up and rebelled against his lord; [7]and certain worthless scoundrels gathered around him and defied Rehoboam son of Solomon, when Rehoboam was young and irresolute and could not withstand them.

Some Important Notes

The chosen text is taken from the account of the reign of Abijah as found in 2 Chronicles 13.1-14.1. Abijah, son of Rehoboam and Micaiah/Maacah[242] is introduced as a king of Judah in the eighteenth year of king Jeroboam in the northern kingdom. It is also mentioned that he reigned for three years in Jerusalem. After this brief introduction, the situation is explained as the time when Abijah engaged in battle with his counterpart in the north (2 Chr 12.16-13.3). It is in this context that the sermon or exhortation of Abijah to the Israelites (the northerners) (2 Chr 13.4-12) is creatively inserted. Paul K. Hooker is of the opinion that the war described in this text is perhaps not a historical battle but the creation of the Chronicler's theological imagination. He argues that it is unlikely that one king delivered a speech or a sermon to another and that the casualty numbers listed in verse 17 are apparently

241 McKenzie, *1-2 Chronicles*, 47-48.

242 Micaiah and Maacah appear to be variant spellings of one name. It is recorded as Micaiah in 2 Chronicles 13.2. But most Septuagint manuscripts and Syriac have it as Maacah which is in line with 2 Chronicles 11.20 (cf.1 Kings 15.2).

exaggerated.[243] Sara Japhet opines that “Unrealistic as this setting is, it provides the Chronicler with an opportunity to take a belated but categorical stand on the issue of the schism.”[244] While accepting certain aspects of this account as historical, H.G.M. Williamson admits that we cannot take all the details of this account in a literal sense and argues that "the account itself bears all the marks of the Chronicler's own ideology and style and must be attributed directly to him in its present form."[245] Therefore, we can say that the details of this account must be seen as the Chronicler’s creative work despite the possibility of connecting this account with certain event.

As the text is situated in the context of war, Abijah is seen to have spoken to his opponents from the slope of Mount Zemaraim, which is in the hill country of Ephraim, the territory claimed by the north. He addressed them as "O Jeroboam and all Israel." While "all Israel" is very often used in an inclusive sense, it seems that the same is used in this context to refer to the people in the northern kingdom (verse 4). The expression "Do you not know" (verse 5) is obviously a rhetorical question where the expected answer is affirmative because the people of the north are presented to have already known the election of David and his sons to be the rulers of his people by God.[246] The use of “covenant of salt” in this verse is apparently an indication of the perpetual nature of the election of the Davidic kingship as salt was the preservative per excellence in ancient times (cf. Lev 2.13; Num 18.19). The nature of Davidic kingship as expressed in verse 5 can be seen as a dynastic credo.[247]

In verse 6, Jeroboam, king of the northern kingdom, is presented as a rebel leader, meaning his claimed kingship is illegitimate. It is also mentioned in verse 7 by the Chronicler that Jeroboam gathered worthless scoundrels to strengthen his rebellion against the legitimate kingship. He is again presented as the one who took advantage of Rehoboam's weakness, as he was young and irresolute at that time. R.J. Coggin is right in saying that the picture of Rehoboam as young and irresolute sounds incompatible with the note that he was already 41 years old at that time (2 Chr 12.13).[248] But,

243 Paul K. Hooker, *First and Second Chronicles*, Westminster Bible Companion (Louisville: Westminster John Knox Press, 2001), 179-180.

244 Sara Japhet, *I & II Chronicles*, Old Testament Library (London: SCM Press Ltd, 1993), 690.

245 H.G.M. Williamson, *1 and 2 Chronicles*, The New Century Bible Commentary (Grand Rapids: Wm. B. Eerdmans Publ. Co./London: Marshall, Morgan & Scott Publ. Ltd., 1982), 250-251.

246 Hooker, *First and Second Chronicles*, 180.

247 Japhet, *I & II Chronicles*, 691.

248 R.J. Coggins, *The First and Second Books of Chronicles*, The Cambridge Bible Commentary. (Cambridge: Cambridge University Press, 1976), 196.

this kind of presentation is required for the Chronicler in order to create a negative picture of Jeroboam as an illegitimate king.

Interpretation

From the above notes, we can come to the conclusion that the Chronicler creatively inserted the speech of Abijah in his writing so that the legitimacy of the kingdom of Judah can clearly be explained. The perpetual character of the election of David and his sons to be the rulers of the people of God is also clearly demonstrated. On the other hand, in order to show the unacceptable nature and character of the northern kingdom, Jeroboam the king of the northern kingdom was presented as a rebel who collected wrong people against the legitimate king.[249] Curtailing the faults of Rehoboam in administration, the Chronicler presented him in this text as a young and irresolute person who could not withstand the rebels, and Jeroboam is presented here as the one who took advantage of the weakness of the legitimate king. From the points of emphasis given by the Chronicler, we can observe that the Chronicler was in a position where the legitimacy of the Davidic kingship stood in a dilemma in the face of other claimants of authority and leadership in the life of the people. In the context of the ideological battle between these two claims – one in the south and another in the north, the Chronicler skilfully constructed and inserted this text in order to promote the acceptability of the Davidic kingship. Even though they had lost their political independence at the time of his writing, the demonstration of the legitimacy of the Davidic kingship would make meaning and significance in terms of leadership amongst them.

Jerusalem Temple

Jerusalem temple occupies a very significant position in the Chronicler's History. Steven L. McKenzie rightly states that "The Chronicler wishes to demonstrate the centrality of Israel's religious life, with its heart in the temple, to its existence as a people."[250] It is understood in this writing that Jerusalem temple is the chosen place of God for his name to be there forever (2 Chr 6.5; 7.12, 16; 12.13; 33.7). Given the time of this writing, one may assume that there was a growing need to give a detailed description of the legitimacy and significance of Jerusalem based on the past history of the people of Israel. In that situation, the Chronicler deliberately emphasized the Jerusalem temple in his writing so that their community based on the temple would realize the restoration of their life.

---

249 Cf. Coggins, *The First and Second Books of the Chronicles*, 195-196.

250 McKenzie, *1-2 Chronicles*, 49.

As mentioned, there is a close connection between the kingship and the temple. Such being the case, the activities of the kings are also seen several times to have interconnected with the temple cult. David is seen to have brought the ark up to Jerusalem (1 Chr 13-16) and, prepared for the construction of the temple and set the worship life therein (1 Chr 22-29). Solomon is seen to have built the temple of the LORD in Jerusalem (2 Chr 2-7). It cannot be denied that David and Solomon attracted more attention than the other kings, at least partly because of their activities towards the temple. In fact, there seems to be a tendency on the part of the Chronicler to evaluate the life of the king on the basis of his commitment to the temple and the religious activities in that place. For example, Hezekiah's commitment to the temple cult helped him get detailed descriptions and positive notes about him and his activities in this writing (2 Chr 29-32). In order to make our points clear, we shall take one text and have a study on the same as given below.

Text: 2 Chronicles 6.3-6

[3] Then the king faced about and blessed all the assembly of Israel, while all the assembly of Israel stood. [4]And he said, "Blessed be the LORD, the God of Israel, who with his hand has fulfilled what he promised with his mouth to David my father, saying, [5]'Since the day that I brought my people out of the land of Egypt, I have not chosen a city from any of the tribes of Israel in which to build a house, so that my name might be there, and I chose no one as ruler over my people; [6]but I have chosen Jerusalem in order that my name may be there, and I have chosen David to be over my people Israel.'"

Some Important Notes

The chosen text is found in a broader sense in the accounts of the dedication of the temple built by Solomon (2 Chr 6.3-7.11) and in a narrower sense in Solomon's blessing upon the people (verses 2-11). At the same time, while we identify the chosen text as part of the blessing of the king upon the people, it can also be seen as a prophetic utterance that talks about the relationship between God and Israel right from the time of the deliverance from Egypt (verse 5).[251] It is on the fulfilment of the promises made by God to David that Solomon is seen to have uttered these words (cf. 1 Chr 17.23-24). In other words, the faithfulness of God upon his covenant is greatly extolled by Solomon. In verses 5 and 6, the election of Jerusalem and its temple out of all other places and the election of Davidic kingship are clearly spelt out.

251 Hooker, *First and Second Chronicles*, 141.

Interpretation

The chosen text tries to explicate the election of Jerusalem and its temple. It explains that the Jerusalem temple was founded as a fulfilment of the promises of God to David. As the election of the Jerusalem temple is intrinsically connected with the election of Davidic kingship, the chosen text also explains that David was chosen to be the ruler of the people of Israel. The use of "Israel" in this context five times can well be interpreted as an inclusive term in the sense that all the descendants of Jacob are included. The election of the Jerusalem temple automatically indicated the unsuitability of other places for worship, and the election of Davidic kingship disapproved of the claimed kingship of others. Therefore, we can say that the Chronicler attempted to express the legitimacy of the Jerusalem temple along with the rightfulness of the Davidic kingship in this text, for that kind of description would be of great help to provide hope and strength to the people in the context where some illegitimate claims of authority and leadership from different corners arose.

All Israel

It is natural that the Chronicler, as a Jerusalemite, gave his attention to the account of the southern kingdom. There is an observation that the northern kingdom got a space in his writing only when it overlapped with the southern kingdom. In this sense, one can assume that emphasis was given to Judah at the expense of Israel, following the style of Ezra-Nehemiah. However, the expression "all Israel" appears to have indicated a very significant point in our study and interpretation of the concerns of the Chronicler since this expression repeatedly occurs with significant implications in his writing. According to Williamson, the Chronicler used the term "Israel" 80 times about the divided monarchy. This word is used to mean the northern kingdom in the majority of these references (e.g. 2 Chr 10.16, 18, 19; 11.1, 13), and the same is employed to specify the southern kingdom in other places (e.g. 2 Chr 10.17; 11.3; 12.1, 6).[252]

Therefore, an expression "all Israel" seems to have been used to imply both the north and the south in an inclusive sense. In fact, the Chronicler included the northern kingdom in his genealogies. It is seen that "all Israel" witnessed the enthronement of both David and Solomon (1 Chr 11.1; 28.1), involved in the conquest of Jerusalem (1 Chr 11.4), took part in the transfer of the ark (1 Chr 13.2), and participated in the construction and dedication of the temple (2 Chr 1.2; 7.8).[253] It can be observed that the Chronicler

252 H.G.M. Williamson, *Israel in the Books of Chronicles* (Cambridge: Cambridge University Press, 1977), 102, 110.

253 McKenzie, *1-2 Chronicles*, 50.

gave importance to the unity of the people of Israel irrespective of their territorial background. Mentioning "The People" as one of the characteristic themes of the Chronicler's History, Williamson asserts that the Chronicler attempted "to mediate between the extreme 'exclusivists' and the extreme 'assimilationists' of his own day."[254] The unity of the people was no doubt a very important concern of this writing. The same can be explained further with the text given below.

Text: 1 Chronicles 11.1-3

[1] Then all Israel gathered together to David at Hebron and said, "Behold, we are your bone and flesh. [2]In times past, even while Saul was king, it was you who commanded the army of Israel. The LORD your God said to you: It is you who shall be shepherd of my people Israel, you who shall be ruler over my people Israel." [3]So all the elders of Israel came to the king at Hebron, and David made a covenant with them at Hebron before the LORD. And they anointed David king over Israel, according to the word of the LORD by Samuel.

Some Important Notes

The chosen text falls under the account of David's accession to the throne of Israel, and this particular text (verses 1-3) talks about the anointing of David at Hebron. It is taken almost verbatim from 2 Samuel 5.1-3 with the exception of one phrase, "according to the word of the LORD by Samuel" (verse 3). Hooker is of the opinion that "By adding this phrase, the Chronicler reminds his readers that David's kingship is neither the result of political machinations nor the accident of historical events but the specific expression of the divine will as articulated by Samuel."[255] Williamson also opines that this phrase is most probably the Chronicler's own addition and maintains that "The addition underlines the implication of *2b* that, as already noted, David's rule was the result of God's election for the sake of Israel."[256]

In addition, while the chosen text greatly resembles the same narrative in the Deuteronomistic History, it is interesting to note that the Chronicler omitted references to war with Ishbosheth and David's reign for seven years and six months in Hebron (2 Sam 2.1-4, 8-32; 5.4-5). Without mentioning David's tussles with Saul and his life struggles, which are elaborated in the Deuteronomistic History (1 Sam 18-30), the Chronicler simply mentioned that David was the commander of the army of Israel during the time of Saul and said that he was the one whom God elected to be the shepherd and ruler

254 Williamson, *1 and 2 Chronicles*, 26.

255 Hooker, *First and Second Chronicles*, 55.

256 Williamson, *1 and 2 Chronicles*, 97.

of his people Israel (verse 2). Therefore, the attempt of the Chronicler to explain the legitimacy of the kingship of David is quite apparent.

The use of "all Israel" in this text has significant implication for the historiography of the Chronicler in writing the history of Israel. It has signified the inclusion of not only all those who were in the north, but also those who were in the south including Judah.[257] The expression "*we are your bone and flesh*" is a language of kinship.[258] The Chronicler skilfully inserted this expression in verse 1 to signify the inherent unity of the people of Israel. It is apparent that the Chronicler attempted to portray as if a united Israel supported David right from the beginning.[259] So, instead of mentioning the political battles between David and other contenders for the authority over Israel, he used an expression "all Israel" to mean that all the people of Israel wholeheartedly accepted the kingship of David right from the beginning as a divinely ordained kingship. This is strengthened by the use of "all the elders of Israel" who made a covenant with David at Hebron before the LORD.

Interpretation

The intention of the Chronicler in describing the anointing of David is quite clear. William Johnstone is right in saying that this text "stresses Israel's unanimity in recognizing David as king."[260] There are three levels of acceptance of his kingship. The first one is his kingship as a divinely ordained one. The second one is the acceptance of his kingship by all of Israel. The third one, which is closely connected with the second one, is the approval of his kingship given by all the elders of Israel. As mentioned above, the use of "all Israel" implies the people both in the south and in the north. The election of David and his sons to be the rulers over Israel by God is mentioned in other places. The specific significance of the chosen text is its description that the kingship of David was approved by all of Israel as they were inherently related to each other. It can well be argued that the Chronicler tried to integrate all the descendants of Israel/Jacob in the context of their vulnerabilities in the face of several destructive forces so that they could realize their unity under the Davidic kingship and have a new hope for restoration.

---

257 Japhet, *I & II Chronicles*, 237.

258 Klein, *1 Chronicles: A Commentary*, 299.

259 Klein, *1 Chronicles: A Commentary*, 298.

260 William Johnstone, *1 and 2 Chronicles: Volume 1*, JSOT Sup Series 253 (Sheffield: Sheffield Academic Press, 1997), 142.

Immediate Reward and Retribution

The Chronicler's History is greatly characterized by the idea of immediate reward and retribution. It is clearly exhibited in this writing that each one is responsible for his or her behaviour. A very clear example is the story of Saul. It is mentioned that Saul died, and his monarchy was transferred to David due to his infidelity, disobedience and consulting a medium instead of seeking guidance from the LORD (1 Chr 10.13-14). In addition, several kings are mentioned to have received rewards following their faithfulness and punishment on account of their unfaithfulness. For example, Asa (2 Chr 14-16), Jehoram (2 Chr 21), Joash (2 Chr 24), Amaziah (2 Chr 25), Uzziah (2 Chr 26), Manasseh (2 Chr 33).[261] It is apparent that these stories try to demonstrate that there is either reward or retribution for everyone based on his or her life and conduct (cf. 2 Chr 12.5). After Solomon finished building the temple and the royal palace, God is said to have expressed thus: "If my people who are called by my name humble themselves, pray, seek my face, and turn from their wicked ways, then I will hear from heaven, and will forgive their sin and heal their land" (2 Chr 7.14). This expression plainly exhibits the theology of reward and retribution in the Chronicler's History. Raymond B. Dillard rightly asserts that "For the Chronicler sin always brings judgment and disaster, while obedience and righteousness yield the fruit of peace and prosperity."[262]

Text: 1 Chronicles 28.9-10

[9] "And you, Solomon my son, know the God of your father, and serve him with single mind and willing heart; for the LORD searches every mind, and understands every plan and thought. If you seek him, he will be found by you; but if you forsake him, he will abandon you forever. [10] Take heed now, for the LORD has chosen you to build a house as the sanctuary; be strong, and act."

Some Important Notes

The chosen text is an instruction of David addressed to his son Solomon, which is part of David's public instructions for the temple (1 Chr 28.1-21). While verse 9 can be seen as a general command, verse 10 can be interpreted as a specific command.[263] It is mentioned in 1 Chronicles 22.6-10 that while David intended to build a house in the name of the LORD, God did not allow him to do so because he shed so much blood. As a result,

---

261 McKenzie, *1-2 Chronicles*, 51-52.

262 Raymond B. Dillard, "Reward and punishment in Chronicles: The Theology of Immediate Retribution," *WTJ* 46/1 (Spr 1984): 165.

263 Johnstone, *1 and 2 Chronicles: Volume 1*, 278.

as per the word of the LORD that came to him, David charged his son Solomon to build a house for the LORD. The Chronicler presented David as having done good preparations in several ways for the construction of the temple even though he himself could not do the actual construction. His instructions to the people and to his son Solomon are parts of David's preparations for the same. There are some significant verbal words used in this text. "Know" in verse 9 does not indicate intellectual knowledge or acquaintance. Instead, it refers to the relationship between God and human beings. David's instruction to "serve" God with a single mind and willing heart in the same verse reflects the command of God to love God with all heart, soul and might, as found in Deuteronomy 6.5.[264]

After mentioning two things that Solomon should do towards God, the Chronicler identified two other things that God does towards human beings, such as to "search" every mind and to "understand" every plan and thought. This expression recalls the sinfulness of humankind before the flood, where it is mentioned that every inclination of the thoughts of their hearts was only evil continually (Gen 6.5). At the same time, while "search" is very often used in a judgmental sense, it can also be used as a connotation of longing which implies that God searches for a positive human response.[265]

Having said the responsibilities of Solomon towards God and God's way of looking at human beings, the Chronicler skilfully inserted a fundamental ideological principle that he will find God if he seeks him and that God will abandon him if he forsakes him. In other words, God will give him rewards for his obedience and faithfulness to him and punishments for his disobedience and unfaithfulness to God. As mentioned above, the Chronicler demonstrated with the accounts of different personalities that everyone is responsible for his or her behaviour and conduct. As Solomon was chosen to build the temple, David is seen in this text as encouraging him to stay strong and act so that he can fulfil his responsibilities as the chosen one for an important task (verse 10). The formula of encouragement found at the end of verse 10 (cf. verse 20 and 1 Chr 22.13)[266] is rendered in the New Jerusalem Bible as "go resolutely to work!"

Interpretation

From the above notes, it is clearly demonstrated that the Chronicler wanted to explain in this text that there is immediately either a positive result or a negative return based on one's behaviour and conduct. God is depicted as the one who looks at the heart and mind and understands every plan and

264 McKenzie, *1-2 Chronicles*, 214.

265 Klein, *1 Chronicles: A Commentary*, 524.

266 Klein, *1 Chronicles: A Commentary*, 524.

thought of human beings. It can be observed that the Chronicler creatively kept the idea of immediate reward and retribution in this text in the context where they were in dire need of emphasizing the importance of giving proper attention to temple worship and religious activities. This text has an implication that failure to fulfil one's responsibilities towards God can lead to the same pathetic situations that others have faced before.

Supporting Themes

Besides the significant concerns of the Chronicler's History mentioned above, there are some supporting themes that deserve to be mentioned. There are many *prophets* mentioned in the Chronicler's History. It is stated that they should not harm the prophets (1 Chr 16.22); instead, they should believe them (2 Chr 20.20). The list of the descendants of *Levi* is clearly found in 1 Chronicles 6 (starting from 5.27 in the Hebrew Bible). Their tasks are elaborated in 1 Chronicles 23-26 and in many other places of the Chronicler's History. *Scripture* is also given importance in this writing (1 Chr 15.15; 29.29; 2 Chr 34.21; 35.6; 36.22). It is also seen that the Chronicler gave importance to the positive attitude of the people (1 Chr 28.9; 29.9, 17, 22; 2 Chr 7.10; 30.25 etc). Also, some characteristic vocabularies in the Chronicler's History include success, rest, willingness, complete heart, unfaithfulness, rebellion, seek, loving-kindness, and others.[267] In spite of the fact that the themes mentioned above can stand on their own, they are seen to have supported the major themes of the Chronicler's History as discussed before.

Chronicler's History as History with a Purpose

The Chronicler's History is not a simple account or record of the history of Israel, as it is apparent that the Chronicler wrote this history from a particular perspective with a definite purpose in mind. Even though the Chronicler's History has some connections with Ezra – Nehemiah, it should be seen as a separate work written by a man of Jerusalem who was well versed with the socio-economic, political and religious life of the people of Israel during the first half or the middle of the fourth century BCE.[268] While he used different sources to write the history of Israel, it is clearly seen that he utilized his sources to convey significant messages to his own context. Despite the absence of well recorded crisis during his time, the Chronicler appears to have encountered different challenges in their socio-economic, political and religious life. It can be argued with a high degree of accuracy

267 McKenzie, *1-2 Chronicles*, 52-58.

268 See Lalawmpuia Hauhnar, "Revisiting the Scope of the Chronicler's History," *Mizoram Journal of Theology* 15/1 (January-June, 2024), 7-34.

that the Chronicler selected certain relevant points in order to preserve and promote his viewpoints.

To write history is to view and interpret the past with and through the eyes of the present. As a historian, the Chronicler did the same thing as he viewed the history of Israel from his own perspective. As a result, there are specific differences between the Chronicler's History and other sources of their history, particularly the Deuteronomistic History. As this writing came into black and white during the Persian domination, we can interpret it as a literature of resistance. In that sense, we can draw the significance of writing history with a purpose for those who are under domination. At the same time, in view of the Chronicler's emphasis on the centrality of the Jerusalem temple and the Davidic dynasty, we can see that the Chronicler himself attempted to perpetuate the cultic life centred around the urban setting and the idea of dynastic rule at the expense of rural areas and commoners. This kind of urban-centred and pro-dynastic mindset should be analyzed in a critical manner. In fact, to give too much emphasis on urban centres at the expense of rural areas and to perpetuate dynastic or hegemonic lines by denying the rights of commoners or others are not conducive to the idea of justice, freedom and equality of all people.

It can be seen that the Chronicler's historiography resulted in confident exclusivistic religious attitude and narrow-minded ethnic nationalism to some extent. Therefore, we can maintain that while the Chronicler's historiography can be seen as a resistance to the empire as well as an attempt to maintain their identity in the context of various challenges, it is also clearly seen that his emphasis on the centrality of Jerusalem temple and Davidic dynasty cannot simply be applied to our present context without critical evaluation. It is only through thorough analysis and understanding of the context of this writing that the implication of the same can meaningfully be drawn for our context today.

Concluding Remarks

From the above discussion on the Chronicler's historiography, we can draw some points as an implication of the same for our present context today. As mentioned before, the Chronicler's History was written during the time of Persian domination and became a recognized writing among the people of Israel during this time. It continued to be so during the time of the Greeks and even afterwards. In other words, the Chronicler's History came into existence as a literature of the subjugated people. In this sense, this writing can be interpreted as a resistance of the weak and vulnerable people to the powers of domination. In fact, literature is always a convenient and powerful tool of resistance for those who are under domination. In the Indian context, where domination is quite rampant in the forms of caste stratification, class distinction and gender discrimination, the Chronicler's historiography can meaningfully be applied to bring forth liberating interpretations of our history and theology.

As Christians belong to a minority group in India, there has always been an attempt from the majority side to conceal their participations and contributions for the nation due to various reasons.[269] In fact, their history is always excluded from the works of the historians in the mainstream.[270] In spite of the enormous contributions of Christians in the freedom movement, education, medical mission, social reformation and upliftment of the country, there has been a majority mindset that tries to label Christians as followers of foreign religions despite their presence in India since ancient times. With the rise of parochial Hindu nationalism under the banner of Hindutva, Christians and other minority groups have been targeted very often to have involved in anti-national activities. For such a time as this, it is an urgent task to write and interpret the history of the nation without sidelining minority groups. The participation and perspectives of minority groups should always be included in the history of the nation.

Furthermore, discrimination and other forms of oppression have crept into the structure of Christianity in India. It is pretty obvious that the Dalits, Tribals and women have been marginalized and oppressed in various ways by their fellow Christians due to their different backgrounds and ascribed status in the society. It is sad that their religious confession of being Christians can hardly provide them liberation from those oppressive social and religious structures within Christianity itself. In such a situation, we need to evaluate the nature of our Christianity and church structures with critical minds so that relevant and liberating interpretations of our history and theology can be provided. As a matter of fact, any historical fact and material can be identified, collected, viewed and interpreted from different perspectives and approaches, which can result in different interpretations and varied understandings of the same topic and event. As the Chronicler gave emphasis on certain significant themes in his writing in order to provide hope, strength and endurance to the people in the context of various forms of oppression and discrimination, we can also identify, select, view and interpret those topics and events that can bring forth liberative measures in our context today.

---

269 Cf. D. Arthur Jeyakumar, *Christians and the National Movement: The Memoranda of 1919 and the National Movement with Special Reference to Protestant Christians in Tamil Nadu: 1919-1939* (Calcutta: Punthi Pustak, 1999).

270 John C.B. Webster, *Historiography of Christianity in India,* Second Impression; (New Delhi: Oxford University Press, 2014).

At the same time, it is noted that the Chronicler wrote this history from the urban perspective in the sense that the centrality of Jerusalem and its temple is given great importance while rural areas are given very less significance. It is also seen that the Chronicler attempted to explain the legitimacy of the Davidic dynasty and the unacceptability of common people to be their ruler. In order to bolster his points, the Chronicler omitted David's adultery, Absalom's revolt, Solomon's negative accounts, etc. in his writing. It is obvious that giving too much emphasis on urban area at the expense of rural areas and perpetuating dynasty by sidelining the commoners cannot simply be applied in our context today. In fact, it is not a healthy approach to show special favour to some group of people at the expense of others. In view of the rise of communalism, Zionism, ethnic nationalism and the like, we need to carefully and sensibly write and interpret the history of Israel as well as our own history so that we can do away with various forms of domination and belligerent activities.

In addition, while the unity of the people and the idea of immediate reward and retribution can be used in a positive sense on the one hand, they can also be used to reinforce domination over others on the other hand. In the situation where everybody realizes the need to remove oppressive structures and domination by advocating equality, justice and freedom, we need to carefully study the biblical texts so that we can provide meaningful and relevant interpretations for our present context.

17

Stirring-Up Rooted Solidarity While Living Alongside Children

Rohan P. Gideon

When they came to the home of the synagogue leader, Jesus saw a commotion, with people crying and wailing loudly. He went in and said to them, "Why all this commotion and wailing? The child is not dead but asleep." But they laughed at him.

(Evangelist Luke)[271]

"But moving along this pole of pain-pathos, we can see the reality of Dalit goddesses or gods as the mortals-turned deities who have been killed in their very act of protecting the village boundaries in times of danger. Majority of the local deities are slaughtered in this process of expressing their solidarity and giving new life to the weak and suffering Dalits."

(K. Jesurathnam)[272]

This article presents what solidarity looks like when working along with children towards advancing and affirming the agency of children. Resources for the arguments are drawn from theological interpretations of solidarity that advance the agency of the marginalized. Solidarity, while working alongside children, necessitates rooted solidarity of adults. The entitled adult mindset has the moral challenge of identifying two conflicting yet

271 Luke10:38-40

272 K. Jesurathnam, "Towards a Dalit Liberative Hermeneutics: Re-reading The Psalms of Lament", *Bangalore Theological Forum*, Volume 34, Number 1, June 2002: 1-34.

potential areas: the area that affirms the space for the agency of the child through solidarity and advocacy and the area which traditionally entitles the adults that impinge on the potential space for the agency of the child.

This article is dedicated to Prof. Kondasingu Jesurathnam, my teacher and respected senior faculty colleague at the United Theological College. As our teacher in Biblical theology, he provoked us to think about why there was commotion and turmoil wherever Jesus went and why Jesus went where there was commotion. My thoughts on rooted-solidarity, especially while living alongside and working with children, are the theological commotions. Solidarity of adult communities stands as one of the foremost liberative methods in the contexts of the violation of the dignity of children and their rightful place in the society. Ironically, the violations are outcomes of the adult communities that prescribe ageism that specifically undermines children's age and age-related capacities. Through ageism, the adults are able to control and colonize the minds and bodies of children in the pretext of socializing the children and help them towards a level of maturity, which is usually favourable to the adults.[273] My bigger argument is that for the agency of child to take a form, manifest and thrive in unfavourable theological and cultural conditions, there must be a robustly supplementing understanding of 'rooted solidarity of the adults' along with a well thought through theology of the 'immanent mystery.'[274] In a world that intimidates children at every possible level and instrumentalizes them, the agency of the children needs the rooted solidarity of the adult community. The combination of the agency of the child and the rooted solidarity can be theologically strengthened by recognizing the immanent mystery that is present in children while addressing the mystery of God and God's manifestations. More specifically, the entitled adult mindset has the moral challenge of identifying two conflicting areas and deliberately stirring up its thought process: the area that affirms the space for the agency of the child through solidarity and advocacy and the area which traditionally entitles the adults that impinge on the potential space for the agency of the child.

The understanding of the agency of the child considers the impact children make by their presence as social and political actors and also by their views and expression. These views and expressions emerge out of their endowed wisdom as complementing and supplementing the conversations

273 Rohan P. Gideon, "Battered Bodies and Scarred Emotions of Labouring Children in India: Interrogating Dichotomies, Envisioning Embodiment" in Martin Tamcke and Gladstone Jathanna eds, *Body, Emotion and Mind: 'Embodying' the Experiences in Indo-European Encounters* (Studies on Oriental Church History/ StudienzurOrientalischenKirchengeschichte), 2013.

274 Rohan P. Gideon, *Advancing the Agency of the Child: Theological and Methodological Principles* (Delhi: Christian World Imprints, 2024). Forthcoming

but also as fierce responses to the desecration of their rights and dignity. The agency of the child can be elucidated at two levels: i. children's capacity to express their views and opinions that affirm the wisdom endowed in them as human beings, and ii. their capacity to interrogate the difficult socio-cultural and political circumstances that affect their being and becoming. Both these understandings have the potential for newness of understanding our existential issues. Nuancing it further, acknowledging the capacity of children to define their agency must consider different age groups of children because of the period of exposure and socializing they have in their contexts. Children's suppressed subjectivity or agency is a cultural and religious product of the adult impositions on children. In such contexts, the opinions and experiences of children are ignored and neglected. For this reason, the understanding of the agency of the child should include children's presence and participation as much as their views and expression coming from certain knowledge systems endowed in them alongside their views that come from their suppressed subjectivity.

It is with a sense of shared humanity that the theological understandings of solidarity work at various intersection of sociological, political, religious and gender definitions. Anselm Min speaks of solidarity as having four interrelated meanings that bridge secular and religious definitions. Firstly, solidarity is an ontological category reflecting the constitutive interdependence of all reality; in other words, solidarity names that all human beings are connected by their very nature. Second, solidarity is a historical process whereby all nations and aspects of life are becoming increasingly interdependent. Third, it is an ethical concept where, realizing one's interrelatedness to others as human beings and the historical process that links one in an even greater web of connection, one is drawn to acts of ethical and political solidarity. Finally, solidarity is a theological principle, described in Christian terms as the "communion of saints" in which all humanity is bound together by the Holy Spirit as children of God.[275]

Delving into the debates on solidarity, we are confronted with the following questions: Where do we draw the necessary lines between advocacy and solidarity? While we advocate on behalf of those whose voices are not heard loudly and well, do our thoughts and words represent the lesser-heard communities adequately well? How well do we feel being one among the representing communities while we advocate? Do our feelings of oneness translate well into the idea and practice of solidarity? Do those in solidarity embody under-privilege as a critique of their own privilege?

---

275 Anselm K. Min, The Solidarity of Others in a Divided World: A Postmodern Theology After Postmodernism (New York: T. T. Clark International, 2004), 140–41.

The Rooted Solidarity of the Adults

Much of the advancing of the agency of the child happens with rooted-solidarity as an adult responsibility. Rooted-Solidarity calls the adult world to empathetically listen to children and be responsibly silent during the act of listening. Empathetic and responsible listening of adults further facilitate them to engage in and embody two narratives: i. the narratives of adults' own childhood experiences and the stories and narratives of children, which could be dissimilar to their own but coming from similar social and cultural contexts that belittle children, put children at risk and make children vulnerable.

In the act of empathetic and responsible listening, the adults would assess the following: to go back to our roots, which is childhood, and see if we were once victimised or wronged against; what were some of the most vulnerable situations we have had been in; and how the memories of such vulnerabilities and subsequent victimisation have conditioned our current mindset to address the situations of victimization of children around us. Equally importantly, as adults, when we are in positions of power to make decisions or even in a position to influence the decisions, what do we become: perpetrators of violence or exhibited a sense of empathy for the victims?; what mindset takes over when we are in a position of power? Will it be a selective amnesia that we were once victims of, and now it is our time to enjoy the power and privilege that we were deprived of? or will it be a sense of deeply rooted solidarity that we will not let recreate a sense of risk or vulnerability because we did not like to be at risk and vulnerable ourselves? The characteristics of rooted solidarity involve a redefined responsibility of not just representing (as in advocacy) but also listening to the extent that finally, what the adult world listens as individuals and groups will convert into a community activity of listening and opening up spaces for the voices of children. Such community activities will create flourishing spaces for more authentic agency of the child.

The theme 'rooted solidarity of the adults' constantly throws up some challenges. Initially, the dominant adult mindset has the moral challenge of identifying two conflicting areas: to create an affirmative space for the agency of the child and, simultaneously, time to create a space for its advocating act and solidarity without impinging on the potential space for the agency of the child.

Immensely nuanced knowledge of our contexts, before defining what is solidarity and what is not, is most important. To understand the context at a broad level, Rowan Williams warns us of at least three forms of activities that could simply pass off as forms of solidarity, which, in fact, are not. In his

Bampton lectures on solidarity[276], Williams calls solidarity as both a condition and an imperative, which, in turn, informs us that communitarianism as a moral priority is presented glorifiedly as disentangled from individualism, the notion of the common good, and the empathy in its simplistic sense of feeling awful or emotional are either projected or prescribed as movements of solidarity. Communitarianism has the tendency to moralize practices to an extent that they get vested in a few entitled families or select communities. While communitarianism, by definition, can interrogate individualism, in effect, it moves towards systems very similar to individualism, as in select families or select communities that define the working ethos. The notion of common good has, historically, not been effectively practiced, thus questioning its relevance. Also, the claims to our ability to empathize with the victims of social structures, both historically and specific-contextually has to be consciously assessed as the pain and suffering of individuals or specific communities are unique.

The openness to contextual knowledge of the adult-child binaries, their challenges and their potentials offer negotiable spaces for theory and praxis. As observed in liberation theologies in India and children-related theologies in general, the advocates of the subalterns delicately, if not impeccably, recognise that grassroot activism at any scale is crucial as it challenges the notion of an established space. This is because the established spaces are rigid and less likely to grasp the availability of liberative resources outside their spaces. These explanations also open up spaces for a critique of the practice of advocacy or solidarity that adult-centric ideologies proclaim.

Advocacy is basically didactic in nature, and its objective is to conscientize the public of discrimination and speak on behalf of the voiceless marginalized. The acts of conscientizing and speaking mean good towards the agency of the marginalized, in our case, the child. The advocates are constantly challenged to journey through a transformative process between their entitled-self and their solidarity-self that represents the child, which finally upholds the agency of the child than the entitled adult-self. Failure to achieve this transformation leads to a failure in sincerely advancing the agency of the child. More specifically, the danger of employing an uncritical didactic method in Christian theology will lead to the traditional didactics of the so-understood Great Commission to tell, preach, proclaim and initiate into certain religious ways of knowledge, which will promote a dominant and vicious circle of advocacy and colonization.[277]

---

276 University Church, The Bampton Lectures 2024 Lecture 1, February 27, 2024, YouTube video, 55.50 https://www.youtube.com/watch?v=vXOeQ1dSkxI&t=2516s

277 Rohan Gideon, "Children's Agency and Edinburgh 2010: The Great Commission or a Greater Omission?" in Mitzi Smith and Jayachitra Lalitha eds. *Teaching All Nations:*

Advocacy, as an act of representing, confronts stumbling blocks before opening up to potential of being in the act of solidarity. Advocacy has the ability to misjudge the power to represent. When the subalterns speak the language of the dominant, the advocates must be able to discern it. Otherwise, it completes a vicious circle where the representers re-hear their own language in the expressions of the children to make it easier for them to represent, speak or preach their own perspective of the narrative. Advocacy may not be truthful to the oppressed narratives thus strangle the advancing of the agency of the marginalized.

Listening to and representing children in the context of advocacy has legal implications. In rights-violated situations, the advocates will have to resort to a legal language that is mostly couched in philosophical debates and probabilities rather than in the languages and emotions of children. The uniqueness of experiences may not find an authentic place in the legalese involving the violated-against children. However, these negative practices allow for a positive turnaround if the advocates are able to open up more careful and responsible listening spaces. Mark Taylor[278] sees mysterious or potentially invigorating spaces for the entitled advocates to move towards being more authentic.

Taylor dwells on the theme of 'delirium' through his account of advocacy. Delirium or the mysterious space is the differential that the engaging spaces offer to the advocating dominant. This mystery subsequently promotes responsible advocacy when the advocates potentially expose themselves to the context of solidarity and explore the liberative resources, which is a movement away from their imperial self. The ability to accept the profound uncertainty in the face of the other enhances the value of the learning spaces. Taylor says:

> I stress that authentic advocacy means embracing such mysteries, but entering this delirium does not replace or sidestep the need for disciplined scholarly endeavor in subaltern studies. By no means. Mystery and delirium concern merely one crucial dimension of subaltern studies, one that is especially crucial to acknowledge if we are to subvert the pretensions and assimilations to which entitled subaltern advocates are especially prone.[279]

Interrogating the Matthean Great Commission (Minneapolis: Fortress Press, 2014): 195-216

278 Mark Lewis Taylor, "Subalternity and Advocacy as Kairos for Theology," in *Opting for the Margins: Postmodernity and Liberation in Christian Theology,* ed. Joerg Rieger (Oxford: Oxford University Press, 2003): 23-44.

279 Mark Lewis Taylor: "Subalternity and Advocacy as Kairos for Theology," 39

To echo Taylor's perspective in this context, it is in the adults interacting actively with the child that advances both the child's agency and sees the agency of the child beyond the restricted realm of the adult-child binary.

Joerg Rieger and Rosemarie Henkel-Rieger's explanation of 'deep solidarity' offers a noteworthy explanation and unpacks our thoughts for deeper questions on solidarity. For Rieger and Henkel-Rieger,

> "Solidarity is no longer a matter of the relatively privileged trying to help the underprivileged and to solve their problems; rather, it is a matter of understanding that nothing will change unless we are addressing the problems of the world together. And deep solidarity is the recognition that we might be in the same boat."[280]

Crucial to Rieger and Henkel-Rieger's thoughts are moving beyond even the nuanced binaries of relatively privileged-underprivileged. They explain their concept in the context of ruthless neoliberal capitalist economics where more people are getting underprivileged by the day only to see that all wealth and privileges are concentrated among a few. Rieger and Henkel-Rieger are mindful of the differences and "where all other forms of oppression along the lines of race, ethnicity, gender, sexuality, etc., are bundled"[281]

Expanding the scope of the metaphor in the context of adult-child binary, the existential journeys and travel of children and childhoods can happen at different levels of luxuries: the privileged in luxurious and secured means, while the underprivileged in the most insecure of and unsafe boats to move across to cities, states and continents. When hit by the same storm or tempest on the same sea, the responses vary depending on degrees of security. The secured means have a greater possibility of reaching the shores than the unsafe ones.

So, a deeper understanding of solidarity for the adult-centric world to exercise and to advance the agency of the child is 'rooted solidarity'. Rooted solidarity begins with the idea that adulthood is an embodiment of childhood experiences. The adults have their roots in their childhood. Their childhood would have experienced deprivation, biases and negligence as much as privileges and protection. For the agency of the child to be advanced, the adult community has to recall its own experiences and narratives of vulnerability and deprivation to help empathize with children who face injustice and vulnerability.

---

280 Rieger, J. & Henkel-Rieger, R., 'Deep solidarity: Broadening the basis of transformation', HTS Teologiese Studies/ Theological Studies 73(3), 2017, a4578. https://doi.org/ 10.4102/ hts.v73i3.4578

281 Rieger, J. & Henkel-Rieger, R., 'Deep solidarity.

18

'Sacred and Fetishized Narratives' Certain Receptive Practices of the Bible

Allan Samuel Palanna

It is with immense joy and deep respect that I dedicate this article in celebration of a remarkable milestone: the Shastiabdapoorthi of Prof. Rev. Dr. K. Jesurathnam, my teacher and colleague. His journey as a teacher and Professor of the Old Testament has been a beacon of inspiration and wisdom to many. His teaching and research are a reflection of the power of faith, education, and service. His commitment to nurturing the intellectual and moral growth of his students has been unwavering. The present article was originally presented as the Mary Jones Lecture, 2024 on the invitation of the Bible Society of India, Bengaluru.

A Society of Walking Women

We gather together because of the inspiring narratives of young women such as Mary Jones, a teenager whose yearning for a Bible and her thirty-mile walk triggered an entire movement of the Bible Society, whose formation day we are commemorating today. Interestingly, there is an Indian connection to Mary Jones in history. Crayden Edmunds, who was secretary of the Calcutta Auxiliary of the Bible Society, recalls thus: "At the afternoon service, I told [the Khasi Christians at Cherra Poonjee] the story of Mary Jones...when Dr Roberts [the translator of the Khasi Old Testament and the reviser of the

New] declared that he had both seen and spoken to Mary herself when he visited the village of Bryncrug many years ago."[282]

There may have been many more nameless young women, such as Mary Jones, who walked too, and that eventually led to the establishment of the Bible Society. Thomas Charles, the facilitator of the Bible Society himself, wrote thus:

> The possession of a Bible produces a feeling among them which the possession of no one thing in the world besides could produce... ***Young females in service have walked thirty miles*** to me with only the bare hopes of obtaining a Bible each; and returned with more joy and thanksgiving than if they had obtained great spoils. *We who have half a doz. (sic) Bibles by us, and are in circumstances to obtain as many more, know but little of the value those put upon one, who before were hardly permitted to look into a Bible once a week.*[283]

The words of Thomas Charles uttered in the early part of the 19th century point to the many nameless women who initiated a movement that has stood the test of time. There is also a hint of self-evaluation on the part of Thomas Charles as he critiqued himself and his companions for not valuing the Bible enough as much as the young women who strived hard for the Bible did. What also appears ironically true today is that the more we have access to the Bible and are in possession of 'many more, know but little of the value' of the Bible, as Thomas Charles had predicted.

The not-so Receptive Practices of the Bible

It is to be recalled that the establishment of Bible societies around the world did not naturally lead to transformation. Such a romanticized view of any history of institutions would mask the dehumanizing narratives associated with the publication and distribution of the Bible around the world. It is to be recalled that there has also been the selective printing of the Bible in order to serve the interests of slave owners who (mis)used the Bible to suit their unjust ends. The notorious "Slave Bible" is one among many instances. Originally designed as a teaching tool for people who were forced into slavery to learn reading and as a means for missionaries to introduce Christianity in British colonies, the primary objective of "The Slave Bible" was to induce theophobia. This involved instilling a fear of God's wrath in

---

282 William Canton, *A History of the British and Foreign Bible Society*, Vol. 1 (London: John Murray, 1904), 469.

283 Thomas Charles, cited in E. Wyn James, *Bala and the Bible: Thomas Charles, Ann Griffiths and Mary Jones*, 77. https://biblicalstudies.org.uk/pdf/eusebeia/05_069.pdf. Accessed on 8th February, 2024. Emphasis mine.

converts to serve the interests of slave owners and supportive governments through missionary efforts. Due to concerns that the contents of the Bible could incite rebellion, a significant portion of the traditional Bible was omitted from "The Slave Bible." Out of the original 1189 chapters, 957 were excluded, and numerous chapters and verses that spoke of liberation within the included books were also left out. Only those chapters that explicitly upheld exploitation were included.[284] Martin Luther once wrote that the human heart is curved in on itself, and that humans have an innate ability to turn anything toward the benefit of themselves, the Bible and even God. Here is how Luther put it in his *Lectures on Romans*:

> Our nature, by the corruption of the first sin, so deeply curved in on itself (*incurvatus in se*) that it not only bends the best gifts of God towards itself and enjoys them…it so wickedly, curvedly, and viciously seeks all things, even God, for its own sake.[285]

The common misconception still prevails in India that the British rule helped the Bible Society in India. However, this was not the case as the missionaries found it difficult to continue their mission due to the lack of support from the colonial authorities.[286] The inception of the Bible Society of India in Calcutta in 1811 was met with stiff opposition from the members of the East India Company. William Canton records that: "In India…missionaries English and American, were forbidden to land. In England appeals were made to political and commercial timidity to eject all missionaries from the Company's territories, and to arrest the translation of the Scriptures into the native languages."[287] The later missionary translations were not without problems since the missionaries were enmeshed in colonial mentality which affected the translations.

That is certainly why a subversive reading of the Bible acts as a prism through which colonialism is called to question. Pandita Ramabai Sarasvati was awakened early to the pitfalls of colonial missionary translation of the Bibles for the Church in India due to its inherent colonial and visibly Sanskritic character. Ramabai, therefore, took on the formidable challenge of translating the Bible from its original Hebrew and Greek versions into local Marathi. This effort aimed to replace the Marathi Bibles of her day, which were either written in the form of Marathi influenced by colonial

284 See Whyte, C. (2020). *Select parts of the Holy Bible for the use of the Negro Slaves in the British West-India Islands* (London, 1807).

285 Martin Luther, *Lectures on Romans*, qtd. in Mark Johnston, *Saving God* (Princeton: Princeton University Press), 88.

286 cf., Timothy J. Gorringe, *Furthering Humanity: A Theology of Culture* (Aldershot: Ashgate Publishing Ltd, 2004), 185-186

287 William Canton, *A History of the British and Foreign Bible Society* Vol. 1, 266.

missionaries or containing highly Brahminicized expressions. Ramabai made significant efforts to steer clear of both influences.[288]

The Bible continues to provide inspiration amidst the suffering realities of our times. The Bible does not necessarily present explicit arguments for God's existence. Instead, it portrays instances of conflict, anger, doubt, anguish, and a feeling of being lost, where individuals struggle to sense God's presence.[289] Rowan Williams says, "Don't imagine that the Bible is full of comfortable and reassuring things about the life of belief and trust; it isn't. It is often about the appalling cost of letting God come near you and of trying to trust him when all the evidence seems to have gone."[290] This, perhaps, is the character of the way in which the church in India has read the Bible.

The Solo-ist Understanding of the Bible

A significant misconception, especially stemming from Protestant missionary influence, concerns the interpretation of 'sola' in the phrase "sola scriptura," or scripture alone. This term has come to represent an absolute, closed, normative, and authoritative understanding of the Bible that continues to shape church doctrines. The concept of sola scriptura presents both challenges and opportunities. When scripture is viewed as the ultimate, self-contained, final, and comprehensive revelation of God, it restricts the possibility of God's ongoing revelation beyond the written text. This perspective challenges the freedom of God to reveal new and surprising aspects of divine truth. However, acknowledging scripture as divinely inspired or God-breathed, as stated in II Timothy 3:16, suggests that the divine breath cannot be confined or absolutised. Limiting this breath can be stifling and diminish its life-giving potential. The life-enhancing breath of God, when controlled by those in charge of canonization and interpretation, risks losing its vitality and inspirational power.

In the Indian context, the understanding of the Bible is notably distinct due to its diverse interpretative traditions. Indian perspectives balance the inspiration ethic with the idea of an unbound word of God (II Timothy 2:9). The concept of sola scriptura in this context represents an unfettered, dynamic word of God that resists dominant canonical and hermeneutical constraints imposed by prevailing powers. This understanding of scripture emphasizes that texts embodying life-affirming values carry the divine

288 Meera Kosambi, 'Indian Response to Christianity, Church and Colonialism: Case of Pandita Ramabai,' *Economic and Political Weekly*, October 24-31, 1992, 65.

289 Rowan Williams, *Tokens of Trust: An Introduction to Christian Belief* (London: Canterbury Press, 2007), 21.

290 Rowan Williams, *Tokens of Trust: An Introduction to Christian Belief*, 21.

breath of God while rejecting interpretations that undermine the inherent worth of the divine image in all humans and the integrity of creation.[291]

The emphasis on sola scriptura emerged as a historical necessity for the reformers who sought to counter the ecclesiastical magisterium's control over scripture. This shift laid the foundation for 20th-century fundamentalism, which also draws from the idea of a sacralized Bible. Weinrich writes that "the exclusivity that was hereby transferred to it (bible) can in a certain sense be understood as a sacralisation of the Bible…it meant a spiritual and theological gain in authority, for now, the Scripture alone, *sola scriptura*, was the source of content and the material criterion *(fons et index)* for the recognition of faith."[292] This shift from church authority to biblical authority did not fully address the politics of scriptural interpretation or the interests influencing translations. Consequently, Protestant fundamentalism in India and the normative interpretations of scriptures can be traced back to a claim of authenticity based solely on scripture.

Crucially, while reformers emphasized the scriptures, they recognized Jesus Christ as the ultimate Word of God—the eternal Logos made flesh. The written text was never intended to overshadow the living Word, whose life, death, and resurrection transcended the written scriptures. When this Christ-centered perspective is embraced, it allows for the recognition of suffering bodies as sacred texts, affirming that '*verbum caro factum est'*—the Word became flesh. John Rogerson's insight remains pertinent: "Any responsible use of the Bible must acknowledge that it comes from a culture completely different from modern Western society. It must also recognize that the Bible does not address many contemporary issues directly. However, this does not mean the Bible cannot contribute to modern discussions. Despite its historical context, the Bible has the potential to bring light and hope to a world still darkened by ignorance and inhumanity."[293]

The Dangers of Fetishization of the Bible in India

There appears to be a contradiction of sorts when analysing the Indian reading of the Bible. While theologians across decades have proposed various Indian readings of the Bible, such as contextual reading of the

291 Allan Samuel Palanna, 'Reformation and Renewal: Scriptures, Justification and Priesthood of All and the End of Priestcraft,' *Bangalore Theological Forum*, Vol. XLIX No.1) June 2017), 163-172.

292 Michael Weinrich, 'The Openness and Worldliness of the Church,' in Wallace M. Alston Jr. and Michael Welker (ed.) *Reformed Theology: Identity and Ecumenicity* (Grand Rapids, Michigan: William B. Eerdmans Publishing Company, 2003), 418. Emphasis original.

293 Cited in Fleur S. Houston, *You shall Love the Stranger as Yourself: The Bible, Refugees and Asylum* (New York: Routledge, 2015), 2.

Bible, Liberation Hermeneutics, Inter-faith Hermeneutics, Dhvani method, community readings and the like.[294] The overt fetishization of the Bible in India must also be addressed.

A fetish is any object regarded by those with superstitions as possessing mystical abilities or any object or action to which one unreasonably attaches irrational devotion to. Certain practices of fetishization of the Bible amongst the ordinary Christian communities in India may bring perspectives as to the glorified, almost idolized status of the Bible or abject disregard of the Bible. In both cases, the Bible is held to the point of irrelevance. Some instances may be shared that may have echoes in our everyday experiences:

a. Stagnant Family Bible/s placed at dedicated places in homes, albeit gathering dust.
b. Bibles were converted into portable museums of old memorabilia.
c. Bibles are used as good luck charms or protective symbols, especially around babies and those suffering from mental health issues, in order to overcome or ward off 'dosha' (mistake/problem).
d. Burying the deceased persons along with their personal bibles.
e. Bibles are used as oath taking or truth-telling devices.
f. Extensive markings of various colours in the Bible show familiarity with texts. (other un-highlighted texts presumably become redundant!)
g. Irreplaceably worn-out leather covers to project piety of personal Bibles.
h. Bibles are kept open under glass cases or at the altar/pulpit, which is almost invariably open to the book of Psalms (purely for balancing the book).
i. Highly adorned Bible cases in churches or display Bibles next to the church gates often becoming final resting places of insects hit by the glaring lights focussed on the open stagnant Bible whose pages are never turned for years.

The above practices are only representational of the many fetishized practices that exist amongst people who associate themselves with a particular nature of the Bible to exert influence through its essentialized physicality. Popular piety and disregard of the Bible go hand in hand in the everyday congregations in India.

294 A more diverse understanding of Indian reading is discussed in Sam P. Mathew, 'Indian Biblical Hermeneutics: Methods and Principles,' *Neotestamentica*, Vol. 38, No. 1 (2004), 100-126.

When Narrative becomes Life

When his father eventually converted to Christianity and wanted to learn more about Jesus, Sadhu Sundar Singh once advised him: "If you want to understand Christ, read the Bible. But if you wish to experience a personal relationship with him, you need to pray."[295] Practice authenticates and vigorously validates confession. Dietrich Bonhoeffer pleads with the faith communities to dwell on 'the deed', that 'the primary confession of the Christian before the world is the deed which interprets itself. If the deed is to have become a force, then the world itself will long to confess the Word'.[296] The Church is never a finished event. It forever challenges faith communities to identify moral and ethical gaps in the use of the Bible, re-imagine the Bible as a living breath of God and resist attempts to make the Bible irrelevant to the cries of the most vulnerable communities and the earth.

295 Cited in A. J. Smiles, 'Sadhu Sundar Singh: His Contribution to Indian Christian Theology.' *Indian Journal of Applied Research*, Vol.11/03 (March, 2021), 71.

296 Dietrich Bonhoeffer, 'The Nature of the Church,' in *A Testament to Freedom: The Essential Writings of Dietrich Bonhoeffer*, Geoffrey Kelly and F. Burton Nelson (ed.) trans. John Bowden (San Francisco: HarperCollins, 1990), 91.

Section - Four

Bible, Ecology, Women and Mission

19

Image and Likeness in Genesis 1:26-28

Chilkuri Vasantha Rao

Tributes

Rev. Dr. Prof. K. Jesuratham, fondly called Jesu, has been a friend and colleague in the Department of Old Testament. His scholarship has constantly enriched me, and I am baffled by his art of guiding students at the Graduate, master and Doctoral levels with high success rates. His commitment to academics is much appreciated. As he turns 60, marking this occasion is a great blessing, and with this write-up, I express my profound appreciation to him and wish him a fruitful life ahead. His often-quoted Bible verse always strengthens me, "Thus far, God has helped us." (I Sam.7:12).

Introduction

Down through the ages, the words 'Image' and 'Likeness' in the book of Genesis[1], have received attention and have been the engagement of scholars in every generation. In recent times, several students from various departments have written many theses. For instance, Imlirenla Aier, "Body Shaming in the Contexts of Young Naga Women: A Feminist Theological Discourse on The 'Image of God' Towards Reaffirming Gender Justice in Socio-Political Cultural and Religious Realms"[2], Wandalin Kharlukhi,

1 Genesis 1:26-28.

2 Imlirenla Aier, "Body Shaming in the Contexts of Young Naga Women: A Feminist Theological Discourse on The 'Image of God' Towards Reaffirming Gender Justice in

"Significance of the Feminist Interpretation of the "Image of God" for Women's Liberation in the Khasi Society"[3], Paulos Gregorious, "Cosmic Man the Divine Presence God-World-Humanity Relationship in Gregory of Nysaa: An Analysis of the Place and … Gregory of Nysaa (Ca. 330-395 AD), Thenzauva, "The Image of God as the Basis of Human Freedom and Responsibility"[4]. M. Shana, "Concept of 'Image of God' in the Creation Account (Genesis 1:26-27) and its Implications to the Lives of the Adivasis in the Wayanadu, Kerala".[5]Apart from these research works, students writing research papers engage with these terms and end up with a philosophical interpretation based on the perspectives repeated over millennia. When we examine these research engagements, we notice that, by and large, making an exegetical study from the Hebrew text is imperative. Hence, a fresh look into the terms is necessitated, the basic text being Genesis 1:26-28. This essay argues that revisiting the phrases' Image and Likeness' will recall God's purpose for the human role in the creation. In addition, it is a call to the faith community to realize their interdependence with the creation and everything in it for sustainable growth.

Text: Genesis 1:26-28

V. 26 And God said, "Let us make humankind[6] in our image, after our likeness, and let them rule[7] over the fish of the sea, and over the birds of the heavens, and over the cattle, and over all ('the beasts of')[8] the earth, and over every creeping thing that moves upon the earth".

Socio-Political Cultural and Religious Realms", unpublished thesis submitted to the Senate of Serampore College (University) in partial fulfilment of the requirements of the Degree of Master of Theology, 2020.

3 Wandahlin Kharlukhi, "Significance of the Feminist Interpretation of the "Image of God" for Women's Liberation in the Khasi Society",", unpublished thesis submitted to the Senate of Serampore College (University) in partial fulfilment of the requirements of the Degree of Master of Theology, 1999.

4 Paulos Gregorious, "Cosmic Man the Divine Presence God-World-Humanity Relationship in Gregory of Nysaa: An Analysis of the Place and … Gregory of Nysaa (Ca. 330-395 AD), Thenzauva, "The Image of God as the Basis of Human Freedom and Responsibility", unpublished thesis submitted to the Senate of Serampore College (University) in partial fulfilment of the requirements of the Degree of Doctor of Theology, 1976.

5 M. Shana, "The Concept of 'Image of God' in the Creation Account (Genesis 1:26-27) and its Implications to the Lives of the Adivasis in the Wayanadu, Kerala", unpublished thesis submitted to the Senate of Serampore College (University) in partial fulfilment of the requirements of the Degree of Bachelor of Divinity, 2004.

6 The text has *('ådåm)* 'man' as the generic term.

7 Several translations have 'Dominion' viz., KJV, RSV, NRSV, etc.

8 'The beasts' here is added. MT, LXX and the Vulgate do not have this word. The Syriac Bible Peshitta adds 'beasts'; the text thus reads 'and upon all the beasts of the earth'.

V. 27 And God created human beings in his image, in the image of God he created them;[9] male and female, he created them.

V. 28 And God blessed them, and God said to them, "be fruitful and multiply, and fill the earth and possess[10] it; and rule over the fish of the sea and over the birds of the heavens and over every living thing that moves upon the earth."

Interpretation of Genesis 1:26

"In the history of biblical interpretation and dogmatic speculation, Gen. 1:26-28 have proved remarkably fecund as a source of exegetical and theological reflection".[11] One strand of interpretation makes this pericope as the foundation for the exploitation of the earth and its resources. Ian McHarg, for instance, in his book *Design with Nature,* says:

the biblical creation story of the first chapter of Genesis, ... in its insistence upon dominion and subjugation of nature, encourages the most exploitative and destructive instincts in man ... there could be no better injunction than this text.[12]

Gen. 1:28 also furnishes the title of a documentary, "Multiply and Subdue the Earth," which stresses the text under consideration for the 'bulldozer mentality'.[13] Lynn White, whose article is cited in almost every writing on ecology, notes that, based on the creation story in Genesis, Christianity insisted that it is God's will that human beings exploit nature for their proper ends.[14] The creation story of Gen. 1:1-2:4(a) as a whole and vv. 26-28 in particular, and the terms *Radah* 'to have dominion' and *Kabash* 'to subdue' are blamed as a basis for the present exploitation of creation. Indeed, such an interpretation is a misreading of the texts, and

---

"The addition of the words' beasts of' in the sense of 'the wild beasts of', will complete the classification of living creatures, as (1) fish; (2) birds; (3) domestic animals; (4) wild beasts; (5) creeping things. This enumeration reproduces the animals previously mentioned (vv. 20-25)" (Herbert E. Ryle, The Book of Genesis, *CBSC*, ed. For OT, A.F. Kirkpatrick. [Cambridge: University Press, 1921), 20.

9 Since the generic term 'man' has been translated to human beings, the pronoun is plural

10 To the standard translation of *Kabash,* 'subdue' is rendered as 'possess', which is taken to be appropriate in the context.

11 Phyllis A. Bird, "'Male and Female He Created Them' Gen. 1:27b in the Context of the Priestly Account of Creation", *HTR* Vol. 74, No.2, (1981), 149.

12 Ian L. McHarg, *Design with Nature.* (Garden City: The Natural History Press, 1969), 26.

13 The colour movie is available from Indiana University, order number CSC-1979, and it is cited by James Limburg as "What Does it Mean to Have Dominion Over the Earth?" *Dialogue* Vol. 10, No. 3, (1971).

14 Lynn White Jr., "The Historical Roots of Our Ecological Crisis", *Science* Vol. 155, (1967), 1205.

Walter Houston says such expressions are frequently found in writers who are not Old Testament scholars.[15]

So, then, the task must be to re-investigate these terms, *Radah* and *Kabash,* in relation to the other terms in the text in their general context of the 'P' writer of the exilic times. U. Cassuto[16] proposes that dominion over living creatures and over the earth as a whole (including the plants) has been given to human beings since they are created in the divine image and likeness. J. Skinner[17] as well as H. E. Ryle[18] suggest the same, thus making it imperative to study the terms *Tselem*' image' and *Demuth*' likeness' concerning Radah to understand the dominion concept better.

Tselem 'Image' and Demuth 'Likeness'

Several interpretations have been given to the question of what this image and likeness were supposed to consist of, and Walter Houston calls it a vexed question.[19] Claus Westermann submitted an elaborate bibliography.[20] H.P. Santmire reiterates the traditional interpretations of gender differentiations, anthropocentrism and domination.[21] Karl Barth[22] has shown how each age has filled Gen. 1:26 with the philosophical content of its times, i.e., the image of God as human beings' immortal soul, reason, and spirituality. James Barr, however, points out that such an interpretation was already present as early as the apocryphal Wisdom of Solomon 2:23,[23] and under this sort of interpretation, he says that the relation of human beings to the rest of nature, and especially the animal world, "tended to be thought of not as the practical question of control, technology and exploitation, but as the

15 Walter Houston, 'And Let Them Have Dominion ....'. Biblical Views of Man in Relation to the Environmental Crisis and Related Themes". (JSOT Supp. Series 11, Sheffield: JSOT Press, 1979), 167, nt. 25.

16 U. Cassuto, *A Commentary on the Book of Genesis* Vol. 1, tr. Israel Abraham. (Jerusalem: The Magnes Press, The Hebrew University, 1961), 58.

17 John Skinner, *A Critical and Exegetical Commentary on Genesis,* ICC. (Edinburgh: T&T Clark, 1910), 30.

18 Herbert E. Ryle, *The Book of Genesis,* (CBSC), 20.

19 Walter Houston, "And Let Them Have Dominion", 166.

20 Claus Westermann, *Genesis 1-11: A Commentary,* tr. John J. Scullion. (Minneapolis: Augsburg Publishing House, 1984), 147-148.

21 H. Paul Santmire, "The Genesis Creation Narratives Revisited. Themes for a Global Age", *Int* Vol. XLV, No. 4, (Oct. 1991), 371.

22 Karl Barth, *Church Dogmatics,* III/1. (Edinburgh: T&T Clark 1960), 123.

23 "For God created us for incorruption and made us in the image of his own eternity" (NRSV).

superiority of the rational beings",[24] with immortal soul, over that which is soulless and mortal.

The phrase' image of God' occurs only three times in canonical scripture (Gen. 1:26, 5:1, and 9:6). To study it, N. Lohfink suggests that the "literature of the ancient oriental world helps us a little. "[25] Indeed, one of the major contributions of recent research has clarified that the notion of a divine image in ancient West Asia was almost invariably associated with kingship.

The Akkadian *Salmu*' image' is said to refer to a visible symbol, usually a representation of the deity set up in a temple as a sign of the authority of the city-state deity to whom the image referred. Moreover, in Akkadian, it is also used of the King.[26]

H. Hehn, as early as 1915, explained, with several suitable references, that the description of a person as the 'image of God' has its roots in the Egyptian and Mesopotamian description of the King. [27] S. Mowinkel, too, in 1948, suggested the same background for Genesis chapter one.[28] W.H. Schmidt has no hesitation in claiming that the motif of the 'image of God' is firmly 'anchored' in this royal tradition,[29] like Hans Wildberger[30] does to illustrate this relationship.

Egypt, which is rich in texts that describe the King as God's image, shows us from the stele of Amenophis II from Amada that the Pharaoh is praised as "the beloved son in bodily form of Re ... the good God, the Creature of Re, the ruler .... image of Horus on the throne of his father,

24 James Barr, "Man and Nature – The Ecological Controversy and the Old Testament", *BJRL* Vol. 55, (1972), 23.

25 Norbert Lohfink, "Growth: The Priestly Document and the Limits of Growth" in his book *Great Themes from the Old Testament,* tr. Ronald Walls. (Edinburgh: T&T Clark Ltd., 1982), 171.

26 W.J. Dumbrell, "Genesis 1-3, Ecology and the Dominion of Man", *Crux* Vol. XXI, No. 4, (Dec. 1985), 17.

27 H. Hehn, "Zum Terminus 'Bild Gottes'", Festschrift E. Sachau, 1915, cited by Claus Westermann Genesis 1-11: A Commentary, 152.

28 S. Mowinkel, Urmensch und Konigsideologie" St.Th. Vol. 2, (1948), pp. 71-89, cited by Claus Westermann, Genesis 1-11: A Commentary, 132.

29 W.H. Schmidt, Die Schopfungsgeschichte der Priesterschrift 2nd ed. (Neukirchen Vluyn: Neukirchener, 1957), 140, cited by Mark G. Brett, "Motives and Intentions in Genesis 1", J. Th. St. Vol. 42, Part 1, (April 1991), 11.

30 Hans Wildberger, "Das Abbild Gottes" TZ Vol. 21, (1965), pp. 245- 259, 481-501 cited by Mark G. Brett, "Motives and Intentions in Genesis 1", 11.

mighty in power ...."[31] Thus, as the image, Pharaoh was the visible representation of the deity God incarnate on earth.[32]

So also in an address of Amon Re to Amenophis III, it is written: "thou art my beloved son, came forth from my limbs, my very own image, which I have put upon the earth. I have permitted thee of rule over the earth in peace".[33]

Thus, as far as the Egyptian writings are concerned, it is clear enough that the context of Gen.1:26-28 belongs to this royal ideology. The same is also attested in Babylonian literature, and this use of *Salmu* from the Babylonian context might have been the most influential of the 'P' writers, having come from exilic times in the land of Babylon.

Wildberger, having established the description of the King as God's image with several quotations from the Babylonian texts, concludes that "the places where the king is spoken of as the *Salmu* or *Mussulu* of his God ... suggest that Gen. 1:26-30 are rooted ultimately in the royal ideology of the Ancient Near East."[34] W.H. Schmidt, too, arrives at the same conclusion, saying that the parallels to Ps. 8 make this more apparent.[35] However, the priestly writer (writers) of Genesis chapter one does not simply recapitulate the traditions but daringly adapts it.[36] B.W. Anderson opines the same.[37] W.M. Clark, too, subscribes to the background of royal ideology and explains that the ideology of the King's rule over the world is transformed into the rule of human beings over the other living elements of creation. He notes that the rule over animals was included in the task of the King, as in Jer. 27:5 and Dan. 2:38f.[38]

In the literature of Mesopotamia, the purpose of being in the image of God was said to be the performer of slave labour.[39] Thus, G. von Rad says that "the decisive thing about Man's similarity to God, therefore, is his

31 Hans Wildberger, "Das Abbild Gottes", 485, cited by C. Westermann, Genesis 1-11: A Commentary, 152.

32 W.J. Dumbrell, "Genesis 1-3, Ecology and the Dominion of Man", 17.

33 W.H. Schmidt, Die Schopfungsgeschichte der Priesterschrift, kap III B 9: "Das Achte Schopfungswerk: die Menschen Gen. 1:26-28", WMANT Vol. 17, (1964), p. 139, cited by C. Westermann, Genesis 1-11: A Commentary, 152.

34 H. Wildberger, "Das Abbild Gottes". 255, cited by C. Westermann, *Genesis 1-11: A Commentary*, 152.

35 W.H. Schmidt, Die Schopfungsgeschichte der Priesterschrift, 140, cited by C. Westermann, *Genesis 1-11: A Commentary,* 153.

36 Mark G. Brett, "Motives and Intentions in Genesis 1", 11.

37 B.W. Anderson, "Subdue the Earth: What Does it Mean?" BRev Vol. 8, (Oct. 1992), p. 10.

38 W.M. Clark, "The Animal Series in the Primeval History", VT Vol. XVIII, No. 4, (Oct., 1968), p. 436, nt. 2.

39 N. Lohfink, "Growth: The Priestly Document and the Limits of Growth", 171.

function in the non-human world."[40] W. J. Drumbrell,[41] and D. T. Asselin[42] Also, this royal function has a mandate from God. V. Steven Parrish calls this function the task of relating to the rest of the created world in a way that reflects a God who interacts with creation by providing and maintaining order—in short, "by sustaining the goodness of the earth."[43] Moreover, the expression for such an exercise lies in using the term *Radah*.[44] The term *Radah* in the context of Genesis chapter one depicts the royalty of human beings.

Conclusion

This essay argues that the image and likeness God bestows upon humankind is to inform a great deal of God's purpose in creating human communities. Further, it enlightens human communities to realize their inviolable relationship with God and creation. God calls humankind to live with nature, cultivating a mutual relationship with everything in it. It is not merely representing God in the creation order but drawing some theological notions about human origin and purposeful living in the world. Humankind must follow the order of nature and relinquish the ideas of dominion and authority over the creation to fulfil God's purpose in and through their significant living in the created world.

40 G. von Rad, *Genesis: A Commentary,* 3rd ed. (London: SCM 1961), p. 60.

41 W.J. Dumbrell, "Genesis 1-3, Ecology and the Dominion of Man", 17.

42 David Tobin Asselin, "The Notion of Dominion in Genesis 1-3", *CBQ* Vol. 16, (1954), pp. 293f.

43 V. Steven Parrish, "From Domination to Eco-Justice Rereading Selected Creation Texts in the Hebrew Bible", *Memphis Th Sem J* Vol. 29, (Sum., 1991), p. 59.

44 G. von Rad, *Genesis: A Commentary,* 60.

20

Dalit Reading of Holiness in the Revelation Narrative of Exodus 19

Dr. Laila Vijayan

Introduction

I am delighted to contribute to this Festschrift in honour of Prof. Dr. K. Jesurathnam, sharing the joy of God's blessings on his life and ministry. As colleagues and friends reflect on his significant contributions to Old Testament studies and contextual readings, particularly his work on Dalit interpretations of the Bible, this article is dedicated to Prof. Dr. Jesurathnam. May God continue to bless him, enabling him to remain a powerful instrument for justice and equality.

Indian society is a caste-oriented patriarchal society. In Indian Society, people, religion, and literature identify something as polluting or unclean, dirty or ugly. They made these as opposite to clean or pure, holy or sanctified and so on. The caste system of the Indian Society made a hierarchy and kept some people outside the caste system. It labelled them as untouchables. The geographical situations they live in and the job-related situations attributed to the intensity of the cause of the untouchability. This paper attempts to reread Exodus 19 using the Dalit liberation hermeneutics, where interpretative tools such as hermeneutics of resistance, hermeneutics of experience and purity (holiness) - pollution ideology are employed.

Holiness is a powerful theme found within the Pentateuch. The P tradition emphasizes holiness like other traditions and reflects its impact on various levels. The holy mountain and the divine presence make the people feel an impactful holiness in and around it, reaffirming human beings' impure nature. By nature, humans need to anticipate acquiring the qualities of clean and pure hearts. One's words, deeds, and actions must reflect holiness. The exodus tradition reaffirms the election and covenant of the people of Israel and the promising call to be a blessing to the rest of the nations. The supremacy of divine election and the liberation from the land of Egypt reaffirms the biblical history of Israel. It further considers the faith and life experience of the people of Israel in the biblical tradition.

The people's experience of God and the mighty acts of God mirrors the divine revelations in various contexts and life situations. The proof of the presence of plague narratives and the Sinai narratives are two examples taken to expose the incomprehensibility of Yahweh and the limitations of human beings, kings and other gods. The book of Exodus and the Exodus event have a greater significance in the liberation readings of the Bible. In Exodus 19, the divine revelation is visible to the people of Israel, and the text clearly describes the separation between the people, Moses, and the mountain. The narration reaffirms sacred and human boundaries, and disobedience can lead to the complete removal of the person, animal, or people. In this article, the author attempts to analyze Exodus 19, which is considered part of the Sinai narrative and is the account of preparation to receive the Decalogue. This paper is not paying attention to the Decalogue; instead, it tries to understand the concept of holiness presented in Exodus 19 and a critique of Indian Society. Exodus 19 is a part of the larger Sinai narrative, which has undergone a series of developmental stages with revisions and additions.[45] Therefore, separating the chapter without paying attention has some limitations, but here, the focus is on holiness and its implications for Indian Society.

Definition of the Terms

Revelation

The Hebrew word גלה means 'uncover'. When this word is used with the phrase גלה אזן, it means to uncover the ear, by implication, 'to hear.'[46] It also conveys an idea as a 'communicate a secret.'[47] The word פתה means 'to open' or 'he opened', and it can also mean 'uncovered.' There are different ways the revelation of God is exposed within the Scriptures / in

45 For further reading, see the assumptions proposed by John I Durham, *Exodus WBC* (Texas: Word Books, 1987), 259.

46 Francis Brown, *The Brown-Driver-Briggs Hebrew and English Lexicon* (Massachusetts: Hendrickson Publishers, 1997), 162f.

47 C F D Moule, "Revelation" in *NIB,* Vol.4 (Nashville: Abingdon Press, 1962), 55.

the biblical tradition. For instance, in 'eyes of Balaam', Balaam was able to experience the revelation of God. The idea of revelation can also mean the manifestations of God in nature (Ps 19:1-6, 29, Rom 1:19-20). The Pauline speeches talk about the revelation of God through the created world (Acts 14:15-17; 17:24ff). There are general and specific ways of expositions about the revelation of God. God reveals God's self in various ways through designs of the world, deeds and actions and most decisively in the climax through Jesus Christ (Am 3:7; Gen. 12:1-3; John 3:16, etc.). God reveals secrets to the prophets (Daniel 10:1), and the ability to discern God's designs and interpret them. There is a need to perceive God's design. 'Revelation is personal rather than Propotional.'[48] In other words, revelation is seen through relationships, communion and confrontation of the Divine with the creation/human.[49] The sitz im leben influences the revelation narratives, so it is possible to see the narrations from different perspectives.

Holy/Holiness

The Hebrew word קדש means 'holiness or set apart or to be sanctified.' For example, when the word "holy" appears for the first time in the creation story, it separates the Sabbath as a distinct day from other days: "God blessed the seventh day and sanctified it" (Genesis 2,3). The verbal translation is sanctified, as its basic root meaning is to set apart, which makes a clear distinction between the so-called profane [50]that the Brahmanical/Priestly tradition considered.

It differentiates between the sacred realm of God and the profane human world. The first six days of creation focus on the profane human

48 C F D Moule, "Revelation" in *NIB,* 55.

49 The biblical traditions present communion or confrontation in various ways. God reveals Godself through nature/creation/actions of justice/righteousness/wrath etc. Creation is an ongoing process that God initiated and continues in the universe. Revelation can be limited to statements for some. As Moule writes, for the Biblical writers, it is a "statement of God's will and purpose. It is more connected with God as a person and people's obedient response' than communication of information" (Gen 35:7); Cf. C F D moule, "Revelation" in *NIB,* 55. In the vision of Jacob (Genesis 38), God's character is the divine presence in the form of strength and protection to a needful person. Samuel's knowledge of Saul's ass (1 Sam 9:6) is a revelation. 1 Sam 3:1, 21 shows the revival of revelation. This divine revelation is a more drastic moral judgement than the beginning of a prophetic ministry. Elisha uses divination by music, but he uses it in the interests of the wars of the Lord (II Kings 3:15). From the 8th century, the Writing or the classical Prophets' account proves that God revealed the secrets to the Prophets (Am 3:7).

50 The terms holy and profane distinguish between the two realms. The biblical tradition distinguishes between the profane and sacred, righteous and wicked, obedience and disobedience, blessing and curse etc. However, defining the term profane is challenging; this article explains it below. The liberative readings of the Bible challenge the idea of holy or profane

world. It is important to note that no act of creation takes place on the seventh day. Here, the focus is on God rather than on creation. In earlier times, interpreters described it as God resting in the divine realm. It is a day of sacred activity (worship) in the human world. However, in modern times, contextual readers identify the holiness of God amid the so-called 'profane realm.' The holiness of the seventh day introduces a separation between God and the created world. It announces that God is separate from the world of human beings. God is the transcendent, "the wholly other" in earlier understanding, but now the creation identifies the holiness amid vulnerable situations as profane. This article holds the paradox of holiness in its thought pattern. When the victims of violence and discrimination attain equality and justice without any binaries and boundaries, the creation experiences holiness. The notion of holiness is an experience of one in every moment of life, and it has to be the gospel for all.

Theophany: An Expression of Holiness

Theophany is the manifestation of God. The manifestations or appearance of God to the people of Israel or the individuals are significant events in the biblical tradition. These events, over time, achieved more mystical values, bringing importance to God's omnipotence and cosmic majesty. The first exposition of the manifestation and divine encounter is explained in the Garden of Eden narrative after the creation accounts. The Garden of Eden narratives exhibit the elements of holiness and vulnerability/profanity. The disobedience of human beings leads to the estrangement between the divine and human. The ancestors' divine encounters receive the climax with the theme of promise and blessing. The dichotomy of divine-human interconnectedness is visible in the ancestral narratives.[51] The theophanic experience of Moses at the burning bush is an essential expression of the manifestation of God (Exod. 3). The experience of Moses at Mount Horeb is a dramatic narration where the angel of Yahweh is visible, and later Yahweh speaks to Moses. The narration shadows the danger of seeing God when Moses asks God to show the glory of God. The theophany experience at Sinai is a unique stratum in the history of Israel.[52] It further explains the purpose of God and the intention of the liberation of the people of Israel in their history. The text exhibits a tripartite relationship. God is in the process and the source of divine communication; Moses is the leader representing the society's social, religious and cultural systems, and the people of Israel are the recipients who complete the triangular relationship. In this tripartite relationship, the Divine manifestations and attributions are vital in the

51 Cf. Genesis 12:1-3, 7; Genesis 18:2-32; Genesis 28:12-19; Genesis 32: 24-30, etc.

52 Martin Noth, *Exodus* (Philadelphia: Westminster Press, 1959), 153.

narrations. Job's experience of theophany reveals a different worldview, such as theodicy. It is a dramatic way of presentation in the Book of Job. Even in these narrations, the divine supremacy and holiness versus the vulnerability of human beings/creation takes a prominent position. The Prophetic Literature emphasizes the transcendent God and theophany experience, which reveals the glory and power of God. Isaiah's experience of cleansing and making pure and holy, Jeremiah's experience of confirmation as God's elected one before the formation in the womb, etc, are some examples of the divine experience. However, within the Prophetic books, one can identify the portrayal of the theophanic experience of God's manifestations in many forms, such as thunder, lightning, a form of judgement, victory, and so on.

Inconsistencies or Tensions Within the Text

The text often emphasizes the mountain's holiness for the divine encounter. Even after Moses received the Ten Commandments, the people of Israel asked Moses to mediate between God and the people of Israel. The number of times Moses ascended and descended the mountain and the repetition of warnings given to keep the distance from the hill.[53] Chapter 19 introduces the Sinai narrative. The presence of explanatory and qualifying materials and the insertion of cultic elements prove the tradition's attempt to establish its authority.[54] Durham also agrees with the inconsistencies and complications within the narrative.[55] Doublets are possible, and the change of the divine name is an example.[56] The following verses of Genesis 19:3a, 17,19;20:1, and 19-21 mention Elohim as the divine name. The speciality of the E narratives is seen as the mighty signs of the divine presence that appear soon after the arrival of the people of Israel in the mountain. The conflict ideology is seen within the text that, by seeing the theophany, the people are in terror and demand Moses to be the mediator (20:18-21). Still, in the beginning of the account, it is a warning to people that they must keep sufficient distance from the mountain and not touch it (19:12f). There is a possibility of J narratives' presence in the account. There is also an addition of materials like explanations of theophany, keeping the covenant and the approach to the mountain (19:3b-9a/ab). Martin Noth says the theophany on Sinai and Decalogue has its own independent and self-contained entity and its traditional history.[57] So, the distinction between the Elohistic Decalogue (Exodus 19-20) and the Yahwistic Decalogue (Exodus 34) suggests that

53 Cf. Brevard S Childs, *Exodus* (London: SCM Press Limited, 1974), 344f.

54 John I Durham, *Exodus WBC*, 258.

55 John I Durham, *Exodus WBC,* 259.

56 Martin Noth, *Exodus,* 153.

57 Martin Noth, *Exodus,* 154.

the Decalogue is not part of theophany on Sinai but a later insertion.[58] G von Rad studied the significance of the festival cult of Jerusalem and its impact on the Yahwistic and Elohistic accounts of Sinai after S Mowinckel's research.[59] Important leading themes in the Pentateuch, such as deliverance from Egypt, entry into Canaan, and the revelation on Sinai, were independent complex traditions in their origin. These were specific expressions of faith rooted in the cult and shaped by the creed.[60] The Yahwist and the Elohist use the common basis (G). Theophany's narrations have a robust and traditional impact on the descriptions, and the ideologies of the source stratums play a significant role in their constructions. Childs writes that the cultic or dominant pattern is seen, culminating in the mosaic cultic ratification of the pact.[61] The E source represents the dominant pattern, and J reflects the minor pattern. The presence of two oral forms of tradition shows the blend of two sources before the literary stage. Even though scholars like von Rad and Mowinckel tried to confirm the setting as a cultic office of Institutional structure, this structure has the E source as the base.[62] The Dueteronomic redactor claims the present form of the text (19: 3b-8).[63] The form of the passage is generally called an introduction to the Sinai Narrative, the Advent of Yahweh, that merged with covenantal and cultic materials. Verse 1-8 is the speech of Yahweh, which serves as a prologue to the Sinai narrative sequence.[64]

Interpretation

Geographical Narrative Plot Scene One: Exodus 19: 1-2

A new history begins with the first phrase, 'third new moon.' The phrase new moon signifies the commencement of a new period in the life of nature, and the third new moon, after the people of Israel came out of the land of Egypt, embarks on the importance of entry into the Sinai.[65] The Sinai event commences a new event in the life of the people of Israel. The writer emphasized the word 'third new moon', which reflects the past two weeks

58 Martin Noth, *Exodus,* 155.

59 Walter Beyerlin, *Origins and History of the Oldest Sinaitic Traditions* (Oxford: Basil Blackwell, 1965), xv.

60 Walter Beyerlin, *Origins and History of the Oldest Sinaitic Traditions*, xvi.

61 Brevard S Childs, *Exodus,* 350.

62 Brevard S Childs, *Exodus,* 355.

63 Brevard S Childs, *Exodus,* 360-361. A summary of source identification by different scholars is found in the book of John I Durham. Cf. John I Durham, *Exodus WBC*, 260, 268, 269.

64 John I Durham, *Exodus WBC*, 260.

65 Cassuto, *A Commentary on the Book of Exodus* (Jerusalem: Magness Press, 1967), 224.

of Nissan and four weeks of Iyyar, so they are in the seventh week when they reach Sinai. In ancient West Asia, seven is considered a unit of time. Six days of work are labour, and the seventh day is a rest. The climax of seven weeks is a time of exaltation and coming closer to God.[66] The later tradition connects it with the Festival of Weeks.[67] These first two verses are attributed to P, and they explain the circumstances of Moses' arrival at Sinai. The writer connects this with Exodus 24, which discusses the 'glory of Yahweh' and Moses' ascent to the mountain to receive the covenant.

The geographical identification of Rephidim and then to the wilderness of Sinai are the two place names found in this narrative. However, confirming its present geographical location is always challenging; traditions try to attribute or identify some places. Rephidim is a place where Israel was stationed during their journey to Canaan. Identification of the place Rephidim is also a challenge, and it may be a place closer to Midian or near Wadi Feiran.[68] The identification of the location of Mount Sinai and the wilderness of Sinai are in contention, and so that is not the importance of this paper; instead, the religious and theological experiences people experienced are of great concern for exposition.[69] Sinai or Horeb (Exodus 3:1) is understood as the mountain of God. It is a sanctified mountain, hallowed with theophany. The boundary of Israel's holiness is a postexilic development that reached fruition after the temple's demise in Rabbinic Judaism and Christianity.[70]

Revelation Plot Scene Two: Exodus 19: 3-6

In response to divine command, Moses ascended to the mountain and performed the sacred task. Childs quotes Muilenburg's view that a 'special

---

66 Cassuto, *A Commentary on the Book of Exodus,* 224. Cf. William H C Propp, *Exodus 19-40 Anchor Bible* (New York: Doubleday, 2006), 154.

67 William H C Propp, *Exodus 19-40 Anchor Bible*, 155.

68 Walter C. Kaiser, *A History of Israel* (Nashville: Broadman & Holman Publishers, 1998), 116. Cf. Frank Moore Cross, *Canaanite Myth and Hebrew Epic: Essays in the History of the Religion of Israel* (Cambridge: Harvard University Press, 2009), 311.

69 Cassuto brings attention to the idea of Scholars who suggest Sinai is near to Kadesh Barnea or in the land of Midian or the southern part of the Peninsula (known as the Sinai Peninsula) and the latest understanding of Jebel Serbal or Jebel Musa. Cassuto, *A Commentary on the Book of Exodus*, 225. Martin Noth writes about the geographical location of Mount Sinai and acknowledges the absence of certainty about the area. He writes, "From the Byzantine period, one of the very high mountains in the southern part of what is today called the Sinai Peninsula has been recognized as the scene of the Old Testament theophany, either the 'Mountain of Moses' or 'Mountain St. Catherine' at whose foot stands the Greek Orthodox monastery of St. Catherine." Cf. Martin Noth, *Exodus* (Philadelphia: Westminster Press, 1962), 155-156.

70 William H C Propp, *Exodus 19-40 Anchor Bible*, 158-159.

covenantal Gattung' is seen here.[71] The literary feature of the Poetic formula is an adaptation from Canaanite poetry. The expression of the formula is 'Thus you shall say to so-and-so, and tell the son of so-and-so.' This is equivalent to the messenger formula, and it is understood as an expression of commissioning.[72] The interchange of the divine name God and Lord is visible here. The mixture of anthropomorphic nature and the transcendence of God is present here. It reflects the presence of two traditions' characteristic features and ideologies. The idea of transcendence reaffirms the holiness of God and the vulnerability of human beings, and it is a more significant challenge to the liberation readings of the Bible. By affirming the background, the narrator reminds the actions of God in history. It is a call to Jacob's house and the people of Israel. The narrator reminds God's mighty deeds and wondrous acts in the land of Egypt and the liberating action of God as a prerequisite to receiving the covenant with God. The remembrance of the history and the willingness of the people to obey God's commandment will provide an opportunity for the people of Israel to have a continuous experience of the special possession status. The earth belongs to God, and God's ultimate authority is also there. According to this covenant agreement, Israel will continue to be a Priestly kingdom and a holy nation. The idea of Israel as a unique treasure or possession reaffirms that Israel's identity is not with the human kings on the land. Instead, the nation exists on the foundation of the covenant ideology which Yahweh made with the people of Israel.[73]

Cassuto defines a holy nation as "a nation dedicated entirely to the service of the Godhead, in the same way as priests are consecrated thereto."[74] The central theme of God's election is a challenge to understand further. This exodus event has projected God's dominion over the universe and other gods. The final statement suggests the need for a covenant relationship, which reaffirms that the people of Israel have a special possession. At the same time, the narrator affirms that God is the God of the whole world. Cassuto writes this as a "proposal which envisages a bilateral covenant, giving Israel an exalted position among the peoples instead of accepting a special discipline."[75] Obedience to the Torah envisages a special relationship that refers to Israel's uniqueness in three areas: Israel as a special possession, a

71 Brevard S Childs, *Exodus,* 366.

72 Cassuto, *A Commentary on the Book of Exodus,* 226.

73 John I Durham, *Exodus WBC,* 263. Cf. Terence E Fretheim, *Exodus Interpretation* (Kentucky: John Knox Press, 1973), 212.

74 Cassuto, *A Commentary on the Book of Exodus,* 227.

75 Cassuto, *A Commentary on the Book of Exodus*, 227.

kingdom of Priests, and a holy nation.[76] This section ends with a concluding formula to communicate this solemn message to the people of Israel.

Revelation Plot Scene Three: Exodus 19: 7-9b

The second scene exposes the tripartite communication within the context. The three connections in this trilateral relationship are Moses, the People and elders of Israel, and the Lord. Moses spoke to the elders and people of Israel. Then, the Lord said to Moses, and Moses exposed the divine presence to the people of Israel. Cassuto explains this relationship as a power dynamic activity.[77] He also maintains that this is a proposal God gives, and the elders and the people receive it. Then, the people reaffirm as they accept the proposal with one mind and spirit. A socio-hierarchical structure is present in this narration. There is a possibility of analyzing the text in two ways. The author wants to carry the tradition of Mosaic leadership as accepted by all people of Israel. Moses is an acknowledged leader, mediator and messenger to the people of Israel. The narrator authenticates Moses' leadership and the acceptance of the people.[78] The ascending and descending phrases communicate the socio-psychological and religiopolitical plot of the narration. In verse nine, the author says that God's form or image or physical form will not be visible to Moses, either. Instead, God affirms that God is present in the thick cloud, and you and people could experience the presence of God. This thick cloud signalizes the Divine Presence.[79]

Revelation Plot Scene Four: Exodus 19:10-15

In this section, the narrator prepares the plot with the theme of 'purity and sanctity,' Moses was with the people during theophany. Wellhausen has attributed this portion (10-19) to E source.[80] The people are expected to wash their garments, a symbolic representation of their inner purity of the soul. If the calculation is about the days, the revelation happens on the sixth day of the month, which is the end of the seventh week. That is why the later traditions which attribute the Festival of Weeks to the Day of the Revelation on Mount Sinai agree with these days' calculations. This theophany experience repeatedly affirms the boundaries between Divine and human spheres. This preparation is an externality of outward washing, but spiritual

---

76 Brevard S Childs, *Exodus*, 367.

77 Cassuto, *A Commentary on the Book of Exodus*, 227.

78 Martin Noth, *Exodus*, 158.

79 Cassuto, *A Commentary on the Book of Exodus*, 228.

80 Childs ' Exodus commentary elaborates on early literary scholars ' views for more detailed discussions on source analysis. Cf. Brevard S Childs, *Exodus*, 345f.

purification is imperative.[81] The advice for physical cleansing and avoiding sexual relationships is more related to infectious situations than the worship context. However, within this narration, the required physical cleanliness is identified as a prerequisite to receiving or experiencing the Divine; if it is not followed, the death punishment is announced.[82]

Torah reaffirms the union of God with nature or any elements because all things in the universe are God's creation, and nothing can be equated to the Creator God. The three references to 'touching the mountain' are characteristics of the literary genre 'repetition,' and the purpose is to emphasize. With the information on sanctification, the plot preparation is completed.

Revelation Event Scene Five: Exodus 19: 16-19

People would expect divine presence in various forms. The thunder and lightning impacted by the thick cloud filled the sky, too. The storm is an expression of theophany.[83]

In the Biblical tradition, thunder often denotes the voice of God, but here, it is not identified as such.[84] In the Canaanite tradition, the voice of Baal is a theophanic revelation. In some biblical narratives, these natural phenomena are considered to be the expression of theophany, and the voice follows after that. The reference to the sound of the horn could be understood as Cassuto writes, "It signifies the strong wind that blows violently through the gorges between the mountains, rending the air with a great noise like the sound of the horn."[85]All the events made the people tremble, and all these were signs announcing God's advent. Therefore, people waited at the foot of the mountain. God and Moses had a dialogue in the midst of a smoking mountain, and God descended in a fire on the mountain.

Divine Revelation Scene Six: Exodus 19: 20-25

Moses ascended to the mountain, and God descended to the mountain. The theophanic encounter took place at the top of the mountain, and people stood at the foot of the mountain. The continuous reminder to Moses to warn the people to keep their distance and the boundary may have a twofold purpose, as Cassuto writes, "(a) to stress still further the thought that the boundary between the two spheres, the human and the Divine, is not to be effaced;

81 Brevard S Childs, *Exodus,*380.

82 John I Durham, *Exodus WBC*, 264-265.

83 Cassuto, *A Commentary on the Book of Exodus,* 230.

84 In Elijah's narratives, God was not present in natural events: Yahweh was not in the wind, not in the earthquake, not in the fire, but came as a still voice (II Kings 19: 11-13).

85 Cassuto, *A Commentary on the Book of Exodus,* 231.

(b) that it was necessary to repeat the warning at the crucial moment when the revelation was about to take place."[86] The continuous reminders about distancing and purifying are identified as triple references, and by doing so, the author gives importance to this matter. The narrator reaffirms the need for the intermediary or the mediator, which makes the people not worthy to meet Yahweh directly. If people attempt to meet Yahweh or try to look through, the punishment will be death.[87] This section reaffirms the credibility of Moses' leadership.[88] The challenge in the later part is the admonition to Moses to go down and warn the people and ascend again with Aaron. This section reflects the mixing of Mosaic and Aaronic tradition.[89]

Dalit Reading of the Text

The Varna Vyavastha (caste system) excluded a group of communities and labelled them untouchables. Indian society gives different names to those people who fall outside of the *Varna Vyavastha* (caste system).[90]

Dalits are the oppressed communities in India. Even though there are varied castes and subcastes within the Dalits, the common factor that unites them is the stigma of untouchability because of the 'so-called polluting' nature of their professions. The pollution of the stigma of untouchability stands in contrast to holiness. As Devasahayam quotes Mary Douglas's views, "Defilement is never an isolated event. It cannot occur except in view of a systematic ordering of index."[91]

In Indian Society, the nature of purity pollution stands synonymous with Brahmins and Dalits, and it has become a curse to the society. All human beings are God's creation and are equal before God. But the election ideology makes the divisions. Brahmins are inherent with the purity notion of sacred, which biblical tradition calls holiness, and one must challenge it. The caste-oriented purity-pollution ideology influences the social, religious and political structures of the society. The sacredness or holiness attributed

86 Cassuto, *A Commentary on the Book of Exodus*, 233.

87 John I Durham, *Exodus WBC,* 272-273.

88 Terence E Fretheim, *Exodus Interpretation,* 215.

89 Exodus 20: 1-17 shows the climax of the event, the receiving of the Decalogue. This paper does not focus on the Decalogue but on the dedication of Exodus 19 as the preparation for the theophany.

90 Cf. V Devasahayam, "Pollution, Poverty and Powerlessness-A Dalit Perspective" in *A Reader in Dalit Theology,* Arvind P. Nirmal (ed.) (Madras: GLTC, n.y), 1-22. For further reading, Cf. V. Devasahayam (ed.), *Dalits and Women: Quest for Humanity* (Madras: GLTC, 1992); V. Devasahayam, *Outside the Camp* (Madras: Gurukul, 1992); V. Devasahayam, *Doing Dalit Theology in Biblical Key* (Madras: Gurukul, 1997); Arvind P Nirmal (ed), A Reader in Dalit Theology, (Madras: Gurukul, n.y).

91 V Devasahayam, "Pollution, Poverty and Powerlessness-A Dalit Perspective", 5.

to different castes, jobs, and places significantly impacts the present Indian Society, too. As Devasahayam writes, "The Brahmins who are at the top of the social hierarchy follow pure professions, eat pure food and worship vegetarian, pure gods, but Dalits who are at the lowest in the hierarchy are considered as impure and untouchable because of the professions, impure food and worship of meat-eating gods."[92]

Social and Religious Stratification in the Revelation Narrative

The authors of the revelation narratives in Exodus 19 emphasize the hierarchical structure, which places the divine revelation and the holiness of God at the top of the ideologies. God, the creator and initiator of the covenant, sits in the heavenly realm and summons the divinely holy and selected leaders to join in the sacred realm. The continuous warning and command given to Moses to communicate to the people not to touch the mountain or break through to look, which can bring death, and therefore, Moses ascends and descends to communicate the urgent need to obey the divine guidance so that the mountain holds it holiness without pollution. Can this holiness ideology be the creation of any tradition that wants to create a hierarchical structure in society? Can this be an attempt to validate the status of the Mosaic tradition? In the faith systems, people believed that the mountains are the dwelling place of God/gods, but here, God does not dwell in the mountain; instead descends to the mountain, where Moses has to ascend to agree with God and the people. The obedience and blessing ideology of Deuteronomists also influences the text. God dwells in the heavenly realms, and it is the place of angels and archangels, cherubim and seraphim, and it is a world of absence of mistakes and presence of holiness. The binaries of above and below, here and there, centre and periphery/ margin lead to division and disparity in society. It creates the society's ideology in contrast to two imaginative worlds, where the disparities continue to prevail. Even though Indian law affirms justice for all, people continue to experience discrimination and dehumanization in the name of caste/purity and pollution. People try to reaffirm that holiness is not part of all individuals but comes as hereditary. The dominant caste people continue to experience the privilege of holiness as their identity symbol, and the Dalits, as untouchables, mark the pollution. The social hierarchical structure in the revelation narratives presents God as the Supreme, who is on the top. Then, the leader, Moses, serves as a mediator between the elders of Israel and the people. God is the God of holiness, and the presence of God makes the mountain holy, which only Moses could experience.

92 V Devasahayam, "Pollution, Poverty and Powerlessness-A Dalit Perspective, "5.

Presence of Smoke and Trembling: A Challenge to Social Mobility

After the consecration, the people stand at the foot of the mountain to experience the revelation of God. The thunder, lightning, the sound of the horn, and the smoke are symbols of the descended God, and here, the author reaffirms the mobility of the people in a restricted mode. Whose ideologies are protected here, and whose movements are restricted? The statements of Srinivas, as quoted by Devasahayam, are very significant, "I am equal to those who think of themselves as my betters, and I am better than those who regard themselves as my equals and how dare my inferiors claim to equality with me?"[93] This view expresses the possibility of social disorder and chaos because of inequality.[94] Why does the account end with Aaron joining with Moses per God's command? The social mobility of the people of Israel as God's special possession and to be a blessing to the rest of the world is an ideology of Israel's election and covenant motif.

Caste conflict death (honour killing)[95] Indian society is the best example of understanding the challenge of holiness and pollution ideologies' impact on society. As per the latest data from the National Crime Records Bureau (NCRB), the number of honour killings reported in India was 25 each in 2019 and 2020, and 33 in 2021 (how many crime events go unnotified in the media). These events continue to bring shame to Indian Society as people still carry the status and pride in the name of caste, sub-caste, culture and religion. The vital reason behind honour killing is the notion of holiness/ purity and pollution and the status of the family.

Conclusion

The binaries and boundaries continue to be the agents of oppression and discrimination. The time has come to recognize the oppressive structures and ideologies which continue to influence the people, church, and traditions. It is essential to revisit critically to ensure everyone receives honour, equality, and happiness. The holiness in the narration is part of faith. The faith communities must challenge the oppressive elements of creating borders and divisions among humankind, and it should never be the guideline for the practice of the church and society.

---

93 V. Devasahayam, "Pollution, Poverty and Powerlessness-A Dalit Perspective," 9.

94 Terence E. Fretheim, *Exodus Interpretation,* 220.

95 Honour killings expose the confluence of religion, caste, other forms of hierarchical social stratification, or sexuality. It is the murder of a man or woman because of the perpetrators' belief that the victim has lost her innocence by bringing dishonour or shame upon the family name, reputation or prestige.

21

Resonance of Women's Resistance
The Exodus Women and the Meira Paibis of Manipur

Nongthombam Alifina

Introduction

The Exodus event is often centred around Yahweh's role in deliverance and Moses as its leader. However, the liberation movement could not have begun without the brave women involved, such as the Hebrew midwives, Moses' mother, Miriam, Pharaoh's daughter, and her maids. These women showed courage, solidarity, and empathy by defying Pharaoh's genocidal decree. This paper examines the Exodus women and the Meira Paibis, focusing on women's leadership, moral courage, and non-violent resistance. The study seeks to uncover the overlooked contributions of these courageous women in the Exodus narrative, who acted beneath society's surface to evade Pharaoh's decree. By rereading the Exodus story from a feminist perspective using hermeneutics of remembrance, the role of women as liberators will be explored. The paper underscores how historical narratives can influence contemporary struggles for justice, peace, and community protection, offering valuable insights into the ongoing efforts of the Meira Paibis and their vulnerability amid the failure of the Manipur state.

Tracing Women's Resistance by Employing Feminist Biblical Hermeneutics

Feminist biblical interpretation is an academic discipline inspired and nurtured by the politics of the second feminist movement in the early 1920s. Since the field's emergence, feminist exegetes have used various methods to interpret biblical literature.[96] A Hermeneutics of Remembrance is employed to remember the memory of our fore sisters' suffering and hope rather than abandoning their memory in the biblical text. A hermeneutics of remembrance reclaims their sufferings and struggles through the subversive power of the "remembered past." This "subversive memory" not only keeps alive the sufferings and hopes of women in the biblical past, present and future yet continues to challenge the victims of religious patriarchy through solidarity and committed remembrance of their hopes and despairs and to reclaim biblical women as our biblical heritage.[97] A hermeneutics of remembrance seeks to expose both the values inscribed in the text and the patriarchal or emancipatory interests of its historical contextualization.[98] Judette A. Gallares suggests "Using one's memory or imagination" while recalling the memory of the past.[99] It is time to write that speaks of women's complete equity, participation, and presence in Reform Judaism's leadership and theology.[100] The early Exodus narrative highlights the critical role of women in liberation, and their actions were essential to the Exodus event. Since this history preserves the memory of women, it is important to actively remember this "remembered past" because recognizing women's contributions in history deepens understanding of biblical roles and offers guiding principles for women facing struggles in today's violence and war.

The Context of Violence and Oppression in the Exodus Event

Genesis 41:57 mentions that it was the severe famine that brought a number of nomads in Egypt and Israelites were one among the nomads.[101] They

96 Susanne Scholz and Shelly A. Matthews, "Feminist Biblical Interpretation," in *The Oxford Encyclopaedia of Biblical Interpretation,* ed. Steven L. Mckenzie (New York: Oxford University Press, 2013), 1:303-313.

97 Elisabeth Schussler Fiorenza, *Bread Not Stone: The Challenge of Feminist Biblical Interpretation* (Boston: Beacon Press, 1984), 19-20.

98 Elisabeth Schussler Fiorenza, *But She Said: Feminist Practices of Biblical Interpretation.* Boston: Beacon Press, 1992), 62.

99 Judette AGallares, *Images of Faith: Spirituality of Women in the Old Testament (*Maryknoll: Orbis Books, 1992), 163-164.

100 Rabbi Sarah Berman, "Shiru: Miriam's Model for Leadership," *Central Conference of American Rabbis* 69, no.3 (Sum 2022): 70-71.

101 Francios Castel, *The History of Israel and Judah: In Old Testament Times* (New York: Paulist Press, 1985), 31.

settled in the region of Goshen (Nile Delta) (Gen.41:1-47:12) and soon (Gen.46:4, 50:24)[102] increases in number, which later was exploited as slaves by the Egyptians rulers.[103] They were reduced to forced corvee labor for various building projects (Exo.1:11). Ultimately the Hebrews pleaded to their God for deliverance (Exo.2:23-25).[104] In Egypt, the Israelites lived together in workers' settlements and followed an internal self-rule by elders, yet they were subservient to the Egyptian pharaoh.[105] The corvee[106] the system was known to have been practised in Egypt in all periods.[107] Hence, the Israelites were one of the victims of corvee under the exploitation hands of Pharaoh Rameses II.[108] Egypt becomes a site of forced labor, religious oppression, and the execution of children.[109] It was in this context that the story of Exodus women appeared in the text, describing their act of saving children. What happened to this child in Exodus 2 could have happened to any Israelite infant, and what these women accomplished could have been done by any Israelite woman.[110] Alice Ogden Bellis affirms that the Israelites' freedom "begins with women, and without these women, there would be no Moses to liberate the Hebrews from bondage."[111] Five women

---

102 Nahum M. Sarna, "Israel in Egypt: The Egyptian Sojourn and the Exodus," in *Ancient Israel: A Short History from Abraham to the Roman Destruction of the Temple*, ed. by Hershel Shanks (New Jersey: Prentice-Hall, 1988), 31-52.

103 John Bright, *A History of Israel* (London: SCM Press, 1980), 120.

104 Allen C. Meyers, "Exodus," in *The Eerdmans Bible Dictionary* (Grand Rapids: William B. Eerdmans Publishing Company, 1987), 363-65.

105 Norman K. Gottwald, *The Politics of Ancient Israel* (Kentucky: Westminster Knox Press, 2001), 37. The Egyptian word for 'Pharaoh' is a combination of 'great' and 'house.' Politically, he carried out economic, diplomatic, and military functions. Religiously, he is the representative of the chief God and the people's intermediary to the gods. Below Pharaoh were the court and the priesthood. The country had a centralized bureaucracy; local administrators were responsible directly to the Pharaoh. 80% of the population (peasants) produced all kinds of foods in Egypt and paid the majority of the taxes Laurel A. Dykstra, *Set Them Free: The Other Side of Exodus* (Maryknoll: Orbis Books, 2002), 105-106.

106 Corvee refers to the imposition of compulsory state service upon the population to accomplish building projects, roads, and canals that were state-operated using free or very cheap labour. D. N. Premnath, *Eight Century Prophets: Social Analysis* (Missouri: Chalice Press, 2003), 83.

107 Sarna, "Israel in Egypt: The Egyptian Sojourn and the Exodus," 41.

108 Dykstra, *Set them Free,* 68.

109 Dykstra, *Set Them Free*, 59.

110 Carmen Joy Imes, "Can I Get a Witness? Miriam's Song in the Literary Design of Exodus," *Bulletin for Biblical Research* 33, no. 4 (2023): 431.

111 Alice Ogden Bellis, *Helpmates, Harlots, and Heroes: Women's Stories in the Bible* (Louisville, KY: Westminster John Knox, 2007), 86.]

are specifically highlighted here to emphasize their role in defying Pharaoh's decree. United in their decision, they chose to resist his command without resorting to violence.

The Israelite Midwives Defying the Death Edict of Pharaoh's (Exodus 1:15-21)

In Exodus 1.15-22, the attention centers on two women who give life in a double sense: By profession, they are midwives, and through their actions, they defy the death edict of Pharaoh.[112] The oppressors move from slavery to genocide, and the agents in this atrocity are to be the midwives.[113] These midwives illustrate the only way to break oppression is to refuse to be oppressed.[114] P. Trible remarks that had Pharaoh anticipated the effectiveness of women in thwarting this decree, he might have commanded all female infants to be killed.[115] The number of two midwives has been taken as a sign of a different literary source since the two midwives would suggest a tiny Hebrew community, a contradiction of the tradition that the Hebrews are too numerous.[116] Pharaoh speaks with the midwives of Israel, Shiphrah and Puah (Exo. 1:16) to kill all the Hebrew male[117] Infants and only leave

---

112 J. Cheryl Exum, "You shall Let Every Daughter Live': A Study of Exodus 1:8-2.10," in *A Feminist Companion to Exodus to Deuteronomy*, ed. Athalya Brenner (England: Sheffield Academic Press, 1994), 45.

113 There are different opinions among scholars regarding the ethnicity of the midwives, some suggesting it is of Egyptian or Hebrew origin. For example, Irene Nowell states that these women may be Egyptian. This gives greater credibility to the Pharaoh's expectation that they would obey his command. Irene Nowell, *Women in the Old Testament* (Minnesota: The Liturgical Press, 1997), 46-47. Even though they are described as Hebrew midwives in the Hebrew text, in the Latin and Greek versions, they are understood to be midwives to the Hebrews. See, Alice Ogden Bellis, *Helpmates, Harlots and Heroes: Women's Stories in the Hebrew Bible* (Louisville: Westminster, 1994), 100. No reason is given to justify the Pharaoh's expectations of these midwives, whether they are Hebrews or Egyptian. Although scholars hold differing opinions about the ethnicity of the midwives, regardless of their background, both served under Pharaoh's authority and were accountable to him. This reflects the general powerlessness of women, who were expected to follow orders. However, these two midwives defied expectations and became powerful by deliberately resisting Pharaoh's decree.

114 Irene Nowell, *Women in the Old Testament* (Minnesota: The Liturgical Press, 1997), 47.

115 Phyllis Trible, "Depatriarchalizing in Biblical Interpretation," *Journal of the American Academy Research* 41 (1973): 34.

116 Kim Elli, Kim Jung-su, Lee Yeung-mee, "Women in the Exodus Story," in *Women of Courage: Asian Women Reading the Bible*, eds. Lee Oo Chung, et al., (Korea: Asian Women's Resource Centre for Culture and Theology, 1992), 125-138

117 The male and female were used for different reasons. The boys must die because boys grow up to fight, to be soldiers; they were the most apparent threat to the empire. Girls were used as slaves and for entertainment, and also the Egyptians intermarried with them.

the girls alive. However, the midwives fear God and do not obey Pharaoh's wishes, letting all the male children live.[118] The midwives faced a serious charge.[119] So the king of Egypt summoned the midwives and said to them in (Exo. 1:18), "why have you done this and allowed the boys to live?" The midwives' response suggests that these Hebrew midwives attended both Hebrew and Egyptian births and found out that the Hebrew women were more vigorous and healthier than any of the women of the Pharaoh's experience.[120] Pharaoh again issued the directive in (Exo. 1:22): "Every boy that is born of the Hebrews (the Samaritan, Greek and Targum lack the word "Hebrew) you shall expose on the Nile, but every daughter you shall let live."[121] Here, the Pharaoh portrays death as the source of life, and the midwives as the source of life.[122] The Bible praises the midwives for saving infants; it is even possible that they have saved many more Hebrew children, but it is essential to remember the danger and potential suffering they faced by defying Pharaoh's orders. Despite the risks, the fear of God, bravery, wisdom, and commitment to life allowed them to resist oppression and protect the vulnerable children.

Defying the Decree: Moses' Mother and the Nile River Rescue (Exodus 2:1-3)

Exodus 1.22 provides the introduction to this text. The failure of his second plan drove the king to acts of open violence.[123] Pharaoh promotes a murderous plan to achieve his goal, which is to eliminate it every male child that comes into the world with a death sentence by throwing them into the Nile River.[124] For the Hebrew women, this new decree could have turned the joy of new motherhood into dreadful tension.[125] The sentence in verse 2, "the woman conceived and bore a son," does not mean that she conceived and gave birth for the first time, but at the very time when Pharaoh issued his decree, it happened that this woman became pregnant and gave birth

---

The boys, however, were dangerous and had to be dealt with immediately and violently. Mckenna, *Not Counting Women and Children,* 41.

118 Janice Nunnally Cox, *Fore-Mothers: Women of the Bible* (New York: The Seabury Press, 1981), 30.

119 Exum, "You shall Let Every Daughter Live," 51.

120 John I Durham, *Exodus: Word Biblical Commentary:* (Dallas: Word Book Publishers, 2002),11.

121 Exum, "You shall Let Every Daughter Live," 49.

122 Exum, "You Shall Let Every Daughter Live," 47.

123 Carl Friedrich Keil and Franz Delitzsch, *Commentary on the Old Testament* (Peabody, MA: Hendrickson Publishers, 2002), 275-276.

124 Terence E. Fretheim, *Exodus*: *Interpretation, a Bible Commentary for Teaching and Preaching* (Louisville: John Knox Press, 1991), 31.

125 GienKarssen, *Her Name is Woman* (Colorado: Navpress, 1992), 80.

to a male child. The mother hid the son for three months. However, at the end of this time, she could hide him no longer. So, she made an ark of bulrushes, daubed it with bitumen and pitch, and placed the ark with the child among the reeds at the river's brink.[126] The writer portrays the intense care with which the basket was prepared to prevent its leaking, it even had a top and placed at the edge of the river's bank.[127] Here, Moses' mother joins in the story of resistance to oppression against the Oppressor.[128] All this activity, on her part, underscores the mother's concern for her child.[129] At first glance, Moses' mother seems to be following the command to expose male infants upon the Nile.[130] Although she appears to obey Pharaoh's order, she is resisting it.[131] Moses mother bravely risked her life to save her son, hiding him for three months despite the danger from Pharaoh's men. She knew that no Hebrew person could save her son, whom she had hidden for three months, as they were all in the same oppressed situation. Her only option was Pharaoh's daughter, who, as part of the ruling class, had the power to protect the child, provided she felt compassion from a maternal perspective. She carefully timed placing her son in the ark on the Nile to coincide with Pharaoh's daughter coming to bathe. Moved by compassion, Pharaoh's daughter adopted Moses, ensuring his survival. Moses' mother's courageous defiance and determination to protect her child with various alternatives stand out as a powerful act of resistance.

Miriam's Role in Liberation: A Young Girl's Watchful Eye and Negotiation with Power (Exodus 2:4,7-8)

Miriam presentation in the Bible is that of an active and controversial female- a family member, leader,[132] and a prophetess.[133] She is a multifaceted

126 U. Cassuto, *A Commentary on the Book of Exodus*, trans. Israel Abrahams (Jerusalem: The Magness Press, 1967), 17-18.

127 Brevard S. Childs, *Exodus: A Commentary* (London: SCM Press Ltd, 1974), 18.

128 Nowell, *Women in the Old Testament*, 49.

129 Exum, "You shall Let Every Daughter Live," 53.

130 Exum, "You shall Let Every Daughter Live," 51-52.

131 Alice Ogden Bellis, *Helpmates, Harlots and Heroes*: *Women's Stories in the Hebrew Bible* (Louisville: Westminster, 1994), 101.

132 See, Rita J. Burns, *Has the Lord Indeed Spoken Only through Moses? A Study of the Biblical Portrait of Miriam*, (Atlanta: Scholars, 1987); Carmen Joy Imes, "Can I Get a Witness? Miriam's Song in the Literary Design of Exodus," *Bulletin for Biblical Research* 33, no. 4 (2023): 428.

133 According to the eighth century prophet, Miriam was no usurper. God had called her. Carmen Joy Imes, "Can I Get a Witness? Miriam's Song in the Literary Design of Exodus," 427.

biblical figure, richly painted in Midrashic literature.[134] P. Trible describes the cultural and class chasm separating two women (Moses's mother, Pharaoh's daughter), bridged by a third woman (Miriam).[135] The mother wanted someone to watch over the fate of the ark and the child, so his sister took her stand at a distance to see what would happen to him.[136] The sister plays a vital role as the agent in the story who joins the introductory theme of the mother and child with that of the princess and child.[137] Recently, scholars have noticed that Miriam is a young girl. Catherine Vialle recognizes Miriam as a girl and associates Pharaoh's daughter with Moses's mother, suggesting they both are young women.[138] When Pharaoh's daughter discovered the baby, she approached her and asked if she would like her to find a Hebrew woman to nurse it.[139] She acted alert and swift as a girl (Exo.2.4, 7-8).[140] The infant's young sister did not hesitate and approached Pharaoh's daughter at once and made a suggestion: Shall I go and call you a nurse from the Hebrew women to suckle the child for you? Here, "you" is used twice to give the impression that she is making her suggestion only for the sake of the princess.[141] By suggesting a nurse from the Hebrews, she prepares the way for the reunion of mother and child but suggests that the princess keep the infant, creating the impression that she makes the proposal for the sake of princesses.[142] Not only is the child saved and returned to his mother with royal protection, but she is even paid for caring for her own child.[143] Miriam's calm and confident negotiation with Pharaoh's daughter on the Nile bank reveals how well her mother had prepared her for this crucial task. Her actions reflect her mother's skill in protecting her child from Pharaoh's decree.

---

134 To understand Miriam's various roles not mentioned in the biblical text but preserved in extra-biblical literature, See Phyllis Silverman Kramer, "Miriam," in *Exodus to Deuteronomy: A Feminist Companion to the Bible*, ed. Athalya Brenner (Sheffield: Academic Press, 2000),104.

135 Phyllis Trible, "Bringing Miriam Out of the Shadows," in *A Feminist Companion to Exodus to Deuteronomy,"* 166–86.

136 Cassuto, *A Commentary on the Book of Exodus*, 19.

137 Childs, *Exodus: A Commentary*, 18.

138 Catherine Vialle, "Des femmes á l'origine de la libération des filsd'Israël: Le rôle des femmes et des filles au début du livre de l'Exode," Melanges de science religieuse 74, no. 3 (2017): 13-14

139 Gallares, *Images of Faith: Spirituality of Women in the Old Testament*, 159.

140 Kramer, "Miriam," 105.

141 Cassuto, *A Commentary on the Book of Exodus*, 19-20.

142 Cassuto, *Exodus*, 20.

143 Childs, *Exodus: A Commentary*, 18.

Pharaoh's Daughter: A Royal Defiance Against Her Father's Decree (Exodus 2:5-10)

Pharaoh's daughter comes down to bathe in the Nile. Since her maids are walking beside the Nile, she sees the ark among the reeds. She sends her maid to fetch it; she opens it and sees the child. Observing his tears, she has compassion for the infant. Surmising the situation, she says, "This is one of the Hebrew children."[144] Pharaoh's daughter, like the Hebrews, she too disobeys the law, the king, and her father by saving and adopting a Hebrew child. There are many questions on why she stands together with the Hebrew women. This woman acts in collusion with a mother and daughter to keep a child alive.[145] She, too, defies her father and even adopts the despised and doomed Hebrew child as her own.[146] Although she recognizes that he is one of the Hebrew children, which ties the story back to the king's decree, she does not hesitate to offer it protection.[147] She follows the young sister's proposal to its logical conclusion by taking responsibility for the child upon herself.[148] Additionally, she offered wages to the wet nurse, Moses' mother (v. 9). She did not exploit her position of authority over the enslaved. She despised her position of authority over the enslaved people who were at the mercy of the Egyptians.[149] The story ends with the princess naming the child, another sign perhaps of her claim of the child. She named him Moses. It has long been recognized that the name Moses is Egyptian in derivation, meaning 'son,' which usually appears in the shortened form of Egyptian names like Thutmose. The author connects the name with the Hebrew root 'to draw out,' deriving it from the passive form ("the one drawn out") to match the story.[150] Pharaoh's daughter's compassion for the child and her defiance of her father's harsh decree serves as a reminder of the "powerful memory of the past" of resistance against injustice. Despite being Pharaoh's daughter, she took a bold stand against her father's oppressive nature. Aware of her power as a member of the ruling class, she used her status to protect the child, crossing ethnic, religious, racial, and economic boundaries to preserve life.

144 Exum, "You shall Let Every Daughter Live," 55.

145 McKenna, Megan, *Not Counting Women and Children: Neglected Stories from the Bible* (New York: Orbis Books, 1994),46-47.

146 Göran Larsson, *Bound for Freedom: The Book of Exodus in Jewish and Christian Traditions* (Peabody, Massachusetts: Hendrickson Publishers, 1999), 19.

147 Childs, *Exodus: A Commentary*, 19.

148 Exum, "You shall Let Every Daughter Live," 58.

149 Larsson, *Bound for Freedom,* 19.

150 Childs, *Exodus: A Commentary*, 19.

A Brief Introduction on the Emergence of Meira Paibis

Meira Paibis, literally known as women torchbearers, is an informal and voluntary organization of Meitei women. They assume the protective and self-sacrificing role of mother. They spend nights outside their homes, patrolling their local streets as social guardians of the community. In Meitei society, Meira Paibis is addressed as *Ima Iben* (*Ima*—mother, *Iben*—grandmother) with a sense of respect.[151] This group massively parades each night with torches.[152] The torch, which became the hallmark of the women's movement, was even articulated as a weapon of just war and a sacred symbol of the resistance movement.[153] Meira Paibis's acts of resistance are categorized into formal and informal conventional strategies. Meira Paibis reached demands using a communication approach such as dialogue or negotiation to convey the legal form's needs. Meanwhile, the informal conventional strategy is carried out through street campaigns.[154] Collectively, they use peaceful communication to negotiate policy amendments. At the grassroots, Meira Paibis is active in fasting or hunger strikes as a form of solidarity for the victims of oppression and discrimination.[155] Chaki-Sircar states that the Meitei women had no political or legal rights during the pre-colonial British period.[156] Women in large groups protested against *lalupkaba* (forced labour) of Manipuri men, and. They and came to be known as "Nupilal" (Women's War/ Women's Uprising in 1904). There was an immediate upheaval of another "Nupilal," (Women's War/Women's Uprising in 1939), when Meitei women loss control of trade and economy and the women protested this economic injustice *chaktangba* (a rise in food prices).[157] Nupilal took place as a resistance against British rule since the

151 Ningombam Rojibala, "Meetei Women in the Political Sphere of Manipur," *Indian Journal of Women and Social Change* (2022):2-5.

152 N. Gaikwad, "Revolting Bodies, Hysterical State: Women Protesting the Armed Forces Special Powers Act (1958)," *Contemporary South Asia 17*, no.3 (2009.):299–311.

153 M. L Veneracion-Rallonza, "Women's Naked Body Protests and the Performance of Resistance: Femen and Meira Paibi Protests against Rape," *Philippine Political Science Journal* 35, no. 2 (2014):251–68.

154 Derina FasligSilitonga, "Meira Paibis Movement Roles in Creating Peace at Northeastern India," in *Jurnal Hubungan Internasional Tahun* XIV, no.1 (Januari - Juni 2021): 116.

155 Laishram Jitendrajit Singh, "Reconstructing Women's Nude Protest in Manipur Manipur through Oral History: Public Memory, Women's Identity," *International Journal of Creative Research Thoughts* 8, no. 9 (2020): 2894 2900.

156 Manjushri Chaki-Sircar, Feminism in a traditional society: Women of the Manipur valley (New Delhi: Shakti Books.1984), 29.

157 Laishram Jitendrajit Singh, "Understanding Women's Activism of Manipur: The Meira Paibis Movement," November 29, 2019. Microsoft Word - 21 Laishram Jitendrajit Singh 55- (krishisanskriti.org)https://www.krishisanskriti.org/vol_

subjects of Manipur had to undergo extreme hardships under their rule. It was an uprising against the dictatorship of British imperialism that could shake the capitalists and aristocratic rule of the Britishers.[158] This kind of social consciousness of Meitei women was seen again in the 1970s, when the society of Manipur became prey to drugs,[159] alcohol and other intoxicants. Women in different localities formed an informal organization named Nisha band (banning intoxicants). The informal organization of women which emerged as Nisha band came to be known as Meira paibi, women torch bearers, in 1975, when Manipur was frequently victimized and oppressed by the Indian military personnel under the Armed Forces Special Powers Act (AFSPA), 1958.[160] Under these circumstances, the Meira Paibi movement became a symbol of resilience fighting against the atrocities meted out to individuals.[161] The Meira Paibis women's movement turning point came in 1980 when security forces under the Armed Forces Act 1958 (AFSPA) were deployed to parts of Northeastern India to control insurgent

---

image/29Nov201911115021%20%20Laishram%20Jitendrajit%20Singh%20%20%20%2055-60.pdf

158 Jamini Devi, *Manipuri Culture and Manipuri Women (Manipuri Sanskriti Amasung Manipuri Nupi)*, trans. Chongtham Narendra Singh (Imphal: C D Byte Computers Yaiskul Police Lane, 2009), 47- 49.

159 Manipur is the border state to Myanmar, which has a long history of psychotropic substance abuse with opium, cannabis, alcohol and medical drugs such as Buprenorphine, Cocktails with antihistamine injections, and sedatives such as Benzodiazepines. These drugs were crossed over from the border and circulated to youths of Manipur. The youths of Manipur trapped in insurgent affected zone, together with poor management of law and order by the government, aggravated the situation. The women were concerned as their children were ruining their life, leading to various problems such as physical, psychological, social, health and occupational problems. Pratima Murthy and S. Bala Shanthi Nikketha, eds. *Introduction in Psychosocial Interventions for Persons with Substance Abuse: Theory and Practice, National Institute of Mental Health and Neuro Sciences (*Bangalore: NIMHANS, 2007). It was in 1975 that women in large numbers started the anti-liquor movement in urban as well as in rural areas when the peaceful social order in the localities was disturbed by the persons involved in selling and drinking liquor. The women in groups at this stage were known as Nisha Bandish, and their organizations as Nisha Bandh organizations. The initial movement against alcoholism progressed to various other issues, such as drug abuse. See, Koni Potsangbam, "A Study on the Social Movements by the Women Civil Society Organizations (Meira Paibis) in Manipur State," Doctoral diss., Department of Social Work at Faculty of Arts, Social Sciences & Commerce at University of Bharati Vidyapeeth Deemed Pune, 2016), 65-66.

160 Rojibala, "Meetei Women," 2-5.

161 Rosy Yumnam, "The Meira Paibi Movement: A Feminist And Educative Perspective," March 2023, (PDF) The Meira Paibi Movement: A Feminist And Educative Perspective (researchgate.net). https://www.researchgate.net/publication/369474179_the_meira_paibi_movement_a_feminist_and_educative_perspective

forces.[162] In 1980, Manipur was declared "disturbed", and the Armed Forces (Special Powers) Act was imposed in the state.[163] With the enactment of AFSPA of 1958, it is used as a pretext for discrimination and violations of human rights by the Armed Forces. Reports of sexual harassment cases, rape, and even murder unilaterally encouraged Meira Paibis as a grassroots women's movement to develop a strategy of resistance.[164] The peak of the movement then occurred in 2004 when twelve elderly women positioned themselves in front of the Kangla Fort Gate with their naked bodies to voice their acts of disillusionment and protest against the AFSPA soldiers and the government.[165] The naked bodies that they show are symbolic of the unrest they have felt since enacting the particular privilege policy on AFSPA soldiers.[166] As Ima LourembamNganbi says, 'When our children are suffering, can we as mothers remain silent?' For the *imas*, the mother's identity is central to their memories of the protest. If my daughter lies naked, how can I be clothed? When Manipur has been stripped of its clothes, how can we, as mothers, be quiet?[167] The aggressive act of stripping oneself successfully pushed the Assam Rifles troops to evacuate the Kangla

162 A. Ranjan, A, "A Gender Critique of AFSPA: Security for Whom?" *Social Change* 45, no. 3 (2015): 440–457.

163 See, Human Rights Watch, "*These Fellows Must Be Eliminated: Relentless Violence and Impunity in Manipur*," also Yumlembam Mema, September 2008, "These Fellows Must Be Eliminated": Relentless Violence and Impunity in Manipur: II. Background: Conflict in Manipur (hrw.org) https://www.hrw.org/reports/2008/india0908/1.htm

164 Silitonga, "Meira Paibis Movement," 110.

165 P. Ray, "Political Motherhood and a Spectacular Resistance: (Re) Examining the Kangla Fort Protest, Manipur," *South Asian History and Culture* 9, no. 4 (2018):435–448. One of the cases committed by AFSPA that received public attention was the Thangjam Manorama case of rape, torture and killing by the Armed Forces in July 2004. See, M. Basnet, "Disrobed and Dissenting Bodies of the Meira Paibi: Postcolonial Counter public Activism," *Communication and the Public* 4, no.3 (2019):239–252.
Using their bodies, Meira Paibis opposed the AFSPA soldiers to come out and gave them the option to rape them in public or protect the people of Manipur. Veneracion Rallonza 2014 [Veneracion-Rallonza, M. L., 2014. "Women's Naked Body Protests and the Performance of Resistance: Femen and Meira Paibi Protests against Rape", Philippine Political Science Journal, 35 (2):251–68.]).

166 Ranjan "A Gender Critique of AFSPA," 440–457.

167 Panchali Ray, "Political Motherhood and a Spectacular Resistance: (Re) Examining the Kangla Fort Protest, Manipur," *South Asian History and Culture* 9, no. 4 (2018):435–448, personal interview by Panchali Ray to Ima LourembamNganbi on 03.09.2016.

battalion base.[168] A month after this protest, the state government withdrew the controversial AFSPA from seven constituencies in Imphal area.[169]

Meira Paibis: Navigating the Complexities of Peace and Blame

Manipur, situated in Northeast India, has experienced violence and conflict for decades. But the present Manipur violence is a complex and tragic phenomenon that has affected the lives of many people.[170] The violence has resulted in thousands of injuries and over 60,000 displacements, as well as widespread destruction of property, infrastructure, and social cohesion. The Supreme Court stated, "There is no law and order left at all" in Manipur, despite 6,500 FIRs registered by the "lethargic" police. There is a breakdown of constitutional machinery" in the state.[171] In Manipur's law and order crisis, it is unclear who is responsible - the Chief Minister, the state government, or the Prime Minister, complicating accountability. The role of the armed forces, whether deployed by the state or central government, is also ambiguous. The Home Minister's comments about cooperation from the CM contribute to the confusion, raising doubts about effective governance. This lack of clarity exacerbates the violence, with the state government failing to provide solutions, forcing citizens to protect themselves in a situation that resembles statelessness.[172] In this current situation, emerging challenges may hinder the Meira Paibis non-violence movement's success in implementing its principles.[173] Several challenges have hindered Meira Paibi's non-violence movement and made it challenging to achieve several goals.[174] The Meira Paibis are now facing accusations of obstructing the army and inciting violence against Kuki-Zo

---

168 V. Arora, "Citizens, the Smoking Guns of AFSPA and Bare Life in Northeast India," *Sociological Bulletin* 69, no. 3 (2020): 351–67]).

169 Singh, Understanding Women's Activism of Manipur, Microsoft Word - 21 Laishram Jitendrajit Singh 55- (krishisanskriti.org)

170 Soroj Mullick SDB, "Manipur: A Frying Pan for the 'Good Friday People Reflections on the Manipur Violence from a Christian Perspective," *Third Millennium XXVI*, no.2 (2023): 42-76.

171 Panchali Ray, "Political Motherhood and a Spectacular Resistance: (Re) Examining the Kangla Fort Protest, Manipur," *South Asian History and Culture* 9, no. 4 (2018):435–448, personal interview by Panchali Ray to Ima LourembamNganbi on 03.09.2016.

172 AngomchaBimolAkoijam Speech, "One Voice Seminar held at Punjab University in Chandigarh on September 16 2023, posted on September 21, 2023, by EastMojo, 1:00:35, Youtube, Meitei JNU professor questions government over continuing violence in Manipur (youtube.com) https://www.youtube.com/watch?v=vts1m3icuac

173 Derina FasligSilitonga, "Meira Paibis Movement Roles in Creating Peace at Northeastern India," in *JurnalHubunganInternasionalTahun*XIV/1 (Januari - Juni 2021): 119.

174 U. Goswami, "Armed in Northeast India: Special Powers, Act or No Act," *Peace and Conflict Review* 4, no. 2 (2010): 1–14.

women, with people questioning whether they are feminist icons or violent vigilantes. In this battle, hundreds of Meira Paibisare out on the highways during the day, and patrolling the streets of their localities by night. They are the first line of defense for their community, a role they take to heart.[175] There is an absolute breakdown of trust between the two communities, with brutal killings occurring on both sides, and the Meira Paibis have completely lost faith in the armed forces as well.[176] Most disturbingly, throughout this conflict, Meira Paibis have been accused of participating in violence against women.[177] This is an issue the Meira Paibis will have to engage with and conduct their own serious post-mortem on their actions; otherwise, it will remain a blot on all Meitei women for a long time.[178] According to the Meitei activists, different groups can use their influence over the Meira Paibis to do their bidding. Since the ethnic clashes between the Meiteis and Kuki-Zo communities, the mistrust between the Meira Paibis and the central security forces has sharpened. However, there are many questions raised about the activity of the MeriaPaibis: How could a women's organization with such a rich history of standing up against injustice be party to crimes against women? Senior Meira Paibis and Meitei civil society leaders cited "lack of organization" and the "decentralized structure" of the movement as a reason for the alleged transgressions. Ema Lungwaleima, a Meira Paibi in her sixties, agreed. "No one was prepared ... no one knew that a warlike situation was imminent. Since it happened suddenly, people took up their ways to protect themselves," she said. However, conversations

175 Tora Agarwala, "Manipur Unrest: Feminist icons or violent vigilantes? The contentious role of Meira Paibis in Manipur's conflict," August 4, 2023, Manipur conflict: The contentious role of Meira Paibis. Feminist icons or community thugs? (scroll.in)https://scroll.in/article/1053761/feminist-icons-or-violent-vigilantes-the-contentious-role-of-meira-paibis-in-manipur-conflict

176 In Itham village in Imphal East district, the Meira Paibis confronted security personnel, forcing them to release 12 cadres of the KangleiYawol Kanna Lup (a Meitei separatist outfit). The cadres had been arrested with arms and ammunition during an operation in Imphal East district. These incidents underscore the evolving nature of the political activism of Meitei women in Manipur. Ophelia Yumlembam, "Manipur Violence: Understanding the Shifts in Meitei Women's Political Activism," August 9, 2023. Manipur Violence: Understanding the Shifts in Meitei Women's Political Activism–The Diplomat. https://the diplomat.com/2023/08/Manipur-violence-understanding-the-shifts-in-meitei-womens-political-activism/

177 Agarwala,"ManipurUnrest,"https://scroll.in/article/1053761/feminist_icons_or_violent_vigilantes_the _contentious_role_of_meira_paibis_in_manipur_conflict

178 Manorama Sharma, "Meira Paibis: How Manipur's peace-keepers became agents provocateur," August 24, 2023.Meira Paibis: How Manipur's peace-keepers became agents provocateur - Frontline (thehindu.com) https://frontline.thehindu.com/the-nation/manipur-conflict-meira-paibis-how-manipurs-peace-keepers-became-agent-provocateurs/articles67212483.ece

with many Meira Paibis made it clear that most of them were not guided by feminist principles. The community took precedence over gender for most women's groups in Manipur. Ema Lungwaleima, the general secretary of the wing, said she went to neighbourhoods asking people not to indulge in mob violence. The other Meitei woman activist in Imphal, who is not actively involved with the Meira Paibis, said there was also disquiet within the Meira Paibi groups.[179]

The conflict in Manipur is driven by numerous unresolved issues, deepening distrust between communities, and hate-filled communal narratives in the media. The failure of state machinery to protect citizens has left many, including women, men, and children, vulnerable and direct victims. In this vacuum, Meira Paibis, as protectors of their community, strive to defend their people, but their actions, driven by ethnicity, risk deepening enmity and intensifying ethnic tensions. Despite their errors, including involvement in violence against women, the Meira Paibis have played a significant role in stopping further violence by acting as the first responders to protests and killings. However, they lack political power and legal influence, making them vulnerable to manipulation by those in power for political gain. There is an urgent need for the state government to rebuild trust and ensure the safety of the Meira Paibis, as they are left unprotected while they safeguard others. Additionally, they require training and resources to better respond to conflict situations.

Contemporary Challenges and Implications: Insights from the Exodus Women Towards Meira Paibis

The resonance of resistance between women in the biblical Exodus and the Meira Paibis movement in Manipur reveals a few implications regarding women's roles in times of crisis, especially in contexts of resistance, protection, and non-violence. Women have always been at the forefront of saving lives in biblical events like the Exodus. They have come together from all ages, races, and occupations to safeguard people who are victims of injustice. Even in ancient times, when Pharaoh ordered the execution of male Hebrew infants, midwives resisted the command, risking their own lives in solidarity to preserve the children. Similarly, Moses' mother resisted Pharaoh's command by concealing her child for three months before placing him in a tightly sealed basket to keep him safe in the river. She was aware of the hazards but took every care, assigning her daughter, young Miriam, to watch over him. When Pharaoh's daughter discovered the basket, her compassion for the Hebrew kid overcame her father's edict, and she adopted

179 Agarwala,https://scroll.in/article/1053761/feminist_icons_or_violent_vigilantes_the_contentious_role_of_meira_paibis_in_manipur_conflict

Moses. In an act of courage, Miriam approached Pharaoh's daughter and suggested a nurse for the child, resulting in Moses' mother being paid to care for him. This narrative powerfully illustrates the bond between women from different backgrounds, built on trust and empathy. Their actions, driven by a shared understanding of suffering and compassion, were carried out with faith and mutual support, especially for the Hebrews, who feared God. Though the women's roles disappear from the story over time, their resilience must be remembered and celebrated because it remains pertinent to contemporary conflict and struggle.

In the Exodus story, women step forward as protectors of life. The midwives, Moses' mother, Miriam and Pharaoh's daughter, defy Pharaoh's decree to save Hebrew infants, highlighting their courage and maternal instincts to preserve lives. Similarly, the Meira Paibis have historically fought against various social evils and injustices perpetrated by British invaders, the imposition of AFSPA military force and other social related issues. The biblical exodus women and the Meira Paibis took charge of their circumstances when the state machinery failed. In Exodus, Hebrew women and Pharaoh's daughter risk their lives to defy Pharaoh's orders to save lives. Similarly, the Meira Paibis have historically challenged injustices despite the risks involved. It is crucial to recognize that their actions are driven by a collective, conscious decision to reject subjugation and risk their own lives to save more lives. In Exodus, Pharaoh's daughter adopts Moses despite knowing he is a Hebrew, demonstrating empathy that transcends political and ethnic boundaries. This illustrates the potential for human empathy and solidarity even within oppressive systems. The Meira Paibis can draw from this Pharaoh's daughter act by embracing solidarity beyond religion, class, and ethnicity. The biblical narrative and Meira Paibis movement emphasize non-violent resistance, with Exodus women using peaceful defiance to save lives and Meira Paibis using slogans and different forms of protest. This tradition highlights women's use of non-violence as a powerful tool in confronting injustice. Women, like the Exodus and Meira Paibis, face vulnerability in male-dominated power structures and political manipulation despite their crucial roles in resistance.

Urgent Call to Action: The Meira Paibis and the Path Forward

Historically, the Meira Paibis have significantly contributed to the welfare of the people of Manipur. However, during the recent conflict, their role has changed drastically. While their active participation in the crisis is undeniable, they feel obligated to protect their communities. Even though women lead the movement, it does not adhere entirely to feminist ideology. Instead, it focuses on addressing the community's broader needs while continuing to combat crimes against women actively. It is essential to recognize how they, too, are victims of the situation, defending and safeguarding their communities in addition to their responsibilities. Despite their community contribution, their guiding ideology needs reassessment to prevent exploitation or scapegoating.

Their earlier accomplishments and contributions should be recalled and remembered, and a more in-depth analysis of what has happened during this conflict and what steps are required should be undertaken both by the state government and the other civil society organizations. In the current ongoing violence in Manipur, women, mainly those directly affected, are using various platforms to plead for peace. These voices, including those of grieving mothers, fathers, wives, and children, highlight a desperate desire for tranquillity rather than revenge. The tragic cycle of violence could have been prevented with timely state intervention, but the state's failure has led people to protect their communities in the best way they can despite lacking proper conflict management skills. Women, notably the Meira Paibis, during this conflict, listened to the voices of the victims and addressed their unjust suffering. Besides criticizing the Meira Paibis for their recent actions, it is essential to understand the historical context and shifts that occurred for the first time in Manipur's history during this unprecedented situation in Manipur. It is crucial to investigate how the situation of the Meira Paibis has evolved, what changes have occurred, and what steps need to be taken to improve the community.

Conclusion

The Exodus liberation movement began with courageous women consciously subverting Pharaoh's decree, spanning racial, religious, gender, and ethnic lines. Their leadership and moral courage were exhibited through non-violent opposition. This mirrors the role of the Meira Paibis, who similarly demonstrate leadership and moral courage in resisting oppression and protecting their communities since the British colonial period. The parallel between the women in the Exodus narrative and the Meira Paibis highlights women's crucial roles in non-violent resistance, moral courage, and community protection. Both examples show how women often take on leadership roles in crises, advocating for peace and defending life when state structures fail. Their activism underscores women's vital role in both historical and contemporary conflicts and their inherent vulnerability when state governance fails to provide adequate support for its citizen.

22

Purity and Pollution in the Dead Sea Scrolls
A Dalit Perspective

B. Silpa Rani

Introduction

The pioneering works by Prof. Rev. Dr. K. Jesurathnamin terms of his books, Dalit Liberative Hermeneutics: Indian Christian Dalit Hermeneutics of Psalm 22 (2010),[180] Exploring Dalit Liberative Hermeneutics in India & the World: Based on An Ancient Hebrew Prophet, Jeremiah of Anathoth (2015),[181] and the recent publication, Introduction to Old Testament: A Dalit Liberative Hermeneutical Perspective (2023),[182] have been my inspiration to contribute an article entitled "Purity and Pollution in the Dead Sea Scrolls: A Dalit Perspective" on the occasion of his 60th-year celebration (Shashtipoorthi). Prof. Jesurathnam has been my teacher (guru) in both my degrees, M.Th. (2015-17) and D.Th. (2021-2025) at the United Theological College, Bangalore.

180 K. Jesurathnam, *Dalit Liberative Hermeneutics: Indian Christian Dalit Hermeneutics of Psalm 22* (Delhi: ISPCK, 2010).

181 K Jesurathnam, *Exploring Dalit Liberative Hermeneutics in India & the World: Based on an Ancient Hebrew Prophet, Jeremiah of Anathoth* (New Delhi: Christian World Imprints, 2015).

182 K. Jesurathnam, *Introduction to the Old Testament: A Dalit Liberation & Hermeneutical Perspective* (Delhi: Christian World Imprints, 2023).

While celebrating his life and contribution, I must acknowledge that it was his encouragement that pushed me to get admission at the UTC during COVID-19, when I did not plan for studies in 2021 due to the break out of COVID and thought of applying for my doctoral program the following year. As the famous quotation goes, "Sometimes the best things in life are unplanned", and indeed, it was true in my case. Though unplanned from my end, purely Prof. Jesurathnam's inspiration pushed me to get admission to the doctoral program, which eventually made me join UTC in 2021. I clearly remember that it was the second wave of COVID-19, and I was infected when I appeared for an online interview with the faculty members of UTC for admission. At this juncture, I am incredibly grateful to him for his guidance through my admission process and his willingness to be my supervisor for my doctoral program.

Currently, Prof. Jesurathnam is my research supervisor who has encouraged me tremendously in my doctoral program. He has supported, guided, and influenced my entire academic journey in various ways. He has offered constructive feedback on my research, helping me refine my ideas, methodology, and content and developing my critical thinking and research techniques. As my research area is the Dead Sea Scrolls, he has invigorated my zeal to explore this area by visiting various libraries on land and abroad. Moreover, he has offered me the opportunity to facilitate exegesis classes on the Dead Sea Scroll texts with the Master's students at the United Theological College, Bangalore, which has been one of the most exciting experiences during my research journey. I will always be grateful for his scholarly guidance, which drives me to explore not only my research area but also delve into the scholarly arena of the Hebrew Bible and the Dead Sea Scrolls. I am privileged to work under him, as I have learned enormously from his expertise. He is an expert in Dalit reading of the Hebrew Bible, and his works concentrate on the Dalit interpretation of the Biblical texts with liberative motifs. Therefore, as a renowned Indian Dalit Biblical scholar, I would like to dedicate this article to him by exploring the concept of purity and pollution in the Dead Sea Scrolls with a Dalit lens.

This article is an attempt to read the Dead Sea Scrolls with its underlying notion of "purity and pollution" from an Indian Dalit lens. The Dead Sea Scrolls, discovered in the mid-twentieth century, shed light on the Qumran community's religious beliefs, customs, and communal life, which were greatly influenced by the Second Temple Period. In these scrolls, "purity and pollution" is frequently associated with ritual cleanliness, moral conduct, and community boundaries. Dalits, one of India's historically oppressed communities, have endured institutionalized discrimination and social exclusion for ages. In this marginalization, the Indian caste system's concept of "purity and pollution" plays an important role. This article will explore the notion of "purity and pollution" in the Second Temple Period, the Dead Sea Scrolls, and the Indian Dalit context.

Purity and Pollution During the Second Temple Period

Purification was practiced in various contexts during the Second Temple era, and the system of purification marked initiations into several forms of Judaism.[183] One of the fundamental principles of ancient Judaism is that the Jewish people are an organic whole chosen by God. Many groups that grew during this time separated from this exaggerated understanding of Israel's purity. Therefore, it was believed that other organizations had either deviated from or fallen short of the utmost standards of Jewish purity.[184] The most striking indication of the temple's status is that questions of purity and impurity, originally confined to the temple space, burst into the everyday lives of different Jewish communities.[185] That is the reason that the Gentiles, resident aliens, and strangers were regarded ritually impure as they failed to observe the Torah consisting of laws of ritual purity. Hence, Israel is separated from other nations/groups to pursue a life of holiness and purity.[186] The attention to matters of ritual purity was so extreme that the impurity caused by an abomination was more difficult for them than the loss of life.[187] Ritual purity is the first and foremost marker of separating Israelites from non-Israelites.[188] This notion of Israel being a separate, chosen, and holy nation has been attested by the scriptural base of the Hebrew Bible, especially the Torah, and by keeping the purity laws Israel was set apart from other nations. In the Israelite religion, this notion was strongly evident as it categorized people, objects, and places as either pure or impure. The Jews considered bodily discharges and corpses as impure (Lev. 11-15; Num. 19).[189] The Jews were purified before meals and prayers.

---

183 Hannah K. Harrington, *The Purity Texts*, Companion to the Qumran Scrolls 5 (London; New York: T&T Clark International, 2004), 7.

184 David Flusser, *Judaism of the Second Temple Period. Volume 2: The Jewish Sages and Their Literature* (Grand Rapids: William B. Eerdmans, 2009), 8.

185 Flusser, *Judaism of the Second Temple Period. Volume 2: The Jewish Sages and Their Literature*, 22.

186 Christine Elizabeth Hayes, *Gentile Impurities and Jewish Identities: Intermarriage and Conversion from the Bible to the Talmud* (Oxford; New York: Oxford University Press, 2002), 19-20.

187 Flusser, *Judaism of the Second Temple Period. Volume 2: The Jewish Sages and Their Literature*, 9.

188 Harrington, *The Purity Texts*, 34.

189 Cecilia Wassen, "Purity and Holiness," in *T&T Clark Companion to the Dead Sea Scrolls*, ed. Charlotte Hempel and George J. Brooke, T&T Clark Companions (London; New York; Oxford; New Delhi; Sydney: T&T Clark, 2019), 513.

Jews regarded the city of Jerusalem as the holy city and purified themselves before participating in the festivals. The priestly portion of the harvest was selected in a state of ritual purity.[190] All these practices were regularized in the Jewish context with the motif of being separated and ritually pure from the Gentiles, strangers and resident aliens.

One of the remarkable contexts in the history of Judaism in the Second Temple period is the time of Ezra and Nehemiah, who urged for the dissolution of the marriages which were between the Jews and the Gentiles (Ezra 6:21; 9:1; 11-14, Neh. 13:30) which led the biblical readers to opine that the foreign wives are ritually impure as the Canaanites, who were considered Gentiles were engaged in morally defiling behaviours which is also articulated in Lev.18.[191] The Second Temple sources, like the biblical sources, were concerned that contact with the idolatrous and non-Israelites would result in a deleterious religious and moral effect on the Israelites. For many Jews, the limitation of social interaction with the Gentile was desirable to refrain from erosion of fidelity and undermining Jewish laws.[192] The Book of Jubilees in the second century BCE is concerned with the matters of purity. Jubilees 3: 8-14 contains the childbirth purity laws of Leviticus 12:2-5. Jubilees 22: 16-22 and 30:13-15 forbid keeping the relationship with Gentile as their ways are defiled, abominable, and detestable.[193] Sirach 11:34 records the suspicion that intimate contact with or hospitality toward a stranger will compromise one's loyalties: "Let the stranger dwell with thee, and he will estrange thy way of life and alienate thee from thine own house."[194] The uniting standard for most of the religious communities during the Hellenistic period was ritual purity. Indeed, the entire Second Temple Period was characterized by the later rabbis as the period when purity burst out in Israel.[195] During this period, Jewish Philosopher Philo's writings were impactful they prioritized moral purity over ritual purity, stressing the defilement of soul over body, which prompted the Jews to resonate with the Torah and to emphasize that moral defilement has on the individual sinner as opposed to the community of Israel as a whole. According to Philo sinners ought to be excluded from the sanctuary as their sins make them unworthy

190 Harrington, *The Purity Texts*, 7.

191 Jonathan Klawans, *Impurity and Sin in Ancient Judaism* (Oxford: Oxford University Press, 2000), 44-45.

192 Hayes, *Gentile Impurities and Jewish Identities: Intermarriage and Conversion from the Bible to the Talmud*, 47.

193 Klawans, *Impurity and Sin in Ancient Judaism*, 47.

194 Hayes, *Gentile Impurities and Jewish Identities: Intermarriage and Conversion from the Bible to the Talmud*, 47.

195 Flusser, *Judaism of the Second Temple Period. Volume 2: The Jewish Sages and Their Literature*, 9.

of encountering the sacred.[196] In the Letter of Aristeas, the Alexandrian Jewish author Aristeas mentions the abomination and the rules of purity in 142: "Therefore, lest we should be corrupted by any abomination or our lives will be perverted by evil communication, he hedged us round on all sides by rules of purity, affecting alike what we eat, drink, or touch, or hear, or see." The purpose of these instructions was to restrict extensive social interactions. Some of the writings have lenient approaches to purity matters. In some texts, contacts for business dealings seem to pose no threat, as long as restrictions based on sabbath observance, *kashrut*,[197] Worship, and so on are taken into consideration, for example, III Maccabees 3:3-7,10. Josephus, too, has a similar approach in that the ancestral laws and customs are in no way intended to offend or alienate non-Israelites.[198]

Some scholars cite texts that refer to Jewish abstention from Gentile foods as evidence of Gentile ritual impurity.[199] Purity censures spread throughout Jewish society, playing the same role in everyday religious observance that would later be allotted to dietary restrictions, *kashrut*. However, there is an important distinction between purity and dietary laws, as the latter applies to all Jews equally, while the adoption of the former, at least outside of the area of the temple, was a matter of personal choice.[200] As a result, different levels of purity emerged: The Pharisees, whose legal doctrines were preserved in the rabbinic corpus, set themselves apart from the impurities of the lay folk and maintained strict rules of purity, including the consumption of non-temple foodstuffs. From a halakhic perspective, the Pharisees were nothing more than a group that maintained a certain level of purity. [201] According to the Mishnah, Yose ben Yo'ezer is referred as the mist pious in the priesthood, or more, literally as "pious within the priesthood" (*hasid she-ba-kehunah*). The word *hasid* here is questionable which refers to his piety or was he perhaps part of Hasidim.[202] It appears from a halakhic

196 Klawans, *Impurity and Sin in Ancient Judaism*, 65–66.

197 כַּשְׁרוּת refers to Jewish Dietary Laws, including the preparation, storing, and eating of food. It also included Laws on slaughtering animals that are permitted for consumption.

198 Hayes, *Gentile Impurities and Jewish Identities: Intermarriage and Conversion from the Bible to the Talmud*, 47–48.

199 Gedaliah Alon, "The Levitical Uncleanliness of Gentiles," in *Jews, Judaism, and the Classical World*, trans. I. Abrahams (Jerusalem: Magnes Press, 1977), 181.

200 Flusser, *Judaism of the Second Temple Period. Volume 2: The Jewish Sages and Their Literature*, 9.

201 Flusser, *Judaism of the Second Temple Period. Volume 2: The Jewish Sages and Their Literature*, 9.

202 The religious community that joined the Hasmonean in the early days of rebellion against the Seleucid empire. A later midrash records that Yose ben Yo'ezer was executed by Eliyaqim (or Yakim), that is, by Alcimus, the Antiochian high priest who served at the

perspective; the purity observance of the Hasidim was stricter than that of the Pharisees and they were defined in terms of their commitment to a certain level of ritual purity.[203]

In short, the concern about purity and impurity during the Second Temple era was not only a religious practice but a defining feature of Jewish identity and separation from other nations. The strict adherence to ritual purity laws underscored the Israelites' commitment to holiness, particularly in their separation from Gentiles, whom they considered ritually impure. Scriptural and historical sources from this period reflect the tension between preserving Jewish purity and engaging with non-Jewish cultures. The emphasis on moral and ritual purity shaped communal boundaries and reinforced the distinct identity of the Jewish people amidst foreign influences. However, these demanding laws and customs on purity and pollution among the Jews paved the way for religious splits among the Jews during the Second Temple Period.

Purity and Pollution Evolvement at Qumran During the Second Temple Period

According to David Flusser, the concept of inclusive Jewish sanctity (purity) engendered religious splits within the Jewish people. These splits led to increased tension between the warring factions, occasionally to political schisms within the broader populace, and eventually to persecution and civil war.[204] Ironically, an ideology of Jewish unity set the stage for separatist tendencies, whose most extreme form is visible in the Qumran sect. This group saw itself as faithful Israel while the rest of the Jewish world was "futility, for futile are those who do not know the covenant. And all those who scorn his word he shall cause to vanish from the world" (1QS 5: 19-20). Thus, the other Second Temple Jewish sect could see itself as the faithful Israel versus Israel even when it broke off from Judaism itself.[205] In the aftermath of the desecration of the temple in the Second Century BCE,

---

outbreak of the Hasmonean revolt.1 Maccabees 7:16 recounts that Alcimus executed sixty of the Hasidim. All these suggest that Yose ben Yo'zer, who was executed by Alcimus, was one of the sixty Hadisim and that Mishnah Hagigah 2:7 reports that this man was a Hasid- a member of the Hasidim who served in the priesthood." Flusser, *Judaism of the Second Temple Period. Volume 2: The Jewish Sages and Their Literature*, 9; G. Alon, *Studies in Jewish History* (Tel Aviv, 1957), 148–76.

203 Flusser, *Judaism of the Second Temple Period. Volume 2: The Jewish Sages and Their Literature*, 10.

204 Flusser, *Judaism of the Second Temple Period. Volume 2: The Jewish Sages and Their Literature*, 8.

205 Flusser, *Judaism of the Second Temple Period. Volume 2: The Jewish Sages and Their Literature*, 8.

the Qumran sect chose to determine its self-dignity by separating from other Jews to a lifestyle of greater purity. This view is supported by 4QMMT, which outlines several cultic and purity complaints against some individuals or groups, which is not rigorous enough in these matters, although it knows better.[206] They followed the laws of ritual purity as the faithful Jews. According to J. Litch:

> "Another group that defined itself in terms of its rules of ritual purity is the Qumran sect, which most scholars identify as Essenes. The centrality of purity is evident throughout the Dead Sea Scrolls."[207]

In line with the same thought, Harrington states:

> "Among all the Jewish groups of the Second Temple Era, the Qumran Community was the most rigorous in maintaining Purity. The Laws of Purity and impurity were a central concern for the authors of the Dead Sea Scrolls."[208]

The community's emphasis on purity is supposed by Josephus' descriptions of the Qumran community and by the site at Qumran, where an ancient channel connected many cisterns and immersion baths. Thus, the report of Josephus on the Essene is very close to the community documents of the scrolls in the area of purity. For example, the sect required baths and a change of clothing before meals.[209] They were known for their strictness on purity, and according to Josephus:

> "They are divided, according to the duration of their discipline, into four grades; and so far are the junior members inferior to the seniors, that a senior, if but touched by a junior, must take a bath, as after contact with an alien." (War 2:150).[210]

The Qumranites were very strict in matters of purity and impurity and believed that ritual impurity is acquired not only through contact with an impure substance but through sin itself. Thus, in the Rule of the Community it states:

> "He should not go into the waters to share in the pure food of the men of holiness for one is not cleansed unless one turns

206 Harrington, "Purity and the Dead Sea Scrolls-Current Issues," 399.

207 J. Licht, *Megillat Ha-Serachim* (Jerusalem, 1971), 294-303.

208 Harrington, *The Purity Texts*, 7.

209 Harrington, *The Purity Texts*, 8.

210 Hayes, *Gentile Impurities and Jewish Identities: Intermarriage and Conversion from the Bible to the Talmud*, 63.

> away from one's wickedness for he is unclean among all the transgressors of his word" (1QS 5:13-14).[211]

Before the immersion, the members of the community had to turn away from their wrongdoing to repent before God, thus removing from their own being the impurity that attends sin. "And by the compliance of his soul with all the laws of God his flesh is cleansed by being sprinkled with cleansing water and being made holy with the waters of repentance" (1QS 3:8-9).[212]

Both the Scrolls and Josephus agree on the period of initiation within the community based on the exclusion of the candidate from pure food and drink until he has been accepted. The common meal is discussed both in Scrolls and Josephus, along with necessary purifications (1QS 6:2-5; War 2:129). Both the impurity of excrement and Gentile are evident in some of the scrolls and Josephus' descriptions of the Essenes. The Damascus document refers to a group of celibates as the 'men of perfect holiness' as opposed to the inferior holiness of those who have families (CD 7: 4-9). Philo states that it is through their purity rituals that the Essenes expressed their love of God.[213] The group at Qumran appears to have been a celibate, monastic group of Essenes who had separated themselves for some time or a lifetime.[214] Purity laws of the Scrolls are a large pillar of the Essene hypothesis, which holds that the members of the Qumran community are in some way connected to the Essenes, as Elisha Qimron's argument on the celibacy of the community[215] and Cross equates the community with the Essenes and eventually with the priestly laws.[216] However, contrary to those ideas, scholars have opined the disconnection between the purity laws of the Jews and the community's behaviour. Norman Golb finds the purity concerns in the Qumran community to be unsure if indeed they stem from a priestly

211 Flusser, *Judaism of the Second Temple Period. Volume 2: The Jewish Sages and Their Literature*, 22.

212 Flusser, *Judaism of the Second Temple Period. Volume 2: The Jewish Sages and Their Literature*, 22.

213 Harrington, "Purity and the Dead Sea Scrolls-Current Issues," 398.

214 Harrington, *The Purity Texts*, 8.

215 Elisha Qimron, "Celibacy in the Dead Sea Scrolls and Two Kinds of Sectarians," in *The Madrid Qumran Congress: Proceedings of the International Congress on the Dead Sea Scrolls, Madrid, 18-21 March, 1991*, ed. Julio C. Trebolle Barrera and Luis Vegas Montaner, vol. 1 of *Studies on the Texts of the Desert of Judah* 11 (Leiden ; New York : Madrid: Brill ; Editorial Complutense, 1992), 287–89.

216 Frank Moore Cross, "The Historical Context of the Scrolls," in *Understanding the Dead Sea Scrolls: A Reader from the "Biblical Archaeology Review,"* ed. Hershel Shanks (New York: Random House, 1992), 20–34.

community.[217] A. Baumgarten regards purity, especially food and drink as a primary distinction of the Qumran sect but he does not equate them with the Essenes.[218] Shemaryahu Talmon too proposes the Qumran community as the community of renewed covenants and calls them covenanters rather than connecting them to the sect of Essenes.[219] Several scholars have questioned and challenged the idea that the Qumran community was celibate, monastic, and Essenes. Therefore, this research highlights the notion of purity and pollution that prevailed within the Qumran community without delving deeper into the community's identity, which has been debated over the period.

Concept of Purity and Pollution in the Dead Sea Scrolls

According to Hannah Harrington, the Dead Sea Scroll community is known for a certain distinctive interpretation of purity: 1. Among the Scrolls there is a tendency to expand the categories of holiness and purity of the Torah and to interpret purity restrictions maximally; 2. Impurity is defined as a more malevolent force than any other ancient Jewish text in terms of sources, contagion, and purification; 3. The pure food and drink of the community, often called 'the purity' becomes a central focus of the community; 4. Ritual and moral impurity are intertwined."[220] She divides the concept of purity and holiness in the DSS into three parts: 1. קֹדֶשׁ קָדָשִׁים (*qodesh qodashim*)-holy of holies, 2.קֹדֶשׁ (*qodesh*)-holy, 3.טָהוֹר(*tahor)*-pure.[221]

1. **קֹדֶשׁ קָדָשִׁים (*qodesh qodashim*):** According to the Temple Scroll, the 'holy of holies' is the entire sanctuary as well as the altar area (11Q19 35:8-9). It refers to all priests (not just the high priest) and the angels. The Community Rule refers to ranks in the 'community of holiness' mentioning two specific groups: 'the house of holiness' consisting of the Israelites who were regarded as the holy community, and the 'most holy congregation' consisting of Aaron from where the community of priests sprung

217 Norman Golb, *Who Wrote the Dead Sea Scrolls?: The Search for the Secret of Qumran* (Scribner, 1995), 34-35.

218 Joseph M. Baumgarten, "The Law and Spirit of Purty at Qumran," in *The Bible and the Dead Sea Scrolls: The Second Princeton Symposium on Judaism and Christian Origins*, ed. James H. Charlesworth (Waco, Texas: Baylor University Press, 2006), 93-106.

219 Shemaryahu Talmon, "The Community of the Renewed Covenant: Between Judaism and Christianity," in *The Community of Renewed Covenant: The Notre Dame Symposium on the Dead Sea Scrolls*, ed. Eugene Ulrich and James VanderKam, vol. 10 of *Christianity and Judaism in Antiquity Series*, ed. Gregory E. Sterling (Notre Dame, Indiana: University of Notre Dame Press, 1994), 8-9.

220 Harrington, *The Purity Texts*, 13.

221 Harrington, *The Purity Texts*, 13.

at the most holy level (1QS 8: 5-6; 9:2-6).[222] The Damascus Document differentiates between the Israelites who lived in the 'camp of holiness'. The **יָחַד** (*yaḥad*) and the sectarians who lived in the other cities called camps. According to L. Ginzberg, along with Elisha Qimron, these people were considered to be the dwellers in the 'camp of holiness', which kept a high degree of purity.[223] The יָחַד (*yaḥad*) was considered a temporary substitute for Jerusalem, and its members maintained a high degree of purity like those they would have maintained in Jerusalem, whereas other Qumran sectarians did not follow such a degree of purity.[224] The difference between the members of the יָחַד (*yaḥad*) and different Qumranians (sectarians) has been stressed by some of the scholars who maintain a lesser or inferior degree of purity.

2. **קֹדֶשׁ (*qodesh*):** Each member of the Qumran Community (יָחַד (*yaḥad*)) was considered איש הקודש(*ish-ha-qodesh*), 'holy man' (1QS 5:13, 18; 8:17,23; 9:8). The Qumran writers identify their community members with the following terms: men of holiness (1QS 8:17), God's holy people (1Q33 14:12), the holy ones (1Q33 6:6), holy council (1QH 15:10; 1QM 3:4; CD 20:25; 1QS 2:25; 8:21; 1Q28a 2:9), assembly of holiness (1QS 5:20; 9:2; 1Q28a 1:9,13; 4Q181 1 ii 4). Along with that, the community refers to itself as the set apart community to read Torah in the desert or wilderness of the settlement (1QS 8:13-15).[225]

3. **טָהוֹר(*tahor*):**Thc writcrs of thc Qumran scrolls admit that not all of the sects are maintaining the same level of purity. Moreover, some of the texts advocate to be more-pure טהוֹר יותר (*tahor yoter)*more-pure or purer (4Q274 3 ii 4) with superior purity and strive to be the 'pure man'איש טָהוֹר (*'ish tahor*) as opposed to the אנשי ישראל (*anshei yisrael*) the 'men of Israel', who were considered average (11Q19 49:8).[226] Some texts suggest that a truly 'pure man' would

222 This concept has been derived from the Hebrew Bible, Exod. 19:6, Lev. 11:44, 1Chronicle 23:13.

223 Elisha Qimron, "Celibacy in the Dead Sea Scrolls and Two Kinds of Sectarians," in *The Madrid Qumran Congress: Proceedings of the International Congress on the Dead Sea Scrolls, Madrid, 18-21 March, 1991*, ed. Julio C. Trebolle Barrera and Luis Vegas Montaner, vol. 1, Studies on the Texts of the Desert of Judah 11 (International Congress on the Dead Sea Scrolls, Leiden; New York: Madrid: Brill; Editorial Complutense, 1992), 290.

224 Qimron, "Celibacy in the Dead Sea Scrolls and Two Kinds of Sectarians," 288.

225 Harrington, *The Purity Texts*, 15.

226 Harrington, *The Purity Texts*, 16–17.

not eat from a vessel though it is sealed in the house of the dead (4Q274 3 ii 4; 11Q19 49:8). Along with that a man who newly enters into this order is not allowed to touch an elder who would then become impure by the new comer's lesser status of purity. Physically impaired persons were excluded from the community as they were considered a hindrance to holiness in the presence of the angels. (CD 15:15-16).[227]

Qumran Community and the Resident Aliens/Outsiders

In the second temple period, there was a widening gap between the Jews and non-Jews. The non-Jews were called the גֵּרִים (*gerim*) and any relationship with them was considered impure. According to Hays, they were the people who lived in the community of גֵּרִים which was not in the vicinity of the Jews. Ritual impurity is a covenantal condition and the non-Jews are excluded from the Israelite's system of purity and impurity because they stand outside of the covenantal relationship between Yahweh and Israel.[228] Such isolation or exclusion is marked by two primary functions: firstly, exclusion separates impure people from pure people and objects, limiting the contagion of impurity, and secondly, exclusion provides the opportunity for the impure people to repent of their sins to ritually purify themselves.[229]

According to Klawans, the outsider's sin is as impure as the outsider who was ritually defiling at Qumran. The outsiders were not permitted to eat the community's pure food, in case they ritually defiled it according to the following verse in the Rule of Community:[230]

> The outsiders must not enter the water in order to touch the purity of the men of holiness. For they cannot be purified (1QS 5:13).

The impurity in the can be contagious, which not only makes the bearer of impurities an impure one but the impurity can be contagious to others. The Temple Scroll mentions the intensity of such contagious impurity.[231] There are three types of impurity regarding the outsiders- the corpse impure, people with skin disease, and genital dischargers must not enter the temple

227 Harrington, *The Purity Texts*, 16.

228 Hayes, *Gentile Impurities and Jewish Identities: Intermarriage and Conversion from the Bible to the Talmud*, 21.

229 Bruce McComiskey, *Rhetoric and the Dead Sea Scrolls: Purity, Covenant, and Strategy at Qumran* (University Park, Pennsylvania: The Pennsylvania State University Press, 2021), 119–20.

230 Klawans, *Impurity and Sin in Ancient Judaism*, 79.

231 Harrington, *The Purity Texts*, 20.

city until they are purified.[232] For example, those who have had sexual intercourse must remain outside the sacred city for three days and bathe on the first and third day of their impurity (11Q19 45:7-12, 15-18).[233] The Temple Scroll restricts the גֵּרִים (*gerim*) from entering into the middle court of the temple until the fourth generation. (11Q19 39:5-7).[234] Apart from that, the possessions of the גֵּרִים (*gerim*) are also impure, and one can contract impurity even by touching the possessions of outsiders.[235] In ordinary cities, women who were menstruating were confined to separate dwelling places till the time of their impurities (11Q19 48: 13-17).[236]

According to the Rule of Community, purity is central to the process of initiation into the יָחַד (*yaḥad*). The individual who remains outside the community:[237]

> "he shall not be reckoned among the perfect; he shall neither be purified by atonement, nor cleansed by purifying waters, nor sanctified by seas and rivers, nor washed clean with ablution." (1QS 3:3-6)

In some other texts, impure individuals were barred from having communal meals (4Q514 4-6; 4Q274 1 i 9).[238] These are a few instances of the many from the Qumran scrolls on the purity and pollution among the Jews and non-Jews.

Purity and Exclusion from the Viewpoint of גֵּרִים (*gerim*) at Qumran

The widening gap between Jews and non-Jews during the Second Temple period reflects a complex interplay of religious, social, and covenantal dynamics. At its core, the issue of purity and pollution served as a defining mechanism for Jewish identity, particularly within the context of covenantal relationships between Yahweh and Israel. Non-Jews, referred to as גֵּרִים (*gerim*), were considered outsiders who fell outside of this covenantal bond, which in turn excluded them from the purity system that governed Jewish life. This exclusion had religious implications, as the non-Jews were seen as ritually impure, and any interaction with them was viewed as a potential

232 Thomas Kazen, *Impurity and Purification in Early Judaism and the Jesus Tradition*, Resources for Biblical Study 98, ed. Davina C. Lopez (Atlanta: SBL Press, 2021), 293.

233 Harrington, *The Purity Texts*, 20.

234 Harrington, *The Purity Texts*, 114.

235 Harrington, *The Purity Texts*, 117.

236 Harrington, *The Purity Texts*, 20.

237 Susan Haber, *"They Shall Purify Themselves": Essays on Purity in Early Judaism*, Early Judaism and Its Literature 24, ed. Adele Reinhartz (Atlanta: Society of Biblical Literature, 2008), 47.

238 Harrington, *The Purity Texts*, 20.

threat to the purity of the community. From the viewpoint of the *gerim* or those considered 'outsiders,' the stringent purity laws, which separated them from the Jewish community, created layers of social, religious, and even economic marginalization. Being labelled ritually impure not only restricted their physical presence within sacred spaces but also placed them in a stigmatized position where they were seen as inherently other, contributing to their social alienation. These purity laws, while intended to maintain the holiness of the Jewish community, perpetuated the othering of the non-Jews including the resident aliens, strangers, gentiles, people with disabilities, and other vulnerable masses. The exclusion of them from communal meals, sacred spaces, and purification rituals deprived them of full membership in the societal and religious order. Considering this, can we connect this to the issues of Dalit exclusion; issues of 'purity and pollution' in the Dalit Context?

Purity and Pollution in the Context of Dalits in India

According to Louis Dumont, the principle of 'purity and pollution' determines the relative position of castes within the hierarchy. Dumont argues that the principle of the fundamental opposition of the pure and the impure permeates all the visible features of a caste system- hierarchy, separation and division of labour.[239] On the other hand, Michael Moffat explains this theory by exemplifying the practices of 'purity and pollution' within the low caste communities.[240] The interlinkage between the notion of 'purity and pollution' and hierarchical exclusion has often been argued to be foundational to the Indian Caste system. Scholars have expressed the idea of purity and pollution as a valid epistemological premise to understand the Indian caste context, especially about the discrimination against the Dalits.[241]

In India, social exclusion is practiced based on caste and untouchability-based exclusion where a group of people is excluded or denied the rights and opportunities which the majority enjoys. According to the *Purusha-Sukta* in Rig Veda, the elite class, Brahmana, was born out of the mouth of God, Kshatriya- the warrior class came out of the arms of God, the Vaishyas- the business class came out of the thighs of God and the Shudras the working class were born out of his feet. Dalits are alien to the very being of the

239 Louis Dumont, *Homo Heirarchicus: The Caste System and Its Implications* (Chicago: University of Chicago Press, 1970), 43.

240 Michael Moffat, *An Untouchable Community in South India* (Princeton: Princeton University Press, 1979).

241 Peniel Rajkumar, *Dalit Theology and Dalit Liberation: Problems, Paradigms and Possibilities*, Ashgate New Critical Thinking in Religion, Theology, and Biblical Studies (Farnham: Ashgate, 2010), 21.

body of God and thus, have no ontological participation with the divine or the transcendence.[242] There was a temple-centred social system, and the Brahmins, due to their association with the temples, captured the apex of the feudal pyramid and dictated the pattern of social and cultural developments. Caste as a theology of soul relegated the validity of the body and also the social positioning of the people who toil in the land. Thus, this theory determines the distance between the social bodies and becomes the crux of the theory of 'purity and pollution.'[243] Dalits continue to live outside the border of Hindu caste society with labels like outcast, untouchable, exterior caste, depressed class, pariah, and so on[244] relating to the meaning of the term 'Dalit,' from the Sanskrit root *dal*, meaning burnt, split, broken or torn asunder, down-trodden, crushed, destroyed, and so on.[245]

Dalits are politically neglected, economically poor, socially discriminated against and excluded, religiously untouchable, symbolically othered people in India. They live on the outskirts of the public living spaces by doing caste-assigned and thus enforced menial jobs like scavenging and animal skinning.[246] According to Y. T. Vinayaraj, "the exclusion or the othering of Dalits is not because of the malfunctioning of welfare measures of the state; rather, it is an epistemological issue that defines ontology and politics discursively."[247] Moreover, the caste system is seen as a social practice that emerges out of some hegemonic social knowledge that determines the social distribution of cultural, economic, and symbolic capital. Caste functions as basic knowledge that legitimizes the subsequent hierarchical ordering of social bodies, unequal distribution of capital, and marginalization of Dalit bodies as untouchables.[248] In Indian

242 Y. T. Vinayaraj, *Dalit Theology after Continental Philosophy*, ed. Joseph Duggan and J. Jayakiran Sebastian, Postcolonialism and Religions (Aargau: Palgrave Macmillan, 2016), 91.

243 Y. T. Vinayaraj, *Re-Imagining Dalit Theology: Post Modern Readings* (Thiruvalla: Christava Sahitya Samithi, 2008), 27.

244 Sathianathan Clarke, Deenabandhu Manchala, and Philip Vinod Peacock, eds., *Dalit Theology in Twenty-First Century: Discordant Voices, Discerning Pathways* (New Delhi: Oxford University Press, 2010), 4.

245 James Massey, *Towards Dalit Hermeneutics: Re-Reading the Text, the History and the Literature* (New Delhi: ISPCK, 1994), 1–6; James Massey, *Down Trodden: The Struggle for India's Dalits for Identity, Solidarity and Liberation* (Geneva: WCC Publications, 1997), 1–3.

246 Y. T. Vinayaraj, *Dalit Theology after Continental Philosophy*, ed. Joseph Duggan and J. Jayakiran Sebastian, Postcolonialism and Religions (Aargau: Palgrave Macmillan, 2016), 89–90.

247 Vinayaraj, *Dalit Theology after Continental Philosophy*, 90.

248 Vinayaraj, *Dalit Theology after Continental Philosophy*, 90.

Vedic epistemology, the human body is made up of certain *gunas* (qualities) that are given and eternal. In this thought, some bodies are insufficient for certain *gunas,* and they cannot come up with highly qualitative bodies. Less qualitative bodies cannot have social spaces, as in the case of higher bodies. The hierarchical ordering of labour, social spaces, and social capital are foregrounded on the epistemology of the ontological separation between the divine/sacred body and the non-divine/impure bodies.[249]

In traditional Hindu society, commensality is closely tied to notions of purity and pollution, where upper castes avoid sharing food with Dalits because of their perceived 'impurity.' This practice of caste-based exclusion in food sharing has historically marginalized Dalits in several ways. Dalits are often prohibited from eating with higher caste groups, reinforcing their 'untouchable' status. In rural areas, they are made to eat separately or denied entry to communal spaces like temples or festivals where food is shared.[250] Along with that, the division of labour in India for the Dalit community has been disgusting as they are assigned unclean occupations like picking up the dead cattle and manual scavenging.[251]

In short, the deeply entrenched caste-based exclusion and dehumanization are rooted in notions of purity and pollution. Dalits are not only segregated from social and religious spaces but also relegated to degrading, menial labour that perpetuates their 'untouchable' status. The epistemological framework of caste, based on hierarchical divisions of labour and bodily purity, reinforces the social, economic, and symbolic marginalization of Dalits. This exclusion is not simply a social failure but a deeply embedded ideological system that perpetuates inequality and oppression across generations.

Assessment of Purity and Pollution at Qumran and in Dalit Context

The concepts of 'purity and pollution' serve as central frameworks of exclusion both in the Qumran community of the Second Temple period and within the Indian caste system, particularly about Dalits. In both cases, these ideas are not merely religious but deeply social and political, legitimizing hierarchical divisions and perpetuating exclusion. At Qumran, purity regulations were grounded in the community's covenantal relationship with Yahweh. Those outside the community non-Jews, referred to as *gerim* were seen as ritually impure, excluded from access to sacred spaces, and often

249 Andre Beteille, *Caste, Class, and Power: Changing Pattern of Stratification in a Tanjore Village* (New Delhi: Oxford University Press, 1965); Vinayaraj, *Dalit Theology after Continental Philosophy*, 90–91.

250 Surinder S Jodhka, *Caste in Contemporary India: Dynamics of Discrimination* (Oxford: Oxford University Press, 2015), 27.

251 Jodhka, *Caste in Contemporary India: Dynamics of Discrimination*, 30.

marked by their inability to participate in communal rites of purification. Similarly, in the Indian caste system, purity and pollution determine the social positioning of individuals, with Dalits being relegated to the lowest rung of the hierarchy, considered inherently polluted, and thus segregated from the higher caste groups.

At Qumran, the ritual was tied to covenantal membership, where those considered impure were excluded from the community's sacred practices and spaces. As the Rule of the Community (1QS 5:13) mentioned, the impure were not allowed to participate in purification rites or share in communal meals, reinforcing their status as outsiders. This reflects a worldview where impurity could be 'contagious,' capable of spreading through contact with the impure. The same logic of contagion is evident in Indian society, where upper castes fear pollution through physical or even spatial proximity to Dalits. Dalits are often excluded from communal spaces like temples and dining areas, and they are socially stigmatized due to their association with unclean occupations like manual scavenging and leatherwork.

The theological foundations of purity and pollution at Qumran and in the Indian caste system are different but share a common outcome of exclusion. At Qumran, impurity was seen as a violation of divine law, deeply connected to covenantal theology, where outsiders and sinners were kept separate from the sacred community. In India, the caste system is rooted in Vedic cosmology, where each caste is born from different parts of the divine body, with Dalits excluded altogether from this ontological hierarchy. The Rig Veda's *Purusha-Sukta* places Dalits outside the divine body, stripping them of any sacred status. This exclusion reinforces their social and religious marginalization, as they are seen as impure by birth and permanently outside the reach of spiritual transcendence.

The social and religious consequences of purity and pollution are profound in both contexts. At Qumran, the impure not only lost access to spiritual privileges but were also excluded from communal life, including the sharing of food and participation in the rites that defined community membership. In India, Dalits are economically marginalized, and relegated to caste-assigned jobs considered unclean by the upper castes. The caste system's division of labour ensures that Dalits remain economically disadvantaged, with little access to upward mobility. The exclusion from commensality and the sharing of food serve as visible markers of their status as untouchables, much like the outsiders at Qumran who were barred from sacred meals.

Moreover, resistance and reform in both settings show a drive toward breaking these systems of exclusion. In India, Dalit movements led by figures like B.R. Ambedkar have challenged the caste system's foundation of purity and pollution, advocating for the annihilation of caste and more significant social equity. Ambedkar's conversion to Buddhism symbolized a rejection of the caste system's theological and social premises. In contrast, Qumran's system of purity remained rigid, but its legacy of exclusion mirrors the systemic nature of caste-based discrimination in India. While reforms have made strides in legal and social equality for Dalits, the enduring epistemological framework of purity and pollution continues to shape their marginalization, just as ritual exclusion reinforced social boundaries at Qumran.

Conclusion

The comparative analysis of purity and pollution in the Qumran community and the Indian caste system reveals a profound intersection of religious, social, and political dimensions of exclusion. Both systems use the notions of purity and pollution to enforce hierarchical structures, excluding marginalized groups from sacred, social, and economic participation. At Qumran, impurity was a barrier to spiritual and communal integration, while in India, caste-based purity and pollution perpetuate systemic marginalization of Dalits. Despite legal and social reforms, these frameworks continue to influence contemporary practices, highlighting the enduring challenge of overcoming entrenched systems of exclusion. Understanding these parallel mechanisms of exclusion underscores the need for ongoing efforts toward genuine inclusivity and equality across diverse contexts.

23

Prophetic Movement During the Period of Hosea and Its Relevance in Today's Context

N. Subramani

Introduction

The book of Hosea is considered the first of the minor prophetic books, otherwise known as "the Book of the Twelve." The book of Hosea distinctively portrays the unforgettable imagery of God's love, which does not let go of God's people. In the book of Hosea, the covenant is essential (6:7, 8:1). Hosea's task was to warn the people that Yahweh intended to enforce the terms of His covenant.[252] The people of Israel continually broke the covenant, and Yahweh was, therefore, determined to punish the people by unleashing the punishments outlined in the law. But he also had a plan to bless his chosen nation. Accordingly, the book of Hosea often reminds the faithful that God will one day bring prosperity to Israel. God promises the victims that there is hope for them now, which is vivid in the present context. How can the mission of God be achieved through the prophet in the present context? The historical context of Hosea was the period of prosperity under Jeroboam II.

In today's context, in Christian circles, the term "protest" is often understood negatively, and unfortunately, society branded the outspoken people as "radicals" or "rebels." However, such a protest, when made

252 Robert B. Chisholm Jr., "A Theology of the Minor Prophets," in *A Biblical Theology of the Old Testament*, 398.

against injustice and oppression, is fundamentally a positive stance because it strives to set right a system that man, in his self-centeredness, has distorted to suit his partisan ends. It helps us to critically understand the eighth-century prophet's situation and compare it with India's present social and economic conditions. It focuses on prophetic protest in the eighth century B.C.E., intending to foster a new understanding of the Christian principle of protest against oppression, suppression, and injustice between the rich and the poor. This essay urges the Church and society towards justice, peace, and equality. The main object of this article is to examine the sociological conditions prevalent in the eighth century B.C.E. and to evaluate the conditions to draw lessons for people in contemporary India. The socio-economic oppression, religio-political corruption, and the gap between the poor and the rich became rather acute and intense in the eighth century B.C.E. Particularly, this essay focuses on the ministry and message of the Prophet Hosea. he prophet Hosea, coming from a rural, desert area of Palestine, had seen the oppression of the poor by the wealthy class of people and the prevailing power structures of society. Therefore, this book is relevant to the issues of oppression and corruption.

The Life and Ministry of the Prophets

Before we analyse the prophetic ministry of Hosea, let us take a look at the prophets and their ministry during the eighth century period in ancient Israel. When we read the prophetic books, we come to a particular understanding that the prophets ministered in times of tragedy and triumph in the history of Israel.[253] The prophets called warning, guidance, rebuke and encouragement to the people and the ruler. The prophetic ministry of the prophets directed toward the people of God carried a strong missionary implication of responsibility for the chosen people of Israel.[254] We read in the Bible that whenever the people of Israel forgot that God had chosen her intending her to speak to the other nations, they turned away from the countries in introverted pride. For example, prophets such as Amos, Jeremiah, and Isaiah lashed out at the people's ethnocentric pretensions and charged them for subverting God's actual intentions. The prophets articulate God's redemptive purposes for the world.[255] `The prophets of Israel grew increasingly aware that not only Israel would share in God's acts of redemption. God would break in to restore His liberating Lordship over

253 Donald Senior, C. P and Caroll Stuhlmueller C. P, *The Biblical Foundations for Mission*, (Maryknoll, Orbis Books, 1995), 67–68.

254 Hedlund, R. E. and Hranghuma (eds.), *Indigenous Missions of India*, (Madras, Church Growth Research Centre, 1980), 92.

255 Walter C. Kaiser Jr., *Mission in the Old Testament*, Grand Rapids, Baker Books, 2006, 49ff.

all the nations of the world.[256] The prophets worked hard to keep this hope alive in Israel, as seen in their prophetic words and actions.[257]

Regarding prophetic attitudes, there is some evidence that, in the life of the prophets, they responded to the problems of idolatry, syncretism, and merely external religion.[258] The prophets warned the people of Israel not to commit adultery and proclaimed the message of the Ten Commandments,[259] 'Thou shall not make unto thee any graven image.' Some Psalms reflect the latter prohibition, which ridicules idolatry and idolatrous practices. That the prophets denouncing of idolatry is seen very clearly during the monarchical period. Reform entailed the removal of idols.[260] The prophets condemned the worship of the idols, as idolatry was a false religion because it entailed the worship of other gods that the Bible regards as false gods, e.g., Exodus 23:24. The prophets warn the people of Israel not to engage in worshipping idols. Further, they guide the people of God to be loyal to the covenant Yahweh made with people. The prophets strongly condemned syncretism. Syncretism is the blending of two or more contradictory belief systems. The prophets spoke against combining the worship of Yahweh and the worship of Baal and the religious practices of nations, which would result in punishment (2 Kings 17:33).[261]

The prophets spoke to the issues of their day. Frequently, they reinforced their verbal message with symbolic actions – one thinks especially of Hosea (Hosea 1:2f), Jeremiah (Jer. 13:1f), Isaiah (Isa. 20:2–4), and Ezekiel (Ezek. 4:1–5:4ff). The object was not sensationalism but spiritual and moral renewal. One can assert that the faith of the people of Israel was seminal for the mission to the nations.[262]

256 John Corrie (ed.,) *Dictionary of Mission Theology Evangelical Foundations*, (England, InterVarsity Press, 2007), 238ff.

257 Walter C. Kaiser Jr., *Mission in the Old Testament, (*Grand Rapids, Baker Books, 2006), 72ff.

258 Donald Senior, C. P and Caroll Stuhlmueller C. P, *The Biblical Foundations for Mission*, (Maryknoll, Orbis Books, 1995), 67.

259 Donald Senior, C. P and Caroll Stuhlmueller C. P, *The Biblical Foundations for Mission*, (Maryknoll, Orbis Books, 1995), 67f.

260 Walter C. Kaiser Jr., *Mission in the Old Testament*, (Grand Rapids, Baker Books, 2006), 22ff.

261 Julian Saldanha, *Mission Today: Themes and Issues*, (Bangalore, Claretian Publications, 2006), 141ff.

262 Walter C. Kaiser Jr., *Mission in the Old Testament*, (Grand Rapids, Baker Books), 2006, 12ff.

Prophets and their Traditions

The prophets played a vital role in their prophecy and the traditions they embedded in it. The prophets report that their passion for prophetic utterance has grown from their personal experience through metaphors and similes, explained clearly in the prophetic literature. They express their message out of their knowledge of disaster, which speaks about the alienation that is coming between Yahweh and Israel, a "break up" that will end in suffering, displacement, and misery. It is evident in the life of the prophet Hosea. Hosea arose from the covenantal background of Deuteronomy, which was deeply committed to the Sinai covenant with its rigorous commandments and inescapable sanctions of blessings and curses. The prophets specifically cite the commandments of Sinai in their prophetic message. The best-known text of Hosea in Christian usage is verse 6:6, which is twice quoted by Jesus (Matt. 9:12–13; 12:7): For I desire steadfast love and not sacrifice, the knowledge of God rather than burnt offerings.

As we see in Amos 5:21–23, Amos looks askance at worship practices that function in Israel, as they often do, to legitimate worship as a substitute for covenantal activity. The pairing of "steadfast love" and "knowledge of God" refers to covenantal practices.[263] In the tradition of Deuteronomy, those covenantal practices pertain to neighbourly generosity and solidarity with a particular regard for the poor, widows, orphans, and immigrants (see Deut. 14:28; 24:19–22). Thus, Hosea links the reality of Yahweh, the Lord of the covenant, to concern for the neighbourhood. In Hosea 4:1–3, the oracle claims violating covenantal commands will disrupt creation. In Hosea 4:2, the prophet uses a version of the pairing in Hosea 6:6, the pairing twice quoted by Jesus: "loyalty . . . knowledge of God." Here, the prophet Hosea lists the offences of Israel related to the covenant at Sinai—swearing, lying, murder, stealing, and committing adultery.[264]

The Prophetic Message

The prophets come from somewhat different circles of tradition. Nonetheless, they all address an everyday socio-economic reality. Our attention focuses on the fact that these prophets have a cluster of familiar terms: Amos spoke about justice and righteousness (Amos. 5:24), Hosea concentrated on the steadfast love and knowledge of God (Hosea 6:6), and Micah's interest was in justice and kindness (Micah. 6:8). Among these terms there are, to be sure, variations in nuance. But in summary, all of these terms point to the same single covenantal mandate of the need for solidarity between influential

263 Freeman, Hobart E. *An Introduction to the Old Testament Prophets*. (Chicago: Moody Press, 1968), 177.

264 Wood, Leon J. *The Prophets of Israel*. (Grand Rapids: Baker Book House, 1979), 292.

people and the vulnerable people upon whom they prey. In self-justifying ideology, the privileged regarded the vulnerable poor as if they were fitting material for exploitation and cheap labour. Against such dominant economic exploitation, the prophets urged an alternate practice grounded in neighbourly solidarity. They raised their voices and spoke with zeal against the way the powerful and the clever exploited every economic possibility against the vulnerable so that the weaker society of the economy had no chance for well-being. The exploiters or rulers of the day were variously allied with and benefitted from the governance of the elite: kings, priests, and scribes. Thus, the prophet Amos collided with the high priest of Bethel. Hosea was against a robust hierarchy of power that Yahweh authorized. They made kings, but not through me; they set up princes but without my knowledge. With their silver and gold, they made idols for their own destruction. (8:4). This verse is of particular importance because it is quoted centuries later in defence of the prophets, who had critiqued the context and the situation of their time and spoke against the practices of their day. It continues to be relevant even today.

The Prophets and Social Justice

The prophets spoke boldly against the social issues of their time. The image of the prophet as a courageous person standing up for social justice is rooted in the ministries of the eighth-century B.C.E. prophets. Isaiah, Hosea, Amos, and Micah delivered fiery, confrontational oracles to the leaders of Israel and Judah. The prophets denounced economic stratification and the ill-treatment of the poor and powerless. Social and economic rifts marked Israelite society in the eighth century and revealed a spiritual sickness.[265] The prophets were courageous in their attention to the poor and powerless, but we must admit that their rhetoric was often undiplomatic. Even though the prophets wrote in gripping and poetic language, they sometimes were downright insulting. The prophets, including Hosea, compared Israel and Judah to prostitutes (for example, Hos. 1–3; Isa. 1:21; Ezek. 16).[266] They threatened the people with God's anger and severe punishment, including the destruction of the kingdom itself. Hosea declares that God's people must be faithful to God as a wife must be to her husband or a child to its parent and not pursue other lovers, the Baals, and foreign nations (Hos. 2:2–13; 8; 11:1–11).

---

265 Aaron Jr., Charles L. *Preaching Hosea, Amos and Micah*, (Chalice Press, U.S.A., 2005), 4.

266 Keil, Carl Friedrich. *The Twelve Minor Prophets*. 2 vols. Translated by James Martin. Biblical Commentary on the Old Testament. Reprint ed. (Grand Rapids: Wm. B. Eerdmans Publishing Co., 1949), 1:93.

Historical Background of Hosea

We know very little about Hosea, son of Beeri, except what we can glean from the collection of his prophetic speeches. It is a challenging task to reconstruct his personality and make inferences from the details contained in the book. However, some observations do help us in the process. For example, he delivered an oracle in the last days of the Northern Kingdom. His prophetic activity extended from the prosperous reign of Jeroboam II to the disappearance of Israel from the political scene. Therefore, one can locate the prophecies of Hoses in the mid-eighth century (750–732 BCE). Wood focuses on the prophet's daily activities; the same is informed in the opening verse that Hosea ministered in the days of Uzziah, Jotham, Ahaz, and Hezekiah, the kings of Judah, and during the reign of Jeroboam, the son of Joash, king of Israel. Such a historical sketch makes one consider Hosea a contemporary of Isaiah, Amos, and Micah.[267] It was a time of spiritual decline of the nation and the people. The political climate in which the prophet ministered was that of political distrust. Hoshea killed Pekah (2 Kings 15:30) and paid tribute to Sahlmener V for some time. Later, Hoshea withheld the tribute to Assyria and sought help from the Egyptians. The situation took a sudden turn, and the king of Assyria arrested Hoshea and captured the city of Samaria. The resultant social and political chaos eventually brought about a collapse of the moral structure of the society.[268] Along with the corrupted political situation, Hosea pictures in the book that the people were observing the Canaanite fertility cult associated with the God Baal. The people of Israel identified Yahweh with Baal and attributed Yahweh's good gifts of land and fertility to Baal. The worship of Baal increasingly attracted the people of Israel, and they started to worship Baal. Hosea's central target was the attack on the worship of Baal. During this time, the priests also failed in their duties. They were assigned to instruct the people, but the priests were greedy and corrupt. The book of Hosea captures the total departure from faithfulness to Yahweh.[269] It helps us understand Hosea's social, historical, religious, and political background. In the Old Testament, the prophets spoke and fought against injustice happening in society, and they played an essential role by warning people to establish justice, peace, equality, and righteousness. Hosea is among them who played a vital role in handling the crisis and prophesied against the evil treatment and injustice to the poor.

---

267 Leon J. Woods, *The Prophets of Israel* (Grand Rapids: Baker Academic Publishing Co, 1979), 282.

268 Hubbard, David Allan. *Hosea: An Introduction and Commentary*. Tyndale Old Testament Commentaries series. (Downers Grove, III and Leicester: InterVarsity Press, 1989), 21.

269 Tozer, A. W. *The Pursuit of God*. Harrisburg, (Pa.: Christian Publications, 1948), 82.

He spoke against the kings, warned them, and prophesied judgment against them. The prophet directly delivered prophecies amid corruption, injustice, and inequality, which acutely demanded justice, equality, and peace.[270] The prophet emphasized God's love more than any other prophet in the Old Testament. He insisted they return to Yahweh, their God, and continue to abide in Him.

Different Forms of Corruption[271]

The princes, prophets, and priests used their positions for selfish ends. The rulers and merchants made money through corrupt means, judges took bribes, and prophets prophesied for selfish gain.[272]

In Israel in the year eight B.C.E., there was another problem – oppression by landlords; the landlords oppressed people with low incomes by bribing the judges.[273] Though the Israeli law favoured the poor and the needy, wealthy landlords found ways to circumvent the rules. When we look at India, there are two disadvantages: first, unlike Israel, our land distribution pattern is very uneven. One does not see many changes in this unequal land distribution between the pre-independence and post-independence eras. Second, our laws and the legal system largely favour wealthy landlords.[274] Another aspect of discrimination that we can find is that caste, as a sociocultural institution, not only has sociocultural and "connection" values but has religious sanctions to "the discrimination" practices based on caste. Then, caste itself became a "discriminator" and a device of the high caste to keep the majority in perpetual slavery. Caste and, along with it, one's social occupation is dictated/determined by birth.

---

270 McComiskey, Thomas Edward. "Hosea." In *The Minor Prophets: An Exegetical and Expositional Commentary*, 1:1-237. 3 vols. Edited by Thomas Edward McComiskey. (Grand Rapids: Baker Books, 1992), 164.

271 such as political graft, bribery, and perversion of laws, were quite prevalent during the time of the eighth-century prophets, especially in the days of Amos and Micah. "corruption" means changing from good to bad, debase, or pervert. From the point of view of a moralist, corruption occurs under particular circumstances. It also depends on the many people of that country who consider an act in specific circumstances corruption. See Leys Colin, 1970, 32. Mosaic instructions and the concept of justice measure the standard in ancient Israel. The public official is said to be corrupt when "... he accepts money or money's worth for doing something that he is under a duty to do anyway, and that he is under a duty not to do or to exercise a legitimate description for improper reasons." McMullan, 1961, 18, 182.

272 Amos 2: 6–8; Micah 3, Ezekiel 13; Jeremiah 21–23.

273 Landowners continued to oppress poor peasants. The government made laws oppressive to low-income people and favourable to landlords.

274 Duarte Barreto, *India's Search for Development and Social Justice: The Indian situation*, 1977, 38–40.

Message of Hosea – An Analysis

Hosea calls the people to repent and to know the Lord — "Let us know, let us press on to know the Lord" (6:3). The people had turned away from God and proper knowledge of God. Hosea calls them back. He borrows language from the people's worship of false fertility gods – "revive us" and "raise us up" are borrowed from the worship of Baal – to call the people back to the true God, who alone can keep promises and who alone can revive the people.

Closeness to God

In the Old Testament, the prophets received authority from God for the prophetic ministry. The eighth-century prophets received the word from God to warn the people and to fight for them in terms of the injustice done to them.[275] They were not only messengers or mouthpieces of God but also mediators between God and people. The prophets did everything according to the command of God without any self-interest. An important message that we learn from them is that they did everything without any self-concern but for the sake of God to reach the people during times of struggle, pain, and suffering. The attachment to God and commensurate detachment from material pursuits empowered the prophets to attack the forces of greed and evil in persons and structures.[276]

The prophet is in a state of being called by God. The prophet is always conscious that he is the object and instrument of God's hand and "will" after the manner of the Servant of God. The prophet Elijah's words "before whom I stand" indicate that a prophet's distinctness lies in the fact that he is in the state of being called by God. In God's proximity, a prophet received the Word of authority to communicate the message of prophetic protest with the force of "Thus says the Lord."

God's Closeness with Humanity

God prepared the prophets for the ministry in specific geographical and sociocultural contexts. Hosea was from the northern kingdom and also ministered to the southern kingdom. It will be difficult for us to understand the message of their prophetic ministry unless we get familiarized with the context of the "war and hostilities." [277] The ministry was directed towards

275 Keil, Carl Friedrich. *The Twelve Minor Prophets*. 2 vols. Translated by James Martin. Biblical Commentary on the Old Testament. Reprint ed. (Grand Rapids: Wm. B. Eerdmans Publishing Co., 1949), 1:19.

276 Amos 7

277 Kidner, Derek. *Love to the Loveless: The Message of Hosea*. The Bible Speaks Today series. (Downers Grove, Ill.: InterVarsity Press, 1981), 97-98.

a specific context, not as if the prophets were separate from the context of oppression but often as men inside the context: seeing the pain, struggle, suffering, hopes, and aspirations of the people and sometimes taking upon themselves the experience of the evils of society. An example of this complete "identification" is seen in Hosea's personal life. God asks the prophet Hosea to symbolically experience the sins of his people by marrying a harlot and by naming his children with names that would point to a judgment of God-forsakenness. So Hosea identified with the people in their God-forsakenness. God asked Hosea to be in solidarity with the oppressed people because God himself is the one who identifies with the oppressed, as we have seen from our study of Exodus and the conquest and monarchy situations. It brings us an understanding of the essential element of God taking a stand against the oppressor. The Word of God is the criterion for discerning which side is the side of justice. The lives of the prophets reflect "hate evil and seek good."[278] Only by seeking good will we be able to hate evil. Justice and righteousness embody the good and are the desired norms of individual and corporate conduct. The prophet's audience was mainly a collective corporate audience, and we should consider the corporate aspect of evil and address the issue of evil.

Through this, the prophet brought change and transformation to society. We need to address individuals as well because they ultimately make up systems and structures. It helps to show solidarity with the oppressed, to have a stance against the oppressor, and to expect change and transformation. These attitudes are vital to the prophetic protest ministry in India today. This study helps to better understand prophetic ministry through the imagery and symbols in the book of Hosea. These critical values are derived from God in the context of closeness with God – to show solidarity with the poor and oppressed and share God's stance against oppressors and oppressive and unjust systems. Hebrew prophecy gives more punch to the demand for change made by the prophets in their context. Given the complex oppression and discrimination in society, it enlightens us to be aware of the need to show love to others. In today's context, society must stand up for social justice, biblical humanism, and the prophetic tradition of laying the foundation for a just society.

The situation in our society is similar to that in Old Testament history in many ways. We are experiencing an abandonment of our devotion to God and chaos in interpersonal relationships. There is militarism, sexism, racism, and human exploitation, as well as immoral and excessive ways

---

278 Hubbard, David Allan. *Hosea: An Introduction and Commentary*. Tyndale Old Testament Commentaries series. (Downers Grove, Ill. and Leicester, Eng.: InterVarsity Press, 1989), 134.

in which we carry ourselves and wrongfully act against our neighbour. However, in our lack of faithfulness as a people—our hatred toward God and neighbour exemplified in our actions—there is hope for divine beauty to infuse our hearts in a manner that brings harmony to society.[279] Though the book of Hosea speaks mostly of Israel, these references allude to the divine *hesed* as a covenant with humanity. Second, the Spirit's showers of love, in cooperation with our willingness to have hearts, make the perfect combination for a life worth living for us and generations worldwide. There is hope for a better world as one finds oneself wholly saturated by divine love, the Spirit of God. Third, there is a certainty that the showers of blessing will come over the earth. The call for us today is to turn our affections toward God and receive this gift of grace by freely living within its bounds of unsurpassed beauty.

Hope and Promise for the Future

Hosea's prophetic book highlights the development that leads to a good outcome for Israel. After the coming catastrophe, which they are specific about, these prophetic witnesses imagine a new scenario of well-being for Israel. Hosea can imagine a recovery of prosperous agriculture and society and a restored future of a safe, thriving life. On the day of the Lord, God will raise the prophets, leaders, and people to rebuild the days of the old. God will restore the fortunes of the people of Israel and rebuild the ruined cities, and they will inhabit them, and the Israelites will plant vineyards and drink their wine. God promises and assures that He will plant them in their land, and they will renew the strength they lost and settle in the land that God has given them.[280] God says they shall be my people, and I will be their God (Hosea 2:21–23). Here, the prophet will witness God's readiness to forgive with compassion, faithfulness, and loyalty. The Old Testament pictures God as a missionary in the opening metaphor in the book of the minor prophet Hosea.[281] In the book of Hosea, it is clear that God is faithful, and He uses unfaithfulness in the form of an unfaithful wife to illustrate God's saving faithfulness to His people, Israel. The book of Hosea picks up two themes: the first is the calling of the unfaithful to return to their faithful God; the second is the theme of impending judgment for those who refuse to return to the Lord.[282] These two concepts focus on the mission's message

279 Tozer, A. W. *The Pursuit of God.* Harrisburg, (Pa.: Christian Publications, 1948), 82.

280 Tozer, A. W. *The Pursuit of God.* Harrisburg, (Pa.: Christian Publications, 1948), 82.

281 See further F. Landy, "In the Wilderness of Speech: Problems of Metaphor in Hosea," *Biblical Interpretation* 3, 1995, 35–39.

282 Tozer, A. W. *The Pursuit of God.* Harrisburg, (Pa.: Christian Publications, 1948), 82.

to the people of Israel.[283] It reminds us that God is a faithful God who calls men and women to return to him, or they will face judgment.

Faithful to the Unfaithful

The book of Hosea's first three chapters records the word of the Lord coming to a prophet and commanding him to 'take an adulterous wife and children of unfaithfulness' Hosea 1:2. The prophet is to live out a metaphor of the Lord's relationship with his people. The book of Hosea states that Hosea loves the wife even though she is entirely unfaithful. This love shows the love of God that He has shown to the people of Israel, even though they turn to other gods. Hosea 3:1. This shows a passionate love for his people. According to Bostrom, no other book in the Old Testament includes such a detailed description of God's inner feelings as Hosea does.[284] He is a God who cares passionately about being united with His people. The book of Hosea makes it clear that God discards the physical nation of Israel, as in the northern kingdom, which takes place in a literary sense in Hosea 8 and that God's people, promised and described in 1:10–11, include far more than just the old covenant people of Judah and Samaria.

It helps us understand the idea of the missionary God, who is passionately concerned with the people with whom he is to be united in the marriage union. In this sense, the marriage metaphor saves fundamental motivation for missions. God is passionately waiting for the return of the lost people of Israel and their return to become His people. For Goldsworthy, this metaphor 'presents a magnificent illustration … of God's covenant love and faithfulness.'[285] This metaphor is not only a magnificent illustration but also a magnificent motivation.

Return to the Lord

The second aspect of this can be seen in Hosea 7:13–16, where it depicts that God longs for these unrepentant people to turn back to him and for them to repent. In the book of Hosea, the call to return to the Lord is explicit, but the concept of return is implied through the attitude of a passionate God and through the promise of that God. According to Bartholomew and Goheen, "The Old Testament prophets bear ample witness to God's patience with his people and to the repeated efforts he makes to call them back to faithfulness

283 Robinson, George L. *The Twelve Minor Prophets*. N.c.: Harper & Brothers, 1926; reprint ed., (Grand Rapids: Baker Book House, 1974), 15.

284 Bostrom in Alexander and Rosner (eds.), *New Dictionary of Biblical Theology*, (InterVarsity Press, Downers Grove, 2003), 237.

285 Goldsworthy, G., *Preaching the Whole Bible as Christian Scripture*, (Intervarsity Press, Leicester, 2000), 173.

within the covenant."[286] It is God's desire for his promises. Hoses 1:10 shows the heart of the Lord wants His people to return and receive restoration. According to John Stott, "the restoration is described in the words which once more echo the promise to Abraham."[287] It also explains that God promises an increase in descendants in verse 10 and that they will be God's children – returning to God and living under God's rule again in verse 11. These images align with God's universal missional promise to Abraham in Genesis 12. With these promises, the unfaithful Israel can understand that God is calling them to return to Him. It shows that God is a missionary calling people to return to Him. It helps us to understand that Hosea ultimately presents the heart of the missionary call as it leaves this implicit message to its readers – that is, the unfaithful are to be reconciled and return to their faithful God.

Mission has a serious concern – that is, for those who reject God's faithful love and choose not to make Him their ruler and king, there is judgment.[288] The judgment is final, and it is for all who disobeyed and went away from the Lord. The obliteration of the northern kingdom, altar, and even the southern kingdom stands as a stern reminder that the God who loves passionately judges harshly because His holy character demands it. The mission's concern is that people should be reconciled with God because, without reconciliation, there is only judgment. It reminds the people that God loves them and is passionate about taking them back and forgiving them for all their iniquities. God expects them to leave other gods, remain faithful to Him, and renew the covenant between God and the people. It reminds the people to renew their covenantal relationship between God and them and escape from judgment. It shows that God is concerned for them and is calling them on a mission. It is called the concern for mission.

The Sorrow and Indignation of Love

The prophecy describes Yahweh's sorrow and anger and His people's (Israel's) faithlessness. Hoses used a peculiar language: emotional and passionate. This emotion and passion bring out feelings of pain. This anguish of love caused by the faithlessness of Israel filled the prophet's mind, expressed through his rich and lively imagination, and explained by a variety of imageries and the return of Israel. The prophet has deep sympathy

---

286 Bartholomew, C. G. and Goheen, M. W., *The Drama of Scripture*, (Baker Academic, Grand Rapids, 2004), 107.

287 Winter, R. D. and Hawthrone, S. C., (eds.), *Perspectives on the World Christian Movement*, William Carey Library, California, 1992, 14.

288 Kaiser, Walter C., Jr. *Toward an Old Testament Theology*. (Grand Rapids: Zondervan Publishing House, 1978), 197.

that gives the reader an idea of the character and excitement of love that Hosea has for his wife.

Hosea and today's Mission of the Church

God called Hosea to a special mission. He was to share the Lord's anguish caused by the people's unfaithfulness and urge them to return to God. Hosea could relate the problem of unfaithfulness to his personal life due to his wife, who was unfaithful and deserted him. The book is replete with sermons that Hosea must have spoken at various times in many places. God's commission enabled Hosea to take up a difficult task. The reason was the people of Israel forgot their God, who had made a covenant with them, and they are His people, and now they have forgotten and have started to follow the Canaanite god called Baal. Yahweh is the one who chose the people of Israel to be his people and made a covenant with them. But God doesn't want His people to follow the Canaanite deity Baal, whom they mistakenly think is the right one. During the time of Hosea, corruption, political crisis, disordered economy, and false religion were real problems in his society. In the book of Hosea, some metaphors describe God's steadfast love towards His chosen people of Israel.

God chose Hosea to be His vessel to preach to His chosen people. The metaphors, such as the husband-wife-father-son relationship, portray the relationship between God and the people of Israel. Many times, the people of Israel have disobeyed the word of the Lord and broken the covenant. But God wants true repentance from the people. Many symbolic actions and metaphors in the book express this in order to show how much Yahweh loves them so that they don't follow after any other god and would follow their God Yahweh, who had made a covenant with them. In this situation, God uses Hosea as His messenger to alert the people of Israel. It was because they had forgotten their covenant with Yahweh that Yahweh reminded them of the covenant that He had made with them. The people of Israel have broken the covenant and followed Baal. Here, God urges them to come back in true repentance.

Social Reform Movements in India

The arrival of missionary movements in India brought social reform to modern India, beginning with the work of Serampore missionaries in the late eighteenth and early nineteenth centuries.[289] The missionaries in India continued to be involved in social protest and agitation from 1850 to 1900, during which significant developments occurred. The arousal of

289 Geoffrey A. Oddie, *Social Protest in India: British Protestant Missionaries and Social Reforms, 1850-1900*, Manohar Publisher, India, 1979, 1.

nationalistic feelings among the educated Hindus made them sensitive about the missionaries' involvement in their nation's socio-religious matters; this ultimately led to the rise of Indian social reform movements. The Indian social reform movement drew inspiration and impetus from the work of Western Christian missionaries and the man-liberating message of the Gospel they preached. The missionaries fought against the social issues of the day and brought awareness among the people, for example, to the practice of *sati* in 1829.

Social Issues: Dalits – Exploitation

In India, the Dalits and tribals remain even today as the ones who are exploited and oppressed. They have remained collectively at the bottom of the hierarchical and stratified Indian society for more than 3,000 years. The Dalits and tribals belong to ancient tribal communities or ‘indigenous' or 'aboriginal' people, who were either conquered or co-opted, excluded or isolated from the particular framework of the society, the caste system. Some religious stories give credence to the legitimacy of this treatment and label them as Dalits and tribals. There are also other reasons. It is not only the sociocultural factors but also the economic structures of the caste-hierarchical Hindu society that have perpetuated this division in the society. The Dalits are a low caste, and the high caste people exploit Dalits in society. Some of how the society exploits Dalits as follows:[290]

a. victimization through caste atrocities and obstructions to their social progress and spiritual growth,
b. violations of their human and cultural rights and suppression of their protests seeking full social membership,
c. social and political patronage and co-option to subserve the power interests of the forward castes and the ruling class,
d. multiple exploitations of their (Dalit) women by social, economic, sexual, and patriarchal domination,
e. deprivation of the fruits of their labour on land which they cultivate, denial of fair wages, reduction in staple food-grain productions, discrimination against the workers and their exploitation by the high-caste leadership and discriminatory interest of trade unions and employers.

Mission

‘Mission is Love’ makes the Church’s solidarity with the poor, the oppressed, and the marginalized not just a preferential option but a prerogative. The weaker sections of our society are the most affected groups. The Church’s

---

290 N. H. Smith. *Distinctive Ideas of the O*.T., (London: Epworth press, 1953), 44ff.

solidarity with the poor should thus now become a real and living everyday Christian experience. A profit-oriented, accumulative, consumeristic, and competitive economic system that pushes aside the powerless and the weak is to be challenged not so much by *words* of love but by *works* of love.[291] It calls for an altering of our lifestyle by identifying totally with the poor, accepting them, and adopting their way of life. Mechanisms that enable us to listen to the voices of the poor, to the pathetic stories of the broken people, need to be established, and we should urge that "solidarity with the poor" be practised at home – by opening the doors of our houses to the poor and the marginalized.

Hence, the Church, established by God, is, by extension, 'a Church-in-mission'. The task is to undertake conscientization of the people about contemporary global concerns so that they become aware of their responsibility to 'evangelize' the world, to participate in God's mission for the liberation of the poor, to safeguard the integrity of creation, and to advance world peace and dialogue between Christians and other religions. These are the primary responsibilities of the Church amid the exploitation, discrimination, religious fundamentalism, and poverty that are prevalent in the whole world, particularly in India. The Church's mission is to the entire world, and, therefore, there is a need for an ecumenical understanding, cooperation, and pursuit of unity among the divided churches. Mutual respect for other religions and cultures is essential for this mission.

The Relevance of the Prophets' Message for Today

In today's context, we pay little attention to the prophetic texts and read them with much emphasis, more than any other biblical texts, as they are contemporary to our own time, place, and circumstances. We must remember that reading these ancient texts for our contemporary contexts is a difficult task. However, it is essential to note that such texts feed our imagination and sometimes encourage us in our social circumstances. Here, the Old Testament emphasizes the minor prophets and their mission to the Israelites. The prophetic imagination speaks with different levels of speech against the social contexts that were answerable to the will of the covenantal God. In traditional Indian society, exchanging goods is a means of transactions. During the early period, bribes took place by exchanging horses, goods, and other means. With the introduction of a money economy, corruption increased in the society. According to O.P. Dwivedi, corruption became institutionalized during colonial times, and society carried over even after

291 Feinberg, Charles Lee. *Hosea*. The Major Messages of the Minor Prophets series. New York: (American Board of Missions to the Jews, N.d.) 10-11.

independence.[292] Colonial masters had two norms: one for Europeans and the other for the native population. "Most of the colonial administrators ignored the acts of nepotism, bribery, and the institution of polygamy. They became apathetic and cynical because of the prevalent corruption in colonial society."[293]

The prophets raised their voice against the imaginations that violated the more pragmatic assumptions of the financiers who dominated that urban culture. They imagined that the economy was answerable to God. The texts or speeches of the prophets are to be appreciated because our circumstances require an act of prophetic imagination whereby the imagination of these ancient texts speaks an important word for our context. There is no doubt that our political economy is somewhat similar to the situation found by the prophets. In present-day society, it is clear that the political economy exploits the economically vulnerable. It is an incredibly privileged, entitled community of the well-off that is so fully conformed to the tune of civil religion that it wilfully lacks the categories for such social analysis. Now, as then, prophetic imagination is to recognize that our present power arrangements and practices work against neighbourly well-being.

292 Dwivedi, O. P., *Bureaucratic Corruption in Developing Countries*, Vol. 7, No. 4, (April, 1967), 245-253, University of California Press, 1967, 246-247.

293 S.M. Chandorikar, *Prophetic Protest Movements in Old Testament and their Relevance in Today's Ministry*, (Delhi: ISPCK, 2011), 63.

24

Reclaiming a Compassionate God
Conceptualizing a Theology of Ahimsa

Arun Kumar Wesley

Introduction

Theology has been always contextual highlighting various aspects of faith and belief. Thus, theology has highlighted certain aspects of doctrines or dogmas and, at other times, aspects of the transformative features or liberation trends of the faith. In its journey through contexts, cultures, plurality of religions, invasions, exploitations, colonization and so on, theology has emphasized certain features as to suit and appeal to the people concerned. Its rationale being, the highlighted feature has to be relevant, significant and appealing to the situation on hand as the following shows.[294]

Cultural Reality

Theological articulation has been born out of the collective responsibility of a community to express itself of its innate faith in congruence with its cultural reality. Each culture may evolve its own values, ethics and morality that would endorse the social, religious and political reality of a community in a particular area. Based on these the community projects its outlook, attitude and relation with others that would govern its existence. Thus, a

294 Paul Duane Matheny, ' Contextual Theology as Practical Theology' in Essays in Contextual Theology, S.B. Bevans,2018 https://brill.com; https://na.eventscloud.com; https://en.m.wikipedia.org; www.theology-Centre.org.uk; https://CAA.org.uk

cultural reality which harbors a negative attitude towards its own members, let alone its outside neighbors, on the basis of birth and berth in social hierarchy, would color its existence in a world of discrimination and division in a binary reckoning. If it is reckoned otherwise in a positive attitude and relationship, its existence is governed by values such as tolerance, love, compassion etc.

Contextual Reality

Cultural reality being thus projected would have been because of various factors, and this stance could have evolved through the years through wars, invasions, migrations etc. However, contextual reality in its reckoning endorses a stabilized stand in expounding a socially acceptable reality that suits the political, economic and religious reality of the day. Thus, the community's collective responsibility takes care of the current trends in socio-political reality in projecting values and trends that are concurrent with the contextual reality, that could be one of positive or negative attitude, relationship or outlook.

Appellant Spirituality

Theological articulation, even incorporating the above, would sometimes be rigid and dry and, at times, devoid of emotional content, with more rational or philosophical underpinnings. Yet, it cannot be devoid of the sentiments of the community of faith with its own understanding of the reality in relation to its religious feelings that appeal to the community members. Thus, theological articulations at times keep the feelings and sentiments of the community in balance with rational arguments and philosophical leanings. Thus, a community steeped in its spiritual evolution expressing itself in an emotional outburst in songs, chants, pilgrimages, and rituals symbolic of its faith cannot but be appealing to all and sundry. However, this need not be homogenous and appealing to one and all with their own or diverse expressions complementary to each other. Taking cognizance of the above parameters - cultural and contextual reality, with the appellant spirituality, for the articulation of the faith of the community in theological categories enables one to comprehend the reality of its cultural diversity, pluralistic social-religious ethos, probably incorporating the economic and fiscal issues and the community members' aspirations, hopes and dreams.

If one analyzes the situation we are in, one cannot gloss over the ethos of hate, envy, exploitation, etc. that undermine the hopes and aspirations of the people which looks for peace and harmony, unity in diversity, reconciliation and negotiation rather than in conflict and clashes, endorsing a spirituality of life-togetherness, neighbourliness, tolerance and peace, while upholding diversity and plurality in life-expressions and articulations.

The context we live in, therefore, warrants a spirituality that endorses a socio-religious expression of love, peace, compassion, etc., that could be articulated in conceptions of faith that embody a power beyond oneself or lies within, as articulations go in a divine category of Ahimsa. As religious expressions go, all of them endorse a compassionate God, though He or She stands against evil, uniformity, homogeneity and so on. Diversity being the order of the day, opinions and views exist side by side in a pluralistic society, as with differing expressions of faith. These expressions depend on the understanding of the limitations of human capacity to order oneself, and thus lead a moral and an ethical life acceptable to society. If this is lacking one has to look for help beyond oneself or strive to find resources within oneself.

We are in a situation of conflicts, discrimination, exploitation, etc., that warrants the highlighting of a divine virtue as Ahimsa as a theological category that would be relevant and significant in resolving the issue. Theology being contextual, it is in conceiving God in Christ as the Ahimsaka that we can work out a theology of Ahimsa as relevant in a situation such as this, compounded as such by clashes, pandemics, suffering, hatred and pain. God's empathy towards the situation, one hopes, opens up a venue for working out a way of peace and salvation in terms of Ahimsa. Given below are a few details of the context.

The Background

As I write this, I am conscious of the communal clash that happened just a few days ago near our house on the 11th of August 2020 in Bangalore. It was a sudden eruption of mob violence allegedly triggered by an offensive FB post. The clash, alleged to be between two religious groups, began with arson, destruction of vehicles, property, the police station and so on. Some were killed and wounded besides policemen; hundreds were arrested, and the case is being probed to find out who was behind the clash, whether it was a conspiracy to malign someone or was it a political plan to score a point etc.[295] We also remember at this time, as we celebrate Independence Day on the 15th August 2020, those of the Freedom Fighters who sacrificed their lives at the altar of Ahimsa, the chief of them being Mahatma Gandhi.[296]

Since then, innumerable events and happenings until now among wars, ethnic conflicts, invasions, etc., have highlighted the need for Ahimsa and

295 Bangalore Riots: 'Bangalore Burns ....', *Bangalore Mirror*, Aug 11 2020;www.opindia.com; 'Bangalore Violence: Section 144.' *Economic Times,* Aug 13 2020, economic times.indiatimes.com; https://en.m.wikipedia.org; *Indian Express*, Aug 12 2020,'Karnataka Bengaluru News Aug 12: Curfew...'

296 Gandhi (Calcutta): 1947 Fast - https://thewire.in(Communalism); https://www.history.com; www.hindustantimes. com

for a peaceful solution to conflicts and issues that haunt humans at large, affecting the ecosystem, harmony among nations and its peoples and thus causing a ripple effect across the world. They include those happenings as Covid pandemic, Palestine and Ukraine invasions, and back home the Manipur ethnic issue, Demonetisation, Lockout Migrations, the erosion of Morality and Ethics concerning the rights of the people, and many more including the Hooch tragedy, the NEET imbroglio, the abuse of governing authorities etc.

A conception of God that depicts him as the compassionate one,[297] and as the one in whom Ahimsa is personified seems relevant to the situation. Ahimsa[298] as a virtue is an overarching and objective feature of a person mature enough to analyse a situation of conflict for example judicially, logically and rationally without being partisan or to be influential so as to cause injustice to anyone, but to bring about peace and love.

Peace and tranquility in love being the chief goals in God's intervention, his incarnation as the Ahimsaka gives credence to all that is close to him in creation. Thus, the God of Ahimsa considers everything as sacred - valuable; redeemable even if it has gone wrong. Even situations of conflict are considered as warranting his intervention as the God of Ahimsa. Thus, the redemption of situations as this rests with God. As the redeemer is God himself, he is the Ahimsaka par excellence. As a divine category, in practice Ahimsa manifests divine presence. In other words, divine presence manifests in Ahimsa. Thus, wherever or whoever practices Ahimsa, divine presence is manifest there in bringing about order, peace and justice. Maybe as the conception of God as the Ahimsaka seems relevant in this situation; one hopes that in resorting to Ahimsa, conflict situations such as this can be resolved.

Culture Specific

Ahimsa is a cultural characteristic embedded in and upholding humane values expressed in doing good. Ahimsa as such is a category that comprises all that is good in the human and doing good to the human, the living, the creation and so on. It is thus a comprehensive term that incorporates all that is good in the human so much as to see in him or her the divine attributes.

---

297 Compassionate: Edwin Arthur Burtt, ed/author, *The Teachings of the Compassionate Buddha*; Anandamurti Guramaa, *The Compassionate Buddha*, Kindle edition; https://www.amazon.in

298 Ahimsa: https://essaysprofessors.com; https://www.slideshare.net; https://www.esamskriti.com - 'Gandhi, Ahimsa and Christianity'; https://www.mkgandhi.org - 'Ahimsa its theory and practice'(Gandhi); https://journals.sagepub.com - 'Gandhi on Non-violence"; https://en.m.wikipedia.org - 'Ahimsa in Christianity'; https://lifehopeandtruth.com - 'Jesus Christ taught peace and non-violence: Life, Hope and Truth'

In the Indian tradition and culture, Ahimsa as a religious tenet and a divine virtue occurs, so much so as to consider anyone resorting to the act of Ahimsa as divine. In other cultures, too Ahimsa is considered a great virtue.

Evolved long ago and recognized since time immemorial, Ahimsa as mere non-violence has had a narrow understanding of action and involvement in doing good. In fact, it is rather a proactive participation in life to bring about good as a divine category. It matches the characteristics of the divine as being good, becoming good and doing good. While it is a divine characteristic and a category, in the human it has to be evolved in making one good, a process that characterizes progressive steps as in becoming, being and doing good.

Ahimsa, as such a divine category, has been manifest in creation in various ways and forms. In creation, Ahimsa brought about order and design; it brought about the various facets of human responsibility towards others and creation. Evolving among humans as non-violence, it was manifested in the Buddha, the Mahaveera, the Christ, and many others in human history. Many of the dominant Indian religions depict God in terms of Ahimsa, as the compassionate one. In modern times, Ahimsa was very effectively used by Gandhi in the freedom struggle to gain liberty from colonial powers. It has been since employed in various times, forms and ways in gaining freedom, in transforming situations and so on around the world.

The Bible

The Bible too evolved through history, and different cultures have featured Ahimsa as a great divine virtue in resolving conflicts and in doing good. Ahimsa is thus a divine attribute as God is good. In the creation narrative, too, after all the work of creation was finished, God found it to be good. God in his goodness brought about order, design and norm in creation. Further, God is depicted in the Bible as good, and that goodness is channelled to humans to continue the good work that God in Christ intends to do. Christ is also depicted in the Gospels as the one who went about doing good.[299] It is in fact in the life and work of Christ that we see in concrete terms God as being conceived as all suffering, compassionate, kind and loving, and the embodiment of Ahimsa.

In imbibing this divine category, the human gets transformed and redeemed by divine grace, compassion and forgiveness as exhibited in and through Christ, to be so, becoming good and to do good, as *missio Dei*, as it is as much a divine leading and activity.

299 Genesis 1: 9,18; Acts 10:38

Divine Origin

Thus, Ahimsa, though manifest because of divine grace, originates in God, who is all compassion, love and grace. God is thus the Ahimsaka, the embodiment of Ahimsa, of non-violence and yet endowed with such attributes as promoting peace and tranquillity, reconciliation, relationship within as in Trinity, and thus with creation, including the human. God is thus depicted as full of compassion and mercy, though at times vengeful with regard to anything evil.[300]

In a world that seemingly appears to be dispassionate, evil, corrupt, and vengeful, a God of compassion and Ahimsa may seem irrelevant and insignificant. But would that sound credible at all otherwise? For a people beset with revenge, greed, exploitation, oppression and so on, a God who is all love and grace, concern, and welfare may be anachronistic and irrelevant. However, would it be appealing? Even then, what about the victims of oppression and evil? Would they be satisfied with a God who appears unconcerned, passive, and indifferent to all that evil and suffering in the world?

Suffering

It is always difficult to understand and explain to the people in suffering, in sickness, job loss and, lack of wages etc., the conception of God in terms of love, concern, peace and justice. It is a challenge as well to entertain such conceptions in the midst of suffering and doubt and try to understand God as the one in charge of all our affairs in his scheme of things and to conceive of him as the Ahimsaka, who would resolve all issues. Would God's solidarity with the suffering and his compassion towards the suffering and those who suffer injustice help mitigate our understanding of him as the one who himself suffered injustice and pain and overcame them with God's grace in Ahimsa?

Facets of Ahimsa

Ahimsa is not mere non-violence, as said earlier. It embodies love, compassion, passion, concern, welfare, justice, peace and so on, of all that is divine. It is good - good deeds, doing good that sets it apart from evil or being indifferent. It manifests as being non-divisive, non-discriminative, and non-derogatory in words and deeds. However, it is being radical in aggressively setting things and situations right for human welfare. Thus, it is the healing arm of the divine being working through human channels. It subdues evil aggression, vengeful reaction and retaliation. Ahimsa provides

300 God is Compassionate: Psalm 86: 15-16 (NIV); Psalm 103:8; https://god.net; https://bible.org

the divine presence in compassion, understanding and mutual respect in conflict situations. This is corroborated in the communal clashes that happened during and after the freedom struggle in Kolkata and other places, as Gandhi exemplified Ahimsa in himself by his presence there.[301] It is in his being non-retaliative to his detractors - those who caused him pain and anguish, suffering on the cross, that Christ's Ahimsa shows through. In other words, it is in his submission to the cross that his Ahimsa is manifest clearly. It is, therefore, in Christ's forgiveness of his people who caused him pain and the cross that the power and effect of Ahimsa shows through.

Positivity

In a world of division, discrimination and disturbance, Ahimsa is characterized by acceptance and peace. By its very divine attribute, Ahimsa, as the attitude of doing good and being good, translates the situation of disturbance to that of peace. It looks at the positive aspect of the situation for transformation, correction and reformation. This is so whether it is in terms of individual transformation or situational or societal transformation. The positivity in action that embodies Ahimsa however does not ignore or sideline that which needs to be corrected, mended and molded to be good, and to do good.

Acceptance

In becoming, being and being good, Ahimsa accepts the situation as it is and analyses the same for any redeemable features were doing good can take hold of towards transformation. Just as in communal disturbances or in mob violence, Ahimsa accepts the situation of difference, of opinion, stance and action, seeking to transform the same in a positivistic involvement. In a world of social divisions and disturbances caused by hatred, discrimination, greed and suffering, Ahimsa the attitude of being good and to do good manifests itself in objectivity, positivity and acceptability in transforming the situation by listening to both the sides, by being patient, evolving a course of action where the parties accept each other but also become humane to do good.

Compassion

Whenever we think of or see a picture of the Buddha, it is one of compassion. He is pictured as Compassion personified, one who is encompassed by peace and tranquility. Ahimsa is the term that characterizes its synonymity, a divine attribute. In the Eastern Orthodox Church tradition, Christ is pictured as the Compassionate one, the one who cannot be moved by violence and the one who will not abrogate non-violence. In some of the Indian expressions of

301 Gandhi's suffering in Calcutta: https://www.timesnow.com; www.aparchive.com

Christ, too, he is depicted as the compassionate one and as being full of humility and grace.

Transformation

Ahimsa transforms the situation of conflict. By showing compassion and concern, the individual, the community, or the society gets transformed - in grasping the mistake, in repenting over it, and in understanding each other and the responsibility towards each other in being non-violent. Ahimsa thus engenders reconciliation and relationship based on love and peace. It is thus a divine action that brings about transformation. It further transforms the binary categories of one and the other, we and them, to one of unity, as children of God in a family, of which Hinduism boasts of as *Vasudeva Kutumbakum*, the world as a family, living together in love and peace.

Tolerance

Ahimsa is synonymous with tolerance, which is being conscious of the aggression or evil engendered due to greed, selfishness, power, and so on. By being objective and analytical, Ahimsa provides a forum or a platform for dialogue, debate and discussion to resolve issues. Justice being the other side of the coin, Ahimsa ensures it; by being non-violative of the norm, the decorum or the law, the culprit is made to learn a lesson in recompense for the damage done in kind, gesture or deed to ensure justice to the victim.

Empowerment

Ahimsa, in practice, empowers one to promote life and living, to mete out peace and justice. Ahimsa, thus, in practice, empowers the one pragmatic and others in relation to him or her. It is thus as though the divine presence in being non-violative as Ahimsa enables the wronged or the victim to claim justice and be empowered. This aspect has been much needed in India as the marginalized - the Dalits, Adivasis, men and women, children, farmers, labourers etc., suffer the most.

Conservation

In the divine scheme of things where Ahimsa stands supreme, the sacredness of things in the world and creation are marked as precious and valuable. Their sacerdotal values are in the plan of divine dispensation, considered as such for future renewal and rejuvenation when the new creation dawns on the horizon. Thus, preservation, conservation and protection of nature, flora and fauna, etc., are to be maintained for the future glory that God has planned for them. Thus, ecological conservation is close to the heart of divine grace, where human responsibility towards the protection of creation is decreed - in not being destructive, exploitative and oppressive of creation.

The Cross[302]

The Cross of Christ as the supreme event of divine grace as Ahimsa epitomizes for all, and for all times passive resistance in suffering, submission to all that is evil in political, social, religious and in economic realms, which in the natural and normal course of thinking and doing would have expected righteous anger and retaliation; a subdued exhibition of divine mercy and forgiveness on those who took recourse in being cruel, rude and in being revengeful; to overcome all that is wicked and evil in the human and in the world, to transform situations as this of conflict, clashes of interest, divisive trends, communalizing and discriminative reactions etc., once and for all to bring about change in the course of human history - to revolutionize thinking and doing, in accordance with the divine plan to inaugurate a new creation[303] based on love, peace and justice through the journey of suffering, self-denial and non-resistance.[304]

Thus, it was not a defeat of Ahimsa on the cross - an exhibition of weakness against evil, nor of indifference to suffering or submission; but a way of Ahimsa, as in the divine scheme of things, to override vengeance and retaliation. This was evident in the resurrection as the love for the human and the world as Ahimsa could not be contained in the grave confines of doing evil to overcome evil, but in transforming the situation in mercy and forgiveness. It was thus a victory,[305] he exhibition of which in rising from the dead and in being raised from the dead endorsed the value of Ahimsa - non-violence, non-retaliation, non-vengeance and so on extolling the virtue of passive resistance as a divine virtue.

302 The Cross: Mt 10:38(Take up one's cross); 1 Cor 1: 18 (Word of the cross folly to..); Eph 2: 16 (reconciles); Col 1: 20 (makes peace)' Heb 12: 2 (endures)

303 The New Creation: 2 Cor 5:17; Heb 10: 20; Gal 6: 15; Col 3: 10; Rev 21: 1,5

304 Self -denial: Ja 5: 10; Heb 2: 10 (submission/suffering).

305 Victory: 1 John 5: 4 (0vercomes the world); 1 Cor 15: 5 (death)

25

Christian Impact on the Modern Indian Renaissance

Swami Raju Tadivaka

Introduction

This article is, indeed, prepared in honour of Prof. Rev. Dr. Kondasingu Jesurathnam to publish in his "festschrift" as he celebrates his 60 years of life journey '*shashtipoorthi*', honouring his valuable services to theological education through United Theological College, Bangalore and Senate of Serampore College (University). Dr. Jesurathnam has been a profound thinker, an ardent reader, a relentless writer, and a source of inspiration to his students over the last three decades. As an Old Testament schooler, he produced many scholars in his field. It is a great privilege for me to write this article to honour such a great scholar. I focussed my attention on presenting how Christians contributed to the rise of a Renaissance in India during the modern era of our country, particularly during the 19th and 20th centuries CE; perhaps it is an attempt to access the impact of Luther's Reformation and modern Christian missionaries.

"Luther's Reformation" is a landmark in the history of Christianity and the history of the Renaissance in modern India. The reformative spirit of the 16th Century was not limited to Germany or Europe; it spread all over the world through the word of God by Protestant Christian Missionaries, who influenced religions, civilizations, cultures, and nations. The Protestant Missionaries who came to India during the modern period, particularly in the 19th and 20th centuries, influenced Indians, exceptionally modern Hindu thinkers, to a greater extent, which perhaps became a motivation and inspiration to reform the socio-religious life of Indians by developing renascent movements in India. Several religious and secular movements developed in India during the modern period, reviving and reforming religious and secular life in the Indian subcontinent. This article is a brief attempt firstly to give some conceptual clarifications on important terms "reformation" and "renaissance"; secondly, the importance of Luther's Reformation, a brief attempt is needed to study internal Indian conditions; and final section is an attempt to understand how the spirit of Reformation influenced Indian socio-religious life.

Conceptual Clarifications

Reformation

The medieval period is remarkable for various new developments in the world and the Church. During this age, it was a period of "new inventions and discoveries" - sea routes, printing press, paper, gunpowder, and many other discoveries. New places and new nations are discovered/located. It was also a period of significant movements and revolutions; for example, the French Revolution and the Industrial Revolution developed in the West, and many bhakti movements developed and brought great revival in Indian religion and society. It is also the period of great Reformation in the Church; indeed, this period of great Renaissance takes place in the history of the Christian Church, marking the era of "Reformation". It was in the 16th Century that thc great movement came to the culmination of reforming the doctrine and practices of the Roman Catholic Church through the deliberate efforts of Dr. Martin Luther, which resulted in the establishment of the Protestant Churches. The roots of the Reformation, perhaps, go back to the 14th Century, with groups such as the Lollards and the Hussites attacking the Church for its wealth and hierarchical structures; the work of humanists such as Erasmus also fuels the movement. Historians and scholars thought that the Reformation began in 1517 in Wittenberg when Martin Luther issued ninety-five theses criticizing the sale of indulgences and launched an attack on papal infallibility, the celibacy of the priesthood, the doctrine of transubstantiation and corruption within religious orders. Luther confirmed his commitment to reform at the Diet of Worms in 1521. In Denmark, Norway, Sweden, Saxony, Hesse, and Brandenburg, supporters broke away and established Protestant Churches, while in Switzerland, Zwingli led a separate movement and later Calvin. The spirit of Reformation spread all over the globe, reawakening the Church from slumber, and its impact went further, paving the way to a renaissance in India, reforming religion and society to a greater extent.[306] This impact of the Renaissance and Reformation helped produce new literature, develop humanitarian concepts, and abolish feudalism and slavery.

Renaissance

"Renaissance" means 'rebirth' or 'revival'. It is a paradigm shift in the perception and approach of people towards religious, cultural, social and political aspects. There are several synonyms used in expressing the meaning of "renaissance", such as reawakening, new birth, new dawn, reappearance, rebirth, recrudescence, re-emergence, renascence, reconstruction, resurrection, regeneration, rejuvenation, renewal, restoration, rekindling, revival, Reformation, and so on. "Renaissance" is a term used to indicate a period when revival, renewal, reawakening and Reformation took place in the history of humankind. "Renaissance", in other words, means the revival of art and learning under the influence of classical models, which began in Italy in the late Middle Ages. It also means rebirth and renewal. It is a revival and renewal of religious, social, and political matters.[307]

It was a period of new growth of interest and activity in art and literature, particularly in the West. Renaissance took place primarily in northern Italy during the 14th to 16th centuries. The "Renaissance" is generally regarded as beginning in Florence in the early 14th Century, where humanist ideas were arising, and there was a revival of interest in the classical age with its association of naturalism and faithfulness to nature. The period from the end of the 15th Century or the beginning of the 16th Century has become known as the "high Renaissance" in art and architecture. The ideas of the Renaissance did not begin to spread beyond Italy until the early 16th Century, but were then important throughout Western Europe for the next hundred years and from the art of the Italian high Renaissance developed "mannerism".[308] Ideas of the Renaissance and Reformation came and changed socio-religious and economic-political life in India. Renaissance brought a modern culture. It encouraged expression, thinking, and ideas, but at an early age, thinking was not encouraged. Religion controlled ideas, but

306 T. Swami Raju, *BharatavaniloAdhunika Chaitanya Udyamalu* (Modern Renascent Movements in India), (Text Book in Telugu, Telugu Theological Literature Board, Hyderabad, first print 2004, second print 2014) and also Judy Pearsall and Bill Trumble (eds.), *The Oxford English Reference Dictionary*, (New York: Oxford University Press, 1995), 1212.

307 Judy Pearsall and Bill Trumble (eds.), *The Oxford English Reference Dictionary*, 1220.

308 T. Swami Raju, *Bharatavanilo Adhunika Chaitanya Udyamalu*, 14f. For more details, refer to the recent publication, *Modern Religious and Secular Movements in India,* Rodinmawia Ralte and T. Swami Raju (eds), (Serampore: Senate of Serampore College, 2023).

the Renaissance and Reformation questioned religious beliefs and doctrines. This affected many areas, particularly religious thinking in the modern age, especially John Calvin and Martin Luther, the reformers who brought revolutionary thinning in the Church and the State. Changes came in India's socio-religious, economic, and political life.

Importance of Martin Luther's Reformation

Martin Luther was born to Hans Luther and Margret Zigler on Saturday, November 10, 1483, in Eiselben, Saxony State of Germany.[309] Luther's parents were devotional, and they brought him up in Christian spirituality and devotional life. Luther did his early education in a Latin School at Eisenach from 1498-1501, and then he joined Erfurt University and attained B.A and M.A. degrees during 1501-1505. Then, he joined St. Augustinian Monastery on July 17 1505.[310] He dedicated his life to Christian ministry and was ordained in Erfurt Church in May 1507. He joined Wittenberg University in 1508 in the teaching ministry. He received a doctorate in theology in 1512. He preached on Psalms, St. Paul's epistle to Romans and Galatians during 1513 – 1516, and he read the Bible carefully, searching for the truth. He was influenced by the word of God, mainly through the following three critical verses:

"Look at the proud! Their spirit is not right in them but the righteous live by their faith" (Habakkuk 2:4)

"For in it the righteousness of God is revealed through faith for faith; as it is written 'The one who is righteous will live by faith'" (Romans 1:17).

"Now it is evident that no one is justified before God by the law; for 'The one who is righteous will lie by faith'" (Galatians 3:11)[311]

With the motivation of these verses, Martin Luther believed that human beings did not get righteousness by his/her works based on the Law, but by faith and grace alone. In 1517, Martin Luther first protested to the Catholic Church about selling indulgences. (the full or partial remission of temporal punishment due to sins already forgiven). Martin Luther argued that faith alone could provide the remission of sin and not monetary payments. The Church was slow to respond to the criticism of Martin Luther, and in this period, Martin became a prolific writer, and his writings were widely distributed throughout Europe. On October 31 1517, Luther posted ninety-five Theses criticizing the practices of the Church on the door of the Castle

---

309 T. John Ratnam, *Life of Martin Luther* (in Telugu), (Narasapuram, AP: Jeevan Jyothi Press and Publishers, 1987), 8.

310 Refer to a chronological table of Martin Luther's life, 117-120.

311 All references are from *the Holy Bible* (The New Revised Standard Version, Catholic Edition for India), (Bangalore: Thomas Nelson for Theological Publications in India, 1989).

Church of Wittenberg. He also posted a handwritten copy to the archbishop of Magdeburg, Albert of Mainz. The 95 Theses of Martin Luther were critical of many practices relating to baptism and the sale of indulgences for the remittance of sin. He also indirectly challenged the Pope's legitimacy; this courageous act of Martin Luther brought great revival and Reformation in the Catholic Church in the 16th Century.[312]

Reformation Opened the Way for Renaissance

It was no coincidence that the Reformation, with its emphasis on Scripture, came on the heels of the invention of the printing press, with the Bible being the first book to get printed. For the first time in history, God's word could be mass-produced and made available to ordinary people. With the word of God now available on a scale hitherto unknown, Luther and other reformers emphasized education for the masses, primarily so they could read the Bible. They saw getting God's word into the hands and hearts of the people as the key to ongoing Reformation throughout the Church. The Reformation and its emphases also opened the way for all the great revivals of the modern era. The invention of the printing press and Luther's success in directing the Church's attention back to Scripture changed the course of history more than any events since the birth of Christ and the conversion of the apostle Paul. Even secular historians understand this, and Time Warner, in the year 2000, named Gutenberg's invention of the printing press and Luther's instigation of the Reformation as the number 1 and number 3 most important events of the past millennia.

As a German monk, Martin Luther became the father of the Protestant Reformation. He is most widely known for criticizing aspects of the Roman Catholic Church. In particular, he believed that the Bible and not the Roman Catholic Church were the sources of legitimacy for interpreting the word of Christ. Martin Luther translated the Bible into German, making it more accessible to the general public. Martin Luther's Reformation was not limited to Germany only; it was widespread all over the world, inspiring and impacting many people, cultures, religions and nations. Though there was no specific evidence for the direct impact of Martin Luther's Reformation on the Indian Renaissance, there is much possibility to trace out the indirect influence through Protestant Christian Missions during the modern period, particularly in the 19th and 20th centuries. It is indeed a fact that Protestant Christian Missions and the British Government were major catalysts and

312 *www.biographyonline.net* (accessed on March 20th 2016).

influencing factors in the Renaissance and Reformation of Indian socio-religious life.[313]

Impact of Luther's Reformation on Indian Renaissance

Indeed, the Reformation impacted the Indian Renaissance during the modern period, though it might have been indirectly through Protestant Christian Missionaries. The meaning of Reformation is "make or become better by the removal of faults and errors", "abolish or cure as abuse or malpractice"[314] In other words, it attempts to " reform " the existing systems, thoughts, concepts, practices, and beliefs to suit their original purity by eradicating wrongs and evils. Martin Luther did precisely the same in his Reformation of the Roman Catholic Church in the 16th Century to protest against the then-existing evil practices contrary to the word of God.

Internal Indian Conditions

Several evil practices and blind beliefs existed in Indian society during the 19th and 20th centuries, which continued in the name of religion with social acceptance. A brief background of the political, economic, religious, and social life of Indian society is needed for a better understanding of why the Reformation was needed and how the Renaissance developed.

Political Instability: India was in a pitiable condition around 1800 AD. Early Hindu governments did not succeed in giving peace to the country. Muslim invasions began in India at the end of the 12th Century. India had not known peace from 1200 to 1800 AD. Even under the best of Moghul emperors, there was frequent fighting. There were no reform movements during that period. There was no unity between small Hindu kingdoms in India. There was no proper education for the people of our country, particularly for the poor and Dalit backgrounds. British ruled our country during the 19th and 20th centuries, especially from 1857 to 1947. Almost our country was under British rule for 90 years.

Economic Exploitation: Economic conditions in India became worse due to economic exploitation by the policies of East India Company and British rule, especially during the 19th and 20th centuries. There were economic inequalities even among Indians. People suffered from the challenges of poverty. There was a big gap between the rich and poor. Before the advent of East India Company to India, Indian people have been living on their skills and earning their livelihood through small-scale industries. East India Company and Colonialism destroyed the Indian economic system

313 T. Swami Raju, *BharatavaniloAdhunika Chaitanya Udyamalu*, 6-22, Allyama Zachariah, *Modern Religious & Secular Movements in India,* (Bangalore: Theological Book Trust, 1992).

314 Judy Pearsall and Bill Trumble (eds.), *The Oxford English Reference Dictionary*, 1212.

and exploited the Indian economy to a greater extent. The country that established colonialism was called a "ruling country", and the country where colonialism was established was called a "colony"; therefore, India became a colony of British rule. The ruling country developed their economic resources, while the colonized country destabilized economically.[315] British East India Company gradually exploited the Indian economy in many places to attain political power in India. It transported the Indian economy and wealth to England. Economic analysts highlighted three kinds of economic exploitation applied in India during the period of East India Company and British rule; they are: a) the period of merchant capital, b) the period of industrial capital and c) the period of financial capital, which pushed India under the poverty line.

Religious Superstitions: Many superstitious practices continued in the name of religion. There was no revival or renewal in Hinduism at that time. Neither new literature was produced in Hinduism, nor revival movements developed in Hindu society. People followed many superstitious practices and had blind beliefs. Animal and human sacrifices were continued in the name of religion, so no one objected, even not identifying that this was wrong.

Social Evils: Some activities began in the name of religion and continued for centuries as traditions and customs with social sanction and community approval. Such traditions greatly influenced society and ordered people's lives after attaining sanctity and holiness with religious approval. While some had a good influence on society, others have continued to be "social evils" that have troubled the country's social life. Many social evils existed in Indian society by the 18th Century, with the approval of Hinduism. Many of them were continued against women. During the 18th Century, there was a very low status of women in Indian society. Manu prescribed in his *dharmasasthra* that a woman should be under the control of her father from birth to marriage, and after marriage, she should be under the control of her husband and in her old age, she should be under the control of her son. Hence, women were not allowed any freedom at any stage. In such a pitiable condition, there were imposed on women many traditions that are religiously superstitious and socially evil practices. Let us examine some of them to understand Indian society.

***Devadasi* System:** It was a custom that continued in Indian society for centuries, unknowingly as a social evil. In the 18th and 19th centuries, perhaps

315 For more discussion on economic exploitation, refer to an article published related to the economy paper of Group-I exams, V. Chiranjeevi, "Bharatadesamulo British Palana – Valasa Dopidi" (British Rule in India: Exploitation of Colonialism) in *Sakshi:* Telugu Daily News Paper, June 26, (2009), 7. T. Swami Raju, *Bharatavanilo Adhunika Chaitanya Udyamalu*, and *Modern Religious and Secular Movements in India*, 21-30.

even today, *the devadasi* system has been prevalent in India. It was a Hindu custom to dedicate girls to serving in Hindu temples. The term *devadasi* means female servant of *deva* or God. The main aim of this system was that the priests dedicate young girls to singing and dancing before the temple's idols. This custom began with a good aim, but it became a social evil in long practice. Over time, *devasasis* became public prostitutes. Once they dedicated to God in temples, they were treated as married to God, hence, public property of that village or town. Temple priests or trusties made them by force to do prostitution. Many *devadasis* believed that prostitution was not wrong, but it was their occupation. They had the freedom to have sex with any person and bore children, but their children became fatherless and, hence, faced many problems in schooling and other activities. Their lives became helpless and hopeless; their children became careless and criminals due to a lack of proper education and parental care/counselling.[316] The lust and desire of men spoiled many young girls' lives. Holy places became places of public prostitution, and the girls dedicated to living holy life were made holy prostitutes. They did not know they were doing wrong or that their lives were spoiled. In other words, *the devadasi* system was transformed into an accepted "sex industry" of the society for the profit of temple authorities. *Devadasis* were, indeed, "slaves of circumstance". Sindhuja Parthasarathy thinks:

> Though outlawed in 1988, the Devadasi system persists, forcing women into a lifetime of sexual exploitation. The Devadasi community in three villages around Bellary district, Karnataka, exemplified the pain and dignity under this regressive practice.[317]

Parthasarathy quoted many examples; for instance, Durgamma married the goddess Yellamma at 10, even before puberty. She was forced to sleep with her maternal uncle and pushed into prostitution. Mudamma’s parents vowed to dedicate their first child to Huligamma, a local goddess if it were a girl. It is a common practice when there are no sons in the family. While Articles 34 and 35 of the Convention on the Rights of the Child called for the State to protect children from all forms of sexual exploitation, organized crime against lower-caste children continues with religious sanction. According to the National Commission of Women, over 2.5 lakh girls, most of whom belong to the Dalit communities, are dedicated to temples on the Maharashtra-Karnataka border.[318]

---

316 T. Swami Raju, *Bharatavanilo Adhunika Chaitanya Udyamalu*, 23-24.

317 “Slaves of Circumstance”, *The Hindu*, August 18 (2013), 5.

318 “Slaves of Circumstance”, in *The Hindu*, 5.

Sati: It has been a custom in India for centuries. It has been known as "burning of widows" with the dead bodies of their husbands. The higher castes believed that the faithfulness of their wives was proved by their jumping into the funeral fire in which the bodies of their husbands were cremated. Mainly *Kshatriya* caste people believed that after the death of the husband, the wife's chastity and faithfulness is proved only by committing sati.[319] There were many instances relating to *sati sahagamana* in Hindu religious and social literature. However, there was no indication of *patisahagamana* – the husband died on the funeral pyre with the dead body of his wife. The custom of sati, as some scholars argue, goes back to the age of *Rigveda*. However, tracing out *sati* custom in Vedic literature is more complicated. It has been referred to in the great epics *Ramayana* and *Mahabharata*. In the *Uttarakanda*of *Valmiki Ramayana* (17:4), we find Vedavathi's mother performing "sati", but this story is more legendary than historical. In *Mahabharata*, there are some references to Madri, the wife of Pandu Raju and the four wives of Vasudeva, namely – Devaki, Bhadra, Rohini and Madira, who died on their husband's funeral pyre. From then onwards, this custom became more popular.[320]

In modern India, this social evil custom has continued to kill many women in the name of sati, from Alokmanjari to Rupkanwar. A recent incident that happened a decade ago witnessed the continuation of this cruel custom in India. On November 11 1999, a Dalit woman, Charan Shahi, was forcefully burned by her husband, Maniram Shahi, dead body in Satpura village of Uttar Pradesh.[321] William Cary, the Christian missionary, first highlighted that sati is a cruel custom against the life of women, and he fought against this custom, but Indian historians did not give him due respect to mention his name in their histories; they credited it to Raja Rammohan Roy, perhaps, he was Indian and from the Hindu community.

Child Marriages: Another social evil prevailed in India during the 18th and 19th centuries, continuing in many places, though not directly but secretly. This custom is also, indeed, an oppressive structure against the

---

319 For more details on the practice of *sati*refer, for example, H. C. Upetri, *The Myth of Sati,* (Bombay: Himalaya Publishing House, 1991); Sakuntala Narasimhan, *Sati*, (Delhi: Penguin Books (India) Ltd, 1990); Arvind Sharma, *Sati,*(Delhi: Motilal Banarsidas, 1988); John Stratton Hawley, *Sati-the blessing and curse,*(New Yor: Oxford University Press, 1994); S. K. Ghosh, *Indian Women Through the Ages,*(New Delhi: Ashish Publishing House, 1989); M.B.Fuller, *The Wrongs of Indian Womanhood, (*Delhi: Inter India Publications, 1900).

320 For a historical background on the origin and development of sati, refer *to The History and Culture of Indian People (Vedic Age),* Vol;1 (Bombay: Bharatiya Vidya Bhavan, n.d).

321 *Inadu*, Telugu Daily News Paper, November 15, (1999), 6. *The Hindu*, Daily News Paper, November 18, (1999), 4.

liberty, dignity and freedom of female children. Some instances revealed that below ten years old were married to men above 50. These girls did not know what marriage is and what married life is. When these girls were grown up with the maturity to have married life with their aged partners, the aged husbands became too older and unable to meet the physical and material needs of their younger wives, particularly these young girls were particularly unhappy in sexual relations with their aged partners. However, for family and society, they have to keep entirely either suppressing their physical desires of youth or commit adultery, which sometimes leads them to mental agony, severe physical persecution, torture, violence and death. Often, the aged husbands died when their wives became mature; the family made her widow shave her head, wear white/saffron clothes, and remove all kinds of ornaments. She had to live as a widow as long as she was alive if she rejected *sati*. Though there was a ban on "child marriages", it still continued secretly, if not publicly.[322] A very recent incident happened in Moinabad of Hyderabad when a 16 years old girl met Ms.J.C. Amrapali, Joint Collector of Ranga Reddy District and requested to stop her marriage as her father had been forcing her to get married.[323]

Dowry: The primary threat to women's extinction is the dowry system, which has troubled Indian women for many centuries till it spread its tenterhooks to kill girls troubling their parents. In some of the castes, dowry was the deciding factor in marriage. Therefore, many parents considered it a liability to have girl babies, for it was the girl's father who had to pay the dowry to the boy's father. This extravagant expenditure led to the cruel practice of letting the girl babies die through infanticide and foeticide. Even after marriage, though parents paid large amounts as dowry in cash and things, many women faced severe persecution and domestic violence from their husbands' families. Pathetically, in many cases, husbands and family members (aunts, uncles and relatives) brutally killed the girls. Some girls committed suicide as the only solution to put an end to this dowry problem. This social evil has been vigorously working in Indian society during the 18th and 19th centuries. It has continued until today, though there were many laws and legal protections in favour of females.[324] The question is why dowry deaths and other social evils still continue in Indian society against

322 For example, 15 a 15-year-old minor girl, Vara Lakshmi, was arranged to marry 30-year-old Narender on June 22, 2007, in Hyderabad, but the Secunderabad Revenue Divisional Officer stopped that child marriage with police protection. Details with photos published in *Eenadu*, Daily News Paper in Telugu, June 23, (2007).

323 "Na Pelli Apeyandi Medam?" in *Sakshi*, (Daily News Paper in Telugu, December 20 (2015), 12.

324 For more details, refer to the recent publication of this author, T. Swami Raju, *Christian Theological Responses: Contemporary Contextual Concerns,* (New Delhi: Christian

women when there are many Laws and Acts taken in favour of female protection. Dowry deaths and violence have continued; in other words, it has been increasing.[325] Many times, girls' parents also end their lives due to the burden of dowry.[326] The NRI husbands, those who have been earning good salaries, are also not exempted from demanding dowry.[327]

Caste System: One of the biggest problems ever solved in India is the caste system, which threatens the unity and integrity of Indian society. It might not be surprising that the caste system worked vigorously as a dividing and conflicting force in India during the 18th and 19th centuries. However, it is surprising that this caste system is troubling Indian society even in 21st Century too. This caste system was codified by Hindu *dharmasastras* and elaborated in Epics, Puranas systematizing Indian social order. Therefore, the hierarchical caste system became the major dividing force in Indian society. People in India are/were divided on caste basis as upper castes, lower castes and outcastes or *panchamas*. This caste system was codified in *varnashrama*, giving rules and regulations of caste duties, which indeed created differences in society and affected social relations in the worst state. The fourfold caste system set the social hierarchical status of major castes – *Brahmanas* shall perform priestly duties; the duty of *Kshatriyas* will be administration/ruling; *Vaisya's* duty is agriculture/business, and *Sudras* duty is service (Gita 18:41-44). Many Dalits were treated as *panchamas* and treated eligible for nothing but for all menial jobs like vetti, scavenging, skinning and so on. This led some sections of people belonging to a lower caste to socio-economic and religiopolitical exploitation, pushing/keeping

---

World Imprints, 2014), particularly the chapter on "Gender Discrimination: Theological Inquiry", 112-131.

325 For example, Mrs Vijaya d/o Koteswara Rao married Mr K. Balagangadhar of Hyderabad, who ended her life in a septic tank with her two children due to a dowry problem. Mrs. Padma married Srinu on May 22 2002, but she was murdered within one month due to dowry by her husband and burned alive on July 7 2002. Details of both incidents were published in "Septic Tanklo Talli Biddalasavalu (The dead bodies of mother and children in septic tank)" and "Katesina Katnam (Dowry Bite)" in *Enadu: Telugu* Daily News Paper, July 8, (2002), 1.

326 The very recent incident reveals the intensity of dowry deaths a father put an end to his life by hanging himself to a tree on the day when he had his daughter's marriage on December 23 2015, due to a lack of money to pay the dowry to the bridegroom. Refer for details, "RathriKuthuriPelli, UdayamAtmahathya (Daughter's marriage in the night Suicide in the Morning)" in *Sakshi:* Telugu Daily News Paper, December 24, (2015), 12.

327 "AdanapuKatnam Kosam Vedimpulu (Troubles for excess dowry)", in *Sakshi,* Hyderabad, 28-11-2009. P. 5. Though the bride's parents paid Rs.30,00,000/- as dowry on marriage day, the husband demanded more dowry.

them in severe poverty, illiteracy, minority, powerless, untouchables and unworthy to approach God/temple.[328]

Untouchability: The inflexible Indian caste system created another social evil which troubled much of the lower caste society during the 18th and 19th centuries. According to Hinduism, one's birth determines a person's caste. There are several castes and sub-castes in India. Some are considered high, and others are low. The Brahmanas were those who belonged to the upper caste and considered themselves divine/gods. They were the only caste people allowed to read and learn Vedas in Sanskrit, but the Sudras and Dalits, who belonged to the lower castes, were denied the right to read and learn Sanskrit/Vedas. Manu, the greatest law-giver of Hinduism, ruled out that the lead should be melted and poured into the ears of the Sudras (Dalits), who were listening to the reading of the Vedas. Besides the low castes, there were large numbers of outcastes who were considered as "untouchables".[329] B.R. Ambedkar had experienced such pathetic untouchability in his lifetime; hence, he had given up "Hinduism" and converted to Buddhism. The caste system denied the fundamental rights of education, economics and dignified religious life to the lower caste people. Social domination and control of knowledge by upper castes kept a vast majority of Indian people as slaves/dalits.[330] One can bring out various superstitious practices that Indian society had during the 18th and 19th centuries. Forced labour, blind belief in travelling outside India and so on. Due to the limitation of space, it is impossible to provide all the details.

Protestant Christian Missions

The significant role played as a major catalyst in bringing Renaissance and renewal in Indian society was the Protestant Christian Missions of the 19th and 20th centuries. Presumably, all Protestant Christian Missions were/are the products of Luther's Reformation. The revival spirit of the 16th Century Reformation has been kindling many hearts throughout the last five

---

328 See for discussion on Indian caste system and Dalit problems, T. Swami Raju, *The Study of Religion: Methods and Perspectives*, (Bangalore: BTESSC/SATHRI, 2004); T. Swami Raju, *Vira Cult in Folk Religion of Guntur District: Dalit Perspective* (New Delhi: ISPCK, 2005); T. Swami Raju, *Chennakesava Cult and Dalits* (Bangalore: BTESSC/SATHRI, 2010).

329 Aleyamma Zachariah, *Modern Religious & Secular Movements in India*.12

330 Refer for more information on "untouchability", for example, R. Barbara Joshi (ed.), *Untouchables Voices of Dalit Liberation Movement*, (New Delhi), 1986; Michael Mahar (ed.), *The Untouchables in Contemporary India* (Arizona: The University of Arizona Press, 1972); James Freeman, *Untouchable: An Indian Life History* (London: 1979); Suresh Narain, Srivastava, *Harijans in Indian Society* (Lucknow: Aminabad, 1980); Prabhati Mukherjee, *Beyond the Four Varnas: The Untouchables in India,* Delhi, 1988.

centuries to take the word of God into peoples and nations, which can bring revival and Reformation in the lives of individuals and communities. It is, perhaps, the right time to re-vision Martin Luther's Reformation from the Indian context, as wc are preparing to celebrate 500 years celebrations of his Reformation in 2017.

Danish Mission began Protestant Missionary work in India, which did great work in Tamil Nadu during the 18th Century. It is, indeed, popularly known as the Serampore Trio – William Cary, Marshman and Ward, who perhaps first awakened Protestant Missions of the British, then America and Europe to the sense of their responsibility to propagate the gospel to non-Christians of the world, especially to Indians. They explained the need for missionary work in India and encouraged Protestant Missionaries. William Cary learned Bengali and Sanskrit languages and translated the Bible into Bengali.

Protestant Missionaries adopted three kinds of works – gospel, education and medical so they established Churches and made them gospel centres, established schools and promoted education, and started clinics and hospitals and provided medical support to the people. The missionary compounds became centres for evangelism, education and medicine. It was chiefly by the winning of the actual converts from Hinduism through schools, newspapers and literature by awakening them from their superstitious Hindu mind and social evil practices. The Serampore Trio used their gifts and talents to bring renewal among Hindus. They opened boarding schools and orphanages, did medical work freely for the poor and downtrodden, and cared for lepers. They were eager to send out native missionaries to preach throughout the country. A college was opened at Serampore to train them, now popularly known as Senate of Serampore College (University), which became a tremendous intellectual and ministerial centre for qualified theological education to prepare the leaders and ministers to the Church in India and other countries like Srilanka. The then king of Denmark gave authority to confer degrees.

Protestant Missionaries realized that many social and religious reforms were necessary to improve the socio-religious life of the people in India and mainly to eradicate social evils and superstitious practices from the society. Due to the excellent work done by the Serampore Trio, the British Parliament granted complete freedom to Protestant Missionaries to come to India and do their missionary work. Soon after, many missionaries – Baptists, Lutherans, Anglicans, Presbyterians, etc., came from Britain, America and Europe and established their mission fields in India. Several individual Europeans came to India and started educational work by establishing schools and colleges, which introduced Western scientific education to Indians. Alexander Duff, for example, a Scottish missionary, opened a school in Kolkata for English teaching.

Duff had two convictions: the first one is that the highest form of education is Christian education, and the second is that modern education can be given to the people of India only through English medium. The vernacular languages do not have the books required to the purpose. Duff's work opened a new era in India. Dynamic young people were attracted by Duff and impressed by his work. While talking about Western influence, Farquhar said, "Western thought caused a great ferment in their minds, breaking down the old ideas with great rapidity, and the daily scripture lesson filled them with Christian thought."[331] Raja Ram Mohan Roy was one of Duff's students who later established Brahmo Samaj to reform Hindu society. He led many of his followers to Duff's influence on English education. Many Protestant Missionaries started similar work, for example, Dr. John Wilson in Bombay and John Anderson in Madras. Christian Missionaries also gave importance to women's education, and for this purpose, several unmarried missionaries arrived in India. Women's work continued to a greater extent under the wing of Zenana workers. Women Medical Missionaries also came to work with women in India. Orphanages and widow homes were started to protect and help people in need.

The impact of Protestant Christian Missionaries was significant on the Indian Renaissance, particularly of Serampore missionaries William Cary and others; indeed, the Indian Renaissance was started in Bengal through the origin and development of Brahma Samaj as a reformed Hindu socicty. Indian reformers like Raja Rammohan Roy, Keshub Chendrasen, and Debendrnath Tagore spoke against superstitious beliefs, evil practices and polytheistic aspects of Hindu society. They initiated reforms in the Hindu religion and Indian society and gave importance to high standards for rational thinking. The social, religious and political life of India was re-examined, and a spirit of rationalism developed in modern Indian thinkers. Indians began to use scientific knowledge to reform themselves and eliminate social and religious evils in Indian society. Reformers arose to purge the Indian society of evils. There were three types of social and religious reforms began:

The first one is the "compromise type" of movements developed. They adopted much from Christianity and attempted to reform religion and society in India. The best examples of this were Brahmo Samaj and Alighar movements. The second type of movement was the "Orthodox movement". These attempted to protest their religion and tried to prove the greatness of their own religion; for example, Arya Samaj and Ahmadiya Movements

331 Quoted by Aleyamma Zachariah, *Modern Religious & Secular Movements in India,* 18.

adopted this kind of method in bringing awareness among their religious masses. The third category was "reform movements", which absorbed Western ideas, concepts and methods but used to reform their religion from within without giving credit to the West. Ramakrishna Mission was the best example of this type. Renaissance enabled Indians in the 19th and 20th centuries to grow their religion out of its mythological, traditionalistic, ritualistic and sociological structural forms. In place of Puranic Hinduism, Philosophical Hinduism was emphasized. Neo-Vedantins like Swami Vivekananda, Gandhi, Aurobindo Gosh and S. Radhakrishnan succeeded in carrying the Hindu message to the West, perhaps due to their ability to reinterpret Vedanta as a religious philosophy independent of the caste system and elaborated mythologies. The impact of the Renaissance made Indian thinkers and reformers pay more attention to the human reality of life on earth. They had much concern about the well-being of human society. Renaissance helped adjust Hindu teachings to the West's scientific thought and socio-political philosophy.

Conclusion

As Christians, we indeed have to re-vision and re-examine the socio-religious life of our Indian Christian community in order to find out if there is any need to reform and the necessity to revive our Church activities. It is, perhaps, a fact that one of the major social evils of Hindu society, called the "caste system", entered into the Christian community and dominated its socioeconomic and religious life even in post-modern days of our time. The caste system is vigorously working among Christians, particularly in Churches in South India, as a dividing force; hence, the Dalit community faced the same caste problem even after their conversion to Christianity, and further, this caste consciousness became strong among Dalit Christians since they were divided based on their Hindu caste origin though they were converted to Christianity.

Social services are another revival area in our Church activities, particularly in the medical and educational sectors. Many missionary hospitals and educational institutions are being closed and neglected in providing services to the poor and needy. Christian service-oriented organizations/institutions are becoming corporatization, making their services inaccessible to the poor. We are facing many challenges from the multi-faith context of our country, particularly from modern *Hindutva* fundamentalism and global issues such as ecological crisis, terrorism as a religious obligatory duty, violence and other forms of corruption in religious and secular institutions. We need to re-vision our Christian missionaries' social services, particularly the educational and medical services they rendered in India, which influenced our Indian society to a greater extent.

26

Rhetorical Reading of Psalm 13:1-6 and *Leshe*
Its Significance of Deciphering Divinity in Laments

Jeviholi Swu

Introduction

The Hebrew Bible encompasses a diverse range of literary forms, including historical narratives, poetry, prophetic oracles, hymns, and songs. This article focuses specifically on the genre of hymns, songs, and poetry found in the Book of Psalms. The Psalms are a distinctive collection of literature that includes prayers, praises, laments, and meditations. It is divided into five books (1-41; 42-72; 73-89; 90-106; 107-150) and is also classified[332] into different categories: i) Hymns, ii) Community Laments, iii) Royal Psalms, iv) Individual Laments, and v) Individual Thanksgiving.

This article, in honour of Prof. Rev. Dr. K. Jesurathnam, who specializes in Psalms,[333] is a venture into how divinity is revealed in times

332 This type of classification has been produced not by investigating the historical background but by identifying the *Gattungen* (German term for "daily life situation of the people") of the song and tracing it back to its origin in the life of Israel. The rudimentary pursuit focused on the *Sitz im Leben* (German term for "setting of life"), which is the situation that brought the particular Psalm into existence. Moses Buttenwiesser, *The Psalms* (Chicago: University of Chicago Press, 1938),321-324; see Arthur Weisure, *The Psalms: An Introduction* (London: SCM,1962); Herman Gunkel, *The Psalms: A Form-Critical Introduction*, trans. T. M. Horner, FBBS 19 (Philadelphia: Fortress, 1967).

333 Kondasingu Jesurathnam, "Towards a Dalit Liberative Hermeneutics: Re-reading the Psalms of Lament," *Bangalore Theological Forum* 34, no. 1 (June, 2002): 1-34; K.

of grief, loss, struggles and suffering. In all honesty, his monograph *Dalit Liberative Hermeneutics: Indian Christian Dalit Interpretation of Psalm 22* has inspired writing this present article on Lament Psalms. Jesurathnam has been passionate about appropriating biblical texts with the Dalit experiences and struggles in the Indian churches. In line with his theology of suffering and struggles,[334] The researcher ventures into Psalm 13:1-6 to decipher divinity in laments. Lament Psalms are rarely used as a means to understand God because grief, loss, suffering, and struggles are viewed as something related to one's actions. As Claus Westermann rightly states, "Lament is seen as a negative way of speaking, unfitted for a prayer to God… most people generally regarded suffering as a consequence of sin and a punishment for sin."[335] Due to such concepts of lament, the individual lament psalms are rarely used to comprehend the intervention of divinity in human lives. The highest point of human lives deciphers the best of humans and what humanity can achieve. Likewise, the lowest point in human lives deciphers who we are and who God is, creatively revealing divinity amid grief, loss, suffering and struggles. For instance, as asserted by Jesurathnam, in the struggles for identity, the Dalits have emerged as a strong force in the history of India.[336] In line with this assertion, the researcher, in this article, intends to delve into the Individual Lament Psalms, which can be the mode of deciphering divinity towards humanity. This poses various queries, such as: How do laments help humans understand divinity? What is the context of the grief, loss, suffering and struggles of the Psalmist? What are the linguistic styles used to convey the most profound lament? How can such rhetorical literature decipher divinity amid tormented situations? Why and how does lament shape the imaginative discerning of humans in their relationship with God? How can we bring the significance of the lament Psalms and *Leshe* in the present context of terminal illness and violence of war? These are a few questions to ponder as the research moves further to understand the divine revelation through the individual lament Psalms and ballads. The researcher will employ rhetorical criticism to find answers

---

Jesurathnam, "Midrash Tehillim 22 and Dalit Christian Women's Interpretation of Psalm 22," *Bangalore Theological Forum* 40, no. 2 (December, 2008): 1-17; Kondasingu Jesurathnam, *Dalit Liberative Hermeneutics: Indian Christian Dalit Interpretation of Psalm 22* (Delhi: ISPCK, 2010); Kondasingu Jesurathnam, *Introduction to the Old Testament: Tracing the History, Culture and Scripture of Ancient Israel* (Delhi: CWI, 2018).

334 Jesurathnam, *Dalit Liberative Hermeneutics*, xv; Kondasingu Jesurathnam, *Old Testament Theology: History, Issues, and Perspectives* (Delhi: CWI, 2022).

335 Claus Westermann, *The Living Psalms*, trans. J. R. Porter (Edinburgh: T&T Clark, 1989), 67.

336 Jesurathnam, *Dalit Liberative Hermeneutics*, xv.

to these queries and interpret the individual lament Psalms to understand divinity amid human struggles. This method aims to analyze the literary style and intensity of the voice in Psalm 13:1-6 and *Leshe* towards deciphering divinity. It seeks to connect the lament Psalm and *Leshe* to divine revelation within the context of human suffering and loss. It persuasively expresses the despair, pain, shame, remorse, love and the being of the composer, which the other modes of music or speech may fail to convey. Amid human despair and tormented situations of prolonged absence of God, Lament Psalms and *Leshe* can be a way to decipher divinity at its best. The article emphasizes the significance of these expressions in moments of turmoil, highlighting the concept of interpreting divinity amidst life's darkest moments.

Rhetorical Criticism

To appropriately interpret biblical texts, every critical study needs a methodology to direct the study. Here, the researcher attempts to employ rhetorical criticism to interpret Psalm 13:1-6 towards deciphering divinity. In the discussion of rhetorical criticism, there is no doubt that James Muilenberg became its pioneer when he called for looking into the text's literary features, which was ignored by form criticism.[337] In line with this, George A. Kennedy rightly states that rhetorical criticism fills the gaps between form and literary criticism.[338] Rhetorical criticism, as Muilenberg states, "is to define the limits or scope of the literary unit, to recognize precisely where and how it begins and where and how it ends."[339] Rhetorical criticism focuses on literary style and composition and its impact on the original audience. It begins by identifying the beginning and end of a unit

337 James Muilenberg, "Form Criticism and Beyond," *JBL* 88, no. 1 (March, 1969): 4-9.

338 George A. Kennedy, *New Testament Through Rhetorical Criticism* (Chapel Hill, NC: The University of North Carolina Press, 1984), 3; Rhetorical criticism is, therefore, an essential part of a literary texture seeking to identify the voices (its elements and expressions) and their arrangements in conveying the meaning of the text. Carl R. Holladay, "Contemporary Methods of Reading the Bible," in *The New Interpreter's Bible* vol I eds. Leander E. K et al. (Nashville: Abingdon Press, 1994), 140.

339 Muilenberg, "Form Criticism and Beyond," 4-9; In defining rhetorical criticism, various scholars analyse it as the concept of the author in pursuance to advance the outline of the characters involved in the text; however, working in the cycle of historical interpretation. T. H. Olbricht asserts that the impression of rhetorical criticism began in the 4th-5th Century ACE. However, it flourished during the Renaissance and Reformation period in the latter half of the 18th Century ACE and evolved through the centuries. T. H. Olbricht, "Rhetorical Criticism," in *Dictionary of Biblical Criticism and Interpretation* ed. Stanley E. Porter (New York: Routledge Taylor & Francis Group, 2007), 325-326; see Holladay, "Contemporary Methods of Reading the Bible," 140.

involving the literary device.[340] Thus, it looks into the persuasive text, situations, and world of the text by identifying the intensity of voices in it. Jack R. Lundbom also opines that rhetorical criticism is distinct from literary criticism since it is not concerned with the permanent value of the literary work but rather with its effect on the original audience and readers.[341] Additionally, W. Rudolph Tate asserts that rhetorical criticism focuses on the interaction between the author, the text, and the audience due to the audience's interest in the product, the process, and the effect of the literature.[342] Rhetorical criticism in analysing Psalms looks for features like parallelism,[343] repetition,[344] chiasm,[345] structure[346] and figurative[347] usage of language as these features make Psalms the best poetry there is. As an art

340 David A. deSilva, "Rhetorical Criticism," in *The Oxford Encyclopedia of Biblical Interpretation* vol. I, ed. Steven L. McKenzie (New York: Oxford University Press, 2013), 274-276.

341 According to him, rhetorical criticism goes from diachronic to synchronic stage to observe emotional and empathetical elements (leading the author, audience and readers) to achieve the task of the text. Jack R. Lundbom, "Methodological Issues in the Study of the Old Testament: Rhetorical Criticism," in *Interweaving Methodology and Praxis: Exploring Disciplinary Options in Today's World* ed. Indukuri Mohan Razu (Bangalore: BTESSC/SATHRI, 2007), 146-147.

342 W. Rudolph Tate, *Biblical Interpretation: An Integrated Approach* (New York: Hendrickson Publishers, 2008), 286; Petr Pokorný states that rhetorical criticism is "the overall term for the synchronic analysis of texts" used for interpretation in a broad sense. Petr Pokorný, *Hermeneutics as a Theory of Understanding* (Grand Rapids, Mich: W.B. Eerdmans Pub, 2011), 141.

343 Parallelism, synonymous, antithetical, and synthetic, is the most pertinent poetic feature of Psalms and is also a feature that is easily grasped. J. Clinton McCann, Jr., "The Book of Psalms: Introduction, Commentary, and Reflections," in *The New Interpreter's Bible* vol. iv eds. Leander E. K et al. (Nashville: Abingdon Press, 1996), 652; see Robert Alter, *The Art of Biblical Poetry* (New York: Basic Books, 1985); Adele Berlin, *The Dynamics of Biblical Parallelism* (Bloomington: Indian University Press, 1985).

344 With the inclusio/envelope structure and step/stair-like feature, repetition is yet another important feature found in Psalms in order to draw the attention of the audience. McCann, "The Book of Psalms: Introduction, Commentary, and Reflections," 653.

345 Chiasm is a unique form of repetition that arranges the elements in patterns like ABBA/ ABCBA which may vary at times. McCann, "The Book of Psalms: Introduction, Commentary, and Reflections," 653.

346 Structure is one of the form criticism elements; however, rhetorical criticism is also interested in understanding the unique and distinct way a poem, especially a Psalm, is structured. McCann, "The Book of Psalms: Introduction, Commentary, and Reflections," 654.

347 These figurative usages of language in Hebrew poetry are the most difficult to grasp since the rhythmical qualities, Hebrew syntax, word orders, and word plays are different and distinct from Hebrew poetry, such as Psalms. McCann, "The Book of Psalms: Introduction, Commentary, and Reflections," 654; see J. R. John Samuel Raj, "Cosmic

of effective communication which is concerned with the composition, the language and its style, rhetorical criticism will enable the study to make the emotional elements of the writer, audience and reader of Psalm 13:1-6 visible, thus allowing the researcher to decipher the voice of the lamenter and divinity amid struggles and tormented situations in the text. A rhetorical reading of this text will enable the reader to observe the situation, condition of the lamenter, the techniques of words used and the effectiveness of lament in accomplishing the task. By exploring the rhetorical situation of Psalm 13:1-6, its interaction with the product and the process of the literature, this method will elevate the interpretation of divinity in times of human laments. While exploring the texts, the rhetorical method will ultimately allow the researcher to relate to the linguistic styles of the Sümi-Naga lament ballad (*Leshe*) and identify the voice of the lamenter and the audience to understand the context of the ballad. Before studying in depth and deciphering the divine revelation in the select text, the study will briefly attempt to understand the lament Psalms in the following discussion.

Lament Psalms

The book of Psalms, as beautiful as it is in its content of songs of praise, is also a book of complaints, laments, and confession. Jesurathnam states that "it defines, inspires, and safeguards worship," and this worship is achieved by lamenting the struggles and looking to Yahweh for deliverance.[348] Almost one-third of the book of Psalms comprises Lament Psalms[349] or in other words, "complaints/prayer for help/petition" either individual or communal. Most Psalms were written for cult purposes in the post-exilic period and are considered to be authored by David because of this literary tradition he was known. The classified psalms are listed according to their literary type with two major forms, lament and hymn (these two forms are either communal or individual).[350]Among these forms, individual lament Psalms are considered one of the most common and most beautiful Psalter[351]arising

---

Judge or Overseer of the World Order? The Role of Yahweh as Portrayed in Psalm 7," *Bangalore Theological Forum* 34, no. 2 (December, 2002): 4.

348 K. Jesurathnam, *Introduction to the Old Testament: A Dalit Liberative Hermeneutical Perspective* (Delhi: CWI, 2023), 371.

349 The individual Psalms of lament include Psalms 3, 5, 6, 7, 13, 17, 22, 25, 26, 27: 7-14, 28, 31, 35, 38, 39, 41, 42, 43, 51, 52, 54, 55, 56, 57, 59, 61, 63, 64, 69, 70, 71, 86, 88, 102, 109, 120, 130, 140, 141, 142, and 143. Page H. Kelley, "Prayers of Troubled Saints," *Review & Expositor*, 81, no. 3 (August, 1984): 377; Jesurathnam, *Introduction to the Old Testament*, 261.

350 Konrad Schaefer, "Psalms," *The Jerome Biblical Commentary for the Twenty-First Century* eds. John J. Collins et al. (London: Bloomsbury, 2022), 665.

351 Westermann, *The Living Psalms*, 65.

as the technique of mastering specific contexts in the writer's life (grief, loss, mockery, warfare, diseases, etc) or the entire community.

Lament Psalms begin with an introductory/invocation cry to Yahweh accompanied by divine exaltation. It defines the crisis in which the Psalmist brings the petition/supplication while presenting the needs and remedies for the situation. Additionally, the lament Psalms also conveys the confidence of the Psalmist in Yahweh, who reveals and is involved in the hopeless situation of humans.[352] Jesurathnam affirms it by stating "in the lament psalms God is conceived by the lamenter both as problem and solution."[353] Individual lament Psalms come in as a desperate query to Yahweh as complaints amid suffering which later ends in confidence in Yahweh for deliverance. Looking into these technicalities of the Psalms of laments, it is evident that laments consist of praising Yahweh while bringing petitions and that space was given to the lamenters in the religious circle. C. Hassell Bullock affirms that "the Hebrew faith drew the circle wide enough to accommodate human complaint"[354] thus, validating the need for laments. Lament became a part of the Hebrew faith, social lives as well as in their personal life. This is so because, as Jesurathnam states, there is no doubt lament Psalms reflect most of the themes concerning the divine-human relationship.[355] Psalms of laments are the most profound expression of the extreme situations undergone in the life of the Psalmist (both communal and individual). Laments are at the core of human feelings, and at such a time as this, humans reach the innermost part of their hearts and minds. Lament enables them to question the existence, creation, beginning or cessation of all good and bad times it goes to the extent of questioning the existence and revelation of divinity. Raising laments over grief, loss, death, mockery or diseases seemingly move towards deciphering divinity by understanding the purpose of the human-divine relationship.

352 Leland Ryken, et al. eds., *Dictionary of Biblical Imagery* (Leicester: Inter Varsity Press, 1998), 484-485.

353 Jesurathnam, *Dalit Liberative Hermeneutics*, 17.

354 C. Hassell Bullock, *Encountering the Book of Psalms: A Literary and Theological Introduction* (Grand Rapids, Michigan: Baker Academic, 2001), 149.

355 Jesurathnam, "Towards a Dalit Liberative Hermeneutics: Re-reading the Psalms of Lament," 12.

Characteristics of Individual Psalm of Lament

The characteristic elements of the individual Psalm of lament consist of: i) introductory address;[356] ii) presentation of the lament;[357] iii) prayer for help;[358] iv) confession of trust in Yahweh;[359] and v) promise to praise Yahweh.[360] These characteristic elements of the individual lament of Psalm ensures and reaffirms the relationship between the Psalmist and Yahweh.[361]However, it should be noted that not all of these elements appear in all the individual lament Psalms. Also, the order of the elements varies. Additionally, some Psalms of laments are longer while others are short. All of these differences contribute to the distinctiveness of each lament Psalm which the rhetorical criticism enables to decipher.[362] With all these characteristic elements, it is obvious that the lament Psalm has three main characters: Yahweh, the lamenter, and the enemy. Claus Westermann affirms that the lament Psalm is complete with these three subjects because the relationship among them reveals the nature of the particular lament.[363] Keeping this in mind, this article further explores the setting and structure of the lament Psalms, especially Psalm 13:1-6 to enable the study to uncover the need for lament situations to reveal the divinity.

---

356 The introductory address establishes the context of dialogue in expectation of Yahweh's response.

357 The lament is an expression of anguish, grief, and pain, as a betrayal by Yahweh or by the friend addressed as the enemy or the actual foe/adversaries. The presentation is mainly about the troubled situation of sickness, loneliness, abandonment, danger, humiliation, and death.

358 This prayer for help depends on the nature of the complaints presented. According to Erhard Gerstenberger, prayer with imprecation is an important element in the laments because it aims to change suffering into divine intervention. Erhard Gerstenberger, *Psalms Part I: With an Introduction to Cultic Poetry* eds. Rolf Knierim and Gene M. Tucker (Grand Rapids, Michigan: Eerdmans, 1988), 9-14.

359 After this, the lamenter confesses trust in Yahweh's actions and reputation in a helpless and hopeless situation with a cry of desperation. However, the Psalmist is aware that the answer is in the hands of Yahweh and thus, is confident that Yahweh has heard the laments and will deliver him from the situation.

360 Peter C. Craigie, *Word Biblical Commentary: Psalm 1-50* vol. 19 eds. David A. Hubbard et al. (Texas: Word Books Publisher, 1983), 141.

361 Walter Brueggemann, *The Psalms and Life of Faith*, ed. Patrick D. Miller (Minneapolis: Fortress, 1995), 70.

362 McCann, "The Book of Psalms: Introduction, Commentary, and Reflections," 645.

363 Claus Westermann, *Praise and Lament in the Psalms*, trans. Keith R. Crim and Richard Soulen (Atlanta: John Knox Press, 1981), 169.

Setting and Structure of Psalms13:1-6[364]

Psalm 13:1-6 is one of the Psalms of lament that presents an individual's complaints about the physical and psychological torment connected with the presentation of petition then with confidence in Yahweh.[365] Thus, this individual lament Psalm is set in the context of fear of death due to illness. It is difficult to affirm the date of this particular Psalm; however, it is assumed to be old, i.e., in the early period of the Hebrew monarchy. This lament goes in line with the Babylonian laments, which havea long history in Israel's worship[366] where laments were used in festival or cultic contexts. In all this, as Jesurathnam rightly asserted, it is obvious that the intended setting of most lament Psalms is getting Yahweh involved in the struggles of the Psalmist.[367] Psalm 13:1-6is an individual Psalm of lament where the Psalmist comes to Yahweh to complain about the situation and ends with confidence in the deliverance.The basic sections of Psalm 13: 1-6 are structured as: i) laments (vv. 2-3); ii) prayer/petition (vv. 4-5); iii) confidence (v. 6).[368] Clinton McCann opines that the complaint appears in vv. 1-2, petition in vv. 3-4 and confidence of deliverance in vv. 5-6.[369] Bullock takes a different direction to structure Psalm 13:1-6, according to him:i) the problem lies in vv.1-2, which is the spiritual anguish; ii) the complaint against God in v. 1, "How long, o Lord?"; iii) the complaint against enemies in vv. 2b, 4; iv) trust in vv. 5-6; and v) petition in vv. 1-4.[370] The lament of the Psalmist begins with more or less the fear of possible near death due to sickness and ends with a twist of hope and confidence in deliverance. The researcher attempts to go on a different structure of the text, taking a standpoint from the rhetorical steps of reading a text, as will be discussed in the following.

364 The English versions of Psalms and the Hebrew Bible differ in their numbering, and thus, the researcher uses the *Biblia Hebraica Stuttgartensia* for exegetical purposes.

365 Schaefer, "Psalms," 666.

366 Craigie, *Word Biblical Commentary*, 141.

367 Jesurathnam, "Towards a Dalit Liberative Hermeneutics: Re-reading the Psalms of Lament," 10.

368 Craigie, *Word Biblical Commentary: Psalm 1-50*, 141.

369 McCann, "The Book of Psalms: Introduction, Commentary, and Reflections," 726.

370 Bullock, *Encountering the Book of Psalms*, 484-485.

Bullock, *Encountering the Book of Psalms*, 149.

Craigie, *Word Biblical Commentary*, 141.

Bullock, *Encountering the Book of Psalms*, 141.

Deciphering Divinity through Rhetorical Techniques in Psalm 13:1-6

With the characteristics and structure understood, the study moves further to exegetically interpret Psalm 13:1-6[371] by employing and incorporating the rhetorical method. This section gears up to understand the voices of the writer, audience, and readers and to grasp the depth of the revelation of divinity amid laments. This rhetorical interpretation of deciphering the divinity in Psalm 13:1-6[372] is interested in what the text is as well as what the text does to achieve the peak of the human-divine relationship. It will delve into interpreting what the texts say and how it is communicated with the power of language used in the text. Such exegetical interpretation is necessary to decipher the divinity in the individual Psalm of lament. This section will succinctly be divided into three sub-sections: i) rhetorical situation (vv. 1-2); ii) rhetorical petition(vv. 3-4); iii) rhetorical effectiveness (vv. 5-6).

Rhetorical Situation (vv. 1-3)

A rhetorical situation is a specific condition or situation of rhetorical criticism which describes the verbal reality (not the historical reality)[373] by looking into the lamenter's verbal complaints to Yahweh. We will look into the actual condition and setting that brought the Psalmist to question Yahweh and what the Psalmist did to overcome his situation. To achieve this, the rhetorical usage of language and its styles in the text will artistically paint the picture of the Psalmist's situation.

עַד־אָנָה "until when/how long" in vv., 1-2 has been repeated, and the tone of it intensified every time it is uttered. In the first utterance of עַד־אָנָה the intention of the question is about Yahweh forgetting the Psalmist and turning away in wrath. This anger of Yahweh seems to be the reason for the anxious questions.[374] The level of frustration and urgency rooted in the

371 Psalm 13:1-6: *To the leader. A Psalm of David.* [1] How long, O Lord? Will you forget me forever? How long will you hide your face from me? [2] How long must I bear pain in my soul, and have sorrow in my heart all day long? How long shall my enemy be exalted over me? [3] Consider and answer me, O Lord my God! Give light to my eyes, or I will sleep the sleep of death, [4] and my enemy will say, "I have prevailed"; my foes will rejoice because I am shaken. [5] But I trusted in your steadfast love; my heart shall rejoice in your salvation. [6] I will sing to the Lord, because he has dealt bountifully with me. *New Revised Standard Version* (Grand Rapids, Michigan: Zondervan, 1989), 429-430.

372 The study, with its limitation of words and pages, will not focus on the Hebrew texts and translation; however, technical terms that highlight the interaction between the author, text, and reader will be used often to translate and interpret.

373 Lundbom, "Methodological Issues in the Study of the Old Testament: Rhetorical Criticism," 189.

374 McCann, "The Book of Psalms: Introduction, Commentary, and Reflections," 726.

Psalmist's lament is heard in the repetition of עַד־אָנָה which torments the soul of the lamenter. עַד־אָנָה[375] is repeated four times in the entire unit (two times each in v. 2 and v. 3), emphasizing the continuous experiences of suffering in the life of the lamenter. These repetitive questions are natural and a very human display of the reality of torments and the existence of anxiety in the heart of the Psalmist.[376] This portrays that the Psalmist was desperate for Yahweh to look towards him and help him out of his desperation. His situation may have been worsening, which is why the Psalmist is running out of patience forcing him to repeatedly ask "how long" his situation is going to go on, "how long" Yahweh is going to be silent and also "how long" he must continue suffering.

The verbs חכשׁ "to forget/wiped memory" and רתס "hide/keep secret," in v. 2, are deemed not suitable to utter to Yahweh because these verbs are usually used in terms of humans forgetting or turning away from Yahweh and not Yahweh from humans. However, the lamenter still addresses the question to Yahweh.[377] This passage does not reveal what torments the Psalmist, but the lamenters' torment can be heard through the linguistic style and power of language. The increasing echoes of the repetition of questions make it evident that the Psalmist's struggles have been long enough and unbearable.

The turmoil in the mind and heart of the Psalmist, in v. 3, is presented in the usage of the terms עֵצֹות "revolt/resist/counsel/pain"[378] and יָגֹון "torment/trouble/sorrow" which are usually used for the death of individuals.[379] The textual studies in *Biblia Hebraica Stuttgartensia*,[380] the wordעֵצֹות has been proposed as עַצֶּבֶת "nervousness" or עַצָּבוֹת "sadness."[381] Such linguistic style and the power of language used by the Psalmist show the intensity of the situation the lamenter is in, that is, grave illness affecting him physically and psychologically. The usage of the words in v. 3, נֶפֶשׁ "soul/life/breath" and לֵבָב "heart/mind/will," also indicates that this troubled/tormented situation has affected the entire being (body/soul) of the Psalmist, but Yahweh

375 Craigie, *Word Biblical Commentary*, 141.

376 Westermann, *The Living Psalms*, 71.

377 Westermann, *The Living Psalms*, 71.

378 It literally means "counsels." However, assuming that the text says, "Put counsels in my soul," would make less sense than "Put pain in my soul," which is the simplest and most satisfactory translation תוֹצֵע תישָׁא. Craigie, *Word Biblical Commentary*, 140; *New Revision Standard Version* (NRSV) translates, "Bear pain my soul."

379 McCann, "The Book of Psalms: Introduction, Commentary, and Reflections," 726.

380 *Biblia Hebraica Stuttgartensia* hereafter will be referred as BHS.

381 K. Elliger and W. Rudolph, *Biblia Hebraica Stuttgartensia* (Stuttgart: Deutsche Bibelgesellschaft, 1990), 1095.

continues to hide away or has forgotten to address the complaints.[382] In this rhetoric text, the Psalmist is seen to be torn between Yahweh (to whom the lament is addressed) and אֹיְבִי "enemy" (who is exalted at that moment). אֹיְבִי[383] has not been specified in this text as to whether it is the personal enemy, the sickness, Yahweh or death. However, it is evident through the preceding and succeeding words that the Psalmist was also tormented deeply because the enemy was exalted/raised above/lifted. Thus, the Psalmist burst into anxiety, loneliness, and feelings of isolation by Yahweh in the face of the enemy without any fault of his. This keeps on and on as the word יוֹמָם" daytime/by day" suggests. It has been translatedinSeptuagint[384] as well as other translations with the addition of the phrase κάί νυκτός "and nights"[385] which translates it as "by day and night" carrying the meaning of struggles that linger each passing moment, both during day and night. Thus, the rhetorical situation of the Psalmist is observed as the unimaginable broken condition of both body, mind and soul, which has been lingering for a long time and is likely to go on forever. Thus, through the usage of the power of language by the lamenter, his tormented situation is sharply portrayed.

Rhetoric petition (vv. 4)

Rhetoric prayer or petition of laments is a method of imploring rather than requesting or pleading for help; in other words, this petition is a transitive one[386] enabling the reader or the audience to prepare for deciphering divinity through structured verbs and phrases.

The word הַבִּיטָה "look/consider/see" in v. 4 is in their imperative form, which indicates that the rhetoric petition of lament here necessarily does not intend to be a request nor a plea but imploring Yahweh from the depth of the tormented situation. The usage of the term הַבִּיטָה shows that the Psalmist wants Yahweh to look into the condition of struggles and consider answering the questions of עַד־אָנָה so that the laments do not go in vain or become pointless.[387] In v. 4, the verb עֲנֵנִי" answer me" is also imperative, which the different versions and translations, such as LXX, Syriac, Targum, Vulgate, and other 6th-century manuscripts of the Psalter puts עֲנֵנִי before the following connecting phrase.[388] The rhetorical petition here is for the restoration of

382 Westermann, *The Living Psalms*, 72.

383 Craigie, *Word Biblical Commentary: Psalm 1-50*, 142.

384 Septuagint hereafter will be referred to as LXX.

385 Rudolph, *Biblia Hebraica Stuttgartensia*, 1095.

386 Westermann, *The Living Psalms*, 73.

387 Craigie, *Word Biblical Commentary: Psalm 1-50*, 142.

388 Rudolph, *Biblia Hebraica Stuttgartensia*, 1095.

health as well as the deliverance from the troubled condition.[389] In this view, Westermann asserts that this petition does not involve deliverance but looks beyond it, i.e., the consequences of divine deliverance.[390] This is evident, as the Psalmist wants Yahweh to look towards him and intervene in the suffering because it would הָאִירָה עֵינַי "brighten my appearance/bring light to my eyes" as Yahweh's face is described as the source of light. At a deeper level, this petition is the urge to become closer to Yahweh once again, thus lamenting to Yahweh for the divine revelation of the face that brings light.[391] This lament is a petition for deciphering divinity amid suffering, grief, pain, and troubles, as well as the consequences of divine revelation, i.e., the brightening up of gloomy and tormented situations. Such imperative petitions become a necessity in tormented situations because they portray the lamenter's deepest feelings and the urgency of divinity.

V. 4 concludes with the phrase פֶּן־אִישַׁן הַמָּוֶת "lest I sleep in death," which is also a rhetorical petition to Yahweh. This phrase intends to paint a picture of the struggles and pain that the Psalmist undergoes on the path to death. Westermann asserts that these lines resonate with the screams of unending death through the languages used.[392] In that with death's scream, his enemy prevails over him, or the enemy could be death itself. According to Craige, the term הַמָּוֶת "the death" is the אֹיְבִי that the Psalmist talks about in v. 2.[393] The idea of death exalting or rising over the Psalmist made him feel the absence of Yahweh and, thus, lamented עַד־אָנָה because the lamenter felt Yahweh would forever hide the face. It is in such a tormented situation of proximity of death that rhetoric petition indicates the urgent need for divine revelation. The rhetoric terms הַבִּיטָה, עֲנֵנִי and הָאִירָהportray that is imploring Yahweh in grave situations can also be another way to establish closeness with divinity, thus, one step closer to deciphering divinity in the tormented situation.

Rhetorical Effectiveness (vv. 5-6)

The rhetorical effectiveness of lament reviews the entire text unit and attempts to understand the impact of the language. It is an articulative way of accomplishing specific tasks of the text. It tends to bring out the findings of the queries made.[394]

389 Craigie, *Word Biblical Commentary: Psalm 1-50*, 142.

390 Westermann, *The Living Psalms*, 73.

391 Craigie, *Word Biblical Commentary: Psalm 1-50*, 142.

392 Westermann, *The Living Psalms*, 73.

393 Craigie, *Word Biblical Commentary: Psalm 1-50*, 142.

394 Lundbom, "Methodological Issues in the Study of the Old Testament: Rhetorical Criticism," 190.

יְכָלְתִּיו "I have conquered him"is the word in v. 5 that is used to portray the victory of the enemy over the Psalmist. In LXX, it is observed that ἴσχυσά πρὸς ἀὐτόν "powers over him" is equal with the Hebrew לוֹיְכָלְתִּי "conquered him."[395] It should be noted that v. 5 mentions the enemy twice with different forms, once in singular אֹיְבִי and the other in plural צָרַי "adversaries/oppressors" indicating human enemies and not death as the enemy. This usage of both singular and plural form of enemy portrays that the Psalmist prays for deliverance from literal death as enemy as well as from human enemy, who overpowered him.[396] Now, the lamenter urges Yahweh to deliver him from the proximity of death and the conquering adversaries who mock him in his tormented situations.

The sudden shift in v.6 with the verb בָטַחְתִּי "I trust/I am confident" portrays the ongoing trust in Yahweh despite the complaints and petitions. Amid complaints of sorrow and petitions for deliverance, the Psalmist shifts to an articulative mode of finding the answers to his laments. This is portrayed clearly in the transition from complaints to expression of his confidence, trust and hope in Yahweh. This rhetoric transition is sharply focused by the repetition of reference to the heart of the lamenter in v.3, which was filled with יָגוֹן but now in v.6, the heart of the lamenter will יָגֵל "rejoice."[397] The actual rejoicing and confidence in Yahweh is heard when the lamenter says אָשִׁירָה "I will sing" despite the tormented situation he is in.The phrase אָשִׁירָה לַיהוָה כִּי גָמַל עָלָי"I will sing to Yahweh because he dealt upon me" supports the fact that the lamenter is now confident in accomplishing the task of deliverance and divinity. Here, the LXX adds κάί ψάλῶ τῷ ὀνόμάτι τοῦ ὑψίστου "I sing to the name of the most high" which is similar to וַאֲזַמְּרָה שֵׁם־יְהוָה עֶלְיוֹן "and I will make music to the name of Yahweh, the most high" from Psalm 7:18b.[398] In v.6, the Psalmist indicates that Yahweh stops hiding the face and reveals the divine character of חֶסֶד "faithfulness/steadfast love" to him. To this, Craigie asserts that the song of praise will burst once deliverance is accomplished and that the lamenter is calm with a sense of confidence knowing that Yahweh will deliver him[399] and divinity is deciphered amid the tormented situation. Such rhetorical effectiveness of transition in the lament displays accomplishing the task of deciphering the revelation of Yahweh in the life of the lamenter.

McCann suggests the readers ask: What is our problem, and who or what is our enemy? Rather than asking, what is the problem of the

395 Rudolph, *Biblia Hebraica Stuttgartensia*, 1095.

396 Craigie, *Word Biblical Commentary*, 143.

397 McCann, "The Book of Psalms: Introduction, Commentary, and Reflections," 727.

398 Rudolph, *Biblia Hebraica Stuttgartensia*, 1095.

399 Craigie, *Word Biblical Commentary*, 143.

Psalmist? Or who was the enemy? These must be the questions to openly understand the theology and history of an individual lament. Through this, the Psalms of lament can be interpreted, and implications can be drawn for understanding human suffering and revelation of God amid suffering.[400] With the careful reading of the rhetorics of Psalm 13:1-6, it is observed that divinity is deciphered and revealed at the deepest of the heart and soul of the laments of suffering humans. Complaints and laments situation allow humans to understand the depth of who one is and what one is incapable of. The rhetorical reading of Psalm 13:1-6 also enables readers to understand that the Psalmist implores Yahweh and questions the absence or hidden moments but that there is nothing aberrant about imploring Yahweh. Rather, it brings him closer to deciphering divinity amid his tormented situation. It is also made clear that in the depths of the moments humans' struggle, the character of God's faithfulness is revealed amid grief, struggles, loss and hopelessness. Thus, ultimate transition helps in deciphering divinity during the lowest point of humans, physically, psychologically and spiritually.

Sümi-Naga *Leshe*: A Lament Ballad

The study now turns to the lament ballad of the Sümi-Nagas known as *Leshe*. By such a shift towards a tribal ballad of lament, the researcher intends to portray that the individual lament Psalms is not just of the biblical literature, but it is the lived experiences of every human in all ages and societies. Being a distinct ballad, *Leshe*[401]needs attention as we study the laments in Psalms to decipher divinity.

Leshe is a Sümi-Naga term used for "poetry/ballad" which has its distinct tune[402] as well as its distinct linguistic style. *Leshe* literally means "chanted/recited song" where *Le* is short for *Ale* "song" and *She* has no English equivalent translation however, "recite/chant" (reciting lines with tunes) can be the closest one, thus forming the term, *Leshe*.[403] The ancient

400 McCann, "The Book of Psalms: Introduction, Commentary, and Reflections," 647.

401 The book of Psalms in Sümi-Naga translation of the Bible is called *Leshele* "songs of ballad," thus, the relation between the two laments can be related.

402 The tune is different from folk songs/*Lejole*. It should be noted that *Leshe* is a part of the bigger umbrella of *Lejole* "folk songs."

403 Like any other Naga tribes, the Sümi-Naga tribe has numerous folk songs. Approximately there is more than thousands of *Lejole Küküngü* (folk tunes). Some of the classified prominent folksongs are *Alu Kümlale* (working song); *Luwule* (jungle clearing for jhum); *Lusale* (clearing after burning of the field); *Aphushele* (plough song); *Athighale* (sludge squashing song); *Shotüghü le* (fore season song); *Akiphi Küsüle* (pounding wood dragging song); *Ghixüle* (sowing song); *Mozale* (weeds uprooting song-late May or early June); *Tixile* (uprooting weeds-August); *Ghilele* (harvesting song); *A-uh shekiisüle* (rice husk pounding song); *Asho kukubole* (indigenous rice flour pounding song); *Aghüle kuku* (war song); *Leshele* (chanting poems); *Lejole* (general folk song); *Anu kümüzü le* (lullaby) etc.

Sümi-Nagas used *Leshe* in order not to convey the direct message also the messages were not conveyed through dialogue but with the usage of tunes with words that had deep-rooted meanings.[404] which only a few could understand. This section will briefly examine the lament ballad *Leshe* of the Sümi-Naga tribe.

Characteristics of *Leshe*

According to Vikato Awomi, *Leshe* composers are often overthinkers who are passionate about music and tunes, as well as those who have suffered grief, pain, and despair. Thus, *Leshe* was initially and commonly meant to be a lament. For instance, raising lament over the departed spouse (by death or other means), by the barren mothers, by suitors in praise of their unfulfilled love.[405]*Leshe* originated out of sadness, grave happenings like sudden unnatural death, beheaded by enemies, loss of loved ones and unfulfilled love. *Leshe* is rhetorical in nature; thus, the listeners have to closely listen to the usage of vocabulary, phrases and tunes of the poetry. *Leshe* is not said nor sung, but it is recited with its distinct tunes filled with sentimental emotions. Thus, the tone differs from the speech tone and song tune. The words used in conversation or dialogue are not the same when chanted or recited as *Leshe*.[406] The tone of the words also changes (higher to lower and lower to higher) when used in *Leshe*. Not just tones but the vocabularies used in *Leshe* are formal and deeply rooted vocabularies[407] which is not commonly used.

K. Ghulakha Pukho Swu (Rtd. Public Prosecutor, Justice & Law Department), interview by the researcher, Dimapur, October 10, 2010.

404 Vikato Awomi (Rtd. Trainer of Teachers, Department of School Education), interview by the researcher, Kohima, July 13, 2023.

405 Awomi, interview: To compose *Leshe*, the composer would first bring out the appropriate words and then fit them in the tunes. These tunes were orally transmitted from composers to singers, parents to children, and generation to generation. Oral literature is unique and has different characteristics: romantic in character, patriotic in nature, factious in essence with a fundamental nature, and spiritual in principle.

406 For instance, the tone of the noun *Aghüpumi* "warrior" when used in conversation stresses the middle syllable with a higher note/tune; however, when used in *Leshe*, the stress on the middle syllables will have a lower note. G. Ghoshili P. Swu (Former Women Secretary, Sümi Aphuyemi Baptist Akukuhou Küqhakulu/SABAK), interview by the researcher, Dimapur, July 14, 2023.

407 For instance, the casual/informal usage *ilomi* "lover/darling/spouse" in *Leshe* uses the deeper vocabulary *ixeu*.

Structure of *Leshe*

The structure of one *Leshe* differs from another.[408] *Leshe* does not have its distinct lines and stanzas but has its unique linguistic style and tunes. As a part of the bigger umbrella of *Lejole*, sometimes a few *Leshe* are used both as poetry as well as folksong.[409] In such cases, it is enveloped with a pause/ caesura term *He/Ho* and *Ishe/Wolo*. Every line begins with a prelude and ends with a postlude. However, the words in the lines do not complete the sentence to show that it continues in the following line. For instance, the study will consider the first four lines of the famous Lazami[410] Sümi-Naga *Leshe/Lejole* of lovers entitled*Ixeu Nikujo Le*[411] "song of my spouse and me" which originally consists of 26 lines:

Ho – ixeu nikujo ishe aki – ho
Ho – akithi lo kukho natha ina akü – ho
Ho – aküxü lau jo ishe kukho – ho
Ho – kukho moni ili ishe kügha – ho

These linguistic and structural styles are unknown to other Naga tribes and are even distinct from another Sümi-Naga *Leshe*. These lines are connected to one another, where the succeeding line carries forward the meaning of the preceding line. There is no specific structure that the *Leshe* follows, no such rules for lines, verses or stanzas nor does it have its set of musical notations, however, it has its distinct tune which the listeners can differentiate *Leshe* from *Lejole*.[412] Having no structure, no rules of lines, verses or stanzas may have been the result of neglecting[413] the ancient literature of Sümi-Nagas. The structure of one *Leshe* differs from another; for instance, the popular Sümi-Naga *Leshe* called *Inakha ngo Ghonili Pama Küyixa,* "Separation of

---

408 Some consists of 8 lines, some of 16 lines and others of 20 lines but most *Leshe* has more than 20 lines.

409 Kiqheho Phucho (GB, Lazami Village), interview by the researcher, Lazami, July 12, 2023.

410 Lazami village, under the Pughoboto Sub-division, is the biggest and oldest Sümi-Naga village in Zunheboto district in Nagaland.

411 This *Leshe* is a lament ballad composed of a lover who part ways with the spouse. It is commonly recited in festivals in the village of Lazami. The translation of *Leshe* is roughly as:

Ho – today my lover and me, in death – ho
Ho – in death we depart, in life – ho
Ho – in life today we part – ho
Ho – we part not, alas! we promised – ho.

412 Awomi, interview.

413 The ancient traditions, culture and values of Sümi-Naga, or any Naga tribe for that matter, have been neglected for many years with the arrival of modernization and Christianity, which viewed them as not modern, uncivilised and non-Christian ways of life.

Inakha and Ghonili."[414] It has 4 stanzas with irregular 27 lines, 1st stanza has 8 lines, 2nd and 3rd stanzas have 7 lines each and the 4th stanza has 5 lines.

Thus, looking into the characteristics and structure of *Leshe*, it is understood that it is a lament, a ballad over the loss of loved ones or grieving over the unfulfilled love and a failed marriage. *Leshe* is a rich literature of expressing one's innermost thoughts and emotions. It persuasively expresses the despair, pain, shame, remorse, love and the being of the composer, which the other modes of music or speech may fail to convey. *Leshe* is the best expression of communicating lament by using words and tunes that avoid direct speech and avoid conveying the message in precision. This way, the composer uses the power of language to convey the feelings, meanings, and emotions that the intended listener/receiver fails to catch if the details in the lines are not listened to and interpreted appropriately. However, the composer intends to express his/her own feelings with figures of speech or distinct linguistic styles. This distinct mode of expression and communication becomes an essential part of life because, as humans live, life unfolds pain, shame, despair and grief in one way or another. In such tormented situations, *Leshe* becomes the best of human expression, which carries the different layers of emotional elements within its lines and tunes through its persuasive powers of language.

Leshe and Lament Psalms towards Deciphering Divinity

The ancestors of the Sümi-Nagas used rhetorical ways of communicating messages to one another to indirectly convey their thoughts, feelings and emotions. As discussed in the above section, *Leshe* is one way of communicating and delivering the message in tormented situations as laments. H. S. Rotokha, in his preface of the book *Apuh-Assü Leshe*,[415] asserts that such a rich and distinct way of communication has been forgotten and lost ever since the arrival of Christianity (20th Century). However, with the emergence of the importance of traditions and cultures, *Leshe* is now being retrieved as it is the root of the distinct identity of Sümi-Naga literature.[416] Contemporary society, while preserving *Leshe*, encourages young people to learn it (memorizing preferred) and recite/chant at gatherings/celebrations of festivals by organising competitions. These rhetorical lines of *Leshe*, with Christianity as a new way of life, are rich in vocabulary with deep-rooted meanings that give significance to understanding personal, religious,

414 This *Leshe* is a lament raised over her husband (Inakha) by Ghonili, who narrates about their initial happy married life, which was ruined by the extramarital affair of her Husband with Chevili. S. V. Sheyepu, "Inakha Ngoh Ghonili Küyixa," *Apuh-Assü Leshe*ed. H. S. Rotokha (Zunheboto: Sümi Literature Board, 2019), 1-2.

415 H. S. Rotokha ed., *Apuh-Assü Leshe*, (Zunheboto: Sümi Literature Board, 2019).

416 Rotokha ed., "Shotügiu," *Apuh-Assü Leshe*, iii-iv.

festive, and social issues. Thus, it should be noted that, in the 21st century, with Christianity already rooted in the lives of the Sümi-Nagas, *Leshe* and its expressions have undergone transition and have been developed as a rhetoric way of communication not just about/among humans but also with the divinity. For instance, *Leshe* is raised as gratitude or petitioning God for the sowing and harvest during the festivals and can be related to the lament of Psalms. Thus, in this research on the individual lament of Psalms to decipher divinity, focusing on *Leshe* on Sümi-Naga is vital as it also deals with deciphering divine comfort in composition and recitation.

In both the Psalmist and ancient Sümi-Nagas tradition, laments were powerfully used to decipher divinity by persuasively expressing one's innermost thoughts and feelings. A few observations have been briefed out in the following on the individual lament Psalm and *Leshe* (lament ballad):i) Like the lament Psalms, *Leshe*is rich in its rhetorical techniques and language usages to convey one's sentimental emotions; ii) Parallelism, repetition and artistic usage of language in lament Psalm portray the emotions and feelings of the lamenter about divinity, humanity and society. On the other hand, the deep-rooted vocabulary and the distinct tone of *Leshe* characterize the tormented experiences of the composer, which, after the arrival of Christianity, now represents personal, religious and social issues as well; iii) the Psalmist uses powerful words of complaints for his pain and despair. However, the composers of *Leshe* seldom make use of strong words to avoid using solid and direct terms *Leshe* is composed to express laments beautifully; iv) Psalm 13:1-6 poses rhetoric questions to Yahweh with no intention to be answered; however, the poetic and rhetorical expressions of *Leshe* are statements and facts about the personal feelings and experiences. Lament Psalm and *Leshe,* as a form of specialized literature, are expressions of feelings and emotions briefly and yet precisely in ways that stories, prose, or hymns/songs cannot. Humans best convey and express their emotions, feelings, or desires through laments, so it also becomes a writing/reciting activity close to humans' hearts and minds. Considering this, the following discussions briefly draw on the study's significance in physical and socially tormented situations.

Significance of Psalm 13:1-6 and *Leshe*

In the context of physically tormented situations, the study draws significance to the person suffering from a terminal illness.[417] In this context, keeping

417 Terminal illness is a condition that cannot be cured and will eventually lead to death (as certified by doctors or health professionals) within a few years. It is also known as chronic illness, actively dying illness, palliative care, end-stage disease, untreatable illness, intractable disease, etc. These terms are commonly used for progressive diseases like cancer, dementia, including Alzheimer's, advanced lung/liver/kidney/heart disease,

the rhetorical setting of the text, the lament Psalms and *Leshe* become significant in deciphering divinity. In such tormenting situations of battling with terminal illness, the one struggling to find answers and continue to question, "How long is God going to hide the face of divine healing or has God forgotten me/us?" is the patient as well as the family members with the continuous fear of the proximity of death overpowering them. In this physically tormented situation, the rhetorical reading of Psalm 13:1-6, and *Leshe* become significant, enabling the lamenter to find comfort and faithful character of divinity. These rhetorical ballads help the lamenter understand that this physically tormented situation is a lived experience from ancient times to the present and will continue in days/years to come. It helps them comprehend the questions in their mind, the pain in their body and soul, and doubts in their faith. Besides understanding and comprehension, the lamenter realizes that there is nothing aberrant about the terminal illness, nothing negative about lamenting or complaining to God about the illness. Additionally, the physically tormented situations are not the consequence of sin/curse but the mode of creatively deciphering divinity amid their lowest point of life. The rhetorical understanding of Psalm 13:1-6and *Leshe* also helps lamenters to express the deepest and strongest feelings of physical pain persuasively and struggles to torment them. With such understanding and comprehension, the lamenter's faith is elevated, and this physically tormented situation becomes their most potent force in maintaining the human-divine relationship. The lamenters do not only learn to express persuasively but also are enabled to look beyond the divine healing, thus enabling the terminally ill person to decipher divinity amid lament.

In the context of socially tormented situations, the study attempts to draw its significance in the present context of India, the ongoing Manipur's[418] violence[419] calls for deciphering divinity amid the tormented situation of war.[420] The people of Manipur have lost their homes, families, and friends

---

neurological diseases like Parkinson's/Huntington's/motor neuron disease (MND), muscular dystrophy, HIV/AIDS, and other degenerative or deteriorating conditions like old age.

418 Manipur is one of the eight sister states of North-East India.

419 The researcher does not intend to name the group of people or side with any in this context of violence but would instead refer to both as lamenters since everyone is struggling and suffering in this tormented situation. The researcher is not an expert on this issue of violence. Rather, this significance is an attempt to decipher divinity amid war and violence, which has been happening with no sign of ending anytime soon. This significance is a way of comforting the people of Manipur that this tormented situation is a mode of deciphering divinity at the most tormented moments of life.

420 Manipur experienced significant ethnic violence in the first week of May 2023, following the 'Tribal Solidarity March' organized by the All Tribal Students' Union Manipur

in the face of this tormented situation.[421] In such a situation, the people of Manipur are torn between their faith and reality, and they constantly ask, "How long will this go on? How long will my enemy overpower me? Why has God hidden its face of divine peace? Has God forgotten us? How long must we bear this pain in our being?" The people of Manipur are in constant fear of the proximity of death, which lingers every day and night because, for them, their enemy has been exalted over them. In such a socially tormented situation, the rhetorical reading of Psalm 13:1-6 and *Leshe* becomes a significant mode of deciphering divinity while presenting the petitions of complaints. These lament ballads are a reminder that complaints are not always negative. Rather, it is another form of prayer imploring God to reveal and intervene in this violent situation. Rhetorically reading Psalms 13:1-6 enables the lamenters to understand that crying out, questioning and imploring God to consider the tormented situation of violence and answer them helps them persuasively express their thoughts, fear, feelings and daily lived experiences. This kind of expression of their deep thoughts helps them realize that divine comfort is deciphered in their laments and complaints since it rebuilds and elevates their faith, which is left in ruin. Their attempt to find the answer to their question of "how long?" becomes their strong force in deciphering divinity and maintaining divine-human relationships in the midst of the prolonged violence.

Lament Psalms and *Leshe* employ elements and power of language that lead the lamenters/readers to look for the goal of divinity. This is through the choice of words by the lamenters and intensifying them with repetitions, which pictures the urgency of the lamenter's voice. When one reads Psalm 13:1-6, it sounds like the Psalmist has no hope nor confidence in the divinity of Yahweh. However, the persuasive linguistic styles allow us to uncover that a series of tormented situations is not the problem of destroying the human-divine relationship. Rather, these situations of illness and violence are the moments that elevate faith, enabling lamenters to decipher the divinity and

---

(ATSUM) in the ten Hill Districts of Manipur on 3 May 2023. The peaceful protest marches turned violent in the Torbung area of Churachandpur district. Suspected Kuki militants attacked the Meitei community, leading to retaliatory attacks and property damage. Violence quickly spread across Kuki and Meitei-dominated districts in the state."Manipur Violence: Assam Rifles Rescues 96 People in Air Evacuation Ops from India Myanmar Border," *The Economic Times*, 15 May 2023; More than a year now, the violence still persists, and at least 178 people have been killed and 50,000 displaced in Manipur since May 3 2023. Neeraj Chauhan, "MHA Bans Several Meitei Extremist Organisations for their Violent Activities," *The Hindustan Times*, Saturday, September 14, 2024.

421 "'Don't Know What our Fault Was': Agonising Tales of Lives at Relief Camps Emerge, "*The Sangai Express* xxiv, no. 222, Monday 8, 2023.

meaning of life. Their voices of lament become their most potent force for deciphering divinity amid their tormented situation.

Conclusion

Lament Psalms and Leshe portray the lamenter's ethos, pathos, and loss, bringing out the best expressions of human hearts throughout the centuries and inspiring contemporary literature. The study explored rhetorical criticism, delving into the verses of Psalm 13:1-6 and noting some parallels with the Sümi-Naga ballad/Leshe. It reveals that both ancient ballads enable lamenters to express their emotions persuasively.

Laments serve as a powerful and distinctive mode of expression, communicating the thoughts and emotions rooted in the human heart and mind, which is more potent than any other form. Complaints towards God reflect the why and how of life during the struggles and hardships of life, bringing the lamenter closer to understanding divinity rather than having a negative meaning. As Jesurathnam rightly stated, laments are powerful theological and religious resources for struggling humans.[422] This is so because lament, as it is, remains the most potent and persuasive mode of communication in deciphering divinity.

Lament Psalms and *Leshe* are voices written or expressed in the tormented situations of the Psalmist and the composer. This is proof that dark times unveil light, struggles uncover trust, challenges reveal strength, and laments decipher divinity.

Laments are the core of a human's heart; the intense feelings are often locked away deep within, but when these are rhetorically expressed, divinity is revealed. Therefore, when humans lament, we elevate ourselves, our conditions, and our faith in God as we attempt to decipher our faith, our existence, the existence of tormented situations and the existence of God. In such context, as we lament, our thoughts and voices become strong, persuasive, and deep-rooted, with powerful language used by God to decipher divinity. Thus, with such deep thoughts, petitions, complaints, and the power of words, we can decipher divinity amid tormented situations. As long as humanity (with tormented situations) lives, the need for deciphering divinity remains, which is perfectly, persuasively, and powerfully interpreted in the rhetorical ballad and laments.

---

422 K. Jesurathnam, *Dalit Liberative Hermeneutics*, 16.

27

The Necessity of Agroecological Prophetism Hope for the Agriculture

K. J. Premavardhan

Introduction

It's my privilege and honour to write this essay for the Festschrift in Honour of Prof. Rev. Dr. K. Jesurathnam. When I started my Master of Theology studies in Old Testament at UTC Bangalore, Prof. Jesurathnam encouraged, inspired and led me to be confident in my studies. I thank Prof. Jesurathnam for his guidance and support during my studies. In gratitude to his mentorship and fellowship over the years, I submit this essay to the Festschrift that honours him.

This essay explores the significance of agroecological prophetism that provides hope for the agriculture. The biblical notion of agriculture helps one to identify ancient practices and productive values that sustained human communities in the ancient days. It is to emphasize how ancient communities survived in the context of migration and severe draught.

Agriculture was fundamental to the development of human civilization and served as the backbone of ancient economies. It provided food and facilitated trade growth and the exchange of goods.[423] The ability to cultivate crops and domesticate animals led to the establishment of permanent

423 M. Eleanor Irwin, "Agricultural Plants in the Ancient Mediterranean" in *A Companion to Ancient Agriculture* edited by David Hollander & Timothy Howe (Moboken USA: Wiley Blackwell, John Wiley & Sons, 2021), 83.

settlements, which fostered the growth of cities and complex societies. A stable food supply provided by agriculture was essential for growth and the development of social structures.[424] Agriculture also influenced the religion and culture of ancient peoples. M. Eleanor Irwin observes that agriculture played a role in shaping cultural practices and religious beliefs. For instance, religious rituals used agricultural products such as wine and cultivating certain plants tied with cultural identity. This close connection between agriculture and spiritual life is evident in various ancient practices. Furthermore, one can notice that ancient agricultural practices preserve ecological knowledge, viewed as ancient wisdom that biblical texts passed on to the generations. These insights offer a valuable understanding of ancient societies and their adaptability to environmental changes.[425] Therefore, agriculture has multifaceted dimensions, and studying and understanding its significance in human history is essential. Additionally, ancient societies adapted to changing environmental conditions, leading to innovations in land management and crop selection. Ultimately, these agricultural practices laid the foundation for modern agriculture, with many techniques and crops from antiquity still in use today.

Agroecology

Agroecology is increasingly recognized as a vital approach to sustainable agriculture, emphasizing integrating ecological principles into farming practices. The sustainability of agriculture relies on environmental management principles. The term "agroecology" holds significant importance in the context of ecological awareness. Wezel et al. explain that Russian agronomist Bensin first introduced the term in the 1930s to describe the application of ecological methods in the study of commercial crop plants, establishing it as a field focused on integrating ecological principles into agriculture. In the 1950s, German zoologist Tischler expanded this concept by analyzing the components of agroecosystems, such as plants, animals, soils, and climate, and their interactions with the surrounding landscape and the effects of agricultural management. The emergence of agroecology as both a movement and a set of practices in the 1970s was a response to the adverse effects of industrialized agriculture on the environment and human welfare. Agroecology thus began to be recognized as the scientific foundation for designing sustainable agroecosystems. Over time, the discipline evolved

424 Alan Farahani, "Paleoethnobotany and Ancient Agriculture" in *A Companion to Ancient Agriculture* edited by David Hollander & Timothy Howe (Moboken USA: Wiley Blackwell, John Wiley & Sons, 2021), 7.

425 David Hollander and Timothy Howe," *A Companion to Ancient Agriculture* edited by David Hollander & Timothy Howe (Moboken USA: Wiley Blackwell, John Wiley & Sons, 2021) 3.

to encompass the entire food system, leading to a broader definition that integrates ecological, economic, and social dimensions.[426] By adopting an agroecological lens that emphasizes sustainable farming practices rooted in ecological principles, we can shift our reading of the Bible towards the agrarian perspective that uncovers the ecological wisdom embedded in its ancient agricultural context, offering insights for addressing environmental and social justice issues today.

Agrarian Reading of the Bible

An agrarian context produced the Bible, and the rural culture reflected in the text likely addressed various social and environmental problems, offering solutions. In light of this rural culture, reading the biblical text can lead us to deeper insights into the real issues faced by ancient societies. Richard L. Rohrbaugh argues that the necessity of an agrarian biblical interpretation stems from recognizing that the writing of the Bible was fundamentally different from the context of the modern industrial world. He postulates that understanding the agrarian context is crucial for accurate interpretation, as many biblical texts reflect agrarian life's social, economic, and cultural realities. Similarly, Ellen F. Davis emphasizes that the agrarian perspective highlights the theological significance of land in the Bible. The concept of *adamah* (Earth or arable land) underscores the inherent relationship between humanity and creation, suggesting that humans are divinely appointed stewards of the Earth. This stewardship mandate calls for responsible care and cultivation of the land, reflecting God's intentions for creation.[427]

Additionally, contemporary discussions and an agrarian reading of the Bible promote ecological awareness and its sustainability. Consequently, agrarian perspective advocates for practices that honour the Earth and promote ecological balance, aligning with biblical care principles and respect for creation.[428] Furthermore, Theodore Hiebert argues that several key points underscore the necessity of an agrarian reading of the Bible. First, it recognizes the agricultural foundation of ancient Israelite society, essential for interpreting biblical narratives deeply rooted in rural life.[429] This perspective highlights how agricultural practices and themes, such as fertility and harvest, shape theological concepts in the Bible, reflecting

426 Konrad Martin & Joachim Sauerborn, *Agroecology* (Springer: New York,2013), 6.

427 Ellen F Davis, *Scripture, Culture, and Agriculture: An Agrarian Reading of the Bible* (New York: Cambridge University Press, 2009), 127 & 178.

428 Ellen F Davis, *Scripture, Culture, and Agriculture*, 127.

429 Theodore Hiebert, *The Yahwist's Landscape: Nature and Religion in Early Israel* (New York: Oxford University Press, 1996), ix.

the relationship between God and the land.[430] Additionally, this reading encourages contemporary readers to reflect on their relationship with nature, providing insights into ethical agricultural practices and ecological stewardship.[431] Finally, understanding the agrarian context is crucial for reconstructing the socio-economic realities of ancient Israel, which informs the development of Israelite identity and biblical narratives.[432] Notably, the scholars' opinions above underscore the significance of an agroecological reading in deepening our understanding of the voices of the eighth-century prophets and their arguments for social justice. It is crucial to consider the origin and development of agriculture in ancient West Asia, its profound impact on the growth of civilization and culture, and how agriculture played a pivotal role in shaping society. Despite this, the agrarian practices of neighbouring cultures undoubtedly influenced the agrarian vision and social justice practices of early Israelites, who adopted alternative models. Let us examine these realities in detail.

Agriculture in Ancient West Asia

Ancient agriculture played a crucial role in the development of early civilizations. This region is recognized as one of the earliest centres of agricultural innovation, beginning around 10,000 BCE with the Neolithic Revolution. The transition period from the hunting-gatherer culture to settled communities and domestication of crops likely started in the context of this revolution.[433] The region's favourable climate and fertile soil allowed for the development of irrigation systems to manage water resources effectively. Agricultural techniques such as ploughing and crop rotation are employed to enhance productivity.[434] The rise of agriculture in the Near East led to significant social and economic changes. As agricultural practices supported larger populations, complex societies emerged, characterized by social hierarchies, trade networks, and the establishment of cities.[435]

David Hollander and Timothy Howe rightly point out that the development of agriculture in ancient societies, particularly in the Near East, is closely linked to the emergence of social hierarchies and exploitative practices. Producing surplus food enabled specific individuals or groups to accumulate wealth, establishing social classes where landowners exerted control over labourers and creating systems of exploitation. As agricultural

430 Theodore Hiebert, *The Yahwist's Landscape*, 63.

431 Theodore Hiebert, *The Yahwist's Landscape*, 63.

432 Theodore Hiebert, *The Yahwist's Landscape*, 85.

433 David Hollander and Timothy Howe, *A Companion to Ancient Agriculture*, 1.

434 Alan Farahani, "*Paleoethnobotany and Ancient Agriculture*", 23.

435 Alan Farahani, "*Paleoethnobotany and Ancient Agriculture*", 23

practices advanced, land ownership became a significant factor in social stratification, allowing landowners to dictate terms to those who worked the land, resulting in unequal power dynamics and exploitative labour practices.[436] The establishment of complex political structures accompanied agricultural development, with rulers using their control over resources to maintain power. Furthermore, these developments often granted religious authorities the power to redefine religious ideologies, which frequently justified social hierarchies and exploitative practices by linking agricultural success to divine favour. They reinforced elite status while marginalizing lower classes.[437] Moreover, the rise of agriculture facilitated labour specialization, creating a dependency on landowners for livelihoods, often leading to exploitative relationships where labourers faced unfair treatment and limited rights.[438] These factors inevitably influenced early Israel, prompting it to redefine its cultural, religious, and agricultural aspects. The agricultural innovations that emerged in ancient West Asia, including irrigation and crop rotation, not only shaped the development of early civilizations but also influenced the agroecological vision of early Israel, where a deep connection between land, social justice, and stewardship of creation became central to their agricultural and cultural practices.

Agroecological Vision of Early Israel:

The agricultural practices of early Israel maintained a deep understanding of local ecosystems and a commitment to sustainable farming. They employed techniques such as crop rotation, intercropping, and soil fertility preservation to ensure the long-term viability of agricultural lands. The land was a divine gift, and stewardship was a communal responsibility. This perspective fostered social cohesion and a shared vision for the community's well-being. The prophets of Israel, including Amos and Micah, emphasized the importance of justice and equity in agricultural practices, critiquing the exploitation of both the land and marginalized people (Amos 5:11-12; Micah 6:8). Their messages serve as a reminder of the ethical dimensions of agriculture and the need for a socio-political framework that prioritizes sustainability and social justice.

Before David Hopkins, Old Testament scholars proposed various models regarding the emergence of the ancient Israelites in Canaan. Most of these models suggest that multiple factors contributed to the formation of

---

436 Alan Farahani, "*Paleoethnobotany and Ancient Agriculture*", 42.

437 M. Eleanor Irwin, "*Agricultural Plants in the Ancient Mediterranean*", 97.

438 Valasia Isaakidou, "Zooarchaeology" in *A Companion to Ancient Agriculture* edited by David Hollander & Timothy Howe (Moboken USA: Wiley Blackwell, John Wiley & Sons, Inc: 2021), 42.

the people known as Israel. However, David Hopkins argues that subsistence agrarian awareness played a pivotal role in the emergence of Israel in the highlands of Canaan through the Subsistence Agrarian Model. Furthermore, Hopkins contends that the community had a strong awareness of producing sufficient food to meet communal needs, which shaped the structure of their agricultural systems.[439]

Adapting to the specific environmental conditions of the highlands of Canaan required communities to select appropriate crops and develop effective land management techniques, thereby enhancing food security. The reliance on subsistence agriculture fostered cooperation among community members, leading to social structures that facilitated collective decision-making and resource sharing.[440] Similarly, Norman K. Gottwald emphasizes that the early Israelite community's agricultural production was more egalitarian. The community adhered to an agroecological model to achieve and sustain this egalitarian ethos. Gottwald argues that established kin relationships and tribal affiliations provided the framework for organizing militias and fostering a sense of belonging. Further, land cultivation fosters the sustenance of community rather than individual profit.[441] The various Israelite groups collectively identified with the theme of land acquisition, which was essential for their survival as a community. It suggests that agricultural output is vital to meeting communal needs rather than for commercial purposes.[442] The allotment of land to tribes allowed for autonomous economic development based on their respective landholdings, with the focus on fulfilling the community's needs rather than producing for external markets.[443] In alignment with this, Albino Barrera suggests that early Israel's social structure differed significantly from the Canaanite system, particularly regarding agrarian models and land tenure practices. The Canaanites practised a mix of prebendal and patrimonial land tenure, wherein the kings granted land to officials and passed down through generations. In Canaanite society, landowners often did not farm their estates themselves. Still, they relied on peasants required to pay substantial taxes and rents, sometimes amounting to more than half of their harvest. This system allowed wealthy landowners to extract surplus from the peasants,

439 David C Hopkins, *The Highlands of the Canaan,* 12.

440 David C Hopkins, *The Highlands of the Canaan,* 15.

441 Norman K Gottwald, *The Tribes of Yahweh: A Sociology of Religion of Liberated Israel 1250-1050 BCE* (New York: Orbis Books, Maryknoll, 1979), 159.

442 Norman K Gottwald, *The Tribes of Yahweh*, 179.

443 Norman K Gottwald, *The Tribes of Yahweh*, 183.

leading to poor living conditions for the latter and fostering an inegalitarian society.[444]

Conversely, the combination of rational agricultural practices and a strong sense of community solidarity enabled these subsistence farming societies to navigate the challenges of their environment effectively. This reliance on mutual aid and cooperation facilitated survival and reinforced values of generosity and care for the vulnerable, which became integral to their national identity.[445] Moreover, the *musha* system is one of ancient Israel's most explicit examples of agroecological practices. The *musha* system refers to communal land tenure or collective farming. This system was characterized by sharing agricultural land among families or individuals, typically within a village or community. The concept of *musha* is closely associated with communal rights to land, which individuals did not own but cultivated collectively. The *musha* system allowed for the pooling of resources and labour, which proved particularly beneficial for managing agricultural activities, sharing risks, and ensuring food security among community members. It also fostered social cohesion and cooperation among farmers as they worked together to cultivate the land and share the harvest. This practice is significant for understanding ancient Israel's social and economic structures, as it reflects the interplay between land ownership, community relationships, and agricultural productivity. The *musha* system is a practical response to the environmental and economic challenges of the region, including droughts and the need for sustainable farming practices.[446] Additionally, agroecology promoted a vision of egalitarianism and influenced ancient Israel's religious practices. Todd LeVasseur, quoting Elaine Solowey, summarizes that the sacred Jewish agricultural traditions are deeply rooted in both religious texts and the cultural practices of Judaism. These traditions reflect a profound connection between faith, land, and the ethical treatment of the environment.[447]

Jewish agricultural practices are often derived from the Torah and other religious texts, which provide guidelines on cultivating the land ethically and sustainably. For instance, the laws of *kashrut* and the concept of *shmita*

---

444 Albino Barrera, "*Biblical Economic Ethics Sacred Scripture's Teachings on Economic Life* (New York: Lexington Books, 2013), 29.

445 Albino Barrera, *Biblical Economic Ethics Sacred Scripture's Teachings on Economic Life*, 31.

446 Philippe Guillaume, *Land, Credit and Crisis Agrarian Finance in the Hebrew Bible* (Sheffield: Equinox Publishing Ltd, 2012), 28-42

447 Todd LeVassur, "Introduction, Religion, Agriculture and Sustainability" in *Religion and Sustainable Agriculture: World Spiritual Traditions and Food Ethics* edited by Todd LeVassur, Pramod ParaJuli and Norman Wirzba (Lexington: The University Press of Kentucky, 2016), 27.

(the sabbatical year) emphasize the importance of treating the land with respect and allowing it to rest, reflecting a deep connection between faith and environmental stewardship. The integration of agricultural practices with ethical considerations is evident in the teachings of the Hebrew Bible, which commands the Israelites to care for the land and its resources. The concept of *bal tashchit* prohibits wastefulness and encourages the sustainable use of resources, highlighting the ethical dimensions of farming within Jewish tradition.[448]

The early vision of Israel's egalitarian society and commitment to social justice was deeply rooted in and sustained by subsistence farming practices, which religious teachings guided them. These practices significantly impacted the community, embedding agroecological concerns within their spiritual and ethical frameworks. The agroecological vision in ancient Israel extended beyond environmental stewardship; it also influenced religious reformers to advocate for social justice, intertwining the principles of agroecology with values of equity and communal well-being. This convergence of environmental and social ethics underscores the integral role of agroecology in shaping the religious and social consciousness of the time.

A Shift from Agroecological Practices to Agribusiness

The transition from subsistence agriculture to agribusiness in the eighth century marked a significant shift in the socio-economic landscape of Israel. The prophets criticized this shift, emphasizing its detrimental effects on the land and the people. The focus on profit maximization led to the exploitation of resources and the marginalization of smallholder farmers, resulting in a loss of social vision and community cohesion. This critique resonates with contemporary concerns regarding industrial agriculture, which often prioritizes corporate interests over environmental sustainability and social equity. The harmful impacts of agribusiness, including soil degradation, loss of biodiversity, and social inequality, echo the prophets' warnings. *In her seminal book 'Who Really Feeds the World?* Vandana Shiva argues the dominance of agribusiness has led to a disconnection from traditional farming practices and a disregard for the ecological knowledge of local communities. This disconnection poses significant challenges to both food security and environmental sustainability. In light of these parallels, examining the social context and factors that led the Israelite community of the eighth century from agroecological concerns to agribusiness practices is essential.

448 Todd LeVassur, "Introduction, Religion, Agriculture and Sustainability", 25-27.

Matthew J.M. Comber, quoting Chaney and Premnath, approaches the socio-economic contexts of ancient agrarian societies, particularly prophetic texts from eighth-century Judah, by applying cultural-evolutionary theory and analyzing the recurring patterns of societal change arising from increased economic activity. Their work emphasizes the parallels between ancient and modern agrarian societies, especially in terms of how they respond to financial pressures and transformations. Chaney and Premnath employ cultural-evolutionary theory to explore the transformation of agricultural societies from subsistence-based farming to more complex political economies. They argue that this evolution often leads to increased social stratification, where wealth and resources become concentrated in a few's hands, resulting in an elite class that controls land and agricultural production. This shift frequently marginalizes most of the population, including subsistence farmers, who may face exploitation as land ownership practices change. As agricultural societies become more commercialized, once communally owned land may be appropriated for profit-driven agriculture, leading to the expulsion of small farmers and a growing reliance on wage labour. Chaney and Premnath underscore that these dynamics of exploitation echoed in the prophetic literature of ancient Judah, which critiques social injustices and addresses the moral decay of society. The grievances expressed in these texts can be understood as responses to the socio-economic transformations of their time, reflecting the broader patterns of cultural evolution and economic change that continue to shape agrarian societies today.[449]

Factors in Shifting Israelites from Agroecological Principles to Agribusiness

Marvin V. Chaney rightly points out that several factors contributed to ancient Israel's shift from agroecology to agribusiness. The transition from communal land management to a system dominated by large estates led to the concentration of land ownership in the hands of a few elites. This shift displaced traditional agricultural practices, which compelled peasants to work on large-scale monoculture farms; consequently, such a compulsion prioritized cash crops over subsistence farming. The growing demand for cash crops, such as wine and olive oil, redirected agricultural focus away from cultivating diverse subsistence crops. This transformation was primarily driven by the elites' desire for profit and luxury goods, leading to

449 Matthew J.M. Commber, *"Re-Reading Prophets Through Corporate Globalization:' A Cultural Evolutionary Approach to Economic Injustice in the Hebrew Bible"* (USA: Gorgias Press LLC, 2010), 235.

a decline in the production of staple crops essential for local food security.[450] To further understand the dynamics of this transition, let us examine the reasons categorically to provide a more precise analysis.

Political Influence:

The emergence of monarchy in ancient Israel brought significant changes to Israelite society. The centralization of power was one of the critical factors that put subsistence farming in a precarious position. Marvin Chaney states that kings like David and Solomon implemented policies that favoured large-scale agricultural production to support their expanding bureaucracies and military needs. This centralization often resulted in the appropriation of land from peasant farmers, consolidating it into larger estates that profit the wealthy and managed more efficiently.[451] Moreover, the monarchy implemented taxation systems that required farmers to produce surplus crops to meet state demands. It often led to the exploitation of peasant labour, as landowners sought to maximize production to fulfil tax obligations. As a result, the shift from communal farming practices to more business-oriented agricultural operations became widespread. The interests of the monarchy frequently aligned with those of wealthy landowners, leading to policies favouring agribusiness and the concentration of land.[452] Norman K. Gottwald rightly points out that the pressure from the monarchy's tax policies, designed to increase revenue to meet market demands, inevitably transformed Israelite society. In addition, the centralization of power consolidated agricultural resources and demanded increased production to ensure surplus generation.[453]

Sociological Influence

In ancient Israel, a subsistence economy characterizes the social structure of peasants, where the peasant household aimed to feed itself rather than produce for the market. Norman K. Gottwald depicts the pre-monarchic Israelite community as fundamentally agrarian, organized around protective kinship and community ties. These ties were essential for subsistence farming, as they provided mutual support in agricultural activities and offered protection from external threats. This collective awareness fostered a sense of community responsibility, enabling them to manage human

---

450 Marvin L. Chaney, *"Peasants, Prophets, & Political Economy:' The Hebrew Bible and Social Analysis"* (Eugene: Wipf and Stock Publishers, 2017), 91.

451 Marvin L. Chaney, *"Peasants, Prophets, & Political Economy"*, 100.

452 Alice A. Keefe, "*Woman's Body and the Social Body in Hosea"* in Journal for the Study of the Old Testament Supplement Series 338, Gender, Culture, Theory 10 (New York: Sheffield Academic Press, 2001), 30.

453 Norman K Gottwald, *"The Tribes of Yahweh*, 100.

resources effectively and maximize productivity, thus ensuring food security for the entire community.[454]

However, several external factors influenced the social structure, including land ownership, credit systems, and the evolving relationship between peasants and landlords. The basic economic unit in ancient Israel was the nuclear family, which focused on subsistence farming. Peasants were not agricultural entrepreneurs; they maintained their households through agriculture, relying on their labour and limited resources. With the rise of agribusiness and urbanization, this social structure began to shift. As urban centres grew and the demand for agricultural products increased, the relationship between peasants and landlords evolved. A mercantile system emerged in which urban landowners or merchants extracted a significant portion of agricultural produce as rent, leading to a more exploitative relationship. This shift often made peasants increasingly dependent on urban markets and moneylenders, further exacerbating their poverty and reducing their autonomy.[455]

Economic Influence

In ancient Israel, market ideologies drove the transition from subsistence farming to agribusiness, increasingly influencing agricultural practices. The shift towards agribusiness involved the commercialization of agriculture, where agricultural production became oriented toward profit rather than meeting the basic needs of local communities. This shift often led to the prioritization of cash crops over subsistence crops, negatively impacting food security for local populations.[456] Similarly, Morris Silver notes that as agribusiness emerged, there was a trend toward consolidating land into larger estates owned by wealthy individuals or corporations. This process displaced small farmers and shifted agricultural production from local subsistence to large-scale commercial operations, often prioritizing efficiency and profit over sustainable practices. Furthermore, the transition to agribusiness created a dependency on market forces, making farmers increasingly reliant on external markets for their livelihoods. This dependency left smallholders vulnerable to fluctuations in market prices and economic downturns, a stark contrast to the self-sufficiency associated with subsistence farming.[457]

---

454 Norman K Gottwald, *"The Tribes of Yahweh*, 213-214.

455 Bernhard Lang, "The Social Organization of Peasant Poverty in Biblical Israel" *Journal for the Study of the Old Testament* (1982): 48-50.

456 Alice A. Keefe, "*Woman's Body and the Social Body in Hosea"*, 30.

457 Morris Sliver, *"Prophets and Markets: The Political Economy of Ancient Israel"* (New York: Kluwer-Nijhoff Publishing, 1983), 74.

Religious Influence

The influence of religious ideology also played a significant role in changing attitudes toward fertility and agricultural production. The religious narratives that emerged during the rise of the elite class in eighth-century Israelite society legitimized the practices of the wealthy. These narratives framed the wealth and success of the elites as signs of divine favour, thus justifying their accumulation of resources. This reinterpretation of land ownership allowed the elites to view their growing control over agricultural resources as a fulfilment of divine will, often at the expense of subsistence farmers.[458]Furthermore, Alice A. Keefe suggests that village peasants, though removed from the politics of the urban world, were heavily influenced by fertility religions. The cult of Asherah and the Yahweh cult were widespread, with communities attributing agricultural fertility, growth, and surplus production to these deities. The state cult supported and reinforced this belief system, which embraced such ideologies.[459] To secure blessings for their land and harvests, communities engaged in various rituals and offerings. These practices included sacrifices, feasts, and other forms of worship to appease the deities and ensure their favour. The gathered community members often performed rituals at local shrines or state-sanctioned temples to express their devotion. These gatherings served a religious purpose and reinforced social cohesion in both Judah and Israel until the Deuteronomist reformers sought to challenge and reform these religious ideologies.[460]Through these ritual and divination practices, the state cult became the locus for religious propagation, enforcing divinely ordained laws related to land ownership and agricultural practices.[461]

However, these socio-political and religious ideologies played a crucial role in the shift from subsistence farming to agribusiness, ultimately contributing to agrarian communities' failure to secure their future. On the other hand, these circumstances gave rise to the voices of the prophets, who proposed solutions and offered hope in times of despair.

Agroecological Concerns in the Prophetic Voices of Eighth-Century Israel

The eighth-century context marks a pivotal moment in the history of ancient Israel, characterized by profound social, economic, and environmental transformations. During this period, prophetic figures such as Amos, Hosea, Isaiah, and Micah emerged as powerful agents of critique and reform,

458 Matthew J.M. Commber, *"Re-Reading Prophets Through Corporate Globalization:' ...,* 233

459 Alice A. Keefe, "*Woman's Body and the Social Body in Hosea*", 92.

460 Alice A. Keefe, "*Woman's Body and the Social Body in Hosea*", 93.

461 Alice A. Keefe, "*Woman's Body and the Social Body in Hosea*", 85.

addressing the pressing issues of their time. Central to their messages was a deep concern for agroecological integrity and social justice, reflecting an acute awareness of the interconnectedness between the land, its people, and the divine.

A complex interplay of agricultural practices, land ownership, and socio-economic structures shaped the agrarian context of ancient Israel. As the region faced the encroachment of market economies and the consolidation of land among the elite, the prophets articulated a vision that challenged the prevailing injustices and advocated for a return to ethical land stewardship. Their prophetic utterances were not merely spiritual exhortations; they mentioned the lived realities of the agrarian community, inextricably linking the people's well-being to the agrarian structure's future.

In their writings, the prophets employed vivid metaphors and poignant imagery to convey the consequences of social and agricultural degradation. They condemned the exploitation of people with low incomes, the manipulation of land boundaries, and the moral decay that accompanied the pursuit of wealth at the expense of communal welfare. By framing their messages within the context of agricultural life, the prophets underscored the importance of sustainable practices and equitable access to resources, advocating for a holistic understanding of justice encompassing ecological and social dimensions.

This introduction sets the stage for a deeper exploration of the agroecological concerns articulated by the eighth-century prophetic voices. By examining their critiques of land ownership, their calls for sustainable agricultural practices, and their advocacy for the marginalized, we can glean valuable insights into the enduring relevance of their messages for contemporary discussions on agriculture, environmental stewardship, and social justice. The prophetic tradition reminds us that the quest for a just and sustainable society is not a modern endeavour but a timeless call that resonates through the ages, urging us to consider our relationship with the land and one another in pursuing a more equitable future.

The Song of the Vineyard: A Critique of Social and Agroecological Injustice in Eighth-Century Israel

The *Song of the Vineyard* has been examined from various perspectives to uncover the social realities of the eighth-century context. However, many attempts may have fallen short in addressing the core concerns of the text, as allegorical readings have often failed to do justice to its deeper meanings. Consequently, Margaret Miller approaches the text by exploring the world behind it, highlighting agrarian families' suffering due to dominant ideologies' influence. Miller argues that the *Song of the Vineyard* reflects a time when traditional agricultural practices and kinship structures were breaking down due to a shift from local to monarchical decision-making. This transition caused significant hardship in rural communities, particularly for the families responsible for sustaining life in these agricultural settings. The *Song of the Vineyard* mirrors the societal transition of its time, responding to the crisis faced by traditional agricultural communities. The song is a lament for the loss of a sustainable way of life and critiques the injustices brought about by new socio-economic realities. Eighth-century Israel witnessed a shift from traditional subsistence farming to agribusiness, driven by the monarchy's demand for cash crops like wheat, olive oil, and wine. Peasants were encouraged to take risks in the face of environmental challenges, as the monarchy promised high returns from market-oriented agricultural production. Royal vineyards converted much land to gain profits, and the presence of wine presses and large-scale wine production bears witness to the high demands placed on agricultural communities.462 Voice of the Text: In Isaiah 5:1-7, the interpretation of the text reveals a nuanced understanding of the voices present, particularly emphasizing the role of a female speaker alongside Yahweh. This analysis posits that the poem features two distinct voices: a woman who introduces the song in verses 1-2 and concludes it in verse 7, and Yahweh, who speaks in verses 3-6. Several lines of evidence support the identification of the female speaker, including her point of reference as an observer of a man labouring to establish a vineyard, which suggests a personal connection and likely indicates that she is the man's wife. The phrase "song of my beloved" further reinforces this interpretation, highlighting her intimacy and personal investment in the vineyard's establishment. The cultural backdrop of rural Israel, where women played vital roles in family and agricultural life, supports the notion that the speaker is narrating her observations and experiences related to establishing a family unit. By highlighting the essential role of the female voice, this interpretation challenges traditional readings of the text. It emphasizes the importance of women's experiences in ancient Israel's cultural and social fabric, suggesting that the essence of the passage is deeply rooted in a woman's perspective and expression.463

The Failure of Israelite Society: The *Song of the Vineyard* critiques Israelite society, particularly its failure to live up to covenant obligations. The commercialization of agriculture led to a breakdown of agroecological vision and contributed to the erosion of justice and righteousness, resulting in moral and ethical decay. This shift widened the gap between the rich

---

462 Margeret Miller, "Let Me Tell You About A Vineyard': Isaiah's Song of the Vineyard and the Green Revolution" *Dalam Teologia: Journal Teologi Interdisipliner:* (2014): 122.

463 Margeret Miller, "Let Me Tell You About A Vineyard',

and the poor, amplifying social inequality and undermining the foundational principles of justice and communal well-being.

Amos: A Voice for Adamah and Agroecological Justice

The teachings of Amos reflect significant agroecological concerns, mainly through the use of the term "adamah," which refers to arable land. This term is deeply rooted in the biblical understanding of the relationship between humanity, the land, and the Creator. Among the many issues drawn from the book of Amos, the concern for "adamah" stands as pivotal for understanding agroecological principles.

"adamah" highlights the intrinsic relationship between humans and the Earth. In Genesis, humanity (*Adam*) is created from the "adamah," underscoring a fundamental connection where humans are stewards of the land. Amos reemphasized this connection, where the people's moral and ethical behaviour presents the land's health (Amos 1:2). The degradation of the land due to injustice reflects a failure to honour this relationship. Furthermore, Amos advocates for sustainable agricultural practices that respect the land and its resources. Exploiting the land through unjust practices—such as over-farming and neglecting the Sabbath—leads to soil degradation and diminished fertility. It aligns with agroecological principles emphasizing the importance of maintaining soil health and biodiversity. Amos' call for justice and ethical treatment of the land serves as a reminder of the need for sustainable practices that ensure the long-term viability of agricultural systems.[464] In addition, Amos highlights the social dimensions of land use, particularly the impact of agricultural practices on the poor and marginalized. The exploitation of the land by the wealthy elite not only harms the environment but also exacerbates social inequalities. Amos condemns practices that lead to economic injustice, emphasizing that the land should be a source of sustenance for all, not just the privileged few. It reflects an agroecological concern for equitable access to resources and the need for social justice in agricultural systems.[465]

However, alongside his criticism, Amos also offers hope for restoration. While he critiques the ideologies of kingship that created a disconnect between the land and the people, he also promises that God will restore the arable land in the future (Amos 9:14-15). This hope for renewal underscores

464 Robert Khua Hnin Thang, *The Theology of the land in Amos 7-9* (Cumbria: Langham Monographs, 2014), 213.

465 Robert Khua Hnin Thang, *"The Theology of the land in Amos 7-9"*, 139.

the possibility of returning to sustainable practices and honouring the relationship between humanity and the land.[466]

Therefore, the teachings of Amos reflect a holistic understanding of the interconnectedness of creation. The community's well-being and the health of the land ("adamah") are the major concerns of the broader ecological system. This perspective aligns with agroecological principles that recognize the importance of biodiversity, ecosystem health, and the relationships between different components of the environment.

Hosea: Prophetic Critique of Agricultural Exploitation and Ecological Degradation

Hosea's prophetic messages reflect deep agrarian concerns, focusing on the ethical treatment of the land and its inhabitants, the consequences of social injustices, and the relationship between the people's behaviour and the fertility of the land. Hosea criticizes the people for following seductive religious ideologies and royal cults that promoted fertility practices at the expense of Yahwism. The official encouragement of these cults, alongside the imperial policies of Assyria, led to unsustainable agricultural practices that neglected the land policies prescribed by Yahwism.[467]

In ancient Israel, the privileged elites threatened sustainable subsistence farming by exploiting both the land and its tenants for personal enrichment. This exploitation often resulted in the displacement of family farms and their replacement with large estates, especially when the land was seized due to debt foreclosure, as noted in Isaiah 5:8 and Micah 2:2. Under the monarchy, the kings imposed the taxes. He seized land to reward officials and fund royal projects, forcing citizens to leave their farms to serve the monarchy in various roles, such as farmers, bakers, and builders (1 Samuel 8; 1 Kings 4:1–5:8). This system of forced labour disrupted traditional agricultural practices, placing immense pressure on farmers, as their surplus wine, grain, and oil were extracted for state needs or international trade, leading to further unsustainable practices. Under the Davidic monarchy, the king was Yahweh's representative and was responsible for ruling the rural families justly, ensuring justice and prosperity for the oppressed while maintaining order and fertility on the land (2 Samuel 7:8–17; Psalms 2, 89, 72). The king's role also included sponsoring the Jerusalem Temple, seen as God's earthly home and a source of blessing and fertility for the people (1

466 Gillingham Susan, "Who Makes the Morning Darkness': God and Creation in the Book of Amos" *Scottish Journal of Theology,* Vol 45. May (1992):182.

467 Ucheawaji Godfrey Josiah and Blessing Jeffrey-Ebhomenmen, "An Afrocentric Eco reading of 'Coloniality of Power' in Prophet Hosea's Narrative" *Religions* Vol.14.1389 (2023): 2.

Kings 8:26–38; 2 Chronicles 7:12–15; Psalm 132). However, the monarchy's singular focus on imperial expansion disrupted the land, creating ecological imbalances and leading to drought, famine, and poor harvests.[468]

Alice A. Keefe rightly points out that Israel's faithfulness to Yahweh was the fertility of the land. When the people turned away from God and engaged in idolatry, they faced consequences such as drought and agricultural failure. During Hosea's time, agrarian practices shifted toward short-term benefits rather than prioritizing sustainable long-term cultivation. This shift resulted in over-farming and soil degradation, placing immense pressure on small farmers. The ethical implications of neglecting the land are evident in Hosea's condemnation of these practices, particularly in Hosea 4:3.[469]During Hosea's time, there was a shift in agricultural practices, and they shifted to short-term benefits from the land rather than prioritize sustainable long-term cultivation. The discussion over agricultural practices implies the consequences, particularly in the context of the exploitation of the land and its resources. The effects of overfarming and soil degradation are related to the pressures small farmers face.[470]The neglect of the land and its needs, along with the consequences of such neglect, can be inferred from the discussions on the ethical implications of agricultural practices (Hosea 4:3).[471] Hosea emphasizes the need for true repentance, warning that greed and exploitation lead to a cycle of ecological degradation. The excessive consumption of resources strains the land's capacity to sustain life, and the punishment for these actions is the loss of fertility, symbolizing the consequences of exploiting both the people and the Earth (Hosea 4:10).[472]

Micah: A Prophetic Call for Agrarian Justice and Ecological Restoration

The prophet Micah raised his voice against the injustices violating agrarian principles, focusing on the abuse of land ownership (Micah 2:1-2). He explicitly condemns those who devise plans to seize land from people with low incomes, expressing deep concern for farming communities. Micah critiques the injustices perpetrated by the urban elite and the exploitation of rural farmers.

His oracles highlight the consequences of corrupt practices in the city, where the wealthy benefit at the expense of the poor. Micah's message

468 Laurie J. Braaten, *"God's Good Land: The Agrarian Perspective of the Book of the Twelve"* in The Oxford Handbook of The Bible and Ecology edited by Hilary Marlow and Mark Harris (New York: Oxford University Press, 2022), 150.

469 Alice A. Keefe, "*Woman's Body and the Social Body in Hosea*", 34.

470 Ellen F Davis, Scripture, Culture, and Agriculture, 121.

471 Ellen F Davis, Scripture, Culture, and Agriculture, 138.

472 Laurie J. Braaten, *"God's Good Land the Agrarian Perspective of the Book of the Twelve"*, 155.

underscores the need for justice and accountability in urban governance, advocating for the rights of those who work the land. He questions how the state-controlled food economy can lead to the exploitation of farmers, revealing the systemic injustices that arise when power is concentrated in a few, leading to the impoverished of the rural population while the urban elite thrive (Micah 6:9-16).[473] Laurie J. Braaten observes that Micah's prophecies are agrarian laments, with the prophet expressing deep sorrow over the intertwined fate of the people and the land. Micah calls upon all creation to witness divine judgment against the corrupt elite, emphasizing the unity of the agrarian community with the Earth. As God enacts judgment on cities like Samaria and Jerusalem, the consequences of human sin disrupt the land, with even the animals sharing in the grief. Micah critiques the elite for their greed and exploitation, which harm both the vulnerable and the land, creating a cycle of decay. He presents a divine lawsuit with the mountains as witnesses, revealing the elite's failure to pursue justice and care for the land. In his closing prayers, Micah expresses a yearning for restoration, likening himself to a farmer lamenting barren fields due to the people's sins, and he envisions a time of healing under divine guidance.[474]

While Micah's concerns reflect the broader issues of the eighth century, his prophecies are remarkable for their emphasis on the hope for the restoration of agroecological awareness. His use of agrarian imagery offers a vision of revival rooted in a return to sustainable practices and communal well-being. Micah envisions a future where every Israelite lives in freedom, with a house on ancestral land, reflecting a return to traditional communitarian structures. This vision aligns with economic justice and societal stability, resonating with wisdom literature such as Proverbs, which advocates for neither extreme wealth nor poverty but rather sufficiency. Micah's approach reflects a balanced economic life that values community well-being over individual wealth accumulation (Micah 4:4).[475]

Furthermore, the prophet envisions a hopeful future where the Earth is restored and used productively, particularly for agriculture, suggesting a return to a more straightforward, more harmonious way of living aligned with God's original intentions for creation. The imagery of people sitting under their vines and fig trees symbolizes well-being and self-sufficiency, free from fear and oppression. This reversion to nature implies restoring the relationship between humanity and the Earth, indicating that when societies

473 Ellen F Davis, Scripture, Culture, and Agriculture, 156-157.

474 Laurie J. Braaten, *"God's Good Land: The Agrarian Perspective of the Book of the Twelve"*, 157-158.

475 Albino Barrera, *"Biblical Economic Ethics Sacred Scripture's Teachings on Economic Life"*, 91.

adhere to God's ways, ecological balance and social justice will flourish, leading to a thriving community where people and the environment coexist harmoniously.[476]

Therefore, the eighth-century agrarian prophets of Isaiah, Hosea, Micah, and Amos reflect a profound engagement with the socio-economic realities of their time. Through agricultural imagery, these prophets articulate a vision of justice, ethical responsibility, and the vital connection between the people and their ancient agroecological principles. They also criticized the royal ideologies that misled the community toward individualism, self-sufficiency, and market-driven practices. Their messages continue to resonate, offering insights into the importance of social justice, stewardship, and the hope that renewal is possible through agroecological principles, both in ancient and contemporary contexts.

The Relevance of Agrarian Prophetism in Light of Vandana Shiva's Critique of Industrial Agriculture

Vandana Shiva, a prominent environmental activist and scholar, argues that the root causes of the current agricultural crisis lie in the industrial agricultural practices that have dominated since the Green Revolution. This paper aims to elucidate Shiva's key arguments and the solutions she proposes to address the failures of agribusiness. Vandana Shiva critically examines the failures of industrial agriculture and agribusiness, highlighting their ecological, social, and economic consequences

She begins her analysis by critiquing the industrial agricultural model, which relies heavily on chemical inputs, monocultures, and mechanization. She argues that this model has led to significant ecological costs, including soil erosion, water depletion, and biodiversity loss. The ecological footprint of industrial agriculture contributes to climate change and undermines the foundations of food production. Furthermore, Shiva highlights the social implications of this model, noting that it has displaced small-scale farmers, exacerbated rural poverty, and led to widespread farmer suicides due to insurmountable debt.[477]

Historical Context and the Green Revolution: In examining agricultural history, she discusses the Green Revolution as a pivotal moment in transforming food production. While it aimed to increase yields and combat hunger, the Green Revolution's reliance on high-yielding varieties and chemical inputs resulted in environmental degradation and social inequities.

476 Keith Innes, God, *"The Earth and Humanity In The Book Of Micah"* in The· JRI ·Briefing· Papers: 28 accessed at K Innes - 2014 - jri.org.uk at 10:30 p.m.

477 Vandana Shiva, "Who Really Feeds the World': *The Failures of Agribusiness and The Promise of Agroecology"* (Berkeley, California: North Atlantic Books, 2016), 93.

Further, she emphasizes that traditional agricultural practices, which were sustainable and resilient, were systematically undermined in favour of industrial methods. This historical context is crucial for understanding the current food crisis and the need for a paradigm shift.[478]

Moreover, she critiques the role of multinational corporations in shaping agricultural policies and practices under the appearance of "free trade," which has benefited wealthy nations and corporations at the expense of small-scale farmers in developing countries. The dismantling of import barriers has made these farmers vulnerable to dumping and exploitation, further entrenching poverty and food insecurity. She contends that the corporate control of seeds and agricultural inputs has led to a loss of biodiversity and farmer autonomy, creating a system prioritizing profit over ecological and social well-being.[479]

Even though in response to the failures of industrial agriculture, she advocates for agroecology as a sustainable alternative. Agroecology integrates traditional ecological knowledge with modern scientific practices, promoting biodiversity, soil health, and local food systems. She argues that agroecological practices can enhance food security, restore ecological balance, and empower local communities. She emphasizes the importance of seed sovereignty, advocating for the preservation of indigenous seeds and establishing community seed banks to ensure farmers have access to diverse and resilient crops.[480]She proposes several policy changes to support the transition to agroecology. These include the establishment of fair-trade practices, the protection of small-scale farmers, and the promotion of local food systems. She calls for reimagining food policies prioritizing ecological health and social equity, urging governments to support sustainable agricultural practices and empower communities to take control of their food systems. Shiva's vision encompasses a "food democracy" where the rules of agriculture are determined by the people, fostering a system that values sharing, caring, and ecological stewardship.

Conclusion: Relevance of Agrarian Prophetism

In light of Vandana Shiva's insights and proposals, the failures of contemporary industrial agriculture mirror the deep-rooted crises within the agricultural sector. The problem remains unseen because land and agriculture are commodities, nurtured by the ideologies of the market and science. As a result, peasant communities face a collapsing agroecosystem, which threatens the land's productive capacity, leading to crop failures, economic

478 Vandana Shiva, "Who Really Feeds the World', 21.

479 Vandana Shiva, "Who Really Feeds the World', 93.

480 Vandana Shiva, *"Who Really Feeds the World'*,18.

crises, and food insecurity. In this context, the church is responsible for raising its voice and advocating for justice. The agrarian prophets of ancient Israel, particularly in the eighth century, offer a valuable model for evaluating the failures of ancient communities while also understanding the pain of the God of the Old Testament. The eighth-century prophets stood firmly against imperial ideologies and policies that created social injustice and ignored essential agroecological principles for sustaining justice and righteousness in society. Amid these failures, the prophets also offered a vision of hope, promising restoration if the community returned to agroecological principles.

Section - Five

Dalit and Tribal Readings

28

Voice of Dissent against the Whitewashed Walls Deciphering Divine Revelation for the Contemporary Indian Churches

Lydia Bujem

Introduction

Biblical studies and its implication in the contemporary Indian context have been enriched immensely through the contribution of Kondasingu Jesurathnam. Particularly, the Dalit-Bible interface has found its articulation in his thoughts and writings, which artistically embodied biblical reflections in concrete Dalit's living experiences. Out of the many hermeneutical principles employed by K. Jesurathnam, the "Voice of Dissent" is one such principle he explores in the course of Bible and Dalit interaction. Using this principle as a perspective, this article, as part of a *festschrift* honoring K. Jesurathnam, will attempt to present the prophetic ministry of Ezekiel as an appropriate example of the voice of dissent in its context. The location of Ezekiel's ministry amidst the overpowering nationalistic concerns of the prophets with their lack of truth telling to the people will be explored through the deliberation of Ezekiel 13:10-16. The exploration of Ezekiel as the dissenter will draw contemporary challenges for the Indian churches to revisit the important role of "Voice of Dissent" and as "Dissenters" in its prophetic ministry.

The Book of Ezekiel: A Brief Introduction

Ezekiel is identified as the son of Buzi (most probably the son of a priest). He was among the officials, princes, military valour, craftsmen, and smiths who were taken captive in 597 BCE by Nebuchadrezzar, the King of Babylon (2 Kgs. 24:14).[1] The location of Ezekiel's ministry is a matter of contention among scholars, as some suggest that his ministry began in Babylonia during the exile of 597 BCE. In contrast, others argue that Jerusalem is the place for Ezekiel's ministry. Still, a third consensus asserts that the ministry took place in both places, beginning in Jerusalem during 593 BCE, followed by the fall of Jerusalem and ministry in Babylonia in 587 BCE. Therefore, Ezekiel is seen to be active in Jerusalem till 597 BCE and then in Babylonia.[2]

Ezekiel's context can be traced to the Neo-Babylonian rise to power and the invasion of Judah in the 6th century BCE. It resulted in the fall of Jerusalem, the end of the independence of Judah and the exile of the people. Though there is a picture of the exiled people as not in a devastating state as imagined through texts such as Ezekiel 3:15; 8:1, 14:1; 20:1 29:5-6, there was anguish and pain experienced by the devastating experience of exile. The whole of Judah was deprived of its central elements in its theological system as all of a sudden, its land, the city, temple, monarchy and its status as the chosen people were taken away.[3] Economic conditions also deteriorated as many of the craftspeople were already in exile, and they were bound to pay tribute to Babylon. In the context of Ezekiel, the depressing political situation brought complications to the religious atmosphere of Judah. There was a loss of reverence for Yahweh as the people suffered defeat, resulting in exile. Also, Judah's existence as a vassal nation under Babylonians would have initiated the adoption of numerous aspects of the cult of more powerful nations (Ezek. 8:3; 5, 14).[4] This brief glimpse of Ezekiel and his times helps to place the further inquiry in chapter 13 in its concrete socio-political and religious milieu.

---

1 John B. Taylor, *Ezekiel: An Introduction and Commentary* (London: Inter-Varsity Press, 1969), 21.

2 This argument is presented in Paul M. Joyce, *Ezekiel: A Commentary* (New York: T&T Clark, 2007), 5-6.

3 Joyce, *Ezekiel: A Commentary*, 3-4.

4 George Arthur Buttrick, Walter Russell Bowie et.al., eds., "Lamentations, Ezekiel, Daniel, Twelve Prophets," Vol VI, *The Interpreter's Bible*(Nashville: Abingdon Press, 1956), 58.

Prophetic Dissent in Ezekiel 13:10-16: Revealing the Deception of False Prophets

Ezekiel 13 as a whole is divided into four parts, and they are: firstly, the denunciation of false prophets by God (vv. 1-7); secondly, the declaration of the judgement of God in two stages (vv. 8-12, 13-16), thirdly, the condemnation of false prophetesses (vv. 17-19) and lastly, God declaration of judgement (vv. 20-23).[5] Particularly, the pericope vv.10-16 consists of oracles against prophets who communicated empty visions to the people, promising peace when there could be none. Ezekiel and Jeremiah follow similar metahistorical frameworks, though they are set in different social conditions.[6] Ezekiel finds himself in a similar context to Jeremiah, where there is the rebuke of a false prophet, yet Ezekiel also has an independent line with features not found in Jeremiah.[7] Here, Ezekiel is seen to prophesy against the prophets who were proclaiming messages that were contrary to what was actually happening.

Prophetic Conflict: False and True Prophets (v. 10, 16)

The phrase in verse 10, "Saying Peace when there is no peace" (לֵאמֹר שָׁלוֹם- -וְאֵין שָׁלוֹם), highlights the false prophets' misleading assurances. The false prophets are an expression connoted not to a class of prophets but their falseness was expressed in their attitude as grasped from their concrete descriptions in the prophetic texts.[8] While only a few names of prophetic shadows besides Jeremiah and Ezekiel are known during the exilic period (Uriah and Hananiah Jer. 26: 20-23; 28: 1-17), there must have been a considerable number of people who claimed to be prophets, making it hard to distinguish the true from the false prophets.[9] These false prophets are seen as leading the people astray with their message of peace when there were moral and political lapses in the nation. They did not provoke the people for their sin and impending judgment but safely caressed them in their false security. Their words, visions, and revelations were a product of their own minds and empty fantasies, and they delivered their oracles for money. They

---

5 Lamar Eugene Cooper Sr., "Ezekiel," in *The New American Commentary*, Vol. 17, edited by E. Ray Clendenen, Kenneth A. Mathews and David S. Dockery (Broadman & Holman Publishers, 1994), 153.

6 Klaus Koch, *The Prophets: The Babylonian and Persian Period,* Vol. 2 (Philadelphia: Fortress Press, 1984), 85.

7 Walter Eichrodt, *Ezekiel: A Commentary,* translated by Coslett Quin (Bloomsbury Street London: SCM Press Ltd, 1970), 161.

8 J. Lindblom, *Prophecy in Ancient Israel* (Philadelphia: Fortress Press, 1965), 212.

9 Taylor, *Ezekiel*, 35.

were themselves held captives by their wickedness and immorality.[10] Though associating false prophets with cultic prophets linked to sanctuaries is a vague assumption and not a concrete criterion for defining false prophets, it does not completely deny that some false prophets could be associated with the sanctuary.[11] The false prophets were not a new phenomenon only during Ezekiel's time; rather it is also observed in Jeremiah's ministerial experience when he countered Hananiah, the prophet from Gibeon (Jer. 28). From such incidences, it can be assumed that the majority of the false prophets were cultic prophets as one of their major professional tasks were to proclaim the oracles of peacekeeping in mind the interest of the royal house and official policy. They used their power to narrate events in their favourable situation.[12] The people's attitude was the primary reason for such a prophecy. For instance, the people in exile were kept in Babylon in places out of cultivation to restore the economy of strips of land. The people experienced a comparatively less restricted environment as they were given a chance to manage their own affairs and worship their own God. Their way of life was not completely abrupt. However, the people's status was reduced to serfs without any right of appeal. Their treatment solely depended on the circumstances of the government, so in such a context, the people could not accept their situation for long and considered it a temporary arrangement. This attitude of the people was supported, therefore, by the promises from nationalistic prophets of victory.[13] Also, the presence of prophetic opponents of Ezekiel who prophesied about peace suggests support for Zedekiah's foreign policy. They preferred establishing a settlement with Egypt and Tyre and then choosing arms to win independence. Therefore, secret negotiations were deliberated as early as 594 between the small states of Palestine for an anti-Babylonian pact.[14] Such nationalistic interest might have been the shaper of the message of peace that the prophets were prophesying.

In the midst of this scenario, Ezekiel's prophecy is deemed as unequivocally negative as he reminds the listeners about their sins and forces them to hold responsibility for the present and coming disaster.[15] Duguid points the differences between Ezekiel and the "prophets of Israel" as the abuse of Yahweh. It is not the message of peace that classify them as false prophets, as particularly Ezekiel also uttered words of peace in chapters 34-

10 Lindblom, *Prophecy in Ancient Israel*, 213-214.

11 Lindblom, *Prophecy in Ancient Israel*, 217.

12 Lindblom, *Prophecy in Ancient Israel*, 215.

13 Eichrodt, *Ezekiel: A Commentary*, 4.

14 Eichrodt, *Ezekiel: A Commentary*, 4.

15 Andrew Mein, *Ezekiel and the Ethics of Exile* (Oxford: Oxford University Press, 2001), 84.

48, but here the contention is their claim that peace is there when peace was not a possibility and their claims of the words as from Yahweh.[16] Peace means a state of prosperity, all is well situation, which is a reflection of the faithfulness in covenant relationships and the people of Israel cannot have it when they have been unfaithful in their covenantal relationship with God and with fellow beings.[17] Ezekiel and his prophetic message was directed not against peace but against the deteriorating situation of the Israelites' society that makes the possibility of peace an arduous task. It directs to the people's attitude to be made right as it is responsible for peace to be established. It was a voice that did not succumb to the other echoing voices and craving of the prophetic message according to the whims of the people.

Plastering the Whitewashed Walls (vv. 10,11,13,14)

Two main terms appear in the phrase, "And he builds a wall, and they plaster it with whitewash" (וְהוּא בֹּנֶה חַיִץ, וְהִנָּם טָחִים אֹתוֹ תָּפֵל). Firstly, "טוּחַ" (*ṭûaḥ*), which the BDB defines as over-spread, over-lay, coating, which specifically in Ezekiel 13 is used to denote superficial coating of the wall to hide its weakness.[18] Secondly, the term "תָּפֵל" (*tāpēl*) has an etymological root that connotes something tasteless or unsavoury in relation to the Arab wor*ld kafala* or "spit" and "stink" and also, particularly as something worthless, foolish or wrong or better still as "whitewash."[19] This term is described in vv. 10,11,13,14, along with the other two instances in the biblical texts (Job 6:6; Lam 2:14), denoting the meaning of vacuity and nonsense.

The concept of vacuity also aligns with plastering a crumbling wall, which is an act of foolishness because the wall will eventually fall.[20] There is also an image of a shabbily built wall daubed with whitewash to give it an appearance of solidity. The image portrayed from such terminology implies a creation of an illusion and a deceptive portrayal of lies that is aimed at concealing the truth or fundamental authenticity.[21]

---

16 Ian M. Duguid, *Ezekiel and the Leaders of Israel*, VTS 56 (Leiden, New York, Köln: Brill, 1994), 95.

17 Millard C. Lind, "Ezekiel," in *Believers Church Commentary,* edited by Elmer A. Martens and Willard M. Swartley (Scottdale, Pennsylvania: Herlad Press, 1996), 109.

18 F.S. Brown and C. Briggs, *The Brown- Driver-Briggs Hebrew and English Lexicon* (Peabody, Massachusetts: Hendrickson Publishers, 2007), 376.

19 Marböck, "לָפַת" in *Theological Dictionary of the Old Testament* Vol. XV, edited by G. Johannes Botterweck and Helmer Ringgren, translated by David E. Green (Grand Rapids, Michigan: William B. Eerdmans Publishing Company, 1988), 743-744.

20 Francesco Arena, *Prophetic Conflicts in Jeremiah, Ezekiel and Micah* (Tübingen, Germany: Mohr Siebeck, 2020), 133.

21 Joseph Blenkinsopp, "Ezekiel," in *Interpretation: A Bible Commentary for Teaching and Preaching,* edited by James Luther Mays, Patrick D. Miller, Paul J. Achtemeier

Ezekiel compares the work of the false prophets to those who whitewash a wall to give it a sense of solidity, giving the people who live in the house a false sense of security.[22] The prophets are accused of being worthless because of their vision of vacuity and lying divination. Though their media of foretelling are legitimate, since they do not have Yahweh as the source of their oracles, they are destined to fail.[23] It can also mean "something lacking an essential ingredient," as, in this case, plaster had nothing to bind it, which, therefore, led to its disintegration, reflecting the prophets' groundless oracles. When these two terms are taken together, they can mean "whitewash with lies" or "coating over with worthless stuff," which is here referring to the prophecies of peace and prosperity.[24]

The prophets cover over or smear the wall the people have made or with the people's false hope and make it appear like an appropriate expectation of true faith through their deceitful promise of salvation. In doing so, they dodge any suggestion of moral commitment and propagate words of encouragement to the people who are distanced from God, not in a way to repent but to enjoy divine protection.[25] In this act of prophesying, there is no utterance of truth as the prophets failed to make known what is failing and conceal the reality with foolishness and false hope. Ezekiel is seen to target the prophets' lack of discernment and courage to tell the truth. He condemns them for establishing their prophecies on lies and masking up words to conceal such shaky foundation of their words. The truth that exposes the reality of the people's attitude, their sins and their accountability to their actions are sidelined in their prophecies, which Ezekiel boldly admonishes.

The Prophet Ezekiel as the Voice of Dissent

As Walter Brueggemann professed, "…peacemaking by God only happens, however, when there is truth-telling – costly, urgent and subversive."[26] The anxiety of the time of exile might have led to the formation of different classes of prophets who were all working to get a popular following and prophesied peace. Ezekiel rebuked such prophets and their message that the doom of Jerusalem would not come and that there was the hope for

---

(Louisville: John Knox Press, 1990), 70.

22 Schunck, "חוּט" in *Theological Dictionary of the Old Testament* Volume V, edited by G. Johannes Botterweck and Helmer Ringgren, translated by David E. Green (Grand Rapids, Michigan: William B. Eerdmans Publishing Company, 1988), 319.

23 Arena, *Prophetic Conflicts in Jeremiah, Ezekiel and Micah*, 145.

24 Marböck, "תָּפֵל" in *Theological Dictionary of the Old Testament*, 743-744.

25 Eichrodt, *Ezekiel: A Commentary*, 168.

26 Walter Brueggemann, "Truth-telling and Peacemaking. A Reflection on Ezekiel," *The Christian Century* (November 301988): 1096.

the speedy restoration of the exiled people.[27] The prophetic content of the so-called false prophets was messages of false assurance, a result of self-induced dreams and visions, that national well-being was assured with freedom from all kinds of invasion and its evils and the combined rebellion against those who oppressed.[28] Ezekiel, on the other hand, was committed to truth-telling before any false assurance of peace. His voice became the voice of dissent amidst the dominant echoes of false assurance of peace to the people. Ezekiel had to carry out his prophetic ministry in exile, where he was placed in a completely different position in comparison with his fellow people, who had a cold attitude towards his message in the matter of their national life.[29] The issue that Ezekiel encountered was not only regarding false hope in the form of peace messages but also the whitewashing of the sins of the people. It was the people's ignorance and unconfrontational attitude towards the sins they committed that resulted in their experiencing exile. The people were accused of going against the laws and defiling the sanctuary (Ezek. 5: 6,11). The people commit numerous civil and cultic sins as the prophet prophesied the destruction of altars and condemnation of the acts of violence, as noted particularly in chapters 5 and 6. The prophet's ecstatic vision tour further clarifies the horrendous sins committed by the people in chapter 8. There were practices of horrendous abomination, the performing of secret rituals in the temple, and wail cries in the temple gates for Tammuz. All of these presented a picture of the ongoing paganizing practices performed in the Jerusalem temple.[30] There is no truth telling of the situation of estrangement between the people and God. There is no recognition of the covenantal stipulations they have failed to adhere, leading to the destruction of the covenantal relationship of the people with God. The prophet Ezekiel, therefore, is relentless in his prophecies against the sins of the people and the false prophecies of the prophets. He did not mask the situation but employed creative rhetoric of everyday life to expose the unconfrontational attitude of the people towards their sins and their raptured relationship towards their covenant with God. Ezekiel, in doing so, did not just negate the scheme of false assurance and whitewashing of the depleting reality which surrounds them, but it was a protest of the truth, a voice of dissent founded on the truth of God.

27 Michael Fishbane, "Sin and Judgment in the Prophecies of Ezekiel," in *Interpreting the Prophets,* edited by James Luther Mays and Paul J. Achtemeier (Philadelphia: Fortress Press, 1987), 174.

28 Joseph Blenkinsopp, *A History of Prophecy in Israel* (Louisville, Kentucky: Westminster John Knox Press, 1996), 155.

29 Eichrodt, *Ezekiel*, 25.

30 Fishbane, "Sin and Judgment in the Prophecies of Ezekiel,"173.

Whitewashed Walls: Reflection in Indian Context

Dissent in any society is crucial, and even in the legal aspect, India as a country grants these rights to the citizens of India under the freedom of speech and expression. It is granted under article 19(1)(a) and is a philosophy, an opinion, or a feeling of disagreement or resistance against the dominant belief or policy that is imposed by the government, political party, or other body or a specific individual. It is not just an act of disagreement but leads further to fresh discussion.[31]In the act of voice of dissent, there is always an element of truth telling which might have been overlooked or suppressed by the discourses of the dominant voices.

This is true of the present situation of media in Indian society. The reality of Indian media corresponds with the whitewashed walls that the prophets during Ezekiel's times presented. Mainly concerning Modi's governance, the pliant journalists and media portray the leader as in charge of a flourishing democracy. The voice of dissent is suppressed suspiciously as there are pictures of the rosy state of affairs in Kashmir. However, civil liberties are breached under the government's manipulation. There is a claim made about minorities, especially Muslims, as "living happily and thriving" in India, a claim which is contrary to reality as there is regular violence documented against the community. There is no mention of Manipur, where the ethnic violence had torn apart the people and the ignorance of the government in addressing this issue.[32]The manner in which the media is controlled and the manipulation of the law to curb the space for dissent create conditions that make it difficult for an alternative narrative to even be generated.[33]In such a scenario, who is responsible for voicing out the truth? Who will expose the whitewashed lies and be the voice of dissent?

Voice of Dissent is not only about exposing the untold truths suppressed by the dominant voices of whitewashed lies. Truth telling is always accompanied by justice, as justice cannot be divorced from the truth.[34] As Ezekiel revealed, not only are there sins of the people, but there is also the need for repentance and restoration of the right relationship with God and with other fellow beings. Similarly, in the present religio-political scenario,

---

31 Naseema Pk and Anjum Saifi, "Right to Dissent under Freedom of Speech and Expression," *Journal of Indian Law Institute,* Vol. 66/1 (2024): 86.

32 Amrita Singh, "The Chilling of the Fourth Estate After 10 Years of Modi" *Foreign Policy.* https://foreignpolicy.com/2024/05/07/modi-media-journalists-freedom-press/ accessed on 23/08/2024.

33 Sharanya Hrishikesh & Vikas Pandey,"Narendra Modi's India: A decade of popularity and polarisation," BBC News, Delhi (17 May 2024)https://www.bbc.com/news/world-asia-india-69010109 accessed on 23/8/2024.

34 Kochurani Abraham, "Is this how Justice Ends?" *The New Guardian: A Christian Journal of Public Affairs* 5/3 (November 2022): 5

there cannot be any proclamation of truth without the demand for justice to be followed. The corruption in society, be it at secular or even ecclesiastical levels, is alarming. In churches, religious practises are commercialized, the glamorous lifestyles of the church leaders are promoted, and there is a greater focus on income generation to tap into resources for personal gains. Alongside, there is a constant covering up of gender-based discrimination and sexual exploitation in the church institutions itself, where manipulation of the truth takes place.[35]In such depleting reality, where do one's commitment with the truth stand? How can the voice of dissent articulate viable practical acts to be followed with truth telling?

Voice of Dissent Against the Whitewashed Walls: Practical Pointers for the Church

K. Jesurathnam considers dissent a crucial part of Dalit consciousness and identity. It attacks anything that negates life to the fullest and protests against the oppression meted to them. Dissent, therefore, is understood as a minority voice opposing the majority's opinion or dogma.[36] Similarly, Ezekiel and his prophetic ministry were no doubt a prophetic voice of dissent that stood for truth telling, which exposed the uncomfortable situation of the people owing to their sins. The truth shook the people out of their comfortable whitewashed spaces, a return to reality from their bubble of false peace. The prophetic admonition of Ezekiel, especially the so-called false prophets, for endorsing the false assurance with which the people console themselves imparts feasible contemporary actions that can be implemented. Some of them are as follows:

Revisit the Role of Religious Leaders

As a religious leader, Ezekiel calls for a significant shift in how religious leadership is understood and practiced in today's context. The role of religious leaders should go beyond providing comfort or maintaining the status quo; they must engage in a transformative prophetic ministry. As a role model, Ezekiel highlights the need for leaders willing to confront the deeper societal and spiritual challenges that plague their communities. This involves addressing the falsehoods and injustices often perpetuated by those in power, both within religious institutions and broader society. Religious leaders are, therefore, urged to become active agents of moral clarity and social justice, challenging false prophets and narratives while offering

35 Kochurani Abraham, "Is this how Justice Ends?" *The New Guardian: A Christian Journal of Public Affairs* 5/3 (November 2022): 6.

36 K. Jesurathnam, "Righteous Dissenters: Job and Dalits," *Bangalore Theological Forum* vol. XLII/1 (June 2010): 74.

guidance rooted in truth and ethical responsibility. This reimagined role has the potential to profoundly influence how religious institutions engage with their followers and with society at large, leading to a more authentic and justice-oriented expression of faith.

Reiterate Prophetic Ministry of the Church as Truth telling

There is no prophetic ministry without the confrontation of lies and proclamation of the truth. The essence of truth telling defines the prophetic ministry. Church exists as the visible prophetic voice that echoes the truth of God. This imperative of the church is gradually toning down as the church itself is falling short of living out the truth it should be proclaiming. Ezekiel, through its prophetic ministry, reminds the church as a messenger of God to find ways to articulate God's truth unapologetically. It is a call to live out the truth in the way of demolishing the whitewashed lies the church herself must have established and echo the same to the situation around it, even though it is a lonesome task.

The church is crucial to empowering marginalized voices where truth is suppressed and false narratives prevail. Like Ezekiel, who stood against the false prophets of his time, the church must challenge systems of oppression and advocate for justice. This involves actively engaging in truth-telling, ensuring the church does not become complicit in perpetuating falsehoods or ignoring the struggles of the marginalized. The church must create spaces for dissent, amplifying the voices of the oppressed and providing support and resources to those who speak out against injustice, ensuring their voices are not silenced by dominant powers.

Redefining Democratic Engagement of the Church

Democratic engagement does not require the church to interfere in every political matter but rather to maintain a vigilant consciousness against state schemes that manipulate public perception, much like the false prophets in Ezekiel's time. The church is called to critically oppose propaganda that distorts democratic processes and upholds the "whitewashed walls" of abuse and lies. This vigilance is essential in protecting the integrity of democracy. Ezekiel critiques how state power can be used to create and sustain false narratives, highlighting the dangers such manipulation poses to public trust and democratic principles. It calls on citizens and leaders to resist these tactics, asserting that dissent is not just a right but a fundamental democratic imperative. By protecting and encouraging dissenting voices, democracy ensures that injustices are exposed and power is held accountable. This redefinition of democratic engagement advocates for a more participatory and equitable society where all voices, especially those on the margins, are heard and respected.

Conclusion

Through the discourse of the paper, there is a recognition of the importance of "Dissent" in the prophetic ministry of the church. The focus that Ezekiel 13:10-16 challenges in the contemporary context is the need to be bold enough to stand against the currents of opposing influences that propagate whitewashed lies. It is a call to articulate an alternative imagination rooted in reality and the truth. The article, much indebted to K. Jesurathnam's work on the role of Dalits as righteous dissenters against the oppression meted out to them, acknowledges the ripples of creative academic pursuits that his works have acted as a catalyst to. The contribution of the voice of dissent among the many has helped tap into the courage, perspective and experience of the biblical text to articulate, empower and drive contextual transformative actions of the church and the oppressed communities in particular.

29

Deciphering the Divine Revelation in Isaiah 27
Reifying Dalit Apocalyptic Vision for Justice and Social Liberation

Gnanam David

Few scholars have made as profound an impact as KondasinguJesurathnam in biblical studies and Dalit theology. His pioneering work "Towards a Dalit Liberative Hermeneutics: Re-reading The Psalms of Lament"[37] has reshaped our understanding of the Bible and its intersection with the experiences of marginalized communities. Jesurathnam's approach emphasizes the need for a Dalit-context-specific reading of biblical texts, with clear goals and objectives to engage grassroots and subaltern communities. Inspired by Jesurathnam's academic mentorship, which guided my pursuit of a master's degree in Old Testament and research focused on minority issues, this article is a presentation as part of a festschrift in his honour. This article explores the apocalyptic imagery in Isaiah 27 and its resonance with Dalit Apocalyptic Thought. By examining symbols such as Leviathan and the vineyard within this framework, we honour Jesurathnam's legacy and contribute to the ongoing discourse on divine justice, social transformation, and the role of memory in shaping collective identity. This exploration underscores the enduring relevance of Jesurathnam's work, its implications for understanding systemic oppression, and the vision for a just future.

---

37 K. Jesurathnam, "Towards a Dalit Liberative Hermeneutics: Re-reading The Psalms of Lament,"*Bangalore Theological Forum*, Volume 34/1 (June 2002): 1-34.

Definition and Characteristics of Apocalyptic Literature

The terms "apocalypse," "apocalyptic," and "apocalypticism," while similar, have distinct meanings and are all derived from the Greek word ἀποκάλυψις (apokalypsis), meaning "revelation," typically given to an apocalyptic in a dream or vision.[38] The term "apocalypse" refers explicitly to a literary genre featuring divine revelations about the end of the world or cosmic judgment. In contrast, "apocalyptic literature" refers to writings that adopt the outlook of apocalypticism and portray its themes through vivid symbolic language.[39] Jesurathnam emphasizes the prophetic and imaginative power of apocalyptic literature, distinguishing it from other prophetic writings by its ability to capture the imagination. Characterized by vivid symbols and imagery, apocalyptic literature often portrays visions of disaster and destruction.[40] This genre goes beyond mere prediction; it evokes a robust emotional and imaginative response in its audience, inspiring hope or provoking action in the face of existential threats, crisis, and trauma.[41] Thus, apocalyptic literature refers to writings that are recognized as depicting apocalypse, apocalypticism, and apocalyptic eschatology through symbolic and imaginative language, as well as other related literature that shares similar features.[42]

Apocalyptic literature derives its imaginative and visionary power from the historical contexts in which it arises. Hanson defines "apocalyptic" as a genre focused on divine intervention in human history, often emerging during periods of crisis, such as those reflected in the postexilic prophecies of the late sixth century BC.[43] Cross further elaborates by describing Old Testament apocalyptic literature as a response to social worlds dominated by powerful empires. These texts serve as stories of resistance against cultural and religious assimilation imposed on minority communities by dominant

---

38 Mitchell G. Reddish, ed., *Apocalyptic Literature: A Reader* (Nashville: Abingdon Press, 1990), 19, 22.

39 Richard A. Taylor, *Interpreting Apocalyptic Literature: An Exegetical Handbook* (Grand Rapids: Kregel Publications, 2016), 34.

40 Kondasingu Jesurathnam, *Introduction to the Old Testament: A Dalit Liberation & Hermeneutical Perspective* (Delhi: Christian World Imprints, 2023), 308.

41 Kondasingu Jesurathnam, *Old Testament Theology: History, Issues, andPerspectives* (New Delhi: Christian World Imprints, 2016), 168.

42 Emmanuel Foster Asamoah, "Interpretation Approaches For Biblical Apocalyptic Literature: An Evaluation,"*ERATS,* Vol.6/4 (July 2020): 237. 236-242

43 Paul D. Hanson, *The Dawn of Apocalyptic: The Historical and Sociological Roots of Jewish Apocalyptic Eschatology* (Philadelphia: Fortress Press, 1975), 32-35, 209.

foreign powers, illustrating how dispersed communities expressed their hopes and fears through faith.[44]

Several unique features distinguish apocalyptic literature. Klaus Koch identified six standard features of the apocalyptic genre: Revelation, Dualism, Determinism, Eschatological Themes, Use of Symbolism and Imagery, and Otherworldly Mediators.[45] According to Hanson, these writings offer hope to threatened communities by revealing a transcendent, heavenly order communicated through a seer, which diminishes the significance of worldly powers. They focus on the end times, portraying divine intervention that transforms reality. Apocalyptic texts frequently use mythological symbols to depict the cosmic struggle between good and evil.[46] However, ancient texts vary in their use of these features. Some strongly exhibit apocalyptic characteristics, while others reflect them only partially. Thus, apocalyptic literature exists on a spectrum, with some texts fully embodying its characteristics while others do so to a lesser degree.[47]

Apocalyptic literature is a distinct genre characterized by its focus on divine revelations, often in response to periods of crisis. It uses vivid symbolism, dualism, and eschatological themes to inspire hope and resistance against oppressive powers. While not all apocalyptic texts display these features to the same degree, they collectively offer visionary responses to existential threats, blending prophecy with a powerful imaginative force.

Isaiah 27 as an Apocalyptic Tradition: Literary and Historical Perspectives

Isaiah 27 is a significant chapter in prophetic literature, recognized for its striking symbolism and contribution to the genre. It combines themes of judgment, renewal, and cosmic struggle, reflecting its complex historical context. The chapter's detailed imagery and emphasis on divine judgment and restoration correspond with fundamental aspects of apocalyptic literature. Examining its literary characteristics and historical context helps reveal Isaiah 27's role within the apocalyptic tradition.

Isaiah 27 as Apocalyptic Literary Genre

Isaiah 27 is often regarded as a prime example of apocalyptic literature within the Old Testament, particularly within what scholars term the "Isaiah Apocalypse" (Isaiah 24-27). Duhm was the first scholar to categorize Isaiah

44 Frank Moore Cross, *Canaanite Myth and Hebrew Epic: Essays in the History of the Religion of Israel* (Massachusetts: Harvard University Press, 1997), 343.

45 Klaus Koch, *The Rediscovery of Apocalyptic: A Polemical Work on a Neglected Area of Biblical Studies and Its Damaging Effects on Theology and Philosophy,* Studies in Biblical Theology 22 (London: SCM Press, 1972), 23-28.

46 Paul D. Hanson, *Old Testament Apocalyptic* (Nashville: Abingdon Press, 1987), 25- 34.

47 Taylor, *Interpreting Apocalyptic Literature*, 28.

24-27 as an apocalyptic genre,[48] noting the presence of cosmic upheavals and divine judgment similar to those in the book of Daniel.[49] Walter Brueggemann currently supports this view.[50] Otto Plöger was a pioneer in identifying parts of Isaiah 24-27 as "early apocalyptic,"[51] a view that Hanson later supported.[52] W. R. Millar characterizes these chapters as proto-apocalyptic, noting their prosodic style and themes.[53] Brian Doyle also designates these chapters as proto-apocalyptic,[54] citing elements such as the cataclysmic overthrow of the existing world order, the dualistic distinction between the end of the current age and history, the punishment of celestial beings, and the anticipated end of the period of evil.[55] However, significant debate exists over whether Isaiah 24-27 should be classified as apocalyptic due to differing definitions of the "apocalyptic" genre and the features of "apocalypse" among scholars. Based on J. J. Collins' definitions of apocalypse,[56] William D. Barker argues Isaiah 24-27 does not fit neatly into the apocalyptic genre. Collins' criteria include the presence of an otherworldly being conveying a message to a human recipient, which is absent in Isaiah 24-27. Instead, this text features a prophetic oracle delivered directly from the prophet to a group without involving supernatural intermediaries. Isaiah 24-27 also lacks references to a mystical or celestial world, typical in apocalyptic literature.[57]

---

48 Cited in Gary V. Smith, *An Exegeticaland Theological Exposition of Holy Scripture Isaiah 1-39,* The New American Commentary, Vol. 15A (Nashville: B&H Publishing Group, 2007),408.

49 Neil O. Skjoldal, "The Function of Isaiah 24-27,"*JETS* 36/2 (June 1993):164.

50 Walter Brueggemann, *Isaiah 1-39* (Louisville: Westminster John Knox Press, 1998), 188.

51 Otto Plöger, *Theocracy and Eschatology,* trans. S. Rudman (Oxford: Basil Blackwell, 1968), 53-78.

52 Hanson, *The Dawn of Apocalyptic*, 313-15.

53 William R. Millar, *Isaiah 24-27 and the Origin of Apocalyptic* (Montana: Scholars Press, 1976), 114.

54 Frederick J. Murphy observes that several prophetic texts written during and after the Babylonian exile share content features with the apocalypse, leading some scholars to refer to them as "proto-apocalyptic." Frederick J. Murphy, "Introducing to Apocalyptic Literature,"*The New Interpreter's Bible,* (Nashville: Abingdon Press, 1994), 2.

55 Brian Doyle, *The Apocalypse of Isaiah Metaphorically Speaking: A Study of the Use, Function, and Significance of Metaphors in Isaiah 24-27*, BETL 151 (Leuven: Leuven University Press, 2000), 24-27.

56 In a literary sense, John J. Collins defines "apocalypse" as a genre of revelatory literature characterized by a narrative framework in which a revelation is mediated by an otherworldly being to a human recipient. This genre focuses on eschatological salvation and explores supernatural realms. Collins, *Towards The Morphology of a Genre,* 1-19.

57 William D. Barker, *Isaiah's Kingship Polemic: An Exegetical Study in Isaiah 24-27* (Germany: Mohr Siebeck, 2014), 6-7.

In light of this debate, it is crucial to consider broader definitions of apocalyptic literature. Scholars like Adela Yarbro Collins[58] and Frank Moore Cross[59] advocate for a broader definition of the genre. They argue that thematic elements and socio-political contexts are crucial in defining apocalyptic literature. According to them, texts can be considered apocalyptic based on their content and themes, even without otherworldly mediators. Collins also notes that not all apocalyptic literature includes a heavenly journey, a feature often associated with the genre but relatively rare, suggesting a broader diversity within it.[60]

Despite lacking a heavenly mediator, Isaiah 27 can still be classified as apocalyptic when viewed through a broader lens. Scholars like Plöger and Hanson view Isaiah 24-27 as an early stage of apocalyptic eschatology, demonstrating early apocalyptic themes and motifs. The text's use of symbolic imagery, cosmic themes, and eschatological visions aligns with key aspects of the apocalyptic tradition. Specifically, the depiction of God's victory over Leviathan underscores themes of divine sovereignty and cosmic order, positioning Isaiah 27 within the proto-apocalyptic category and highlighting its role in the evolution of apocalyptic literature.

The Literary and Politico-Historical Context of Isaiah 27

Understanding Isaiah 27 within apocalyptic tradition requires consideration of its historical and literary context. Scholars like Paul Hanson suggest that the composition of Isaiah 27 could have originated relatively late in the sixth century, possibly during the temple controversy around 520 BC.[61] W. R. Millar dates the entire Isaiah Apocalypse, including Isaiah 27, to the latter half of the sixth century BC, during which the apocalyptic movement began to take shape. This movement reflected the profound theological and existential crises of the time.[62] Isaiah 27 is best understood within the broader historical and literary context of the late exile or immediate post-exile period, a time marked by the Babylonian exile and the subsequent hope for restoration.

The literary context of Isaiah 27 further supports its classification as apocalyptic literature. The chapter opens by depicting God's defeat of Leviathan, a sea monster symbolizing chaos and evil in ancient West Asian mythology. This motif parallels Babylonian myths, such as those

---

58 A. Y. Collins, "The Apocalypse: The Morphology of a Genre," In *Apocalypticism in the Mediterranean World and the Near East* (Cambridge University Press, 1984), 51-68.

59 Cross, *Canaanite Myth and Hebrew Epic*, 343-346.

60 Collins, *Towards The Morphology of a Genre,* 14.

61 Hanson, *The Dawn of Apocalyptic*, 314.

62 Millar, *Isaiah 24-27 and the Origin of Apocalyptic,* 120.

involving Tiamat, a primordial sea goddess representing chaos.[63] The use of cosmic imagery, symbolic narratives, and the vineyard song within the text interprets the suffering of the exilic and postexilic periods as part of a larger divine plan, offering hope and reassurance by framing current hardships as temporary and leading to ultimate divine intervention and restoration.[64]With its eschatological visions of destroying evil and establishing a new righteous order, this chapter's apocalyptic tone aligns with the broader themes of Isaiah 24-27.

Historically, Isaiah 27 is situated within the context of the Babylonian exile, a period when the people of Judah grappled with the destruction of Jerusalem and the temple and their dislocation from their homeland. The Babylonian exile (586-538 BC) significantly disrupted the Jewish people. The destruction of the First Temple and forced displacement led to a profound crisis of identity and faith. The Israelites in Babylon faced cultural and religious assimilation pressures and the loss of sovereignty and cultural dominance.[65] D. Johnson situates the setting of Isaiah 27 after the fall of Jerusalem and just before the fall of Babylon in 539 BC. He suggests that the nation experienced divine wrath through Babylon's conquest and needed to maintain faith and patience in exile until God would ultimately destroy Babylon.[66] The apocalyptic themes of divine retribution and restoration in Isaiah 27 mirror the context of subjugation and displacement.[67] The chapter addresses the challenges of the Babylonian exile and, though composed later in the postexilic period, offers a vision of hope and renewal, affirming divine justice and the promise of restoration.

Isaiah 27, viewed through the apocalyptic lens, vividly captures the genre's core features: cosmic imagery, symbolic language, and eschatological visions. The depiction of God's triumph over Leviathan symbolizes divine sovereignty and cosmic order, situating the text within proto-apocalyptic literature. Its use of extravagant language and emphasis on God's direct intervention in human affairs further solidifies its

---

63 John Day, *God's Conflict with the Dragon and the Sea* (Cambridge: Cambridge University Press, 1985), 10-12; S. Dalley, *Myths from Mesopotamia: Creation, the Flood, Gilgamesh, and Others* (Oxford University Press, 1989), 58-60.

64 Sweeney, *Isaiah 1-39*, 318-19.

65 Joseph Blenkinsopp, *Isaiah 1-39: A New Translation with Introduction and Commentary,* The Anchor Yale Bible 19 (London: Yale University Press, 2000), 348; S. W. Holloway, "The Babylonian Exile and Restoration," In *The Cambridge History of Judaism, Volume 1* (Cambridge University Press, 1992), 78-80.

66 Dan G. Johnson, *From Chaos to Restoration: An Integrative Reading of Isaiah 24-27* (Sheffield: JSOT Press, 1988), 69-70.

67 J. H. Walton, *Ancient Israelite Literature in Its Cultural Context* (Michigan: Zondervan, 2003), 121-23.

apocalyptic character. Reflecting the political, social, and religious crises of Babylonian domination, Isaiah 27 offers a powerful vision of divine justice and restoration, resonating with the socio-political struggles of the late sixth century BC.

Apocalyptic Visions and Dalit Resistance: Correspondence in Literature as Protest against Oppression

Apocalyptic literature often arises when a minority group witnesses the collapse of a well-ordered worldview that once defined their values and structured their universe, leading to chaos and uncertainty. While the majority continues to adhere to established norms, the apocalyptic minority perceives signs of impending destruction and offers a new vision of life's values.[68] Similarly, When the Aryans invaded India, the social order of the Dalits, along with their symbolic world and socio-cultural realms, collapsed.[69] Once rich with potential symbols and meaningful value systems, the Dalits were subjected to persistent discrimination and exclusion.[70] This "collapse of a well-ordered worldview" mirrors the breakdown of the caste system's moral legitimacy in the eyes of the Dalit community. For the Dalits, this caste system, which has long dictated societal values, is fundamentally unjust and oppressive. While the majority clings to entrenched norms, Dalits, as the apocalyptic minority, recognize the system's inherent flaws and foresee its inevitable downfall.

In response, Dalit literature emerges as a powerful oppositional force, rich in symbolism and unique in genre, embodying realistic, metaphysical, philosophical, and imaginative elements.[71] The relationship between literature and politics has been a strand in much of the discourse surrounding Dalit literature.[72] This literature serves as both a sociological and political record of Dalit struggles, capturing the lived experiences, resistance, and aspirations of the Dalit community.[73] Dalit literature stands as potent protest literature, envisioning a future grounded in liberation, equality, and justice and offering a profound critique of the systemic injustices perpetuated by the

68 Hanson, *The Dawn of Apocalyptic*, 2.

69 Anupama Rao, *The Caste Question: Dalits and the Politics of Modern India* (California: University of California Press, 2009), 12-15.

70 Clarinda Still, "Dalits in Neoliberal India: An Overview," in *Dalits in Neoliberal India* (New Delhi/London: Routledge, 2014), 1-43.

71 Thummapudi Bharathi, *A History of Telugu Dalit Literature* (Delhi: Kalpaz Publications, 2008), 9.

72 Ravi Shankar Kumar, "The Politics of Dalit Literature," edited by Joshil. K. Abraham, Judith Misrahi-Barak, in *Dalit Literatures inIndia* (London: Routledge, 2018), 49-52.

73 Judith Misrathi-Barak, K. Satyanarayana, & Nicole Thiara, ed., *Dalit Text: Aesthetics and Politics Re-imagined* (London: Routledge, 2020), 3.

caste system. The correspondence between apocalyptic and Dalit literature highlights a shared spirit of resistance against oppressive systems. Both forms of literature serve as powerful vehicles for envisioning a more just and equitable future, challenging the status quo, and inspiring transformative change.

Dalit Apocalyptic Thought: Theoretical and Contextual Framework

Dalit Apocalyptic Thought emerges as a robust framework that intersects the symbolic narratives of divine justice in apocalyptic literature with the resistance and aspirations found in Dalit literature. This approach draws on the vivid symbols of Biblical apocalyptic visions and Dalit symbolic resistance to deepen the understanding of God's solidarity with the oppressed. Sandi John connects Dalit and Biblical apocalyptic symbolism to deepen the knowledge of God's solidarity with the oppressed, emphasizing both traditions' shared ethos of protest and resistance. Dalit literature, with its apocalyptic symbolism,[74] engages in a creative dialogue with Biblical apocalyptic themes, focusing on justice, liberation, and the critique of dominant powers while envisioning a new, egalitarian society.[75] Both traditions use vivid symbols to offer hope amidst oppression—apocalyptic literature emphasizes resistance, divine sovereignty, and justice. In contrast, Dalit literature embodies a powerful protest and resistance against caste-based oppression.

In apocalyptic literature, the oppressed utilize creative visions and symbolism to challenge and transform oppressive systems. These symbolic visions empower the oppressed to counter the dominance of caste or colonial powers, even within limited politico-cultural space.[76] This approach allows marginalized groups, such as Dalits, to subvert caste and colonial dominance

---

74 Dalit literature is rich in symbolism, mirroring the protest and resistance seen in apocalyptic literature. It uses symbols like stars for martyrs, animals to depict dignity and oppression, and elements of nature to symbolize revolutionary struggles. Memory and martyrdom are central, challenging dominant narratives and commemorating the oppressed. Through everyday life symbols, Dalit literature expresses pain and suffering while embodying hope for liberation and justice, rooted in nature's and the community's resilience. Jesurathnam, *Introduction to the Old Testament*, 328-348.

75 Sandi John, "Re-deciphering Apocalyptic Symbolism as a mode of Protest and Resistance with special Reference to the book of Daniel," (D.Th Dissertation, Senate of Serampore University, 2020), 276-78. Jesurathnam cites Sandi John's work and notes his contribution towards apocalyptic thought and symbolism for Dalit liberation and emancipation. See, Jesurathnam, *Introduction to the Old Testament*, 328.

76 Maria Arul Raja, S. J, "A Castles World is Possible: Building Dalit Horizons from Apocalyptic Ethos," in *Dalit World-Biblical World an Encounter*, edited by Leonard Fernando, S.J. and James Massey (New Delhi: Centre for Dalit/Subaltern Studies and Vidyajyoti College of Theology, 2007), 174.

through symbolism like memory, martyrdom, and agricultural metaphors. Dalit Apocalyptic Thought employs these vivid symbols to critique existing power structures and advocate for radical societal change.[77]Jesurathnam's insights into Dalit Apocalyptic Thought underscore how this framework rejects traditional manifestations of the caste system, including the karmic justification and internalization of caste hierarchies. Instead, it envisions a new world order characterized by justice and equality.[78] This thought process critiques existing hegemonies and serves as a visionary call for a just social order.

By integrating historical insights, symbolic resistance, and a vision for radical transformation, Dalit Apocalyptic Thought provides both a critique of current injustices and a pathway for meaningful change.[79] It advocates for active resistance against caste oppression, drawing strength from a belief in divine justice. In particular, the symbolic language and vision of Isaiah 27 offer a template for reimagining social structures. This vision calls for a future where equality and dignity prevail, inspiring activism and social and political structures reconfiguring to pursue justice and equality. Through this framework, Dalit Apocalyptic Thought addresses the plight of marginalized groups and empowers them to envision and work towards a radically transformed and just society.

Deciphering the Divine Revelation in Isaiah 27: Dalit Apocalyptic Thought

Verse 1- Leviathan's Defeat: Symbolizing Liberation from Oppression

Isaiah 27:1 uses the apocalyptic imagery of "Leviathan" and the phrase "On that Day" to illustrate divine intervention and the promise of liberation from oppression.[80] In this context, the defeat of Leviathan symbolizes the downfall of oppressive powers, akin to Babylon, marking Yahweh's decisive action against tyranny and chaos.[81] The Leviathan, depicted as a monstrous sea serpent or dragon, symbolizes these oppressive forces.[82] Yahweh's victory over Leviathan, a creature of immense power and terror, metaphorically signifies the end of such oppressive regimes.

The destruction of Leviathan in Isaiah 27:1 is part of the polemic against Yamm and the establishment of Yahweh's cosmic kingship over

77 Jesurathnam, *Introduction to the Old Testament*, 328-348.

78 Jesurathnam, *Introduction to the Old Testament*, 328.

79 Jesurathnam, *Old Testament Theology*, 173.

80 Brevard S. Childs, *Isaiah* (Louisville, Westminster John Knox Press, 2001), 196.

81 Day, *God's Conflict with the Dragon and the Sea*,143.

82 Smith, *An Exegetical and Theological Exposition of Holy Scripture Isaiah 1-39*, 456.

every enemy.[83] This act of defeating Leviathan is part of a broader challenge against the ancient West Asian deities and the hierarchical systems that oppress marginalized communities. Leviathan, in this context, transcends its mythic origins to embody any system that perpetuates social and economic inequalities, including the caste system. Yahweh's victory over this formidable creature is a metaphor for the struggle against caste-based oppression, transforming a symbol of chaos into one of divine justice and liberation.

In Dalit Apocalyptic Thought, memory shapes collective identity and resistance. The apocalyptic imagery of Leviathan as a symbol of oppressive systems can be seen as a reflection of the historical trauma and collective memory of caste-based discrimination. The defeat of the Leviathan can thus be interpreted as a metaphor for the reclamation and transformation of historical memory, where the oppressive past is confronted and reinterpreted through the lens of divine justice and liberation. This interpretation aligns with the broader theme of liberation in Dalit Apocalyptic Thought, highlighting how apocalyptic symbols resonate with the struggle against systemic injustice and envisioning a redeemed future.

The serpent-like imagery of Leviathan mirrors the consuming and overwhelming nature of caste-based discrimination. Yahweh's triumph over such a creature signifies a radical overthrow of these oppressive systems, akin to the hoped-for dismantling of the caste system. For the Dalit community, this vision offers a potent metaphor for liberation. Leviathan, representing the oppressive caste system, becomes a symbol of the ultimate triumph of divine justice over social inequality and discrimination.

Dalit Apocalyptic Thought employs this animal imagery of Leviathan to critique and challenge existing social hierarchies, similar to how Isaiah 27 challenges Babylon. The defeat of Leviathan inspires resistance and envisions a world where justice and equality prevail. This apocalyptic vision, driven by the divine intervention symbolized by the sea serpent's defeat, offers hope and motivation for a future free from caste-based oppression.

Verses 2-6- The New Vineyard Song: Judgement to Restoration

These verses portray Israel as a vineyard flourishing under divine care,[84] despite its history of suffering and oppression during Babylonian captivity. Once nurtured by Yahweh, Israel was punished and exiled for turning to Baal. Now, like the Dalits yearning for divine deliverance, Israel seeks

83 William D. Barker, "Isaiah 24-27: Studies in A Cosmic Polemic,"*Tyndale* 60/2 (2009): 320.

84 Hans Wildberger, *Isaiah 13-27: A Continental Commentary,* Translated by Thomas H. Trapp (Minneapolis, Fortress Press, 1997), 449.

Yahweh's intervention. This text reinterprets the earlier vineyard song from Isaiah 5, which depicted an unfruitful vineyard destined for destruction due to God's anger. In Isaiah 27, however, Yahweh shifts from an angry judge to a diligent caretaker, moving the narrative from judgment to restoration.[85]

The vineyard, once marked for drought and barrenness, is now perpetually watered by God's care. The once unproductive land, symbolized by thorns and thistles, is transformed into a fruitful and well-tended garden. Thorns and thistles, previously symbols of sin's harsh consequences, are reimagined as divine tools to repel adversaries. The renewed vineyard, nourished by abundant rain, now yields a bountiful harvest.[86]The imagery of harvest and fruitfulness highlights a shift from desolation to abundance. Where there was once oppression and barrenness, there is now peace and prosperity. Yahweh's declaration, "I have no wrath," signals the end of divine anger and the dawn of a new era of growth and flourishing.[87] This transition from judgment to restoration sharply contrasts with previous narratives of punishment, offering a hopeful promise of future renewal with eschatological significance.

The vineyard song in Isaiah 27, depicting the shift from barrenness to abundance, parallels agricultural metaphors in Dalit literature that symbolize growth and renewal despite systemic oppression. This imagery reflects how divine restoration in Isaiah mirrors the aspirations for social and economic flourishing within Dalit communities. The flourishing vineyard in Isaiah represents a future where the marginalized are empowered and their potential fully realized. Isaiah 27:2-6 aligns with Dalit Apocalyptic Thought by rejecting the idea that suffering results from divine judgment or karma, instead framing oppression as the outcome of human-made injustices. The transformation from a barren to a flourishing vineyard emphasizes the necessity of addressing social injustices, such as caste oppression. Yahweh's promise of restoration underscores a divine mandate for justice, advocating for activism against systemic oppression.

Babylon, symbolizing oppressive power similar to the caste system in the Dalit context, faces a choice: reconcile with God and receive His protection or face destruction. The imagery of the restored Israel as a flourishing vineyard filled with abundant fruit parallels the Dalit vision of liberation and flourishing in a just society. Just as the exiles were once marginalized and deprived, Yahweh's promise of renewal and protection echoes the Dalit aspiration for divine justice and social equality.

---

85 Childs, *Isaiah*, 196.

86 Christopher R. Seitz, *Isaiah 1-39,* Interpretation: A Bible Commentary for Teaching and Preaching (Louisville: John Knox Press, 1993), 198.

87 Seitz, *Isaiah 1-39,* 198.

This new vineyard song symbolizes a transition from desolation to abundance and oppression to divine protection. It highlights Yahweh's power to renew and restore, offering hope and liberation for the oppressed. This imagery is a political and theological assertion, envisioning a future where divine justice prevails over human-imposed hierarchies. Just as Yahweh promises to restore Israel, there is a sacred promise of justice and equality for Dalits, presenting a powerful narrative of hope and transformation.

Verses 7-11-Slayer and the Slain: Sowing Seeds of Justice

The oracle opens with a sceptical question: "Has the slayer been slain as he slew others?" This question addresses Israel's enemies, whom Yahweh used to punish Israel but who have not yet faced retribution for their injustices. Yahweh's actions, which led to Israel's desolation and exile, reflect the political destruction by Assyria in 722 BC and Babylon in 587 BC[88] Despite enduring divine punishment, Israel held onto hope for the future. The promise of the destruction of pagan altars suggested that their punishment would be lifted and their relationship with Yahweh restored (v. 9).[89] This initial question becomes a powerful metaphor for the challenge against the caste-based social order. The "slayer" symbolizes the oppressive structures and individuals who perpetuate the caste system and marginalize Dalits. Thus, the question "Has the slayer been slain as he slew others?" mirrors the Dalit community's demand for accountability and justice against those who benefit from and maintain caste-based oppression. Yahweh's desolation of Israel parallels the systemic and historical injustices faced by Dalits. Just as Israel's exile was a result of their perceived sins, the marginalization of Dalits stems from a deeply entrenched social hierarchy. However, the promise of future hope after the destruction of pagan altars symbolizes the potential for Dalit liberation through the dismantling of oppressive systems and practices.

The mention of Jacob's name in verse 9 is a powerful statement of empowerment and self-determination, symbolizing a future where Jacob/Israel is destined to flourish. In the 6th century, the "Jacob-Israel" community was politically inactive and lacked self-determination, reflecting the absence of the Davidic kingdom and the dominance of Babylon.[90] It echoes the aspirations of the Dalit community, which, like the historically disenfranchised "Jacob-Israel," seeks political empowerment, social justice,

88 R. E. Clements, *Isaiah 1-39,* New Century Bible Commentary (London: Marshall, Morgan& Scott Ltd, 1980), 221.

89 Page H. Kelley, "Isaiah," in *The Broadman Bible Commentary: Proverbs - Isaiah* Vol 5, edited by Clifton J. Allen (Nashville: Broadman Press, 1971), 267-69.

90 John L. McKenzie, S. J, *Second Isaiah: Introduction, Translation, and Notes,* The Anchor Bible (New York: Doubleday & Company, Inc., 1968), xvii.

and cultural resurgence. The vision that "Jacob shall take root, and Israel will bloom" signifies a profound transformation and resurgence. It mirrors the Dalit aspiration for a just and equitable society where they can thrive and contribute meaningfully. The prophecy of the destruction of the fortified city, which foreshadows Babylon's downfall, parallels the anticipated dismantling of caste-based power structures. This imagery resonates deeply with the Dalit's hope for dismantling oppressive systems and the emergence of a new social order where they are recognized and empowered.

Verses 12-13- Gathering the Exiles: Bridging Isaiah's Vision with Dalit Dreams

These verses bring chapters 24-27 to a hopeful conclusion, portraying Yahweh as the harbinger of redemption, renewal, and Israel's return to Zion.[91] On "that day," Yahweh's actions—judgment of kings, destruction of Leviathan, restoration of Israel, expiation of guilt, and gathering of exiles—signal a divine reversal of fortunes.[92] The imagery of harvest and the trumpet call symbolize Yahweh's gathering of the exiled, separating the just from the unjust. The lack of reference to Babylon hints at a focus on the future, where the dispersed Israelites reunite in Jerusalem to worship Yahweh's holy mountain.[93]This absence might reflect that Jerusalem was under Babylonian control at the time. The author was addressing the Babylonian-captive Israelites, envisioning a time when, after Babylon's destruction, they would reunite in Jerusalem to confront the consequences and rebuild.[94]

Yahweh's judgment and the gathering of Israel mirror the Dalit struggle against systemic injustice and the aspiration for a transformative future. The ingathering of exiles symbolizes the unification and empowerment of the Dalit community, which has been marginalized and oppressed by the caste system. The harvest imagery—where good grain is separated from the chaff—reflects the hope for a future where the Dalit community, long treated as the discarded trash, is finally recognized for its inherent worth and dignity. The trumpet call acts as a divine summons for liberation and justice, calling the oppressed to reclaim their rightful place in society.

The omission of Babylon emphasizes a vision that transcends immediate oppressors, aligning with Dalit apocalyptic thought's focus on envisioning a just society where the marginalized can thrive. Just as the dispersed Israelites are expected to reunite in Jerusalem after Babylon's

91 Hanson, *The Dawn of Apocalyptic*, 23.

92 John D. W. Watts, *Isaiah 1-33,* Word Biblical Commentary, Vol 24 (Waco, TX: Word, 1985), 351.

93 Kelley, "Isaiah," 267-69.

94 Watts, *Isaiah 1-33,* 351.

fall, Dalits aspire to rebuild their community after the dismantling of caste-based oppression. As a symbol of divine justice and renewal, Jerusalem represents a new social order where once scattered and oppressed, Dalits come together in solidarity to celebrate their liberation and reclaim their spiritual and cultural heritage. Dalit apocalyptic thought envisions a future where the oppressed are gathered, redeemed, and restored to honour and dignity, overcoming the historical injustices inflicted by the caste system.

Reimagining Isaiah 27's Dalit Apocalyptic Thought as a Catalyst for Justice and Social Transformation

Reinterpreting Biblical Apocalyptic Narratives for Contemporary Justice Movements

Reinterpreting Isaiah 27 through Dalit Apocalyptic Thought reveals the transformative potential of biblical narratives for modern justice movements. Connecting the ancient text to the lived experiences of marginalized Dalit communities offers a powerful tool for social empowerment. The parallels drawn between the defeat of Leviathan and the dismantling of the caste system allow Dalits to see their struggles reflected in scripture, affirming that their fight for justice is part of a divine narrative. This approach challenges traditional interpretations that overlook the oppressed, instead centring their experiences and providing theological resources for advocacy. The victory of Yahweh over Leviathan serves as a symbol of hope, demonstrating that even the most formidable forces of oppression can be overcome through divine justice, thereby inspiring religious communities to engage with scripture in ways relevant to contemporary movements for equality.

Challenging Oppressive Structures and Advocating for Radical Social Transformation

Dalit Apocalyptic Thought, reimagining Isaiah 27's defeat of Leviathan as dismantling the caste system, calls for overthrowing oppressive structures, advocating for radical transformation rather than mere reform. This framework, rooted in apocalyptic visions of divine justice, argues that true justice can only be achieved by eradicating systems that perpetuate caste-based discrimination. The imagery of Leviathan's destruction resonates with those who have experienced the dehumanizing effects of the caste system, challenging the status quo and inspiring a prophetic imagination for a world free of hierarchical divisions. This theological perspective urges believers to participate actively in the struggle for justice, rejecting passive acceptance and embracing a commitment to social engagement as a divine mandate.

Integrating Dalit Apocalyptic Thought for Empowering Marginalized Communities Through Theological Reflection

Integrating Dalit Apocalyptic Thought with Isaiah 27 empowers marginalized communities by centring their experiences in theological reflection. This approach validates their struggles, offering a spiritual and moral framework that affirms their dignity and worth. By framing the fight for justice as part of a divine plan, it challenges dominant ideologies that have historically justified their marginalization. The vineyard imagery in Isaiah 27, depicting a transformation from desolation to abundance, serves as a metaphor for the potential flourishing of Dalit communities freed from the constraints of the caste system. This theological reflection becomes a source of strength, helping marginalized groups maintain hope and determination in the face of systemic oppression and urging the broader religious community to align their theology with the pursuit of justice.

Promoting a Vision of Collective Liberation and Social Renewal

When interpreted through Dalit Apocalyptic Thought, Isaiah 27's imagery, particularly the vineyard song and the gathering of exiles, promotes a vision of collective liberation and social renewal. This vision underscores the interconnectedness of individual and communal liberation, asserting that true justice requires freedom from oppression for all members of society. The transformation of the vineyard symbolizes the renewal and growth possible within Dalit communities, both physically and spiritually, when liberated from caste-based oppression. The gathering of exiles resonates with the Dalit experience of fragmentation and marginalization, calling for a reimagined society where the oppressed are central to the community's flourishing. This vision emphasizes the need for solidarity and collective action among marginalized groups to dismantle oppressive systems.

Affirming the Role of Divine Justice in Social Struggles

Dalit Apocalyptic Thought, combined with the eschatological themes in Isaiah 27, affirms divine justice as central to social struggles. It portrays God as an active participant in the fight against oppression, providing hope and assurance to those struggling for justice. The defeat of Leviathan, symbolizing the overthrow of oppressive systems, is not just a future hope but a present reality that calls believers to participate in the praxis of eradicating the caste system. This theological perspective encourages a proactive stance in pursuing social change, viewing it as a sacred duty aligned with God's will. By rejecting the notion that suffering and oppression are divinely ordained, this framework empowers believers to confront and dismantle human-made injustices. It offers confidence that their efforts are part of God's ultimate plan for a world where justice, equality, and dignity prevail.

To conclude, the analysis of Isaiah 27 within the framework of Dalit Apocalyptic Thought reveals a profound and layered interpretation of biblical imagery, reflecting both historical and contemporary struggles against oppression. The Leviathan's defeat and the vineyard's transformation serve as potent symbols of divine intervention and restoration, mirroring the aspirations for justice and liberation within Dalit communities. Jesurathnam's contribution to Dalit hermeneutics highlights the importance of engaging with biblical texts through a liberative and praxis-oriented lens. By retelling biblical texts to address contemporary issues and incorporating grassroots perspectives, Jesurathnam's work has profoundly influenced our understanding of apocalyptic thought and its application to real-world injustices. As we honour his scholarly contributions through this festschrift, it is clear that his insights into apocalyptic imagery—used to critique oppressive systems and envision a future of equity—continue to resonate deeply. Jesurathnam's work remains a guiding light, inspiring research focused on minority experiences and underscoring the crucial role of biblical scholarship in the pursuit of justice and liberation. This article extends his vision and scholarship, demonstrating the lasting impact of his thought on biblical exegesis and the quest for a more just world.

30

From Exile to Emancipation
Dalit Resonances in Psalm 137

Sam T. Rajkumar

Introduction

Psalm 137 is a hymn that captures the deep yearning of the Jewish people during their Babylonian exile. This psalm expresses a profound longing for Jerusalem and a vehement hatred for the city's enemies, using vivid and violent imagery. It reflects the emotional struggle of the Israelites, who, despite being forcibly displaced from their homeland, cling to their memory of Zion. The psalm symbolizes the endurance of faith and cultural identity amidst adversity, underscoring how integral faith, homeland, and memory are to one's identity. Psalm 137 has inspired numerous musical interpretations, resonating with the question, "How shall we sing the Lord's song in a strange land?" Its depiction of Babylon can symbolize any oppressive force or injustice, whether political, cultural, or spiritual. Initially resonating with early Anglo-Americans, the psalm's more recent history aligns it with antiracist and anticolonial movements.[95] It captures the universal human experience of longing for home and coping with displacement.

Rev. Dr. Kondasingu Jesurathnam is a significant figure in contextual biblical interpretation, emphasizing the importance of understanding biblical texts within their cultural, social, and historical contexts. He advocates for

95 David W. Stowe, "Babylon Revisited: Psalm 137 as American Protest Song," *Black Music Research Journal* 32/1 (Spring, 2012): 95-112.

a hermeneutical approach that transcends literal readings, encouraging scholars to engage with the Bible through their own contexts, including those of marginalized communities. Jesurathnam's work aligns with Dalit readings of biblical texts, which seek liberation, justice, and empowerment for marginalized communities. By applying contextual hermeneutics, he amplified the voices of Dalits, emphasizing their dignity and agency. Psalm 137, with its themes of exile, suffering, and longing, particularly resonates with Dalit experiences. Jesurathnam's approach highlights the psalm's relevance for those facing oppression, encouraging resistance against injustice while nurturing hope for transformation.

Dalit readings of Psalms employ hermeneutics of suspicion and retrieval. They challenge oppressive aspects of the text while recovering its liberative potential.[96] Psalm 137 expresses the suffering, resistance, and hope of the exiled Israelites in Babylon, mirroring the Dalits' own experiences of oppression, alienation, and loss of dignity.[97] The psalmist's lament over Jerusalem's destruction reflects the Dalits' enduring struggle under the caste system. The refusal to mock their faith parallels the Dalits' resistance to dehumanization.[98] The psalm's passionate love for Zion and commitment to homeland resonate with the Dalits' pride, resilience, and longing for justice.[99] Psalm 137 offers a message of hope and liberation, affirming marginalized communities' inherent worth, dignity, and rights. Its powerful imagery and emotive language provide a voice of lament and resistance, empowering the oppressed to tell their own stories of suffering and struggle.

Historical and Contextual Background of Psalm 137

Historical Context

Psalm 137 captures the grief and longing of the Jewish people during their Babylonian exile, which began after Jerusalem's destruction in 586 BCE. This psalm is a powerful lament, reflecting the deep emotional and spiritual crisis faced by the exiles, far from their homeland and sacred practices. Its structure includes an address, lament, contrasts, petition, double request,

96 Kondasingu Jesurathnam, "Towards a Dalit Liberative Hermeneutics: Re-reading The Psalms of Lament," *Bangalore Theological Forum* 34/ 1 (June, 2002): 1-34.

97 Adele Berlin, "Psalms and the Literature of Exile: Psalms 137, 44, 69, and 78," in *The Book of Psalms. Composition and Reception,* edited by Peter W. Flint and Patrick D. Miller (Leiden: Brill, 2005), 65-86.

98 John Mathew Attuvasseryil, "A Reading of the Psalms of Lament with a Dalit Focus," *Academia,* accessed 23 July 2024, https://www.academia.edu/29711534/A_Reading_of_the_Psalms_of_Lament_with_a_Dalit_Focus_John_Mathew_Attuvasseryil.

99 Daniel Simango, "A Comprehensive Reading of Psalm 137,"*Old Testament Essay* 31/1 (March, 2018): 217-242.

and a vow of praise, showcasing a range of emotions from sorrow and anger to a desire for retribution. Hans-Joachim Kraus suggests that Psalm 137 is the only psalm reliably dated to the exile period, highlighting its historical significance.[100]

The Babylonian exile marked the end of the First Temple period, with Jerusalem falling to the Babylonians under King Nebuchadnezzar. This led to the destruction of the city and Temple, the centre of Jewish worship, and the deportation of a large portion of the population to Babylon. The exiles experienced profound physical and spiritual displacement, grappling with the loss of their homeland, temple, and national identity under God's covenant.[101] The psalm captures the exiles' sorrow and longing for their lost city and spiritual centre. The act of weeping and hanging up their harps symbolizes their deep despair and alienation from their cultural practices in a hostile land.[102]

The psalm also reflects the mocking of the captors who demanded that the exiled Jews sing songs of Zion, highlighting the Babylonians' lack of understanding of these songs' significance. The exiles' response, "How shall we sing the Lord's song in a foreign land?" encapsulates their profound sense of loss and dislocation.[103] The latter part of Psalm 137 shifts from lament to a cry for vengeance against Babylon and Edom, reflecting the exiles' deep-seated anger and desire for justice.[104] The psalm concludes with a shocking expression of retribution against Babylonian children, revealing the complexities of the exiled community's emotions, encompassing both grief and a yearning for justice.

Psalm 137 is not just a historical document but a profound reflection of the human experience of loss, identity, and the struggle to maintain faith in adversity. Stripped of their homeland and sacred spaces, the exiles found themselves in a foreign land, dislocated from their cultural and spiritual practices. The psalmist's lament, "By the waters of Babylon, there we sat

---

100 John Ahn cites Hans-Joachim Kraus in "Psalm 137: Complex Communal Laments," *Journal of Biblical Literature* 127/2 (Summer, 2008): 267-289.

101 Scott Aniol, "The Historical Context of Psalm 137, "*Religious Affections,* accessed 23 July 2024, https://religiousaffections.org/articles/articles-on-culture/the-historical-context-of-psalm-137.

102 Joe Palekas, "Bashing Babies on Boulders? Making Sense of Psalm 137,"*The Washington Institute,* accessed 23 July 2024, https://washingtoninst.org/bashing-babies-on-boulders-making-sense-of-psalm-137.

103 Simango, "A Comprehensive Reading of Psalm 137…, 217-242.

104 David W. Stowe, *Song of Exile: The Enduring Mystery of Psalm 137* (New York: Oxford Academic, 2016), 119-178.

down and wept," captures their profound sorrow and disorientation.[105] The sense of loss transcended the physical destruction of their city and Temple. They mourned the loss of their spiritual connection to their homeland, community, and covenant relationship with God. This led to a deep existential crisis, compounded by the belief that their suffering was a consequence of their collective failings, such as idolatry and social injustice.[106]

Literary Structure and Themes

Psalm 137, with its complex structure and themes, is classified as a communal lament, a modified Zion psalm, and a malediction against Edom and Babylon. Its symmetrical structure features an introduction (verses 1-2) and a conclusion (verses 8-9), with a body (verses 3-7) centred around a nucleus (verses 4-6).[107] Psalm 137 employs various literary devices to convey its themes. Parallelism is evident in verses 5-6: "If I forget you, Jerusalem, may my right hand forget its skill. May my tongue cling to the roof of my mouth if I do not remember you." Personification is used in verse 6: "May my tongue cling to the roof of my mouth." The imprecation in verse 9: "Happy is the one who seizes your infants and dashes them against the rocks" adds a stark and shocking element. These literary elements effectively convey the depth of the Israelites' grief, their loyalty to Jerusalem, and their desire for justice against those who destroyed their city and temple.

The Dalit Experience: Contextual Parallels

Historical Context of Dalits in India

Dalits face lifelong discrimination, exclusion, and human rights violations due to their low rank in the caste system,[108] Leading to a collective struggle against caste-based oppression. Dalit literature is a crucial tool in this fight, providing a platform to express their lived experiences and counter the unrealistic portrayals by upper-caste writers through poems, stories,

105 Shayna Zamkanei, "Justice for Jews from Arab Countries and The Rebranding of The Jewish Refugee,"*International Journal of Middle East Studies* 48/3 (August, 2016): 511-530.

106 Rupen Das, "Migration and Displacement Woven into the Fabric of the Biblical Narrative," *Langham Publishing,* accessed 23 July 2024, https://langhamliterature.org/blog/migration-and-displacement-woven-into-the-fabric-of-the-biblical-narrative.

107 Morris Halle and John J. McCarthy, "The Metrical Structure of Psalm 137,"*Journal of Biblical Literature* 100/2 (June, 1981): 161-167.

108 "The Dalit: Born into a life of discrimination and stigma," *United Nations Human Rights,* accessed 23 July 2024, https://www.ohchr.org/en/stories/2021/04/dalit-born-life-discrimination-and-stigma.

folklore, dramas, and non-fiction.[109] Historically known as "untouchables," Dalits have endured severe discrimination and social exclusion within Hindu society. The term "Dalit," meaning "broken" or "oppressed," was popularized by social reformers like Jyotiba Phule and Bhimrao Ramji Ambedkar, a key leader in the Dalit rights movement and the architect of the Indian Constitution. The caste system, which categorizes people based on birth and occupation, places Dalits outside this hierarchy, denying them access to education, land, and basic human rights, thereby perpetuating poverty and exclusion.

The Indian Constitution of 1950 acknowledged Dalits' plight by designating them as Scheduled Castes, outlawing untouchability, and implementing affirmative action measures such as reserved seats in education and government.[110] Despite these legal protections, systemic oppression persists, manifesting in social ostracism, violence, and economic exploitation. The Untouchability (Offenses) Act of 1955 aimed to address such discrimination, but weak enforcement and slow societal change have limited its effectiveness.[111]

In recent decades, Dalit activism has resurged, focusing on asserting identity and rights. Movements have emerged to challenge historical narratives that marginalize Dalit experiences and to promote a collective Dalit identity. Scholars and activists emphasize the importance of Dalit historiography, documenting and analyzing Dalit experiences often overlooked in mainstream accounts.[112] Despite constitutional protections, caste-based violence against Dalits persists, manifesting in physical attacks, social exclusion, and denial of basic rights. Incidents like the killing of a Dalit child for drinking water from a pot meant for upper-caste teachers highlight

---

109 Aparna Vyas, "A Cultural Psychological Reading of Dalit Literature: A Case Study of *Joothan* by Om Prakash Valmiki,"*CASTE: A Global Journal on Social Exclusion* 1/2 (October, 2020): 157-168.

110 "Dalit," *Encyclopaedia Britannica*, accessed 23 July 2024, https://www.britannica.com/topic/Dalit.

111 Radhika Kapur, "Understanding the Historical Background of Dalits," *Academia,* accessed 23 July 2024, https://www.researchgate.net/publication/376140791_Understanding_the_Historical_Background_of_ Dalits.

112 Monika Browarczyk, "WE are Dalit History. Hindi Dalit Autobiographies and Their Engagements with India's Past and Present," *Cracow Indological Studies* XXIII/2 (February, 2021): 1-39.

the extreme discrimination they endure.[113]Social stigma discourages Dalits from participating in government schemes or accessing resources.[114]

While affirmative action policies have opened opportunities in government service and education, many areas of freedom remain limited.[115] Dalits continue to advocate for their rights, challenging the entrenched caste system, but the struggle for equality and justice is ongoing. They face significant social discrimination, including restrictions on movement, access to public spaces, and social interactions with upper castes.[116] Economic marginalization is also critical, with Dalits often confined to low-paying, unskilled labor, perpetuating poverty. Efforts to improve their economic status are frequently resisted by dominant caste groups.[117]

Political representation for Dalits has improved, but they remain underrepresented in decision-making processes, hindering effective advocacy for their rights. The struggle for cultural identity and empowerment is ongoing, with Dalits increasingly asserting their heritage and challenging dominant caste narratives, often facing backlash.[118] Dalit women face unique challenges that intersect with caste and gender discrimination, enduring violence and exploitation as both Dalits and women.[119] Addressing the contemporary issues facing Dalit communities requires a multifaceted approach, including social, economic, and political reforms, and a commitment to cultural recognition and empowerment.

Parallels with the Exilic Experience

The experiences of Dalits in India and the Israelites during their Babylonian exile share significant parallels in terms of oppression, identity, and the struggle for dignity. Both groups have faced systemic marginalization. The

---

113 Kavita Chowdhury, "Seven Decades After It Was Abolished, 'Untouchability' Continues to be Practiced in India,"*The Diplomat,* accessed 23 July 2024, https://thediplomat.com/2022/08/seven-decades-after-it-was-abolished-untouchability-continues-to-be-practiced-in-india.

114 Parameswar Mallik, "Understanding the Dalit Communities in Contemporary India: Prospects and Challenges," *International Journal of Social Science and Economic Research* 9/2 (February, 2024): 476-483.

115 Sagarika Ghose, "The Dalit in India," *Social Research* 70/1 (Spring, 2003): 83-109.

116 Paramjit S. Judge, "Between Exclusion and Exclusivity: Dalits in Contemporary India," *Polish Sociological Review* 2/178 (2012): 265-279.

117 Nutan Maurya, review of *Dalits in Contemporary India, Vol. I* by Nandu Ram, *Indian Anthropologist* 38/2 (July-December, 2008): 96-98.

118 Vivek Kumar, "Situating Dalits in Indian Sociology," *Sociological Bulletin* 54/3 (September-December, 2005): 514-532.

119 Meera Velayudhan, "linking radical traditions and the contemporary Dalit women's movement," *Feminist Review* 119 (July, 2018): 106-125.

Israelites, during the Babylonian exile were forcibly removed from their homeland, leading to significant psychological and social upheaval as they grappled with their faith and hoped for an eventual return.[120] Similarly, Dalits have been historically relegated to the lowest strata of the Indian caste system, enduring extensive social, economic, and political marginalization. This deeply entrenched oppression leads to a loss of dignity and identity similar to that experienced by the Israelites in exile.[121]

The exile led the Israelites to re-evaluate their identity and faith, maintaining cultural and religious practices in a foreign land. This period prompted theological reflection, emphasizing hope and restoration, as seen in the prophetic texts of the time.[122] For Dalits, the struggle for identity has been crucial. Some communities, like the Bene Ephraim in Andhra Pradesh, draw parallels between their status as Dalits and the historical plight of the Israelites, using these narratives to foster pride and belonging. This reinterpretation empowers Dalits by linking their struggles to a broader historical framework of oppression and resilience.

The publication of the Al-Yahudu Documents in 2014, which shed light on the lives of Judean exiles and West Semites in Babylonia, underscores these shared experiences. The Babylonian exile significantly impacted the Israelites' identity and religious practices.[123] Similarly, Dalits experience a metaphorical exile characterized by social and economic disenfranchisement, similar to the Israelites mourning their lost homeland.[124] Both contexts involve negotiating cultural boundaries and preserving distinctiveness. The Al-Yahudu Documents, alongside Hebrew Bible compositions, reveal hidden narratives of struggle and adaptation. Scholars like Benedict Anderson and Robin Cohen emphasize the diaspora's role in shaping collective identity and ancestral roots.[125]

---

120 Dalit Rom-Shiloni, "Exile in the Book of Isaiah," in *The Oxford Handbook of Isaiah,* edited by Lena-Sofia Tiemeyer (Oxford: Oxford University press, 2018), 295-313.

121 Vincent Manoharan John Packianathan, "Towards A Practical Dalit Theology: A Study on The Status and Relevance of Dalit Theology Among Grass Roots Dalit Christians in Their Struggle Against Caste Oppression," (PhD. Thesis, University of Burmingham, 2012).

122 Daniel Smith-Christopher, "Exile: History, Interpretation, and Theology," *St Andrews Encyclopaedia of Theology,* accessed 24 July 2024, https://www.saet.ac.uk/Christianity/ExileHistoryInterpretationandTheology.

123 Dalit Rom-Shiloni, "Psalm 44: The Powers of Protest," *The Catholic Biblical Quarterly* 70/4 (October, 2008): 683-698.

124 Leonard P. Mare, "Psalm 137: Exile - Not the Time for Singing the Lord's Song," *Old Testament Essays* 23/1 (2010): 116-128.

125 Dalit Rom-Shiloni, "The Untold Stories: Al-Yahūdu and or versus Hebrew Bible Babylonian Compositions,"*Die Welt des Orients* 47/1 (2017): 124-134.

Dalit theology emphasizes liberation from oppressive structures, advocating for the recognition of their humanity and rights, much like the Israelites' plea for divine intervention against their oppressors.[126] The longing for liberation is central to both the Dalit experience and Psalm 137. The psalmist's lamentation can be seen as a cry for deliverance from oppression, mirroring the Dalit aspiration for freedom from caste-based injustices. This longing is not merely for physical liberation but also for a restoration of identity and dignity, historically denied to them. The Dalit movement seeks to reclaim this lost identity, much like the Israelites' desire to return to Jerusalem and restore their cultural and spiritual heritage.[127]

A Dalit Hermeneutic Approach to Psalm 137

The Lament and Cry for Justice

Psalm 137 captures the lament and suffering of the exiled Israelites, resonating deeply with the experiences of marginalized communities like the Dalits in India. The psalm begins with the Israelites weeping by the rivers of Babylon as they remember Zion, symbolizing profound loss and collective trauma akin to the historical oppression faced by Dalits. The mocking demands from the Israelites' captors to sing songs of Zion reflect the humiliation and dehumanization experienced by oppressed groups, similar to the ridicule and social exclusion faced by Dalits under the caste system. The concluding verses, expressing a desire for retribution against the Babylonians, underscore the yearning for justice rather than a literal call for violence. This plea highlights the hope for dignity and restoration central to Dalit liberation theology.

Psalm 137 captures the sorrow of the Israelites in exile, mourning their homeland while enduring the scorn of their captors. This parallels the experiences of Dalits, who have faced systemic oppression and social exclusion for centuries. The psalm's depiction of collective grief and yearning for justice resonates with the Dalit community's ongoing fight against caste-based discrimination and violence.[128] The systemic injustices faced by Dalits, including violence, economic deprivation, and social ostracism, echo the feelings of despair in Psalm 137. The ongoing atrocities

126 Christopher Robert Conway, "Liberative Service: A Comparative Theological Reflection on Dalit Theology's Service and Swami Vivekananda's Seva," (PhD. Dissertation, Boston College, 2014).

127 KondasinguJesurathnam, "Contextual Reading of Psalm 22 with Special Reference to Indian Christian Dalit Interpretations," (PhD. Thesis, University of Edinburgh, 2006).

128 Shiv Visvanathan, "The Race for Caste: Prolegomena to the Durban Conference," *Economic and Political Weekly* 36/27 (July, 2001): 2512-2516.

against Dalits and their often-unheard pleas for justice parallel the Israelites' cries for recognition and vindication in a foreign land.[129]

This shared experience of being marginalized and dehumanized fosters solidarity among Dalit communities, who draw strength from their collective suffering. The concluding verses of Psalm 137 express a longing for justice and retribution, seen as a desire for the restoration of dignity. This theme is relevant to Dalit struggles, where the quest for justice involves reclaiming identity and humanity. The Dalit movement emphasizes the need for recognition and respect within the broader societal framework, advocating for historically denied rights.

Memory and Identity

Memory plays a crucial role in preserving identity and fostering resistance among oppressed communities. It maintains cultural identity and mobilizes collective action against oppression, helping communities see themselves as cohesive entities responsible for their past and future.[130] This sense of shared history strengthens communal bonds and provides a foundation for collective action. Collective memory shapes national consciousness and identity, framing perceptions of a community's past. By honouring their history, communities foster pride and resilience.[131] In postcolonial contexts, memory addresses the cultural and political legacies of colonialism, allowing communities to reclaim their narratives and resist erasure. This process is fundamental to postcolonial resistance and identity formation.[132]

Memory encompasses shared experiences, narratives, and histories that bind individuals together, fostering belonging and continuity. For example, in the Civil Rights Movement, collective memory serves as a nonviolent resistance tool, affirming the humanity of both oppressed and oppressor. This underscores the importance of community in shaping memory to support justice efforts.[133]

---

129 Ambrose Pinto, "Badanvalu: Emerging Dalit Paradigm,"*Economic and Political Weekly* 30/15 (April, 1995): 797-799.

130 James Booth, "Communities of Memory: On Identity, Memory, and Debt," *The American Political Science Review* 93/2 (June, 1999): 249-263.

131 Kazuya Fukuoka, review of *Power and the Past: Collective Memory and International Relations,* by Eric Langenbacher and Yossi Shain, *Georgetown Journal of International Affairs* 12/1 (Winter/Spring 2011): 142-148.

132 Michael Rothberg, "Remembering Back: Cultural Memory, Colonial Legacies, and Postcolonial Studies," in *The Oxford Handbook of Postcolonial Studies*, edited by Graham Huggan (Oxford: Oxford Academic,2013), 359-379.

133 Chijioke John Ojukwu, "Collective memory and nonviolent resistance," *Irenees,* accessed 6 August 2024, https://www.irenees.net/bdf_fiche-analyse-998_en.html.

Reclaiming and reconstructing memories of past injustices challenge dominant narratives and assert identity, particularly in oppressive systems like caste in India. However, commodifying these memories into mere knowledge can dilute their potential for fostering genuine community and belonging.[134] While memory can empower, it also risks legitimizing cycles of violence if not properly channelled. Memories from oppression can lead to distrust and bitterness, perpetuating violence rather than constructive social change. Thus, collective memory must be framed within reconciliation and mutual understanding to avoid reinforcing divisions.[135]

The remembrance of Zion by the Israelites and the cultural memory of Dalits in India highlight the significance of memory in shaping collective identity and mobilizing resistance. Zion represents a symbolic homeland for the Israelites, anchoring their identity and aspirations,[136] while Dalits reclaim their historical narratives and cultural heritage marginalized by dominant groups. Both groups use memory to foster resilience and resist oppression, emphasizing dignity and identity.[137]

Psalm 137 encapsulates the Israelites' remembrance of Zion, expressing deep sorrow and longing during their Babylonian exile. This psalm reflects their determination to keep the memory of Zion alive, resisting cultural assimilation and loss.[138] Similarly, Dalits' cultural memory, shaped by centuries of oppression, serves as a source of strength and resistance against the caste system, articulated through literature, music, and social movements.

Resistance and Hope

The psalm begins with a longing for Zion, symbolizing hope and a future return to their homeland. This hope acts as spiritual resistance, maintaining faith in adversity. The harsh imprecations also reflect a belief in divine justice, trusting that God will ultimately right the wrongs done to them.[139] The

134 Trevor Jeyaraj, "Memory, Identity, and Violence," *Inheritance,* accessed 7 August 2024, https://www.inheritancemag.com/stories/memory-identity-and-violence.

135 Christine M. Koggel, "Relational Remembering and Oppression,"*Hypatia* 29/2 (Spring, 2014): 493-508.

136 Avraham Sela and Alon Kadish, "Israeli and Palestinian Memories and Historical Narratives of the 1948 War - An Overview,"*Israel Studies* 21/1 (Spring, 2016): 1-26.

137 Mooli Brog, "Victims and Victors: Holocaust and Military Commemoration in Israel Collective Memory,"*Israel Studies* 8/3 (Fall, 2003): 65-99.

138 Josiah B. Andor, "PSALM 137: Israel's Remembrance of Zion in Exile,"*International Journal of Innovative Studies in Sociology and Humanities* 2/1 (January, 2017): 21-29.

139 Brandon Thomas Crowley, "Psalm 137: An Exegetical Study on The Psalm and its Relationship to Ancient Babylonia Exile of the Hebrew People," *Brandon Thomas Crowley,* accessed 7 August 2024, https://www.brandoncrowley.com/new-blog/2018/1/6/

repeated verb "remember" in verses 1, 6, and 7 emphasizes the community's determination to keep their suffering and oppression forefront.[140] Psalm 137 expresses the pain and anger of the Israelites in exile while reflecting their resistance to oppression and hope for justice and restoration. This mirrors the experiences of Dalits, who channel their historical grievances and injustices into resistance. Their anger is about reclaiming dignity and asserting rights, with collective memory and shared suffering serving as unifying forces. Vocalizing struggles and preserving history helps Dalits resist the erasure of their identity and culture.[141]

The longing for Zion in Psalm 137 parallels Dalits' aspiration for a society free from caste-based discrimination, sustaining their struggle with a vision for equality and justice. The trust in divine justice seen in Psalm 137 is mirrored in Dalits' spiritual resilience, with many movements drawing strength from faith, believing divine intervention will bring justice and liberation.[142] Dalit literature and life narratives often reflect themes of resistance and hope, critiquing dominant cultural narratives and asserting Dalit identity and agency. This literature serves as a powerful tool for social critique and transformation, much like the imprecations in Psalm 137.[143] By drawing parallels between the Israelites' experience and their own, Dalits find resilience and hope that fuel their ongoing struggle for liberation and justice

Theological Implications and Liberative Potential

Theology of Liberation

A Dalit reading of Psalm 137 reveals profound theological implications, especially around themes of suffering, exile, and the hope for justice. The psalm, which expresses the deep sorrow of the Israelites during the Babylonian captivity, resonates with the experiences of Dalit communities who have faced marginalization and oppression within India's caste system.

---

psalm-137-an-exegetical-study-on-the-psalm-and-its-relationship-to-ancient-babylonia-exile-of-the-jewish-people.

140 Eliana Ah Rum Ku, "Lament as Resistance and Rage: An Asian Woman Immigrant's Reading of Psalm 137 in the Light of Anti-Asian Hate Crimes of North America,"*Asian American Theological Forum,* accessed 7 August 2024, https://aatfweb.org/2021/06/03/lament-as-resistance-and-rage-an-asian-woman-immigrants-reading-of-psalm-137-in-the-light-of-anti-asian-hate-crimes-of-north-america.

141 John C. B. Webster, "Understanding the Modern Dalit Movement,"*Sociological Bulletin* 45/2 (September, 1996): 189-204.

142 Sreya Chatterjee, "Dialectics and Caste: Rethinking Dalit Life-Writings in the Vernacular, Comparing Dalit Narratives,"*Comparative Literature Studies* 53/2 (2016): 377-399.

143 Shweta Majumdar Adur and Anjana Narayan, "Stories of Dalit Diaspora: Migration, Life Narratives, And Caste in the Us,"*Biography* 40/1 (Winter, 2017): 244-264.

The psalm's lamentation acts as a protest against injustice, mirroring Dalits' own cries against caste-based discrimination and violence.

Psalm 137, through a Dalit lens, highlights shared experiences of lament and suffering, emphasizing God's solidarity with the oppressed. It invites Dalits to engage deeply with their faith, fostering a sense of identity and hope that transcends their current realities. The psalm becomes a source of empowerment, offering theological insights that resonate with the Dalit struggle for justice and liberation. The psalm gives voice to the pain of being uprooted from one's homeland, resonates with the struggles of oppressed peoples, and symbolizes the importance of holding onto cultural and spiritual foundations.[144]

A key aspect of Dalit theology is the portrayal of God as an ally of the oppressed. In Psalm 137, the Israelites' cries are seen as a plea for divine intervention, affirming that God is present with the suffering and marginalized. The psalm's imprecations against Babylon are viewed as assertions of hope for divine justice, paralleling Dalit aspirations for liberation.[145]The psalmist's desire for vengeance against Babylon, though controversial, recognizes the need to confront evil and oppression, resonating with marginalized groups seeking accountability for injustices.[146]

Divine Solidarity and Justice

The psalm illustrates the complex relationship between suffering and divine justice, with the psalmist invoking God's memory to assert trust in His commitment to right the wrongs committed against His people. Despite the harshness of the language, the psalm is fundamentally an expression of hope, intertwining the call for justice with the belief in God's eventual deliverance. The act of lamenting becomes a form of faith, acknowledging suffering while trusting in God's future intervention.

Psalm 137 serves as a powerful testament to divine solidarity with the oppressed, articulating the pain of exile, the longing for justice, and the hope for restoration. Through its vivid imagery and emotional depth, the psalm invites readers to engage with the complexities of suffering and faith, affirming that God hears the cries of the oppressed and will act in accordance with His promises. This psalm remains relevant, resonating with contemporary struggles for justice and the enduring hope for divine intervention in times of despair.

144 Jesurathnam, "Towards a Dalit Liberative Hermeneutics..., 1-34.

145 Stowe, *Song of Exile: The Enduring Mystery of Psalm 137*, ix-xiii.

146 Susan Gillingham, "Jewish and Christian Approaches to Suffering in the Reception of Psalm 137," *Old Testament Essays* 32/2 (2019): 444-463.

Implications for Contemporary Faith Communities

Psalm 137, with its themes of remembrance, lament, and longing for liberation, resonates deeply with the Dalit community's struggle against cultural erasure and marginalization. For Dalits, reclaiming their history and identity is crucial, and Psalm 137 serves as a powerful text that affirms their experiences and aspirations for justice. Despite its tone of sorrow and anger, the psalm offers a message of hope and resistance, affirming Dalit identity, dignity, and the pursuit of equality.By interpreting Psalm 137 through a Dalit hermeneutic, faith communities are encouraged to validate the experiences of marginalized groups, fostering a more inclusive and empathetic faith practice. This reading also inspires concrete actions towards social justice, challenging both Dalit and non-Dalit Christians to confront caste oppression and engage in liberative practices. The psalm's emotional depth, particularly its call for vengeance, symbolizes the Dalit demand for justice and recognition in a society that has historically marginalized them. In this way, Psalm 137 becomes a tool for empowering Dalit communities and promoting a more just and equitable society.[147]

The communal aspect of the psalm, where the collective memory and suffering of the Israelites are shared, mirrors the communal struggles of Dalits. This fosters a sense of solidarity and collective action within faith communities, urging them to stand with marginalized groups in their fight for justice.[148]In the pluralistic context of India, a Dalit reading of Psalm 137 can foster dialogue between different faith and cultural communities. This can promote mutual understanding and cooperation in addressing social injustices. By integrating these insights, contemporary faith communities can draw on the rich resources of Dalit theology to create a more just and compassionate society.

Engaging with contextual and liberative readings of the Bible provides profound insights, particularly when examined through the lens of marginalized communities. Indian biblical hermeneutics emphasizes the importance of interpretations that resonate with the specific cultural and social realities of the Indian context. This approach often incorporates perspectives from Latin America, Asia, and South Africa, drawing parallels with the experiences of the poor and oppressed.[149] Understanding the "world in front of the text" reveals how historical, social, and cultural contexts

---

147 Jesurathnam, "Towards a Dalit Liberative Hermeneutics…, 1-34.

148 Andrew Ronnevik, "Dalit Theology and Indian Christian History in Dialogue: Constructive and Practical Possibilities," Religions 12/ 180 (2021): 1-15.

149 Sam P. Mathew, "Indian Biblical Hermeneutics: Methods and Principles," *Neotestamentica*38/1 (2004): 100-126.

influence the reading and interpretation of biblical texts.[150] Liberationist readings of the Bible prioritize the experiences and struggles of marginalized communities and are often conducted in communal settings that encourage active involvement and the pursuit of justice.[151]

Considering the historical and contemporary influences on reading the Bible through the perspective of the poor necessitates critical dialogue with current lived experiences and the economic systems that perpetuate poverty and dispossession.[152] This perspective highlights the Bible as a multifaceted text, warranting interpretation not only in a literal sense but also within its broader historical and cultural contexts. Such readings illuminate the socio-political circumstances of the time, shedding light on the text's meanings and their implications for contemporary issues.[153] Furthermore, a comparative study of biblical and critical readings suggests that these approaches can mutually inform one another. Contextual readings often emphasize how historical and cultural contexts shape the text, while critical readings provide analytical tools that enhance understanding and interpretation.[154]

These frameworks often challenge traditional interpretations of the Bible, advocating for readings that liberate marginalized voices and perspectives. This approach encourages readers to question established norms and consider how the text can speak to issues of justice and equity today.[155] Engaging with the Bible through both theological and critical lenses allows for a richer understanding of its themes, particularly those related to liberation and social justice. This dual approach can foster a more inclusive reading that resonates with diverse communities and their struggles.[156]

---

150 Jeremy Punt, "Inhabiting the world in front of the text: the New Testament and reception studies,"*Neotestamentica*34/1 (2000): 207-224.

151 Christopher Rowland, "Liberationist Readings of the Bible," in *The New Cambridge History of the Bible*, edited by John Riches (Cambridge: Cambridge University Press, 2015), 249-260.

152 Jessica C. Williams and Susan M. Yelich Biniecki, "Historic and Contemporary Influences on Reading the Bible with the Poor: Liberation Theology and Poor People's Movements," *Dialogues in Social Justice* 6/1 (June, 2021): 50-64.

153 Brenda Deen Schildgen, "The Bible as Literature, History and Art," *Religion & Literature* 47/1 (Spring, 2015): 189-195.

154 Cheu-Jey Lee, "Biblical Reading and Critical Reading: How Do They Inform Each Other in Interpreting the Text?"*The Journal of Educational Thought* 49/2 (Spring, 2016): 144-159.

155 George Aichele, Peter Miscall and Richard Walsh, "An Elephant in the Room: Historical-Critical and Postmodern Interpretations of the Bible," *Journal of Biblical Literature* 128/2 (Summer, 2009): 383-404.

156 Shelley L. Birdsong and Serge Frolov, eds., *Partners with God: Theological and Critical Readings of the Bible in Honor of Marvin A. Sweeney* (California: Claremont Press, 2017), 1-12.

In today's context, solidarity with marginalized communities remains crucial. It involves standing against social structures responsible for global oppression and working towards transformative social ethics.[157] This ongoing need for solidarity is not just a theoretical concept but a practical necessity for achieving justice and liberation in our societies. Marginalized groups, such as the Criminal Tribes in colonial India and young people in society, face systemic oppression and barriers to achieving basic human capabilities. However, these marginalized communities, including girls and boys in South Asia, are actively challenging inequalities and advocating for social justice. To achieve true justice and liberation, it is crucial to engage in collective solidarity between marginalized groups. This involves acknowledging the historical context of marginalization,[158] recognizing the paradoxes in society's attempts to control or socialize marginalized individuals,[159] and ensuring that even the most marginalized people can attain the necessary thresholds for basic human capabilities.[160] By supporting the agency and activism of marginalized communities[161] and fostering a practice of collective solidarity,[162] we can work towards a more just and equitable society.

Conclusion

The Dalit reading of Psalm 137 offers a transformative approach to biblical interpretation, especially in contexts of oppression and marginalization. By highlighting themes of suffering, justice, and resistance, this reading reinterprets the psalm through the lived experiences of Dalits in India, challenging traditional interpretations. Psalm 137 becomes a powerful voice for those who have faced dehumanization and loss, resonating deeply with the Dalit struggle against caste discrimination.This interpretation raises complex ethical questions, particularly regarding the imprecatory verses that call for retributive justice, prompting reflection on the nature of divine justice and the ethics of anger in seeking justice. The focus on memory as a tool of resistance parallels Dalit efforts to reclaim their identity, urging faith

157 Sharon D. Welch, *Communities of Resistance and Solidarity: A Feminist Theology of Liberation* (Eugene: Wipf and Stock Publishers, 2017).

158 P. S. Narasimha, "Justice for the Marginalized in a Constitutional Democracy," *CASTE: A Global Journal on Social Exclusion* 5/2 (April, 2024): 302-313.

159 Annette Coburn And Sinéad Gormally, "Social Justice and Equality," *Counterpoints* 483(2017): 51-76.

160 Ann Ferguson, "Feminist Paradigms of Solidarity and Justice," *Philosophical Topics* 37/2(Fall, 2009): 161-177.

161 Claire O'Kane, "Marginalized Children as Social Actors for Social Justice in South Asia," *The British Journal of Social Work* 32/6 (September, 2002): 697-710.

162 Anthony J. Knowles, "Universal Basic Income, Social Justice, and Marginality," *Social Justice*48/4 (2021): 1-32.

communities to support marginalized voices.Ultimately, a Dalit reading calls faith communities to move from reflection to active engagement in social justice, reimagining theological discourse to prioritize the marginalized and translate faith into action. The Dalit interpretation enriches our understanding of Psalm 137, demonstrating the enduring relevance of biblical texts in inspiring contemporary movements for liberation and justice.

31

Divine Revelation and Marginalization A Liberative and Social Identity Reading of 1QHa XII:6-10 in Dialogue with Dalit Struggles

Mede Jeevan Sagar

Introduction

The Dead Sea Scrolls, discovered in the mid-20th century, provide valuable insights into late second-temple Judaism's religious and social settings. The Hodayot (Thanksgiving Hymns) from Qumran offer a unique window into the spiritual experiences and social dynamics of a marginalized community in the Second Temple period. This paper focuses on a specific passage, 1QHa XII: 6-10, examining it through textual analysis, Social Identity Theory, and Liberative Hermeneutics. The Hodayot, with their obscure mixture of personal lamentation and communal expression, present a complex representation of a group transforming its identity in the face of observed opposition and divine favour. 1QHa XII: 6-10, in particular, provides a dreadful account of rejection and exile juxtaposed with assertions of divine justification. This tension between human marginalization and divine approval raises fascinating questions about the nature of religious identity and the experience of the sacred in the context of social exclusion. By applying Social Identity Theory to this ancient text, this study aims to uncover the group dynamics at play in the Qumran community's self-understanding. How did the experience of marginalization shape their collective identity? How did their perception of divine favour serve to reinforce group boundaries and maintain a positive self-image despite external rejection?

Furthermore, this study employs a Liberative Hermeneutical approach to bridge the ancient context with contemporary experiences of marginalization, particularly those of Dalit communities in India. This comparative analysis prompts us to consider the following question: How can the experiences of the Qumran community, as reflected in 1QHa XII: 6-10, inform our understanding of the divine revelations among Dalit communities today? What insights does this text offer about contemporary struggles for dignity and recognition? Through a multidimensional analysis of 1QHa XII: 6-10, this paper aims to demonstrate the enduring relevance of ancient texts in addressing contemporary issues of social justice and religious identity. By examining the interplay between textual analysis, social identity theory, and Liberative hermeneutics, this study aims to contribute to ongoing discussions about the role of sacred texts in empowering marginalized communities and challenging dominant narratives of social exclusion.

1. Methodology

This study employs a multifaceted approach to analyze 1QHa XII: 5-10, combining textual analysis with social identity theory to develop a Liberative reading applicable to Dalit communities. The methodology comprises three main components:

Textual and Historical Analysis

The researcher begins by closely reading the text and examining its linguistic features, structure, and literary devices. The works of scholars such as Holm-Nielsen, Tanzer, and Kittel, who have contributed to understanding the Hodayot genre and function, inform such analysis.[163] The researcher then considers the historical context of the Qumran community by drawing on textual evidence to situate the passage within its Sitz im Leben.

Social Identity Theory Application

The Researcher will interpret the text using the social identity theory developed by Henri Tajfel and colleagues.[164] This theoretical framework allows us to explore how the Qumran community constructed and maintained

163 Hans Bardtke, 'Considérations Sur Les Cantiques De Qumrân', *Revue Biblique* 63, no. 2 (1956): 220–33; Sarah Jean Tanzer, 'The Sages at Qumran: Wisdom in the Hodayot' (Ph.D, Harvard, Harvard University, 2000); Svend Holm-Nielsen, 'The Importance of Late Jewish Psalmody for the Understanding of Old Testament Psalmodic Traditions', *Studia Theologica* 13 (1960): 1–53.

164 Henri Tajfel, *Differentiation Between Social Groups: Studies in the Social Psychology of Intergroup Relations* (London: Academic Press, 1978); J.C Turner, 'Social Categorization

its group identity concerning outsiders. The researcher focuses on concepts such as

i. The continuum between personal and social identities
ii. The role of positive distinctiveness in group formation
iii. Strategies to maintain positive social identity in low-status groups

This approach is particularly relevant, given the acknowledged group-oriented nature of ancient Mediterranean cultures and the competitive nature of religious groups.[165]

Liberative Hermeneutics

Building on textual and social identity analyses, we develop a Liberative reading of texts. This approach parallels the experiences of marginalization and divine revelation in the Qumran and contemporary Dalit communities. The research then examines how one can interpret the text's themes of rejection, divine approval, and possession of special knowledge in light of Dalit experiences.

2. Analyzing the 1QHa XII: 6-10

2.1. Text and Translation[166]

English	Hebrew Qumran Sectarian Manuscript
6. *Blank* I thank you, O Lord, For you have enlightened my face according to your covenant and [… …]	6.[··] [[ ]] אודכה אדוני כיא֯ האירותה פני לבריתכה ומ°[··][167]
7. [with all my heart] I seek you and like a sure dawn, with [perf]ect light you have shone for me.	7. [··] אדורשכה וכשחר נכון לאו֯ר[תו]ם֯ הופעתה לי. והמה עמכה [יתעו] .

and the Self-Concept: A Social-Cognitive Theory of Group Behavior', in *Advances in Group Processes: A Research Annual.*, vol. 2 (Greenwich: JAI Press, 1985).

165 Jutta Jokiranta, 'Social Identity Approach: Identity-Constructing Elements in the Psalms Pesher', in *Defining Identities: We, You, and the Other in the Dead Sea Scrolls: Proceedings of the Fifth Meeting of the IOQS in Gröningen*, ed. Florentino García Martínez and Mladen Popović, vol. 70, Studies on the Texts of the Desert of Judah (Leiden: Brill, 2008), 91–97.

166 The author will translate the text unless indicated otherwise.

167 J. Licht, 'The Doctrine of the Thanksgiving Scroll', Israel Exploration J*ournal 6, no. 1 (1956): 91.*

8. But they, your people [...] (8) [for the wor]ds they made smooth for themand spokesmen of deceit caused them to err;and they are brought down without understandingfor [they carry out]	8. כי[א] דברים החליקו למו ומליצי רמיה התעום וילבטו בלא בינה. כיא[··]
9. in foolishness their deeds. For I have been rejected by themnor do they esteem me when you exert your might through me.	9. בהולל מעשיהם כי נמאסו למו. ולא יחשבוני בהגבירכה בי כיא ידיחני מארצי
10. For one drives me from my land. like a bird from its nestand all my friends and my relatives have been driven away from me and they esteem me like a broken vessel.	10. כצפור מקנה. וכול רעי ומודעי נדחו ממני ויחשבוני לכלי אובד . והמה מליצי

2.2. Sitz-Im Leben

The debate over the *Sitz im Leben* (setting in life) of the Hodayot scrolls, particularly 1QHa XII:5-10, has been a subject of scholarly discussion for decades. While some scholars[168] argue for purely individual and non-liturgical use, compelling evidence suggests that this passage may have had a communal and possibly liturgical function within the Qumran community. The passage contains language that tells a communal context. For instance, the phrase "*All those who gathered in thy Covenant enquire of me*" (1QHa XII 24–25 [IV 23–24]) implies a group setting in which the speaker addresses or represents the community.The terminology used in this passage bears similarities to that found in the Rule of the Community (1QS), a text known to have played a significant role in community life. This linguistic parallel suggests that 1QHa XII:5-10 may have had a comparable function.While not negating a possible liturgical use, wisdom elements in the Hodayot, as noted by scholars like Tanzer, could indicate an instructional role.[169] It aligns with Holm-Nielsen's argument that a balanced distinction should be made between learning and worship in the community's practices.[170]Kuhn's

168 Bardtke, 'Considérations Sur Les Cantiques De Qumrân', 220–33; Tanzer, 'The Sages at Qumran: Wisdom in the Hodayot'; Holm-Nielsen, 'The Importance of Late Jewish Psalmody for the Understanding of Old Testament Psalmodic Traditions', 1–53.

169 Tanzer, 'The Sages at Qumran: Wisdom in the Hodayot'.

170 Svend Holm-Nielsen, *Hodayot: Psalms from Qumran* (Aarhus: Universitetsforlaget I Aarhus, 1960), 328,344.

identification of "*soteriological confession*" and "*meditation on misery*" as crucial elements of the Community Hymns suggests a connection to the annual covenant renewal ceremony.[171] If 1QHa XII:5-10 contains these elements, it strengthens the case for its use in communal rituals.Although Kittel's analysis focused on other passages, her work demonstrates the importance of poetic structure in understanding the functions of these texts.[172] Closely examining the poetic features of 1QHa XII:5-10 can reveal similarities to other compositions believed to have undergone communal or liturgical use.However, it is essential to note that this interpretation is not without challenges. As Nitzan highlights, many liturgical texts from Qumran include explicit titlesthat indicate their functions.[173] The absence of such markers in 1QHa XII:5-10 could suggest a non-liturgical use.The passage's first-person singular "*I*" could be interpreted as reflecting an individual's experience rather than a communal voice, although this remains a point of debate among scholars.In conclusion, while the exact *Sitz im Leben* of 1QHa XII:5-10 remains open to interpretation, the evidence suggests that it likely served to bridge individual reflection and communal practice within the Qumran community. Its language, thematic content, and structural similarities to other essential community texts indicate that it may have played a role in communal instruction, meditation, and possibly liturgical practices rather than being solely used for private purposes.

Textual Analysis

The passage opens with "*But they, your people*," immediately establishing a communal context. It aligns with Holm-Nielsen's argument that the Hodayot has a function in community life.[174] The text then introduces the concept of "*spokesmen of deceit*" (מליצי רמיה), a term that Holm-Nielsen suggests indicates someone with unique insight, possibly referring to rival law teachers.[175] The phrase "*words they made smooth*" (החליקו) may be an allusion to Isaiah 30:10, which links these false teachers to biblical critiques

171 Heinz Wolfgang Kuhn, *Enderwartung Und Gegenwärtiges Heil. Untersuchungen Zu Den Gemeindeliedern von Qumran, Mit Einem Anhang Über Eschatologie Und Gegenwart in Der Verkündigung Jesu*, Studien Zur Umwelt Des Neuen Testaments 4 (Göttingen: Vandenhoeck & Ruprecht, 1966), 80–85.

172 Bonnie Pedrotti Kittel, *The Hymns of Qumran: Translation and Commentary* (Chicago: Scholars Press, 1981), 78.

173 Bilhah Nitzan, *Qumran Prayer and Religious Poetry*, trans. Jonathan Chipman (Leiden: Brill Academic Pub, 1994), 321–26.

174 Holm-Nielsen, *Hodayot*, 80, n.1.

175 Holm-Nielsen, *Hodayot*, 35, n.29.

of false prophets.[176] This portrayal of deceptive leaders as misleading the community sets up a stark contrast between the speaker and these adversaries.

A central theme in this passage is the dichotomy between knowledge and foolishness. The text emphasizes that the people are "*brought down without understanding*" (בלוא בינה) and perform their deeds "*in foolishness*" (בסכלות). This contrast between wisdom and folly is a recurring motif in the Hodayot, reflecting a vital aspect of the sectarian worldview.[177] The implication is that the speaker possesses proper understanding, while those led astray by the "spokesmen of deceit" lack this crucial insight.

The speaker claims to have been "*rejected*" by the community, creating a sense of isolation and persecution. However, divine approval nullifies human rejection, expressed through the phrase "*when you exert your might through me*" (בהגבירכה בי). This juxtaposition of human rejection and divine validation is a common motif in sectarian literature, reinforcing the speaker's authority and righteousness despite opposition.[178] Further, it suggests that the divine sanctioned the speaker's teachings or leadership, though rejected by some.

The text employs powerful imagery of exile and abandonment. The metaphor "like a bird from its nest" introduces the motif of exile, which could be linked to later allusions to Ezekiel in the composition, suggesting a typological interpretation of the speaker's experience.[179] It followed with clear allusions to Psalm 31:11-12 in the phrases "all my friends and my relatives have been driven away from me" and "like a broken vessel".[180] These biblical echoes align the speaker's experience with that of the

176 According to Isaiah 42:6, God has given Israel as a covenant to the people and a light to the nations. Psalms 19:8 and Ecclesiastes 8:1 echo the same idea. Holm-Nielsen suggests that the expression may be understood in analogy with the shining of God's countenance, as mentioned in Numbers 6:25, Psalms 31:17 and 67:2. The priestly benediction appears to have been significant to the community, as evidenced in 1QS II 2. SeeHolm-Nielsen, *Hodayot*, 80.

177 Carol A. Newsom, *The Self as Symbolic Space: Constructing Identity and Community at Qumran* (Atlanta: Society of Biblical Literature, 2007), 319, 322–23.

178 Julie Hughes, *Scriptural Allusions and Exegesis in the Hodayot*, vol. 59, Studies on the Texts of the Desert of Judah (Leiden: Brill, 2006), 109.

179 Proverbs 27:8, Isaiah 16:2, and Psalm 11:1 use similar expressions to describe a state of misery or suffering. While some scholars have interpreted these passages as references to the author's exile or persecution, the context of these verses does not explicitly support such a specific interpretation. These phrases are more likely part of a broader literary tradition in the Old Testament, used to convey feelings of distress and helplessness. See Holm-Nielsen, *Hodayot*, 81, 307.

180 Hughes, *Scriptural Allusions and Exegesis in the Hodayot*, 59:108.

righteous sufferer in the Psalms, thus lending scriptural authority to the speaker's lamentation.

The strong contrast between the speaker and the "*spokesmen of deceit*" and the themes of rejection and divine approval reinforces a sectarian worldview. The composition skilfullyintertwines personal laments, communal concerns, and theological assertions. This complex interplay reflects Hodayot as texts that function on individual and communal levels. The rhetorical purpose appears to be twofold: to validate the speaker's authority within the community and to reinforce the community's sense of possessing unique, divinely granted insight in a world of deception and foolishness.

3. Social Identity in the Context of Divine Revelation and Oppression

The passage under consideration reflects the lamentation of an individual rejected and ostracised by their community. It is a profoundly personal account of exclusion, in which the speaker describes being cast out "like a bird from its nest" and esteemed no more than a "*broken vessel.*"[181] This text is part of a broader tradition in the Hodayat Psalm that highlights the suffering of marginalized individuals in their social or religious communities.[182] The rejection experienced by the speaker aligns with themes of social alienation, marginalization, and personal lamentation, which are recurrent in other biblical texts, such as the laments of the Psalms or the prophetic narratives of Jeremiah.[183]Such social exclusion is often connected with the loss of identity, where the individual's relationship with their community is fractured, leading to isolation.Such dynamics make the application of SIT particularly fruitful for interpreting this passage, as SIT allows the exploration of how identity, group membership, and social categorization play a role in both rejection and the speaker's struggle for recognition.

In-Group and Out-Group Dynamics in the Text Social Identity Theory, developed by Henri Tajfel and John Turner, posits that individuals derive a sense of self and belonging from their membership in social groups. Group identity distinguishes between the in-group (those who belong) and the out-group (those who do not) [184] This categorization process often results in tension because the in-group seeks to maintain positive distinctiveness

181 Hughes, *Scriptural Allusions and Exegesis in the Hodayot*, 59:95.

182 Michael C Douglas, 'Power and Praise in the Hodayot: A Literary Critical Study of 1QH 9:1–18:14.' (Ph.D. diss, Chicago, University of Chicago, 1998), 100.

183 Douglas, 'Power and Praise in the Hodayot: A Literary Critical Study of 1QH 9:1–18:14,' 258-264, supports his arguments with detailed analysis, including biblical usage in 1QHa, Ben Sira 10:2, and 4Q374 7 2.

184 Jokiranta, 'Social Identity Approach: Identity-Constructing Elements in the Psalms Pesher', 90.

by devaluing or excluding others.The above text clearly shows that the speaker is part of an out-group. The lamentation describes a community that has rejected the speaker, portrayed as being driven out of their land and abandoned by their social network friends and relatives.[185] The metaphor of the bird cast from its nest vividly embodies the vulnerability and dislocation accompanying such exclusion. By rejecting the speaker, the community strengthens its in-group boundaries, opposing the speaker's perceived lack of worth.

The reference to "*spokesmen of deceit*" further reinforces the divide between the speaker and the in-group. These deceitful leaders have misled the people, casting the speaker into an out-group characterized by misunderstanding and folly.[186] Here, the speaker's rejection is linked not only to social exclusion but also to a broader ideological divide. The in-group aligns itself with false knowledge and deceit, while the speaker remains aligned with divine truth and wisdom.

Identity Threat and Stigma

The lens of identity threat, a central concept in SIT, describes the process of exclusion in the text. When individuals are cast out of their social group, their sense of self-worth and identity is threatened. The speaker articulates this threat through the imagery of being treated as a "broken vessel."[187] This metaphor suggests a loss of value and functionality, reflecting how the community views the speaker as worthless and irrelevant.Identity threat often leads to stigmatization, where individuals or groups are marked as inferior or deviant. In the text, the speaker's rejection is a form of stigmatization, where the community no longer esteems or recognizes the speaker's worth or contributions. It parallels the experiences of marginalized communities, both in Qumran and in contemporary contexts, such as the Dalits in India, who are often degraded and excluded by dominant social groups.

Social Identity and Divine Validation While the speaker is rejected by the community, the text also powerfully asserts divine validation. The phrase "*when you exert your might through me*" suggests that the speaker's rejection by the human community contrasts with their acceptance by God.[188] This divine validation serves as a form of identity repair, in which

185 Holm-Nielsen, *Hodayot*, 35; Menahem Mansoor, *The Thanksgiving Hymns: Translated and Annotated with an Introduction*, Studies on the Texts of the Desert of Judah 3 (Leiden: Brill, 2018), 123.

186 Hughes, *Scriptural Allusions and Exegesis in the Hodayot*, 59:104.

187 Hughes, *Scriptural Allusions and Exegesis in the Hodayot*, 59:109.

188 Douglas, 'Power and Praise in the Hodayot: A Literary Critical Study of 1QH 9:1–18:14.', 7.

the speaker's sense of self-worth is restored not through the recognition of the in-group but through their relationship with God.

In SIT, individuals or groups that face rejection often seek alternative sources of validation or belonging. For the speaker in the text, divine approval offers an alternative social identity that exceeds human in-group and out-group boundaries. This dynamic is significant in religious contexts where human society marginalizes individuals. However, they often find comfort and affirmation in their relationships with the divine.The speaker's experience interprets social distinctiveness as a form of positive move. Despite their rejection, the speaker maintains a sense of superiority through their alignment with divine wisdom, contrasting themselves with the "spokesmen of deceit". In this way, the speaker transforms their out-group status into a source of positive distinctiveness, drawing strength from their association with divine truth rather than societal approval.

Liberative Reading: Applying to Dalit Communities

Deciphering Diverse Divine Revelations

The experience of marginalization described in the text, in which the speaker is rejected and exiled, resonates deeply with the struggles of the Dalits in India. As noted in Dalit Liberative hermeneutics, marginalized voices uncover unique insights into divine revelation, challenging dominant interpretations of the scriptures that often overlook the realities of oppression.[189] The speaker's exclusion from society and their isolation and rejection reveals a profound moment of divine engagement, in which the margins of society experience God's manifested presence.[190] It aligns with the Dalit perspective that divine revelation often occurs in the context of struggle and suffering.

Social Identity Theory (SIT) helps reveal how God reveals himself to the marginalized by analyzing group dynamics of exclusion and inclusion. In the text, the human community's rejected speaker finds solace and identity in their relationship with the divine.[191] This transformation reflects a broader spiritual truth: a divine revelation is often unnoticed by dominant groups but becomes central for those who are marginalized. SIT allows us to observe how those excluded from societal groups find alternative validation,

189 Kondasingu Jesurathnam, *Dalit Liberative Hermeneutics: Indian Christian Dalit Interpretation of Psalm 22* (Delhi: ISPCK, 2010), 3–6; Kondasingu Jesurathnam, 'Towards a Dalit Liberative Hermeneutics: Re-Reading The Psalms of Lament', *BTF* 34, no. 1 (June 2002): 3.

190 Hughes, *Scriptural Allusions and Exegesis in the Hodayot*, 59:108,114.

191 Holm-Nielsen, 'The Importance of Late Jewish Psalmody for the Understanding of Old Testament Psalmodic Traditions', 307.

a process mirrored in the divine acceptance the speaker receives despite human rejection. This validation is a source of hope, signalling God's commitment to the marginalized, a revelation of liberation.

Liberative Hermeneutics emphasizes God's alignment with marginalized communities, offering a robust framework through which one can interpret Qumran texts. The text's lamentation of rejection mirrors the experience of Dalits, who continue to face caste-based oppression and exclusion in India. By drawing connections between the rejected biblical speaker and the Dalit community, one can observe how the text serves as a liberative message, affirming that divine intervention is not only available but central to the experiences of the oppressed. Dalit hermeneutics, as outlined by K. Jesurathnam, highlights the need to interpret scripture from the perspective of those at the margins of society. The Psalms of Lament, for instance, provide a rich context for understanding how the cries of the oppressed are addressed to God, emphasizing divine involvement in the struggles of the marginalized.[192] Similarly, the rejected speaker in the above passage turns to God for his recognition and restoration, paralleling the Dalit struggle for liberation and dignity. This Liberative reading invites contemporary oppressed communities to find hope in God's commitment to justice and freedom.

Connecting the Marginalized Speaker to Contemporary Marginalized Communities

The speaker's experience of being cast out "like a bird from its nest" reflects the collective displacement and exclusion experienced by Dalits and other marginalized groups. In Dalit theology, this exile resonates with the reality of being pushed out of societybut finding strength and hope in the presence of God.[193] The image of being treated as a "broken vessel" mirrors the way Dalits are often devalued and stigmatized by dominant caste systems. However, the text suggests that the brokenness is not the final word. Instead, it becomes a space where divine revelation and liberation occur. It is not merely a theological assertion but a call to action for oppressed communities, encouraging them to see their struggles as integral to the divine narrative of liberation. God's validation of the rejected speaker offers hope to contemporary marginalized groups, affirming that divine justice is on the side of those who suffer injustice.

192 Jesurathnam, 'Towards a Dalit Liberative Hermeneutics: Re-Reading The Psalms of Lament', 8–15.

193 Faustina, 'From Exile to Exodus', in *Frontiers of Dalit Theology*, ed. V Devasahayam (Madras: ISPCK/Gurukul, 1997), 92–98.

In conclusion, through the lens of Social Identity Theory and Liberative Hermeneutics, this text reveals that God is not only aware of the struggles of the marginalized but is also actively involved in their liberation. This passage offers hope and encouragement for contemporary marginalized communities, especially Dalits. It affirms that divine revelation offers the Dalit communities a transformative vision of justice, healing, and liberation while suffering and exclusion threaten them.

Conclusion

This study of 1QHa XII: 6-10 through the lens of Social Identity Theory and Liberative Hermeneutics reveals profound connections between ancient texts and contemporary struggles for justice and dignity. By examining the experiences of marginalization and divine revelation in the Qumran community, we uncover potent parallels with the struggles of Dalit communities and other marginalized groups today. This analysis demonstrates the importance of inclusively embracing diverse voices in biblical interpretation. The perspectives of those on the margin often yield fresh insights into divine revelation, challenging dominant interpretations that may overlook the realities of oppression and injustice. This approach enriches one's understanding of ancient texts and provides a source of hope and empowerment for Dalit communities facing similar challenges.

These diverse viewpoints can provide fresh theological insights into addressing pressing social issues, such as inequality, systemic injustice, and marginalization. In this endeavour, we acknowledge the significant contributions of scholar Prof. Rev. Dr. Kondasingu Jesurathnam, whose contextual biblical interpretation serves as a model for re-examining scripture considering contemporary struggles. His legacy recalls the transformative power of reading sacred texts through the lens of lived experiences, particularly in Dalit communities. Let us continue to draw inspiration from both ancient wisdom and contemporary struggles. By doing so, one can develop interpretations of scripture that deepen theological understanding and contribute to the ongoing work of justice, liberation, and human dignity in our world today.

32

Administrative Pattern of Joseph in Genesis 47:13-26 A Dalit Perspective on Historical and Contemporary Inequities

Monalisha Tandi

Prof. Rev. Dr. Kondasingu Jesurathnam is a renowned scholar whose work in Old Testament studies has profoundly influenced the understanding of Dalit theology and Dalit biblical hermeneutics. His scholarly contributions emphasize the liberative themes within the Old Testament, drawing parallels between the struggles of marginalized communities in biblical times and the contemporary Dalit experience. Dr. Jesurathnam's focus on justice, liberation, and social equality has provided a powerful lens through which the oppressed can find empowerment and identity within biblical narratives. His commitment to academic rigour and social justice underscores his profound influence, inspiring countless scholars and activists in theology and human rights.

Introduction

The narrative of Joseph in Genesis 47:13-26 is a powerful depiction of administrative cleverness during a crisis. However, it also presents a complex portrait of economic policies that, while ensuring survival, resulted in significant exploitation and loss of freedom for the Egyptian populace. This duality offers a rich ground for socio-political analysis, especially in understanding how power and economic policies can sustain and oppress communities. Warren Carter's socio-political reading of the biblical text is employed. Then, this paper attempts to draw an intersection between Joseph's policies and the Indian administrative policies. The study also seeks to evoke re-imagining from Dalit Lense, which advocates for justice and equitable policies in modern-day India.

Socio-Political Reading

This paper employs socio-political reading to explore the life situation of the Egyptians during the time of famine in Egypt and the political organization in Genesis 47:13-26. According to Walter Brueggemann, sociological analysis "seeks to understand the forces through which communities and societies order their life through arrangements of power and symbol."[194] Norman K. Gottwald, in his book *The Tribes of Yahweh: A Sociology of the Religion of Liberated Israel 150-1050 B.C.E.,* used the sociological method to reveal the socio-political realities behind the text.[195] He tries to understand the social organization and the different mechanisms in this system's processes to understand its functions in system regularity.[196] This study considers Warren Carter's socio-political reading of the biblical text. In *Mathew and Margins: A Socio-Political and Religious Reading*, Carter proposes socio-political reading as "a work of resistance written from and for a minority community... It strengthens this community to resist the dominant."[197] This reading works as a counter-narrative, as a form of resistance, opposing the dominance of imperial power and advocating for change. Thus, this study employs Carter's socio-political reading, which explores and analyzes the dominant or supreme authority of the administrative system in Genesis 47 and compares it to the contemporary Indian context.

The Setting of Genesis 47:13-26

Genesis 41:13-26 deals with Joseph's relationship to the Egyptian populace rather than to his own family. One can argue that J source produces this section (13-26). It dwells on the increasingly acute effects of the prolonged famine and highlights the importance of Joseph's preventive measures.[198] This narrative depicts Joseph as an administrator with great wisdom.[199]However, Joseph's administrative policies and economic

194 Walter Brueggemann, *Theology of the Old Testament: Testimony, Dispute, Advocacy* (Minneapolis: Fortress Press, 1997), 49.

195 Norman K. Gottwald, *The Tribes of Yahweh: A Sociology of the Religion of Liberated Israel 150-1050 B.C.E.* (Sheffield: Sheffield Academic Press, 1979), 591-665.

196 Gottwald, *The Tribes of Yahweh,* 212-217.

197 Warren Carter, *Matthew and Margins: A Socio-Political and Religious Reading* (New Delhi: Theological Publication in India, 2007), 2.

198 E.A. Speiser, "Genesis," in *The Anchor Bible* Vol.1 (New York, Doubleday, 1964), 353.

199 *The Interpreter's Study Bible* (Nashville: Abingdon Press, 2003), 79.

conditions at the time of famine (crisis) led the Egyptians into slavery and laid heavy taxation on them. This report of the enslavement of the Egyptian peasant is a shocking proof of Joseph's inhumanity.[200] According to Philo's opposing point of view, Joseph represents a corrupt politician who gains power through manipulation, like a disloyal person. Here, Joseph symbolizes selfish politicians who use tricks to get ahead.[201] Joseph's procedure was to provide the grain Egyptians needed, but they had to pay a price each time, and the cost kept changing. First, they paid their money until it ran out in Egypt and Canaan. Then, the Egyptians traded their stock for grain while the Canaanites went elsewhere. Finally, Egyptians sold themselves and their land to Pharaoh. [202] However, handing over their livestock, land, and themselves was an administrative order, and the people had no option but to give away everything they had without voicing their concerns.

Exploitative Administrative Policies of Joseph

One of the main themes in Joseph's story is his relationship with the Egyptian empire. The passage in Genesis 47:13-26 is connected to the story of Jacob but doesn't focus on family matters. Instead, it highlights Joseph's cleverness and loyalty to Pharaoh. Joseph will use his family to increase Pharaoh's power (as seen in chapters 41:46-49 and 53-57). Initially, this text might have reflected changes in taxes and land ownership, but now it focuses on Joseph's administrative skills. His cleverness shows that working for the empire brings risks. The Egyptian empire offered food and survival but also involved exploitation, oppression, and slavery. This passage seems to prepare for the Exodus, as Joseph's tax reforms lead people to sell themselves into slavery to the crown (which contrasts with the laws in Leviticus 25:35-55). Joseph is innovative; this may be a negative thing from an Exodus viewpoint. Joseph seems torn between serving his family and the empire, and it's not always clear where his loyalty lies. The food reserves, while helpful, can also be used for oppression (as seen in Exodus 16:2-3, Deuteronomy 8:3, 1 Kings 4:20-28, and Mark 8:15). The strict system described here is similar to the oppressive policies in Exodus 5:5-19.[203] "Questions might be raised about the ways in which a vast economic apparatus keeps its promises and what the costs and hazards are.

---

200 Speiser, "Genesis," 353.

201 Samuel Sandmel, *Philo of Alexandria an Introduction* (U.K.: Oxford University Press, 1979), 63-64.

202 *The Broadman Bible Commentary* vol. 1 (Nashville: Broadman Press, 1969), 276-277.

203 Walter Brueggemann, *Genesis, Interpretation: A Bible Commentary for Preaching and Teaching* (Atlanta: John Knox Press, 1982), 356.

The people of promise might ask if there are alternatives to imperial modes of nourishment (cf. Mark 8:15; John 6:35)."[204]

Biblical Perspectives on Economic Systems

The Bible provides the legal and social principles that promote human freedom. When followed by both leaders and citizens, this framework leads to the development of what is now called the free enterprise system. Essentially, biblical economics aligns with the principles of free enterprise. Biblical economics is free enterprise economics.[205] The economic system described is neither anarchistic,[206] nor aligned with Keynesian,[207] or Marxist economics. Marxist principles. It advocates free enterprise, where voluntary exchanges, like Esau trading his birthright for stew, are honoured by God. When authorities try to undo such exchanges, as Isaac did, those affected may legitimately take steps, including deception, to protect their rights and property. Joseph's actions in Egypt, where he brought the nation into state bondage, serve as a cautionary tale and should not be emulated by Christian societies. It reflects the importance of preserving individual freedom and ownership, rejecting any system that undermines voluntary agreements or leads to state control over people's lives and property. Ultimately, the biblical perspective upholds free enterprise as a critical economic principle, emphasizing personal responsibility and voluntary exchange.[208]

Ethical Dilemmas in Joseph's Economic Policies

Commentators like Y. W. Fung have questioned the ethics of the policy that Joseph carried out, which involved the enslavement of the general Egyptian

---

204 https://idoc.pub/documents/genesis-interpretation-a-bible-commentary-for-teaching-and-preaching-2nv5zgx3o0lk.

205 Free enterprise economics, or capitalism, is an economic system in which voluntary exchanges in an open market determine the production, distribution, and prices of goods and services. Its key features include private property, economic freedom, competition, voluntary exchange, and limited government intervention.

206 Anarchistic economics, also known as anarchist economics, is an economic system rooted in the principles of anarchism. It advocates for a society without hierarchical structures, including the state, and emphasizes voluntary cooperation, mutual aid, and self-management.

207 Keynesian economics is an economic theory and approach based on the ideas of British economist John Maynard Keynes. It emerged during the Great Depression of the 1930s as a response to the inability of classical economic theories to explain and address prolonged periods of high unemployment and economic stagnation. Keynesian economics emphasizes the role of government intervention in stabilizing the economy and promoting growth.

208 Gary North, *Sovereignty and Dominio. An Economic Commentary on Genesis,* Vol.1 of *A Cosmic Commentary on the Bible* (Dallas: Point Five Press, 2012), 319.

populace. Two stages of acquisition by Joseph on behalf of the king occur: first, the people (including Canaan, v. 15) give their money and livestock for grain in the beginning year (vv. 14-17); and second, they barter their land and their freedom in the second year (vv. 18-21). The future arrangement involved a form of land tenure in which the state provided seed, the debtor returned a fifth of the yield to the Pharaoh, and the Egyptian priests were exempt from Joseph's policies. (vv. 20-26). On the first matter, some commentators have charged that Joseph oppressed the Egyptian people by his bartering schemes, which led to the forfeiture of all possessions and ended in servitude to the crown.[209] For this, Athala Brenner poses some questions, such as, "How could Joseph take the surplus from the people and then sell it back to them? Worse, how could Joseph systematically force the people into servitude by, first, having to pay for their surplus; second, having to exchange their livestock for food; and third, having to sell their land and themselves into slavery for food?"[210] John H. Walton discusses the ethical implications of Joseph's actions and notes that while Joseph's management effectively saved lives, it also resulted in significant ethical dilemmas. [211] The Egyptians' cry is a challenge to the morality of exploiting a crisis for economic gain.

Genesis 47:15: A Voice of Resistance

Genesis 47:15 reads, "When the money of the people of Egypt and Canaan was gone, all Egypt came to Joseph and said, 'Give us food. Why should we die before your eyes? Our money is used up' (N.I.V.). This verse can be interpreted as a voice of resistance when viewed through the lens of power dynamics and social justice. Rashi comments that the Egyptians' cry directly resulted from their desperation. They had spent all their money and could not buy more food. It reflects the severe power imbalance between Joseph, who controlled the food supply, and the people, who were left helpless and dependent.[212] Nahum Sarna highlights how Joseph's economic policies during the famine ultimately led to the centralization of power in Pharaoh's hands. He writes that the famine "was a situation he exploited to the full." [213] The people's plea underscores their helplessness and the concentration

209 Kenneth A. Mathews, *The New American Commentary,* Vol. 1B (Nashville: Broadman and Holman Publisher, 2005), 850.

210 Athala Brenner, *Genesis: Texts and Contexts* (Minneapolis: Fortress Press, 2010), 182.

211 John H. Walton, *Genesis: The N.I.V. Application Commentary* (Michigan: Zondervan, 2001), 749-751.

212 Rashi, *Commentaries on The Pentateuch* (New York: W.W. Norton & Company INC., 1970), 70-79.

213 Nahum M. Sarna, *Understanding Genesis: The world of the Bible in the light of History* (New York: Jewish Theological Seminary, 1966), 219.

of economic control. Robert Alter points out that the narrative critiques the consolidation of power and wealth. The people's plea, "Why should we die before your eyes?" can be seen as a powerful protest against the socio-economic policies that have left them destitute.[214] Brueggemann interprets the Egyptians' cry as a lament against an unjust economic system.[215] Gerhard von Rad explains that this verse reflects historical practices, such as rulers manipulating grain distribution during famines to consolidate political power. The people's plea serves as a historical critique of these practices and highlights the human cost of such policies.[216] Therefore, the Egyptians' plea to Joseph is a cry for help and a subtle protest against an economic system that has rendered them powerless and impoverished.

The Intersection between Joseph's Administrative Policy and Indian Administrative Policy:

Joseph's strategy, although ensuring survival, came at the cost of social justice, resulting in the population's enslavement. In India, policies that favour the wealthy and powerful while disadvantaging the poor can be seen as modern parallels; land acquisition, corporate favouritism, and economic reforms prove this claim. Policies such as the Land Acquisition Act of 2013 and subsequent amendments have often favoured so-called higher caste and influential people and their industrial and infrastructural development at the expense of displacing farmers and Dalit Indigenous communities. These policies centralize land ownership in the hands of the state or private corporations, often leading to loss of livelihood and autonomy for the rural populace.[217] Joseph's strategy involved taking money from the Egyptians in exchange for grain, their livestock, and finally, their land and themselves; on the other hand, priests were privileged to enjoy life, resulting in a complete transfer of economic power to the state. The demonetization (2016) policy aimed to curb black money and corruption but disproportionately affected small traders, farmers, and daily wage workers who rely on cash transactions. The centralization of economic control through demonetization had severe short-term impacts on the livelihoods of marginalized communities,

---

214 Robert Alter, *The Five Books of Moses: A Translation with Commentary* (New York: W.W. Norton & Company, 2004), 453-461.

215 Brueggemann, *Genesis,* 356.

216 Gerhard von Rad, *Genesis. A Commentary* (Philadelphia: The Westminster Press, 1972), 410.

217 Juhi Senguttuvan, "A Comparative Analysis of the Land Acquisition Laws in India: 1894, 2013 and 2015," *Legal Service India E-Journal,* accessed July 10th 2024. https://www.legalserviceindia.com/legal/article-2511-a-comparative-analysis-of-the-land-acquisition-laws-in-india-1894-2013-and-2015.html.

highlighting issues of economic justice and equity.[218] The Indian government reduced corporate tax (2019) rates to stimulate investment and economic growth. However, these tax cuts primarily benefited large corporations, while social welfare programs and subsidies for the poor faced budget cuts.[219] This policy widens the gap between the rich and the poor, and Dalits mirroring the exploitative nature of Joseph's economic measures. The recent agricultural reforms, including the controversial farm laws in 2020, aimed at liberalizing the agricultural market but were perceived as favouring large agribusinesses over small farmers. The resulting farmer protests highlighted fears of exploitation and losing control over their livelihoods, similar to the Egyptian peasants' plight under Joseph's administration.

Indian Administrative Policies:

Kalia Yojana

Once a year, some farmers receive Rs 10,000 annually through the Kalia Yojana scheme, which is not equivalent to a security guard's monthly salary. However, when these farmers work all year in their fields to produce paddy and attempt to sell it at a reasonable price, the market prices drop. So, what does a farmer truly need, Rs 10,000 annually or fair compensation for their hard work?

Biju Swathya Kalyan Yojana

This scheme aims to provide financial assistance for healthcare to about 3.5 crore people in Odisha, offering annual health insurance coverage of Rs 5 lakhs. However, some hospitals do not accept this card. In Balangir district, there is only one multi-speciality government hospital within a 30-kilometre radius, and the smaller hospitals are inadequate, lacking even proper beds. As a result, people avoid these smaller hospitals, and even in serious emergencies, the government forces people to go to the government-run hospital. If someone meets with an accident, they don't go to a nearby hospital because it's useless; instead, they must rush to the central government hospital. Due to issues like traffic or unavailability of vehicles,

---

218 Ajay K. Singh, "Impact of Demonetization (2016) on Small-scale Enterprises in India: Evidence from Available Literature and Field Survey," *ResearchGate* (July 2017), accessed July 10th 2024.
https://www.researchgate.net/publication/344326031_Impact_of_Demonetization_2016_on_Small-scale_Enterprises_in_India_Evidence_from_Available_Literature_and_Field_Survey.

219 Aditya Narwekar, "Corporate Tax Rate Reductions and Its Hidden Challenges," *Taxmann* (December 04th 2019), accessed July 05th 2024. https://www.taxmann.com/research/income-tax/ top-story/ 105010000000017097/ corporate-tax-rate-reductions-and-its-hidden-challenges-experts-opinion.

some people leave their final breath on the way. Therefore, what do the people need a good hospital or a Biju Swasthya Yojana Card?

Schemes for Dalit's Upliftment

On May 02nd, two groups, the Ambedkar Reading Circle in Bengaluru and Bahutva Karnataka, released a report called 'Guarantee Check: B.J.P.'s Hollow Promises of Social Justice'. This report reviews the promises and actual results of the B.J.P.'s focus on social justice during the last 10 years of the N.D.A. government. The B.J.P. claims to support marginalized groups and ensure social justice, but the report shows its actions have yet to live up to its words. In a larger picture, it ignores the rights and welfare of the Scheduled Caste (S.C.), Scheduled Tribe (S.T.), and Other Backward Class (O.B.C.) communities.

The report compared B.J.P.'s 2014 and 2019 election promise to the actual outcomes and found neglect, discrimination, and continued caste-based prejudice. For example, despite promises to protect SC/ST communities from violence, cases of crimes against them increased by 48% between 2010-2022, and there was a nearly 50% rise in rapes against Dalit women from 2015-2019. In terms of funds, the B.J.P. pledged proper funding for S.C. and S.T. groups to promote social and economic justice. However, the distribution of promised actual funds has yet to take place. For example, between 2015 and 2020, the government allocated ₹5.23 lakh crores to the S.C. community but received ₹2.55 lakh crores. Similar gaps existed for S.T.s, with much money left unused or spent on unrelated projects.

Regarding manual scavenging, a harmful and dangerous practice, the B.J.P. vowed to end it and protect *safaae karmachaaree* (sanitation workers). However, many areas still practice it, and workers' safety remains at risk. Rehabilitation efforts have been poor, with only a small percentage of affected workers receiving help. The B.J.P. also promised better representation for S.C. and S.T. communities, but it delayed collecting important caste data. Many government positions reserved for these communities remain unfilled. Lastly, while the B.J.P. claimed to support tribal rights and development, the report shows insufficient funds, and many tribal claims under the Forest Rights Act rejected their rights. Only about half of the planned schools for tribal children are operating, and health indicators for tribal people remain poor.[220]

The report highlights a wide gap between the B.J.P.'s promises and the actual situation, showing ongoing challenges for marginalized communities under their governance.

220 https://en.themooknayak.com/dalit-news/fact-check-48-spike-in-scst-atrocities-cases-exposes-bjps-misleading-guarantees

Through The Dalit' Lens

Analysing Joseph's administrative policies in Genesis 47:13-26 through the lens of Dalit theology brings forward perspectives on power dynamics, social stratification, and oppression. Dalit theology, emerging from the lived experiences of marginalized and oppressed Dalit communities (formerly referred to as "untouchables") in India, critiques systems of injustice and the dehumanization of people through hierarchical social orders.[221] In Genesis 47:13-26, Joseph implements a series of policies during a severe famine in Egypt:

Land and Resource Consolidation:

As the famine worsens, Joseph, the administrator under the Pharaoh, first exchanges food for money. When the people's money runs out, he exchanges food for livestock and, eventually, for land. The people surrendered their lands to the Pharaoh and became tenants, effectively transferring ownership of all the land (except for that of the priests) to the Egyptian state.[222]

Slavery and Serfdom:

With no property left, the people agree to become Pharaoh's servants in exchange for food and survival. They become state-owned labourers, and Joseph sets up a system in which the people must give one-fifth of their produce to Pharaoh, keeping the rest for themselves.[223]

Dalit Reading of Joseph's Policies

Concentration of Power and Wealth

From a Dalit perspective, Joseph's actions reinforce hierarchical power structures. The concentration of wealth and land in the hands of the Pharaoh

---

221 A. Sathianathan Clarke, *Dalits and Christianity: Subaltern Religion and Liberation Theology in India* (New York: Oxford University Press, 1998), 150. In this book, Clarke explores how Dalit theology critiques systems of power and oppression, connecting the experiences of marginalized communities in India with biblical stories of social and economic injustice. Specifically, Dalit theology offers a perspective that can be applied to Genesis 47:13-26, highlighting the power dynamics and social stratification evident in Joseph's administrative policies.

222 V. Devasahayam, *Frontiers of Dalit Theology* (Pune: ISPCK, 1997), 302. In this work, Devasahayam discusses how Dalit theology critiques socio-economic exploitation and the dehumanization of marginalized communities. The themes presented in Genesis 47:13-26 resonate with the theological reflections on power and oppression that Devasahayam discusses about Dalit experiences in India.

These texts can provide a robust theoretical framework for analyzing biblical narratives like Joseph's policies through the lens of Dalit theology, focusing on themes such as power concentration, exploitation, and social stratification.

223 Devasahayam, *Frontiers of Dalit Theology*..., 303.

reflects the upper-caste control of resources in India and the denial of land, education, and economic power to the Dalits. Though initially an outsider, Joseph becomes a vital enforcer of this system, aligning himself with the ruling class and further marginalizing the vulnerable.[224]

Exploitation of Vulnerability

Dalit theology critiques systems that exploit people's vulnerabilities, particularly during times of crisis. In Genesis 47, Joseph's policies, though seen as pragmatic from an administrative standpoint, capitalize on the desperation of the famine-stricken people. It mirrors the way Dalits and other marginalized groups have been historically exploited during times of social or economic crisis, with their labour and resources taken without fair compensation, often trapping them in cycles of poverty and dependency.[225]

Servitude and Bondage

The servitude into which the Egyptian populace falls is the bondage that many Dalits experience. The people's transition into serfdom under Joseph's policies mirrors the way Dalits have been subjected to various forms of servitude, whether through bonded labour, caste-based discrimination, or systemic economic exclusion. Joseph's system institutionalizes a form of economic oppression that parallels the caste system's enforcement of generational poverty and subjugation for Dalits.[226]

Religious Exemption and Priestly Privilege (Favouritism)

Interestingly, in Genesis 47, the Egyptian priests are exempt from Joseph's policies. This highlights the religious justification for inequality—something Dalit theologians often critique. Just as the Egyptian priests retained their privilege, higher castes in India frequently used religious ideology to maintain their dominance and denied Dalits religious, economic, and social rights.[227]

Ambivalence in Joseph's Role

Joseph's position as a former outsider (a Hebrew sold into slavery) but now aligned with Pharaoh's power adds complexity to the story. A Dalit reading could explore this ambivalence—how a marginalized person, when in power, may perpetuate the same systems of oppression that once oppressed them. Joseph's actions raise questions about the responsibility of those who

---

224 Clarke, *Dalits and Christianity...*, 156.

225 Sathianathan Clarke, *Dalits and Christianity...,*156.

226 Devasahayam, *Frontiers of Dalit Theology...*, 304.

227 Devasahayam, *Frontiers of Dalit Theology...*, 306.

ascend to power: Should they align with the dominant structures or subvert them in the name of justice for the oppressed?[228]

Re-Imagining from Dalit Lense:

In Prophetic Imagination, Walter Brueggemann analyzes the theme of prophetic imagination by focusing on the achievements of Moses, Solomon, Jeremiah, Second Isaiah, and Jesus. In all these, he says, the prophet understands the politics of language: its capacity to bring newness on the one hand and dehumanization on the other.[229]

Discerning between What People Require and what Rulers Give

Financial experts and highly placed economic institutions in the country have been continuously issuing warning bells regarding the gravity of the situation into which the nation's economy has plunged due to the irresponsible use of taxpayer money and politicized decisions of successive governments. The caption etched in golden letters on the front wing of the Vidhana Soudha[230] Bangalore, the capital of Karnataka, boasts, "Government work is God's work." It is a genuinely appreciable slogan that aims to evoke a sense of responsibility among every government servant. But is the government playing the role of God? Would God give a thing that benefitted the people only for a short period, and in the long run, people must suffer for those things? Would unemployed youth need a monthly stipend of Rs.3000/- per month or jobs? Would older women want to suffice themselves with a sum of Rs. 1000 or prefer affordable healthcare?

All the jobs that lower a person's status, like sanitation work, are given to Dalits. Even though the government claims this is to uplift Dalits, it only reinforces societal divisions, with better jobs reserved for so-called higher castes. Even when Dalits work hard and achieve higher-level positions, they don't receive the same respect as those from higher castes. For example, the Chief Minister of Odisha, who is from a Dalit community, is not allowed to enter the Puri Jagannath Temple despite his high position. So, the question is: do Dalits need jobs like sanitation in the name of upliftment, or should they have equal opportunities and genuine respect in all professions?

---

228 Clarke, *Dalits and Christianity...,*155.

229 Walter Brueggemann, *The Prophetic Imagination* (Minneapolis: Fortress Press, 2001), 23.

230 The Vidhan Souda is the Assembly House of the State of Karnataka. Built by Kengal Hanumanthaiah, this imposing structure stands directly opposite the High Court of Karnataka on Ambedkar Road.

Voicing Against the Ruling Powers

Prophets in the Bible often spoke against the ruling powers and advocated for the oppressed. Religious and social leaders must voice the concerns of communities affected by unfair policies and economic exploitation. There is a need for advocacy that promotes equitable economic policies, land reforms, and protection of rights for all citizens, especially the poor, Dalits and marginalized—empowering the affected through education, legal awareness, and economic opportunities to break the cycle of exploitation. Movements such as the anti-corruption protests led by Anna Hazare, the anti-CAA protests, and the farmer protests have emerged as voices of resistance against policies perceived as unjust. These movements represent modern-day prophetic works, advocating for social justice and equity in the face of centralized and exploitative power.

Implication

A Dalit reading of Genesis 47:13-26 reveals a stark parallel between Joseph's administrative policies during the Egyptian famine and the systemic marginalization of Dalits in contemporary India. In the biblical account, Joseph's strategies for survival—grain centralization, redistribution, and eventual land consolidation—result in the population's dependency on Pharaoh's authority, stripping individuals of autonomy and land ownership. From a Dalit perspective, this mirrors the historical and ongoing subjugation faced by Dalits, who are often landless, economically vulnerable, and excluded from social and political power structures.

The Dalit critique emphasizes that Joseph's policies while ensuring short-term survival, entrenched hierarchical inequities and created a permanent underclass, not unlike the socio-economic barriers faced by Dalits. The concentration of resources in the hands of a few, whether Pharaoh or elite classes, perpetuates cycles of dependency and deprivation. The narrative urges a rethinking of governance in ancient and modern contexts, advocating for policies that ensure survival and actively dismantling oppressive systems, enabling accurate equity and empowerment for marginalized communities. For Dalits, this means moving beyond mere survival toward full participation, ownership, and dignity in society, challenging the entrenched hierarchies that have long perpetuated their oppression.

A Dalit reading of Genesis 47:13-26 critiques Joseph's administrative policies for perpetuating structural inequality, much like the systemic oppression faced by Dalits in India. Joseph's actions brought many benefits to the administration during the famine, but they also resulted in the exploitation and subjugation of the Egyptian people, stripping them of land and freedom. From a Dalit theological perspective, this mirrors the caste-based discrimination and socio-economic marginalization that Dalits continue to face in India. The reality is that a few privileged people control and confiscate resources.

Drawing on Warren Carter's socio-political reading of biblical texts, this analysis exposes how economic policies, even those designed to ensure survival, can reinforce unjust power dynamics. The consolidation of resources under Pharaoh's control in the narrative reflects the concentration of wealth and power in the hands of dominant castes in India, leaving marginalized communities trapped in cycles of poverty and dependence. This reading challenges modern-day governance to move beyond mere survival strategies and toward policies that dismantle oppressive systems and promote equity. It calls for justice and inclusion, urging leaders to advocate for the empowerment of the marginalized, ensuring their full participation in society rather than upholding hierarchical structures.

Conclusion

The narrative of Joseph in Genesis 47:13-26 illustrates his administrative prowess during the famine but also highlights significant ethical issues, as his policies led to the exploitation and enslavement of the Egyptian populace. This duality mirrors contemporary Indian administrative practices, such as temporal schemes, land acquisition acts, demonetization, corporate tax cuts, and agricultural reforms, which often centralize economic power and disadvantage the marginalized. The study criticizes and resists unjust policies to promote long-term justice and equity. The paper calls for a discerning approach to governance, highlighting the timeless relevance of socio-political critique in addressing power dynamics and economic policies to build a more equitable society.

In this essay, Dalit reading exposes conniving Joseph's administrative policies in Genesis 47:13-26 reinforcing structural inequality, exploitation, and systemic oppression. While Joseph may be seen as a successful administrator from one perspective, from the lens of Dalit theology, his actions perpetuate a cycle of subjugation and concentration of power, much like the caste system in India. This reading invites reflection on how marginalized people, like the Dalits, navigate systems of power and oppression and what ethical responsibilities leaders have to challenge unjust structures rather than uphold them.

33

Ideological Critique of the Construction of the Jerusalem Temple and Its Implications for Dalit Christian Communities in India

Barre Daniel Anurag

Introduction

It is with immense joy and gratitude that I present this article in honour of Prof. Rev. Dr Kondasingu Jesurathnam, a distinguished scholar and mentor. As a student at the United Theological College, it is a privileged opportunity to contribute to the scholarly discussions that Prof. Jesurathnam has significantly shaped through his work in contextual readings of the Old Testament. This article draws inspiration from Prof. Jesurathnam's commitment to examining biblical texts through a lens that addresses social justice, marginalization, and upliftment issues. His profound contributions have deepened the understanding of how one can interpret biblical narratives in light of contemporary struggles, particularly for marginalized communities like the Dalits in India.

The construction of large and lavish church buildings has complex and multifaceted impacts on Dalit Christian communities. The allocation of substantial sums of money to such projects diverts resources away from more pressing needs, such as poverty alleviation, education, and healthcare. It also sends a message that the Church prioritizes physical grandeur over addressing the needs of its most vulnerable members. The imposed ideologies drive the construction of these monumental buildings that often benefit a few. Similarly, Solomon's master plan to construct an expensive temple utilizes certain ideologies that benefit Solomon while imposing significant burdens on the lives of ordinary people.

This article seeks to uncover the ideologies behind such constructions, demonstrating how dominant groups generate ideologies to serve their interests. In doing so, it employs Ideological Criticism[231] to investigate the dominant ideologies that drove temple construction. Socio-Historical Method helps one [232] to explore the socio-economic, political, and religious context of ancient Israel. The article then analyzes a contemporary case and draws implications for Dalit Christians.

Socio-Historical Background of Ancient Israel during the Temple Construction

Political Background

By the time Solomon came to power, a sophisticated administrative system had developed around the monarchy, as described in I Kings 4:7-19. The monarchy, originally centralized by David, was further strengthened and systematically organized by Solomon. He implemented significant changes that altered the administrative structures and redrew the territorial boundaries of Israel.[233]According to Niels Lemche, this process of centralization had profound effects on the social and political fabric of Israelite society, leading to substantial shifts in how power and governance were distributed.[234]

Once Solomon secured control of the kingdom, one of his first moves was to restructure the territorial divisions of Israel. He established administrative districts that intentionally disregarded the traditional tribal boundaries that had defined Israelite society for generations.[235] These new districts were not simply a redrawing of lines; they reflected a broader strategy of consolidating power. While the traditional tribal system largely preserves its outlying regions, the central hill country, a critical political and geographical area, underwent significant reorganization.Ishida argues

231 Christopher Rowland, "Ideological Criticism," *The Oxford Encyclopedia of Biblical Interpretation*, vol. 1, ed. Steven L. McKenzie,et al., (Oxford: Oxford University Press, 2013), 435-444; Gale A. Yee, "Ideological Criticism: Judges 17-21 and the Dismembered Body," *Judges and Method: New Approaches in Biblical Studies*, ed. Gale A. Yee (Minneapolis: Fortress Press, 1995), 147-149.

232 Marcel V. Macelaru, "Sociology and Biblical Interpretation Part One: The Concept of Charishma," *Pleroma Anul* 12 no. 1(2010): 14.

233 Rainer Albertz, *A History of Israelite Religion in the Old Testament Period: From the Beginning to the end of Monarchy* vol. 1,(Kentucky: John Knox Press 1994), 111.

234 Niels Lemche, *Ancient Israel: A History of Israelite Society* (Sheffield: JSOT, 1988),124.

235 Simon John DeVries, "I Kings," *Word Biblical Commentary*, vol. 12. 2nd ed. (Texas: World books, 1985), xxiii.

that Solomon's decision to alter the territorial divisions aimed at weakening the influence of the House of Joseph. This powerful entity had historically held considerable sway over the northern tribes of Israel.[236] By reshaping the boundaries and redistributing administrative control, Solomon sought to dilute the tribal loyalties that could challenge his centralized authority and, in doing so, ensure a more unified and controlled kingdom under his rule.

Religious Background

During Solomon's reign, the Israelites experienced a significant transformation in their religious practice, most notably with the construction of the Temple (as recounted in I Kings 5-8). DeVries notes that the people of Israel recognize the Temple as the majestic dwelling place of Yahweh, along with its political territories.[237] Such a recognition signalled the centralization of religious worship and a move away from worshipping other deities.[238] However, despite this centralization, syncretism, the blending of various religious practices, persisted during Solomon's time, as indicated by archaeological evidence from the Temple site.[239] Although Solomon worshipped Yahweh, he also paid respect to foreign gods, a practice criticized by the Deuteronomistic historian (I Kings 11:5-7).The bronze pillars at the Temple present an example of this syncretism, which mirrored Phoenician standing stones known as *Masseboth*, adopted from Canaanite traditions.[240]

Solomon's foreign wives and concubines influence and promoted the emergence of syncretism during his rule. However, viewing his large harem and religious inclusivity as parts of a broader political strategy is more accurate. This policy aimed to integrate his diverse subjects, including Israelites, Canaanites, and foreign allies, into a unified national and religious system. Though it deviated from strict Yahwist beliefs, Solomon's approach was a pragmatic response to governing an expansive and diverse

---

236 Tomo Ishida, "Solomon," *The Anchor Bible Dictionary* vol. 6, ed. David Noel Freedman (New York: Double Day, 1992), 108.

237 DeVries, "I Kings," xxvi.

238 Robert Karl Gnuse, "No Other Gods: Emergent Monotheism in Israel,"*JSOT Supplement* vol.241 (Sheffield: Sheffield Academic Press, 1997), 22.

239 Roland DeVaux, *Ancient Israel: Its Life and Institutions,*trans. John McHugh (London: McGraw-Hill Book, 1961), 317.

240 Andre Parrot, *The Temple of Jerusalem*, 2nd ed. Biblical Archaeological 5 (New York: Philosophical Library, 1955), 57.

empire.[241] Scholars like Amihai Mazar[242] and William G. Dever[243] suggest that the Temple played a pivotal role in understanding Solomon's economic policies, which intertwined religion (syncretism as discussed in I Kings 11:1-3) with political and economic concerns such as taxation, bureaucracy, forced labour, and foreign diplomacy (I Kings 4:1-19; 5:13-19; 9:26-28).

Economic Background

Solomon was a highly influential ruler in Syria-Palestine, primarily known for his diplomacy and international trade. His marriages to foreign women were politically aimed at securing peace agreements, with his marriage to Pharaoh's daughter showcasing his diplomatic skill. His treaty with Hiram, king of Tyre, was particularly significant for advancing his state's building projects.[244] These various alliances opened up many economic opportunities for Solomon, whose economy was primarily based on agriculture.[245] The economy's foundation lay in the many agricultural workers who farmed small plots around villages and tended livestock in open pastures.[246] According to Gottwald, Yahwism was the dominant ideology guiding this communal system of production, which relied on highland farming and pastoralism without extracting surpluses.[247] Solomon also gained wealth through trade, tribute, and gifts from foreign leaders, primarily through his alliance with Hiram. These partnerships allowed him to expand his business ventures (I Kings 9:26; 10:2). Marvin Chaney suggests that the kingdom's focus on import and export trade disrupted the agricultural production of the peasant population, leading to growing economic disparities.[248]

The heavy taxes collected from the ordinary people were used to fund Solomon's grand construction projects, such as the Temple, and to support the

241 Michael Grant, *The History of Ancient Israel* (New York: Scribner, 1984), 90.

242 Amihai Mazar, *Archaeology of the Land of the Bible, 10,000-586 BCE* (New York: Doubleday, 1992), 368-402.

243 William G. Dever, "Archaeology of the 'Age of Solomon:' A Case Study in Archaeology and Historiography," *The Age of Solomon: Scholarship at the turn of the Millennium* ed. L. K. Handy, Studies in the History and Culture of the Ancient Near East 11 (Leiden: Brill, 1997), 217-251.

244 Ishida, "Solomon," 109.

245 Oded Borowski, *Agriculture in Iron Age Israel* (Indiana: Eisenbrauns, 1987), 8.

246 L.K. Handy, "Solomon,"*Dictionary of the Old Testament Historical Books* ed. Bill T. Arnold and H.G.M. Williamson (Illinois: InterVarsity, 2005), 925.

247 Noman K. Gottwald, *The Tribes of Yahweh: A Sociology of Religion of Liberated Israel 1250-1050 B.C.E.* (London: SCM Press Ltd., 1979), 35-41.

248 Marvin L. Chaney, *Peasant, Prophets & Political Economy: The Hebrew Bible and Social Analysis* (Eugene: CASCADE Books, 2017), 150.

royal court's lavish lifestyle and maintain his large army.[249] This economic burden contributed to social injustice, including forced labour. Forced labour was already established during David's reign (2 Samuel 20:24), but it became a fundamental state policy under Solomon.[250] Solomon implemented corvée labour, forcing his subjects to work on significant projects like the Temple, his palace, and other infrastructure. This system significantly strained the population and led to unrest among certain groups.[251] During Solomon's reign, he did not distribute the generated wealth evenly. The royal court, priestly class, and merchant elites likely enjoyed considerable luxury, while most of the population, mainly rural peasants, did not share in this prosperity. This unequal distribution of wealth led to increased social stratification and inequality.[252]

Ideological Exploration of Temple Accounts: The Deuteronomic History

As part of the Deuteronomistic history, I Kings reflects its time's theological and political concerns. The Deuteronomic historians compiling these temple accounts and Solomon's prayer in chapter 8 reveal their distinctive style and ideology. Through these writings, the author not only aims to present Yahweh as righteous but also conveys a political agenda that glorifies Israel while condemning certain practices and people.[253] The accounts in the Book of Kings are predominantly from a Judahite perspective, but I Kings also draws attention to countries beyond Palestine.[254]

The Deuteronomistic historian used source materials with a clear agenda. Numerous documents were incorporated, such as the throne succession accounts in II Samuel 9–20 and I Kings 1–2. However, the redactor made significant contributions by inserting comments and composing extensive passages, such as Solomon's prayer in I Kings 8. These programmatic sections, such as the prayer, reveal a strong connection to the language and ideology of the Deuteronomistic reform, further reflecting the historical and religious context in which they were written.[255]

249 David C. Hopkins, "The Dynamics of Agriculture in Monarchical Israel,"*Society of Biblical Literature 1983 Seminar Papers* ed. Kent Richards (California: Scholars Press, 1983), 196.

250 Millers and Hayes, *A History of Ancient Israel and Judah* (Philadelphia: Westminster Press, 1986), 207.

251 Patrick Nolan and Gerhard Lenski, *Human Societies*: *An Introduction to Macrosociology* (New York: McGraw Hill College, 1999), 216-19.

252 Philip King and Lawrence Stager, *Life in Biblical Israel* (Westminster: John Knox, 2001), 194.

253 DeVries, "I Kings," xxxiii- xxxv.

254 DeVries, "I Kings," xx.

255 DeVries, "I Kings," xl.

The author relied heavily on sources like the Book of Solomon's Acts (also known as Acts of Solomon) to construct the temple accounts, including references such as I Kings 5:15 and 24-26 (in Hebrew), and v.1 and 1-12 (in English). These sections were interpolated by the Deuteronomistic historians, especially in chapters 5 and 6, to emphasize the idea that the building of the Temple was the perfect fulfilment of the Exodus narrative. This material reflects the historian's theological aim of aligning Solomon's temple construction with the divine promises and laws given in earlier scriptural traditions.In composing chapter 8, the author employed an ancient *hero'slogos* (a legitimization recital), expanding much of the content to serve the author's ideological purposes. Verses 14-66, in particular, are attributed to the author's expansions, including the introductory note about the events surrounding the transport of the Ark and Solomon's hymn of dedication. Even the original conclusion of the temple dedication ceremony was extended to include a second warning to Solomon, recalling his earlier encounter at Gibeon.[256] This final section underscores the Deuteronomistic emphasis on divine approval of Solomon's reign while simultaneously warning against disobedience.

Scholars have argued that when the Temple accounts in I Kings are simplified, they can be traced back to the original temple source.[257] The Deuteronomist gives significant weight to Jerusalem as the city chosen by God for the Temple, and anything related to the Temple and Jerusalem as Yahweh's seat is treated at great length, often to the exclusion of other important political issues of the time.[258] This disproportionate focus reflects the Deuteronomistic historian's theological commitment to legitimizing Jerusalem as the central location for Yahweh's worship and authority.

The Deuteronomistic historian also made great efforts to legitimize Solomon's reign, evident in his presentation of Solomon's dream at Gibeon (I Kings 3:4-15).[259] This divine encounter serves as a narrative tool to confirm Solomon's role as a divinely appointed ruler, further reinforcing the Deuteronomist's theological and political agenda. Compared to the elaborate descriptions of the Temple's construction and furnishings, other issues, including political matters, are introduced sporadically and dealt with briefly. While the furnishing of other buildings during Solomon's reign was handled in much the same way as the Temple, the Deuteronomist chose to

256 DeVries, "I Kings," xliv.

257 James A. Montgomery, "The Book of Kings,"*A Critical and Exegetical Commentary* (Edinburgh: T& T. Clark, 1960), 37.

258 John Gray, "I & II Kings," *A Commentary* (Bloomsbury: SCM Press, 1964), 19.

259 Gray, "I & II Kings," *A Commentary,* 26.

emphasize the Temple over all else, showcasing the centrality of the Temple in the narrative.[260]

Therefore, the Deuteronomist's presentation of the Temple and Solomon's reign reveals a deeper ideological agenda. The Temple is portrayed as a physical structure and the ultimate fulfilment of divine promises. Solomon's reign was legitimized through divine encounters and the construction of the Temple. These accounts are carefully crafted to reflect the theological priorities of the Deuteronomistic historians, with the Temple and Jerusalem at the heart of their message.

The Temple as a Tool of Oppression and Burden (Ch. 5)

Solomon's Temple was a monumental construction project, and its completion required vast resources. Solomon negotiated with Hiram, the king of Tyre, to build this grand structure, using materials such as cedar wood and skilled labor. The contract between Solomon and Hiram involved a significant economic exchange between the two kingdoms, with Israel providing agricultural products in return for building materials and labour. Biblical sources indicate that Solomon lavishly used metals to construct the Temple. I Kings 6 states that he used large amounts of gold, silver, and bronze to build and furnish the Temple. Alan Millard points out that the account in the Hebrew Bible regarding the use of precious metals in the Temple follows the known patterns of ancient temples in Egypt and Mesopotamia and is not an exaggeration.[261] The question then arises: how did Solomon manage all these expenses? He did so through forced labour and taxation, as seen in Chapter 5. By gifting the land to the people of Israel and accepting their request for a king, Yahweh gave the king responsibility over the people. The king was to be closely associated with the Torah, and this association brought various tasks, such as, as Brueggemann points out, the prohibition of images, the observance of the Sabbath, and the care for brothers and sisters.[262] Therefore, imposing heavy taxes or forced labour (corvée) was against the principles of the Torah.

Solomon's reign deviated from Israel's social tradition in numerous ways. Neither tribal autonomy nor the public election of a charismatic leader, as Saul and David had done, appears to have received any consideration from Solomon.[263] While the biblical historians recorded Solomon's piety in building Yahweh a great temple, this Temple ultimately served as a tool of

---

260 Gray, "I & II Kings," *A Commentary,* 19-20.

261 Alan Millard, *Treasures for the Bible Times* (Oxford: Lion Press, 1985), 106.

262 Brueggemann, *The Land,* 58-62.

263 DeVries, "I Kings," xxiii.

oppression and burden for the people, rather than protecting them as the Torah intended the king to do.

The Temple as a Centralized Economic Hub (Ch. 5 & 6)

Solomon's Temple was more than a religious tower; it was a dynamic economic institution. Its involvement in livestock ownership, skilled craftsmanship, and wealth accumulation through various means positioned it as a critical player in the financial landscape of ancient Israel (7:1). Leroy Waterman suggested that the "additional structures" (I Kings 6:5) not only served for the use of Temple staff but also as store-houses, shops and storagespace, similar to other eastern temples.[264] While the biblical texts did not mention specific details of trade and commerce, the broader economic significance of the Temple in Jerusalem is undeniable. The concentration of wealth, resources, and financial activities within such institutions can further exacerbate existing disparities and marginalize those who are less privileged. Religious festivals and pilgrimages to the Temple brought wealth to the city, benefiting the urban elite, but may have imposed additional burdens on the rural population, who had to travel long distances to participate in these religious activities.[265]

With the building of the Temple, Solomon's religious horizon also expanded. Solomon allowed foreign elements into the Temple through the doorway from his harem. Due to this, an unusual development of religions took place in Israel[266] which later gave rise to religious syncretism. Solomon's openness to other spiritual practices encouraged cultural exchange and broadened commercial networks. By incorporating foreign influences, Solomon might have hoped to attract merchants and traders from different regions, which boosted the economy through increased imports, exports, and tribute.

The Temple as a Pillar of Political Stability (Ch. 8)

In I Kings 8:23-26, Solomon's prayer at the temple dedication reveals his political ideology centred on divine legitimacy, covenant fulfilment, and the use of religious symbolism to ensure political stability. By constructing the Temple, Solomon seeks to anchor his rule in divine promises, reinforcing his authority and securing the loyalty of his people.[267] Verse 23: Solomon

---

264 Leroy Waterman, "The Treasures of Solomon's Private Chapel," *Journal of Near Eastern Studies* 6 (1947): 161-63.

265 Benjamin D. Sommer, "The Impact of Temple Centralization on Jewish Socio-Economic Structures," *Journal of Ancient Judaism* 10 no. 2 (2020): 45-56.

266 John Endres, S. J., *Temple, Monarchy and Word of God* (Wilmington: Michael Glazier, 1988), 119.

267 Montgomery, "The Book of Kings," 195.

begins his prayer by acknowledging the uniqueness of Yahweh, who "keeps covenant and steadfast love with your servants who walk before you with all their heart." Solomon implicitly affirms his legitimacy as king by emphasizing God's covenantal faithfulness. He positions himself as the divinely chosen leader and considers that God sanctioned him through the covenant God made with his father, David.[268] Verses 24-25: Solomon emphasizes that the Temple's construction fulfils God's promise to his father, David, that David's lineage would continue on the throne of Israel. By doing so, Solomon was solidifying his political position as king. The Temple is a testament to God's favour towards Solomon and his house, making it a cornerstone of the king's strategy for maintaining political stability.[269]Walter Brueggemann also asserts Solomon's move as his social ideology. It serves as a reminder to the people that their prosperity and security are tied to the Davidic line, encouraging them to support Solomon's reign.[270]

The Temple as a Centralized Power

According to DeVaux,the Temple was built primarily to house the ark of Yahweh and as a centre of worship of Israel. However, because it was built adjacent to the palace, its function was under royal influence. Thus, despite its religious significance, the Temple operated under the monarchy and signified the complex relationship between religion, politics and economics.[271] By building the Temple in Jerusalem, Solomon sought to centralize religious worship in the capital city, effectively consolidating religious authority under his reign. This move helped to unify the diverse tribes of Israel under a single religious and political centre, reducing the influence of local shrines and priests across the kingdom. Centralized worship in the Temple reinforced Jerusalem's status as the spiritual and political heart of Israel.[272] The Temple's construction emphasized Solomon's role as the divinely appointed ruler, with the Temple as a physical manifestation of his power and legitimacy. The Temple housed the Ark of the Covenant, symbolizing God's presence, and associated Solomon's rule with divine favour, thus reinforcing his authority over the kingdom. The construction of a grand and lavish temple was a statement of Israel's wealth, power, and cultural sophistication to neighbouring nations. Solomon's Temple intended

---

268 G. H. Jones, *The New Century Bible Commentary: 1 and 2 Kings* vol. 1, (Grand Rapids: Wm. B. Eerdmans Publishing Company, 1984), 184.

269 Gray, "I & II Kings," *A Commentary*, 148.

270 Walter Brueggemann, *The Prophetic Imagination* (Minneapolis: Fortress Press, 2018), 28.

271 DeVaux, *Ancient Israel:Its life and Institutions*, 320.

272 Hopkins, "The Dynamics of Agriculture in Monarchical Israel," 198.

to enhance Israel's prestige internationally, positioning the kingdom as a significant regional power. Temple, in turn, supported Solomon's broader diplomatic and economic strategies, including his alliances with powerful neighbours like Egypt and Phoenicia.[273]

Case Presentation

A small village in the state of Andhra Pradesh, consisting of 110 families belonging to Dalit communities, was influenced by the local Pastor and the President of the Church (Baptist). The villagers, Christians by faith, were encouraged to build a massive church, comparatively more significant than the mainline Church in a nearby town. The villagers are primarily farmers and daily labourers. Motivated by the pastor and president's ideology to construct a more considerable church than those in the surrounding regions, they proceeded with the plans, and the construction was completed after four years.

The total expenditure on the construction was 70 lakhs (as of 2017), of which 22 lakhs were collected from other churches and employees. The remaining amount was taken as loans from various banks, facilitated by the president, a businessman. As a result, the congregation is expected to collect monthly offerings of Rs. 48,000/- as a monthly EMI (Equated Monthly Instalment) to the bank, which has become a significant burden for the villagers. Moreover, there has been no improvement in the social mobility of the villagers; many continue to live in thatched houses, and the village needs proper cement concrete roads, drainage system and water facilities.[274]

Case Analysis

The President of the Church, who hails from a wealthy class but is a Dalit, holds authority over the governance of the Church. Driven by his interest in building a huge church, he imposed his ambitions upon the villagers. His ideology is centred on gaining fame through the construction of the Church under his leadership. Since he was responsible for securing the loan, he claimed the right to remain the president of the Church for life. Due to the insecure governance policies that the Church holds regarding pastors, the pastor agrees with the president in every matter. As a result, the construction of the Church has led the villagers into bondage, both in terms of church administration and finances. The villagers were also involved in labouring for the construction of the Church. In this situation, the president exercised his power for personal profit by exploiting the poor and vulnerable, much

273 Carlo Meyers, "Temple, Jerusalem," *The Anchor Bible Dictionary*vol. 6, ed. David Noel Freedman (New York: Image Books Doubleday, 1992), 362.

274 Interview with P. Martha Rani, elder of the Church, a Baptist church ofcostal Andhra, July 19 2024.

like Solomon abused his authority. Solomon, being one among the Israelite populace, more definitely a brother of them, oppressed them and imposed a heavy burden on them. So also, the president, belonging to the same Dalit community who is a brother to them, out of greed for popularity and fame, led the villagers into economic oppression.

Spending vast sums of money on constructing places of worship continues to thrive in modern times. Across almost all religions, building churches, temples, mosques, and gurdwaras demands a lot of investment in spending billions of dollars. Often, religious communities compete with one another, seeking to demonstrate the superiority of their deity or faith through the grandeur of these buildings. However, the original teachings of the founders of these religions typically emphasized the importance of adhering to moral and ethical principles rather than the physical manifestation of worship spaces. For example, Yahweh repeatedly reminded the Israelites and their kings to prioritize obedience to Yahweh's laws and maintain devotion to Yahweh through righteous living rather than through lavish structures. This emphasis on moral conduct over material displays is a common theme in many religious traditions, though often overshadowed by the modern focus on monumental religious architecture.[275] Indukuri John Mohan Razu compares King Solomon and present leaders and states that "construction has become the major preoccupation of the leaders who govern the Centre or the state or the churches. These leaders at the helm- both Dalits and non-Dalits- behave like Solomon, squandering public money for an unproductive show of their bloated ego."[276]

Huge Churches: From Symbols of Dalit Identity to Agencies of Oppression and Burden

Dalits have faced centuries of discrimination, exclusion, and oppression within India's caste-based system, historically being denied access to public spaces, temples, education, and fundamental rights. In response to this marginalization, many Dalits sought new avenues for spiritual recognition, including the construction of large church buildings. Churches became essential spaces for Dalits to express their collective identity and reclaim their self-worth. These grand churches symbolized visibility, spiritual and cultural assertion, and breaking social hierarchies. For Dalit communities, the construction of large churches served as a source of pride, representing resilience, achievements, and a long struggle for dignity and equality. These churches also reflected the growing economic mobility of Dalits, many of

275 Indukuri John Mohan Razu, "1 & 2 Kings,"*One Volume Dalit Bible Commentary Old Testament* ed. James Massey(New Delhi: Centre for Dalit/Subaltern Studies, 2015),455.

276 John Mohan Razu, "1 & 2 Kings,"456.

whom advanced through education and migration. The significant financial investment in these buildings demonstrated progress in overcoming economic barriers. Additionally, these churches acted as centres of social activism, education, and community support, further strengthening the Dalit social fabric.

Gradually, however, all these constructive elements have turned inside out, and grand churches have become agencies of oppression and burden, as seen in the case presented. Initially, the construction of large churches was a source of pride and reflected the growing economic mobility of Dalit communities. However, as the need to fund, maintain, and expand these large institutions grew, they became a significant financial burden on the community. The resources required to sustain these structures, from upkeep to ceremonies, often exceed what local Dalit communities can afford. As a result, the financial burden pressurizes Dalit families to contribute financial support, leading to economic strain. Such a financial burden negatively impacts their social mobility, such as infrastructure for their homes and localities, education for children, and health care.

The very institutions meant to liberate Dalits from caste-based oppression have created new hierarchies within the Church. Leadership positions became a severe issue, as only wealthy or employed Dalits could hold them since the grand churches function primarily as a matter of money. In this situation, many Dalits from working-class backgrounds may need access to leadership roles, leading to internal divisions. The divisive politics create a situation where power and resources within the Church are concentrated in the hands of a few, recreating a system of exclusion.As the Church grew in influence and size, it became an institution of social control. Church leaders exert power over their congregations in ways that do not always align with the original message of liberation. Exercising power includes enforcing certain social norms and financial contributions and making participation in the Church burdensome rather than empowering. The larger the institution, the greater the possibility of corruption. Leaders within the Church prioritize their authority and benefit, becoming gatekeepers to access and resources, much like the caste structures the Church initially sought to dismantle. It is also a common notion that planning gigantic church buildings reveals and serves personal interests and facilitates financial corruption.

Social Mobility as an Alternative Identity for Dalits

Brueggemann opines that God's presence before the Temple also existed. God responded to the people's pleas in the wilderness and provided food. This act asserts God’s presence as a sustainer. God’s presence was with the people also in the form of clouds.[277] He states that wilderness is "the place of all lacks, because Yahweh is present, is where nothing is lacking."[278] The biblical histories attested to Solomon's piety in erecting a magnificent temple for Yahweh. The same historians documented the Temple's destruction, who saw it as God's punishment for Judah's preference for the shrine rather than its living Lord.[279] Reading Solomon's building of the Temple, Christians are encouraged to build huge church buildings with a lot of infrastructure, but it cannot be so. John Endres opines that "the text hardly seems to justify such a naive reading, for they point to the possibility of seeing indications of the divine in all of earth's materials."[280] Because God's presence was with Israel in the wilderness through clouds and fire and had no worldly structures, the Temple accounts in I Kings 6-8 imply that not everyone enjoyed the Temple's splendour, and many suffered for its construction.[281]

Solomon's rule informs affluence and the centralization of power, which Brueggemann contrasts with the egalitarian and justice-oriented Mosaic community, emphasizing the Torah.[282] The construction of the Temple represents an attempt to domesticate the divine, making God's presence controllable and aligning it with the royal agenda. Such an agenda contrasts with the Mosaic tradition, which emphasizes God's uncontrollable freedom and a religion that serves the marginalized, not the powerful.[283] Brueggemann notes Solomon's regime stifled the prophetic tradition by aligning religious practices with the state's interests.[284] It is essential to critique injustice and envision alternative identities in such a context.

Jeeva Kumar, in his work,[285] emphasizes the importance of land inheritance as a crucial factor in shaping the identity of Dalits in India. He argues that possessing a piece of land is not merely a matter of ownership but a powerful symbol of dignity and autonomy, offering Dalits a tangible way to establish their place in society. The idea of land inheritance ties into broader issues of socio-economic mobility, as land ownership historically provided individuals and communities with economic stability and a

---

277 Walter Brueggemann, *The Land: Place as Gift, Promise, and Challenge in Biblical Faith* 2nd ed. (Minneapolis: Fortress Press, 2002), 38.

278 Brueggemann, *The Land,* 41.

279 DeVries, "I Kings," xxiii.

280 Endres, S. J., *Temple, Monarchy and Word of God*, 119.

281 Endres, S. J., *Temple, Monarchy and Word of God*, 119.

282 Brueggemann, *The Prophetic Imagination,* 30-33.

283 Brueggemann, *The Prophetic Imagination,*25-28.

284 Brueggemann, *The Prophetic Imagination,* 36-39.

285 Jeeva Kumar Ravela, *Struggle for Land Rights in 1 Kings 21: A Dalit Hermeneutic Perspective* (Delhi: ISPCK, 2012), 83-95.

sense of belonging. For Dalits, who have been marginalized for centuries, owning land represents a significant step toward reclaiming their rights and self-worth. This perspective aligns with Dr. B. R. Ambedkar's famous slogan, "Educate, Agitate, Organize," which he proclaimed at the All-India Depressed Classes Conference in Nagpur on July 20, 1942. Ambedkar emphasized the transformative power of education in breaking the chains of caste-based oppression. He urged Dalits to prioritize education as the primary tool to challenge the deeply entrenched social hierarchies that kept them subjugated. For Ambedkar, education was the first step towards empowerment, followed by political and social activism ("Agitate") and the formation of collective movements ("Organize") to secure equality and justice.

In addition to education and land possession, access to fundamental rights such as healthcare and infrastructure is equally vital for Dalits to assert their identity in society. While grand churches may serve as symbolic spaces for spiritual and social gatherings, they should not be the sole markers of Dalit identity. Identity is not limited to the grandeur of a church, where people spend only a few hours every Sunday; it is also profoundly connected to the everyday realities of living conditions, local communities, and the availability of essential infrastructure like healthcare, schools, and roads. These elements are crucial in allowing Dalits to participate in society fully and claim their rightful place.

Access to land, education, healthcare, and infrastructure is necessary for Dalits to build a sustainable and meaningful identity. True liberation for Dalits, as envisioned by leaders like Ambedkar, lies not just in spiritual or symbolic representations but in tangible improvements to their quality of life. The argument highlights that a Dalit's identity must be grounded in their ability to thrive in everyday life, in the neighbourhoods they live in, and in the systems of support, both social and physical, that they can access.

Conclusion

The paper critiques the ideological motivations behind the construction of large religious buildings, drawing parallels between Solomon's Temple and a modern church in a Dalit Christian village in Andhra Pradesh. It argues that such projects often serve the interests of the powerful, imposing financial burdens on marginalized communities while failing to improve their social conditions. The paper calls for a shift in religious practices away from grand construction projects and towards addressing the real needs of low-income people, advocating for a prophetic approach that prioritizes justice, equity, and community welfare over prestige and grandeur.This article critiques the ideological motivations behind the construction of large religious buildings, drawing parallels between Solomon's Temple and a modern church in a

Dalit Christian village in Andhra Pradesh. It employs Ideological Criticism and the Socio-Historical Method to examine the economic, political, and religious contexts of ancient Israel during Solomon's reign. The article reveals how the construction of Solomon's Temple, driven by dominant ideologies, benefited the elite while imposing economic burdens on the ordinary people. Similarly, in the contemporary case presented, the Dalit Christian community is burdened by financial strain due to the construction of a grand church. This parallels Solomon's imposition of forced labour and heavy taxation. The article argues that such projects, while symbolizing identity and pride, often become instruments of oppression. It calls for religious practices to prioritize justice and equity and address the real needs of marginalized communities over the construction of massive buildings.

34

A Geo Trauma Reading of Jeremiah 12:7-12 Reclaiming the Importance of the Land and Wounded Psyche of the Margins

John Matthew

Introduction

Several scholars have explored the use of trauma theory as an interpretive lens to understand some of the most challenging and painful texts in the Bible. Trauma theory does not constitute a method of interpretation but a frame of reference that, when coupled with other methodologies (post-colonialism, refugee studies, Dalit Interpretation 3etc.). The impact of trauma is a significant component of the human condition when it comes to the people on the margins. Some questions are crucial and pertinent, such as who owns, has authority over land, and whose rights are protected. In this context, Jeremiah can be appropriated to read the land ideology, loss of land and the people's profound grief. These disturbing questions would continue to be ignored or rejected in the teaching and reflection of the faith communities many of us belong to. So, this suggests that the narrative can raise awareness concerning land abuse and violence and challenge readers of any era to resist it. Thus, this article intends to employ reclaiming spatial contexts and relations around traumatized people and the wounded psyche of the marginalised and contribute to re-traumatization or help to establish freedom and the rebuilding of life after traumatic events.

Violent Geography: An Assessment in Jeremiah's World

The cultural world of Jeremiah imageries to meet the experience of military violence of Assyrian invasion, which traumatizes its recipients. The symbolic world of text images the actual world of historical events, in this case, the plundering and burning of land and cities together with the killing of an urban population and displacement of the survivors.[286] In this context, the prophetic voice has the chance to express traumatization in the face of national danger: a process which makes the landscape the bearer of urban trauma, a traumascape. For Maria Tumarkin, the significance of such a site is that it permits the utterance of inner anguish because "thinking, grieving, remembering, need the right kind of spaces to unfold."[287] In Violent Geographies, Derek Gregory and Allan Pred consider the nature of imaginative geographies "through which politic violence works"[288]. They argue that geography can be a tool for expressing communal fear. "Landscapes can embody traces of blood, sweat and tears, deliberately written on the face of the earth to inspire fear." Therefore, confessions in Jeremiah may "serve as ready-made prayers for victims of trauma and disaster."[289]

Hermeneutics of Trauma as a Methodological Tool for Biblical Interpretation

A concept of trauma as a powerful interpretive lens. In 2013, the Society of Biblical Literature established the program unit titled "Biblical Literature and the Hermeneutics of Trauma" for its Annual Meeting. Acknowledging the diverse definitions and applications of trauma within biblical interpretation, the unit's organizers emphasized three primary areas for critical reflection. 1) how an interpreter defines trauma and particular aspects of it 2) The interpretative mechanism of such a definition, in the connection between personal and communal aspects of trauma 3) particular methods through which trauma hermeneutics in biblical interpretation can enhance various theological fields. Biblical scholars acknowledge various dimensions of trauma, encompassing the immediate repercussions of events or persistent circumstances and the processes that promote survival, healing, and

---

286 Jer 6:1–8. There is an interweaving of land and city boundaries in this passage, and rural images of shepherd and flock are used to depict the actions of foreign armies

287 Maria Tumarkin, *Traumascapes: The Power and Fate of Places Transformed by Tragedy* (Carlton: Melbourne University Publishing, 2005), 36.

288 Derek Gregory and Allan Pred, "Introduction," in *Violent Geographies: Fear, Terror and Political Violence*, eds., Derek Gregory and Allan Pred (New York: Routledge, 2007), 1-7.

289 Kathleen M. O'Connor, *Jeremiah: Pain and Promise* (Minneapolis: Fortress, 2011), 82.

resilience. Trauma hermeneutics serves as a tool for analysing texts within their historical frameworks and for examining how these texts are utilized in both historical and contemporary contexts.[290]

As it is in today's context, three primary frameworks shape the field of biblical trauma hermeneutics: psychology, sociology, and literary and cultural studies. Psychology enhances our comprehension of how trauma impacts individuals and the mechanisms that promote survival, healing, and resilience. Sociology offers valuable perspectives on the communal aspects of traumatic experiences. Meanwhile, literary and cultural studies facilitate examining how texts represent and bear witness to traumatic suffering while creating discursive and aesthetic environments supporting recovery and resilience. In such a way, it represents the sources for doing hermeneutic of trauma seeks to offer an interpretative framework that is focused on a) fractured memories, b) wordlessness: trauma unable the individual or community to talk about what happened or difficulty of the word d) numbness: it destructs the productivity of emotional responsiveness e) Loss of faith: in God and in community e) sense of powerlessness f) frozen experiences of biological beings. In terms of trauma hermeneutics, this appropriation of sources can be understood in terms of the critical task of defining victims on their trauma roots and reframing ever new challenges posed by their current devastating circumstances. The recurring themes in Jeremiah's book are inheritance, pluck up and build, which may relate to what O'Connor refers to as the "repetitive retelling of the catastrophe." This process assists survivors in regaining a sense of control over their experiences by transforming traumatic events into a series of "standardized narratives." Victims of trauma frequently grapple with distressing memories that can be evoked by various stimuli, such as sights, sounds, or smells, plunging them into an overwhelming state of panic and fear that is difficult to process in its entirety.[291]

To understand the nature and effects of trauma, O'Connor carefully delineates four. First, disaster fragments memory. Victims of violence and disaster often have trouble recalling the precise events or their proper sequence. In effect, 'trauma survivors can experience violence as a kind of stunning non-event, or more aptly, as such an overwhelming experience that they cannot receive it or assimilate it into consciousness". Memory of the disaster event is little more than "glimpses of horror" that distort reality. Second, disaster leads to the 'loss of language'; that is, victims of disaster are unable to articulate their experiences. In fact, "pain does not merely

290 Elizabeth Boase and Christopher G. Frechett, ed., *Bible through the Lens of Trauma* (Atlanta: SBL Press, 2016), 2.

291 O'Connor, *Jeremiah: Pain and Promise*, 21.

resist being put into language; it destroys both language and the power to think symbolically". This is really a direct outgrowth of the fragmentation of memory. Third, the experience of disaster leads to what O'Connor labels "numbness." That is, people lose the ability to feel any emotion. True "grief and anger become unreachable" and the grieving process is prematurely foreclosed. Disaster victims exist "in a shut-down, half-alive state ... no longer fully alive in the world". Fourth, disaster leads to a loss of faith. O'Connor explains: "like a solar eclipse blotting out the sun, calamity blots out God because death and destruction obscure any sense of God's protective and faithful presence."[292]

Hermeneutics of trauma is attuned to the fact that language can encode and respond to traumatic experiences in ways that correspond to the effects of trauma as well as to mechanisms of survival, recovery, and resilience. Trauma hermeneutics has the potential to uncover justifications for identifying meanings that have not been previously acknowledged, or that may challenge current interpretations. Understanding how texts embody traumatic experiences can reveal a depth of meaning that transcends the literal interpretation of the language. By focusing on how trauma narratives depict past occurrences through fragmented or impressionistic representations, sometimes utilizing affective or bodily imagery, the interpreter is freed from the presumption that such imagery requires a straightforward explanation of events. Hermeneutics of trauma examines how texts connect experiences of suffering, as well as the structures of both subjective and collective experiences, alongside their discursive and aesthetic forms.[293] This theory is particularly attuned to encoding the unknown and unassimilated, allowing it to elucidate the gaps and disjunctions present within texts. It highlights the effects of the often violent disruptions that underlie the textual world. Biblical Scholars who recognize the historical contexts surrounding biblical texts can apply trauma hermeneutics to explain specific textual characteristics. They achieve this by being mindful of how the text may engage in a rhetorical framework to represent and interpret trauma, thereby serving as a mechanism for promoting recovery and resilience among individuals and communities. Interpreters may use insights from contemporary trauma studies to interpret characters about situations of trauma as constructed in the world of the biblical text. An important aspect of trauma Hermeneutics that is to be taken as valid, seemingly disparate elements of the biblical text that trauma hermeneutics illuminates are depictions of the behaviours and attitudes of YHWH that seem violent and even abusive, especially when

292 O'Connor, *Jeremiah: Pain and Promise*, 21-26.

293 Elizabeth Boase and Christopher G. Frechett, *Bible through the Lens of Trauma*, 1-17.

considered alongside other biblical depictions that appear compassionate and merciful.[294]

Multiple Temporalities of Geo Trauma: A Definition

Kai Erikson characterizes collective trauma as a significant disruption to the fundamental structures of social life, which undermines the connections that bind individuals together and diminishes the overall sense of community.[295] In contrast, Jeffrey Alexander views collective trauma as a social phenomenon in which a group embraces a specific narrative of trauma. This narrative serves four primary functions: it recognizes a collective seen as having endured severe suffering; it articulates the nature of that suffering; it identifies the perpetrators responsible for inflicting the suffering; and it seeks to engage a broader audience in solidarity with the victimized group. Once this narrative is embraced, it becomes a cornerstone of the group's identity.[296] Drawing on longstanding structural analyses, it highlights the typical role of oppressive power relations in various collective forms of trauma. It pays special attention to lived experience and the repositioning of survivors as experts in narrating trauma, and it recognizes the work of reclaiming space after dispossession. The term geotrauma has appeared sporadically in ecological philosophy and literary analysis. The theory of trauma contends that what is traumatizing to a person is not simply the experience of violence or threat to life and security. Instead, it is also what is symbolically evoked by the experience, including the community's response to the person who has been traumatized. A contextual and sociological approach to trauma recognizes that the violence and resulting trauma is symptomatic of a social pathology and, therefore, moves the locus of the problem of interpersonal violence from its historical location in a victim's personality to the misogyny of the culture expressed through the actions of perpetrators of violence. This approach to trauma also highlights the fact that experiences of violence, subjugation, and pain result not from the inadequacies of an individual but from how the culture, through its various hierarchies and textual traditions, defines identity, silences, dominates, invalidates, and rejects a member by his/her status within a minoritized group in that culture. Thus, Geotrauma describes multiscalar, intersecting and mutual relations between trauma and place. The aspect of Geo trauma theory that is particularly suited to the process of reframing and/or re-symbolising the traumatic events underlying the book

294 Elizabeth Boase and Christopher G. Frechett, *Bible through the Lens of Trauma*, 18-20.

295 Kai Erikson, *A New Species of Trouble: Explorations in Disaster, Trauma, and Community* (New York: Norton, 1994); also see Erikson, in *Trauma: Explorations in Memory*, ed., CathyCaruth (Baltimore: Johns Hopkins University Press, 1995), 187.

296 Jeffrey Alexander, *Trauma: A Social Theory* (Cambridge: Polity, 2012), 6.

of Jeremiah is the notion of Geo trauma proposed by trauma theorists like Ron Eyerman and Jeffrey Alexander[297]. Jeremiah 12 is a master narrative of trauma that helps his audience face the devastating effects of the Babylonian invasion and exile. The threat of being plucked off from the land is a theme of a God who sees injustice and trauma and who hears the cries of those in pain, the marginalised. On the one hand, one sees that the Babylonians are the perpetrators, who, in an incredible show of imperial force, burned down the place of the people's city that they were invading, and many of its inhabitants were forcefully removed to Babylon. As O'Connor explains it, trauma becomes a disaster when "violence reigns down upon a whole society. When suffering and loss heaped upon one person is no more than a minuscule moment in the massive destruction of a society and its habitat, violence magnifies its effects in uncountable ways."[298]

Alexander argues that representing trauma depends on constructing a framework of cultural classification. Trauma representation constructs a narrative that persuades the audience collectively that they have been traumatized. Four representations are essential in the creation of this narrative:

- the nature of the pain: what happened and to whom;
- the nature of the victim: who was affected;
- the relation of the trauma victim(s) to the broader audience: the extent to which the trauma narrative prompts a broader audience that has not experienced the victim group's suffering to identify with the immediately victimized group; and
- attribution of responsibility: who caused the trauma299.

Through such representation, a new plurality is constructed; it is a collective we that identifies itself as a traumatized community.[300]

Identifying geo trauma as a process in which an interlocking mechanism in terms of mutuality of the grip of place and trauma makes sense to see the causative events connected to the people's lives. Such events as memorial places, retraumatizing places, layered places, hardwired places, mobile places, places of repossession and healing places are embodied components to frame the traumatic experience, place and memory. Through geo trauma interpretative method, the social and psychic maladies that ensued, which are bound up in memory, image, contamination and a frozen temporality

297 Kathleen M. O'Connor, *Jeremiah: Pain and Promise*, 31-36.

298 Kathleen M. O'Connor, *Jeremiah: Pain and Promise*, 3.

299 Jeffrey C. Alexander, *Trauma: A Social Theory*, 6.

300 Ron Eyerman, Jeffrey C. Alexander, and Elizabeth Breese, eds., Narrating *Trauma: On the Impact of Collective Suffering* (Boulder, CO: Paradigm, 2014), Introduction, xiii.

and its repositions. Repositioning survivors as experts in narrating and understanding trauma enables recognition of resistance and the mobilization of place in addressing trauma. Therefore, Geo trauma is a tensive topology.

Temporalities, as Land points out, the notion of trauma corresponds to a breach or invasion, the emergence of something into the conscious system, which that system struggles to assimilate.[301] A What Nick Land terms geotrauma gives a discourse on Geo Trauma symptomatic splitting or displacement in which its meaning alternates to denote the inexorable laws of absolute territorialization.[302] Geo-trauma helps us to rethink the relationship between the human and the interconnectedness of the land. Geotrauma in the context of the then immiscible and indeterminate harms of being other specificities of the geological and its imbrication in geographies of harm, that which might be categorized as Geotrauma.[303] Thus, Geotrauma results from epistemic and material partitions in the relation between subjective attachments and inorganic forces, such as the dispossession of land, ecologies, and lifeworld. We understand geo truama as a 'wound' in a wider 'whole', in a 'cosmos' that embraces bodies, organisms, materials and nature. Beyond an individual and isolated experience, it belongs to a physical and material reality- in which the entire life on earth is inscribed.

Mary Mills has also addressed the concept of using trauma theory as a vehicle for exploring the textual construction of Jeremiah. Mills works with those aspects of trauma theory which have been engaged by cultural geographers, suggesting that Jeremiah be read as a traumascape. In her chapter on reading Jeremiah as a Deathscape (2013), she explores the memorialization of space, as a withered landscape found in passages within Jeremiah 1–25 provides a suitable literary site for communal mourning over the loss of land and the horrors of war. She draws on studies in the geography of violence as an entry into the concept of traumatization in the face of national danger. This opens into the nature of trauma studies[304].

301 Nick Land, *Fanged Noumena: Collected Writings* (UK: Urbanomic Sequence Press, 2011), 333.

302 Nick Land, *The Thirst for Annihilation: Georges Bataille and Virulent Nihilism* (London: Routledge, 1992), 496.

303 Kathryn Yusoff, "Afterword Geotrauma, or Geology as a Praxis of Struggle, "*Environmental Humanities* 15/3 (2023): 284–291.

304 Mary E. Mills, "Deathscape and Lament in Jeremiah and Lamentations," in *Jeremiah Invented: Constructions and Deconstructions of Jeremiah*, eds., Else K. Holt, Carolyn J. Sharp (Bloomsbury: Tand T Clark, 2015), 66, 74.

Jeremiah 12 for Traumatic Reading: Appropriating Geo Trauma and Experiences of Marginals and Land

One could say that Jeremiah 12 serves as a prime example who seeks to frame the traumatic events of the Babylonian invasion and exile in such a way as to help his audience, on the one hand, face the traumatic events they had lived through while also finding some meaningful way of moving beyond disaster. We need to be critical look and to take the words in Jer12: 7-13, which expresses the words of exhausted grief, as Brueggemann says, "one who so treasures the land and now finds it so abused that it must be abandoned."[305] It expresses the whole story of traumatic reading in terms of the story of land and people. Therefore, this is a powerful text that overtures the whole story of the land and people, and it is described as a second confession of Jeremiah.

Verse 7-8 begins with a threefold use of "inheritance" *nahalah*; the land of the people had been Yahweh's unique; the land is possessed by none other; it belongs to the people of the land. The land is autonomous, and the use of inheritance is again affirmed in Jer 12:10. The heritage is inalienable to the land of the people. The rapacious attitude of King which was resulted in a destructive way to abuse it. Then the land- the inheritance of Israel has been destroyed and ruined by those whom Jeremiah describes as many shepherds.[306] This hostile situation signals the brokenness, antagonism, and alienation in the land and the people. Abuse of the land aborted the community experience; it has made them heritage to desolation. Abusers have overturned the life-giving potential of the land and the life-celebrating quality of the community. Thus, the good land is made desolate land. It is used to denote the extreme vulnerability people experience in foe face of disaster.[307] As Dalit Rom-Shiloni observes, the loss of the land designates a terminal break in both the physical existence of the people. The people are doomed to death within the land—physical and mental obliteration. It puts them under emotional stress and leads to loss of identity of the psyche. This ongoing stress can be viewed in terms of geo trauma one who experiences the dislocation. One of the results of traumatic experiences is 'splintered memories. Prophet arguing and intensifying the power of the contrast is

---

305 Walter Brueggemann, *A Commentary on Jeremiah: Exile and Homecoming*(Michigan, Wb. Eerdmans Publishing Co, 1998) 121, and see Walter Brueggemann, *To Pluck Up, To Tear Down: A Commentary on the Book of Jeremiah* (Grand Rapids: Wb. Eerdmans Publishing Co, 1988), 125, 115.

306 R. E. Clements, *Jeremiah, Interpretation: A Bible Commentary for Teaching and Preaching* (Atlanta: John Knox Press, 1988), 84.

307 L. Juliana Claassens, "The Rhetorical Function: The Woman in Labor Metaphor in Jeremiah 30-31: Trauma, Gender and Postcolonial Perspectives," *Journal of Theology for Southern Africa* 150 (November 2014): 68, 67-84.

like dwelling in the threat of the ominous jungle of the Jordan. The life of the people is driven by isolation; experiences of this isolation seem to impact their consciousness as it overpowers the senses. Then, the brain of such people undergoes fragmented or pieced events, or they inflict injury on the human psyche. The land and the body are discursive and nondiscursive modes of representing collective suffering sites of simultaneous land-based violence[308] and we feel the land-body trauma in our bodies, because we are the land, land is us. Loss of land and body and grieving of it changes the people those who are at the margins as humans, because it connects them to the life and things they value.

Jeremiah's persona describes pathos and a pathetic identity. Pathos here is defined as the fully embedded experience of grief, not an outsider, taking the suffering of the people as a felt reality. Prophetic confession bears the stress and emotional and physical pain. In brief, the prophetic persona can be narrated as the collective voice of those who are traumatised. This persona of Jeremiah is revealed in the confessions and represents an embodiment of the wider community and its traumatic temperament. Based on human emotions, there is also a deepening of a catastrophic sense of isolation and social deterioration. In this sense, we need to define a crisis on the basis of the language of spatiality, which is in terms mostly in tune with trauma. Here, trauma can be defined as, in this context, the crisis of struggle with life as liminality and to envisage space in this regard, Kathleen O'Connor suggests that the book of Jeremiah's wide-ranging collection of poems, metaphors and stories seeks to find language to name this world undone by trauma. The book of Jeremiah is thus a quest for meaning, an ongoing attempt to help the people of Judah survive as a people.[309]

Regarding Jeremiah 12, we can see the memorial place as one of the focal points to arrive at Geo-trauma Hermeneutics, as a specific site to elaborate issues around collective displacement and the loss of place. The term inheritance can be viewed as a site of subjective interpretation, rendering the haunting of politicized fields of power more visible as it comes

---

308 Ayesha Ahmad, Victoria Pratt, and Samrawit Gougsa, "Where is the land and Indigenous knowledge in understanding land trauma and land-based violence in climate change?" *British Medical Journal* November 379/22(2022): 2790.

309 Kathleen M. O'Connor, *Jeremiah: Pain and Promise*, 31, Louis Stulman and Hyun Chul Paul Kim, *You are My People: An Introduction* (Nashville Abingdon, 2010), 9-26, 97-112. Cf also Louis Stulman argues that as part of the rebuilding process, the prophet is seeking to sculpt new theological formulations out of "the rubble of devastation" that may assist the survival of the people, *Order amid Chaos Jeremiah as SymbolicTapestry* (Sheffield: Sheffield Academic Press, 1998), 185. Similarly, Bauer writes, "Viewed from this perspective, Jeremiah is a work of resilience, a book of massive theological reinvention, and a kind of survival manual for a destroyed society" Bauer, Gender in Jeremiah, X.

from the Babylonian empire. Congruously, one could argue and forges an irradiated territory with the Earth that pushes the "land of hope" to "hope of land". Therefore, the idea of inheritance changes land as its territory. The breakthrough of the land as no productivity depicted in verse "ungrounds", the earth from its moorings and it's viewed from the background of fertile land promised to the ancestors, now is impaired and in ruins as a result of empire.[310] When we see Chapter 12: 7-12, metaphors are used to represent the people and land that are under attack. The shifting of metaphor from wild beasts to shepherds, and heritage (people) to vineyard (land). The metaphor of the shepherd indicates that, in a suggested way, the pastoral nomads destroy the labour of the people of the land. Here, the vineyard is the land of Judah. For Bewer, shepherds are figures of invaders whose forces ravage the land.[311] It is an archaeological fact that some of the cities of Judah show two levels of destruction at the end of the 7th century. Moreover, Yahweh's pathos is due to the non-productivity of the land, which has lost its potential due to the systemic injustice perpetuated by the figure of invaders. Then, the text creates a landscape of vast desolation.[312] as it is that total barrenness that signifies the role of the land as a place capable of carrying and making sense of the weight of social trauma.[313] By indicating the land in which ruin will be manifest, the text produces a context appropriate to traumatic events. So, Jeremiah may well have had in mind some severe attack that was already over when these words were written.[314] We can take Zizek's metaphor to appropriate verses 2 and 4; Zizek suggests: "We must really accept how we are rootless. He uses a wonderful metaphor, boat. Boat is the solution; boat in the sense of, you accept rootless, free floating. This philosophical sense of cutting of roots and the acceptance of drifting at sea, rendered imperative in seeing geo-traumatised, functions with the intensification in horror.[315] Therefore, themes of rejection, pathos, and tragedies can be taken as serious content, as well as how the land was being rootless by vicious aggression. The confession narrated in Jeremiah 12 fleshes out the trauma of the community. The tragic aspect of the mourning of the land is that the whole community can be caught up in the web of hurt and hurting. It is this

310 Mary E. Mills, *Alterity, pain and suffering in Isaiah, Jeremiah and Ezekiel* (New York: T and T Clark, 2007), 110-134.

311 Julius August Bewer, *The Book of Jeremiah* (New York: Harper, 1951), 167-175.

312 Julius August Bewer, *The Book of Jeremiah*, 167-175.

313 Robert P. Carroll, *Jeremiah: A Commentary* (London: SCM, 1986), 170.

314 J. A. Thompson, *The Book of Jeremiah* (Michigan: William B. Eerdmans Publishing Company.1980), 358.

315 Slavoj Zizek, *Monologue in film 'Children of Men'. Alfonso Cuarón* (United Kingdom: Universal Pictures, 2007).

reality which confronts the community in the face of the death of other in the land.[316] The mourning earth imagery in Jeremiah invites human beings to view the disorder that exists or is about to engulf both earth and society. Although the subject of these passages is land, the mourning earth metaphor is set within an overall literary landscape, warning an urban community of the fate awaiting it. The metaphor sets up a memorial to Jerusalem, under threat, by engaging in extended imagery in which a piece of land widens out to the whole earth and thence to the whole cosmos. Therefore, death scape is achieved by combining the seasonality of land failure with the ultimate failure of the entire created order.[317] The land mourns is a representation for communication, conversation, and verbalization on land-based violence, loss, land-body trauma, and grieving. It is a language that reflects everything it evokes. It is multiple modes of expression of verbalization or impulses of language in the wake of trauma, as seen in v. 7. v. 8.

Pluck up and Build: A Trauma Narrative-Rhetoric for Reclaiming the Wounded Psyche of the Margins

The Confession texts are both rhetorically and effectively linked to the surfeit of affective language.[318] In this context, O'Connor suggests that these standardized narratives may assist survivors in coming to terms with the trauma that has intruded upon their lives.[319] The presence of the confession texts means for O'Connor that the 'rhetoric of (human) responsibility' is 'not a definitive interpretation of the disaster but one among many'. In effect, as a 'counterview' of the disaster, the Confessions 'generate questions about causes and complicate interpretation of disaster.'[320] So, we read in Jer 12 :14 to describe the trauma narrative that captures well the trauma and recovery associated with the exile: these words pluck and build is to describe the effects of trauma; the prophet is creating a shared vocabulary for the people that helps them come to terms with the violence that had broken into their lives, so helping the people to face toe trauma on both an emotional and spiritual level.[321] Thus, Trauma Narrative-Rhetoric studies affirm the

316 Mary E. Mills, *Alterity, pain and suffering in Isaiah, Jeremiah and Ezekiel* (New York: T and T Clark, 2007), 110-134.

317 Mary E. Mills, *Alterity, pain and suffering in Isaiah, Jeremiah and Ezekiel*, 78.

318 Robert P. Carroll, *Jeremiah: A Commentary*, 170–173.

319 Kathleen M. O'Connor, *Jeremiah: Pain and Promise*, 22–23.

320 Kathleen M. O'Connor, *Jeremiah: Pain and Promise*, 88-95.

321 O'Connor writes that by constructing memories of the invasion in an imaginative space, the prophets invent other ways of speaking of the traumatic events: "They revise a vocabulary of experience and build common language to name what has happened, to give it shape, and to revisit it emotionally and spiritually", Kathleen M. O'Connor, *Jeremiah: Pain and Promise*, 57.

importance of creating a trauma narrative, a coherent narrative capable not only of processing past trauma but also of fostering resilience against further traumatization. Such narratives construct identity and solidarity in ways that can restore healthy assumptions about the self and the world. Thus, the prophet offers a restoration from the painful loss of the land. Verse 15 is an act of imagining the future in the midst of foe trauma, which can be understood as an act of resistance that forms a vital part of surviving trauma. The texts in the confession narrative in Jeremiah 12 that imagine a future in which foe survivors once more will engage in everyday life of the building, planting, and going back to their own inheritance all attest to foe survivors' enduring hope for redemption, for a future in which they will once more go on woof the everyday task of living one's life. Therefore, the words of Jeremiah intensify with Judith Hermann; it identifies three stages that form a vital part of the recovery process as follows: (1) Reaching safety, (2) Remembrance and Mourning, (3)Reconnecting with ordinary life Judah's restoration[322] that is imaged in terms of the everyday activities mentioned above can be understood in terms of this third stage of recovery by identifying *Nahalah (inheritance)* the land mourns (*abbal*), language used in this text in conjunction with the land is an attempt to voice the trauma experienced by the people. Thus, the phrase 'the earth mourns' provides a metaphor for the effects of warfare in ravaging the land as well as a symbol for the cosmic dysfunctionality, the return to chaos, which human violence shares with a reciprocating divine aggression[323].

The language of the land expresses the rape of the land experienced as a society. It captures a wide variety of experiences regarding the painful reality of trauma. The case of land mourners fits with traumatic experience as a struggle in terms of land and pathos of the marginal community into a dialogue with the biblical text. Therefore, Jesuratnam suggests that to clarify the decentred world of Jeremiah and Dalits, the interpretation and appropriation of the biblical text, in this case, has to take place in a measured to improvise the meaning of the biblical text.[324] The confession in Jeremiah may reflect and resonate with the pain and pathos of marginals. Therefore, these are the prayers of people in anguish and distress, and they are probably put in the mouth of Jeremiah as prayers of anticipation of God's

---

322 Judith Herman, *Trauma and Recovery: The Aftermath of Violence-From Domestic Abuse to Political Terror* (Portsmouth: Hachette Book Group, 2022), 3.

323 Katherine Murphy Hayes, *The Earth Mourns: Prophetic Metaphor and Oral Aesthetic* (Atlanta, GA: Society of Biblical Literature, 2002), 89-117.

324 K. Jesurathnam, "Before I Formed you in the womb of your mother: The Decentered World of Jeremiah and Dalits", *Bangalore Theological Forum* Vol XLIII/1(2011): 5.

intervention and deliverance.[325] The question, how long are the events born out of personal trauma experience and unbearable pain, which is asked in the context, if the land is part of our bodies, then acts of violence against the land are a form of self-harm.

In brief, the task of uprooting and planting is to be seriously noted in the case that land acts as a broader symbol for a just life in which Dalits are allowed to have both physical and social space - the space to claim ownership and navigate life freely and peacefully without fear of violence. Uprooting the social landscape defined by the cast driven hierarchy and planting to regain the psyche, intangible sense of status, belonging and voice in the community. The words pluck, and plant is charts functioning like a grid to galvanize the inanimate life of the marginals, who were the hopeless exiles. It is this socio-political reality which underlies the book and which is focalized in the rhetoric of characterization by the depiction of Jeremiah as the man of pain, as in the prophetic laments where the prophet speaks to God about his intolerable burden of pain and suffering and his reluctance to announce this message of pain to his fellow citizens, as in Jer. 12.7-17. It is then the internal symbolic world of violence which is under consideration in rhetorical interpretation. From the angle of rhetorical exegesis, the literary world is discussed in its own right. This approach covers both the experiences of an original audience and those of modern readers: modern wartime experiences of traumatic disorder can be used to construct a suitable reading methodology.

In this context, the book of Jeremiah is viewed as a text that manages social disruption by employing robustly violent metaphors to provide a means of coming to terms with painful reality. Building on a similar insight, literary scholar Michelle Satterlee proposes that when a traumatic instance ruptures a person's or a community's social world and framework, reconnection must occur before memory, narrative composition or even the ability to address the experience of violence and fight for justice. Moreover, Satterlee argues that trauma 'is rooted within a cultural context, and tie(d) to specific landscapes.[326]. As survivors map the fractured memory of their suffering onto the world around them, all possibilities for, and visions of justicc, begin to grow out of the inhabited landscape. Thus, Dalit Geo trauma narrative rhetoric would then work as liberating psyche to rebuild and plant the lands of the shattered and lives of the scattered people.

325 Patrick D Miller, *The Book of Jeremiah* in New Interpreter's Bible, 666–667.

326 Michelle Satterlee,"Landscape Imagery and Memory in the Narrative of Trauma: A Closer Look at Leslie Marmon Silko's Ceremony", *Interdisciplinary Studies in Literature and Environment* 13/2(2006): 77, 73-92.

Traumatizing the Experiences of Dalit/Marginal/Individual/Community: Land as a Contested Space for Reflective of Geo Trauma as a Reality

The right to land is denied to the Dalits. The crucial elements in the landlessness of Dalits are the inability to access the land and forced evictions. Landlessness is a pervasive feature of Dalits through social oppression and caste oppression. Landlessness is foundational to the existence of Dalits as a distinct social group in rural areas; it forms the material basis for the domination and exploitation of Dalits in the non-economic spheres as well in this context, it is no surprise that the efforts of upper caste groups to sustain "cultural differentiations" transgress into the non-cultural spheres, including the economic sphere.[327] This lies the trauma events in the name of cultural trauma; it has been careful to notice how the tactics of dominance can be brought to impose psychological oppression based on cultural differentiations. A substantial proportion of the land distributed to Dalits is not in their possession, owing to encroachment by non-Dalits. In exceptional instances where Dalits do get to own land, they are dispossessed of it sooner or later. There is a strong correlation between land and atrocities. Land remains an issue of contention and the major cause of atrocities. Access to justice is delusional for marginalized Dalits. When these atrocities are taken into serious consideration, geo-trauma is an outcome of land alienation. For Dalits, land is the lifeline of low-income people and the sole means of livelihood. There is a need to recognize Dalits' Right to Land as a birthright. The experience of anger and helplessness, violence and fortitude, pain and sorrow, humour and pathos, despair and hope has shown that there is a traumatic impact on the psyche of marginals that would evoke significant symptoms of distress in almost everyone." So, Cultural, collective trauma occurs when members of a group feel that they have been subjected to terrible treatment over time, which leaves "indelible marks upon their group consciousness."[328] Dalits have experienced moments of closeness to death; they are destined to feel the pain as imperfect moments inland. And Dalits are in the midst of desperation. Discomfort with the anaemic forces and abysmal situations.

Intersections of Dalit experiences and Trauma: Towards Dalit Geo Trauma Reading

Embodied and emotional experiences of trauma always intersect with wider societal discourses, constructing a geo trauma hermeneutics to intersect with Dalit experiences, shattering the identity and well-being of the marginalised

327 Guru (2012), Notes on the caste system in India, "cultural difference may subsume within itself elements of both material and social hierarchy".

328 Jeffrey C. Alexander, *Trauma: A Social Theory*, 6.

people's emotions in the public sphere. K. Jesuratnam, in his article, 'Dalit and Subaltern Hermeneutics,' makes clear that the importance of Dalit hermeneutics is a more specific way to address the dynamics of power, socio-political and economic religious concerns.[329] As this interpretation of seriously developing Geo trauma hermeneutics based on the interpretive community enhancement, thus it reveals that Dalits are denied of God-given human dignity and denial of their rightful space in terms of their resources, opportunities sand, justice and acceptance.[330] Developing the Dalit Geo Trauma Hermeneutics acts as making- meaning process.[331] The intersections at the heart of each intricacy, dynamics and convergences of race, class, memory, and politics use formal intersections with traumatic narratives in terms of denial and of their land as well, overlaying disparate genres to narrate the land, violent inscriptive processes and rendering more visible the haunting of depoliticized fields of power'. Thus demonstrating the persistent relevance of the literary and imperial past. The land is ontologically significant for Dalits. Abandoning their ancestral inheritance is anathema. As a matter of discussion, I have drawn an idea from one of the trends in trauma literature as identified by Michelle Balaevis: the important role played by place. "Descriptions of the geographical place of traumatic experience and remembrance situate the individual about a larger cultural context that contains social values that influence the recollection of the event and the reconfiguration of the self". The place does not mean the geographical location alone, but is the coming together of culture and nature, and includes both their relationship to the geographical space and how they were treated there.[332] Therefore, Dalit Geo trauma can be classified as collective trauma that is found "between the poles of the individual and liminality of land. Dalit Geo trauma is also intergenerational, which is just one of the several reasons Dalits identify and sympathise with African-American victims of slavery and racism. The importance of the intergenerational quality of trauma that is to be connected is that "significant lessons can be learned and passed between generations through the recital of a story about loss and

329 K. Jesurathnam, "Dalit and Subalterns Hermeneutics in Conversation with reader Response Method: I kings 22 A Casc in report," *Bangalore Theological Forum*vol.58/1(2016): 49-51.

330 K. Jesurathnam, "Dalit and Subalterns Hermeneutics in Conversation with reader Response Method: I Kings 22 A Case in report,"49.

331 For an overview of the literature on meaning-making, especially in the wake of shattered memories, see Crystal L. Park, "Making Sense of the Meaning Literature: An Integrative Review of Meaning Making and Its Effects on Adjustment to Stressful Life Events," in Psychological *Bulletin* 136 (2010): 257–301.

332 Michelle Balaev, ed., Contemporary *Approaches in Literary Trauma Theory* (New York: Palgrave Macmillan, 2014), 149-151.

suffering." The shared land-body trauma experience profoundly affects a community's ability to respond collectively, as the damage is both social and individual.[333] Here, it is ascribed to the expressions of exhausted Grief: the one who treasures the land is seen as abused. At this juncture, we must return to those root wounds and listen to the stories of fear, helplessness, silence and isolation. The intersectional approach means re-shaping the stories about human relationships with the land. However, today, in the present Indian context, like that during the time of the prophet Jeremiah, we see so much of the exploitation and misuse of land, looking at the continuity between the past and the present state from a Dalit point of view, it does not come as a surprise that ideas about monarchy then, and elite land owners and privileged class people now maintained their continuing influence. The opulent and unjust leaders and rulers identified are blinded by wealth and power and fail to lead the people toward a right in the book of Jeremiah. These are linked with the failure of the landowners who understand the cause of the decay of the land. Rulers and elites continue to display power and status, whereas socially underprivileged strata, by contrast, continue to suffer oppression and suppression. It is at such a juncture that the strong voice of the prophet countering the power, status, wealth, and misappropriation should resonate with the prophetic ideology of land promulgated in the book of Jeremiah, which can serve as a catalysing factor and a vantage point to raise voice against the misconception and misuse of land and provide new insights or stimulation to rethink specific issues about land in the margins.

Conclusion

The land is more than just any piece of property, which one, without ado, could exchange for something else or manipulate at one's own will. The land is the symbol of restoration, security and life-giving. The argument presented here suggests that the experience of acquiring land under the providence of God as the ultimate owner generates a unique land ideology. Jeremiah's articulation of land as God's *Nahalah* and how this *nahlah* is polluted by those in power, resulting in the loss of land, is remarkable. The words and deeds of Jeremiah and the arrangement of the materials to articulate the Prophetic Ideology of land enhance the book's function in guiding the readers to be in a prophetic vision that embraces a common bond of human kinship, spatial repossession and healing and cosmic justice.

333 Kai Erikson, "Notes on trauma and community," in Cathy Caruth, ed., *Trauma: Explorations in Memory* (Baltimore/London: John Hopkin University Press, 1995), 185.

35

From Exclusion to Embrace
Dissecting Deuteronomy 10:17-18 through Tribal Lenses

Hukholu Yhobu

Introduction

Deuteronomy 10:17-18 presents an important theological paradigm about God's nature- supreme sovereignty, impartiality, and compassion toward the marginalized. For the marginalized tribal communities in North-East India, who often face systemic exclusion and discrimination, this scripture offers profound insights into God's call for justice and inclusivity. Through a tribal hermeneutical lens, this study seeks to understand the biblical text of Deuteronomy and explore its relevance for tribes in the region. The tribal communities are geographically isolated, economically marginalized, and culturally distinct from mainstream Indian society, and they have often struggled with exclusion in various dimensions of life. The analysis also reflects on the internal challenges that disrupt tribal unity, especially the growing class disparities within these communities.

"From Exclusion to Embrace" signifies the theological move from systemic exclusion and marginalization towards embracing divine justice and compassion. This work delves into the social, cultural, and spiritual realities of tribal communities while juxtaposing them with the Biblical call for impartiality, justice, and the protection of the vulnerable.

Overview of Tribal Communities in North-East India

K. Thanzauva suggested that tribals are a community characterized by speaking a shared language, adhering to consistent social rules, and collaborating for collective welfare. According to him, the tribal have a commonality of names with contiguous territory, a relatively uniform culture or way of life, and a tradition of common descent.[334] Thanzauva also noted that these groups often share names within their neighbouring regions, have a relatively uniform culture or lifestyle, and have a tradition of common ancestry. Thanzauva further viewed that "tribe" and "tribal" denote those with relatively isolated lives and technological backgrounds.[335] Wati Longchar rightly points out that the term tribal has been imposed on the people by anthropologists, missionaries and later by the Indian constitution, where people are preferable by identifying them as Khasi, Mizo, Naga, etc.[336] Hence, the deliberative study will focus on the inhabitants of Northeast India, who are isolated and alienated by mainland India and are socially, economically, and politically disadvantaged.[337] Tribals are geographically isolated or semi-isolated, identified with a particular territory, and have distinct social, economic and cultural traditions and practices. The main criteria adopted for specifying communities as the scheduled tribes include: a) traditional occupation, b) distinctive culture, which includes the whole spectrum of tribal way of life, i.e., language, customs, traditions, religious beliefs, arts and crafts, etc., c) primitive traits depicting occupational pattern, economy and d) lack of educational and techno-economic development.[338]

Marginalization and Exclusion faced by Tribal communities

Marginalization and exclusion refer to the absence of participation in society and emphasize the issue's multi-dimensional, multi-layered, and

334 K. Thanzauva, *Theology of Community: Tribal Theology in the Making* (Aizawl; Mizo Theological Conference, 1997), 1.

335 Thanzauva, *Theology of Community: Tribal Theology*, 1.

336 Wati Longchar, "Tribal Theology- Issues, Method and Perspective," *In Search of Identity and Tribal Theology: Attribute to Dr. Renthy Keitzer,* ed. A. Wati Longchar (Jorhat: Tribal Study Centre), 50.

337 The term "tribal" today is reappropriated by ethnic communities as a symbol of identity, pride, and honour, shedding its colonial connotations. While alternative terms like "indigenous" or "ethnic group" exist, they fail to encapsulate the kinship, socio-cultural, and political consciousness that the word "tribal" represents for these communities. Zhodi Angami, *Tribals Empire and God – A Tribal Reading of the Birth of Jesus in Matthew's Gospel* (London: Bloomsbury T&T Clark, 2017), 10.

338 Pradesh V. Subramanyam and S.Narayana Rao, "Cultural Identity, Exclusion and Inclusion of Tribes in India: An Empirical Research Study in Visakha Agency of Andhra Pradesh," *Skylines of Anthropology* 2, no.2 (December 2022): 144.

dynamic nature. This concept also involves both the process and result of excluding a social group from power centres and resources. It represents a significant form of discriminatory practice.[339] Exclusion has taken the form of segregating a group from the social, political, economic, cultural, educational and religious domain of societal life. Further, it also culminates into a system of domination and subjugation. All these processes not only lead to oppression and exploitation, but also keep certain social groups away from the mainstream development.[340] Marshall Wolfe identifies several types of social exclusion: exclusion from livelihood, exclusion from social services, welfare and security networks, exclusion from political choice, exclusion from popular organization and solidarity, and exclusion from understanding of current events.[341] It results in denying access to opportunities, public goods, public offices, institutions, and self-respect in public spheres. Socially excluded people lack social recognition, self-respect, and social values. The basis of exclusion can be race, ethnicity, gender, religion, language, region, caste, etc. Each form of exclusion has its nature and manifestation. The issue of social exclusion is usually related to the problem of equal opportunity.[342]

Geographical and Spatial Exclusion

Spatial exclusion is a significant concern in the framework that contributes to the social exclusion of tribal communities in India. Many tribal areas live in remote, inaccessible regions such as hills, forests, deserts, and islands. This spatial isolation has several critical impacts due to limited access to Development Programs and services.[343] The majority tribal population's non-participation in many ongoing development programmes and administrative bottlenecks have also contributed to slow development over the years. The physical isolation of tribal communities frequently makes them less reachable for government development initiatives and services. This seclusion obstructs crucial services such as healthcare, education, and infrastructure. For instance, tribes residing in mountainous areas might struggle to reach schools or hospitals at a considerable distance, leading

339 Tarun Gogoi, "Social Exclusion and Ethnic Mobilization: A Perspective from North East India," *IOSR Journal Of Humanities And Social Science* 27, no. 1, Series 1 (January 2022): 17.

340 Tarun Gogoi, "Social Exclusion and Ethnic Mobilisation in Northeast India: Understanding the Role of Elites," *Scholars Journal of Arts, Humanities and Social Sciences* 9, no. 12 (December 2021): 632.

341 Cited in Kumar, "Social Exclusion and Ethnicity in Northeast, 21-22.

342 V. Biju Kumar, "Social Exclusion and Ethnicity in Northeast India," *The NEHU Journal* XI, no. 2 (July 2013): 21-22.

343 Kumar, "Social Exclusion and Ethnicity in Northeast, 21-22.

to reduced educational achievements and worse health outcomes.[344] Thus, this spatial exclusion perpetuates a cycle of poverty and marginalization by reinforcing the divide between tribal communities and the mainstream population. It contributes to the slow pace of development in tribal areas and prevents these communities from benefiting from national economic growth and modernization.

Exclusion from Livelihood and Economic Opportunities

Tribal communities often experience lower income, poor living conditions, and limited access to healthcare, education, and various services. They also face challenges accessing labour, land, and capital markets, leading to diminished work returns and weaker political representation. This poverty and social exclusion are primarily the result of historical and ongoing discrimination at both social and institutional levels, starting from the colonial period and continuing into the post-independence era. Such discrimination restricts their economic opportunities. The lack of infrastructure, including roads and communication networks, further hampers their ability to access markets, sell products, or engage in broader economic activities. This economic marginalization limits their participation in economic activities and access to essential resources. It often results in inadequate job opportunities, discriminatory employment practices, and restricted ownership or control over land and productive assets. Isolated tribes may also have limited access to resources such as agricultural land or forest wealth. Consequently, tribal communities face enduring poverty and economic instability, which exacerbates their exclusion from mainstream economic development and opportunities.[345]

Cultural and Social Segregation

Tribal communities often face significant cultural and social exclusion, which deepens their marginalization. This exclusion is evident in various ways: tribal groups typically have unique cultural practices, languages, and social norms that distinguish them from the mainstream population. These differences can lead to social segregation and reinforce stereotypes, making it challenging for tribal people to integrate into broader society. The effort to preserve traditional practices and maintain cultural identity can sometimes lead to further isolation from economic and social opportunities. Social and cultural isolation also affects political representation. Tribal communities may lack the political connections or knowledge to advocate for their rights

344 Subramanyam and Rao, "Cultural Identity, Exclusion and Inclusion, 144.

345 Tanuja Mohapatra, "Tribes of Odisha: Issues of social inclusion, exclusion and cultural assimilation," *An Interdisciplinary Journal* 5 (2011):16-17.

or engage in political processes. This underrepresentation in decision-making bodies limits their ability to influence policies that impact their lives and continues their exclusion from national development. As a result, cultural and social isolation perpetuates systemic inequalities by hindering tribal communities from fully participating in the social, economic, and political spheres of the country.[346] It undermines their ability to access opportunities and resources that could improve their living conditions and integrate them into the broader societal framework.

Thus, isolation and exclusion significantly contribute to the marginalization of tribal communities. Addressing these issues requires targeted policies that bridge the gap between tribal and mainstream populations, enhance access to essential services, and promote inclusive development practices that respect and integrate tribal cultures while ensuring equitable opportunities for all.

Internal Challenges within Tribal Societies: Disparity and Social Hierarchies

Western Penetration and the Disruption of Communitarian Life

Historically, tribal societies in North East India were known for their peaceful and cohesive communitarian living, anchored in mutual respect, shared resources, and collective responsibility for land and sustenance. However, the arrival of Western colonial forces and modernity began to redefine this way of life. Western ideologies, emphasizing economic competition, individualism, and market-driven systems, clashed with the deeply ingrained communal values of tribal societies.[347] These external influences transformed the social structure, reshaping tribal life into fragmented economic and social inequalityclusters.

Once a collective resource, it is no longer a communal land as per commodification. Legal frameworks, resource extraction for external markets, and the displacement of Indigenous people for development projects further entrenched divisions within the community. The impact of these changes was not just economic but also deeply social, leading to the rise of classes within previously egalitarian societies.[348] As communities fractured, social hierarchies emerged, creating a scenario in which economic disparities began to define relationships within the tribe, making class a new marker of power and privilege.

346 Mohapatra, "Tribes of Odisha: Issues of social inclusion, 17.

347 Paoyoshang Kashung, "A Hermeneutics of Identity – Justice Perspectives," *Journals of Tribal Studies* 19, no. 2 (December 2014): 26-27.

348 Wati Longchar, *Returning to Mother Earth – Theology, Christian Witness and Education: An Indigenous Perspective* (Kolkata: PTCA, 2012), 15-16.

The Thorns of Classes in Tribal Society

The paradigm shifts brought by these external forces introduced the "thorns of classes" within tribal societies. Over time, the once-egalitarian community was divided into hierarchical layers, with a small elite class emerging at the top, enjoying access to resources, while the majority remained marginalized. The following sections explore the critical consequences of these shifts.

Widening Economic Gaps and the Rise of the Tribal Elite

In the past, land and natural resources were communal treasures shared and maintained by all. However, the gradual infiltration of modern economic practices and external interference tilted this balance in favour of a select few, typically those with access to education, political power, or external resources. This small elite group, often called the tribal elite – has managed to control most of the land, forest resources, and development opportunities. Consequently, the wealth disparity between the elite and the broader population has grown significantly, leaving the majority in poverty, struggling to meet basic needs while watching their lands and livelihoods shrink under elite control.

This stark economic gap mirrors the capitalist tendencies introduced through external influences, where resources become concentrated in the hands of a few, leaving the majority behind.[349] The erosion of communal ethics favouring individualism has deepened these divides, splitting tribal society into two distinct groups: privilege and deprivation. The wealthier elite no longer view the land as a collective resource but as a tool for personal profit, exacerbating economic inequalities and creating an underclass within the tribal population.

Social Fragmentation and the Loss of Unity

As economic disparities widened, so too did the fractures in the social fabric of these once-united communities. Trust, cooperation, and mutual aid, which had long been pillars of tribal life, were replaced by suspicion, competition, and exploitation. The elites, increasingly isolated from the rest of the community due to their economic standing and access to government aid or external resources, began to distance themselves from the traditional communal ethos.[350]

This shift has led to a breakdown in kinship ties and communal solidarity, with the wealthy few prioritizing their gain over the welfare of the

---

349 Nikhil Kumar, *Economic Disparities in Tribal Societies: A Case Study of North East India, Journal of Tribal Affairs* 15, no. 2 (2023): 45-47.

350 Arup Jyoti Das, "The Erosion of Communal Values and the Rise of Elite Tribalism in North East India," *Journal of Indigenous Studies* 18, no. 1 (2022): 89.

broader community. Leadership positions, once a collective responsibility for the tribe's well-being, have now become avenues for personal enrichment. As a result, traditional values of unity and mutual care erode under the pressure of class divisions, creating an atmosphere of mistrust and division that undermines the strength of tribal life.[351]

Political Control and Elite Manipulation

The rise of the tribal elite has altered social and economic dynamics and reshaped political control within these societies. The elites have gained control over local governance structures by leveraging their newfound wealth and influence. By manipulating government schemes and development programs intended for the upliftment of the entire tribe, they have further entrenched their dominance, leaving the majority of the population even more marginalized.[352]

This process of "elite capture" is not unique to Northeast India but reflects a broader global trend in which development initiatives intended to empower marginalized communities are co-opted by those with power. As a result, the gap between the wealthy elite and the impoverished majority continues to grow, leaving the marginalized needing a voice in local governance and excluded from meaningful participation in the development process.[353]

Cultural Disconnection and the Crisis of Identity

Perhaps one of the most painful consequences of class divisions is the erosion of tribal identity and cultural cohesion. As the elites become more integrated into the mainstream economy and society, they distance themselves from traditional tribal customs, values, and practices. Cultural traditions that once emphasized respect for the environment, communal living, and collective responsibility were replaced by focusing on individual wealth accumulation and power.[354]

This disconnection from tribal heritage is particularly evident among the younger generations, who want to maintain their tribal identity and aspire to the elites' material success. The result is a cultural fragmentation that threatens the foundation of tribal life as younger members struggle

351 Das, "The Erosion of Communal Values and the Rise of Elite Tribalism in North East India," 90-91.

352 Bimol Akoijam, "Elite Capture and the Subversion of Tribal Development Schemes in India's North East," *South Asian Tribal Review* 10, no. 3 (2021): 123-124.

353 Longchar, *Returning to Mother Earth – Theology, Christian Witness and Education An Indigenous Perspective,* 74-76.

354 Lakshmi Purnima, "The Crisis of Tribal Identity: Cultural Fragmentation in North East India," *Indigenous Heritage Journal* 20, no. 4 (2020): 35-37.

with the tension between upholding their traditions and navigating a society increasingly defined by class divisions. These internal conflicts further deepen the divides within the community as tribal identity becomes another casualty of class stratification.[355]

Connecting the Paradigm Shifts

These paradigm shifts in the relationship between tribes and nature, and between tribal members themselves, illustrate how deeply Western penetration has altered the social fabric of tribal communities in North East India. The commodification of land, driven by external capitalist influences, has widened economic disparities and led to a loss of communal solidarity. The rise of the tribal elite, the manipulation of political power, and the erosion of traditional values have transformed once-egalitarian societies into fragmented communities marked by competition and inequality. As the "thorns of classes" continue to pierce through the heart of tribal life, the social, economic, and cultural cohesion that once defined these communities slowly unravels, leaving a complex landscape of internal conflicts and challenges.

Social and Historical Context of the Text

In Deuteronomy, Moses addresses the Israelites standing on the edge of the Promised Land, marking a crucial transition from their wilderness wanderings. Based on the covenant made at Mt. Sinai, Moses addresses the people, emphasizing obedience. The previous generation failed to follow Yahweh's commands, leading to their downfall and eventual death in the wilderness. Moses' farewell address, delivered from the land of Moab, includes three main parts: a review of their past experiences, a restatement of the laws and the covenant, and a final call to obedience. In this context, Moses stresses that Yahweh is impartial, caring for the marginalized, such as orphans and widows, and expects the Israelites to embody these values. The historical context highlights a shift from exclusion to embrace, where Moses instructed the Israelites to reject the pagan practices of the Canaanites and instead uphold justice and inclusivity as central to their covenant with Yahweh. Covenant renewal intends to prepare the Israelites to live a just and faithful life in their new land, ensuring they maintain their unique identity and relationship with Yahweh amidst their new surroundings.[356] Top of FormBottom of Form

---

355 Kashung, "A Hermeneutics of Identity – Justice Perspectives," *Journals of Tribal Studies* 19, no. 2 (December 2014): 27-28.

356 Jeffrey Audirsch, "Historical Background: The Book of Deuteronomy," Accessed on September 10, 2024, https://www.academia.edu/2583364/Historical_Background_The_Book_of_Deuteronomy.

Interpretation of God's Impartiality in Deuteronomy 10:17-18

God's Unique Sovereignty and Supreme Nature

Verse 17 is the accumulation of titles for God, emphasizing the uniqueness, absolute sovereignty and supremacy over all other powers in the universe. The phrases הָאֱלֹהָאֲדֹנִיםהָאֱלֹהִיםאֱלֹהֵי "God of gods and Lord of lords," serve as superlative expressions that emphasize the supreme and absolute nature of God's authority. The statement here may well be the ultimate source of the phrase "Lord of lords and King of kings," as Craigie noted.[357] The awesome transcendent of God, whose nature is beyond human comprehension, has been revealed as the great, mighty, and awesome one who is impartial. On the term הַגִּבֹּר "the mighty" presents Yahweh as a warrior or "mighty man" a "man of war."[358] Israelite's supreme God deeply cares about the needy in Israel; thus, the Israelites must live out the same compassion for the alien, orphan and widow. Moses gives attention to Yahweh's unparalleled character (10:17), where the title "The Lord your God" highlights the role of Israel's covenantal Lord and all-powerful creator. Moses ascribed three descriptive terminologies to delineate various aspects of Yahweh's uniqueness: "the great God, mighty and awesome," "great God the awesome one" and "great God the mighty one,"[359] It reinforces God's role as a powerful protector and defender of justice. Thus, Yahweh is the transcendent and Supreme Being whose extraordinary nature is beyond human comprehension but who also reveals at the same time as impartial and just.

In the tribal context, the attribution of God as "Supreme" or "Almighty" is interpreted less through the lens of dominion and more through a communitarian hermeneutic. For example, the Ao Naga tribe refers to the Supreme Being as *Lijaba*, with "*Li*" meaning earth and "J*aba*" meaning to indwell, symbolizing God's immanence in nature and humanity. This worldview emphasizes God's presence within creation rather than focusing solely on His transcendence. Nonetheless, the notion of God's supremacy is still acknowledged. Like the Israelites, understanding a supreme God who cares deeply for the needy, the Ao Naga believe that Lijaba, who indwells with the earth, provides for all people, regardless of social class. This symbiotic relationship highlights the tribal perception of divine care for communal needs.

---

357 Cited in Duanel L. Christensen *Word Biblical Commentary: Deuteronomy 1-11,* vol.6,ed. David A. Hubbard and Glenn W. Barkert (USA: Library of Congress Cataloging-in-Publishing Data, 1991), 206.

358 Christensen *Word Biblical Commentary*, 206.

359 Michael A. Grisanti, "Deuteronomy,"*The Expositor's Bible Commentary Revised Edition,* ed. Tremper Longman III & David E. Garland (USA: Zondervan, 2012), 601.

Moses' portrayal of Yahweh in Deuteronomy 10:17 further underscores God's unparalleled nature. Titles such as "The Lord your God" and descriptive phrases like "great God, mighty and awesome" reflect Yahweh's role as Israel's covenantal Lord and the sovereign creator. In the same way, tribal leaders and elders, often holding significant influence within their communities, were reminded that their power and authority were ultimately subordinate to God's supreme will. The attributes of "great, mighty, and awesome" were not just theological constructs but served as practical reminders that Yahweh's governance and justice applied equally to all members of the tribal community. Such divine governance reinforced a sense of collective responsibility among tribal leaders to ensure their decisions and actions aligned with God's universal principles of justice and care, thereby preserving harmony within the community.

Impartiality and Integrity in Justice

God is "no partial and takes no bribes," "He does not lift up faces," the Hebrew idiom for giving particular regard to a person; the meaning is that God cannot be corrupted in his administration of justice as is possible too often in the human court. Regarding penalties for wrongdoing, God remains completely impartial; before his court, every person has an equal standing regardless of his position in the community.[360] In Deuteronomy 1:17, human judges were to possess the same quality because God requires a whole-hearted commitment of his followers, where God sees what is in the heart and cannot be persuaded or bribed into reducing his requirements in any way.[361] Unlike Aristotle, for example, justice is not distributive according to a man's importance or contribution to the community. Being impartial, God provides justice for the weak and the less fortunate in the community, whom human assistance neglects often. [362]Overall, God cannot be enticed or coerced into any partiality through influence peddling and is especially advocated for defending fewer people who are so often victims of such unscrupulous behaviour.[363] In the tribal worldview, the concepts of partiality and bribery are absent in the God-Human-Nature relationship. Relationships involve a mutual responsibility between God, humanity, and nature. This shared responsibility reflects the core of tribal life, where respecting the balance and nature of these relationships is crucial. For the

360 G. Ernest Wright, "The Book of Deuteronomy," *The Interpreter's Bible* vol. 2, ed. George Arthur Buttrick (New York: Abingdon Press Nashville, 1953), 400-401.

361 Grisanti, "Deuteronomy," *The Expositor's Bible Commentary*, 601.

362 Wright, "The Book of Deuteronomy," *The Interpreter's*, 400-401.

363 Eugene H. Merrill, *The New American Commentary: An Exegetical Theological Exposition of Holy Scripture* (USA: Broadman & Holman Publishers, 1994), 204.

tribal communities, the path to a peaceful, fruitful life lies in honouring this interconnectedness, where the God of the tribes, like their own, acts without partiality or corruption. This God upholds justice by recognizing and preserving the integrity of relationships, a highly contextualized understanding of divine justice. The principle of divine impartiality plays an essential role in maintaining harmony and justice among different tribal clans. In societies where internal conflicts and disputes were present, the idea that God "does not lift up faces" – showing no favouritism – served as a critical reminder of the need for fairness in tribal councils and legal proceedings. This impartiality reinforced the importance of unbiased judgment, ensuring that tribal decisions aligned with equality, justice, and respect for all, regardless of one's status or influence within the community.

Inclusive Compassion for the Vulnerable and Marginalized

God's impartiality is a stern expression in terms of his גֵּרוְאֹהֵבוְאַלְמָנָהיָתוֹםמִשְׁפַּט "justice for the fatherless and the widow" and the love for "the sojourner, providing food and clothing."[364] Yahweh "executes justice for the orphan and widow, members of Israel whom society often treats unjustly. Further, Yahweh loves and cares for the aliens as though they were members of the covenantal community.[365] In short, God is particularly concerned for those whose socioeconomic status makes them most vulnerable in human affairs.[366]

In the context of tribal Israel, God's inclusive compassion extended to the most vulnerable members of society, reflecting the same principles of impartiality discussed earlier. Although each tribe operated within its social structures and hierarchies, God's impartial nature demanded empathy and support beyond tribal or social boundaries. This expectation of justice, rooted in the divine care for orphans, widows, and sojourners, resonated deeply within the tribal worldview. Just as God's justice in Deuteronomy transcended human influence and favouritism, it calls tribal communities to adopt practices that fostered equality and care for all, regardless of status. This alignment of divine justice with tribal communal ethics ensured every individual had access to justice, reinforcing a symbiotic relationship between divine principles and tribal responsibilities. Thus, the divine impartiality described in Deuteronomy was not just theological but a practical framework for maintaining social harmony and ensuring that justice reached every corner of the community.

364 Christensen, *Word Biblical Commentary*, 206.

365 Grisanti, "Deuteronomy," *The Expositor's Bible Commentary*, 601.

366 Christensen *Word Biblical Commentary*, 206.

From Divine Justice to Tribal Renewal

To embrace tribal cultures and traditions again, one must recognize the deep connection between the values in Deuteronomy 10:17-18 and the ethics that historically guided tribal societies. As emphasized in the passage, God's impartiality and justice align closely with the communal values of fairness, equality, and integrity that tribal communities have long upheld. The idea that God shows no partiality and cannot be corrupted calls to reflect on how these divine attributes mirror the need for impartial governance and collective responsibility in tribal life. It reaffirms that justice should reach everyone, especially the marginalized and vulnerable, much like in the biblical context where God defends the fatherless, widow and sojourner.

Tribal societies have already taken significant strides in addressing these challenges and issues despite facing external pressures that have led to the erosion of traditional values. Many tribal communities have initiated efforts to reclaim their heritage and restore the balance that once defined their way of life. Through local governance, social movements, and cultural revitalization programs, tribals are working to return to fairness, inclusion, and care for the vulnerable. This movement shows a strong resilience and commitment to the integrity of tribal values in the face of modern influences that often foster inequality and social stratification. Tribals assert their role as protectors of justice and communal harmony, reviving their age-old practices while adapting to contemporary realities. This proactive leap is both an affirmation of their cultural resilience and a response to the challenges of modernity.

The Deuteronomistic God advocates for justice and equality in a way that speaks powerfully to the challenges of our times. By calling the Israelites to defend the marginalized, care for the sojourner, and uphold justice without favouritism, God sets a model for us to approach our communities today. Tribal societies grappling with marginalization, inequality, and erosion of traditional values must embrace these divine principles. God's justice is not static but invites an active engagement in the world, challenging us to restore fairness, equality, and compassion. By drawing from the timeless teachings of Deuteronomy, we can confront contemporary societal divides and foster a more profound sense of communal responsibility, ensuring that justice and equality reach every corner of our societies.

Conclusion

The message of Deuteronomy 10:17-18 is clear: God is supreme and impartial, and His justice extends to all, particularly the marginalized and vulnerable. This biblical principle, when interpreted through tribal lenses, offers a powerful call for justice and inclusivity in the context of North-

East Indian tribes. For these communities, who face external exclusion and internal fragmentation, the text provides theological and practical guidelines for building a more just and unified society.

The challenges faced by the tribals, such as geographical exclusion, economic marginalization, cultural segregation, and the rise of internal class hierarchies, find their resolution in the biblical call for impartial justice and communal care. By embracing these principles, tribal communities can work towards overcoming their divisions and creating a society that reflects the divine ideals of fairness, compassion, and inclusivity. The text invites tribal leaders to recognize their responsibility in upholding justice while urging communities to resist the forces that divide them and instead embrace their shared values of communal living and mutual care. In doing so, they can move from a state of exclusion to one of embrace, where the marginalized are cared for and the community thrives.

36

A Dog's Life better than a Dead Lion
A Dalit Liberative Reading of Ecclesiastes 9:1-6

Sam Thomas Arisapogu

Introduction

When I started my theological journey in 2010, I was introduced to studies on Dalits, Dalit Theology, and Dalit Reading of the Biblical Text. While I was pursuing my bachelor's degree program under the Senate of Serampore, I was deeply inspired by the works and contributions of Rev. Dr. K. Jesurathnam. His writings inspired me to relate faith and theological endeavours relevant to my experience and background. When I joined the Master's program at the United Theological College, Bengaluru, I began to widen my thought and view the world from a Dalit perspective. Dr. Jesurathnam's mentorship also influenced me to write my thesis, which focused on Dalit Liberative reading of the text. It enabled me to explore my own identity as a Dalit and discover the complexities of being a Dalit. During my Master's program, I learned about the atrocities of discrimination and exploitation towards the Dalit communities through the Dalit Course offered by Dr. Jesurathnam. I decided to be a Dalit voice and read and write from a Dalit Liberation perspective.

This article came to life because of the influence of Dr. Jesurathnam. This article focuses on reading the text to understand animal imagery in the book of Ecclesiastes, chapter 9:1-6. One of the significant images that I will reflect on is the dog imagery. The imagery of the Dog must be read from a Dalit point of view to understand the nuances of symbols and imageries that contribute to meaning-making in day-to-day life. Employing the Dalit liberative hermeneutics, I will draw on the implications of dog imagery used in the book of Ecclesiastes for the Dalits. Dalits are often regarded as dogs in Indian society, and although the reference to dogs is often derogatory, I wish to explore the understanding of dog imagery in a favourable light of affirmative resistance. The imagery of the Dog in Ecclesiastes is presented in comparison to the dead Lion. Although the living Dog is said to be better, the comparison itself suggests the Dog is often accepted as the 'underdog'. Dalits are regarded as dogs because of socially imposed categories that relegate them to the bottom of the structure. However, a Dalit reading of the text suggests that the imagery of the Dog presents intricacies in understanding its symbolic meanings.

Take Life as It Comes Ecclesiastes 9:1-6 Exegesis

Vs. 1 For[367] all this I gave my heart,[368] examining[369] all this, that[370]

367 I agree with Craig Bartholomew in translatingכִּי as casual. [Craig G. Bartholomew, Ecclesiastes, Baker Commentary (Grand Rapids, MI: Baker Academic, 2009), 296.] Longman considersכִּי as an asseverative.He translates it as “indeed.” [Tremper Longman III, *Ecclesiastes*, NICOT (Grand Rapids, MI: William B. Eerdmans Publishing Company, 1998), 224.] Most commentators debate on whether v. 1 continues the previous idea or starts a new one. I agree with Bartholomew that v.1 continues from the previous idea in chapter 8. [Craig G. Bartholomew, Ecclesiastes, Baker Commentary (Grand Rapids, MI: Baker Academic, 2009), 296.]

368 MT hasאֶל־לִבִּי, Bartholomew suggests that the more common construction would be with the direct object markerאֵת. [Bartholomew, *Ecclesiastes*, 296.]. Longman suggests emending it with אֵת, a similar idiom is seen in 7:2 and a similar usage in 2 Sam. 13:33; 19:20. [Longman III, *Ecclesiastes*, 224.]

369 This verb לָבוּר is not an easy word to interpret. The MT suggests the rootבור, “to examine, make clear, explain” BDB, Bartholomew explains this word occurs only here in the OT. [Bartholomew, *Ecclesiastes*, 296.] Seow says the root word בור is attested in Arabic and Akkadian. [C. L. Seow, *Ecclesiastes*, The Anchor Yale Bible (New Haven: Yale University Press, 1997), 297.] However, Peter Enns describes that the Hebrew root here is debatable. It is either בור (“to explain”), which only occurs in Ecclesiastes, or ברר, which is seen in 3:18 (“to test”). The difference in the root word does not affect the interpretation. [Peter Enns, *Ecclesiastes* (Grand Rapids, MI: William B. Eerdmans Publishing Company, 2011), 93-94.]

370 Bartholomew suggests the word אֲשֶׁר is nominalized here in use. [Bartholomew, *Ecclesiastes*, 296.]

the righteous and the wise and their deeds[371] are in the hand of God, whether[372] it is love or hate one does not know. Everything before them[373]

Vs. 2 everything is the same for everyone,[374] one fate for the righteous and the wicked, for the good,[375] and the clean and the unclean, and for those who sacrifice and those who do not. As the good person, so is the sinner, the one who swears like those who shun[376] an oath.

Vs. 3 This is an evil in all that is done under the sun, for there is one fate for all,and also the heart of humans is full of evil, and vexation is in their hearts while they live, and after that[377] to the dead.

---

371 Schoors points out thatמֶהֵיַדְבָעו is an Aramaism in its morphology, suggesting an ancient Near Eastern influence. [Antoon Schoors, *The Preacher Sought to Find Pleasing Words: A Study of the Language of Qoheleth* (Leuven: Peeters, 1992), 60-61.]

372 Translating the phrase האֱנְשׂ־מַג הָבָהאַ־מַגis complicated, and its literal meaning is "both love and also hate." Seow suggests it refersto "their deeds," noting that in v. 6 it refers to human activities and not to God. [Seow, *Ecclesiastes*, 298.] I argue that it refers to God and that humans cannot know the acts of God as well as God's emotions.

373 The literal meaning of מֶהֵינְפלis"before them."Bartholomew explains that it can be understood temporally (in advance) or spatially (before their eyes). He says, though there were difficulties in determining what it means, LXX reads the preceding wordלכֹּה asלָבָה, so that the end of v. 1 reads "all before them is enigmatic." By taking love and hate to refer to God, Bartholomew thinks מֶהֵינְפלmust be read temporally to refer to what awaits humans. Bartholomew, *Ecclesiastes*, 296.]

374 It is because of challenges in readingלכהמֶהֵינְפל in the previous verse. Few commentators emend לכֹּהat the start of v. 2 to read לָבָה, thus connecting with the previous two words "all before them is enigmatic." However, this emendation is not necessary. Bartholomew suggests the Hebrew phrase read as "everything is as for all," meaning "everything is the same for everyone." [Bartholomew, *Ecclesiastes*, 296.]

375 בוֹטל stands alone in the verse, unlike the other comparisons, which have a dichotomy. So, most commentators see this as a problem. Fox considered it as haplography at this point in the MT. He follows the LXX in adding "and the bad." [Michael V. Fox, *Qoheleth and His Contradictions*, BLS 18 (Sheffield: The Almond Press, 1989), 257.] Longman considers the word as a later addition to the text. [Longman III, *Ecclesiastes*, 225.] Robert Gordis suggests that the absence of "and the evil" is due to the rhythmic aspect of the text. However, there is a theological issue, and the MT reading has been retained in the text. [Robert Gordis, *Koheleth: The Man and His world* (New York: The Jewish Theological Seminary of America, 1951), 300.]

376 The word ארָי means "fear." Seow translates "the one who reveres the oath" in opposition to "the one who swears." However, the Hebrew text does not indicate false swearing. Based on an Akkadian parallel, he points out that the contrast here is between one who swears falsely and respects the nature of making oaths [Seow, *Ecclesiastes*, 299.]. Similarly, Enns suggests it may be a contrast between who does and does not swear oaths. Even though the text is ambiguous, I will be reading the text with contrasting ideas of who does and does not. [Enns, *Ecclesiastes*, 93-94.]

377 The word וְאַחֲרָיו literally means "after it." It has the third masculine singular suffix. It has confused most commentators due to its use after a series of plural suffixes. LXX and Syr

Vs. 4 For[378] whoever is allied[379] with all the living, there is hope, [380] for a living dog[381] is better than a dead lion.[382]

Vs. 5 For the living know that they will die, but the dead know nothing, and they have no more reward[383], the memory of them is lost.

Vs. 6 Their love, their hate their envy has already perished, forever they have no share in all that is done under the sun.

---

have Plural suffixes. Seow suggests that because of the singular suffix, the last three words in the verse were wrongly arranged from the following verse. So, Seow interchanges these three words to the end of v. 4 and translates them there as "and unto dead is finality" [Seow, *Ecclesiastes*, 300.]. But Bartholomew suggests taking the singular "it" to refer to the madness of human life viewed as a whole. [Bartholomew, *Ecclesiastes*, 296.]. And Longmanreads וְאַחֲרָיו adverbially. [Longman III, *Ecclesiastes*, 225.] Enns describes that Qoheleth means to say the heart of humanity is corrupt and then comes death. [Enns, *Ecclesiastes*, 93-94.]

378 Like v. 1 the כִּי is taken in its casual sense.

379 Most commentators suggest that it is difficult to translate the verb יְבֻחַר and it is the Pual imperfect third masculine singular of בחר meaning "choose, select."Seow in retains Ketib and translates the opening of this verse as "For whoever is chosen" [Seow, *Ecclesiastes*, 300.] However, the textual notes suggest reading with Qere along with twenty Hebrew MSS, LXX, Symm, and Syr, יְחֻבַּר, from the root חבר, meaning "be allied with, be joined to." Reading it as "be allied with" makes sense with the context.

380 According to Seow, בִּטָּחוֹן means not "hope" but "confidence" like the meaning found in 2 Kings 18:19 and Isa. 36:4 I agree with most commentators in recognizing that in 2Kings and Isaiah the context is that of military threat. It is not the same as 9:4. It is better to translate בִּטָּחוֹןas "hope." [Seow, Ecclesiastes, 300.]

381 According to Fox, theלְ before כֶּלֶב which means Dog. He says it has occasioned much debate, but it could function as a preposition. It can be translated as "it is better for a live dog than …" [Fox, *Qoheleth*, 258.] However, Bartholomew suggests it could mark Dog as a *casus pendens*(dislocated), or it could be an insistent word that he considers. [Bartholomew, *Ecclesiastes*, 296.] I agree with Fox in taking it as a proposition.

382 Botterweck asserts that the ancient Near Eastern world used the lion imagery to describe a ruler and, in some cases, gods. The lion imagery has prominence in the ancient world. Even in ancient Israel, the Lion is considered the mightiest. The roars of the Lion are associated with Yahweh in the Hebrew Bible. So, lion imagery was very essential to the ancient world. [Johannes Botterweck, "אֲרִי," *Theological Dictionary of the Old Testament: Volume I*, edited by G. Johannes Botterweck and Helmer Ringgren (Grand Rapids, MI: William B. Eerdmans Publishing Company, 1990), 374-88.]

383 Seow suggests that שָׂכָר may mean in an economic sense as "wages." So, he translates it as "recompense." [Seow, *Ecclesiastes*, 301.] However, in the verse, "reward" is the better translation. Longman explains that it was chosen because of its assonance with זֵכֶר, which means memory. [Longman III, *Ecclesiastes*, 226.] I prefer to read it as a "reward" for a better translation.

Boundaries and Literary Context

The boundaries of the text are placed between Qoheleth's determination to inform the wise that no one can comprehend the work done by God. In Roland Murphy's words, "There is no wisdom, no understanding, no counsel, against the Lord"[384] and Qoheleth's strong commands (9:7-10) for humans to enjoy life. Murphy emphasizes Qoheleth's proposal that it is better to enjoy now as it will be impossible in Sheol.[385] It is also known as carpe diem, wherein Qoheleth teaches people to live their lives to the fullest with the things they have Ecclesiastes 9:1-6 portrays Qoheleth's assertion of the human mortal boundaries. The conclusion is in Ecclesiastes 9:11-12, the inescapable death. Julie Ann Duncan suggests that Qoheleth concludes his saying by reminding the conditional nature of human attempts, with inevitable death as the result.[386] Additionally, Michael V. Fox proposes that humans' talents and merits do not help them achieve the deserved or expected results. He suggests that the text determines that everyone is subject to the quirks of chance.[387] No matter what a person does, they cannot escape death. So Qoheleth commands one to enjoy life and asserts that one should be happy without thinking of the future.

The literary context of the text (9:1-6) suggests that the same fate befalls all. Murphy explains that the text laments how humans do not know if God loves or hates them, for the same fate happens to all. There is no distinction between the good and the bad; he says everyone is treated the same.[388] In other words, there is no dominant or marginalized, everyone's fate is the same. It resonates with what has already been said in 8:14, "there are righteous men who get what the actions of the wicked deserve, and there are wicked men who get what the actions of the righteous deserve." So, v. 1 rightly points out that God is the author, and no one can know what will happen in their lives. According to Seow, Ecclesiastes confirms that people cannot determine the consequence of their works. He says that what seems good for humans is bad in the sight of the divine and what seems bad is good in the sight of the divine.[389] A straightforward answer for readers is that they cannot escape death no matter what they do. This is unlike the Karmic teaching of the Hindu religious tradition, which states that if a person does good deeds, he/she will gain the ability to reincarnate as something better

384 Roland Murphy, *Ecclesiastes*, WBC 23A (Dallas, Texas: Word Books, 1991), 86.

385 Murphy, *Ecclesiastes*, 90.

386 Julie Ann Duncan, *Ecclesiastes*, AOTC (Nashville: Abingdon Press, 2017), 129.

387 Fox, *Qoheleth*, 260.

388 Roland Murphy, *Ecclesiastes*, 89.

389 Seow, *Ecclesiastes*, 303.

than the previous life. But if they are involved in evil deeds, they incarnate as lesser beings.

Backtracking further into the earlier chapters, in the words of J. A. Loader, the idea of human predestination authored by God occurs in Ecclesiastes 1:9, 15; 3:1-9, 14-15. Loader says Qoheleth is convinced that all is futile and believes God has not turned God's back on the world, but God is inaccessible and distant. God intervenes in the lives of people on earth.[390]Therefore, the overall theme is God's authority over humans, and people, no matter what they do, cannot change their fate because all is futile.

Thus, chapter 9: 1-12 conveys a gloomy position by revisiting the theme of death, a significant theme in the literary structure. Peter Enns suggests this concept is not only confined to this chapter; it is in 11:1-12:7. So, death comes to all, and it is the end. Enns says other themes come and goin the book, but the "inevitable levelling effect of human mortality remains an active concept, directly or indirectly, in nearly all his monologues."[391] However, the concept dials down at the end of verse 12 and shifts to a different subject.

Structure, Flow, Plot

The text 9:1-10 according to R.N. Whybray, discusses how humans ought to live their lives in the face of the knowledge that they will all die and suffer a common fate.[392] Section 9:1-6 has twice the phrase "בכל אשר־נעשׂה תחת השמש" (vs. 3 and 6), which seems to divide it into two roughly equal parts: the first part observes that all people suffer the same fate, death, whereas the second part underlines that "a living dog is better off than a dead lion."[393]Also, using animals is unique in Ecclesiastes, and Qoheleth does not shy away from using domestic and wild animals. According to Murphy, Qoheleth's exploration of death leads to ironic praise of the dead, who are spared the troubles of those who live, for they no longer know love or hatred (v. 6 inclusion with v. 1).[394]

Outline Ecclesiastes 8:16-9:1-6

Ch. 8, Vs. 16: When I give my mind to know wisdom and to see the task that is done on earth his/her eyes do not see sleep in the day and in the night

390 J. A. Loader, *Ecclesiastes*, A Practical Commentary (Grand Rapids, MI: William B. Eerdmans Publishing Company, 1986), 107.

391 Enns, *Ecclesiastes*, 93-94.

392 R. N. Whybray, *Ecclesiastes*, Old Testament Guides (Sheffield: JSOT Press, 1989), 36.

393 Antoon Schoors, Ecclesiastes, Historical Commentary on the Old Testament (Leuven: Peeters, 2013), 650.

394 Murphy, *Ecclesiastes*, 89.

Vs. 17: I saw all the work of God, that a person cannot find the work that is done under the sun. However much an individual toils to seek out, he/she cannot find its meaning; even if the wise person claims to know, he/ she cannot find it

Ch. 9, Vs. 1: For all this I gave my heart, examining all this, that the righteous and the wise and their deeds are in the hand of God, whether it is love or hate one does not know. Everything before them

Vs. 2 everything is the same for everyone, one fate for the righteous and the wicked, for the good, andthe clean and the unclean, and for those who sacrifice and for those who do not sacrifice. As the good person, so is the sinner, the one who swears,is like those who shun an oath.

Vs. 3 There is evil in all that is done under the sun, for there is one fate for all, and the heart of humans is full of evil, and vexation is in their hearts while they live, and after that to the dead.

Vs. 4 For whoever is allied with all the living, there is hope, for a living dog is better than a dead lion.

Vs. 5 For the living know that they will die, but the dead know nothing, and they have no more reward, the memory of them is lost.

Vs. 6 Their love, their hate their envy has already perished, forever they have no share inall that is done under the sun.

Though most commentators assert that 8:16-17 and 9:1-6 are two separate topics, I correspond with Michael V. Fox's connection of 8:16-17 with 9:1-10.[395] The above passage has two sections. In chapter 8:16-17, the emphasis on a person's mind to know wisdom directly reflects the Qoheleth's quest for knowledge. Graham S. Ogden expresses the verb "to know" as the relationship or understanding based on experiences.[396] The sages have been prominent since the second temple period and taught the Jews from their experiences. Though Qoheleth strives for a deeper understanding of being a wise person, the works done by God cannot be comprehended by anyone, including Qoheleth. The phrase "Under the sun" in Ogden's explanation refers to the works that God has done on earth. So, Qoheleth assures that no matter what a person does, one cannot know the works of God.

Chapter 9:1-6 continues with the claim and describes that a person cannot know what God loves or hates. In verses 1-3, Fox suggests that these are God's emotions, not human ones. He says that looking at the unjust allocation of fates, one cannot know what God likes or dislikes.[397] In verses

395 Michael V. Fox, *Ecclesiastes*, The JPS Bible Commentary (Philadelphia: The Jewish Publication Society, 2004), 60-64.

396 Graham S. Ogden and Lynell Zogbo, *A Handbook on Ecclesiastes* (New York: United Bible Societies, 1997), 310.

397 Fox, *Ecclesiastes*, 61.

4-6, William P. Brown suggests Qoheleth acknowledges that there is hope among the living through the evocative proverb, "A living dog is better than a dead lion."[398] It points to the notion that a person alive can strive to live better, unlike a person who is dead. Fox says, "love, hate, and jealousy," which humans intensely care about, have completely evaporated. Though the earth lives on, the memory of the wise, dominant, or elite does not remain.[399] Thus, passages 8:16-9:6 give constructive knowledge about the events that are happening in the lives of humans. He says people cannot know God's works, humans can strive but cannot comprehend whether God loves or hates something, and the persons alive can strive to change their lives, unlike those who died.

Form and Genre

Wisdom texts in the Bible are present in a unique way. The author teaches the reader lessons on moral lifestyle with the help of narration, story, prose, and poetry. Most commentators suggest that Qoheleth wrote Ecclesiastes during the later stages of his life, in which he expresses his message through a wide range of literary forms. The text 9:1-6 according to Ed Hindson is in the form of a reflection speech.[400] Further, Sibley Towner asserts that this section blends two of the book's major themes. First, the same fate occurs to all. Second, carpe diem means "seize the day" and enjoy life. He says this passage consists of traditional proverbs with fresh reflections by Qoheleth. For him, it is a combination of prose and poetry. The overarching slogans of Qoheleth, "all is vanity" and "under the sun," are evident in this text.[401] This text is unique and has the essential theological teaching of human mortality and God's authority.

Historical, Social, and Cultural Context

According to Towner, the whole book distinctly exhibits the Hellenistic period's philosophical spirit more than any other book of the Hebrew Bible. But Qoheleth's teachings are separate from Greek literature.[402] Samuel Adams states that the language used in Ecclesiastes is Late Biblical Hebrew.[403] Similarly, Ian Young comments that this late language is closer

---

398 William P. Brown, *Ecclesiastes*, Interpretation (Louisville: John Knox Press, 2000), 92.

399 Fox, *Ecclesiastes*, 63.

400 Ed Hindson and Gary Yates, *The Essence of the Old Testament: A Survey* (Nashville: B&H Publishing Group, 2012), 273.

401 W. Sibley Towner, *Ecclesiastes*, TNIB, 12 Volumes (Nashville: Abingdon Press, 1997), 339.

402 Towner, *Ecclesiastes*, 271.

403 Samuel L. Adams, "Qoheleth," in *The Eerdmans Dictionary of Early Judaism*, edited by John J. Collins and Daniel C. Harlow (Grand Rapids, MI: William B. Eerdmans

to the Mishnaic Hebrew, which is of Aramaic influence.[404] It is unlike most Hebrew Bible texts that are available to us. Moreover, Graham S. Ogden affirms the mention of two Persian loanwords, *Pardes* ("garden," 2:5) and *pitgam* ("sentence," 8:11), indicating the work belonged to as early as the third century BCE.[405]

In addition, Brown clarifies that the book was produced during a cultural context that gripped much of the ancient world, beginning with the Persian period (539-337 BCE). Socioeconomic developments changed the society of Palestine. The economy became commercialized, and a standardized monetary currency was introduced. According to him, this was to facilitate commerce from Egypt to Persia. In addition, taxation was implemented under Persian hegemony; the rich became more affluent, and the poor struggled. Brown suggests that middle-class people felt overwhelmed due to the redundant economic opportunities and risks. A wealthy person can be seen in the dumps the next day. The economy was unstable during this time.[406] So Qoheleth probably reflects the anxiety and hopes of the people during this economic upheaval. As a result, Seow describes in 1:3 that Qoheleth speaks about the "toil which people toil under the sun" (cf. 3:9 and 5:16). Further in the text, we see Qoheleth speaking about people toiling hard and their wealth is left to others (2:19-21; 6:1-2).[407] This information suggests that Qoheleth was also influenced by the surrounding societies, literature, and his sociocultural context.

Compositional Context

Most commentators believe that the wisdom books parallel ancient Near Eastern literature. Ecclesiastes is one of these wisdom books. Brown suggests that the author writing Ecclesiastes might have referred to the Epic of Gilgamesh which is a Mesopotamian tale. The Epic is considered the greatest literary composition of prebiblical times. Brown asserts like Gilgamesh, Qoheleth is on a journey to search for meaning and purpose in his life.[408]

In addition, Towner explains that throughout the first Millennium, the Mesopotamian wisdom tradition was available to writers and thinkers in

---

Publishing Company, 2010), 1125.

404 Ian Young, *Diversity in Pre-exilic Hebrew* (Tübingen: J.C.B Mohr (Paul Siebeck), 1993), 140.

405 Graham S. Ogden, *Qoheleth: Second Edition* (Sheffield: Sheffield Phoenix Press, 2007),19.

406 Brown, *Ecclesiastes*, 7.

407 Seow, *Ecclesiastes*, 25.

408 Brown, *Ecclesiastes*, 2.

Israel. Assyria, Babylon, and Persia dominated Israelites during this period. Towner says, Ecc. 3:11 resembles v. 24 of the Babylonian text, "A Dialogue About Human Misery," or "The Babylonian Ecclesiastes." It says, "the mind of the god, like the center of the heavens, is remote; His knowledge is difficult, men cannot understand it."[409] Among the Egyptian literature, Towner suggests that Qoheleth was familiar with "The Instruction of Amenemope." He says there are other commonalities; the work of "The Song of the Harper", which teaches about carpe diem, is influential on Qoheleth. For instance, "Fulfil thy needs upon earth, after the command of thy heart, until there come for thee that day of mourning" (cf. Ecc. 7:14). Similarly, "The Instruction of Ani," offers admonitions about the proper approach to God like those found in Ecc. 5:1-7.[410] Fox confirms that Qoheleth shared the quest of Greek philosophy in general: to help humans live happily in a world that is not very friendly to human happiness. [411] Thus, the exegetical text teaches that humans are finite beings with no access to God's wisdom, and their striving yields them nothing. So, they must enjoy life with what they have.

Canonical Context

A study of the entire Bible suggests that the current exegetical text has similarities with other texts. For instance, the composition at the end of 9:3 emphasizes the focus on death. But the rest of 9:3 assumes what is described in Gen. 6:5. Treier says the human hearts are inclined to evildoing based on the story of the pre-flood generation. It does speak about total depravity and humans can do both good and evil.[412] In the next section, vs. 4-6 the description of the Dog is unique to Qoheleth. The term "dog" was a term that was frequently associated with hatred in biblical tradition (e.g., 1 Sam. 17:43; Ps. 22:16, 20; Matt. 15:26-27). Especially in Prov. 26:11; 2 Peter 2:22, it portrays "Like a dog that returns to its vomit is a fool who reverts to his folly" another derogatory use of the term dog. Brown suggests the Lion is symbolically associated with intelligence, might, and majesty, but the Dog is symbolically associated with folly, weakness, and lowliness. He goes on to say that sages ascribed reputation as an individual's legacy for future generations and it is the immortalized self. However, Qoheleth writes that the dog has the advantage over a dead lion. Brown says, "Life cannot be

409 Towner, *Ecclesiastes*, 274.

410 Ibid, 275.

411 Fox, *Qoheleth*, 16.

412 Daniel J. Treier, *Proverbs & Ecclesiastes*, Brazos Theological Commentary on the Bible (Grand Rapids, MI: Brazos Press, 2011), 205.

lived for the sake of the future." It means a dog at least receives the crumbs that fall from heaven (Matt. 15:27).[413]

Use of Dog Imagery

Dog Imagery in the Iconography and Art

According to Ann C. Gunter, animal imagery was used in ancient Anatolian art and iconography to express the divine realm and celebrate it in a cultic way.[414] In contrast to Egypt, Mesopotamia, and Iran, Gunter says Anatolia has no evidence of animals portrayed as human companions or subservient labourers to human beings. He says wild animals dominate most of the art and iconography. However, dogs and other animals, such as sheep, goats, cattle, etc., were domesticated in south-central and southeastern Anatolia as early as the aceramic Neolithic period (ca. 7000 B.C.E). So, dog imagery is of little importance, but it is part of the figurines of domestication.[415] Thus, for Anatolia, dogs are believed to have a neutral notion.

Patrick F. Houlihan explains that human-animal relations have a long history in Egypt. Petroglyphs executed on rock faces in western and eastern deserts bordering the Nile Valley present some of their interactions.[416] One of the images is the Dog, which this animal was considered a faithful companion. He says ancient Egyptians considered the dogs as the pet "*par excellence.*" Several images of this animal are found in Egyptian iconography, and they were given attention and affection. For example, the oldest securely dated appearance of the domestic Dog from Egypt occurs on a widely known ceramic bowl from the Amratian period (ca. 4000-3500 BCE). Further, he says that during the Eighteenth Dynasty dogs (esp.

---

413 Brown, *Ecclesiastes*, 92.

414 Ann C. Gunter, "Animal in Anatolian Art," in *A History of the Animal World in the Ancient Near East*, edited by Billie Jean Collins (Leiden: Brill, 2002), 79-80. For Gunter, since the seventh millennium BCE, several visual records of animal imagery were preserved in a "variety of media and formats including wall painting, ceramics, stone sculpture and glyptic, wooden furniture, and stone architectural decoration." He says the art depicted animal imagery as the representation of divine beings. Their attributes were conceptualized and envisioned in the form of a particular animal.

415 Gunter, "Animal in Anatolian Art," 81.

416 Patrick F. Houlihan, "Animal in Egyptian Art and Hieroglyphs," in *A History of the Animal World in the Ancient Near East*, edited by Billie Jean Collins (Leiden: Brill, 2002), 97-98, 102. Animal imagery dominated early Egyptian art before and during the emergence of phonetic writing in the Nile Valley. Animal imagery served as a symbolic language. Houlihan says the imagery communicated theoretical concepts of kinship and the unification of their country under one ruler. The ancient Egyptians depicted non-domesticated animals with divine attributes. Many of the gods and goddesses could manifest themselves in animal appearance and have a human body.

saluki) appears at the side of royalty or wealthy citizens in Egyptian art.[417] Therefore, dogs were favored pets and popular among Egyptians. According to Catherine Breniquet, humans began to depict animals in art around 35,000 B.C.E. Mesopotamian society also included animal imagery in art and iconography. However, the available documents of Mesopotamia do not fully illustrate the evolution of animal representation.[418] In Mesopotamian glyptography, dogs appear as pets and powerful watchdogs. Even the late Babylonian murals depict Ashurbanipal using dogs for hunting. Figures of dogs guard the gates and doors against the incursion of demons.[419] Thus, dogs were common among the societies of the ancient Near East. These societies have domesticated dogs; most art and iconography present dogs as pets or part of the household.

Use of Animal Imagery in Levant Society[420]

Borowski explains that Levant literature and art had rich sources of animal images and symbols. The animals possessed the potential to convey

---

417 Houlihan, "Animal in Egyptian Art and Hieroglyphs," 116.

418 Catherine Breniquet, "Animals in Mesopotamian Art," in *A History of the Animal World in the Ancient Near East*, edited by Billie Jean Collins (Leiden: Brill, 2002), 145. Mesopotamian animal art is closely connected to gods and religion. Breniquet states that Mesopotamian animal imagery depicts the first appearance of divinities. For example, bull imagery acts as a symbol of either gods or deified kings.

419 G. Johannes Botterweck, "כֶּלֶב," *TDOT* 7:146-57.

420 Animal images are prominent in describing the divine; for Syrio-Palestinians, they have a symbolic role. She says some elites sponsored the artistic creation and imagery based on their ideology. So, animals were present in the imagination as well as in people's everyday lives. Therefore, animal images have prominence in the ideology, as symbols of kingship or as representatives and companions of significant deities.[Caubet, "Animals in Syro-Palestinian Art," 211, 234.] It must be noted that, like other societal arts mentioned, those in Syria-Palestine gave importance to animals and considered them part of their daily lives. Animals became imagery and were associated with the divine and humans. Thus, animal imagery in art is not confined to ANE, it is evident in Syria-Palestine. In addition, Borowski suggests that written materials from ancient Syria-Palestine have been preserved in the texts from the Late Bronze Age city of Ugarit (modern Ras Shamra in Syria) and the Hebrew Bible. He says practical documents (texts dealing with sacrifices and taxes) discuss animals. For him, Animal imagery plays an essential role in literary genres such as poetry and prose narratives and myths, wisdom literature, and historical documents. He says the texts provide limited consideration to human-animal interactions in Syro-Palestinian antiquity. It is due to scarce written Canaanite sources and our limited knowledge of biblical writers and their manipulation of animal images. [Oded Borowski, "Animals in the Literatures of Syria-Palestine," in *A History of the Animal World in the Ancient Near East*, edited by Billie Jean Collins (Leiden: Brill, 2002), 289.] Although the animal world is given prominence in literary and historical records, the biblical writers focus on religious teachings and only slightly mention animals regarding sacrifices and offerings made to God. A careful reading of Ecclesiastes shows how animals were closely

symbolic meaning.[421] For him, the Syro-Palestine animals are divided into clean and unclean in the biblical literature (e.g., Lev 11; Deut 14:3-21), and there are instructions concerning sacrifices (e.g., Lev 1-6; Num 7:87-88).[422] He presents a possibility of understanding the animal imagery by saying,

"From a land 'flowing with milk and honey' (Exod 3:8), one might expect numerous literary references to animals in daily life. The biblical sources do not disappoint: Donkeys, camels, cattle, mules, and sheep all figure in lists of treasure, and numerous references to their daily use demonstrate that they were the mainstay of the economy of ancient Syria-Palestine."[423]

Borowski suggests that Israel's sages utilized animal behaviour to teach proper human conduct.[424] According to Benjamin A. Foreman, animal imagery elucidates human behaviour in ways plants or inanimate objects cannot. Animals, unlike flora, live and move in time and space.[425] So, animals functioned as paradigms of wisdom and knowledge. Especially in prophetical literature, animal imagery is correlated to the 'Day of the Lord.' Borowski expounds that the day is explained with dangerous animals at their eschatological worst. For instance, Amos says, "Why do you want that day of the Lord? it is darkness, not light; as if someone fled from a lion and was met by a bear; or went into the house and rested a hand against the wall and was bitten by a snake." (Amos 5:18-19).[426] Thus, animal imagery in art and literature is profound.

Dalit Reading of the Dog Imagery in Hindu Religious Tradition

Animal imagery has prominent significance in the Hindu Religious Tradition. Several animal imageries are seen as vehicles of the deities. In some instances, the deities incarnate as animals. Many Hindu scriptures use animal imagery to describe various teachings to human beings. However, the focus will be limited to the dog imagery found in the Hindu scriptures. Dog imagery has different nuances in the Hindu Scriptures. In some texts, it is portrayed positively; in others, it portrays impurity and pollution, alluding to dogs as unclean or of a lower animal/being. According to Wendy Doniger,

---

associated with humans or human nature and how animal imagery can provide significant lessons for humans.

421 Borowski, "Animals in the Literatures of Syria-Palestine," 297.

422 Borowski, "Animals in the Literatures of Syria-Palestine," 290.

423 Borowski, "Animals in the Literatures of Syria-Palestine," 290.

424 Oded Borowski, "Animal in the Literature of Syria-Palestine," 295.

425 Benjamin A. Foreman, *Animal Metaphors and the People of Israel in the Book of Jeremiah* (Göttingen: Vandenhoeck & Ruprecht, 2011), 3.

426 Borowski, "Animals in the Literatures of Syria-Palestine," 298.

some texts sometimes talk about the lower castes in correlation to narratives about dogs. The lower castes described are now generally called Dalits, formerly called untouchables. She says there are instances where many Dalit groups were also known to be 'dog-cookers.' It is because dominant caste Hindus thought that these people ate dogs.[427] Because dogs eat anything and everything, and in Hinduism, there is a saying, you are what you eat.

Dog Imagery in Vedas

Doniger suggests that the Vedas indicate that dogs are famous and not portrayed as evil. This period is approximately between 2000 and 1500 BCE. During the era when the Rig Veda was written (around 1500-1000 BCE), dogs were commonly kept with families, either inside the home or nearby. However, by the time the Brahmanas were composed a few centuries later (around 900 BCE), increased emphasis on social hierarchy and stricter purity rules led to the Dog being seen as a symbol of impurity due to its omnivorous diet. Additionally, the declining reverence for Vedic deities such as Indra, Yama, and Rudra, who were linked to dogs, may have contributed to the Dog's diminished status.[428]

Dog Imagery in Sanskrit Epics

For some with strict caste beliefs, dogs are regarded as unclean as pigs are to orthodox Jews and Muslims. They also represent the people referred to in Sanskrit texts as 'dog cookers.' The Mahabharata (c. 300 BCE to 300 CE) essentially reinforces this prejudice against dogs.[429] One of the well-known stories expressed at the end of the Mahabharata is about King Yudhishthira and his companion dog. In the story, Indra, the king of the gods, arrives in his chariot and invites Yudhishthira to join him. Yudhishthira responds that he wants the Dog to accompany him. He does not wish to be cruel by leaving it behind. Indra explains that as Yudhishthira has achieved immortality and the joys of heaven, he must leave the Dog behind because the heavenly realm does not accommodate dog owners. According to Indra, offerings and sacrifices are considered tainted if a dog has looked at them; thus, the Dog must be abandoned to gain entry to the gods' world. Doniger suggests that Yudhishthira objects, arguing that abandoning someone loyal is a grave sin and is comparable to killing a Brahmin. When the god Dharma, who had been disguised as the Dog, hears this, he reveals his proper form and praises Yudhishthira for his compassion. Dharma explains that because Yudhishthira chose to prioritize the Dog's devotion over celestial rewards,

427 Wendy Doniger, *On Hinduism* (New York: Oxford University Press, 2014), 488.

428 Wendy Doniger, *On Hinduism* (New York: Oxford University Press, 2014), 490-91.

429 Wendy Doniger, *On Hinduism* (New York: Oxford University Press, 2014), 493.

he has achieved the highest honour and will enter heaven with his body. The Dog serves as a test at the threshold of the afterlife.[430] This story from the Mahabharata also reflects a more negative view of dogs, associating them with pollution and impurity.

In Śaṅkara interpretation of *Bhagavad Gītā* 5.18,

In a Brahmin, in whom sattva predominates and who has the best latent mental impressions (saṃskāra), in an intermediate being like a cow, which is dominated by rajas and is without [such] impressions, and in [beings] such as elephants, which are wholly dominated by tamas alone—those wise ones are "equal-visioned" whose habit is to see equally the one immutable Brahman. *(BhGŚ 5.18)*[431]

The Brahmins and cows are seen alike and considered as the highest class of beings, while dogs are relegated to the status of the untouchables and stigmatized as unclean.[432] Thus, dogs and the untouchables share common attributes, mainly alluding to being a pollutant of the sacred. The imagery of the Dog as a polluting agent reflects symbolically the caste hierarchy that continues to oppress and stigmatize marginalized Dalits.

Dog Imagery in Puranas

Doniger asserts that in the *Skanda Purana* (c. 700-1150 CE), dogs are portrayed in a different light. They are seen as instruments of salvation for sinners to achieve redemption.[433] A notable story from the *Vamana Purana* (c. 450-900 CE) illustrates this transformation in perception. It recounts the tale of the wicked king Vena:

Vena, seeking purification, heads to the sacred bathing place of Shiva the Pillar (Sthanu). However, the gods forbid him from bathing there. At the site, there is a dog who was once a man but was reborn as a dog due to past sins. This Dog swims in the Sarasvati River, which cleanses him of his impurities and quenches his thirst. Feeling hungry, the Dog enters Vena's hut. Despite his fear of the Dog, Vena gently touches it, and the Dog then showers him with water from the tirtha. Vena, in turn, plunges into the

---

430 Wendy Doniger, *On Hinduism* (New York: Oxford University Press, 2014), 494.

431 Lance Nelson, "Cows, Elephants, Dogs, and Other Lesser Embodiments of *Ātman*: Reflections on Hindu Attitudes Toward Nonhuman Animals," in *A Communion of Subjects: Animals in Religions, Science and Ethics*, edit by Paul Waldau and Kimberley Patton (New York: Columbia University Press, 2006), 185-186.

432 Lance Nelson, "Cows, Elephants, Dogs, and Other Lesser Embodiments of *Ātman*: Reflections on Hindu Attitudes Toward Nonhuman Animals," in *A Communion of Subjects: Animals in Religions, Science and Ethics*, edit by Paul Waldau and Kimberley Patton (New York: Columbia University Press, 2006), 185

433 Wendy Doniger, *On Hinduism* (New York: Oxford University Press, 2014), 497.

sacred water, and through the shrine's power, he is purified. Shiva, pleased with Vena's actions, grants him a boon. Vena requests that the Dog who helped him also be blessed. Shiva agrees, promising that the Dog will be freed from sin and ascend to heaven, and Vena will also enjoy a temporary stay in Shiva's heaven.[434]

In this narrative, the Dog's act of transferring water to Vena—shaking itself and scaring Vena into the water—demonstrates an unusual form of salvation. The story suggests that Vena could only enter the sacred water after being sprinkled by the Dog, highlighting a paradox: Vena's sinfulness would pollute the shrine before the shrine could purify him. It reflects a more resounding theme of how the unclean Dog paradoxically becomes a vessel for purification.

Engaging Dalit Liberative Perspective: Subversive Reading of Dog Imageries

Looking at the text Ecclesiastes 9: 1-6, and the Hindu scriptures, the dog imagery plays a vital role in explaining wisdom teaching to human beings. Dogs were considered guardians in the ancient Near East, especially in the Egyptian context. The Anatolian iconography and arts of the ancient Near East describe that dogs were also seen as companions and pets and were found in every household. However, when it comes to the Israelite societies, dogs were seen in a derogatory way; at times, they were considered unclean animals, and at times, they were excluded and seen with disgust due to their carnivorous nature. This notion of dogs as unclean can also be found in the gospels, which often allude to gentiles. From a Dalit perspective, a subversive understanding of the dog imageries aims to challenge the selective meaning-making patterns favouring one group over the other. It challenges the notion that a group of people can be likened to a particular animal and say that this group of people have the negative characteristics of that animal and uses the concept in a way to make them stay at the bottom of society and continue to suppress and oppress them based on such a notion. On the other hand, it is also essential to see that dogs are loyal, faithful and loving. However, the comparison between Dalits and dogs is based on the negative characteristics of the Dog.

Resistance to Live

Qoheleth says that only God knows what happens "under that sun", and striving to learn about God is futile. The ethical lesson taught here is to live life to the fullest and strive to make things right in their lives. A dead person

434 Wendy Doniger O'Flaherty, *The Origin of Evil in Hindu Mythology* (Delhi: Motilal Banarsidas, 1988), 321-331.

cannot enjoy life or make amends. Daniel Fredericks asserts that living has the confidence of a profit (9:5) and portion (9:6). This is to say that there is an advantage to one's labours.[435] It is not a future reward, but one should experience it now while alive and be able to appreciate such a reward. Qoheleth's suggestion that a living dog is better than a dead lion means to enjoy what little life one has and appreciate it rather than be frustrated about it or worry about the future. Through the dog imagery, Qoheleth intends to describe that there is a possibility that a person will eventually die no matter the class, creed, caste, or ethnicity. However, the person alive has a chance to live life to the fullest, or in other words, to strive to make it better and possibly work to acquire wisdom.

Reading Ecclesiastes with a Dalit Lense would let one know that though death is inevitable, everyone will experience it the same. However, being alive like a dog assures the Dalits that they can strive to live life to the fullest and make amends to acquire knowledge and wisdom. The sacred texts and education were restricted to the Dalits, who were exploited by the dominant caste. There was a massive disparity between the priestly caste and the untouchables and outcastes, having limited access to scriptures. Unlike ordinary people, the priests and the sages can access all this knowledge to know God. The Dalits were denied of such knowledge. Suppose they heard the scriptures and experienced punishment with the molten lead poured into their ears.[436] The possibility of being alive allows Dalits to equip themselves with knowledge and wisdom.

Conclusion

Imageries and symbols are potent means of perceiving the world, making meanings and adding value. Associating the Dalits with the imagery of the Dog is a symbol of prejudice and stigma that dominant castes imposed on the Dalits. However, it is possible to rediscover positive connotations in the life of Dogs and Dalits and challenge biased concepts to delineate forms of resistance and liberation. Top of FormBottom of Form

435 Daniel C. Fredericks and Daniel J. Estes, *Ecclesiastes and Song of Songs*, Apollos Old Testament (Nottingham: Apollos, 2010), 207.

436 Peniel Rajkumar, *Dalit Theology and Dalit Liberation: Problems, Paradigms and Possibilities* (England: Ashgate Publishing Limited, 2010), 74.

37

Empowering Spirit of Yahweh
Reading the Story of Othniel in the Book of Judges

S. Wilson Naveen Kumar

Dr Kondasingu Jesurathnam is an ordained minister of the Telugu Baptist Churches. He earned his Ph.D. in Old Testament from the University of Edinburgh in 2006. He is Friedmann Golka Professor of Old Testament at the United Theological College, Bangalore, teaching us in the Department of Biblical Studies. Prof. Jesurathnam is keen to understand the discrimination, suppression, and alienation the Dalits face. However, he does not shy away in responding to those messy realities with prophetic voices. His teaching and writings encourage and are more beneficial to the interpreters of the Bible and activists who voice against injustices that Dalits and marginalized communities experience. Taking a cue from Prof. Jesurathnam's liberative hermeneutics, as his student, I am privileged to write this article for the Festschrift in his honour.

Introduction

In the Ancient Israel's history, every period is essential. The period of Judges is prominent, as there are no kings and leaders, but Judges led the people. Several different judges ruled the people of Israel for several years. According to 1 Kings 6:1, for around 480 years, the people of Israel are under the rule of judges. Since there is no leader to unite people and lead, Israel degenerates into a cycle of disobedience and punishment. Nevertheless, God heard Israel's cry, raised some among Israel, and strengthened them to liberate the people of Israel. This paper discusses the Spirit of Yahweh that it empowers the leaders to liberate Yahweh's people, who experienced suffering and marginalization during the period of Judges.

Definition: Judge

One can understand the profound meaning of concept of Judge from Ancient West Asia (AWA) and Old Testament perspectives. The Hebrew term for Judge is *shaphat* (שָׁפַט), the root word is *Shapat*. According to Akkadian literature, *shaphat* means to 'threaten' or 'warn.' The *shaphat*, "judge," as an undifferentiated executive, performed many other functions, including deciding cases of litigants under his jurisdiction. From Extra-Biblical Literature, the king appoints *a shaphat* to perform particular tasks; he might assist in the administration of a territory or in conducting military campaigns.

The term *shaphat* is a participle of the verb *sapat* (שׁפט), which, because it is multifarious in meaning, is translated as "decide," "judge," "rule," "govern," "vindicate," "deliver". The substantive *shaphat* refers to both God and humans. The Spirit of Yahweh that descended on a person is an indication that God selected him to serve as a *shaphat* (Judg. 2:16; 3:9). Yahweh had the authority to appoint and depose a *shaphat*, "judge" (cf. Ps 82:1-8). The Judges' main task was to maintain harmonious relations among the Israelites to be concerned with the welfare of the poor, the widow, the orphan, and the stranger (Psalm 82; Jer. 5:28-29; 22:15; Deut. 1:16-17.) and to be an arbitrator to restorers of peace (Gen 16:5; 19:9; Judg. 11:27).

The Prologue of the Book of Judges

The prologue of the book of Judges (1.1-3.6) narrates and establishes the stories of the Judges (3.7-16.31). The first section (1.1-2.5) describes the conflicts that continue between the people of Israel and the Canaanites after the death of Joshua. The tribes of Israel started to secure their land by driving out the remaining Canaanites, but many of the tribes failed to do so. God (Yahweh) criticizes the people of Israel, declaring that their failure is a result of their sin, disobedience, worshipping other gods and violation of the covenant (2.1-5). Thus, God told them, 'I will not drive them out before you, but they shall become adversaries to you, and their gods shall be a snare to you' (2.3). The second part of the prologue (2.6-3.6) talks about Israel forgetting Yahweh and turning to idolatry by breaking the covenant and adopting the Canaanite's practices. The behaviour of Israel provokes Go to anger, and then God punishes them by handing them over to an oppressive enemy. Then Israel cries out to God for help; God hears their cry and raises a judge to lead the people and deliver them from their oppressors, and the land enjoys a time of peace. Although each appearance of the cycle incorporates a unique combination of elements.[437] There are just two fundamental movements in the cycle. First, Israel rebelled, and God punished them. Second, Israel cried to God, and He liberated and delivered them. The theological tension between God's justice and mercy merges with these two movements into a single recurrent cycle (cf. Exod. 34.6-7).[438]

The Prologue of Judges Chapter 3

Firstly, Judges chapter 3 starts with a list of the undefeated nations and tests the people of Israel of the future, who grew up without knowing war. These nations included the Hivites, the Sidonians, the five Philistine lords, and the Canaanite nations (Judges 3:1–4). Secondly, the people of Israel started to disobey God by living alongside the Canaanites in captured territories. It gives rise to the temptation of idolatry and all that it entails. Human and child sacrifice, as well as sexual practices, were all part of the worship of these false gods. Despite Joshua's high warnings, the people of Israel intermarried with women from other nations and worshipped their gods (Judges 3:5–6). Also, God punishes God's people for doing this evil. When the people forget God and serve the false gods known as Baal and Asheroth, God sells them into the hand of Cushan-rishathaim, the king of Mesopotamia. He ruled over the people of Israel for eight years. Finally, the people of Israel cried out to God, and God raised the first judge, Othniel.[439] The Spirit of the Lord came upon Othniel, and he led the Israelites into battle against the Mesopotamians and to defeat them. So the land lasted forty years until Othniel, son of Kenaz, died (Judges 3:7–11).

---

437 The variations are charted in detail by Robert H. O'Connell, *The Rhetoric of the Book of Judges* (Leiden: E.J. Brill, 1996), 22-25. Julius Wellhausen, *Prolegomena to the History of Israel*, translated by J. Sutherland Black and Allan Menzies (Edinburgh: Adam & Charles Black, 1885), 231, lists the elements of the cycle as 'rebellion, affliction, conversion, peace'. Instead of the impersonal taxonomy of Wellhausen (and other scholars), I would prefer to use the more relational language of the biblical text, which presents the cycle in the form of concrete verbal clauses: Israel did evil; Yahweh sold them; Israel cried out; Yahweh raised a judge.

438 Most interpreters, unwilling to retain the theological tension, have chosen to describe the cycle as one of justice, in which the deliverance of the Israelites demands their repentance, or one of mercy, in which his compassion eclipses the anger of God. I contend, however, that an essential theological claim of Judges is that the tension between God's justice and his mercy never dissolved. See ch. 7 of Martin, *The Unheard Voice of God*. Welker claims these deliverances are 'experiences of the forgiveness of sins,' and they may be, but forgiveness language is absent from Judges. See Michael Welker, *God the Spirit*, translated by John Hoffmeyer (Minneapolis: Fortress Press, 1994), 65.

439 The son of Caleb's younger brother, he captured a city from the Canaanites on behalf of Caleb. In return, Caleb gave Othniel his daughter in marriage (Judges 1:12–13).

Othniel the Judge (3:7-11)

The first two chapters of the book give an overview, and then from chapter 3, the narrative of judges begins. Where the first judge, Othniel, the narrative is in five verses, this story tells about the repeated behaviour of the people of Israel's sin, cry, and deliverance; from there, the first judge, Othinel, delivers the people of Israel, and the land was quiet for 40 years.[440]

Othniel the Deliverer

Othniel's story starts with God's punishment for their evil. Welker states that whenever the people of Israel forget God and serve other gods (Baal and the Asherah), Israel loses coherence and power and loses in war.[441] Then, the Israelites served Cushan-rishathaim for eight years, and they cried out to God. Here, two Hebrew words bring attention; one is to describe the servitude of Israel (עבד) and express cry (זעק). Both are used in Egyptian bondage (Exod. 1.13-14) and (Exod.2.23), respectively. In Judges, just as in Exodus, amid pain and suffering, the people of Israel cry out to Yahweh; as Yahweh raised Moses, the liberator, the Spirit of Yahweh came upon Othniel, and he gave rest to the land. Yahweh, who liberates (delivers) the people of Israel from the servitude of Egypt, now hears their cries and liberates them from the servitude of Cushan-rishathaim.[442] The Spirit of Yahweh strengthens Othniel to break the community-threatening power of oppression.[443] With the coming of the Spirit, a 'process of emergence set sin, a process that in an unforeseen manner constitutes a new beginning, new relations, a new reality.'[444]

The Spirit of Yahweh in Torah

The Hebrew term *Ruach*(רוּח) has different meanings, such as 'wind', 'breath', 'air', 'disposition', 'vigour', and 'spirit.'[445]–25. It is not easy to

---

440 See Lawson Grant Stone, "From Tribal Confederation to Monarchic State: The Editorial Perspective of the Book of Judges," (Ph.D. Diss., Yale University, 1988), 260-89.

441 Welker, *God the Spirit*, 63.

442 Walter Brueggemann shows the significance of the exodus tradition and how it explains Yahweh's redemption. See Walter Brueggemann, *Theology of the Old Testament: Testimony, Dispute, Advocacy* (Minneapolis: Fortress Press, 1997), 173-81.

443 Although the Spirit enables the judges to lead Israel into battle, Welker argues that the Spirit is not a 'spirit of war.' Welker, *God the Spirit*, 52-58.

444 Welker, *God the Spirit*, 64-65.

445 Francis Brown, et al., *The New Brown, Driver, Briggs, Gesenius Hebrew and English Lexicon: With an Appendix Containing the Biblical Aramaic*, translated by Edward Robinson (Peabody, MA: Hendrickson, 1979), 924

choose the meaning of *ruach* (רוּחַ) according to the context,[446] Although there is some value in establishing an original core meaning, such as 'air in motion' or the like,[447] Such a broad definition is of little use in determining the meaning of *ruach* (רוּחַ) in a specific text. The context of *ruach* (רוּחַ) must take precedence over any diachronic or etymological reconstructions when determining the meaning of *ruach* (רוּחַ) in each context.[448]

The Spirit of Yahweh is Uncontrollable

In the Exodus, Israel's primal liberation is affected by Yahweh's direct intervention, sometimes through the agency of the mysterious and powerful *ruach*. Here, Yahweh uses an east wind to bring the locust plague, a west wind to drive them into the sea (Exod. 10.13, 19), and the east wind to divide the waters (Exod. 14.21). Dale Moody contends, "Israel's faith promoted *ruach* as the metaphor or God's direct action in nature and history."[449] This powerful *ruach* appears in the Exodus story as God's invading presence. Michael Green writes, 'The Beyond has come into our midst, and we can neither organize nor domesticate him.'[450] A person who listens to the biblical narrative from Genesis to Judges would have some awareness of the nature and functions of the Spirit about humanity, the community, and leadership.[451] The texts seem to suggest that in the Torah,

---

446 Furthermore, in some texts, the meanings may interchange and merge into dynamic wordplay. E.g., Ezek. 37 and Isa. 40-42. On the nuances of (רוּחַ) in the latter text, see John Goldingay, "The Breath of Yahweh Scorching, Confounding, Anointing: The Message of Isaiah 40-42," *Journal of Pentecostal Theology* 11 (1997): 3-34.

447 Ludwig Kohler, *Old Testament Theology*, translated by A. S. Todd (Philadelphia: Westminster Press, 1957), 140; cf. J. Barton Payne, (רוּחַ), *Theological Dictionary of Old Testament*, edited by R. Laird Harris, Gleason L. Archer, and Bruce K. Waltke, vol. 2 (Chicago: Moody Press, 1980), 836. See also Walter C. Wright, "The Use of Pneuma in the Pauline Corpus with Special Attention to the Relationship between Pneuma and the Risen Christ," (Ph.D. Diss., Fuller Theological Seminary, 1977), 10–16, who argues that the original meaning of (רוּחַ) is probably 'breath'; and Harold D. Hunter, *Spirit-baptism: A Pentecostal Alternative* (Lanham, MD: University Press of America, 1983), 23, who prefers 'wind' as the most fundamental meaning.

448 Alphonsus Benson, "*The Spirit of God in the Didactic Books of the Old Testament*," (STD Diss, Catholic University of America, 1949), 71.

449 Moody, *Spirit of the Living God*, 13-14.

450 Michael Green, *I Believe in the Holy Spirit* (Grand Rapids, MI: Eerdmans, 1975), 19-20.

451 The abiding presence of Yahweh's Spirit sustains human life (Gen. 6.3); the Spirit gives Joseph the ability to interpret dreams (Gen. 42.38), thus saving Israel (Gen. 50.20); the Spirit enables artisans to construct the priestly garments (Exod. 28.3) and the tabernacle (Exod. 31.3; 35.31); Yahweh's Spirit is upon Moses and is given to seventy elders who prophesy and who then serve as assistants to Moses (Num. 11.17-29); the Spirit of God inspires the prophecy of Balaam (Num. 24.2); When Moses chooses Joshua as a

the Spirit of God relates to humans as the untamable gift of Yahweh's energizing presence.[452]

The Spirit of Yahweh in the Judges

Like the Torah, the Book of Judges clarifies the nature and function of the Spirit of Yahweh in the story of Othniel and other judges like Gideon and Samson. The people of Israel might be surprised by this first biblical appearance of the phrase.[453] Since the Spirit-empowered previous leaders (Joseph, Moses, the Seventy, and Joshua), Israel might assume that Spirit empowerment is a necessary qualifier for leadership in Israel and that the 'personal encounter is not for its own sake but for the sake of the community.'[454] Thus, the importance of Othniel's reception of the Spirit becomes more apparent as the 'mark of God's chosen' leader.[455] And he was considered a past hero of Israel. The phrase (רוּח יהוה) refers to Yahweh's presence.[456] Also, the book of Judges. 2.18 says that Yahweh will be 'with' the judges that he raises the Spirit of Yahweh comes upon Othniel (3.10),[457] The Spirit of Yahweh 'clothed' Gideon (6.34). Therefore, the Spirit's coming

successor, the Spirit is 'in' him (Num. 27.18); and when Moses lays his hands, Joshua is 'filled' with the Spirit (Deut. 34.9).

452 Gordon D. Fee, *God's Empowering Presence: The Holy Spirit in the Letters of Paul* (Peabody, MA: Hendrickson Publishers, 1994), 8. Gordon D. Fee concludes that the Spirit functions in the Old Testament as God's 'empowering presence'. While the trinitarian nature of the Spirit is not a concern of these texts, it notes that Yahweh is the only ancient Near Eastern deity with a spirit. Other gods may control the ruach (wind) but have no *ruach* (Spirit). Lloyd R. Neve, *The Spirit of God in the Old Testament* (Tokyo: Seibunsha, 1972), 1.

453 The phrase רוח יהוה occurs 27 times in the Hebrew Bible. Although the phrase is not in the canon before Judges, two texts have the word the Spirit by a possessive pronoun whose antecedent is Yahweh. Yahweh speaks of 'my Spirit' (Gen. 6.3), and Moses remarks, 'would that all of the people of Yahweh were prophets and that Yahweh would put his Spirit upon them' (Num. 11.29).

454 Brueggemann, *Theology of the Old Testament*, 571. Cf. Welker, *God the Spirit*, 75; Welker insists, 'in no instance is the descent of the Spirit merely a private affair'; and Benson, "The Spirit of God," 72.

455 Herbert Wolf, *Judges*, The Expositor's Bible Commentary, vol. 3, edited by F. E. Gaebelein (Grand Rapids, MI: Zondervan, 1992), 398.

456 Yahweh says to Moses, 'I will be with you' (Exod. 3), and later we hear that Yahweh's Spirit is upon Moses (Num. 11).

457 See Yaira Amit, *The Book of Judges*: Art of Editing (Leiden: Brill, 1999), 161. She recognizes the correlation between 2.18 and 3.10 since she places the two verses opposite each other in a chart.

corresponds to the promise that God will be 'with' his chosen leader. [458] The Spirit is a manifestation of the presence of Yahweh.[459]

The Spirit of 'Yahweh' rather than the Spirit of 'God'

In the presence of Yahweh, the Spirit that comes upon Gideon and the other judges is the Spirit of 'Yahweh' (יהוה) rather than the Spirit of "God' (אלהים). This consistent use of 'Yahweh" over 'God' adds a personal quality to the narrative, since Yahweh is the distinctive personal name of Israel's covenant God.[460] The book of Judges prefers 'Yahweh', which appears 175 times, over the broader name 'God' (used 15 times).[461] In Judges, the name 'Yahweh' is used in every reference to the God of Israel except in the speech of Adoni-bezek (1.7). Yahweh led Israel.[462] Consequently, it is the Spirit of Yahweh which comes upon Othniel in order to ensure the realization of Yahweh's commitments.[463]

The Spirit of Yahweh is free to Bestow Saving Power

In the book of Judges, God's name 'Yahweh' is used because he created an egalitarian community which stood the oppressive regimes of Egypt and Canaan.[464] Yahweh is the God who stands outside every human system of power, control, and oppression and delivers his people from domination.[465] The Spirit of God is not beholden to human centres of power.[466] The Spirit of Yahweh, therefore, comes upon Othniel to resist the Canaanite oppressive system under Cushan-rishathaim. The Spirit of Yahweh is free to bestow his

---

458 Barry G. Webb, *The Book of the Judges: An Integrated Reading* (Sheffield: Sheffield Academic Press, 1987), 127.

459 Moody, *Spirit of the Living God*, 12.

460 Stanley M. Horton, "The Holy Spirit in the Book of Judges," Par 3 (1969): 9–14.

461 The number 15 does not include the ten places where the phrase אלהים יהוה occurs because, in those cases, the more general name (אלהים) is subordinate to the personal name (יהוה).

462 Yahweh who swears to give the land to the Israelites (2.1); it is Yahweh who brings them up out of Egypt (2.1); it is Yahweh who promises to keep the covenant forever (2.1); it is Yahweh who directs the tribes in the conquest (1.1-2); it is Yahweh who gives the Canaanites and Perizzites into the hand of Israel (1.4); it is Yahweh who gives victories to Judah and Joseph (1.19-22); it is Yahweh who sends his angel (2.1); it is Yahweh to whom the Israelites make sacrifice (2.5); it is Isracl's idolatry that causes Yahwehs's anger (2.14); and at the same time, it is Yahweh who promises to raise judges (2.16).

463 The phrase *ruach Yahweh* demonstrates that 'it is Yahweh himself who came to the rescue by raising the judge/deliverer'. Barnabas Lindars, *Judges* 1-5: A New Translation and Commentary (Edinburgh: T&T Clark, 1995), 134.

464 George E. Mendenhall, "Hebrew Conquest of Palestine," BA 25 (1962): 66–87, 73–86.

465 Bruce C. Birch et al., *A Theological Introduction to the Old Testament* (Nashville: Abingdon Press, 1999), 113f.

466 Welker, *God the Spirit*, 51.

saving power upon whoever he will, who is faithful to his covenant people and passionately embraces those who suffer and suffer with them.[467] The Spirit of Yahweh strengthens Othniel as a warrior judge who accomplishes Yahweh's liberation (3.9).

The Spirit of Yahweh Empowers to enter a Larger Arena

Only Othniel's name is in the first chapter; as a victorious man who knows the struggles of his people, he fought for his people, defeated the town of Kiriath-Sepher and achieved notoriety as a local leader (Judg. 1.11-15).[468] Therefore, Yahweh chooses Othniel to save Israel from Cushan-rishathaim; from that movement, Yahweh rises Othniel from the level of clan leader to the status of national deliverer.[469,470] Therefore, the first judge is recognized as a local leader but is subsequently authorized and empowered by the Spirit of Yahweh to enter a larger arena of influence.

The Spirit of Yahweh Comes down to Liberate

The text declares that 'the Spirit of Yahweh came upon Othniel', and the Hebrew phrase 'came upon him' (עליוהיתו) is suggestive of several points: 1. It is the Spirit who is the active subject of the verb, and Othniel is a recipient of the action; 2. The Spirit is not a part of Othniel but comes to him from outside; 3. The Spirit's action registers Yahweh's movement from perceived absence to perceived presence;[471]. And v4. The phrase 'came upon' is a vivid speech that signifies a theological concept. The theological concept is that the Spirit of Yahweh empowers, energizes, and equips Othniel to deliver Israel. One can assert almost universally that the work of the Spirit in Judges is temporary and external rather than lasting inward.[472]

---

467 Samuel Solivan, *The Spirit, Pathos and Liberation: Toward A Hispanic Pentecostal Theology* (Sheffield: Sheffield Academic Press, 1998), 72-77, highlights the biblical witness to God's redeeming compassion and maintains that the Spirit-filled church will imitate God's compassion in forming a redemptive community.

468 Welker, *God the Spirit,* 51

469 Historical evidence indicates that the judges ruled as tribal chieftains over small regions, and the narrative of judges portrays them as national leaders.

470 Wellhausen, *Prolegomena to the History of Israel*, 234.

471 In "The Holy Spirit in the Book of Judges," 14, Horton writes that the Spirit is not a mere influence coming from a distance God.

472 Given the persistent diversity of interpretations of the more abundant New Testament data regarding the Spirit, it should not be surprising that scholars differ in their interpretations of the Old Testament data regarding the Spirit.

The Spirit of Yahweh is an Endowment

The text indicates that the Spirit continued to be with them for the duration of the Spirit's presence. For instance, it says that Yahweh is 'with' the Judge, and Yahweh delivers Israel 'all the days of the judge' (Judg. 2:18). Once Yahweh chooses the judges and strengthens them by the Spirit, those judges continue to serve for several years. Yahweh decides to strengthen Othniel, making him a human participant in Yahweh's liberating plan.[473] Sometimes Yahweh works against Israel by selling them into the hands of their enemies, and in the process, he strengthens' the enemy (Judge. 3.12). However, at no time do we hear that the Spirit of Yahweh comes upon one of the enemy leaders.[474] Whenever Yahweh decides to liberate Israel, he recruits a human partner who will serve in an active leadership role, a human partner who will 'succeed in restoring loyalty, solidarity, and the capacity for communal action among the people.'[475] Therefore, the story of Othniel witnesses the 'important role of humans in partnership with the liberating activity of God.'[476]

The Spirit of Yahweh Moves to Take part in Liberating work

Yahweh raises human beings; their strength comes from the Spirit of Yahweh as endowment. Moreover, there is no indication in the text that Othniel seeks the position of Judge. Yahweh takes the initiative to choose Othniel and is the active subject in the phrase, 'Yahweh raised a saviour' (3.9). Then it is the Spirit of Yahweh who is subject in the phrase, 'the Spirit of Yahweh came upon him' (3.10). Humans cannot control or domesticate the Spirit of Yahweh. Initially, Yahweh takes action in choosing Othniel, then the Spirit of Yahweh comes upon him, and then Othniel takes action to judge Israel and go to war. The Spirit of Yahweh moves Othniel to participate in Yahweh's divine liberating work. Yahweh, therefore, is moved by the cries of Israel, and the coming of the Spirit moves Othniel.

Denial of Right to Eating Beef

India is home to many religions, each with its dietary laws. For some communities (Dalit), eating Beef is a part of their culinary tradition and identity. However, at present, people are restricted from eating Beef because, in Hinduism, cows are considered sacred, and cattle farming is a livelihood, leading to solid opposition against beef consumption in many

473 Horton, "The Holy Spirit in the Book of Judges," 35.

474 The Spirit, however, comes upon non-Israelites like Balaam (Num) and Cyrus as the Lord's 'anointed' (Isa. 45.1).

475 Welker, *God the Spirit*, 53, 56.

476 Birch, *A Theological Introduction to the Old Testament,* 122.

communities.[477] It may be sacred now, but it was not before. Regarding this, Swami Vivekananda, a Hindu philosopher, while addressing a meeting at the Shakespeare Club, Pasadena, California, USA (February 2, 1900) on the theme of 'Buddhistic India, declared: "You will be astonished if I tell you that, according to old ceremonials, he is not a good Hindu who does not eat Beef. On certain occasions, he must sacrifice a bull and eat it."[478] In continuation of this, C. Kunhan Raja mentioned that a prominent authority on the history and culture of the Vedic period said, "The Vedic Aryans, including the Brahmanas, ate fish, meat and even Beef. A distinguished guest was honoured with Beef served at a meal. Although the Vedic Aryans ate Beef and sacrificed many cows."[479] It shows that politics uses religion for its benefit. Therefore, after the BJP government, some states in India have strict laws prohibiting beef consumption and slaughter, leading to legal repercussions for those who partake. Punishments for eating Beef depend on the state and can range from heavy penalties to life imprisonment. For example, the state government of Gujarat announced a bill to introduce life imprisonment and vehicle seizure as punishment for killing a cow.[480] Moreover, in Other states, the punishment for killing a cow or transporting Beef is usually a hefty fine or up to 10 years in prison. In addition to legal penalties, there is also a rise in vigilante violence against people suspected of eating Beef or slaughtering cows. Once Uttar Pradesh Chief Minister Yogi Adityanath said, the Congress wants to give minorities the right to eat Beef, adding that this amounted to allowing cow slaughter. "These shameless people promise to provide the right to eat 'gaumaans' (cow's meat), whereas our scriptures call the cow mother. They wish to give cows into the hands of butchers. Will India ever accept this?"[481]

---

477 Brigitte Sebastia, ed., *Eating Traditional Food: Politics, identity and Practices* (London: Routledge, 2017), 114.

478 Swami Vivekananda, *The Complete Works of Swami Vivekananda*, vol. 3 (Calcutta: Advaita Ashram, 1997), 536.

479 C. Kunhan Raja, "Vedic Culture," in *The Cultural Heritage of India*, vol. 1, edited by Suniti Kumar Chatterji (Calcutta: The Ramakrishna Mission, 1993), 217.

480 Hiral Dave, "Cow slaughter now punishable with life in jail in BJP's Gujarat," *Hindustan Times*, accessed on September 16, 2024, https://www.hindustantimes.com/india-news/cow-slaughter-now-punishable- withlife-in-jail-as-gujarat-assembly-passes-amendments/story-w6HhvEAqTU86dsLJC0NhOM.html.

481 "Congress wants to give minorities right to eat beef: CM Adityanath," *The Economic Times*, April 26, 2024, accessed on September 17, 2024, https://economictimes.indiatimes.com/news/elections/lok sabha/Uttar Pradesh/congress-wants-to-give-minorities-right-to-eat-beef-cm adityanath/article show/109630825.cms.

The Spirit of Yahweh Strengthens the Suppressed Community

Eating Beef is a personal choice for Dalits. In some regions, eating Beef is a luxury, but it is a common food source for Dalits and marginalized communities. Because of dominant cultural and religious views, people who eat Beef, especially those from Dalit communities, may experience discrimination or social exclusion. Violence against people or groups that trade or consume Beef has occurred; these occurrences are frequently the result of religious fanaticism. In such a context, the rights of Dalits, the poor and the marginalized, are denied. People are looking for a leader who will fight for their rights. The story of Othniel (who fights for people's rights) teaches that God strengthens the will of a person who gives voice to the suppressed as a liberator. In the case of Judges, Yahweh raised leaders from those oppressed communities to stand for people's rights. Thus, wherever communities suffer and are denied their rights, God is ready to choose a leader from that community to fight for the people's rights.

Denial of Farmers' Rights

Many of India's exports are based on agricultural products, such as jute, tea, tobacco, coffee, spices, and sugar. These help increase foreign exchange. Agriculture is the primary occupation for the majority of workers in India, and a large number of rural women are also engaged in it.[482] According to the 2022-23 census of India, 45.76% of the primary workers engage in agricultural and allied activities.[483] Many industries are agro-based, such as jute, cotton, sugar, and tobacco. Agricultural produce supplies the raw materials for these industries. However, the present situation has changed; instead of producing more products, farmers are struggling for many reasons, such as lack of marketing and storage facilities, poor adoption of mechanization, credit availability, poor irrigation facilities, soil fertility depletion, inadequate access to crop insurance schemes, the impact of climate change, price volatility and poor training and extension facilities. When formers have been struggling with these issues, In September 2020, the Parliament enacted three bills:[484]

a) The Farmers' Produce Trade and Commerce Bill.
b) The Farmers Agreement on Price Assurance and Farm Services Bill.

---

482 "Agriculture and Food Industry and Exports," *IBEF*, accessed on September 16, 2024, https:// www.ibef.org/ exports/agriculture-and-food-industry-india.

483 In 2001, 56.6% and in 2011, 54.6% of the primary workers in India were engaged in agricultural and allied activities.

484 S. K. Goyal, Shree Ram Singh and Jai P. Rai, "Indian Agriculture and Farmers-Problems and Reforms," *Indian Agriculture and Farmers* (2016): 79–87.

c) The Essential Commodities Bill.

According to the administration, these measures would increase opportunities for the private sector and reduce government participation in agriculture. The farmers feared that companies would have more access to their protective measures if the government removed its protective measures. Thus, farmers protested against these laws in 2021. More than 200 farmer groups attended the protest.

The Spirit of Yahweh Empowers the Oppressed Community

People defend their rights to get a law that guarantees a minimum price for all crops, debt waiver (in losses), and compensation when the government takes away their lands for development projects. They seek the state's support and fear the growing privatization of electricity. In the event of farmers' protests for their rights, the police put up barricades and sealed the borders to stop the tens of thousands of farmers who were marching towards Delhi with their thousands of tractors. Section 144 was in effect for a month, prohibiting any meeting of three or more individuals. Police also deployed rubber bullets and tear gas. Seven Haryana districts suspended internet service. There were also blockages at the borders between Delhi and Haryana. Amidst these struggling, painful and dominating situations, people expect a leader who will fight for their rights. Here, the story of Othniel encourages and teaches that God is ready to empower his people towards liberation, who step forward for their suffering and painful communities. Thus, wherever the rights are denied to a community, God empowers the ordinary person to fight for liberation from that same community.

Denial of Right to Occupation

In India, manual scavenging and "untouchability" are prohibited by constitutional and legislative means.[485] Men and women as manual scavengers clean human excrement from public and private dry toilets, open defecation areas, closed gutters, and sewers. "These people usually resort to this perpetual malpractice due to the caste-based traditional bigotry, and the situation is aggravated by the poor implementation of laws and policies prohibiting Manual Scavenging."[486] Historically, the caste system regulates people's civil and social life in India.[487] Customs and traditions govern

485 Article 17, the Constitution of India, 1950.

486 S. Silliman Bhattacharjee, *Cleaning Human Waste: Manual Scavenging* (New York: Human Rights Watch, 2014), 11.

487 "Equality at work: The continuing challenge," *Geneva*: ILO, 2011, accessed August 3, 2024, http:// www.ilo.org/ wcmsp5/groups/public/---ed_norm/---eclaration/documents/ publication/wcms_166583.

caste-based social organizations.[488] The Constitution of India provides equal status to all citizens and outlaws untouchability practices, but this practice persists.[489] Various political as well as social movements have broken the shackles of caste-based discrimination. However, Caste remains the primary tool to justify cruel, inhuman and illogical treatment imposed on people, and this is more prevalent in the rural part of the country. Caste plays a significant role in deciding an individual's moral and social duties. Within the caste structure, Dalits who work as manual scavengers are usually from the Hindu Valmiki sub-caste, which is the lowest Caste among regionally named groups such as Chuhada, Rokhi, Mehatar, Malkana, Halalkhor, and Lalbegi, or the Muslim Hela sub-caste.[490] 'There is a link between the caste system and the practice of manual scavenging in India where the so-called lower caste people are engaged in this malpractice,' according to a UN report.[491] "The International Labour Organization (ILO) distinguishes three forms of manual scavenging: 1) removal of human excrement from public streets and dry latrines, 2) cleaning septic tanks, and 3) cleaning gutters and sewers."[492] The dispute arises over giving an exact figure for the number of people engaged in this practice, as the government's data is always less than the data collected by social organizations.[493] Due to the lack of alternative livelihood opportunities, the people forcefully engaged in manual scavenging. These people, in most cases, belong to the poorest and most marginalized communities in India, where even food security is a crucial problem. The people engaging in manual scavenging are routinely denied access to communal water sources and public places of worship and prevented from purchasing goods and services. Also, these people are

488 Sukhadeo *Thorat, Caste, Social Exclusion, & Poverty* (New Delhi: Gautam Printers, 2013), 6–7.

489 India's Constitution abolishes the practice of "untouchability" in articles 17 and 14, 19, 21, 23, and 47.

490 Vibhawari Kamble, "Steps towards the Elimination and Eradication of Manual Scavenging Practices: Advocacy Manual for NGOs, CBO's and other related organizations," accessed August 3, 2024, https:// view. Office apps. live.com/op/ view.aspx?src=https%3A%2F%2Fidsn.org%2Fuploads%2Fmedia%2FMan ual_for_ advocacy_2.doc&wdOrigin=BROWSELINK.

491 Chetanya Mallapur, "Manual Scavenging is illegal, but it persists," *Business Standard*, accessed on September 16, 2024, https://www.business-standard.com/article/news-ians/ manual-scavenging-is-illegal-but still persists-116052700776_1.html.

492 Gita Ramaswamy, *India Stinking: Manual Scavengers in Andhra Pradesh and their work* (Delhi: Navayana Publishing, 2005), 3.

493 Aastha Srivastava, "Safai Karamchari Andolan V. Union of India," *Writ Petition* (Civil) 1/583 (2003), judgment given on March 27, 2014, accessed September 16, 2024, https:// legalvidhiya.com/safai-karamchariandolan v-union-of-india/.

privately discriminated against by the so-called 'upper caste' people of the society.

The Spirit of Yahweh Chooses the Untouchable Community

Manual scavenger practice and discrimination have been continuing in India. According to the Union Minister of State for Social Justice and Empowerment, over 400 people died while cleaning sewers and septic. Died person's family going into struggle and continually facing discrimination and untouchability. The government may proclaim that India has digitalized, but Dalit groups and marginalized people have cleaned up human waste. They are crying about the issues and problems in society. Among the many health risks that manual scavengers must deal with are toxic compounds and harmful bacteria, which can cause respiratory infections, skin illnesses, and other more severe diseases. In compelling situations, many choose to work in this field because they have no other options. The stigma and harsh realities of their work can lead to mental health challenges, including depression and anxiety. They were expecting liberation from this caste, class, profession, financial and social stigmas. The story of Othniel encourages and teaches that God chooses an ordinary person to liberate untouchable communities from their suffering and pain. In 1993, Bezwada Wilson started the Safari Karamachari Andolan (SKA) movement; he was born into a family of manual scavengers and had seen the injustices meted out to them all his life. Wilson approached the Employment Exchange Office seeking a job after graduating from school; the officers told him that he would be given the job of a sanitation worker because of Caste. Angered by this, he decided to go to the people in his region (Kolar) and motivate them to revolt against this caste-imposed occupation. He was introduced to Ambedkar's ideas: to educate, organize, and agitate. Therefore, wherever the rights are denied for a community in the name of Caste and untouchability, God chooses and moves by the Spirit of Yahweh to enter a larger arena of influence to fight for liberation from that same community.

Reflection and Conclusion

There have been numerous social, political, economic and religious issues in India regarding Dalits. Although the law provides them safety in India, many Dalit communities face cultural discrimination in the workplace and schools, and they are becoming more victims of violence. When it comes to women, there is a high rate of sexual assault, domestic abuse, and harassment, and obstacles to equal employment opportunities. When it comes to Adivasi and tribal, land is being taken for mining, infrastructure development, and agriculture, often without their consent. In many cases, they frequently endure extreme poverty and do not have access to essential amenities like clean water, healthcare, and education.

Religious fundamentalism rises to its peak. Hatred and anger towards Dalit Christians increase every day, including attacks on congregations and churches. Some states have passed anti-conversion legislation that disproportionately targets Christians. Especially discrimination and marginalization of Scheduled Castes and Tribes are evident in the present Indian context. Religious minorities experience crimes and attacks. Biased application of the law is a source, especially concerning matters like citizenship and anti-terrorism regulations.

The agricultural industry is in crisis as a result of the difficulties faced by farmers, including unpredictable weather, low prices, and debt. High unemployment rates remain a serious problem, particularly for young people. Many recent grads need help landing positions that utilize their skills. Rising costs, several taxes, new education policies and many other problems from all directions, there is an expectation for social, political, economic and religious liberation and liberator. However, the story of Othniel encourages us that the Spirit of Yahweh is untamable, given as endowment, through that he empowers us to enter a larger arena to work for liberation, the Spirit of Yahweh ready to bestow liberating power to whoever is willing to work for Dalit, woman, Adivasi and tribal. The Spirit of Yahweh is ready to strengthen one who is ready to fight for justice, equality, liberation, peace and harmony. As the Spirit of Yahweh moves Othinel to take part in liberating work, it works among the people even today to empower and strengthen them to achieve liberation and justice.

Contributors

Varaprasad Gosala is Professor of the Old Testament, and is an ordained minister of the Andhra Evangelical Lutheran Church. He is currently the Principal of the Andhra Christian Theological College (ACTC), Hyderabad. Prior to this, he served as the Faculty at the Gurukul Lutheran Theological College & Research Institute, Chennai and Master's College of Theology, Visakhapatnam. He also served as the Treasurer for the Society of Biblical Studies in India (SBSI) from 2019-2022. He has published many articles both in Academic Journals and Church Magazines both in English and Telugu. He has also coedited a book entitled "Identity and Community in Biblical World: A Collection of Essays." His email is vara.gosala@gmail.com

Jeeva Kumar Ravela is Professor in the department of Biblical Studies teaching Old Testament at UTC, Bangalore and formerly taught at Andhra Christian Theological College, Hyderabad. He is an ordained pastor of Telugu Baptist Churches. His areas of interest are the Contextual Interpretation of the Hebrew Bible, Dalit hermeneutics and sociology of religion studies. He is the author of book entitled, *Struggle for Land Rights in 1 Kings 21: A Dalit Liberative Hermeneutics*, (New Delhi: ISPCK, 2012). He has published many articles in academic journals and Church Magazines both in English and Telugu. He has recently contributed three chapters: (1) 'The Context of Dalit Christians in Rural Andhra Pradesh: Christian Faith, Caste and Culture; (2) Encountering the Bible: Listening to the Voices of Madiga Christians; and (3) Why are Times not kept by the Almighty? - Job, Violence and God: A Dalit Contextual Reading of Job 24' in the book entitled, *Encountering Diversity in Indian Biblical Studies-A Biblical Masala,* ed by David J Chalcraft and Zhodi Angami (London: Routledge, 2023). He is on the editorial board of Bangalore Theological Forum published by the United Theological College, Bangalore, and also serves as the editor of Masihi Sevak: A Journal of Christian Ministry, UTC. ravela.jeevakumar@gmail.com

C. I. David Joy is a presbyter of the Church of South India, South Kerala Diocese, currently Principal at the Kerala United Theological Seminary, Trivandrum. He is the Liaison for India of SBL-ICI and A member of the board of the International Cooperative Initiative for Biblical Studies of SBL. David Joy is also a Senate Member of the Serampore College, Convener of the Board of Studies, NT, Serampore, Member of the Academic Council of Serampore and Executive Committee Member of Kerala Auxiliary of Bible Society of India. He is also a South Kerala Diocese administrative committee member and president of SCM centre Trivandrum. He serves FFRRC as its co-chairman. He has authored/edited 27 books and published 30 plus Articles in Academic Journals and more than 100 articles in Church magazines both in English and Malayalam. In addition, he has regularly contributed lessons for textbooks published by the Women's Fellowship, Pastoral Aid Department of CSI synod, Christian Education Department of South Kerala Diocese, and Youth Department of South Kerala Diocese. He has delivered academic lectures and presentations at the University of Birmingham, Exeter, Liverpool Hope, Westminster College, and Cambridge, UK. djoy29@gmail.com

B. Lalnunzira is an ordained minister of the Presbyterian Church of India, who taught at Bishop's College & Aizawl Theological College, Aizawl for the past 12 years. He earned his PhD from Graduate Theological Union, Berkeley (CA) USA. Presently he is Administrative Secretary of the Presbyterian Church of India, Shillong, President of the North East India Society for Biblical Studies, and Vice President of the SBSI. He lives in Shillong with his family. blalnunzira@gmail.com

Sam Peedikayil Mathew is Professor of New Testament at The United Theological College, Bangalore. He did his doctoral studies in the Senate of Serampore, West Bengal. He has authored three books, edited two books and published several articles in Journals in India and abroad. His major works include Temple-Criticism in Mark's Gospel: The Economic Role of the Jerusalem Temple in the First Century CE (Delhi: ISPCK, 1999) and Method and Message of Gautama Buddha and Jesus Christ: Explorations in Cross-scripture Hermeneutics (Delhi & Bangalore: ISPCK & CISRS, 2020). He has been a theological educator for more than three decades in varied cultural contexts in North East India, North India, East India and South India. He has served at Serampore College, Serampore, Gurukul Lutheran Theological College, Chennai, and later at Sam Higginbottom University of Agriculture, Technology and Sciences, Allahabad. His main areas of interest are contextual Biblical interpretation and Subaltern Biblical Hermeneutics. He belongs to the Madhya Kerala Diocese of the Church of South India.

Johnson Thomaskutty, PhD., is Professor of New Testament and Chairperson of Biblical Studies at The United Theological College, Bengaluru, India. He is author of Dialogue in the Book of Signs: A Polyvalent Analysis of John 1:19-12:50 (Brill, 2015), Saint Thomas the Apostle: New Testament, Apocrypha, and Historical Traditions (Bloomsbury T&T Clark, 2018), and editor of An Asian Introduction to the New Testament (Fortress, 2022). He also serves as editor of Bangalore Theological Forum. jesusandjohnson@gmail.com

Y. T. Vinayaraj is the Director of Christian Institute for the Study of Religion and Society, Bangalore. He serves as the visiting faculty at the Henry Martin Institute, Hyderabad, United Theological College, Bangalore and the Federated Faculty of Research in Religion and Culture (FFRRC), Kerala. His books include Dalit Theology after Continental Philosophy (2016 Palgrave) and Faith in the Age of Empire (2020 CWM / ISPCK). yvinayraj@gmail.com

Laurence Culas is a Catholic priest of the Archdiocese of Trivandrum. He has secured Master's Degree in History (Kerala University, Trivandrum), Biblical Theology (St. Peter's Pontifical Institute, Bangalore) and Doctorate in Biblical Theology (Catholic Institute of Toulouse, France). He serves as Visiting Professor of New Testament at Bodhi Institute of Theology, Tillery, Kerala. He is the author of *Good News Amidst Crises: Antioch and the Gospel of Matthew* (Delhi: ISPCK, 2010); *Pastoral Ministry: A Shift in Paradigm* (Trivandrum: CIPH, 2019); *Treasures New and Old: Matthew's Message for His Community* (Trivandrum: CIPH, 2021); and others. He has contributed several articles in various journals and edited books. He also works as the executive secretary of KRLCBC Commission for Bible and as the Coordinator of Ministries and Commissions in the Archdiocese of Trivandrum. lalujculas@gmail.com

Indukuri John Mohan Razu, Professor of Christian Ethics taught Christian Ethics, Church and Society, and societal analysis for about seventeen years at the United Theological college, Bengaluru, two years at Clarke theological College, Mooching, Nagaland, at ACTS Academy of Higher Education, Bengaluru, for a couple of years, and coordinated the Research Unit of the Indian Social Institute, Bangalore—a Jesuit Unit Currently serves as a Consultant and Research Fellow at ACTS Academy of Higher Education, Bangaluru. Engaged in the empowerment of the Dalit and Urban poor communities in Chennai, Chingleput District of Tamil Nadu, BUILD, Bombay, and CIEDS, Bangalore, for several years. Served as a Consultant to HEKS, NOWIB, and a number of funding agencies. Availed the sabbatical as William Paton Fellow to the Department of Theology, University of

Birmingham, and as a Visiting Scholar to the Divinity Scholl of Princeton University, New Jersey, USA. Prolific writer published and edited a number of books and booklets on varied areas and issues that concern humanity. Presented research papers, both nationally and internationally. Known for his stance as a public critic and is also a journalist. Posts full-fledged articles and small write ups in academia.edu in his post John Mohan Razu. Phone: +91 99453 90014; E-mail: ijmrazu@gmail.com; ijmrazu@yahoo.com.in ASIAN DOMAIN

David J Chalcraft, is Professor of Sociology, Liverpool John Moores University, UK. He recently edited, with Zhodi Angami, *Encountering Diversity in Indian Biblical Studies.* London: Routledge, 2023. D.J.Chalcraft@ljmu.ac.uk

P. Joseph Titus is a Catholic priest of the Archdiocese of Pondicherry-Cuddalore, and Professor of the Hebrew Bible. He served as President of St. Peter's Pontifical Institute (Bangalore) from 2017-2023. He is the Director of the Board of Doctoral Studies at St. Peter's Pontifical Institute, Bangalore from 2022. He holds a Sacrae Theologiae Doctor (S.T.D.) from the Catholic University of Paris, France and a Ph.D. from the Catholic University of Leuven, Belgium. He received *nihil obstat* from the Dicastery for Culture and Education, Rome, in 2013 and was raised to the rank of a permanent professor. He serves as Editor of the pace setting Indian Theological Studies and is a member of the Editorial Board of Transversalités, a French Theological Journal published by the Catholic University of Paris, France. He previously held leadership positions with the Society for Biblical Studies in India (SBSI), serving as its secretary (2012-2014) and President (2014-2016). A prolific writer, he is a regular contributor to various theological journals in India and abroad. His published works include: The Second Story of Creation (Gen 2:4-3:24): A Prologue to the Concept of Enneateuch? (Frankfurt: Peter Lang, 2010); In Search of Light to My Path: Reflections on Psalms (Bangalore: ATC, 2012); Like a Tree by Streams of Water: Meditations on the Life-Shaping Torah (Bengaluru: TPI, 2016): Missio Dei: Biblical Perspectives on Mission (Bangalore, TPI, 2023). josephtitus72@gmail.com.

Wungtei Buchem did his PhD at the University of Sheffield UK and is currently teaching at Trinity Theological College, Dimapur in the Department of Biblical Studies (OT). He currently holds the chair for Aboghū: Indigenous Studies and Research Centre (ISRC), TTC. wbuchem2009@gmail.com

Ms. S. Esther Ao is currently pursuing a Doctorate in Theology (Old Testament) at the United Theological College, Bengaluru. estherao1904@gmail.com

Lalawmpuia Hauhnar is an Ordained Minister of the Presbyterian Church of India, Mizoram Synod. He is currently serving as Associate Professor in the department of Old Testament at Aizawl Theological College, Mizoram. awpahauhnar18@gmail.com

Rohan P. Gideon is Professor of Christian Theology at the United Theological College, Bengaluru. He is a Presbyter of Karnataka Northern Diocese (CSI). His areas of research and interest are Children-focussed theologies & Methods' and 'Human Sexuality & Christian Theologies'. rohanpgideon@gmail.com

Allan Samuel Palanna is an Ordained Presbyter of the Church of South India, Karnataka Southern Diocese. Dr. Palanna is Professor and Chairperson of the Department of Theology and Ethics at the United Theological College, Bengaluru. The paper was presented as the Mary Jones Lecture, 2024 at the invitation of the Bible Society of India at Bengaluru. allan_samuel@rediffmail.com

Chilkuri Vasantha Rao is an ordained Presbyter of the Church of South India Medak Diocese. He received his B.D. and M.Th. at the United Theological College, Bangalore and Doctorate from the Hamburg University, Germany. He was Principal of ACTC (2010-2014). He is the current Principal of the United Theological College, Bengaluru, and is Professor of the Old Testament. Prof. Chilkuri Vasantha Rao is a Senator and also the Treasurer of the Senate of Serampore College (University). utcvasantharao@gmail.com

Laila L. Vijayan is a communicant member of the Church of South India, South Kerala Diocese and currently serves as the Professor of Old Testament in the Department of Biblical Studies at United Theological College in Bangalore. She is also the Treasure of Society for Biblical Studie in India. Her contact email ID: lailalvijayan@gmail.com

Ms. Nongthombam Alifina Nongthombam Alifina, hailing from the Meitei community in Manipur, is currently undertaking Doctoral Studies at the United Theological College, Bengaluru. alifinanong1@gmail.com

B. Silpa Rani is an ordained presbyter of the Church of North India and an Assistant Professor of the Old Testament at Bishop's College, Kolkata. She is currently pursuing her doctoral research program in the

Department of Old Testament at the United Theological College, Bangalore. bsilparani68@gmail.com

N. Subramani has received his Doctor of Theology degree in Old Testament from Senate of Serampore College (University). He serves as Associate Director Translation and Translation Consultant trained by the United Bible Societies. He served as Coordinator with the World Vision India. At present, he is serving as an Assistant Pastor at the Tamil Evangelical Lutheran Church, Bangalore. He published 'Imagery of Love in the Old Testament: A Socio-Rhetorical Reading of the Book of Hosea. (New Delhi: CWI, 2020); and 'Love and Covenant in the Old Testament with Special Reference to the Book of Hosea (New Delhi: CWI, 2022). He also teaches and preaches the Bible at the grassroots and ecclesiastical levels through Didasklia. subramani11@gmail.com

Arun Kumar Wesley, a former Presbyter of the CSI Karnataka Central Diocese was the Editorial Consultant at CISRS, Bangalore. arun.wesley2010@gmail.com

Swami Raju Tadivaka is an ordained pastor of Andhra Evangelical Lutheran Churches. He taught in the Department of Religion, Culture and Philosophy and is former Principal of Andhra Christian Theological College, Hyderabad. He was the Dean of Advanced Institute for Research on Religion and Culture (ARRC) a joint organized program of Andhra Christian Theological College, Calvin Institute of Theology and Henry Martyn Institute of Hyderabad, which is affiliated to the Senate of Serampore College (University). swamiraju@yahoo.com

Ms. Jeviholi Swu is pursuing Doctor of Theology in the Department of Biblical Studies (Old Testament) at The United Theological College (UTC), Bengaluru, Karnataka. She formerly worked as Associate Pastor (Women) in Pughoboto, Nagaland, as a lecturer of Old Testament in Danishpet, Tamil Nadu, as a Research Scholar at CISRS, Bengaluru, Karnataka and as visiting faculty in three theological colleges in Dimapur as well as was involved in the Music Ministry in her church at Dimapur, Nagaland. jvpukho@gmail.com

K. J. Premavardhan is an ordained minister of Church of South India, Diocese of Rayalaseema. He is currently teaching Old Testament at Andhra Christian Theological College, Hyderabad. kjpvardhan@gmail.com

Ms. Lydia Bujem is from Nagaland. Currently she is pursuing her Doctor of Theology in Old Testament at the United Theological College, Bengaluru. lydiabujem@gmail.com

Gnanam David is an ordained pastor from the South Andhra Lutheran Church (SALC), Andhra Pradesh. He completed his Bachelor of Divinity and Master of Theology (OT) at the United Theological College, Bangalore. Currently, he is serving as a pastor in SALC. gnanamdavid@gmail.com

Sam T. Rajkumar is an ordained pastor, pursuing Master of Theology in the Old Testament at the United Theological College, Bengaluru. str4christ@gmail.com

Mede Jeevan Sagar is an ordained Deacon of the Church of South India by Diocese of Krishna Godavari, Andhra Pradesh. At present, he teaches in the Department of Old Testament at the Bishop's College as an Assistant Professor, Kolkata. binnylakshmi17@gmail.com

Ms. Monalisha Tandi belongs to the Church of North India, Bileikani, Balangir (Odisha). At present she is doing Master of Theology in Old Testament at the United Theological College, Bengaluru. monatandi1996@gmail.com

Barre Daniel Anurag hails from pithapuram, a town in Andhra Pradesh and belongs to the Baptist Church. He received his B.D. degree from the Senate of Serampore College (University). At present he is pursuing Master of Theology (M.Th) in the department of Old Testament at The United Theological College, Bengaluru. danielanuragb@gmail.com

John Mathew, is an Ordained Minister of Marthoma Church. He completed BD from United Theological College, Bangalore. Now he is pursuing his Master of Theology in Old Testament at UTC. johnmathewthalavoor@gmail.com

Ms. Hukholu Yhobu, a member of the Chakhesang Baptist Church Council, hails from Nagaland and is currently pursuing her Master of Theology in Old Testament at United Theological College, Bangalore. hyhobu@gmail.com

Sam Thomas Arisapogu completed his Master of Theology in Old Testament at the United Theological College, Bengaluru. Currently he is pursuing higher studies in the United States of America. arisapogu.sam@gmail.com

S. Wilson Naveen Kumar hails from Pannur, Chittor District, Andhra Pradesh and belongs to Church of South India Diocese of Madras. He is currently pursuing his Master of Theology in Old Testament at the United Theological College, Bengaluru. wilsonsamsonrichardlivingston@gmail.com

A List of Publications of Prof. Kondasingu Jesurathnam

Education

2003-2006: PhD (Doctor of Philosophy in Old Testament) at the School of Divinity, University of Edinburgh, United Kingdom

1994-1996: MTh (Master of Theology in Old Testament) at Senate of Serampore University

1986-1990: BD (Bachelor of Divinity) at Serampore University

1980-1983: BSc (Bachelor of Science in Zoology) at Madras University

Languages Known

Telugu (speak, read and write fluently, mother tongue)

Tamil (speak, read and write fluently)

English (speak, read and write fluently)

Kannada (speak, read and write fluently)

Biblical Hebrew (advanced reading knowledge)

Biblical Greek (intermediate reading knowledge)

Academic Experience and Honors

1. August 2017: Conferred with the Friedemann Golka professor (chair) of Old Testament at the United Theological College, Bangalore by the UTC Society.
2. January-July 2014: Visiting Scholar at the Columbia Theological Seminary, Decatur, Georgia, US.
3. August- December 2014: Visiting Professor at the Lutheran Theological Seminary at Philadelphia, US.

4. June 2010-till date: Professor of Old Testament at the United Theological College. Teaching Old Testament Literature and Theology and Biblical Hebrew at the MDiv/BD and MTh levels. Also guiding doctoral research students.
5. 2006-2009: Associate Professor of the Old Testament. Teaching Old Testament Literature and Theology and Biblical Hebrew at the BD and MTh levels at the United Theological College, Bangalore.
6. 2000-2003: Lecturer in Old Testament at the United Theological College, Bangalore. Teaching Old Testament Literature and Theology and Biblical Hebrew at the BD level.
7. 1996-2000: Lecturer in Old Testament at the Hindustan Bible Institute & College, Chennai. Teaching Old Testament Literature and Theology and Biblical Hebrew at MDiv level.
8. 1992-1994: Lecturer at the Acts Institute, Bangalore. Teaching Old Testament and New Testament subjects at the Bachelor of Theology (B.Th) level.
9. 1990-1992: Lecturer at the Hindustan Bible Institute &College, Chennai. Teaching Old Testament and New Testament subjects at the B.Th level.

Academic Administrative Experience

1. Currently, Dean of Doctoral Studies and Non-degree research at the United Theological College, Bangalore
2. November 2020 Acting Principal and Dean of Doctoral Studies and Non- Degree research at the United Theological College, Bengaluru.
3. 2019-21 Convener, Publications committee at UTC, Bangalore
4. 2016-2018 Chief Hostel Adviser (Warden) at UTC, Bangalore
5. 2018-2022 Vice-President and currently (2022-2024) President of Society for Biblical Studies in India (SBSI)
6. November 2016: Elected as a member of the Executive Committee of the Society for Biblical Studies in India (SBSI).
7. 2012 June: Elected as a member of the Executive council of the Society of Asian Biblical Studies (SABS), meeting in Malaysia
8. 2011-2013: Secretary, the Society for Biblical Studies in India (SBSI)
9. 2011-2014: Dean of Postgraduate Studies at the United Theological College, Bangalore
10. 2009-2011 and 2019-2021: Editor, *Bangalore Theological Forum*, an academic and scholarly journal of the United Theological College, Bangalore

11. 2009-2011: Chairperson, Biblical Department at the United Theological College, Bangalore
12. 1998-2000: Faculty Advisor to the Library at the Hindustan Bible Institute &College, Chennai
13. 1998-2000: Dean of MA in Biblical Studies at the Hindustan Bible Institute &College, Chennai

Pastoral Experience

1. From 2015 to till date: Guest Preacher in and outside Bangalore in Baptist and Non-Baptist Churches on Sundays and other special occasions.
2. July-August 2014: Visiting Missionary in Residence at United Church of Christ Common Global Ministries, Cleveland, Ohio, US.
3. 2007-2008: Honorary Pastor, Hope Baptist Church, Bangalore
4. 1996-2000: Associate Pastor at Calvary Baptist Church, Chennai
5. 1992-1994: Pastor at the Acts Institute, Bangalore
6. 1992: Ordained as a Baptist pastor in Bangalore by the Indian Baptist Mission
7. 1990-1992: Associate Pastor at Madras Telugu Baptist Church

Publications

A. Books

1. Introduction to the Old Testament: A Dalit Perspective. New Delhi: CWI, 2023.
2. Introduction to the Old Testament: Tracing the History, Culture & Scripture of Ancient Israel. New Delhi: Christian World Imprints, 2018.
3. Old Testament Theology: History, Issues and Perspectives. New Delhi: Christian World Imprints, 2016.
4. Exploring Dalit Liberative Hermeneutics in India & the World: Based on an Ancient Hebrew Prophet, Jeremiah of Anathoth. New Delhi: Christian World Imprints, 2015.
5. Dalit Liberative Hermeneutics: Indian Christian Interpretation of Psalm 22. New Delhi: ISPCK, 2010.

Books Edited

1. Liberation Hermeneutics in the Indian Interpretation of the Bible. Bangalore: SBSI and CSS, Tiruvalla, 2012. Edited book along with Abraham Saggu and Hrangthan Chhunghi.

B. Articles - Parts of Books

1. "Rebuilding Lives in Conflict Situations: Biblical Perspectives. The Formation of Israelite Community during and after the Exodus and Wilderness experience (Deut 8:1-10)." In Laila L. Vijayan, Johnson Thomaskutty, Suresh Gunti (eds) *Justice Kindness Humility* A Festschrift to the Rev. Dr. Prof. Chilkuri Vasantha Rao on his Sixtieth Birthday. (Delhi. Bangalore, Arizona, Delhi: UTC, UCCI, ISPCK, 2023), pp. 238-268.
2. “Methodological Issues and Trends in Old Testament Studies with Special Reference to Dalit and Queer Interpretation,” in *Methodological Issues in Theological Research: An Exploration* Volume 4 Serampore: Department of Research (SATHRI), 2020, pp. 7-32.
3. “Quest for Identity in community formation: Ancestral narratives for model communities in the book of Genesis,” in *Identity and community in Biblical world: Collected essays on Identity and Community from Biblical Perspectives* Eds. B. Lalnunzira & Varaprasad Gosala New Delhi: Christian World Imprints, 2020, pp. 19-36.
4. “M. M. Thomas’ Hermeneutical quest for the Church and Society: Rereading the book of Ecclesiastes in today’s world.” C. I. David Joy and P. Mohan Larbeer (Eds) *Journeys into the Deep: Hermeneutical Patterns of M. M. Thomas* Bangalore: BTESSC, 2016, pp. 11-28.
5. “Elijah and Elisha, the Reformers of Socio-political and religious System in Ancient Israel: Implications for the Indian Context.” in *Re-imagining Reformation: Essays in Honor of P. G. George.* y Y.T. Vinayaraj, Dexter Maben, Woba James (Eds) Delhi: ISPCK, 2017, pp. 238-255.
6. “Being Together: Liberation, Justice and Peace: Contesting Voices and Competing Identities in the Indian Church and Society.” Santhosh S. Kumar (ed) *The Great Commission in Context: Being Together with God’s Creation* Bangalore/New Delhi: The United Theological College/Christian World Imprints, 2016, pp. 113-128.
7. “Ecological Concerns in Wisdom Literature.” In Limatula Longkumer, Philip V. Peacock and Rodinmawia Ralte (eds) *Good News to the Whole Creation: A Festschrift to the Rev. Dr. V. J. John* Delhi/Kolkata: ISPCK/Bishop’s College, 2016, pp. 45-68.
8. “The Book of Joshua,” in Wintle, Brian et al (eds)., *South Asia Bible Commentary: A One-Volume Commentary on the Whole Bible* Grand Rapids: MI., Zondervan, 2015.
9. “A Dalit interpretation of Wisdom Literature with special reference to the underprivileged groups in the Hebrew society: a Mission perspective”. Peniel Jesudason Rufus Rajkumar, Joseph Prabhakar Dayam and I.

P. Asheervadham (eds), *Mission at and from the Margins: Patterns, Protagonists and Perspectives* (Oxford: Regnum Books International, 2014), pp. 179-199.

10. "Dalit Concerns of CISRS", in Vincent Rajkumar (ed) *Revisit to revision: contribution of CISRS to church and society*. Bangalore: Christian Institute for the Study of Religion and Society, 2013, pp. 115-130.
11. "Education in Ancient Israel: Challenges and Implications for a Multi-religious context in India in J. R. Paul Singh (ed) *Even now and not yet-Kingdom tensions and contemporary concerns: Essays in Honour of Rev. Dr. Cherian Thomas* (Bangalore: Ecumenical Christian Centre, 2013), pp. 142-159.
12. "Daniel's Experience of God and his encounter with the Persian Empire," in Paul Mohan Raj et al (eds) *Learn to Live: Essays in Honour of Dr Ken Gnanakan*. Bangalore: Theological Book Trust, 2012, pp. 99-118.
13. "Sabbatical Year and Jubilee Year as Eco-justice principles for human and non-human liberation," in Kondasingu Jesurathnam, Abraham Saggu and Hranagthan Chhunghi (eds) *Liberation Hermeneutics in the Indian Interpretation of the Bible*. Bangalore/Tiruvalla: Society for Biblical Studies in India & Christava Sahitya Samithi, 2012, pp. 195-216.
14. "Dalit Christian Biblical Hermeneutical Stance through Job and Jeremiah and its sensibility in the current theological debate," in T. K. John and James Massey (eds) *Theology for a new community: Dalit consciousness with a symbolic universe and meaning systems*. New Delhi: Centre for Dalit/Subaltern Studies, 2013, pp. 222-259.
15. "Dalit Christian Biblical Hermeneutical Stance through Job and Jeremiah and its sensibility in the current theological debate," in Joseph Prabhakar Dayam and P. Mohan Larbeer (eds), *Margins in conversation: methodological discourses in theological disciplines* (Bangalore: BTESSC, 2012), pp. 17-46.
16. "Land, Dalits and Human Rights: Yours Sincerely, Naboth, Ahab, Jezebel and Elijah," in Dalit Daniel Gnanasekaran (ed), *Let me own my Land: Dalit voices in India* (Tiruvannamalai: Department of Dalit Concerns, Arcot Lutheran Church, 2009), pp. 28-42.
17. "Re-reading Psalm 22 from a Dalit Christian Perspective," in James Massey, Indukur John Mohan Razu (eds), *Revisiting and Resignifying Methodology of Dalit Theology* (New Delhi/Bangalore: CDS/UTC, 2008), pp. 187-226.
18. "Is there not a prophet of the LORD among you?: Micaiah ben Imlah, Ahab and Jehoshaphat," in Israel Selvanayagam (ed.) *Light on our dusty*

path: essays for a Bible lover (Bangalore: BTESSC/SATHRI, 2008), pp. 156-166

19. "Transforming Praxis: God, Community, Church—Rereading Jeremiah 7:1-15 (Temple Sermon) with special focus on Dalit Christian Response," in C.I. David Joy (ed.) *Transforming Praxis: God, Community, Church* (Bangalore: UTC, 2008), pp. 111-132.
20. "Charisma, renewal and spiritual gifts: An Old Testament Perspective," in W. S. Milton Jeganathan (ed.) *The Third shift: towards a charismatic community* (Delhi: ISPCK, 2002), pp. 1-18.
21. "Amos indictment on Israel for the protection of human rights (Amos 2:6-8)," in I. John Mohan Razu & Anne Pattel-Gray (eds.) *Struggle for Human Rights: Towards a New Humanity* Biblical Perspectives Vol. 1 (Nagpur: NCCI, 2000), pp. 65-86.

Journal Articles

1. "Land, Dalits and Human Rights: Yours Sincerely; Nathan, Ahab, Jezebel and Elijah" *Bangalore Theological Forum* 53:1 (2021), pp. 19-32.
2. "Education for nurturing discipleship: inculcating the ethos of responsible citizenship in the light of Israelite wisdom." *Bangalore Theological Forum* 52:1 (2020), pp. 203-214.
3. "You shall not oppress a resident alien': Immigrant Theology in the Old Testament." *Bangalore Theological Forum* 51:2 (2019), pp. 94-109.
4. "Resignifying 'Wandering Aramean' concept for Dalit Theology: A Biblical Theological and Hermeneutical Perspective." *Bangalore Theological* Forum 51:1 June 2019, pp. 165-183.
5. "Dalit and Subaltern Hermeneutics in Conversation with Reader-Response Method: 1 Kings 22 A case in point." *Bangalore Theological Forum* 48:1 (2016), pp. 46-60.
6. "You are the Salt of the Earth and the Light of the World: Matt 5:13-16." *Masihi Sevak* 40:1 (2015), pp. 91-97.
7. "A Dalit Prophetic Messiah of 21st Century India." *SATHRI Journal* 9:1 (2015), pp. 110-118.
8. "Am I my brother's keeper? Corruption from an Old Testament Perspective." *Bangalore Theological Forum* 47:1 (2015), pp. 1-22.
9. "Socio-economic and Politico-religious Horizons of Covenant Community of Israel: Some Ethical Implications." *Master's Journal of Theology* 4:2 (2014), pp. 24-46.
10. "Yerraguntala Peraiah: an Honorable Dalit Christian Missionary." *Journal of Subaltern and Cultural Theology* Inaugural Issue (2013), pp. 20-23.

11. "The Task of Old Testament Theology in the Indian Context: Some Methodological Explorations and Proposals." *Bangalore Theological Forum* 45:1 (2013), pp. 1-30.
12. "A Dalit interpretation of Wisdom Literature with special reference to the underprivileged groups in the Hebrew society: a Mission perspective." *Asia Journal of Theology* 25: 2 (2011), pp. 334-357.
13. "Before I formed you in the womb of your mother: the Decentered world of Jeremiah and Dalits." *Bangalore Theological Forum* 43:1 (2011), pp. 1-40.
14. "Agriculture and Labor in the Bible: An ecological interpretation." *Bangalore Theological Forum* 42:3 (2010), pp. 60-76.
15. "Righteous Dissenters: Job and Dalits." *Bangalore Theological Forum* 42:1 (2010), pp. 74-103.
16. "A time to tear down and a time to build." *Masihi Sevak* 34:3 (2009), pp. 92-103.
17. "Thus says the LORD: The Dynamism of the Hebrew Prophetic message and its implications for the contemporary Dalit prophetic discourse." *Bangalore Theological Forum* 41:2 (2009), pp. 179-197.
18. "Maccabean revolt and Dalit revolution: can they intersect?" *Bangalore Theological Forum* 41:1 (2009), pp. 135-158.
19. "Midrash Tehillim 22 and Dalit Christian Women's Interpretation of Psalm 22." *Bangalore Theological Forum* 40:2 (2008), pp. 96-130.
20. "The Socio-economic, Religious and Political Tensions in the Community of Ezra-Nehemiah and its implications for the Marginalized Communities in India." *Bangalore Theological Forum* 40:1 (2008), pp. 1-30.
21. "Towards a Dalit Liberative Hermeneutics: Rereading the Psalms of Lament." *Bangalore Theological Forum* 34:1 (2002), pp. 1-34.
22. "Behold I create a new heaven and a new earth: Isaiah 65: 17-25." *Masihi Sevak*, Bangalore: UTC, 2001

Important Conferences Attended and Papers Read

1. An international conference on science and religion in Pune, December 2001.
2. An international conference of Asian theologians in Jogjakarta, Indonesia, August 2001.
3. Baptist World Alliance Congress in 2005 in Birmingham, UK.

4. Attended Society of Asian Biblical Studies Biennial Conference in Seoul, South Korea and read a paper entitled: "Psalm 22 and Dalit Christology," July 14-16, 2008.
5. Symposium on Dalit Theology at the Bishop's College, Calcutta, presented a paper entitled: "Land, Dalits and Human Rights: Yours Sincerely: Naboth, Ahab, Jezebel and Elijah," September 26-28, 2008.
6. The Biennial conference of the Society for Biblical Studies in India, Trivandrum, Kerala, presented a paper entitled: "Dalit Prophets and Hebrew Prophets," December 27-30, 2008.
7. Baptist Global Peace Conference in Rome and read a paper entitled: "Conflict resolution and Dalit Protest movements," February 9-14, 2009.
8. University of Osnabreuck, Germany, read a paper entitled: "Dalit Liberative Hermeneutics: Towards a theology of the Untouchables," February 16, 2009.
9. Centenary Conference on Lesslie Newbigin in the CSI Diocese of Madras, read a paper entitled: "Lesslie Newbigin's Missionary Ecclesiology," December 8, 2009.
10. Society for Asian Biblical Studies in the Chinese University of Hong Kong reading a paper entitled: "Ecological concerns in the Wisdom Literature of the Hebrew Bible," June 14-16 2010.
11. A national consultation on *Emerging India –View from Below* in CISRS House, New Delhi, jointly organized by CISRS and NCCI, November 26-28, 2010.
12. Professorial lecture entitled: *Before I formed you in the womb of your mother: Decentered world of Jeremiah and Dalits,* to mark the occasion of being promoted as Professor of Old Testament, January 19, 2011.
13. Malaysia in Society of Asian Biblical Studies meeting on the topic: *The experience of exile in ancient Israel and in Southeast Asia: rereading Psalm 137,* delivered a conference paper, June 13-15, 2012.
14. Delivered several lectures at different conferences during my sabbatical in the United States of America through the year 2014.
15. Presented a paper in a National Seminar on Nationalism with a title: "Nationalism in the Old Testament and its Implications in the Present Indian Context." In September 2016 at Indian Social Institute, Bangalore.
16. Presented a paper in a National Biennial Seminar of the Society for Biblical Studies in India (SBSI) entitled: "Rhetorical critical and Dalit Reading of Jeremiah 30:12-17 in the light of present Indian Context: Few Challenges and Proposals" In November 2016 at Chennai.

17. Presented a paper in SATHRI DTh methodology Seminar in May 2018 entitled: "Nationalism in the Old Testament and its Postmodern Interpretation in the Present Indian Context." At Serampore, West Bengal.
18. Presented an academic paper entitled: "Land, Dalits and Human Rights: yours sincerely: Naboth, Ahab, Jezebel and Elijah." In SBSI, Regional Seminar at Madras Diocese, Laity Centre on February 6-7, 2020.
19. Presented an academic paper entitled: "Suffering in the Book of Job," in a Webinar on June 3, 2020 organized by the Ecumenical Christian Centre, Whitefield, Bangalore.
20. Presented a research methodology paper at SATHRI methodology seminar entitled: "Rhetorical Critical and Dalit Reading of Jeremiah 30:12-17 in the light of Present Indian Context: Few Challenges and Proposals." August 2020.
21. Presented a paper (in absentia) entitled: 'Maccabean Revolt and Dalit Revolution: Can they intersect?' in Yusan, Taiwan during biennial meeting of Society of Asian Biblical Studies in July 2024.

Forthcoming Papers/Presentations and Books

1. Writing on the book of Joshua in *South Asia Study Bible* published by Langham International, London in collaboration with Open Door Publications, India. Forthcoming in March 2025.
2. Working on a book Hebrew Prophets and Sages and Parallels to Dalit Prophets and Sages, Forthcoming.
3. Prophets in ancient Israel and implications derived from their message for the Indian socio-political and ecclesial context to be presented in the annual refresher's course of UTC in September 2024.
4. Migration from the Old Testament Perspective ed. I. John Mohan Razu by Candid Publications, Bangalore, January 2025.